Lecture Notes in Computer

T0230197

Commenced Publication in 1973
Founding and Former Series Editors:
Gerhard Goos, Juris Hartmanis, and Jan van Leeuwen

Rocco De Nicola Davide Sangiorgi (Eds.)

Trustworthy Global Computing

International Symposium, TGC 2005
Edinburgh, UK, April 7-9, 2005
Revised Selected Papers

Springer

Volume Editors

Rocco De Nicola
Università degli Studi di Firenze
Dipartimento di Sistemi e Informatica
Viale Morgagni 65, 50134 Firenze, Italy
E-mail: denicola@dsi.unifi.it

Davide Sangiorgi
Università di Bologna
Dipartimento di Scienze dell'Informazione
Mura Anteo Zamboni, 7, 40126 Bologna, Italy
E-mail: davide.sangiorgi@cs.unibo.it

Library of Congress Control Number: 2005936337

CR Subject Classification (1998): C.2.4, D.1.3, D.2, D.4.6, F.2.1-2, D.3, F.3

ISSN 0302-9743
ISBN-10 3-540-30007-4 Springer Berlin Heidelberg New York
ISBN-13 978-3-540-30007-6 Springer Berlin Heidelberg New York

Springer is a part of Springer Science+Business Media

springeronline.com

Printed in Germany

Typesetting: Camera-ready by author, data conversion by Scientific Publishing Services, Chennai, India
Printed on acid-free paper SPIN: 11580850 06/3142 5 4 3 2 1 0

Preface

Computing technology has become ubiquitous, from global applications to minuscule embedded devices. Trust in computing is vital to help protect public safety, national security, and economic prosperity. A new area of research, known as global computing, has recently emerged that aims at defining new models of computation based on code and data mobility over wide area networks with highly dynamic topologies, and that aims at providing infrastructures to support coordination and control of components originating from different, possibly untrusted, sources. Trustworthy global computing aims at guaranteeing safe and reliable network usage, also by providing tools and framework for reasoning about behavior and properties of applications.

An International Symposium on Trustworthy Global Computing (TGC 2005), was held in Edinburgh, UK, April 7–9, 2005. The symposium contained presentations and discussions dealing with issues such as:

- resource usage,
- language-based security,
- theories of trust and authentication,
- privacy, reliability and business integrity,
- access control and mechanisms for enforcing it,
- models of interaction and dynamic components management,
- language concepts and abstraction mechanisms,
- test generators, symbolic interpreters, type checkers,
- finite state model checkers, theorem provers,
- software principles to support debugging and verification.

The themes of the workshop were inspired by the activities of the IST/FET proactive Initiative on Global Computing funded by the European Union. Indeed, TGC 2005 can be considered as the evolution of the previous Global Computing Workshops held in Trento (see, for example, LNCS 2874) and the workshops on Foundation of Global Computing held as satellite events of ICALP or Concur (see, for example, ENTCS Vol. 85)

The format of the symposium was not that of a classical conference, but one structured to leave room for discussions stimulated by a conspicuous number of invited talks and by the papers selected after standard refereeing.

At the symposium we had 10 invited talks, and 11 contributed papers selected by the Program Committee (PC) after a call for contributions and a selective refereeing process (each paper was reviewed by four researchers). The invited talks were delivered by the following distinguished researchers, chosen by the PC members: Michele Bugliesi (Univ. of Venice, Italy), Luis Caires (Univ. Nova of Lisbon, Portugal), Matthew Hennessy (Univ. of Sussex, UK), Peter Van Roy (Univ. Catholique de Louvain, Belgium), Elsa Gunter (New Jersey Inst. of Technology, USA), Joshua Guttman (Mitre, Bedford, USA), Greg Meredith (CTO,

Djinnisys Corporation, USA), Mark Miller (HP, USA), Benjamin Pierce (Univ. of Pennsylvania, USA), Wolfram Schulte (Microsoft, USA).

This volume contains revised versions of the accepted papers which took into account both the referees' reports and the discussions that took place during the symposium. The volume contains also 8 papers contributed by the invited speakers.

The organization of TGC 2005 was stimulated by the IFIP Working Group (WG) 2.2. (`http://www.irisa.fr/s4/wg22/`). In the past, this WG organized a general working conference every 4 years. Members felt that the format should change, and the conference should be more focused. TGC 2005 was the first thematic conference promoted by the WG. The symposium had the co-sponsorship of IFIP TC-2 (Technical Committee 2 "Software: Theory and Practice"), to which WG 2.2 belongs.

The Program Committee included coordinators of EU Global Computing projects, organizers of past events similar to TGC 2005, and a few external experts on security and GC: Luca Cardelli (Microsoft Cambridge, UK), Giuseppe Castagna (ENS Paris, France), Adriana Compagnoni (Stevens Institute, USA), Rocco De Nicola (Florence, Italy, Chair), José Luiz Fiadeiro (Leicester, UK), Roberto Gorrieri (Bologna, Italy), Jean-Jacques Levy (Inria, France), Huimin Lin (Chinese Academy of Sciences, China), Eugenio Moggi (Genoa, Italy), Mogens Nielsen (Aarhus, Denmark), Flemming Nielson (Lyngby, Denmark), Joachim Parrow (Uppsala, Sweden), Corrado Priami (Trento, Italy), Julian Rathke (Sussex, UK), Davide Sangiorgi (Bologna, Italy, Chair), Don Sannella (Edinburgh, UK), Vladimiro Sassone (Sussex, UK), Jean-Bernard Stefani (Inria, France), and Martin Wirsing (Munich, Germany).

We would like to thank all the members of the Program Committee, and their subreferees, for putting together the selective program of the conference.

TGC 2005 was co-located with the events of ETAPS 2005, in Edinburgh. Special thanks is due to the Local Organizing Committee from Edinburgh University, in particular Don Sannella and Massimo Felici, who helped us patiently through our (almost endless) email messages. We would also like to thank Lorenzo Bettini (University of Florence) for his help during the periods of paper submission and preparation of the LNCS proceeedings.

July 2005

Rocco De Nicola
Davide Sangiorgi
TGC 2005 Co-chairs

Table of Contents

Harmony: The Art of Reconciliation
(Invited Talk)

Benjamin C. Pierce

University of Pennsylvania
http://www.cis.upenn.edu/~bcpierce

The Harmony system is a generic framework for reconciling disconnected updates to heterogeneous, replicated XML data. It can be used, for instance, to synchronize the bookmark files of several different web browsers, allowing bookmarks and bookmark folders to be added, deleted, edited, and reorganized by different users running different browser applications on disconnected machines.

A central theme of the Harmony project—and of this talk—is bringing ideas from programming languages to bear on a set of problems more commonly regarded as belonging to the purview of databases or distributed systems. In particular, a major component of the proposed work concerns developing the foundations of *bi-directional programming languages* [1], in which every program denotes a pair of functions—one for extracting a *view* of some complex data structure, and another for "putting back" an updated view into the original structure. Bi-directional programs play a crucial role in the way the system deals with heterogeneous structures, mapping between diverse concrete application data formats and common abstract formats suitable for synchronization. Similarly, the issue of *alignment* during reconciliation—that is, of determining which parts of divergent replicas are intended to represent "the same information"—can be addressed by focusing on the type structure of the data being reconciled [2].

Further information and an open-source implementation can be found on the Harmony home page: `http://www.cis.upenn.edu/~bcpierce/harmony`.

References

1. Foster, J.N., Greenwald, M.B., Moore, J.T., Pierce, B.C., Schmitt, A.: Combinators for bi-directional tree transformations: A linguistic approach to the view update problem. In: ACM SIGPLAN–SIGACT Symposium on Principles of Programming Languages (POPL), Long Beach, California. (2005) Extended version available as University of Pennsylvania technical report MS-CIS-03-08. Earlier version presented at the *Workshop on Programming Language Technologies for XML (PLAN-X)*, 2004.
2. Foster, J.N., Greenwald, M.B., Kirkegaard, C., Pierce, B.C., Schmitt, A.: Schema-directed data synchronization. Technical Report MS-CIS-05-02, University of Pennsylvania (2005) Supercedes MS-CIS-03-42.

R. De Nicola and D. Sangiorgi (Eds.): TGC 2005, LNCS 3705, p. 1, 2005.

A Theory of Noninterference for the π-Calculus*

Silvia Crafa[1] and Sabina Rossi[2]

[1] Dipartimento di Matematica, Università di Padova
crafa@math.unipd.it
[2] Dipartimento di Informatica, Università Ca' Foscari di Venezia
srossi@dsi.unive.it

Abstract. We develop a theory of noninterference for a typed version of the π-calculus where types are used to assign secrecy levels to channels. We provide two equivalent characterizations of noninterference based on a typed behavioural equivalence relative to a security level σ, which captures the idea of external observers of level σ. The first characterization involves a universal quantification over all the possible *active attacks*, i.e., malicious processes which interact with the system possibly leaking secret information. The second definition of noninterference is expressed in terms of an unwinding condition, which deals with so-called *passive attacks* trying to infer confidential information just by observing the behaviour of the system. This unwinding-based characterization naturally leads to efficient methods for the verification and construction of (compositional) secure systems. Furthermore, we characterize noninterference in terms of bisimulation-like (partial) equivalence relations in the style of a stream of similar studies for other process calculi (e.g., CCS and CryptoSPA) and languages (e.g., imperative and multi-threaded languages).

1 Introduction

A central issue of multilevel security systems is the protection of sensitive data and resources from undesired access. Information flow security properties have been proposed as a means to provide strong guarantees of confidentiality of secret information. These properties impose constraints on information flow ensuring that no information can flow from a higher to a lower security level. Since Denning and Denning's work [7], information flow analysis has been studied for various programming languages, including imperative languages [7,21,24], functional languages [11,19] and concurrent languages [1,5,8,15,16,17,18,20,23,26].

One of the most successful approaches to information flow security relies on the notion of *Noninterference* [10]. The basic idea is that a system is interference free if the low level observation of the system is independent from the behaviour of its high components. Recently, various type-based proof techniques for the π-calculus have been proposed [12,15,16,17,18]. In these works type systems are actually part of the definition of noninterference, in that both the observation of the system and the observed processes are constrained by types. A soundness theorem is then proved stating that if a

* Supported by the EU-FET project IST-2001-32617 and the FIRB project RBAU018RCZ.

R. De Nicola and D. Sangiorgi (Eds.): TGC 2005, LNCS 3705, pp. 2–18, 2005.

system is well-typed, then no change in the behaviour of its high components can affect the low level view of the system.

In this paper we wish to define a general theory of noninterference for the π-calculus, where the use of types is much lighter. In particular, the only typing constraint we impose is that values at a given security clearance cannot flow through channels with a lower security level. Such a typing discipline ensures that information does not explicitly flow from high to low. Instead, implicit flows are not dealt with the type system, and then we cannot use it as a proof technique for noninterference. On the contrary, we characterize noninterference in terms of the actions that typed processes may perform.

Our approach intends to generalize previous ideas, mainly developed for CCS, to the π-calculus, where new difficulties arise due to the presence of scope extrusion. The contribution of this paper is twofold: (i) we develop a rich and elegant theory of noninterference intrinsic of the π-calculus, almost independent of types, and (ii) we find a number of sound and complete characterizations of secure processes leading to efficient verification techniques.

The noninterference property we are going to study is based on the notion of process behaviour relative to a security level σ, taken from a complete lattice $\langle \Sigma, \preceq \rangle$ of security annotations. We define typed equivalences for the π-calculus relative to an observation level σ, namely σ-reduction barbed congruences (see [13]). Two processes P, Q are σ-equivalent in the type environment Γ, written $\Gamma \models P \cong_\sigma Q$, if they exhibit the same σ-level behaviour, i.e., they are indistinguishable for a σ-level observer.

A σ-level observer is formalized as a σ-context, i.e., a well typed context which can interact with the observed process only through channels of level at most σ. We require $\cong_\sigma$ to be a congruence for all σ-level contexts.

We also develop a proof technique for $\cong_\sigma$ in terms of a quite natural bisimilarity on σ-actions defined on typed labelled transition systems. A typed LTS is built around typed actions of the form $\Gamma \triangleright P \xrightarrow{\alpha}_\delta \Gamma' \triangleright P'$ indicating that in the type environment Γ, the process P performs the action α of level δ and evolves to P' in the possibly modified environment Γ'. We prove that two processes are σ-barbed congruent if and only if they are bisimilar on typed actions of level σ.

Relying on this equational theory for the π-calculus, we introduce the noninterference property $\mathcal{NI}(\cong_\sigma)$ for typed processes, which is inspired by the *P_BNDC* property defined in [9] for CCS. We say that a process P in a type environment Γ satisfies the property $\mathcal{NI}(\cong_\sigma)$, written $\Gamma \triangleright P \in \mathcal{NI}(\cong_\sigma)$, if for every configuration $\Gamma' \triangleright P'$ reachable from $\Gamma \triangleright P$ in the typed LTS, and for every σ-high level source H (that is a process which can perform only actions at level higher than σ) it holds

$$\Gamma' \triangleright P' \cong_\sigma \Gamma' \triangleright P' \mid H.$$

This definition involves a universal quantification over all the possible *active attacks*, i.e., high level malicious processes H which interact with the system possibly leaking secret information. Moreover, it is *persistent* in the sense that if a configuration satisfies $\mathcal{NI}(\cong_\sigma)$ then also all the configurations reachable from it in the typed LTS satisfy $\mathcal{NI}(\cong_\sigma)$. As discussed in [9], persistence is technically useful since it allows us to apply inductive reasoning when proving security results (e.g., compositionality), but it is also intuitively motivated by the need for mobile processes to be secure at any computation step.

We provide a first characterization of $\mathcal{NI}(\cong_\sigma)$ in terms of an *unwinding* condition in the style of [3]. The unwinding condition aims at specifying local constraints on process transitions which imply the global security property. More precisely, we require that whenever a configuration C performs a typed action of level higher than σ moving to C', then a configuration C'' can also be reached through an internal computation such that C' and C'' are indistinguishable for a σ-level observer. In other words, the unwinding condition ensures that the σ-high actions are always simulated by internal computations, thus becoming invisible for the low level observers.

It is interesting to observe that the unwinding condition characterizes security with respect to the so-called *passive attacks*, which try to infer information about the classified behaviour (σ-high actions) just by observing the σ-level behaviour of the system. Thanks to this characterization, the noninterference property $\mathcal{NI}(\cong_\sigma)$ becomes decidable for finite state processes, i.e., processes whose typed LTS is finite. Furthermore, we show that $\mathcal{NI}(\cong_\sigma)$ is compositional with respect to most of the operators of the π-calculus. In particular, if P and Q satisfy $\mathcal{NI}(\cong_\sigma)$ then $P \mid Q$ and $!P$ also do.

We further develop two quantifier-free characterizations of noninterference based on bisimulation-like (partial) equivalence relations. More precisely, we first introduce a partial equivalence relation $\dot{\approx}_\sigma$ (*per* model) over configurations and, inspired by the definitions in [21] for imperative and multi-threaded languages, we prove that $\dot{\approx}_\sigma$ is reflexive only on the set of secure processes. Hence, we obtain that a typed process P is secure if and only if P is $\dot{\approx}_\sigma$-equivalent to itself. Then we investigate the impact of name restriction on noninterference. Let $(\boldsymbol{\nu}^\sigma)P$ be the process P where all its σ-high free names are restricted. We define the equivalence relation $\ddot{\approx}_\sigma$ and prove that a typed process P is secure if and only if P and $(\boldsymbol{\nu}^\sigma)P$ are $\ddot{\approx}_\sigma$-equivalent. Finally we show that two well typed processes P and Q are equivalent on σ-actions if and only if $(\boldsymbol{\nu}^\sigma)P$ and $(\boldsymbol{\nu}^\sigma)Q$ are equivalent on every action. This property allows us to precisely relate the standard bisimulation equivalence $\approx$ for the π-calculus with our bisimulation on σ-actions and also to express our noninterference property in terms of the equivalence relation $\approx$.

The rest of the paper is organized as follows. In Section 2 we present the language, its semantics and the type system. In Section 3 we study typed observation equivalences relative to a security level. In Section 4 we introduce the notion of σ-noninterference and provide a number of characterizations based on typed actions. In Section 5 we illustrate the expressivity of our approach through a couple of examples. Section 6 concludes the paper discussing some related work.

All the proofs of the results presented in this paper are available in [6].

2 The Language

In this section we introduce the language, its operational semantics and the type system with which we will be concerned.

We presuppose a countably-infinite set of names and a countably-infinite set of variables ranged over by $n, .., q$ and by $x, .., z$, respectively. We often use a, b, c to range over both names and variables. We also assume a complete lattice $\langle \Sigma, \preceq \rangle$ of security annotations, ranged over by σ, δ, where $\top$ and $\bot$ represent the top and the bottom el-

Table 1. Syntax

Prefixes		*Processes*	
$\pi ::= \overline{a}\langle b\rangle$	output	$P ::= \pi.P$	prefix
$\mid\ a(x:T)$	input	$\mid$ if $a = b$ then P else P	matching
		$\mid\ P \mid P$	parallel
Types		$\mid\ (\nu n : T)P$	restriction
$T ::= \sigma[\,]$		$\mid\ !P$	replication
$\mid\ \sigma[T]$		$\mid\ \mathbf{0}$	inactive

ements of the lattice. The syntax of processes and types is shown in Table 1. It is a synchronous[1], monadic, calculus with the match/mismatch operator. As explained in [13], the matching construct is essential for the coinductive characterization of the reduction barbed congruence shown in Section 3.

As usual, the input construct $a(x : T).P$ acts as a binder for the variable x in P, while the restriction $(\nu n : T)P$ acts as a binder for the name n in P. We identify processes up to α-conversion. We use $\text{fn}(P)$ and $\text{fv}(P)$ to denote the set of free names and free variables, respectively, in P. We write $P\{x := n\}$ to denote the substitution of all free occurrences of x in P with n, and we often write $a(x{:}T), \overline{a}\langle b\rangle$ omitting trailing $\mathbf{0}$'s. In this paper we restrict to *closed* processes, i.e., processes containing no free occurrences of variables; in Section 6 we discuss how to extend our theory to open terms.

Types are used to assign security levels to channels. More precisely, if $\sigma \in \Sigma$, then $\sigma[\,]$ is the type of channels of level σ which carry no values, while $\sigma[T]$ is the type of channels of level σ which carry values of type T. We consider the function Λ associating to types the corresponding level, that is $\Lambda(\sigma[\,]) = \sigma = \Lambda(\sigma[T])$.

Semantics. The operational semantics of our language is given in terms of a labelled transition system (LTS) defined over processes. The set of labels, or actions, is the following:

Actions	$\alpha ::= \overline{n}\langle m\rangle$	send a name
	$\mid\ (\nu m{:}T)\,\overline{n}\langle m\rangle$	send a fresh name
	$\mid\ n(m)$	receive a name
	$\mid\ \tau$	internal action

We write $\text{fn}(\alpha)$ and $\text{bn}(\alpha)$ to denote the set of free and bound names occurring in the action α, where $\text{bn}(\alpha) = \{m\}$ if $\alpha = (\nu m{:}T)\,\overline{n}\langle m\rangle$, and $\text{bn}(\alpha) = \emptyset$ otherwise. The LTS is defined in Table 2 and it is entirely standard; we just omitted the symmetric

[1] We consider the synchronous calculus since it allows for more interferences. Nevertheless, our results can be adapted to the asynchronous, polyadic calculus.

Table 2. Labelled Transition System

(OUT)
$$\frac{}{\overline{n}\langle m\rangle.P \xrightarrow{\overline{n}\langle m\rangle} P}$$

(IN)
$$\frac{}{n(x:T).P \xrightarrow{n(m)} P\{x:=m\}}$$

(MATCH)
$$\frac{}{\mathsf{if}\ n=n\ \mathsf{then}\ P\ \mathsf{else}\ Q \xrightarrow{\tau} P}$$

(MISMATCH)
$$\frac{n\neq m}{\mathsf{if}\ n=m\ \mathsf{then}\ P\ \mathsf{else}\ Q \xrightarrow{\tau} Q}$$

(PAR)
$$\frac{P \xrightarrow{\alpha} P' \quad \mathrm{bn}(\alpha)\cap\mathrm{fn}(Q)=\emptyset}{P\,|\,Q \xrightarrow{\alpha} P'\,|\,Q}$$

(COMM)
$$\frac{P \xrightarrow{\overline{n}\langle m\rangle} P' \quad Q \xrightarrow{n(m)} Q'}{P\,|\,Q \xrightarrow{\tau} P'\,|\,Q'}$$

(CLOSE)
$$\frac{P \xrightarrow{(\boldsymbol{\nu} m:T)\,\overline{n}\langle m\rangle} P' \quad Q \xrightarrow{n(m)} Q' \quad m\notin\mathrm{fn}(Q)}{P\,|\,Q \xrightarrow{\tau} (\boldsymbol{\nu} m:T)(P'\,|\,Q')}$$

(OPEN)
$$\frac{P \xrightarrow{\overline{n}\langle m\rangle} P' \quad m\neq n}{(\boldsymbol{\nu} m:T)P \xrightarrow{(\boldsymbol{\nu} m:T)\,\overline{n}\langle m\rangle} P'}$$

(RES)
$$\frac{P \xrightarrow{\alpha} P' \quad n\notin\mathrm{fn}(\alpha)\cup\mathrm{bn}(\alpha)}{(\boldsymbol{\nu} n:T)P \xrightarrow{\alpha} (\boldsymbol{\nu} n:T)P'}$$

(REP-ACT)
$$\frac{P \xrightarrow{\alpha} P'}{!P \xrightarrow{\alpha} P'\,|\,!P}$$

rules for (SUM), (PAR), (COMM) and (CLOSE) in which the role of the left and right components are swapped.

Type System. Our type system corresponds to the basic type system for the π-calculus (see [22]). The main judgements take the form $\Gamma \vdash P$, where Γ is a type environment, that is a finite mapping from names and variables to types. Intuitively, $\Gamma \vdash P$ means that the process P uses all channels as input/output devices in accordance with their types, as given in Γ. The other, auxiliary, judgments are $\Gamma \vdash a : T$ stating that the name/variable a has type T in Γ, and $\Gamma \vdash \diamond$ stating that the type environment Γ is well formed. The typing rules are collected in Table 3, and they are based on the following rules of type formation, which prevent a channel of level δ from carrying values of level higher than δ.

(EMPTY TYPE)
$$\frac{}{\vdash \delta[\,]}$$

(CHANNEL TYPE)
$$\frac{\vdash T \quad \Lambda(T)\preceq\delta}{\vdash \delta[T]}$$

Notice that the type formation rules guarantee the absence of any explicit flow of information from a higher to a lower security level: for instance, the process $\overline{pub}\langle passwd\rangle.\mathbf{0}$ where a secret password is forwarded along a public channel, is not well-typed.

Table 3. Type System

$$\text{(EMPTY)}\ \frac{}{\emptyset \vdash \diamond} \qquad \text{(ENV } a\text{)}\ \frac{\Gamma \vdash \diamond \quad \vdash T \quad a \notin Dom(\Gamma)}{\Gamma, a : T \vdash \diamond} \qquad \text{(PROJECT)}\ \frac{\Gamma, a : T \vdash \diamond}{\Gamma, a : T \vdash a : T}$$

$$\text{(OUTPUT)}\ \frac{\Gamma \vdash a : \delta[T] \quad \Gamma \vdash b : T \quad \Gamma \vdash P}{\Gamma \vdash \overline{a}\langle b \rangle.P} \qquad \text{(INPUT)}\ \frac{\Gamma \vdash a : \delta[T] \quad \Gamma, x : T \vdash P}{\Gamma \vdash a(x : T).P}$$

$$\text{(MATCH)}\ \frac{\Gamma \vdash a : \delta[T] \quad \Gamma \vdash b : \delta[T] \quad \Gamma \vdash P \quad \Gamma \vdash Q}{\Gamma \vdash \mathsf{if}\ a = b\ \mathsf{then}\ P\ \mathsf{else}\ Q} \qquad \text{(PARA)}\ \frac{\Gamma \vdash P \quad \Gamma \vdash Q}{\Gamma \vdash P \mid Q}$$

$$\text{(RES)}\ \frac{\Gamma, n : T \vdash P}{\Gamma \vdash (\nu n : T)P} \qquad \text{(REPL)}\ \frac{\Gamma \vdash P}{\Gamma \vdash !P} \qquad \text{(DEAD)}\ \frac{\Gamma \vdash \diamond}{\Gamma \vdash \mathbf{0}}$$

3 Observation Equivalences Relative to a Security Level

In this section we introduce the notion of σ-level observation equivalence and we develop an equational theory for the π-calculus which is parametric on the security level (i.e., the observational power) of the observers.

Our equivalences are reminiscent of the typed behavioural equivalences for the π-calculus [2,13,15,22]: they are equivalences indexed by a type environment Γ ensuring that both the observed process and the observer associate the same security levels to the same names. Our equivalences, however, are much simpler than those in the above mentioned works since we do not consider subtyping nor linearity/affinity.

Our type-indexed relations are based on the notion of configuration. We say that $\Gamma \triangleright P$ is a *configuration* if Γ is a type environment and P is a process such that $\Gamma \vdash P$ [2]. A type-indexed relation over processes is a family of binary relations between processes indexed by type environments. We write $\Gamma \models P \mathcal{R} Q$ to mean that P and Q are related by $\mathcal{R}$ at Γ and $\Gamma \triangleright P$ and $\Gamma \triangleright Q$ are configurations.

To define our σ-level observation equivalences, we will ask for the largest type-indexed relation over processes which satisfies the following properties.

Reduction Closure. A type-indexed relation $\mathcal{R}$ over processes is *reduction closed* if $\Gamma \models P \mathcal{R} Q$ and $P \xrightarrow{\tau} P'$ imply that there exists Q' such that $Q \Longrightarrow Q'$ and $\Gamma \models P' \mathcal{R} Q'$, where $\Longrightarrow$ denotes the reflexive and transitive closure of $\xrightarrow{\tau}$.

[2] The two notations $\Gamma \triangleright P$ and $\Gamma \vdash P$ are essentially the same; however, we prefer to keep them distinct to make it uniform with the literature.

σ-Barb Preservation. Let $\sigma \in \Sigma$, P be a process and Γ a type environment such that $\Gamma \vdash P$. We write $\Gamma \models P\downarrow_n^\sigma$ if $P \stackrel{\overline{n}\langle m\rangle}{\longrightarrow}$ with $\Lambda(\Gamma(n)) \preceq \sigma$. We also write $\Gamma \models P \Downarrow_n^\sigma$ if there exists some P' such that $P \Longrightarrow P'$ and $\Gamma \models P' \downarrow_n^\sigma$. A type-indexed relation $\mathcal{R}$ over processes is *σ-barb preserving* if $\Gamma \models P \mathcal{R} Q$ and $\Gamma \models P\downarrow_n^\sigma$ imply $\Gamma \models Q \Downarrow_n^\sigma$.

σ-Contextuality. Let a typed context be a process with at most one typed hole $[\cdot_\Gamma]$. If $C[\cdot_\Gamma]$ is a typed context and P is a process such that $\Gamma \vdash P$, then we write $C[P]$ for the process obtained by replacing the hole in $C[\cdot_\Gamma]$ by P. In order to type contexts, the type system of Table 3 is extended with the following rule:

$$\text{(CTX)} \quad \frac{}{\Gamma, \Gamma' \vdash [\cdot_\Gamma]}$$

Proposition 1. *Let $\Gamma \vdash P$ and $\Gamma, \Gamma' \vdash C[\cdot_\Gamma]$, then $\Gamma, \Gamma' \vdash C[P]$.*

We are interested in σ-contexts that capture the idea of σ-level observers. Intuitively, a σ-context is an evaluation context which may interact with the process filling the hole just through channels of level at most σ.

Definition 1 (**σ-context**). *Let $\sigma \in \Sigma$. A context $C[\cdot_\Gamma]$ is a σ-context if there exists a type environment Γ' such that $\Gamma, \Gamma' \vdash C[\cdot_\Gamma]$ and $C[\cdot_\Gamma]$ is generated by the following grammar*

$$C[\cdot_\Gamma] \ ::= \ [\cdot_\Gamma] \ | \ (\boldsymbol{\nu} n{:}T)C[\cdot_\Gamma] \ | \ C[\cdot_\Gamma] \,|\, P \ | \ P \,|\, C[\cdot_\Gamma]$$

where P is a process such that $\forall n \in \mathrm{fn}(P)$ we have $\Lambda(\Gamma, \Gamma'(n)) \preceq \sigma$.

Example 1. Let Γ be the type environment $h : \top[\bot[]]$, $\ell : \bot[]$ and $\sigma \prec \top$. The context $(\boldsymbol{\nu} h)(\overline{h}\langle\ell\rangle \mid [\cdot_\Gamma])$ is not a σ-context since the process $\overline{h}\langle\ell\rangle$ in parallel with the hole has a free occurrence of the high name h. This context does not represent a σ-level observer since it can interact with a process filling the hole through the high channel h. On the other hand, $(\boldsymbol{\nu} h)(\overline{h}\langle\ell\rangle) \mid [\cdot_\Gamma]$ is a σ-context.

We say that a type-indexed relation $\mathcal{R}$ over processes is *σ-contextual* if $\Gamma \models P \mathcal{R} Q$ and $\Gamma, \Gamma' \vdash C[\cdot_\Gamma]$ imply $\Gamma, \Gamma' \models C[P] \mathcal{R} C[Q]$ for all σ-contexts $C[\cdot_\Gamma]$.

Definition 2 (**σ-Reduction Barbed Congruence $\cong_\sigma$**). *Let $\sigma \in \Sigma$. The σ-*reduction barbed congruence*, denoted by $\cong_\sigma$, is the largest type-indexed relation over processes which is symmetric, σ-contextual, reduction closed and σ-barb preserving.*

The following proposition is immediate.

Proposition 2. *Let $\sigma \in \Sigma$, Γ be a type environment and P, Q be processes such that $\Gamma \vdash P, Q$. If $\Gamma \models P \cong_\sigma Q$ then $\Gamma \models P \cong_{\sigma'} Q$ for all $\sigma' \preceq \sigma$. In particular, $\Gamma \models P \cong_\top Q$ implies $\Gamma \models P \cong_\sigma Q$ for all $\sigma \in \Sigma$.*

3.1 A Bisimulation-Based Proof Technique

In this section we develop a proof technique for the equivalences $\cong_\sigma$ defined above. More precisely, following [2,12,13], we define a LTS of *typed actions* (called typed

LTS) over configurations. As in [12], actions are parameterized over security levels and take the form

$$\Gamma \triangleright P \xrightarrow{\alpha}_{\delta} \Gamma' \triangleright P'$$

indicating that the process P in the type environment Γ can perform the action α to interact with some δ-level observer. In this case, we say that α is a *δ-level* action.

The rules of the typed LTS are obtained from those in Table 2 by taking into account the type environment Γ which records the security levels of the channels used by the process. Differently from [12], our typed actions are built around just a single type environment Γ constraining the observed process P. This differs from [12] where, due to the presence of subtyping, two distinct type environments are needed, one for the observer and the other for the observed process.

The rules of the typed LTS are reported in Table 4; note that there is an additional input action of the form $(\boldsymbol{\nu} m{:}T)\, n(m)$ occurring when the process receives a new name m generated by the environment.

Relying on the typed LTS, we now introduce the *bisimilarity on σ-actions* which provides a coinductive characterization of σ-reduction barbed congruence $\cong_\sigma$.

With an abuse of notation, we write $\Longrightarrow$ for the reflexive and transitive closure of $\xrightarrow{\tau}_{\delta}$. We also write $\stackrel{\alpha}{\Longrightarrow}_{\delta}$ for $\Longrightarrow \xrightarrow{\alpha}_{\delta} \Longrightarrow$, and $\stackrel{\hat{\alpha}}{\Longrightarrow}_{\delta}$ for $\Longrightarrow$ if $\alpha = \tau$ and $\stackrel{\alpha}{\Longrightarrow}_{\delta}$ otherwise.

Definition 3 (Bisimilarity on σ-actions $\approx_\sigma$). *Let $\sigma \in \Sigma$. Bisimilarity on σ-actions is the largest symmetric relation $\approx_\sigma$ over configurations, such that whenever $(\Gamma \triangleright P) \approx_\sigma (\Gamma \triangleright Q)$, if $\Gamma \triangleright P \xrightarrow{\alpha}_{\sigma} \Gamma' \triangleright P'$, then there exists Q' such that $\Gamma \triangleright Q \stackrel{\hat{\alpha}}{\Longrightarrow}_{\sigma} \Gamma' \triangleright Q'$ and $(\Gamma' \triangleright Q') \approx_\sigma (\Gamma' \triangleright P')$.*

In the following, for a given relation $\mathcal{R}$ over configurations, we write $\Gamma \models P \;\mathcal{R}\; Q$ whenever $(\Gamma \triangleright P) \;\mathcal{R}\; (\Gamma \triangleright Q)$.

Theorem 1. *Let $\sigma \in \Sigma$, Γ be a type environment and P, Q be processes such that $\Gamma \vdash P, Q$. $\Gamma \models P \cong_\sigma Q$ if and only if $\Gamma \models P \approx_\sigma Q$.*

4 Noninterference

In this section we introduce a notion of noninterference for processes of the typed π-calculus which uses the σ-reduction barbed congruence $\cong_\sigma$ as observation equivalence. This property, called $\mathcal{NI}(\cong_\sigma)$, is inspired by the *P_BNDC* property defined in [9] for CCS processes; it requires that no information flow should occur even in the presence of *active* malicious processes, e.g., Trojan Horse programs, that run at the classified (higher than σ) level.

We start by introducing the following notations:

- We say that a configuration $\Gamma' \triangleright P'$ is *reachable* from a configuration $\Gamma \triangleright P$, written $\Gamma \triangleright P \rightsquigarrow \Gamma' \triangleright P'$, if there exist $n \geq 0$, $\alpha_1, \ldots, \alpha_n$ and $\sigma_1, \ldots, \sigma_n$ such that $\Gamma \triangleright P \xrightarrow{\alpha_1}_{\sigma_1} \xrightarrow{\alpha_2}_{\sigma_2} \cdots \xrightarrow{\alpha_n}_{\sigma_n} \Gamma' \triangleright P'$. (Notice that the concept of reachability is independent from the levels σ_i.)

Table 4. Typed LTS for π-calculus

(OUT)
$$\frac{\Gamma \vdash n : \delta_1[T] \quad \delta_1 \preceq \delta}{\Gamma \triangleright \overline{n}\langle m \rangle.P \xrightarrow{\overline{n}\langle m \rangle}_{\delta} \Gamma \triangleright P}$$

(IN)
$$\frac{\Gamma \vdash n : \delta_1[T] \quad \Gamma \vdash m : T \quad \delta_1 \preceq \delta}{\Gamma \triangleright n(x{:}T).P \xrightarrow{n(m)}_{\delta} \Gamma \triangleright P\{x := m\}}$$

(WEAK)
$$\frac{\Gamma, m : T \triangleright P \xrightarrow{n(m)}_{\delta} \Gamma' \triangleright P'}{\Gamma \triangleright P \xrightarrow{(\nu m:T)\, n(m)}_{\delta} \Gamma' \triangleright P'}$$

(PAR)
$$\frac{\Gamma \triangleright P \xrightarrow{\alpha}_{\delta} \Gamma' \triangleright P' \quad \mathrm{bn}(\alpha) \cap \mathrm{fn}(Q) = \emptyset}{\Gamma \triangleright P \mid Q \xrightarrow{\alpha}_{\delta} \Gamma' \triangleright P' \mid Q}$$

(RED)
$$\frac{P \xrightarrow{\tau} P'}{\Gamma \triangleright P \xrightarrow{\tau}_{\delta} \Gamma \triangleright P'}$$

(OPEN)
$$\frac{\Gamma, m{:}T \triangleright P \xrightarrow{\overline{n}\langle m \rangle}_{\delta} \Gamma' \triangleright P' \quad m \neq n}{\Gamma \triangleright (\nu m{:}T)P \xrightarrow{(\nu m:T)\, \overline{n}\langle m \rangle}_{\delta} \Gamma' \triangleright P'}$$

(RES)
$$\frac{\Gamma, n{:}T \triangleright P \xrightarrow{\alpha}_{\delta} \Gamma', n{:}T \triangleright P' \quad n \notin \mathrm{fn}(\alpha) \cup \mathrm{bn}(\alpha)}{\Gamma \triangleright (\nu n{:}T)P \xrightarrow{\alpha}_{\delta} \Gamma' \triangleright (\nu n{:}T)P'}$$

(REP-ACT)
$$\frac{\Gamma \triangleright P \xrightarrow{\alpha}_{\delta} \Gamma' \triangleright P'}{\Gamma \triangleright !P \xrightarrow{\alpha}_{\delta} \Gamma' \triangleright P' \mid !P}$$

- Given a type environment Γ, we say that a process P is a *σ-high level source* in Γ, written $P \in \mathcal{H}^{\sigma}_{\Gamma}$, if $\Gamma \vdash P$ and either $\Gamma \triangleright P \stackrel{\alpha}{\not\longrightarrow}_{\delta}$ (i.e., $\Gamma \triangleright P$ does not perform any action) or if $\Gamma \triangleright P \xrightarrow{\alpha}_{\delta} \Gamma' \triangleright P'$ then $\sigma \prec \delta$ and $\Gamma' \triangleright P'$ is a σ-high level source. In other words, a σ-high level source can only perform δ-level actions with $\sigma \prec \delta$. Notice that this definition does not prevent a σ-high level source from communicating σ-low values (along σ-high channels).
- Given a security level $\sigma \in \Sigma$, we write $\Gamma \triangleright P \xrightarrow{\alpha}^{\sigma} \Gamma' \triangleright P'$ (with a superscript σ) if whenever $\Gamma \triangleright P \xrightarrow{\alpha}_{\delta} \Gamma' \triangleright P'$ then $\sigma \prec \delta$. In this case we say that $\Gamma \triangleright P$ has performed a *σ-high level action*. We define $\stackrel{\hat{\alpha}}{\Longrightarrow}^{\sigma}$ accordingly.

A process P in a type environment Γ satisfies the property $\mathcal{NI}(\cong_\sigma)$ if for every configuration $\Gamma' \triangleright P'$ reachable from $\Gamma \triangleright P$ and for every σ-high level source H, a σ-level user cannot distinguish, in the sense of $\cong_\sigma$, $\Gamma' \triangleright P'$ from $\Gamma' \triangleright P' \mid H$. The formal definition of $\mathcal{NI}(\cong_\sigma)$ is as follows.

Definition 4 (σ-**Noninterference**). *Let $\sigma \in \Sigma$, P be a process and Γ be a type environment such that $\Gamma \vdash P$. The process P satisfies the* σ-noninterference property *in Γ,* *written* $\Gamma \triangleright P \in \mathcal{NI}(\cong_\sigma)$, *if for all* $\Gamma' \triangleright P'$ *such that* $\Gamma \triangleright P \rightsquigarrow \Gamma' \triangleright P'$ *and for all* $H \in \mathcal{H}^\sigma_{\Gamma'}$ *it holds* $\Gamma' \models P' \cong_\sigma P' \mid H$.

Example 2. In the following examples, we assume just two security levels: H and L with $\mathsf{L} \prec \mathsf{H}$; let also h be a high level channel and ℓ, ℓ_1, ℓ_2 be low level channels. Let Γ be the type environment $h : \mathsf{H}[\,],\ \ell : \mathsf{L}[\,],\ \ell_1 : \mathsf{L}[\,],\ \ell_2 : \mathsf{L}[\,]$ and $\sigma = \mathsf{L}$.

Let us first consider the following simple insecure process: $P_1 = h().\ell() \mid \overline{h}\langle\rangle$. To show that $\Gamma \triangleright P_1 \notin \mathcal{NI}(\cong_\sigma)$ it is sufficient to consider the configuration $\Gamma \triangleright P_1'$ with $P_1' = h().\ell()$ that is reachable from $\Gamma \triangleright P_1$ after performing the output action $\overline{h}\langle\rangle$. The process P_1' is clearly insecure in the type environment Γ since the low level, observable, action $\ell()$ directly depends on the high level input $h()$. Indeed, by choosing $H = \overline{h}\langle\rangle$ one can easily observe that $\Gamma \models P_1' \not\cong_\sigma P_1' \mid H$.

Let us consider a further classic example of insecure process, that is $P_2 = h(x : T).\mathsf{if}\ x = n\ \mathsf{then}\ \overline{\ell_1}\langle\rangle\ \mathsf{else}\ \overline{\ell_2}\langle\rangle$ in the type environment $\Gamma' = h : \mathsf{H}[T],\ \ell_i : \mathsf{L}[\,],\ n : T$ (here the security level of n is irrelevant). To show that $\Gamma' \triangleright P_2 \notin \mathcal{NI}(\cong_\sigma)$ one can choose $H = \overline{h}\langle n\rangle$, where $H \in \mathcal{H}^\sigma_{\Gamma'}$ independently on the level of n, and observe that $\Gamma' \vdash P_2 \not\cong_\sigma P_2 \mid H$. Intuitively, when n is a high level name, a low level observer may infer from P_2 the value of the high level variable x, which is clearly unsound.

Finally, consider the process $P_3 = P_2 \mid \overline{h}\langle n\rangle \mid \overline{h}\langle m\rangle$, where the variable x can be nondeterministically substituted either with n or m. P_3 is still an insecure process since an external attack can destroy the nondeterminism causing an interference: for instance, if $H = h(y).h(z).\overline{h}\langle n\rangle$, then $\Gamma' \models P_3 \not\cong_\sigma P_3 \mid H$.

Building on the ideas developed in [3] for a class of persistent noninterference properties for CCS processes, we provide a characterization of $\mathcal{NI}(\cong_\sigma)$ in terms of an unwinding condition. Intuitively, the unwinding condition specifies local constraints on the typed actions of the system which imply the global security property. More precisely, our unwinding condition ensures that no σ-high action α leading to a configuration C is observable by a σ-low user, as there always exists a configuration C', σ-equivalent to C, that the system may reach without performing α.

Definition 5 (σ-Unwinding Condition). *Let* $\sigma \in \Sigma$, P *be a process and* Γ *be a type environment such that* $\Gamma \vdash P$. *The process* P *satisfies the* σ*-unwinding condition in* Γ, *written* $\Gamma \triangleright P \in \mathcal{W}(\cong_\sigma)$, *if for all* $\Gamma' \triangleright P_1$ *such that* $\Gamma \triangleright P \rightsquigarrow \Gamma' \triangleright P_1$

- *if* $\Gamma' \triangleright P_1 \xrightarrow{\alpha}{}^{\sigma} \Gamma' \triangleright P_2$ *with* $\alpha \in \{\overline{n}\langle m\rangle,\ n(m)\}$, *then* $\exists P_3$ *such that* $\Gamma' \triangleright P_1 \Longrightarrow \Gamma' \triangleright P_3$ *and* $\Gamma' \models P_2 \cong_\sigma P_3$;
- *if* $\Gamma' \triangleright P_1 \xrightarrow{\alpha}{}^{\sigma} \Gamma', m{:}T \triangleright P_2$ *with* $\alpha \in \{(\boldsymbol{\nu} m{:}T)\,\overline{n}\langle m\rangle,\ (\boldsymbol{\nu} m{:}T)\,n(m)\}$, *then* $\exists P_3$ *such that* $\Gamma' \triangleright P_1 \Longrightarrow \Gamma' \triangleright P_3$ *and* $\Gamma' \models P_3 \cong_\sigma (\boldsymbol{\nu} m{:}T)P_2$.

This unwinding-based schema characterizes a notion of security with respect to all *passive attacks* which try to infer information about the classified behavior just by observing the σ-level behaviour of the system.

Both properties $\mathcal{NI}(\cong_\sigma)$ and $\mathcal{W}(\cong_\sigma)$ are persistent, as stated in the following proposition.

Proposition 3 (Persistence). *Let* $\sigma \in \Sigma$, P *be a process and* Γ *be a type environment such that* $\Gamma \vdash P$. *For all* $\Gamma' \triangleright P'$ *such that* $\Gamma \triangleright P \rightsquigarrow \Gamma' \triangleright P'$ *it holds*

– *if* $\Gamma \triangleright P \in \mathcal{NI}(\cong_\sigma)$ *then* $\Gamma' \triangleright P' \in \mathcal{NI}(\cong_\sigma)$.
– *if* $\Gamma \triangleright P \in \mathcal{W}(\cong_\sigma)$ *then* $\Gamma' \triangleright P' \in \mathcal{W}(\cong_\sigma)$.

The equivalence of properties $\mathcal{NI}(\cong_\sigma)$ and $\mathcal{W}(\cong_\sigma)$ is stated below.

Theorem 2. *Let* $\sigma \in \Sigma$, *P be a process and* Γ *be a type environment such that* $\Gamma \vdash P$. $\Gamma \triangleright P \in \mathcal{NI}(\cong_\sigma)$ *if and only if* $\Gamma \triangleright P \in \mathcal{W}(\cong_\sigma)$.

The unwinding-based characterization of σ-noninterfering processes provides a better understanding of the operational semantics of secure processes. Moreover, it allows one to define efficient proof techniques for σ-noninterference just by inspecting the typed LTS of processes. Notice that the σ-unwinding condition $\mathcal{W}(\cong_\sigma)$ is decidable over the class of finite state processes, i.e., processes whose typed LTS is finite. Moreover, by exploiting the following compositionality results, the unwinding condition $\mathcal{W}(\cong_\sigma)$ can be used to define methods, e.g., proof systems, both to check the security of complex systems and to incrementally build processes which are secure by construction.

Theorem 3 (Compositionality of $\mathcal{W}(\cong_\sigma)$). *Let* $\sigma \in \Sigma$, P *and* Q *be processes and* Γ *be a type environment such that* $\Gamma \vdash P, Q$. *If* $\Gamma \triangleright P \in \mathcal{W}(\cong_\sigma)$ *and* $\Gamma \triangleright Q \in \mathcal{W}(\cong_\sigma)$ *then*

– $\Gamma, \Gamma' \triangleright \overline{a}\langle b\rangle.P \in \mathcal{W}(\cong_\sigma)$ *where* $\Gamma, \Gamma' \vdash a : \delta[T]$, $\Gamma, \Gamma' \vdash b : T$ *and* $\delta \preceq \sigma$;
– $\Gamma, \Gamma' \triangleright a(x : T).P \in \mathcal{W}(\cong_\sigma)$ *where* $\Gamma, \Gamma' \vdash a : \delta[T]$ *and* $\delta \preceq \sigma$;
– $\Gamma, \Gamma' \triangleright \mathsf{if}\ a = b\ \mathsf{then}\ P\ \mathsf{else}\ Q \in \mathcal{W}(\cong_\sigma)$ *where* $\Gamma, \Gamma' \vdash a : T$ *and* $\Gamma, \Gamma' \vdash b : T$;
– $\Gamma \triangleright P \mid Q \in \mathcal{W}(\cong_\sigma)$;
– $\Gamma' \triangleright (\boldsymbol{\nu} n : T)P \in \mathcal{W}(\cong_\sigma)$ *where* $\Gamma = \Gamma', n : T$;
– $\Gamma \triangleright !P \in \mathcal{W}(\cong_\sigma)$.

Example 3. Let P and Q be finite state processes and Γ be a type environment such that $\Gamma \vdash P, Q$. Although $R = !P \mid Q$ might be an infinite state process, one can easily check whether $\Gamma \triangleright R \in \mathcal{NI}(\cong_\sigma)$ just by exploiting the decidability of $\Gamma \triangleright P \in \mathcal{W}(\cong_\sigma)$ and $\Gamma \triangleright Q \in \mathcal{W}(\cong_\sigma)$ and the compositionality of $\mathcal{NI}(\cong_\sigma)$ with respect to the parallel composition and replication operators.

4.1 Noninterference Through a Partial Equivalence Relation

In [21,20] the notion of noninterference for sequential and multithreaded programs is expressed in terms of a partial equivalence relation (*per* model) which captures the view of a σ-level observer. Intuitively, a configuration C, representing a program and the current state of the memory, is secure if $C \sim_\sigma C$ where $\sim_\sigma$ is a symmetric and transitive relation modeling the σ-level observation of program executions. The relation $\sim_\sigma$ is in general not reflexive, but it becomes reflexive over the set of secure configurations.

Below we show how this approach can be adapted to the π-calculus to characterize the class of σ-noninterfering processes. We first introduce the following notion of partial bisimilarity up to σ-high actions, $\dot{\approx}_\sigma$. Intuitively, $\dot{\approx}_\sigma$ requires that σ-high actions are simulated by internal transitions, while on the remaining actions it behaves as $\approx_\sigma$.

Definition 6 (Partial Bisimilarity up to σ-high actions $\dot{\approx}_\sigma$). *Let* $\sigma \in \Sigma$. *Partial bisimilarity up to* σ*-high actions is the largest symmetric relation* $\dot{\approx}_\sigma$ *over configurations, such that whenever* $\Gamma \models P \dot{\approx}_\sigma Q$

– *if* $\Gamma \triangleright P \xrightarrow{\alpha}_{\sigma} \Gamma' \triangleright P'$, *then there exists* Q' *such that* $\Gamma \triangleright Q \stackrel{\hat{\alpha}}{\Longrightarrow}_{\sigma} \Gamma' \triangleright Q'$ *with* $\Gamma' \models Q' \dot{\approx}_{\sigma} P'$.
– *if* $\Gamma \triangleright P \xrightarrow{\alpha}^{\sigma} \Gamma \triangleright P'$ *with* $\alpha \in \{\overline{n}\langle m\rangle, n(m)\}$, *then there exists* Q' *such that* $\Gamma \triangleright Q \Longrightarrow \Gamma \triangleright Q'$ *with* $\Gamma \models Q' \dot{\approx}_{\sigma} P'$.
– *if* $\Gamma \triangleright P \xrightarrow{\alpha}^{\sigma} \Gamma, m : T \triangleright P'$ *with* $\alpha \in \{(\boldsymbol{\nu} m{:}T)\,\overline{n}\langle m\rangle, (\boldsymbol{\nu} m{:}T)\, n(m)\}$, *then there exists* Q' *such that* $\Gamma \triangleright Q \Longrightarrow \Gamma \triangleright Q'$ *with* $\Gamma \models Q' \dot{\approx}_{\sigma} (\boldsymbol{\nu} m : T)P'$ *and* $\Gamma, m : T \models P' \dot{\approx}_{\sigma} P'$.

The relation $\dot{\approx}_{\sigma}$ is a partial equivalence relation, i.e., it is not reflexive. In fact, if we consider the process $P = \overline{h}\langle\rangle.\overline{\ell}\langle\rangle.\mathbf{0}$ and the type environment $\Gamma = h : \top[], \ell : \bot[]$ we get $\Gamma \models P \not\dot{\approx}_{\sigma} P$ when $\sigma = \bot$.

The next theorem states that relation $\dot{\approx}_{\sigma}$ is reflexive on the set of well typed noninterfering processes. The proof exploits a sort of persistence property of $\dot{\approx}_{\sigma}$, that is: if $\Gamma \models P \dot{\approx}_{\sigma} P$, then for all $\Gamma' \triangleright P'$ such that $\Gamma \triangleright P \rightsquigarrow \Gamma' \triangleright P'$, it holds $\Gamma' \models P' \dot{\approx}_{\sigma} P'$.

Theorem 4. *Let* $\sigma \in \Sigma$, P *be a process and* Γ *be a type environment such that* $\Gamma \vdash P$. $\Gamma \triangleright P \in \mathcal{NI}(\cong_{\sigma})$ *if and only if* $\Gamma \models P \dot{\approx}_{\sigma} P$.

4.2 Noninterference Through Name Restriction

In [9] the *P_BNDC* property for CCS processes is characterized in terms of a single bisimulation-like equivalence check. We show that the same idea can be applied to the π-calculus. Let us first introduce the following definition.

Definition 7. *Let* $\sigma \in \Sigma$, P *be a process and* Γ *be a type environment such that* $\Gamma \vdash P$. *We denote by* $(\boldsymbol{\nu}^{\sigma})P$ *the process* $(\boldsymbol{\nu} m_1{:}T_1)\ldots(\boldsymbol{\nu} m_k{:}T_k)P$ *where* $m_1, \ldots m_k$ *are all the free names occurring in* P *such that* $\Gamma(m_i) = T_i$ *and* $\Lambda(T_i) \succ \sigma$.

Definition 6 of partial bisimilarity up to σ-high actions can be modified as follows in order to obtain an equivalence relation.

Definition 8 (Bisimilarity up to σ-high actions $\ddot{\approx}_{\sigma}$). *Let* $\sigma \in \Sigma$. *Bisimilarity up to* σ*-high actions is the largest symmetric relation* $\ddot{\approx}_{\sigma}$ *over configurations, such that whenever* $\Gamma \models P \ddot{\approx}_{\sigma} Q$

– *if* $\Gamma \triangleright P \xrightarrow{\alpha}_{\sigma} \Gamma' \triangleright P'$, *then there exists* Q' *such that* $\Gamma \triangleright Q \stackrel{\hat{\alpha}}{\Longrightarrow}_{\sigma} \Gamma' \triangleright Q'$ *with* $\Gamma' \models Q' \ddot{\approx}_{\sigma} P'$.
– *if* $\Gamma \triangleright P \xrightarrow{\alpha}^{\sigma} \Gamma \triangleright P'$ *with* $\alpha \in \{\overline{n}\langle m\rangle, n(m)\}$, *then there exists* Q' *such that either* $\Gamma \triangleright Q \stackrel{\hat{\alpha}}{\Longrightarrow}^{\sigma} \Gamma \triangleright Q'$ *with* $\Gamma \models Q' \ddot{\approx}_{\sigma} P'$ *or* $\Gamma \triangleright Q \Longrightarrow \Gamma \triangleright Q'$ *with* $\Gamma \models Q' \ddot{\approx}_{\sigma} P'$.
– *if* $\Gamma \triangleright P \xrightarrow{\alpha}^{\sigma} \Gamma, m : T \triangleright P'$ *with* $\alpha \in \{(\boldsymbol{\nu} m{:}T)\,\overline{n}\langle m\rangle, (\boldsymbol{\nu} m{:}T)\, n(m)\}$, *then there exists* Q' *such that either* $\Gamma \triangleright Q \stackrel{\hat{\alpha}}{\Longrightarrow}^{\sigma} \Gamma, m : T \triangleright Q'$ *with* $\Gamma, m : T \models Q' \ddot{\approx}_{\sigma} P'$ *or* $\Gamma \triangleright Q \Longrightarrow \Gamma \triangleright Q'$ *with* $\Gamma \models Q' \ddot{\approx}_{\sigma} (\boldsymbol{\nu} m : T)P'$ *and* $\Gamma, m : T \models P' \ddot{\approx}_{\sigma} (\boldsymbol{\nu}^{\sigma})P'$.

We can now characterize $\mathcal{NI}(\cong_{\sigma})$ in terms of a single equivalence check between P and $(\boldsymbol{\nu}^{\sigma})P$ through $\ddot{\approx}_{\sigma}$. The proof of the next theorem exploits the fact that if $\Gamma \models P \ddot{\approx}_{\sigma} (\boldsymbol{\nu}^{\sigma})P$, then for all $\Gamma' \triangleright P'$ such that $\Gamma \triangleright P \rightsquigarrow \Gamma' \triangleright P'$, it holds $\Gamma' \models P' \ddot{\approx}_{\sigma} (\boldsymbol{\nu}^{\sigma})P'$.

Theorem 5. *Let $\sigma \in \Sigma$, P be a program and Γ be a type environment such that $\Gamma \vdash P$. $\Gamma \rhd P \in \mathcal{NI}(\cong_\sigma)$ if and only if $\Gamma \models P \ddot{\approx}_\sigma (\boldsymbol{\nu}^\sigma)P$.*

Corollary 1. *Let $\sigma \in \Sigma$, P be a process and Γ be a type environment such that $\Gamma \vdash P$ and $\forall n \in \mathrm{fn}(P)$, $\Lambda(\Gamma(n)) \preceq \sigma$ (i.e., P has no free σ-high level names). Then $\Gamma \rhd P \in \mathcal{NI}(\cong_\sigma)$.*

Example 4. Let us consider the processes $P_1 = h().\ell() \mid \overline{h}\langle\rangle$ and $P_3 = h(x{:}T).\mathsf{if}\ x = n\ \mathsf{then}\ \overline{\ell_1}\langle\rangle\ \mathsf{else}\ \overline{\ell_2}\langle\rangle \mid \overline{h}\langle n\rangle \mid \overline{h}\langle m\rangle$ and the type environments Γ and Γ' of Example 2. We have seen that $\Gamma \rhd P_1 \notin \mathcal{NI}(\cong_\sigma)$ and $\Gamma' \rhd P_3 \notin \mathcal{NI}(\cong_\sigma)$. Now, by Corollary 1, we can immediately state that both $\Gamma \rhd (\boldsymbol{\nu}h)P_1 \in \mathcal{NI}(\cong_\sigma)$ and $\Gamma' \rhd (\boldsymbol{\nu}h)P_3 \in \mathcal{NI}(\cong_\sigma)$.

Notice that a process whose free names have a security level higher than σ is, in general, not secure. For instance, let Γ be the type environment $h : \top[\bot[\,]],\ \ell : \bot[\,]$ and P be the process $h(x{:}\bot[\,]).\overline{x}\langle\rangle$. Assuming that $\sigma \prec \top$, we have that the only free name h occurring in P has a security level higher than σ. It is easy to see that $\Gamma \rhd P \notin \mathcal{NI}(\cong_\sigma)$: in fact, by choosing $H = \overline{h}\langle\ell\rangle$, we have $\Gamma \models P \not\cong_\sigma P \mid H$, that is P is insecure.

We conclude this section observing that, as in [8] for CCS, the definition of σ-noninterference can be also expressed in terms of bisimilarity on $\top$-actions over well-typed processes whose σ-high level names are restricted. This comes as a corollary of the following property.

Proposition 4. *Let $\sigma \in \Sigma$, P and Q be two processes and Γ be a type environment such that $\Gamma \vdash P, Q$. $\Gamma \models P \approx_\sigma Q$ if and only if $\Gamma \models (\boldsymbol{\nu}^\sigma)P \approx_\top (\boldsymbol{\nu}^\sigma)Q$.*

Corollary 2. *Let $\sigma \in \Sigma$, P be a process and Γ be a type environment such that $\Gamma \vdash P$. $\Gamma \rhd P \in \mathcal{NI}(\cong_\sigma)$ if and only if for all $\Gamma' \rhd P'$ such that $\Gamma \rhd P \rightsquigarrow \Gamma' \rhd P'$ and for all $H \in \mathcal{H}^\sigma_{\Gamma'}$ it holds $\Gamma' \models (\boldsymbol{\nu}^\sigma)P' \approx_\top (\boldsymbol{\nu}^\sigma)(P' \mid H)$.*

5 Examples

In this section we show a couple of examples that illustrate the expressiveness of our approach. In the following, we use a CCS-style for channels that do not carry values, writing simply n and $\overline{n}$ instead of $n()$ and $\overline{n}\langle\rangle$. Moreover, we assume just two security levels: H and L with $\mathsf{L} \prec \mathsf{H}$ and we let $\sigma = \mathsf{L}$.

Example 5. Consider the process $P = (\boldsymbol{\nu}h{:}\mathsf{H}[\,])(\overline{h} \mid !\,h.k.\overline{h}) \mid \overline{k}.\ell$ in the type environment $\Gamma = k : \mathsf{H}[\,], \ell : \mathsf{L}[\,]$. The process P is secure since $\Gamma \models P \ddot{\approx}_\sigma (\boldsymbol{\nu}^\sigma)P$. Indeed, let $\mathcal{S}$ be the symmetric closure of the following relation:

$$\begin{array}{l}\{\ (P, (\boldsymbol{\nu}^\sigma)P),\ (P_1, (\boldsymbol{\nu}^\sigma)P_1),\ (P_2, (\boldsymbol{\nu}^\sigma)P_2),\ (P_3, (\boldsymbol{\nu}^\sigma)P_3),\ (P_4, (\boldsymbol{\nu}^\sigma)P_4),\\ \quad (P_5, (\boldsymbol{\nu}^\sigma)P_5),\ (P, (\boldsymbol{\nu}^\sigma)P_1),\ (P_3, (\boldsymbol{\nu}^\sigma)P_4),\ (P_2, (\boldsymbol{\nu}^\sigma)P_5)\ \}\end{array}$$

where

$$\begin{array}{ll} P_1 = (\boldsymbol{\nu}h)(k.\overline{h} \mid !\,h.k.\overline{h}) \mid \overline{k}.\ell & P_4 = (\boldsymbol{\nu}h)(k.\overline{h} \mid !\,h.k.\overline{h}) \\ P_2 = (\boldsymbol{\nu}h)(\overline{h} \mid !\,h.k.\overline{h}) \mid \ell & P_5 = (\boldsymbol{\nu}h)(k.\overline{h} \mid !\,h.k.\overline{h}) \mid \ell \\ P_3 = (\boldsymbol{\nu}h)(\overline{h} \mid !\,h.k.\overline{h}) & \end{array}$$

It is straightforward to prove that $\mathcal{S}$ is a bisimulation up to high actions, i.e. $\mathcal{S} \subseteq \ddot{\approx}_\sigma$.

Example 6. Job Scheduler. Assume that there are n jobs $P_1, \ldots, P_n$ whose execution must be scheduled. We implement the scheduler as the parallel composition of two threads: the first one produces a numbered token and assigns it to the next job. The second thread consumes a token checking if its number corresponds to the next scheduled job. Let be $Scheduler = Produce \mid Consume$, with

$$\begin{aligned} Produce &= (\nu p{:}T)(\overline{p}\langle 1\rangle \mid !\,p(x{:}\mathsf{L}[\mathsf{L}[]]).enqueue(y{:}\mathsf{L}[\mathsf{L}[]]).(\overline{y}\langle x\rangle \mid \overline{p}\langle x+1\rangle)) \\ Consume &= (\nu c{:}T)(\overline{c}\langle 1\rangle \mid !\,c(x{:}\mathsf{L}[\mathsf{L}[]]).check(y{:}\mathsf{L}[\mathsf{L}[]]). \\ &\qquad \mathsf{if}\ x = y\ \mathsf{then}\ (\overline{y}\langle ok\rangle \mid ack.\overline{c}\langle x+1\rangle)\mathsf{else}\ (\overline{y}\langle no\rangle \mid \overline{c}\langle x\rangle)\ ) \end{aligned}$$

where the channels *enqueue* and *check* are used by jobs respectively to get a token and to exhibit it to the scheduler. Jobs are then written as follows:

$$\begin{aligned} Job_i = (\nu j{:}\mathsf{L}[\mathsf{L}[]])(\overline{enqueue}\langle j\rangle.j(y{:}\mathsf{L}[\mathsf{L}[]]). \\ (\nu l{:}\mathsf{L}[])(\overline{l} \mid !\,l.\overline{check}\langle y\rangle.y(z{:}\mathsf{L}[]).\mathsf{if}\ z = ok\ \mathsf{then}\ P_i.\overline{ack}\ \mathsf{else}\ \overline{l})) \end{aligned}$$

First, a job asks for a token and waits for it along the private channel j. The job then starts a loop where it repeatedly exhibits the token to the scheduler, waiting for its turn to be executed. The loop ends when the job receives the *ok* message, so that it can run the process P, and signal its end using the *ack* channel.

The system $Scheduler \mid Job_1 \mid \cdots \mid Job_n$ can be proved to be secure if we rely on the following type assignment, where the two private channels c and p are high-level, while tokens are low level value (of suitable arity), and the channels *enqueue* and *check* are low level as well.

$$c, p : T \triangleq \mathsf{H}[\mathsf{L}[\mathsf{L}[]]],\quad enqueue, check : \mathsf{L}[\mathsf{L}[\mathsf{L}[]]],\quad 1, 2, \ldots : \mathsf{L}[\mathsf{L}[]],\quad ok, no, ack : \mathsf{L}[]$$

The fact that the system is secure comes easily by Corollary 1 since there are no free high level names.

6 Conclusion and Related Work

In this paper we develop a theory of noninterference for processes of the typed π-calculus. In the literature there are a number of works which study type-based techniques for noninterference. A few of them are discussed in the following.

Hennessy and Riely [14,12] consider a typed version of the asynchronous π-calculus where types associate read/write capabilities to channels as well as security clearances. They study noninterference properties based on may and must equivalences. A similar study is conducted by Pottier [18] relying on the synchronous π-calculus and bisimulation equivalence. Honda, Yoshida, Vasconcelos and Berger [15,16,25] consider advanced type systems for the linear/affine π-calculus and express noninterference in terms of typed bisimulation equivalences. Their type systems guarantee that every communication on a linear channel must eventually succeed, and so its success alone does not carry any information. For instance, the process $h().\overline{\ell}\langle\rangle$, which waits an input on the secret channel h and then performs the low-level output $\overline{\ell}\langle\rangle$, is considered secure as long as h is a linear channel. Similarly, Zdancewic and Myers [26] propose a type system dealing with linear channels in a concurrent language with (a restricted form of) join-patterns as synchronization primitives. Furthermore, their type system controls the temporal ordering of communications on linear channels. Kobayashi [17] presents an even more flexible type system which can deal with arbitrary usage of channels, so that programs using various concurrency primitives (including locks) can be encoded into the π-calculus and analyzed.

The typing constraints imposed by the type systems discussed above allow one to reason only on a limited class of processes and contexts. For instance the process $!x(y).P|!x(y).Q$ is rejected by the type system of, e.g., [16] and thus it is considered insecure independently of the security level of its channels. As another example, when h is a nonlinear channel, the process $(\boldsymbol{\nu} h)(h().\ell() \mid \overline{h}\langle\rangle)$ is never typed in most of the mentioned type systems. However, this process does not leak any secret information, as shown in Example 4.

Our approach relies on a much simpler typing discipline which does not deal with implicit information flow. Instead, we characterize secure processes in terms of the actions they perform. The use of a lighter type system leads to stronger noninterference properties, that check the security of processes against a bigger class of attackers. Compared with the literature discussed so far, such properties could be considered too restrictive. Nevertheless, they are more suitable in contexts with partial trust, where it would be not realistic to assume that attackers are well typed in a strong way. Interestingly, we can increase the flexibility of our approach by admitting mechanisms for *downgrading* or *declassifying* information as done in [4] for CCS. This would allow the process $h().\overline{\ell}\langle\rangle$ to be deemed secure by declassifying the high action $h()$.

Another difference with respect to previous works is that they deal with open terms, while our theory applies to closed processes. However, the results presented in this paper scale to open terms by: (1) introducing the open extension of $\cong_\sigma$ as the type-indexed relation $\cong_\sigma^o$ over terms such that $\Gamma \models T \cong_\sigma^o U$ if and only if $\Gamma' \models T\rho \cong_\sigma U\rho$ for all closing substitution ρ which respects[3] Γ with Γ', and (2) saying that a term T satisfies the *σ-noninterference property in Γ* if for all closing substitution ρ which respects Γ with Γ', it holds $\Gamma' \triangleright T\rho \in \mathcal{NI}(\cong_\sigma)$.

References

1. C. Bodei, P. Degano, F. Nielson, and H. Riis Nielson. Static analysis for the pi-calculus with applications to security. *Information and Computation*, 168:69–92, 2001.
2. M. Boreale and D. Sangiorgi. Bisimulation in Name-Passing Calculi without Matching. In *Proc. of 13th IEEE Symposium on Logic in Computer Science (LICS'98)*, pages 165–175. IEEE Computer Society Press, 1998.
3. A. Bossi, R. Focardi, C. Piazza, and S. Rossi. Verifying Persistent Security Properties. *Computer Languages, Systems and Structures*, 30(3-4):231–258, 2004.
4. A. Bossi, C. Piazza, and S. Rossi. Modelling Downgrading in Information Flow Security. In *Proc. of the 17th IEEE Computer Security Foundations Workshop (CSFW'04)*, pages 187–201. IEEE Computer Society Press, 2004.

[3] We say that $\rho = \{x_1 := m_1, \ldots, x_n := m_n\}$ *is a substitution which respects* Γ *with* Γ' if $\Gamma = \Delta, x_1{:}T_1, \ldots, x_n{:}T_n$ and there exists Δ' such that $\Gamma' = \Delta, \Delta'$ and $\Gamma' \vdash m_i : T_i$ for $i = 1, \ldots, n$.

5. S. Crafa, M. Bugliesi, and G. Castagna. Information Flow Security for Boxed Ambients. *ENTCS*, 66(3), 2002.
6. S. Crafa and S. Rossi. A Theory of Noninterference for the π-calculus. Technical Report CS-2004-8, Dipartimento di Informatica, Università Ca' Foscari di Venezia, Italy, 2004. `http://www.dsi.unive.it/~silvia/CS-2004-8.ps.gz`.
7. D.E. Denning and P.J. Denning. Certification of programs for secure information flow. *Communications of the ACM*, 20:504–513, 1977.
8. R. Focardi and R. Gorrieri. Classification of Security Properties (Part I: Information Flow). In R. Focardi and R. Gorrieri, editors, *Proc. of Foundations of Security Analysis and Design (FOSAD'01)*, volume 2171 of *LNCS*, pages 331–396. Springer-Verlag, 2001.
9. R. Focardi and S. Rossi. Information Flow Security in Dynamic Contexts. In *Proc. of the IEEE Computer Security Foundations Workshop (CSFW'02)*, pages 307–319. IEEE Computer Society Press, 2002.
10. J. A. Goguen and J. Meseguer. Security Policies and Security Models. In *Proc. of the IEEE Symposium on Security and Privacy (SSP'82)*, pages 11–20. IEEE Computer Society Press, 1982.
11. N. Heintze and J. G. Riecke. The SLam Calculus: Programming with Secrecy and Integrity. In *Proc. of ACM SIGPLAN-SIGACT Symposium on Principles of Programming Languages (POPL'98)*, pages 365–377. ACM Press, 1998.
12. M. Hennessy. The security picalculus and non-interference. *Journal of Logic and Algebraic Programming*, 63(1):3–34, 2004.
13. M. Hennessy and J. Rathke. Typed Behavioural Equivalences for Processes in the Presence of Subtyping. *Mathematical Structures in Computer Science*, 14(5):651–684, 2004.
14. M. Hennessy and J. Riely. Information Flow vs. Resource Access in the Asynchronous Pi-calculus. *ACM Transactions on Programming Languages and Systems (TOPLAS)*, 24(5):566–591, 2002.
15. K. Honda, V.T. Vasconcelos, and N. Yoshida. Secure Information Flow as Typed Process Behaviour. In *Proc. of European Symposium on Programming (ESOP'00)*, volume 1782 of *LNCS*, pages 180–199. Springer-Verlag, 2000.
16. K. Honda and N. Yoshida. A Uniform Type Structure for Secure Information Flow. In *Proc. of ACM SIGPLAN-SIGACT Symposium on Principles of Programming Languages (POPL'02)*, pages 81–92. ACM Press, 2002.
17. N. Kobayashi. Type-Based Information Flow Analysis for the Pi-Calculus. Technical Report TR03-0007, Dept. of Computer Science, Tokyo Institute of Technology, 2003.
18. F. Pottier. A simple view of type-secure information flow in the π-calculus. In *Proc. of the 15th IEEE Computer Security Foundations Work shop*, pages 320–330, 2002.
19. F. Pottier and V. Simonet. Information Flow Inference for ML. In *Proc. of ACM SIGPLAN-SIGACT Symposium on Principles of Programming Languages (POPL'02)*, pages 319–330. ACM Press, 2002.
20. A. Sabelfeld and H. Mantel. Static Confidentiality Enforcement for Distributed Programs. In *Proc. of Int. Static Analysis Symposium (SAS'02)*, volume 2477 of *LNCS*, pages 376–394. Springer-Verlag, 2002.
21. A. Sabelfeld and D. Sands. Probabilistic Noninterference for Multi-threaded Programs. In *Proc. of the IEEE Computer Security Foundations Workshop (CSFW'00)*, pages 200–215. IEEE Computer Society Press, 2000.
22. D. Sangiorgi and D. Walker. *The pi calculus: A theory of mobile processes*. Cambridge, 2001.
23. G. Smith and D. Volpano. Secure Information Flow in a Multi-threaded Imperative Language. In *Proc. of ACM SIGPLAN-SIGACT Symposium on Principles of Programming Languages (POPL'98)*, pages 355–364. ACM Press, 1998.

24. D. Volpano, G. Smith, and C. Irvine. A Sound Type System for Secure Flow Analysis. *Journal of Computer Security*, 4(3):167–187, 1996.
25. N. Yoshida, K. Honda, and M. Berger. Linearity and Bisimulation. In *Proc. of the International Conference on Foundations of Software Science and Computation Structures (FoSSaCS'02)*, volume 2303 of *LNCS*, pages 417–434. Springer-Verlag, 2002.
26. S. Zdancewic and A. C. Myers. Observational Determinism for Concurrent Program Security. In *Proceedings of the 16th IEEE Computer Security Foundations Work shop*, pages 29–45, 2003.

Typed Processes in Untyped Contexts *
(Abstract)

Michele Bugliesi and Marco Giunti

Dipartimento di Informatica, Università Ca' Foscari di Venezia

1 Background

The use of types to control the behavior of processes in the pi-calculus is a long known and well established technique. The idea was first introduced by Pierce and Sangiorgi in their seminal work on the subject [9], and is best illustrated by their motivating example:

$$S = (\nu s)!\overline{d}\langle s\rangle \,|\, !s(x).\overline{print}\langle x\rangle \qquad\qquad C = d(x).\overline{x}\langle j\rangle$$

S is a print spooler serving requests from a private channel s that it communicates to its clients via the public channel d. C is one such client, that receives s and uses it to print the job j.

While the intention of the specification is clear, reasoning on its properties is subtler. For instance, given the initial configuration $S\,|\,C$, can we prove that the jobs sent by C are eventually received and printed? Stated in more formal terms: is there a proof of the following equation?

$$S\,|\,C \quad \overset{?}{\cong} \quad S\,|\,\overline{print}\langle j\rangle \tag{1}$$

Here we take $P \cong Q$ to mean that P and Q are behaviorally indistinguishable, i.e. they have the same observable behavior when executed in any arbitrary context. Back to our example, (1) is easily disproved by exhibiting a context that interferes with the intended protocol between S and C. A first example is the context $\mathscr{C}_1[-] = -\,|\,d(x).!x(y).\mathbf{0}$, that initially behaves as a client, to receive s, but then steals the jobs intended for S. A second example is the context $\mathscr{C}_2[-] = -\,|\,(\nu s')\overline{d}\langle s'\rangle$, which may succeed in transmitting to C a dead-ended channel that will never serve the purpose C expected of it.

As shown in [9], hostile contexts such as those above can be ruled out by resorting to a system of capability types to control the transmission and/or reception of values over channels based on the possession of corresponding type capabilities. In our example, that system allows us to protect against contexts like $\mathscr{C}_1$ by requiring that clients be only granted write capabilities on the channel s, and by reserving read capabilities on s to the spooler. Similarly, we may build safeguards against attackers like $\mathscr{C}_2$ by demanding that clients only have read access on d.

Both the requirements are expressed formally by the typing assumption $d : ((T)^{\mathsf{w}})^{\mathsf{r}}$: this typing grants read-only access on d and write-only access to any name received on d, as desired. We may now refine the equation in (1) into its typed version below (where $print : \top$ indicates that

$$d : ((T)^{\mathsf{w}})^{\mathsf{r}} \models S\,|\,C \cong S\,|\,\overline{print}\langle j\rangle. \tag{2}$$

* Work supported by EU FET-GC project 'MyThS' IST-2001-32617

R. De Nicola and D. Sangiorgi (Eds.): TGC 2005, LNCS 3705, pp. 19–32, 2005.

Typed equations of the form $I \models P \cong Q$ express behavioral equivalences between processes in any context that typechecks in the type environment I. Here I represents the context's view of the processes under observation, given in terms of a set of typing assumptions on the names shared between the processes and the context itself. Incidentally, but importantly, the typing assumptions on the shared names may in general be different –in fact, more accurate– for the processes than they are for the context. To illustrate, in (2), a context is only assumed to have read-capabilities on d, while for the system to typecheck the name d must be known at the lower (hence more accurate) type $((T)^{\mathsf{w}})^{\mathsf{rw}}$, so that to allow S to write and C to read. Similarly, for the system $S\,|\,C$ to typecheck, the name s must be known at the type $(T)^{\mathsf{rw}}$ including both a write-capability, granted to S, and read-capability, granted to any process that receives s: the context, instead, will only acquire s at the super-type $(T)^{\mathsf{w}}$ determined by the type of the transmission channel d.

2 Typed Equivalences Fail in Untyped Contexts

Given the type for d available to the context, it is not difficult to be convinced that (2) above (under appropriate hypotheses on the context's view of the name *print*, see Section 4) represents a valid equivalence as no context that typecheks under $d : ((T)^{\mathsf{w}})^{\mathsf{r}}$ may tell the two processes apart.

Typed equivalences like these are very useful, and effective in all situations in which we have control on the contexts observing our processes, i.e. in all situations in which we may assume that such contexts are well-typed, hence behave according to the invariants enforced by the typing system.

The question we address in this abstract is whether the same kind of reasoning can still be relied upon when our processes are to be deployed in distributed, open environments. Stated more precisely: can we implement our typed processes as low-level agents to be executed in arbitrary, open networks, while at the same time preserving the typed behavioral congruences available for the source processes?

One is readily convinced that no implementation with the desired properties may rely on static typing alone, as distributed and open networks do not validate any useful assumption on the trustworthiness, hence the well-typedness, of the contexts where (the low-level agents representing) our typed processes operate. Rather than *assuming* that a context satisfies the constraints imposed by a typing assumption, our implementations should *enforce* them.

The implementation schema we envision here is one in which the statically checked possession and distribution of type capabilities in the source-level processes is realized in terms of the possession and the dynamic distribution of corresponding term-level capabilities in the implementation agents. For instance, each channel could be implemented by means of a pair of cryptographic keys representing the write and read capabilities. If designed carefully, and instrumented with adequate measures to protect against hostile contexts (cf. [1,3,7]) this represents a viable idea to pursue.

The problem remains, however, to make sure that the implementation preserves the desired typed equations of the source calculus: for that to be the case, one must guarantee that for each name, the distribution of the term capabilities in the low-level agents match the corresponding type capabilities in the source level process. While this is possible for the names that are statically shared with the context, ensuring such correspondence is much harder, if at all possible, for the names that are dynamically acquired by the context. There are two fundamental difficulties:

- first, as we have observed, the type at which the context acquires a name depends on the type of the channel over which the name is communicated;
- secondly, the type of the transmission channel may vary dynamically in ways that cannot be predicted statically.

The dynamic evolution is particularly problematic in a calculus with matching because, as noticed by Hennessy and Rathke in [8], matching makes it possible to progressively refine the type at which a name is known during the computation. This is best illustrated by the following typed labelled transition, borrowed from [8], that formalizes the effect of emitting a name on a public channel.

$$\frac{\mathrm{I}^{\mathsf{r}}(a)\downarrow}{\mathrm{I}\triangleright\overline{a}\langle n\rangle.P \xrightarrow{\overline{a}\langle n\rangle} \mathrm{I}\sqcap n:\mathrm{I}^{\mathsf{r}}(a)\triangleright P}$$

The configuration $\mathrm{I}\triangleright P$ represents a process P operating in a context that typecheks under I, and $\mathrm{I}^{\mathsf{r}}(a)\downarrow$ indicates that I (hence the context) has a read capability on the name a. The meet $\mathrm{I}\sqcap n:\mathrm{I}^{\mathsf{r}}(a)$ in the resulting configuration represents the ability of the context to "merge" its current type for n with the type determined by receiving n on a: as explained in [8], taking the meet mimics the ability of the context to match n with the names already known to it (possibly, at different types), and obtain a more informative type based on that. The problem is that the effect of this type refinement may propagate dynamically in ways that cannot be determined statically. To illustrate, let I and P be the typing environment and the process defined as follows:

$$\mathrm{I} = n:((T)^{\mathsf{w}})^{\mathsf{r}}, a:(((T)^{\mathsf{r}})^{\mathsf{r}})^{\mathsf{r}}$$
$$P = \overline{a}\langle n\rangle \mid (\nu p:(T)^{\mathsf{rw}})\overline{n}\langle p\rangle$$

We have $\mathrm{I}^{\mathsf{r}}(n) = (T)^{\mathsf{w}}$ and $\mathrm{I}^{\mathsf{r}}(a) = ((T)^{\mathsf{r}})^{\mathsf{r}}$, and from this we compute $\mathrm{I}' \triangleq \mathrm{I}\sqcap n:\mathrm{I}^{\mathsf{r}}(a) = a:(((T)^{\mathsf{r}})^{\mathsf{r}})^{\mathsf{r}}, n:((T)^{\mathsf{rw}})^{\mathsf{r}}$. Now we see that a context that typechecks under I will acquire p at the type $(T)^{\mathsf{w}}$ or at the type $(T)^{\mathsf{rw}}$ depending on which one of the two names p and n it receives first in its interactions with process P. This is reflected by the following two transition sequences available from $\mathrm{I}\triangleright P$.

$$\mathrm{I}\triangleright P \xrightarrow{(\nu p)\overline{n}\langle p\rangle} \mathrm{I}, p:(T)^{\mathsf{w}}\triangleright\overline{a}\langle n\rangle \xrightarrow{\overline{a}\langle n\rangle} \mathrm{I}\sqcap n:((T)^{\mathsf{r}})^{\mathsf{r}}, p:(T)^{\mathsf{w}}\triangleright\mathbf{0}$$
$$\mathrm{I}\triangleright P \xrightarrow{\overline{a}\langle n\rangle} \mathrm{I}'\triangleright(\nu p:(T)^{\mathsf{rw}})\overline{n}\langle p\rangle \xrightarrow{(\nu p)\overline{n}\langle p\rangle} \mathrm{I}', p:(T)^{\mathsf{rw}}\triangleright\mathbf{0}$$

Clearly, this dynamic evolution of the typing knowledge of the context is problematic, as a fully abstract implementation would need to tune the distribution of the term-capabilities associated with n on the types available dynamically to the context: as the example shows, this is in general impossible to achieve at compile time, by simply inspecting the structure of the source level processes.

3 Dynamic Typing to the Rescue

While the problem with the previous example is a direct consequence of the presence of matching, a more fundamental obstacle against full abstraction is in the very structure of the capability types adopted in the source calculus, and in the way that structure determines the acquisition of new capabilities on a name. As we have shown, acquiring a name, say n, at a type not only informs on how n will be used, but also determines how other names transmitted over n will be circulated and used in the system. These invariants are all encoded in the static type of the channel at which n is received, and clearly they will not be guaranteed if that channel is shared with an untyped context.

To make a fully abstract implementation feasible, the solution we propose here is to adopt a new typing discipline for the source calculus, based on a combination of static and dynamic typing to control the interaction with the context.

We formalize our approach by introducing a typed variant of the (asynchronous) pi-calculus. In this calculus, named API@, the types at which the emitted values are to be received by the context are decided the output sites. This is accomplished by introducing a new output construct, noted $\overline{a}\langle v@T\rangle$, that relies on type coercion to enforce the delivery of v at the type T, regardless of the type of the communication channel a. A static typing system will ensure that v has indeed the type T to which it is coerced, while a mechanisms of dynamically typed synchronization guarantees that v is received only at supertypes of T, so as to guarantee the type soundness of each exchange of values.

By breaking the dependency between the types of the transmission channels and the types of the names transmitted, in API@ we may safely dispense with the nested types of [9,8], and rely instead on channel types with a flat structure that only exhibits the read/write access rights associated with the channels, regardless of the types of the values they transmit. Needless to say, the resulting discipline of static typing is much looser: to compensate for that one then needs a dynamically typed operational semantics to ensure type soundness.

What is more interesting and relevant for our present concerns is that the new typing discipline makes it possible to recover fully abstract implementations, i.e. implementations for which the typed congruences of the source calculus are preserved even in the presence of untyped, and potentially hostile contexts. We give a brief overview of how that can be accomplished in Section 6. Before that, we introduce the source calculus formally, and look at the consequences of the new typing discipline on the ability to reason about process behavior.

4 A Pi-Calculus with Dynamic Typing

API@ is a typed dialect of the asynchronous pi-calculus [5]. The choice of an asynchronous calculus is only meant to ease the implementation in [7], and has no effect or consequence on our present development.

We presuppose countable sets of names and variables, ranged over by $a - n$ and $x, y, \ldots$ respectively. We use bv todenote basic values, and u, v to range collectively over names, variables and basic values whenever the distinction does not matter. The structure of processes is defined by the following productions:

$$
\begin{array}{llll}
P, Q, \ldots & ::= & \mathbf{0} \mid P|Q \mid (\nu n : A)P \mid !P & \textit{pi-calculus} \\
& \mid & [u = v]P; Q & \textit{matching} \\
& \mid & \overline{u}\langle \tilde{v}@\tilde{A} \rangle & \textit{type-coerced output} \\
& \mid & u(\tilde{x}@\tilde{A}).P & \textit{typed input}
\end{array}
$$

We use $\tilde{u}$ and $\tilde{A}$ to note (possibly empty) tuples of values and types, respectively, and the notation $\tilde{v}@\tilde{A}$ as a shorthand for $v_1@A_1, \ldots, v_n@A_n$. As in companion calculi, the typing system rules out meaningless terms, like $bv(x).P$, that use basic values in positions where names are expected.

The reading of the process forms is standard, with the exception of the constructs for input/output. As we anticipated, $\overline{u}\langle \tilde{v}@\tilde{A} \rangle$ represents the output of the values $\tilde{v}$ at the types $\tilde{A}$: the rules of the operational semantics will ensure that outputs at this type only synchronizes with input prefixes expecting values at types higher than (or equal to) $\tilde{A}$.

The types of API@ include types for basic values, a top type and capability types for names. As promised in Section 3, the channel types we use have the flat structure defined in Table 1, that informs on the access rights associated with the channel: read (r), write (w) or both (rw). The subtyping relation, also in Table 1, is the preorder that satisfies the expected relationship over capability types, and admits a partial meet operator $\sqcap$.

4.1 Typing System

Most of the typing rules are standard and self explained, with the two exceptions we discuss next. The typing of matching is inherited, unchanged, from [8]: as in that case, it requires a few preliminary definitions to formalize the structure of typing environments. We build type environments, noted Γ, by using the operator $\sqcap$: $\Gamma \sqcap u : A = \Gamma, u : A$ if $u \notin dom(\Gamma)$, otherwise $\Gamma \sqcap u : A = \Gamma'$ where Γ' differs from Γ only at u, since the capability of this identifier is extended to be $\Gamma(u) \sqcap A$ (if $\Gamma(u) \sqcap A$ is undefined, then so is $\Gamma \sqcap u : A$). We use the notation $\Gamma \sqcap (v_1, \ldots, v_n) : (A_1, \ldots, A_n) \triangleq \Gamma \sqcap v_1 : A_1 \sqcap \ldots \sqcap v_n : A_n$, and in case $\mathrm{dom}(\Gamma) \cap \mathrm{dom}(\Gamma') = \emptyset$, we write Γ, Γ' to indicate the type environment containing all mappings in Γ and in Γ'. Subtyping is extended to type environments as expected. We write $\Gamma <: \Gamma'$ if $\Gamma(u) <: \Gamma'(u)$ for all $u \in dom(\Gamma)$. If the type environment Γ at n has a type of the form r or rw then $\Gamma^{\mathsf{r}}(n)$ is defined (written as $\Gamma^{\mathsf{r}}(n) \downarrow$). Similarly for the dual case of write capabilities.

The typing of input/output is characteristic of our present calculus, and is a direct consequence of the structure of the channel types. In particular, notice that the rules (T-OUT) and (T-IN) do not expect/impose any relationship between the type of the channel u and the types associated with the values transmitted (in (T-OUT)) or expected (in (T-IN)). The only constraint, at the output sites, is that the types at which the emitted values

Table 1. The typing system

Types

$$A, B, \ldots ::= \mathsf{rw} \mid \mathsf{r} \mid \mathsf{w} \quad \textit{capabilities}$$
$$\mid \mathsf{B} \quad \textit{basic values}$$
$$\mid \top \quad \textit{top}$$

Subtyping

$$\mathsf{rw} <: \mathsf{r} \quad \mathsf{rw} <: \mathsf{w} \quad A <: \top$$

Typing Rules

(T-Pro)
$$\frac{\Gamma(u) <: A}{\Gamma \vdash u : A}$$

(T-Tuple)
$$\frac{\Gamma \vdash v_i : A_i \quad \forall i \in 1..n}{\Gamma \vdash (v_1, \ldots, v_n) : (A_1, \ldots, A_n)}$$

(T-New)
$$\frac{\Gamma, n : A \vdash P}{\Gamma \vdash (\nu n : A)P}$$

(T-Par)
$$\frac{\Gamma \vdash P \quad \Gamma \vdash Q}{\Gamma \vdash P \mid Q}$$

(T-Repl)
$$\frac{\Gamma \vdash P}{\Gamma \vdash !P}$$

(T-Nil)
$$\frac{}{\Gamma \vdash \mathbf{0}}$$

(T-Match)
$$\frac{\Gamma \vdash Q \quad \Gamma(u) = A \quad \Gamma(v) = B \quad \Gamma \sqcap u : B \sqcap v : A \vdash P}{\Gamma \vdash [u = v]P; Q}$$

(T-Out@)
$$\frac{\Gamma^{\mathsf{w}}(u) \downarrow \quad \Gamma \vdash \tilde{v} : \tilde{B}}{\Gamma \vdash \overline{u}\langle \tilde{v} @ \tilde{B} \rangle}$$

(T-In@)
$$\frac{\Gamma^{\mathsf{r}}(u) \downarrow \quad \Gamma, \tilde{x} : \tilde{A} \vdash P}{\Gamma \vdash u(\tilde{x} @ \tilde{A}).P}$$

are coerced must be valid. As we mentioned earlier, this rather loose form of static typing is complemented by dynamic type checks to be performed upon synchronization.

4.2 Operational Semantics

The dynamics of the calculus is defined by means of a labelled transition system built around the following actions:

$$\textit{Actions} \quad \alpha ::= \tau \mid u(\tilde{v} @ \tilde{B}) \mid (\tilde{c} : \tilde{C})\overline{u}\langle \tilde{v} @ \tilde{B} \rangle$$

Most of the transitions, in Table 2, are standard. The output action $(\tilde{c} : \tilde{C})\overline{u}\langle \tilde{v} @ \tilde{B} \rangle$ carries a type tag along with the output value: it represents the output of (a tuple, possibly including fresh) values $\tilde{v}$ at the types $\tilde{B}$. Dually, the input action $u(\tilde{v} @ \tilde{B})$ represents the input of $\tilde{v}$ at the types $\tilde{B}$. As anticipated, synchronizing input and output requires a dynamic type check: in (Pi-Com@), complementary labels synchronize only if they agree on the type of the values exchanged. The subject reduction theorem below follows routinely thanks to these dynamic checks.

Table 2. LTS for the source calculus

(PI-OUTPUT)

$$\frac{}{\overline{a}\langle\tilde{v}@\tilde{B}\rangle \xrightarrow{\overline{a}\langle\tilde{v}@\tilde{B}\rangle} \mathbf{0}}$$

(PI-OPEN)

$$\frac{P \xrightarrow{(\tilde{c}:\tilde{C})\overline{a}\langle\tilde{v}@\tilde{B}\rangle} P' \qquad b \neq a,\ b \in fn(\tilde{v})}{(\nu b:B)P \xrightarrow{(b:B,\ \tilde{c}:\tilde{C})\overline{a}\langle\tilde{v}@\tilde{B}\rangle} P'}$$

(PI-INPUT@)

$$\frac{}{a(\tilde{x}@\tilde{B}).P \xrightarrow{a(\tilde{v}@\tilde{B})} P\{\tilde{x} := \tilde{v}\}}$$

(PI-COM@)

$$\frac{P \xrightarrow{(\tilde{c}:\tilde{C})\overline{a}\langle\tilde{v}@\tilde{B}\rangle} P' \quad Q \xrightarrow{a(\tilde{v}@\tilde{B}')} Q' \quad \tilde{B} <: \tilde{B}' \quad \tilde{c} \cap fn(Q) = \varnothing}{P \mid Q \xrightarrow{\tau} (\nu\tilde{c}:\tilde{C})(P' \mid Q')}$$

(PI-MATCH)

$$\frac{a = b}{[a = b]P;Q \xrightarrow{\tau} P}$$

(PI-MISMATCH)

$$\frac{a \neq b}{[a = b]P;Q \xrightarrow{\tau} Q}$$

(PI-PAR)

$$\frac{P \xrightarrow{\alpha} P' \quad bn(\alpha) \cap fn(Q) = \emptyset}{P \mid Q \xrightarrow{\alpha} P' \mid Q}$$

(PI-RES)

$$\frac{P \xrightarrow{\alpha} P' \qquad a \notin \mathrm{n}(\alpha)}{(\nu a:A)P \xrightarrow{\alpha} (\nu a:A)P'}$$

(PI-REPL)

$$\frac{P \xrightarrow{\alpha} P'}{!P \xrightarrow{\alpha} P' \mid !P}$$

Theorem 1 (Subject Reduction). *Suppose* $\Gamma \vdash P$. *Then*

1. $P \xrightarrow{\tau} P'$ *implies* $\Gamma \vdash P'$
2. $P \xrightarrow{a(\tilde{v}@\tilde{B})} P'$ *implies* $\Gamma^{\mathrm{r}}(a)\downarrow$ *and if* $\Gamma \sqcap \tilde{v} : \tilde{B}$ *is defined then* $\Gamma \sqcap \tilde{v} : \tilde{B} \vdash P'$
3. $P \xrightarrow{(\tilde{c}:\tilde{C})\overline{a}\langle\tilde{v}@\tilde{B}\rangle} P'$ *implies* $\Gamma^{\mathrm{w}}(a)$ *defined,* $\Gamma, \tilde{c} : \tilde{C} \vdash \tilde{v} : \tilde{B}$ *and* $\Gamma, \tilde{c} : \tilde{C} \vdash P'$

4.3 Observational Equivalence

As usual in typed calculi, the notion of observational equivalence is based on typed (reduction) barbed congruence. Barbs arise as expected: we let $P\downarrow_a \triangleq \xrightarrow{(\tilde{c}:\tilde{C})\overline{a}\langle\tilde{v}@\tilde{B}\rangle}$ denote the predicate true of any process P ready to output on a public channel $a \notin \tilde{c}$, and define $P \Downarrow_a \triangleq P \Longrightarrow P' \downarrow_a$.

An interesting aspect of our congruence relation, that we inherit from [8], is that we look at the behavior of processes by means of contexts that have a certain knowledge of the processes. As we noted, the typing information available to the context may be different (less informative) than the information available to the system. Thus, while the system processes may perform certain action because they posses the required (type) capabilities, the same may not be true of the context. We formalize these intuitions below.

Given two type environments Γ and I, we say that Γ is compatible with I if and only if $\mathrm{dom}(\Gamma) = \mathrm{dom}(\mathrm{I})$ and $\Gamma <: \mathrm{I}$.

Definition 1 (Type-indexed relation). *A type-indexed relation $\mathscr{R}$ is a family of binary relations between processes indexed by type environments. We write $\mathrm{I} \models P \mathscr{R} Q$ to mean that (i) P and Q are related by $\mathscr{R}$ at* I *and (ii) that there exist Γ and Δ compatible with* I *such that $\Gamma \vdash P$ and $\Delta \vdash Q$.*

We define contexts as the set of terms defined by the following productions, where $[\cdot]$ denotes a typed hole: $C ::= [\cdot_\Gamma] \mid (\nu a{:}A)C \mid C|P \mid P|C$. Contexts defined in this way, which do not include replication and prefixes, are normally referred to as *evaluation contexts*. The definition of typed behavioral equivalence is now standard. We first lift the notion of barb to the typed case, defining $\mathrm{I} \models P \Downarrow_a \triangleq \mathrm{I}^{\mathsf{r}}(a) \downarrow \wedge P \Downarrow_a$. Then we have:

Definition 2 (Typed behavioral equivalence [8]). *Typed behavioral equivalence, noted $\cong$, is the largest symmetric type-indexed relation such $\mathrm{I} \models P \mathscr{R} Q$ implies*

- *if $\mathrm{I} \models P \Downarrow_n$ then $\mathrm{I} \models Q \Downarrow_n$*
- *if $P \xrightarrow{\tau} P'$ then $Q \Longrightarrow Q'$ and $\mathrm{I} \models P' \mathscr{R} Q'$ for some Q'*
- *$\mathrm{I} \models C[P] \mathscr{R} C[Q]$ for every evaluation context $C[\cdot_\Gamma]$ such that $\mathrm{I} \vdash C[P], C[Q]$*

As a simple illustration of the calculus and its behavioral theory we give the API@ version of our running example. Letting J be the type of jobs, the two processes S and C may be defined as follows:

$$S = (\nu s : \mathsf{rw})!\overline{d}\langle s@\mathsf{w}\rangle \mid !s(x@\mathsf{J}).\overline{print}\langle x@\mathsf{J}\rangle \qquad C = d(x@\mathsf{w}).\overline{x}\langle j@\mathsf{J}\rangle$$

The important thing to note is the type $s@\mathsf{w}$ chosen by S for the output on d to make sure that the spooling channel will only be received with output capabilities. Then we can prove the desired equivalence by assuming that contexts may only read on d, and have no control on the channel *print*, namely:

$$j : \mathsf{J}, print : \top, d : \mathsf{r} \models S \mid C \cong S \mid \overline{print}\langle j@\mathsf{J}\rangle \tag{3}$$

As usual, proving such equivalences takes some effort and is often not easy, as it requires induction to capture all the typed contexts. Luckily (but not surprisingly), the construction from [8] works just as well for our calculus in providing a purely coinductive characterization for reduction barbed congruence.

4.4 A Coinductive Proof Technique

The characterization draws on the definition of a set of typed labelled transitions in which the interaction between a process and its context is mediated by the type capabilities that the context possesses on the shared names. The typed actions, in Table 3,

Table 3. Typed Actions

(G-OUT)

$$\frac{\mathrm{I}^{\mathsf{r}}(a)\downarrow \qquad \tilde{A} <: \tilde{B}}{\mathrm{I} \triangleright \overline{a}\langle \tilde{v}@\tilde{A}\rangle \xrightarrow{\overline{a}\langle \tilde{v}@\tilde{B}\rangle} \mathrm{I} \sqcap \tilde{v} : \tilde{B} \triangleright \mathbf{0}}$$

(G-OPEN)

$$\frac{\mathrm{I}, b : \top \triangleright P \xrightarrow{(\tilde{c})\overline{a}\langle \tilde{v}@\tilde{A}\rangle} \mathrm{I}' \triangleright P' \qquad b \neq a,\ b \in fn(\tilde{v})}{\mathrm{I} \triangleright (\nu b : B)P \xrightarrow{(b,\, \tilde{c})\overline{a}\langle \tilde{v}@\tilde{A}\rangle} \mathrm{I}' \triangleright P'}$$

(G-IN@)

$$\frac{\mathrm{I}^{\mathsf{w}}(a)\downarrow \qquad \mathrm{I} \vdash \tilde{v} : \tilde{A}' \quad \tilde{A}' <: \tilde{A}}{\mathrm{I} \triangleright a(\tilde{x}@\tilde{A}).P \xrightarrow{a(\tilde{v}@\tilde{A}')} \mathrm{I} \triangleright P\{\tilde{x} := \tilde{v}\}}$$

(G-WEAK@)

$$\frac{\mathrm{I}, b : B \triangleright P \xrightarrow{(\tilde{c}:\tilde{C})a(\tilde{v}@\tilde{A})} \mathrm{I}' \triangleright P' \qquad b \notin \{a, \tilde{c}\}}{\mathrm{I} \triangleright P \xrightarrow{(b:B,\, \tilde{c}:\tilde{C})a(\tilde{v}@\tilde{A})} \mathrm{I}' \triangleright P'}$$

(G-REDUCE)

$$\frac{P \xrightarrow{\tau} P'}{\mathrm{I} \triangleright P \xrightarrow{\tau} \mathrm{I} \triangleright P'}$$

(G-PAR)

$$\frac{\mathrm{I} \triangleright P \xrightarrow{\alpha} \mathrm{I}' \triangleright P' \qquad bn(\alpha) \cap fn(Q) = \emptyset}{\mathrm{I} \triangleright P \,|\, Q \xrightarrow{\alpha} \mathrm{I}' \triangleright P' \,|\, Q}$$

(G-RES)

$$\frac{\mathrm{I}, a : \top \triangleright P \xrightarrow{\alpha} \mathrm{I}', a : \top \triangleright P' \qquad a \notin \mathrm{n}(\alpha)}{\mathrm{I} \triangleright (\nu a : A)P \xrightarrow{\alpha} \mathrm{I}' \triangleright (\nu a : A)P'}$$

(G-REPL)

$$\frac{\mathrm{I} \triangleright P \xrightarrow{\alpha} \mathrm{I}' \triangleright P'}{\mathrm{I} \triangleright !P \xrightarrow{\alpha} \mathrm{I}' \triangleright P' \,|\, !P}$$

encode transitions over configurations of the form $\mathrm{I} \triangleright P \xrightarrow{\alpha} \mathrm{I}' \triangleright P'$, and identify actions by the process P that are only possible if they are allowed by the environment I. Not surprisingly, most of the typed transitions in our system are derived directly from their companion transitions in the system of [8], to which we refer the reader for the underlying intuitions and full details.

The only differences are in the transitions for the input and output forms, as these reflect the nature of the interactions with the context distinctive of our calculus. Specifically, the (G-OUT) rule formalizes the fact that a context willing to observe an output action performed by a process may only do so by guessing a super-type of the actual type used in the type coercion: that supertype is also the type at which the context acquires the values emitted. Dually, the (G-IN) rule shows that an input by a process may in general only be observed at a lower type than actually performed by the process. All this is a consequence of the format of our subtype-based synchronization rule (PI-COMM@) in Table 2.

The resulting notion of asynchronous bisimilarity arises as expected [4].

Definition 3 (Typed labelled bisimilarity). *A symmetric type indexed relation $\mathscr{R}$ over processes is an asynchronous bisimulation if whenever* $\mathrm{I} \models_a P \mathscr{R} Q$*, one has:*

– *if* $\mathrm{I} \triangleright P \xrightarrow{\alpha} \mathrm{I}' \triangleright P'$ *and* α *is* $(\tilde{c})\overline{a}\langle\tilde{v}@\tilde{A}\rangle$ *or* τ *then* $\mathrm{I} \triangleright Q \overset{\hat{\alpha}}{\Longrightarrow} \mathrm{I}' \triangleright Q'$ *with* $\mathrm{I}' \models_a P' \mathscr{R} Q'$
– *if* $\mathrm{I} \triangleright P \xrightarrow{\alpha} \mathrm{I}' \triangleright P'$ *and* α *is* $(\tilde{c} : \tilde{C})a(\tilde{v}@\tilde{A})$ *then*
  – $\mathrm{I} \triangleright Q \overset{\alpha}{\Longrightarrow} \mathrm{I}' \triangleright Q'$ *with* $\mathrm{I}' \models_a P' \mathscr{R} Q'$ *or*
  – $\mathrm{I} \triangleright Q \Longrightarrow \mathrm{I} \triangleright Q'$ *with* $\mathrm{I}, \tilde{c} : \tilde{C} \models_a P' \mathscr{R} Q' \,|\, \overline{a}\langle\tilde{v}@\tilde{A}\rangle$.

Asynchronous labelled bisimilarity, noted $\approx$, *is the largest type indexed asynchronous bisimulation.*

Perhaps interestingly, the reader will notice that the types $\tilde{C}$ and $\tilde{A}$ chosen to match the input transition are, in both cases, exactly the types occurring in the label of the transition to be matched. Labelled bisimilarity, as defined above, can be shown to coincide with barbed congruence. We omit the proof, which is mostly standard and can be found in [6], and only state the result.

Theorem 2 (Soundness and Completeness). $\mathrm{I} \models_a P \approx Q$ *if and only if* $\mathrm{I} \models P \cong Q$.

Using this characterization, our equation (3) can now be proved coinductively. We leave the details to the interested reader, and focus instead on some distinguishing equations for API@. As we show below, the presence of typed synchronization has some noticeable consequences on the behavioral theory.

A first law we examine is the following generalization of a standard fact about replication.

$$a : \mathsf{r} \models \overline{a}\langle n@T\rangle \,|\, !\overline{a}\langle n@S\rangle \cong\, !\overline{a}\langle n@S\rangle \qquad \text{whenever } S <: T \tag{4}$$

That this law holds also in case $S \neq T$ is a consequence of our subtype-based synchronization rule. The proof of this equivalence follows by coinduction by verifying that the relation $\mathscr{R}$ below is a bisimulation:

$$\begin{aligned} \mathscr{R} \triangleq\ & Id \cup \{a : \mathsf{r} \models_a \overline{a}\langle n@T\rangle \,|\, !\overline{a}\langle n@S\rangle \approx\, !\overline{a}\langle n@S\rangle\} \\ & \cup \{a : \mathsf{r}, n : S' \models_a \overline{a}\langle n@T\rangle \,|\, !\overline{a}\langle n@S\rangle \approx\, !\overline{a}\langle n@S\rangle \;\mid\; S <: S'\} \end{aligned}$$

Another interesting consequence of the typed semantics is observed in the behavior of *forwarder* processes like $a(x).\overline{b}\langle x\rangle$. In particular, we show that one of the distinguishing equations of the asynchronous pi calculus holds only in very specific cases in API@. Specifically, we have:

$$a : rw \models a(x@T).\overline{a}\langle x@T\rangle \cong \mathbf{0} \qquad \text{iff } T \text{ is minimal}$$

The "if" direction can be proved by co-induction, showing that $\mathscr{R}$ below is an asynchronous bisimulation.

$$\begin{aligned} \mathscr{R} \triangleq\ & \{a : rw \models_a a(x@T).\overline{a}\langle x@T\rangle \approx \mathbf{0}\} \cup \\ & \{a : rw, n : T \models_a \overline{a}\langle n@T\rangle \approx \overline{a}\langle n@T\rangle \;\mid n \text{ name}\} \end{aligned}$$

Note that n may only be received at T as T has no proper subtypes. For the "only if" direction, it is enough to exhibit a distinguishing context:

$$C_S[-] \triangleq - \,|\, \overline{a}\langle v@S\rangle \,|\, a(x@S).\overline{\omega}\langle\rangle$$

It is easy to see that this context tells the two processes apart if S is a proper subtype of T. Let $P \triangleq a(x@T).\overline{a}\langle x@T\rangle$. For all $S <: T$, we have $C_S[\mathbf{0}] \xrightarrow{\tau} \overline{\omega}\langle\rangle$ with one reduction internal to the context. If S is a proper subtype of T this move cannot be matched by $C_S[P]$, as a case analysis shows. We only have two possible cases: either $C[P] \Longrightarrow C[P]$, or $C_S[P] \stackrel{\tau}{\Longrightarrow} \overline{a}\langle n@T\rangle \mid a(x@S).\overline{\omega}\langle\rangle$, and in neither case the process reached by the weak action is congruent to $\overline{\omega}\langle\rangle$.

5 Relationships with Statically Typed Pi-Calculi

Having presented our calculus in detail, we are in a position to draw more precise comparisons with the statically typed pi calculus of [8] to which we have referred throughout.

It is a very simple observation that the typed pi-calculus can be encoded in API@. Below we give the relevant clauses of a type-directed translation from well-typed pi-processes to processes of API@. If A is a fully fledged capability type, we let $|A|$ denote the outermost capability in A, and define:

$$[\![\overline{u}\langle\tilde{v}\rangle]\!]_\Gamma = \overline{u}\langle v@|\Gamma^{\mathsf{w}}(u)|\rangle$$
$$[\![u(\tilde{x}).P]\!]_\Gamma = u(\tilde{x}@|\Gamma^{\mathsf{r}}(u)|).[\![P]\!]_{\Gamma,\tilde{x}:\Gamma^{\mathsf{r}}(u)}$$

This encoding has some of the good properties on expects: it is type-preserving, and sound, in the following sense. Let $\Gamma \vdash_\pi P$ and $\mathrm{I} \models_\pi P \cong Q$ denote the typability relation and the asynchronous version of the typed congruence of [8], respectively. Then we have:

Theorem 3. *Let Γ, Γ' be two type environment compatible with* I *and such that $\Gamma \vdash_\pi P$ and $\Gamma' \vdash_\pi Q$. Then $|\mathrm{I}| \models [\![P]\!]_\Gamma \cong [\![Q]\!]_{\Gamma'}$ implies $\mathrm{I} \models_\pi P \cong Q$.*

Not surprisingly, however, the translation is not fully abstract. To see that, simply take $Q = \mathbf{0}$, and $P = [\![a(x).\overline{a}\langle x\rangle]\!]_\Gamma$ with $\Gamma = a : ((T)^{\mathsf{r}})^{\mathsf{rw}}$, so that $[\![P]\!]_\Gamma = a(x@\mathsf{r}).\overline{a}\langle x@\mathsf{r}\rangle$. Then, $a : ((T)^{\mathsf{r}})^{\mathsf{rw}} \models_\pi P \cong Q$ while $a : \mathsf{rw} \not\models a(x@\mathsf{r}).\overline{a}\langle x@\mathsf{r}\rangle \cong \mathbf{0}$, as we have showed previously.

While we do not have a formal separation result between the two calculi, it appears that achieving a fully abstract encoding is just as hard as giving a fully abstract implementation of the pi-calculus. In fact, as we observed, the flat capability types of API@ provide much looser control over the dynamic invariants of execution than the the fully fledged capability types of [8]. Clearly, this affects the notion of typed equivalence, as the representation of contexts in terms of the typing assumptions they satisfy is much less informative on the behavior of those contexts that it is with traditional typing systems. This loss of control is compensated by the type coercions available for API@ processes to determine the types at which a context receives the emitted values: still, as the example above shows, the underlying equational theory remains affected.

On the other hand, just because its typing system makes looser assumptions on the structure of the typed contexts, API@ lends itself to be behavior preserving implementations into low-level calculi. We give a brief overview of how that can be achieved in the following section.

6 Towards a Fully Abstract Implementation

The obstacles and challenges hidden in the implementation of high-level process calculi into low-level environments are well understood [1]. The crux of the problem is that low-level network infrastructures provide very limited reliability for communication. Thus, for instance, while in the source-level calculi we write processes like $(\nu n)(\, \overline{n}\langle m\rangle \,|\, n(x).P\,)$ with the understanding that no context will have access to n, this assumption makes little sense in low-level environments. It is therefore wiser to implement channels meant to deliver private information with lower level mechanisms, such as an encrypted connection over the public *net*work.

$$(\nu n)(\, \overline{net}\langle\{m\}_n\rangle \,|\, net(y).\mathsf{decrypt}\ y\ \mathsf{as}\ \{x\}_n\ \mathsf{in}\ [\![P]\!]$$

The knowledge of n is still confined here, but its role is different: n is an encryption key, rather than a channel. The message is encrypted and communicated along *net*; even though the encrypted packet is intercepted, only the intended receivers, which possess the key n, may decrypt it to obtain m.

In a calculus with capability types, this schema may be refined by associating each channel with a pair of asymmetric keys: an encryption key to transmit and a decryption key to receive data. In our source calculus, this leads us readily to the following correspondence between high-level type capabilities, and low-level term-capabilities associated with a name: $[\![n@\mathsf{w}]\!] = n^+$ and $[\![n@\mathsf{r}]\!] = n^-$. Given this representation, one may try and devise an implementation for API@ based on the following translation:

$$\begin{aligned} [\![\overline{n}\langle m@A\rangle]\!] &= \overline{net}\langle\{[\![m@A]\!]\}_{n^+}\rangle \\ [\![n(x).P]\!] &= net(y).\mathsf{decrypt}\ y\ \mathsf{as}\ \{x\}_{n^+}\ \mathsf{using}\ n^-\ \mathsf{in}\ [\![P]\!]\ \mathsf{else}\ \mathbf{0} \end{aligned}$$

While this translation scheme is appealing in its simplicity, it suffers from a number of shortcomings and attacks, first made explicit by Abadi in [1]. In subsequent work [3], Abadi, Fournet and Gonthier have shown how to counter these shortcomings and recover full abstraction for an implementation of the join calculus.

The fundamental obstacle against using the join implementation for our purposes is related to the property known as *forward secrecy*. The problem is best illustrated with the following example, that we adapt from [1]. Let P and Q be the following API@ processes (where we omit the type coercions whenever irrelevant):

$$P = (\nu n)(\overline{n}\langle m\rangle \,|\, n(x).\overline{p}\langle n@\mathsf{r}\rangle) \quad Q = (\nu n)(\overline{n}\langle m'\rangle \,|\, n(x).\overline{p}\langle n@\mathsf{r}\rangle)$$

It is not difficult to see that these two processes are barbed congruent (essentially under any typing assumption), as m and m' are sent over an secret channel and no API@ context may recover the content of messages sent. On the other hand, a low-level context may tell $[\![P]\!]$ and $[\![Q]\!]$ apart by buffering the message sent on n and then decipher it when n^- is published.

In [3], this problem is avoided altogether, as the join calculus does not allow names to be communicated with read capabilities. In our case, to recover forward secrecy in API@, we need a less naive representation of the type capabilities to make sure that distributing a read capability does not correspond to leaking any description key. We show how this can be accomplished in [7], where we give a fully abstract translation of our source calculus into an asynchronous version of the Applied pi calculus [2].

We refer the reader to [7] for full details, and content ourselves here with few intuitions. Briefly, the idea is to implement each channel with a process that serves input and output requests so that each exchange of messages over the channel is the result of two separate protocols that the server runs with the writer and the reader clients. All channels are associated with two separate key-pairs, that the channel server uses in its protocols with the clients that read from/write to the channel. In the write protocol, the client sends data, and the server buffers it on private queue; on the read protocol, a client sends a session key server returns data encrypted with session key. The translation enforces the following invariants. The channel server possesses the decryption keys associated with the channel and never leaks them; the clients posses (and may eventually release) the encryption keys. Given the structure of the protocols, publishing a read/write capability on a channel corresponds to publishing the read/write encryption keys associated with the channel. Since the decryption keys remain secret with the channel server, the translation should guarantee the *forward* secrecy of messages.

7 Conclusions

Typed behavioral theories provide a powerful technique for reasoning on the behavior of typed processes in typed contexts. However, they are of little use in the more general case of typed processes interacting with untyped contexts. That is unfortunate, as the gap translates directly into a fundamental impediment to fully abstract implementation of the typed calculi.

We have proposed a new dialect of the asynchronous pi-calculus for which this gap can be filled, and fully abstract implementations recovered. As in previous attempts of this kind, filling the gap has a price (in [3] we must give up the ability to communicate read access rights, in our case we need dynamic typing): on the other hand, it is worthwhile, as reasoning on the high-level calculus is feasible, and relatively simple, while reasoning on the implementation is utterly complex.

References

1. M. Abadi. Protection in programming-language translations. In *Proceedings of ICALP'98*, number 1443 in Lecture Notes in Computer Science, pages 868–883. Springer-Verlag, 1998.
2. M. Abadi and C. Fournet. Mobile values, new names, and secure communication. In *Proc. of the 28th ACM Symposium on Principles of Programming Languages (POPL '01)*, pages 104–115. ACM Press, 2001.
3. M. Abadi, C. Fournet, and G. Gonthier. Secure implementation of channel abstractions. *Information and Computation*, 174(1):37–83, April 2002.
4. Roberto M. Amadio, Ilaria Castellani, and Davide Sangiorgi. On bisimulations for the asynchronous pi-calculus. *Theor. Comput. Sci.*, 195(2):291–324, 1998.
5. G. Boudol. Asynchrony and the π-calculus. Research Report 1702, INRIA, Available from http://www-sop.inria.fr/mimosa/personnel/Gerard.Boudol.html, 1992.
6. M. Bugliesi and M. Giunti. A pi-calculus with dynamic typing. Technical Report, University of Venice, June 2005.

7. M. Bugliesi and M. Giunti. Secure implementation of type access control in the pi-calculus. submitted, July 2005.
8. M. Hennessy and J. Rathke. Typed behavioural equivalences for processes in the presence of subtyping. *Mathematical Structures in Computer Science*, 14(5):651–684, 2003.
9. B. Pierce and D. Sangiorgi. Typing and subtyping for mobile processes. *Mathematical Structures in Computer Science*, 6(5), 1996.

Model-Based Testing of Cryptographic Protocols

Dean Rosenzweig[1,2], Davor Runje[2], and Wolfram Schulte[1]

[1] Microsoft Research
schulte@microsoft.com
[2] University of Zagreb
dean@math.hr, davor.runje@fsb.hr

Abstract. Modeling is a popular way of representing the behavior of a system. A very useful type of model in computing is an abstract state machine which describes transitions over first order structures. The general purpose model-based testing tool SpecExplorer (used within Microsoft, also available externally) uses such a model, written in AsmL or Spec#, to perform a search that checks that all reachable states of the model are safe, and also to check conformance of an arbitrary .NET implementation to the model. Spec Explorer provides a variety of ways to cut down the state space of the model, for instance by finitizing parameter domains or by providing predicate abstraction. It has already found subtle bugs in production software.

First order structures and abstract state machines over them are also a useful way to think about cryptographic protocols, since models formulated in these terms arise by natural abstraction from computational cryptography.

In this paper we explain this abstraction process, 'experiments as structures', and argue for its faithfulness. We show how the Dolev–Yao intruder model fits into SpecExplorer. In a word, the actions of the Dolev–Yao intruder are the 'controllable' actions of the testing framework, whereas the actions of protocol participants are the 'observable' actions of the model. The unsafe states are the states violating say Lowe's security guarantees. Under this view, the general purpose software testing tool quickly finds known attacks, such as Lowe's attack on the Needham–Schroeder protocol.

1 Introduction: Why Yet Another Formal Model

A new 'behavioral' theory of algorithms has been developed in recent years in a series of papers by Y.Gurevich, A.Blass [Gur00, BG03, BG04a, BG04b, Gur05], and also B.Rossman and the authors [RR05]. The gist is that algorithms can be mathematically captured at their own native level of abstraction - ex. the native level of abstraction of the Euclidean algorithm is that of Euclidean rings. Algorithms operate over abstract first-order structures, well studied and familiar in mathematical logic, algebra and abstract mathematics in general.

The techniques developed for behavioral theory suggest a natural representation of Dolev-Yao assumptions in first-order structures, and a natural mapping

R. De Nicola and D. Sangiorgi (Eds.): TGC 2005, LNCS 3705, pp. 33–60, 2005.

of ad-hoc notations present in abstract models of cryptography. Unlike the static abstract models, which necessarily invoke additional proof-theoretic devices to capture dynamic aspects, the behavioral theory explicitly targets the dynamic behavior of algorithms semantically. By recent work on behavioral theory [BG04a, BG04b, RR05, Gur05], this also includes interactive algorithms talking to an environment between steps, and within a step, allowing us to represent the abstract content of oracle algorithms and adversary games typical of computational cryptography directly. In the framework of intra-step interactive algorithms exact abstract representations of computational security notions, defined in terms of adversary games, emerge clearly. The experiments of asymptotic computational cryptography can be naturally represented in terms of interactive algorithms over first-order structures, this is our experiments-as-structures paradigm, providing a setting for soundness/completeness proofs. The abstract content of these proofs gets more clearly separated from the probabilistic aspects.

In this paper we execute a small initial segment of this program, in case of confusion-free symmetric encryption. Abstract models for the standard asymptotic security notions in this case are provided, with proofs of their soundness (under the assumption of acyclicity) and completeness. The relation of these proofs to proofs in the literature [AR02, MW04a, AJ01, Ban04, ABS05] can best be described as extraction of abstract content. We also briefly indicate how the assumptions of confusion-freeness and acyclicity can be relaxed in our setting. Partially establishing the exact relation to existing models of abstract cryptography, we show how a variant of Abadi-Rogaway expressions with explicit coins naturally embeds into our framework.

Section 2 is a (necessarily cursory) overview of the behavioral theory of algorithms, essentially referring the reader to the literature. Section 3 is a brief summary of the relevant assumptions of asymptotic computational cryptography in the asymmetric (public key) case. Section 4 presents the experiments-as-structures paradigm and our abstract model of cryptographic adversary games. Section 5 contains sketches of soundness and completeness proofs, and how the Abadi-Rogaway expression language variant embeds into our framework. Testing model for public key protocols is in Section 6, together with an example of rediscovery of Lowe's attack on the Needham–Schroeder protocol by SpecExplorer.

In addition to quoted cryptographic literature, some understanding of the framework as presented in [RR05] is expected of the reader.

2 Behavioral Theory of Algorithms

The behavioral theory of algorithms is *not* an attempt to question the Church-Turing thesis, saying that every computable function over natural numbers can be computed by a Turing machine, or the stronger implicit thesis, actually argued for by Turing, that every algorithm can be simulated by a Turing machine. The aim of the behavioral theory is to make semantical distinctions finer than that precise.

While algorithms get implemented (simulated) exclusively over bits these days, they are often intended to operate over much more abstract objects, abstract data-structures of algebraic or geometric or analytic or even not explicitly mathematical character. The behavioral theory aims to capture algorithms as they are intended, at their own level of abstraction.

The requirement of "capturing algorithms at their own level of abstraction" is made precise as the requirement of simulation step-by-step. The technology to achieve this is using first-order structures, well known to capture faithfully arbitrary static mathematical situations, as states of algorithms. The dynamics, the step, is also defined in terms of the abstract state.

This philosophy leads to a sharp mathematical definition, technically developed in [Gur00] and overviewed in [BG03], computationally realized in the theoretical programming language of Abstract State Machines [Gur00] and the implemented programming languages AsmL [AsmL] and Spec# [Spec#]. Models written in these modelling languages are used by a model-based software testing tool SpecExplorer, also developed at Microsoft Research [SpecExp].

2.1 Interactive Algorithms

Interactive algorithms issue *queries* to the environment, which contain labels and data, and receive replies, which are data, elements of algorithm's state, within a step. This mechanism allows a clean separation of computational (the algorithm) and declarative (the environment) aspects, and naturally models nondeterminism, function calls, interaction with oracles, input and output,... The full theory of (ordinary) interactive algorithms is developed in [BG04a, BG04b]; overviews are given in [Gur05] and [RR05].

All algorithms in this paper are assumed to be small-step ordinary interactive algorithms in the sense of [BG04a, BG04b, Gur05].

2.2 Accessibility, Reachability and Indistinguishability

The notions of accessibility of objects, reachability and indistinguishability of states, as introduced in [RR05], will be important here. An object is *accessible* at a state if it is the value of a term there. A state Y is *reachable* from a state X if there is an algorithm turning X to Y. Two states X, Y are *distinguishable* if there is an algorithm turning them into states distinct by values of a specific term. Structures X, Y of the same vocabulary are *similar*, written $X \sim Y$ if they induce the same equivalence on ground terms:

$$Val(t_1, X) = Val(t_2, X) \text{ iff } Val(t_1, Y) = Val(t_2, Y)$$

Precise definitions and the theory behind these notions can be found in [RR05]. Here we shall repeatedly use the following results from [RR05](where $Y - X$ is the set of differences of two states over the same carrier, see [Gur00, BG04a, RR05] for definitions):

Theorem 1. *State Y is reachable from state X iff*

- *X and Y have the same base set; and*
- *$Y - X$ is finite and every element in $Y - X$ is accessible.*

Theorem 2. *State X and Y are indistinguishable by small–step algorithm iff $X \sim Y$.*

2.3 Background Structures and Importing/Creating

An algorithms often needs to create a new object. A Turing machine often needs to access a new tape location never used before.

In the TM case it obviously doesn't matter whether we conceive its tape as finite, creating new locations as needed, or as infinite, with all locations possibly needed given in advance. In the latter case locations get activated as the TM visits them for the first time.

The case of a first-order structure is the same, a reserve pool ("the heap") of sufficiently many fresh amorphous objects can be given in advance, to be accessed as needed. For interactive algorithms, they are available to the environment to be returned in reply to an appropriate query (get me a new ...). The reserve elements are amorphous in the sense that no "significant" functions are defined on them, or denote them as values. For abstract cryptography the amorphous reserve objects will represent random coins.

But if we have some infrastructure defined on all objects, such as ordered pairs and/or finite sets and/or encryptions, it would be both unnatural and very boring to have to establish all the infrastructure over a new element each time one is introduced, brought forward from the reserve.

The notions of *background structure* and *background class* [BG00] serve exactly this purpose: the axioms for a background class of [BG00] specify what kind of structure can exist over amorphous atoms without imposing any specific properties on them except for identity.

See [BG00, RR05] for definitions of background classes, background of algorithms, exposed elements, active part, reserve.

A structure X is *explicitly atom–generated* if the smallest substructure of X that includes all atoms is X itself. All background structures in the paper are assumed to be explicitly atom-generated. *Atomic support* of a set S of elements of a structure X from a background class $\mathcal{K}$ is the set of atoms of the *envelope* of S, the smallest $\mathcal{K}$-substructure containing S.

Corollary 1. *If the atomic support $Sup_X(\{x\})$ of an element x is accessible in a state X, then x is accessible in X.*

We assume that the set of exposed elements is finite, but not necessary uniformly bounded, in every state. Remember that the foreground of an algorithm is its (generalized) memory, storing input data and results of previous calculations. As such, after a finite number of algorithm steps, only a finite number of locations can be changed.

Let $\mathbf{0}_X$ denote the reduct of X to the background vocabulary, the structure obtained by "forgetting" all foreground functions in state X. We assume that all states have an infinite but countable reserve. It follows immediately from the axioms of [BG00] that if X and Y are $\mathcal{K}$-states over the same carrier, then their background reducts are isomorphic $\mathbf{0}_X \cong \mathbf{0}_Y$.

Theorem 3. *Let X be a state with background BC. Then there is an algorithm A and an injective answer function α appropriate for $\mathbf{0}_X$ with only reserve elements in its codomain such that $X = A(\mathbf{0}_X, \alpha)$.*

3 Computational Cryptography

3.1 Encryption Schemes

An *asymmetric encryption scheme Π* is a tuple of polytime algorithms $(\mathcal{K}, \mathcal{I}, \mathcal{E}, \mathcal{D})$

$$\mathcal{K} : \texttt{Parameter} \times \texttt{Coins} \longrightarrow \texttt{DecryptionKey}$$
$$\mathcal{I} : \texttt{DecryptionKey} \longrightarrow \texttt{EncryptionKey}$$
$$\mathcal{E} : \texttt{EncryptionKey} \times \texttt{String} \times \texttt{Coins} \longrightarrow \texttt{Ciphertext} \cup \{\bot\}$$
$$\mathcal{D} : \texttt{DecryptionKey} \times \texttt{String} \longrightarrow \texttt{Plaintext} \cup \{\bot\}$$

where `String` denotes the set of finite strings over $\{0,1\}$, domains `EncryptionKey`, `DecryptionKey`, `Ciphertext`, `Plaintext` are subsets of `String`, $\bot$ is a distinguished string representing failure of the algorithm, and `Coins` is the set of all infinite strings over $\{0,1\}$. The polytime assumption for $\mathcal{K}$ means time polynomial in η (not the size of its string representation) and ignores the `Coins` argument representing random coin flips. Suppressing the `Coins` argument $\mathcal{K}, \mathcal{E}$ become probabilistic polytime algorithms, and $\mathcal{K}(\eta, c), \mathcal{E}(k, m, c), \mathcal{D}(K, m)$ are, according to tradition, often written as $\mathcal{K}(\eta), \mathcal{E}_k(m), \mathcal{D}_K(m)$ respectively.

The key-inversion algorithm $\mathcal{I}$ returns an encryption key matching the decryption key.

Remark 1 (Usual Assumptions). We require that

- $\mathcal{D}_K(\mathcal{E}_k(m)) = m$ whenever $k = \mathcal{I}(K)$, for every key K sampled from $\mathcal{K}(\eta)$ and every plaintext m such that $\mathcal{E}_k(m)$ doesn't fail;
- the `Plaintext` domain is the set of all m for which, for some `EncryptionKey` k, $\mathcal{E}_k(m)$ doesn't fail; `Ciphertext` is the corresponding codomain;
- if K, K' are two outputs of $\mathcal{K}(\eta)$ for the same η, then
  - K, K' have the same length;
  - $k = \mathcal{I}(K), k' = \mathcal{I}(K')$ have the same length;
  - if m, m' are strings of the same length, then $\mathcal{E}_k(m)$ doesn't fail if and only if $\mathcal{E}_{k'}(m')$ doesn't fail, and then the encryptions have the same length.

Remark 2. Syntax of an asymmetric encryption scheme is usually defined as a triple of algorithms $(\mathcal{K}, \mathcal{E}, \mathcal{D})$, where $\mathcal{K}$ returns a pair of both encryption and decryption keys [BDPR98]. But then $\mathcal{I}$ is simply a projection and the decryption algorithm simply ignores one of the parameters. We find our variant more convenient for the purpose of abstract modeling.

We also assume a (polytime) encoding of ordered pairs, which means a triple of functions $\Sigma = (\mathcal{P}, \mathcal{F}, \mathcal{S})$, where $\mathcal{P}$ is a binary pairing function on strings, and $\mathcal{F}$ and $\mathcal{S}$ are unary projections, with the usual properties. We also assume a type-flaw preventing tagging scheme, ensuring that the codomains of $\mathcal{K}, \mathcal{E}, \mathcal{I}, \mathcal{P}$ are pairwise disjoint, and that neither of them contains $\perp$.

3.2 Notions of Security

Notions of security of encryption schemes are typically based on a notion of indistinguishability, represented by two sequences of oracles of the same length, the good-oracles $O_1^{\mathcal{G}}, \ldots, O_n^{\mathcal{G}}$ and the fake-oracles $O_1^{\mathcal{F}}, \ldots, O_n^{\mathcal{F}}$. Each of the sequences gets initialized by randomly generating a sequence of keys to be used by respective oracles, good-init and fake-init. The oracles and the initializations are implicitly paremeterized by the encryption scheme Π and possibly the pairing scheme Σ, but we shall drop this from the notation. Some data resulting from the initialization can be passed to the adversary algorithm as parameters—we consider this to be a part of the initialization. Let us call the initialization and oracle data just ATT, and let the notion of security defined by ATT be IND-ATT. The idea is that no PPT-limited adversary can distinguish whether she is working with the good or the fake oracles:

Definition 1. Let A be an algorithm working with n oracles. Its *advantage* for IND-ATT is

$$\begin{aligned}\mathsf{Adv}_{\Pi}^{\text{ind-att}}(A) = \Pr[&\mathsf{good\text{-}init} : A(\ldots)^{O_1^{\mathcal{G}},\ldots,O_n^{\mathcal{G}}} = 1] - \\ \Pr[&\mathsf{fake\text{-}init} : A(\ldots)^{O_1^{\mathcal{F}},\ldots,O_n^{\mathcal{F}}} = 1]\end{aligned}$$

The encryption scheme Π is IND-ATT secure if no probabilistic polytime algorithm A can guess which set of oracles it is provided with probability negligible in the security parameter η: $\mathsf{Adv}_{\Pi}^{\text{ind-att}}(A)$ is negligible.

The $A(\ldots)$ notation denotes the adversary algorithm called with any parameters that the initialization chooses to provide. Thus the notion of security is completely characterized by the initializations and the oracles selected.

By *negligible* we mean, throughout this paper, *polynomially negligible* functions: $f(n)$ such that for every c for all sufficiently large n we have $f(n) \leq \frac{1}{n^c}$, and by *overwhelming* those negligibly close to 1.

We define oracles characterizing notions of securities called *indistinguishability under chosen–plaintext attack* and indistinguishability under adaptive chosen–ciphertext attack, denoted with IND-CPA and IND-CCA, respectively.

Example 1 (IND-CPA).

- Let good-init be $K \leftarrow \mathcal{K}(\eta)$, passing along to the adversary algorithm $k = \mathcal{I}(K)$.
- Let good-oracles be $\mathcal{O}$ with $\mathcal{O}(m_1, m_2) = \mathcal{E}_k(m_1)$.

– Let fake-init be as good-init.
– Let fake-oracles be $\mathcal{O}$ with $\mathcal{O}(m_1, m_2) = \mathcal{E}_k(m_2)$, where $k = \mathcal{I}(K)$.

This defines the notion of security known as IND-CPA, "security under known plaintext attack".

Example 2 (IND-CCA).

– Let good-init, fake-init be as for IND-CPA.
– Let good-oracles be $\mathcal{O}, \mathcal{O}_d$ where $\mathcal{O}$ is as good-oracles of IND-CPA, and $\mathcal{O}_d(e) = \mathcal{D}_K(e)$ given that e is not an output obtained from $\mathcal{O}$; if it is, then $\mathcal{O}_d(e)$ fails.
– Let fake-oracles be $\mathcal{O}, \mathcal{O}_d$, with $\mathcal{O}$ as fake-oracle of IND-CPA and $\mathcal{O}_d$ as in good-init.

This defines a strictly stronger notion of security known as IND-CCA or IND-CCA2, "security under known ciphertext attack".

Nonces. Nonces are random values enclosed with some formating data generated with a nonce generation algorithm $\mathcal{N}$. They serve as a source of fresh, unguessable data exchanged in protocols. Nonce generation algorithms can be stateful, which somewhat complicates the appropriate definition of their security. We define the advantage of an arbitrary algorithm A of breaking the security of nonce generation algorithm $\mathcal{N}$ as a probability of succeeding in the following game: $k+l+1$ nonces are sequentially generated with $\mathcal{N}$ and then the algorithm A is run on the first k and the last l nonces with the task to guess the value of $k+1$-th nonce:

$$\mathsf{Adv}^{\mathrm{nonce}}_{\mathcal{N}}(A) = \Pr[\boldsymbol{m}, n, \boldsymbol{p} \xleftarrow{\$} \mathcal{N}(\eta) : A(\boldsymbol{m}, \boldsymbol{p}) = n]$$

If this advantage is negligible in η for every PPT algorithm A, then $\mathcal{N}$ is secure.

In practice, this type of security is achieved by simply enclosing η long uniformly sampled string with formating data.

3.3 Confusion Freeness and Weak Key Authenticity

Neither the syntax of an encryption scheme nor the typical notions of security, such as the one defined above, say much about what happens if we attempt to decrypt an encryption with a key distinct from the decryption key. Syntax of an encryption scheme allows for such decryption to fail, but it does not insist on it. If it does not fail, notions of security forbid that the result is in any *meaningful way* related to the underlying plaintext — a PPT algorithm has no way of distinguishing it from any other potential plaintext with non-negligible probability.

As a reader might already suspect, a failure to detect such situations would affect the completeness of an abstract model of cryptography. It is implicitly assumed that an abstract agent recognizes undecryptable encryptions in most if not all abstract models; if a PPT agent in the computational model is strictly weaker, then the abstract model would be incomplete.

We might require that decrypting an encryption with independently generated fresh key fails with all but negligible probability (as a function of security parameter η). This property was defined in [MW04a] and called *confusion freeness*. It is sufficient to prove the completeness of an abstract model. Similar and independent definition can also be found in [AJ01].

However, confusion freeness is a quite strong requirement on an encryption scheme. It turned out not to be a necessary one: a strictly weaker notion called *weak key authenticity* was defined and shown to be both necessary and sufficient for proving completeness [HG03]. Weak key authenticity requires only that an attempt to decrypt an encryption with incorrect decryption key fails with non-negligible probability.

4 The Abstract Model

4.1 Messages as Experiments

The act of creating a cryptographic message, in view of the probabilistic character of cryptographic algorithms, is a probabilistic experiment. Say the message is $\mathcal{E}_k(\mathcal{P}(n,0))$. Without any contextual assumptions on the key k and nonce n, meaning that they should be freshly generated, this implies the following cryptographic experiment:

$$[K \xleftarrow{\$} \mathcal{K}(\eta);\, k \longleftarrow \mathcal{I}(K);\, n \xleftarrow{\$} \mathcal{N}(\eta);\, m \longleftarrow \mathcal{P}(n,0);\, e \xleftarrow{\$} \mathcal{E}(k,m) : e]$$

While it is easy to formalize the above notation for experiments directly, we skip it here. It should suffice to say that an experiment is a sequence of actions delimited with semicolon; if the experiment has an output, then it is separated from preceding actions by a colon. Left arrows are assignment operators, sometimes decorated with \$ to emphasize the use of randomized algorithms on the right hand side.

Expanding the shorthand for probabilistic algorithms, the above experiment would take the form of

$$\begin{aligned}&[c_1 \xleftarrow{\$} \texttt{Coins};\, K \longleftarrow \mathcal{K}(\eta, c_1);\, k \longleftarrow \mathcal{I}(K);\, c_2 \xleftarrow{\$} \texttt{Coins};\\ &n \longleftarrow \mathcal{N}(c_2);\, m \longleftarrow \mathcal{P}(n,0);\, c_3 \xleftarrow{\$} \texttt{Coins};\, e \longleftarrow \mathcal{E}(k,m,c_3) : e]\end{aligned}$$

We shall in the sequel assume that all experiments are so expanded, that $\xleftarrow{\$}$ appears only at the left of `Coins`.

4.2 Experiments as Terms

Here we develop a more systematic notation for representing cryptographic probabilistic experiments, with well-known and widely used *terms* of first-order logic.

In logic every function symbol comes equiped with its arity and, optionally, can be marked as relational. We in addition mark some function symbols as *probabilistic* and some as *parameterized.*

Here we list all vocabularies that will be used throughout this paper.

Vocabularies:

- Υ_{log} is the vocabulary of logical constants, containing nullary symbols true, false and undef, the usual boolean operators and the equality $=$.
- Υ_{exp} contains unary symbols key, inv, fst, snd and nonce, binary decrypt and pair, and ternary encrypt. Symbols key, nonce and encrypt are marked as probabilistic and symbols key and nonce are also marked as parameterized.
- Υ_{const} contains nullary symbols for some constants, at least for bits 0 and 1.
- Υ_{fun} contains unary relation symbols PriKey, PubKey, Ciphertext, Pair, unary len and a binary relation symbol sameKey.
- $\Upsilon = \Upsilon_{log} \cup \Upsilon_{exp} \cup \Upsilon_{const} \cup \Upsilon_{fun}$.

For experiment-representing terms the vocabulary $\Upsilon_{exp} \cup \Upsilon_{const} \cup \{\mathsf{undef}\}$ will suffice, together with some set of additional constants to denote some coins.

Definition 2. Let C be a set of constants. The set of *experiment-representing terms*, in short e-terms, of vocabulary $\Upsilon_{const} \cup \Upsilon_{exp} \cup \{\mathsf{undef}\}$ over C, is defined inductively as:

- nullary symbols in Υ_{const} and undef are e-terms;
- if n-ary symbol $f \in \Upsilon_{exp}$ is not marked as probabilistic and $t_1, \ldots, t_n$ are e-terms, then $f(t_1, \ldots, t_n)$ is an e-term; and
- if n-ary symbol $f \in \Upsilon_{exp}$ is marked as probabilistic, $t_1, \ldots, t_{n-1}$ are e-terms and $c \in C$, then $f(t_1, \ldots, t_{n-1}, c)$ is an e-term.

Given an assignment of infinite strings to constants in C and a concrete value of security parameter η, we can assign a concrete string to every e-term.

Definition 3. Let t be an experiment-representing term of vocabulary $\Upsilon_{const} \cup \Upsilon_{exp} \cup \{\mathsf{undef}\}$ over C, $\Pi = (\mathcal{K}, \mathcal{E}, \mathcal{D})$ an encryption scheme, $\Sigma = (\mathcal{P}, \mathcal{F}, \mathcal{S})$ a pairing scheme, $\mathcal{N}$ a nonce generation algorithm, and σ an assignment of infinite strings to constants in C. Then a string $[\![t]\!]_{\eta,\sigma}^{\Pi,\Sigma,\mathcal{N}}$ is defined inductively as follows (when $\Pi, \Sigma, \mathcal{N}$ are known, we drop them from the notation):

- undef is interpreted as the failure string

$$[\![\mathsf{undef}]\!]_{\eta,\sigma} = \bot$$

- if g is neither marked as probabilistic nor marked as parameterized, then

$$[\![g(t_1, \ldots, t_n)]\!]_{\eta,\sigma} = \mathcal{G}\left([\![t_1]\!]_{\eta,\sigma}, \ldots, [\![t_n]\!]_{\eta,\sigma}\right)$$

- if g is marked as probabilistic but not as parameterized, then

$$[\![g(t_1, \ldots, t_{n-1}, c)]\!]_{\eta,\sigma} = \mathcal{G}\left([\![t_1]\!]_{\eta,\sigma}, \ldots, [\![t_{n-1}]\!]_{\eta,\sigma}, \sigma(c)\right)$$

– if g is marked as both probabilistic and parameterized, then

$$[\![g(t_1,\ldots,t_{n-1},c)]\!]_{\eta,\sigma} = \mathcal{G}\left(\eta, [\![t_1]\!]_{\eta,\sigma},\ldots,[\![t_{n-1}]\!]_{\eta,\sigma},\sigma(c)\right)$$

for every $(g,\mathcal{G}) \in \{(\mathsf{key},\mathcal{K}),(\mathsf{encrypt},\mathcal{E}),(\mathsf{decrypt},\mathcal{D}),(\mathsf{pair},\mathcal{P}),(\mathsf{fst},\mathcal{F}),(\mathsf{snd},\mathcal{S}),(\mathsf{nonce},\mathcal{N})\}$ and every $c \in C$.

Thus taking any e-term t, sampling for σ from the uniform distribution we obtain a probability distribution $\Pr\left[\sigma \xleftarrow{\$} \mathcal{U} : [\![t]\!]_{\eta,\sigma}\right]$; varying η we obtain an ensemble.

The assumptions on the encryption scheme force that

$$\Pr\left[c,c' \xleftarrow{\$} \mathcal{U} : \mathcal{D}(\mathcal{K}(\eta,c),\mathcal{E}(\mathcal{I}(\mathcal{K}(\eta,c)),m,c')) = m\right] = 1$$

must hold for any message string m, while the confusion-freeness assumption forces

$$\Pr\left[c,c',c'' \xleftarrow{\$} \mathcal{U} : \mathcal{D}(\mathcal{K}(\eta,c),\mathcal{E}(\mathcal{I}(\mathcal{K}(\eta,c')),m,c'')) = \bot\right]$$

to be overwhelming for every message string m. Similar equivalences are forced by assumptions on the pairing function and projections.

We show that these equivalences carry over to formalization by e-terms, for instance that

$$\Pr\left[\sigma \xleftarrow{\$} \mathcal{U} : [\![\mathsf{decrypt}(\mathsf{key}(c_1),\mathsf{encrypt}(\mathsf{inv}(\mathsf{key}(c_1)),t,c_2))]\!]_{\eta,\sigma} = [\![t]\!]_{\eta,\sigma}\right]$$

must be overwhelming for every e-term t.

Definition 4 (Equivalence of E-Terms). Let T be a set of e-terms of vocabulary $\Upsilon_{const} \cup \Upsilon_{exp} \cup \{\mathsf{undef}\}$ over C. Then $\doteq$ is the smallest equivalence over T induced by the clauses

– for every pairwise distinct $c_1,c_2,c_3 \in C$ and every e-term t

$$\mathsf{decrypt}(t_k,t_e) = \begin{cases} t_m & \text{if } t_k = \mathsf{key}(c_k) \wedge t_e \doteq \mathsf{encrypt}(\mathsf{inv}(t_k),t_m,c_e) \\ \mathsf{undef} & \text{otherwise} \end{cases}$$

– for all e-terms t_1,t_2,t, where $t \neq \mathsf{pair}(x,y)$ for all x,y, then

$$\mathsf{fst}(t) = \begin{cases} t_f & \text{if } t \doteq \mathsf{pair}(t_f,t_s) \\ \mathsf{undef} & \text{otherwise} \end{cases} \qquad \mathsf{snd}(t) = \begin{cases} t_s & \text{if } t \doteq \mathsf{pair}(t_f,t_s) \\ \mathsf{undef} & \text{otherwise} \end{cases}$$

Let $[t]_{\doteq}$ be the standard notation for the class of $\doteq$ equivalent terms. The above definition justifies the common representation of cryptographic messages with terms without decrypt, fst and snd symbols:

Corollary 2. *For every e-term t there is an e-term t_0 in which* decrypt, fst *and* snd *do not occur and $t_0 \doteq t$.*

Finally, we will show that the equivalence just introduced is justified by its computational interpretation.

Lemma 1. *Let t_1, t_2 be experiment-representing terms of vocabulary $\Upsilon_{const} \cup \Upsilon_{exp} \cup \{\mathsf{undef}\}$ over C, $\Pi = (\mathcal{K}, \mathcal{E}, \mathcal{D})$ a confusion-free encryption scheme, $\Sigma = (\mathcal{P}, \mathcal{F}, \mathcal{S})$ a pairing scheme, $\mathcal{N}$ a nonce generation algorithm. If $t_1 \doteq t_2$, then*

$$\Pr\left[\sigma \xleftarrow{\$} \mathcal{U} : [\![t_1]\!]_{\eta,\sigma} = [\![t_2]\!]_{\eta,\sigma}\right]$$

is overwhelming in η.

Proof. The proof is by induction on the definition of equivalence $\doteq$. Use the assumptions on Π, Σ, the confusion freeness property of Π and the fact that negligible functions are closed under addition. □

Remark 3. A corresponding statement can be made in the case of weak key authenticity. Under this assumption, the statement of the above lemma becomes

$$\Pr\left[\sigma \xleftarrow{\$} \mathcal{U} : [\![t_1]\!]_{\eta,\sigma} = [\![t_2]\!]_{\eta,\sigma}\right]$$

is not negligible in η. The proof is (almost) the same.

We shall often assume the following properties of encryption schemes:

$$\Pr\left[c_1, c_2 \xleftarrow{\$} \mathcal{U} : \mathcal{K}(c_1) = \mathcal{K}(c_2)\right]$$
$$\Pr\left[c_k, c_1, c_2 \xleftarrow{\$} \mathcal{U} : \mathcal{E}(\mathcal{K}(\mathcal{I}(c_k)), m, c_1) = \mathcal{E}(\mathcal{K}(\mathcal{I}(c_k)), m, c_2)\right]$$

are both negligible in η. We shall name these properties, which easily follow from the usual security notions such as IND-CPA, but are themselves much weaker, as "random keys" and "random encryption" properties.

Lemma 2. *Let Π be a confusion-free encryption scheme with random keys and random encryption properties, Σ a pairing scheme, $\mathcal{N}$ a secure nonce generation algorithm and t_1, t_2 e-terms. If $[t_1]_{\doteq} \neq [t_2]_{\doteq}$ then*

$$\Pr\left[\sigma \xleftarrow{\$} \mathcal{U} :\ [\![t_1]\!]^{\Pi,\Sigma}_{\eta,\sigma} = [\![t_2]\!]^{\Pi,\Sigma}_{\eta,\sigma}\right]$$

is negligible in η.

Proof. By Lemma 1 and Corollary 2, it suffices to show that

$$\Pr\left[\sigma \xleftarrow{\$} \mathcal{U} :\ [\![t_1]\!] = [\![t_2]\!]\right]$$

is negligible for terms t_1 and t_2 in which $\mathsf{decrypt}, \mathsf{fst}$ and snd do not occur. The rest of the proof is straightforward simultaneous induction on the structure of construction terms t_1 and t_2. □

4.3 Experiments as Structures

Given a set of abstract representatives of coins to interprete constants from C, we can organize the e-terms modulo $\doteq$ to a first-order structure. What it buys us is possibility to harness the well-developed theory of interactive algorithms of [BG04a, BG04b], which operate over such structures as their states.

If elements of the structure are essentially equivalence classes of e-terms, and $\doteq$ is closed under substitution, the interpretation of any function g in the vocabulary $\Upsilon_{const} \cup \Upsilon_{exp} \cup \{\mathsf{undef}\}$ is naturally defined as

$$g([t_1]_{\doteq}, \dots, [t_n]_{\doteq}) = [g(t_1, \dots, t_n)]_{\doteq}$$

The logical part of the structure is defined in the usual way. Some additional relations are added to the interpretation, reflecting the assumptions on the tagging scheme $\mathcal{T}$, holding in codomains of functions key, encrypt, pair and nonce.

We proceed with a verbose definition of an isomorphism-closed classes of structures $\mathcal{K}$.

Definition 5. Let $\mathcal{K}$ be an isomorphism closed class of Υ–structures such that $X \in \mathcal{K}$ if and only if there is a uniquely defined set Coins_X such that:

- true, false and undef denote distinct elements; elements in domains and codomains of all logical constants except equality are *logical elements* in X; the interpretations of logical connectives in Υ_{log} are the usual ones, and
- each $k \in \Upsilon_{const}$ denotes a unique non-logical element, we denote the set of such elements Const;
- domains and codomains of functions in Υ_{const} and Υ_{exp}, and the set Coins_X contain non-logical elements only;
- the non-logical part of X is freely generated with functions key, inv, encrypt, pair and nonce from $\mathsf{Coins}_X \cup \mathsf{Const}$;
- PriKey, PubKey, Ciphertext, Pair and Nonce hold on codomains of functions key, inv, encrypt, pair and nonce respectively,
- sets Coins_X, Const, PriKey, PubKey, Ciphertext, Pair, Nonce are pairwise disjoint, and we define $\mathsf{Msg} = \mathsf{Const} \cup \mathsf{PriKey} \cup \mathsf{PubKey} \cup \mathsf{Ciphertext} \cup \mathsf{Pair} \cup \mathsf{Nonce}$;
- functions key, inv, encrypt, pair, nonce are injective, with the domains Coins_X, PriKey, $\mathsf{PubKey} \times \mathsf{Msg} \times \mathsf{Coins}_X$, $\mathsf{Msg} \times \mathsf{Msg}$, Coins_X, respectively;
- decrypt, fst and snd are defined as

$$\begin{aligned} \mathsf{fst}(\mathsf{pair}(m_1, m_2)) &= m_1 \\ \mathsf{snd}(\mathsf{pair}(m_1, m_2)) &= m_2 \\ \mathsf{decrypt}(\mathsf{key}(c_1), \mathsf{encrypt}(\mathsf{key}(\mathsf{inv}(c_1)), m, c_2)) &= m \end{aligned}$$

  for every $m, m_1, m_2 \in \mathsf{Msg}$ and every $c_1, c_2 \in \mathsf{Coins}_X$; elsewhere these functions take the value undef;

– function len assigns an integer to each $m \in \mathsf{Msg}$ such that, assuming $\mathsf{len}(m_1)=\mathsf{len}(m'_1), \mathsf{len}(m_2) = \mathsf{len}(m'_2)$, we have:

$$\begin{aligned}
&\mathsf{len}(\mathsf{pair}(m_1, m_2)) = \mathsf{len}(\mathsf{pair}(m'_1, m'_2))\\
&\mathsf{len}(\mathsf{encrypt}(\mathsf{inv}(\mathsf{key}(c_1)), m_1, c_2)) = \mathsf{len}(\mathsf{encrypt}(\mathsf{inv}(\mathsf{key}(c'_1)), m'_1, c'_2))\\
&\mathsf{len}(m_1) + \mathsf{len}(m_2) \leq \mathsf{len}(\mathsf{pair}(m_1, m_2))\\
&\mathsf{len}(m_1) \leq \mathsf{len}(\mathsf{encrypt}(\mathsf{inv}(\mathsf{key}(c_1)), m_1, c_2));
\end{aligned}$$

for every $m_1, m'_1, m_2, m'_2 \in \mathsf{Msg}$ and every $c_1, c'_1, c_2, c'_2 \in \mathsf{Coins}_X$;if the argument is not in Msg, len takes the value undef.

– relation sameKey holds in e_1, e_2 iff $e_1 = \mathsf{encrypt}(\mathsf{inv}(\mathsf{key}(c)), m_1, c_1)$ and $e_2 = \mathsf{encrypt}(\mathsf{inv}(\mathsf{key}(c)), m_2, c_2)$ for some $c, c_1, c_2 \in \mathsf{Coins}_X$, $m_1, m_2 \in \mathsf{Msg}$.

Defining the structure, we have used e-terms with set of constants $C = \mathsf{Coins}_X$.

What exactly is the relation of e-terms and structures just defined? Elements of Coins_X are not accessible by ground terms in a structure $X \in \mathcal{K}$, and therefor e-terms cannot be directly evaluated in X. But if we expand the structure X with constant symbols denoting Coins_X, then non-logical elements can be seen as a class of $\doteq$ equivalent terms. For $X \in \mathcal{K}$, we will denote with X^+ its unique expansion with constants Coins_X denoting themselves in X^+. Since the non-logical part of X is freely generated by key, inv, encrypt, pair, nonce from $\mathsf{Const} \cup \mathsf{Coins}_X$, there is a unique ground term t_x^X of vocabulary $\{\mathsf{key}, \mathsf{inv}, \mathsf{encrypt}, \mathsf{pair}, \mathsf{nonce}\} \cup \Upsilon_{const} \cup \mathsf{Coins}_X$ denoting every non-logical x in X^+. Denote with T_x^X the set of all ground terms denoting x in X^+. Then T_x^X is exactly $[t_x^X]_{\doteq}$. This reading of the definition allows us to attach the computational interpretation to elements of structures as well.

Definition 6. *Let $X \in \mathcal{K}$, x a non-logical element in X and σ an assignment of infinite strings to Coins_X. Then*

$$[\![x]\!]_{X,\eta,\sigma} = [\![t_x^X]\!]_{\eta,\sigma}.$$

If any of the parameters is determined by the context, we might suppress it and ultimately write $[\![t]\!]$ and $[\![x]\!]$ if all parameters are understood from the context.

By Lemma 1 and Lemma 2, both equality and inequality on non-logical part are preserved with overwhelming probability. If we fix some distinct coding of the logical elements, then we can extend the computational interpretation to all elements of the structure. The abstract interpretation will be preserved with overwhelming probability by the computational representation.

Corollary 3. *Let $\Pi = (\mathcal{K}, \mathcal{I}, \mathcal{E}, \mathcal{D})$ be a confusion-free encryption scheme with random keys and random encryption properties, $\Sigma = (\mathcal{P}, \mathcal{F}, \mathcal{S})$ a pairing scheme, $\mathcal{N}$ a secure nonce generation algorithm, $X \in \mathcal{K}$ and t_1, t_2 terms of X^+. Then $Val(t_1, X^+) = Val(t_2, X^+)$ if and only if $[\![t_1]\!]_{\eta,\sigma} = [\![t_2]\!]_{\eta,\sigma}$ with overwhelming probability.*

4.4 Experiments and Algorithms

If we wanted to capture full static logic of asymptotic computational cryptography, we would need much more involved logical constructions. But full static logic is not what we are after, capturing equality and inequality suffices for our purposes. Equality and inequality, which means similarity, suffices to determine the behavior of abstract interactive algorithms of [BG04a, BG04b].

Under the computational interpretation, concrete PPT Turing machines operating on concrete cryptographic messages can simulate abstract algorithms operating over structures representing such messages. A concrete PPT Turing Machine, run on a tape containing a finite set of cryptographic messages, can analyze the messages by running deterministic algorithms such as decryption $\mathcal{D}$ and projections of pairs $\mathcal{F}$ and $\mathcal{S}$, testing parts of analyzed messages for equality etc. It can also create new messages by running probabilistic key and nonce generation algorithms $\mathcal{K}$ and $\mathcal{N}$, encryption algorithm $\mathcal{E}$, or deterministic algorithms such as the pairing algorithm $\mathcal{P}$.

The fact that concrete PPT Turing machines can do essentially no more than the abstract algorithms will be forced by security assumptions on the encryption schemes.

Abstract algorithms represent all possible internal actions of an algorithm with evaluation of terms, and external actions, such as receiving of input messages, with an answer function attached to a state. Internal memory of the abstract algorithm will be modeled with additional functions expanding the structures. The modeling choices we just made are quite obvious and sufficient for everything but coin flipping, e.g. creation of fresh nonces, encryptions etc.

The behavioral theory of algorithms has a well developed theory of importing of fresh objects. Almost every non-trivial application of the theory use importing over a background structure. There is nothing fundamentally different in extending the working space of an algorithm with a fresh atom used to build hereditarily finite sets, or with a fresh atom representing a fresh coin flip used for probabilistic functions. Only atoms that are not used in any meaningful way in the state can be imported, and the exact choice of the atom imported is irrelevant since they all produce isomorphic states.

The isomorphism-closed class of structures $\mathcal{K}$ is a background classes with $Atoms(X) = \mathsf{Coins}_X$ for every $X \in \mathcal{K}$. We will denote it by BC_{CPA}.

Let A be an ordinary interactive small–step algorithm with background BC_{CPA}. In every state X, A evaluates a finite set of terms, possibly using results of interaction with its environment α, and finally, based of the result of the evaluation, generates an update set $\Delta_A^+(X, \alpha)$. We will make no limitations on coins that can be imported by α, except the usual one that an imported coin must be a reserve atom.

Definition 7. *Let A be an ordinary interactive small-step algorithm with background BC_{CPA} and X its state. Let Π an encryption scheme, Σ a pairing scheme and $\mathcal{N}$ a nonce generation algorithm. Then*

– $[\![X]\!]_{\eta,\sigma}$ *is a concatenation of strings* $[\![x]\!]_{\eta,\sigma}$ *for all accessible* $x \in X$.
– $[\![A]\!]_{\eta}$ *is a Turing machine that evaluates computational interpretations of abstract terms evaluated by* A.

Example 3. An abstract algorithm modeling the first action of responder B in the Needham–Schroeder protocol:

$$A \xrightarrow{\{k_A, n_A\}_{k_B}} B$$
$$\xleftarrow{\{n_A, n_B\}_{k_A}}$$

is given with the following ASM program:

$$
\begin{array}{l}
\texttt{let}\ p = \mathsf{decrypt}(\mathsf{B}, \mathsf{in}), k_A = \mathsf{fst}(p),\ n_A = \mathsf{snd}(p)\ \texttt{in} \\
\quad \texttt{if}\ \mathsf{PubKey}(k_A)\ \texttt{and}\ \mathsf{Nonce}(n_A) \\
\quad \texttt{then} \\
\quad\quad \texttt{import}\ \mathsf{c}_1, \mathsf{c}_2\ \texttt{in} \\
\quad\quad\quad \texttt{let}\ n_B = \mathsf{nonce}(\mathsf{c}_1)\ \texttt{in} \\
\quad\quad\quad\quad \mathsf{a} := k_A \\
\quad\quad\quad\quad \mathsf{n} := n_A \\
\quad\quad\quad\quad \mathsf{m} := n_B \\
\quad\quad\quad\quad \mathsf{out}(\mathsf{encrypt}(k_A, \mathsf{pair}(n_A, n_B), \mathsf{c}_2))
\end{array}
$$

The program is executed in a state X with background BC_{CPA} and a context α. State X contains a constant B denoting the private key K_B, and undefined constants n, m, and a. Context α is

$$\alpha = \{(\mathsf{c}_1, c_1), (\mathsf{c}_2, c_2), (\mathsf{in}, e_1), (\mathsf{out}[e_2], \mathsf{ack})\}$$

for some $c_1, c_2 \in \mathit{Reserve}(X)$ and encryptions $e_1, e_2 \in X$. Queries in and out are used for communicating for the environment, while c_1 and c_2 represent internal coin flips made by the algorithm—environment replies to queries $\mathsf{c}_1, \mathsf{c}_2$.

The corresponding Turing machine $[\![A]\!]_{\eta}$ operates on three tapes. The first tape represents the internal memory of the algorithm and contains the string $[\![K_B]\!]_{\eta,\sigma}$. The second one represents internal randomness needed by the algorithm, it is an infinite sequence of random bits. The third tape represents interaction with an environment, containing $[\![e_1]\!]_{\eta,\sigma}$ at beginning and $[\![e_2]\!]_{\eta,\sigma}$ at the end of the calculation.

The interpretation of actions of an abstract algorithm with experiments deserve some additional attention. The (abstract) work performed by an algorithm is measured in ground terms it evaluates. Evaluation of a term is inductively defined as:

1. interpretation of a background function,
2. interpretation of a foreground function, and
3. querying and receiving an answer from the environment.

Work performed in (1) amounts to evaluation of the appropriate function $\mathcal{G}$ represented by a background function g. Foreground functions represent the internal memory of an algorithm, and therefore (2) is usually a simple memory lookup. Work performed by the environment (3) is not done by the algorithm, as it simply creates queries and uses the answers provided. This view has the following simple consequence when A is instantiated with a concrete implementation working on strings:

Corollary 4. *Let A be a small–step algorithm with background BC_{CPA}, Π an encryption scheme, and Σ an pairing scheme. Then $[\![A]\!]_\eta$ is a* PPT *Turing machine.*

As already said, we will assume that every algorithm is capable of performing experiments on its own, and therefore we will pose no restriction on importing of fresh coins from the reserve of a state. However, algorithms might also receive, within a step, results of experiments from its environment, such as answers obtained by oracles. Specific modeling circumstances, such as a specific notion of security, will determine our restrictions on such answer functions.

Theorem 4 (Completeness). *Let $\Pi = (\mathcal{K}, \mathcal{I}, \mathcal{E}, \mathcal{D})$ be a confusion-free encryption scheme with random keys and random encryptions, $\Sigma = (\mathcal{P}, \mathcal{F}, \mathcal{S})$ a pairing scheme and $\mathcal{N}$ a secure nonce generation algorithm. Furthermore, assume that for all but a finite number of values of η:*

- $\mathsf{len}(x) = \mathsf{len}(y)$ *in X iff $|[\![x]\!]_{\eta,\sigma}| = |[\![y]\!]_{\eta,\sigma}|$ for every state X with background BC_{CPA};*
- *encryption scheme Π is equipped with a* PPT *algorithm that can distinguish two encryptions created with different keys.*

Let X and Y be states with background BC_{CPA}. If $X \not\simeq Y$ then there is a PPT *algorithm distinguishing $[\![X]\!]_\eta$ and $[\![Y]\!]_\eta$ with overwhelming probability.*

Proof. If $X \not\simeq Y$, then there are ground terms t_1 and t_2 such that $Val(t_1, X) = Val(t_2, X)$ and $Val(t_1, Y) \neq Val(t_2, Y)$. By Corollary 3, the equality and inequality of terms is preserved with overwhelming probability by the computational interpretation. Let A be an algorithm outputting true when $t_1 = t_2$ and false otherwise. Then $[\![A]\!]_\eta$ distinguishes $[\![X]\!]_\eta$ and $[\![Y]\!]_\eta$ with overwhelming probability. By Corollary 4,, $[\![A]\!]_\eta$ is a PPT algorithm. □

4.5 Abstract Notions of Security

Abstract interactive algorithms of [BG04a, BG04b] allow us to model the oracle adversary games defining cryptographic security notions directly on the abstract level!

The security of an encryption scheme is completely characterized with the corresponding oracles attached to a PPT algorithm trying to break the security of an encryption scheme, as described in section 3.2. The oracles attached to the algorithm also perform experiments, and the results of the experiments are already representable by elements of the base set of the background classes BC_{CPA}. From the algorithm's point of view, actions of oracles are actions of its environment. Interaction of an algorithm and environment is well studied in the behavioral theory of algorithm. It is represented with a collection of answer functions attached to a state completely characterizing all possible reactions of environment.

We will show how to view definitions of the notions of security from section 3.2 abstractly as a set of abstract answer functions attached to a state of an algorithm. Recall the IND-CPA notion of security given by Definition 2. Its abstract representation is as follows, minding that $\mathsf{n}, \mathsf{pk}, \mathsf{eo}(x, y)$ are *queries* asking the environment for a new nonce, a new private key, an encryption of one of the two messages respecitvely:

Definition 8. Let X be a state with background BC_{CPA}. Then

- a context α of an ordinary interactive small–step algorithm A in X is *IND-CPA good* if there are distinct elements $c^k, c_1, \ldots, c_n, c_1^e, \ldots, c_k^e$ in the reserve of X such that

$$\alpha(\mathsf{n}_i) = c_i$$
$$\alpha(\mathsf{pk}) = \mathsf{inv}_X(\mathsf{key}_X(c^k))$$
$$\alpha(\mathsf{eo}_j(x_j, y_j)) = \begin{cases} \mathsf{encrypt}_X(\mathsf{inv}_X(\mathsf{key}_X(c^k)), x_j, c_j^e) & \text{if } \mathsf{len}_X(x_j) = \mathsf{len}_X(y_j) \\ \mathsf{undef} & \text{otherwise} \end{cases}$$

  for some $x_j, y_j \in X$, $i = 1, \ldots, n$, $j = 1, \ldots, k$; and
- a context β of an ordinary interactive small–step algorithm A in X is *IND-CPA fake* if there are distinct elements $c^k, c_1, \ldots, c_n, c_1^e, \ldots, c_k^e$ in the reserve of X such that

$$\alpha(\mathsf{n}_i) = c_i$$
$$\alpha(\mathsf{pk}) = \mathsf{inv}_X(\mathsf{key}_X(c^k))$$
$$\alpha(\mathsf{eo}_j(x_j, y_j)) = \begin{cases} \mathsf{encrypt}_X(\mathsf{inv}_X(\mathsf{key}_X(c^k)), y_j, c_j^e) & \text{if } \mathsf{len}_X(x_j) = \mathsf{len}_X(y_j) \\ \mathsf{undef} & \text{otherwise} \end{cases}$$

  for some $x_j, y_j \in X$, $i = 1, \ldots, n$, $j = 1, \ldots, k$.

Let $\mathcal{A}$ be the set of all IND-CPA good contexts and $\mathcal{B}$ the set of all IND-CPA fake contexts in state X. Then $\mathcal{A}, \mathcal{B}$ is *the abstract model of IND-CPA oracle interaction* in X.

Instantiations of these answer functions with concrete encryption schemes are exactly the experiments defined with the IND-CPA notion of security in Definition 2.

Both IND-CCA good and fake contexts are extension of IND-CPA good and fake contexts with additional queries and answers representing the decryption oracles

$$\alpha(\mathsf{do}(x_l)) = \beta(\mathsf{do}(x_l)) = \mathsf{decrypt}_X(\mathsf{key}_X(c^k), x_l)$$

for some x_l such that x_l *is not* one of the answers to encrypt queries in α or β, for $l = 1, \ldots, m$.

The abstract model of interaction of IND-CPA notion of security induces an equivalence relation on states in the following way. We say that a small–step algorithm A *reduces* state X to state Y for answer functions α, β if $X = A(\mathbf{0}_X, \alpha)$ and $Y = A(\mathbf{0}_Y, \beta)$. State X is *reducible* to Y for α, β if such a small–step algorithm exists.

Definition 9. Let $\mathcal{A}, \mathcal{B}$ be the abstract model of IND-CPA interaction. Then X is reducible to Y for IND-CPA, denoted with $X \xrightarrow{\text{CPA}} Y$, if X is reducible to Y for some $\alpha \in \mathcal{A}$ and $\beta \in \mathcal{B}$. If both α and β are parameterized with the same oracle encryption key K, then we also write $X \xrightarrow{K} Y$.

The equivalence induced by the reducibility relation for IND-CPA relation, its transitive and symmetric closure, is denoted with $X \overset{\text{CPA}}{=} Y$.

Lemma 3. *Let Π be a confusion-free IND-CPA secure encryption scheme, Σ a pairing scheme and $\mathcal{N}$ a secure nonce generation algorithm. Let X and Y states with background BC_{CPA}. If $X \overset{\text{CPA}}{=} Y$, then $[\![X]\!]_\eta$ is indistinguishable from $[\![Y]\!]_\eta$ by probabilistic polynomial time algorithms with all but negligible probability.*

Proof. Since computational indistinguishability is an equivalence, it is sufficient to show that $[\![X]\!]_\eta \approx [\![Y]\!]_\eta$ when $X \xrightarrow{\text{CPA}} Y$.

We argue by contradiction. Suppose there is a PPT algorithm $\mathcal{A}$ distinguishing $[\![X]\!]_\eta$ and $[\![Y]\!]_\eta$ with non-negligible probability. We will use this algorithm to distinguish oracles characterizing IND-CPA security.

Denote with α an IND-CPA good context and with β an IND-CPA fake context such that for some algorithm A we have $X = A(\mathbf{0}_X, \alpha)$ and $Y = A(\mathbf{0}_Y, \beta)$. Run the algorithm $[\![A]\!]_\eta$ with an IND-CPA oracle to create $[\![X]\!]_{\eta,\sigma}$ or $[\![Y]\!]_{\eta,\sigma}$, depending on whether you are provided with a good oracle or a fake one. Run $\mathcal{A}$ on the resulting state. If $\mathcal{A}$ can distinguish $[\![X]\!]_{\eta,\sigma}$ from $[\![Y]\!]_{\eta,\sigma}$ with non-negligible probability, then we can break IND-CPA security of the encryption scheme used. □

The above lemma tells us that certain challenges are indistinguishable as a simple consequence of the notion of security. If two inputs of a challenge can be generated by the same abstract algorithm, but using two different oracles, then it is clear that this algorithm, if successful, would break security of the underlying encryption scheme.

Remark 4. Given some enumeration of coins $c_1, c_2, \ldots$ in a state X, we will often use the following notation for elements of X: n_i for $\mathsf{nonce}_X(c_i)$, K_i for $\mathsf{key}_X(c_i)$, k_i for $\mathsf{inv}_X(\mathsf{key}_X(c_i))$, $\langle m_1, m_2\rangle$ for $\mathsf{pair}_X(m_1, m_2)$ and $\{m\}^i_{K_j}$ for $\mathsf{encrypt}_X(k_j, m, c_i)$. If a state has a single nullary foreground symbol, then we will identify the state with the unique element the symbol is denoting in it. E.g. a state X with f denoting $\mathsf{encrypt}_X(\mathsf{inv}_X(\mathsf{key}_X(c_2)), \mathsf{key}_X(c_1), c_3)$ for some coins $c_1, c_2, c_3 \in \mathit{Reserve}(X)$ is identified with $\{K_1\}^3_{K_2}$.

Example 4. We will show that

$$\{\{K_1\}^4_{K_2}, K_3\}^5_{K_1} \xrightarrow{K_2} \{\{0\}^4_{K_2}, K_3\}^5_{K_1} \xrightarrow{K_1} \{0\}^5_{K_1}$$

for IND-CPA security (assuming that 0 denotes a zero string of an appropriate length). Let A_1 and A_2 be algorithms with programs Π_1 and Π_2:

$$\begin{aligned}
\Pi_1 \quad = \quad & \texttt{import } \mathsf{c}_1, \mathsf{c}_3, \mathsf{c}_5 \\
& \quad \texttt{let } K_1 = \mathsf{key}(\mathsf{c}_1),\ K_3 = \mathsf{key}(\mathsf{c}_3),\ k_1 = \mathsf{inv}(K_1) \texttt{ in} \\
& \quad\ \mathsf{f} := \mathsf{encrypt}(K_1, \mathsf{pair}(\mathsf{eo}(K_1, 0), K_3), \mathsf{c}_5) \\
\Pi_2 \quad = \quad & \texttt{import } \mathsf{c}_2, \mathsf{c}_3, \mathsf{c}_4 \\
& \quad \texttt{let } K_2 = \mathsf{key}(\mathsf{c}_2),\ K_3 = \mathsf{key}(\mathsf{c}_3),\ k_2 = \mathsf{inv}(K_2) \texttt{ in} \\
& \quad\ \mathsf{f} := \mathsf{eo}(\mathsf{pair}(\mathsf{encrypt}(k_2, 0, \mathsf{c}_4), K_3), 0)
\end{aligned}$$

and let IND-CPA positive α_1, α_2 and IND-CPA negative β_1, β_2 be

$$\begin{aligned}
\alpha_1 &= \{(\mathsf{c}_1, c_1), (\mathsf{c}_3, c_3), (\mathsf{c}_5, c_5), (\mathsf{eo}[K_1, 0], \{K_1\}^4_{K_2})\} \\
\beta_1 &= \{(\mathsf{c}_1, c_1), (\mathsf{c}_3, c_3), (\mathsf{c}_5, c_5), (\mathsf{eo}[K_1, 0], \{0\}^4_{K_2})\} \\
\alpha_2 &= \{(\mathsf{c}_2, c_2), (\mathsf{c}_3, c_3), (\mathsf{c}_4, c_4), (\mathsf{eo}[\langle\{0\}^4_{K_2}, K_3\rangle, 0], \{\langle\{0\}^4_{K_2}, K_3\rangle\}^5_{K_1})\} \\
\beta_2 &= \{(\mathsf{c}_2, c_2), (\mathsf{c}_3, c_3), (\mathsf{c}_4, c_4), (\mathsf{eo}[\langle\{0\}^4_{K_2}, K_3\rangle, 0], \{0\}^5_{K_1})\}
\end{aligned}$$

Then

$$\begin{aligned}
A_1(0, \alpha_1) &= \{\{K_1\}^4_{K_2}, K_3\}^5_{K_1} & A_1(0, \beta_1) &= \{\{0\}^4_{K_2}, K_3\}^5_{K_1} \\
A_2(0, \alpha_2) &= \{\{0\}^4_{K_2}, K_3\}^5_{K_1} & A_2(0, \beta_2) &= \{0\}^5_{K_1}
\end{aligned}$$

By Lemma 3, we can conclude that

$$\begin{aligned}
\mathsf{Adv}(\mathcal{A}) = \Pr &\left[K_1, K_2, K_3 \xleftarrow{\$} \mathcal{K}(\eta); e \xleftarrow{\$}: \mathcal{E}_{k_1}(\mathcal{P}(\mathcal{E}_{k_2}(K_1), K_3)) :\ \mathcal{A}(e) = 1\right] \\
&- \Pr\left[K_1 \xleftarrow{\$} \mathcal{K}(\eta); e \xleftarrow{\$} \mathcal{E}_{k_1}(0^\ell) :\ \mathcal{A}(e) = 1\right]
\end{aligned}$$

is negligible for every PPT algorithm $\mathcal{A}$ (we use $k_i = \mathcal{I}(K_i)$).

5 Soundness and Completeness of the Abstract Model

5.1 Indistinguishability

If we prove that state X and Y are indistinguishable by small–step algorithms, what have we proved? We hope that than there is no probabilistic polytime algorithm that can distinguish strings produced by experiments encoded by X and Y with all but negligible probability.

For the IND-CPA notion of security, the background class BC_{CPA}, an encryption scheme Π, a pairing scheme Σ and a nonce generation algorithm $\mathcal{N}$, we have three equivalence relations on abstract states with background BC_{CPA} representing experiments

1. computational indistinguishability;
2. abstract indistinguishability; and
3. abstract reducibility.

If $[\![X]\!]_\eta$ and $[\![Y]\!]_\eta$ are indistinguishable by PPT algorithms, we write $X \overset{\Pi}{\approx} Y$. Computational indistinguishability is the semantical relation on states, defined independently from our formalism in terms of capabilities of probabilistic polynomial time Turing machines.

If X and Y are indistinguishable by small–step algorithms, we write $X \sim Y$. Abstract indistinguishability articulates our intention about what an encryption scheme should achieve. It can also be seen as the power explicitly given to an agent by an encryption scheme: if an agent can distinguish two states with an abstract algorithm, then she can use an instantiation of the program to distinguish instantiations of the states, all with the concrete instantiated encryption scheme. This property is usually called *completeness*, and it can be phrased as "whatever an abstract algorithm can do, a concrete instantiation can do with overwhelming probability as well". The proof given in Theorem 4 is quite straightforward, but it involves some simple reasoning about probabilities. This is necessary, since it relates an abstract relation with semantics defined in terms of PPT algorithms. We get

$$X \not\sim Y \;\Rightarrow\; X \overset{\Pi}{\not\approx} Y,$$

or equivalently

$$X \overset{\Pi}{\approx} Y \;\Rightarrow\; X \sim Y. \tag{1}$$

Abstract reducibility tells us what a concrete PPT algorithm *cannot do* as a direct consequence of the notion of security. The proof given in Lemma 3 is again very simple, it is nothing more than expressing what is the true meaning of a particular notion of security. We get

$$X \overset{\text{CPA}}{=} Y \;\Rightarrow\; X \overset{\Pi}{\approx} Y \tag{2}$$

From equations (1) and (2), we have

$$X \overset{\text{CPA}}{=} Y \;\Rightarrow\; X \overset{\Pi}{\approx} Y \;\Rightarrow\; X \sim Y \tag{3}$$

If we could relate *abstract notions of equivalence* by showing that

$$X \sim Y \;\Rightarrow\; X \overset{\text{CPA}}{=} Y, \tag{4}$$

we could, using (3), conclude that all three notions are equivalent

$$X \sim Y \;\Leftrightarrow\; X \overset{\text{CPA}}{=} Y \;\Leftrightarrow\; X \overset{\Pi}{\approx} Y.$$

The theorem establishing (4) is the essence of the computational soundness of abstract wrt computational cryptography. It is also the most difficult one to prove. However, it is expressed and proved completely in abstract terms, with no mention of Turing machines and their probabilities to distinguish concrete strings in PPT time.

A state X is said to be in (IND-CPA) *normal form* if every accessible encryption with inaccessible decryption key has zero string (of appropriate length) as a subject.

Let $\mathcal{A}, \mathcal{B}$ be the model of interaction for IND-CPA security in $\mathbf{0}_X$. If an inaccessible key k is not a subject of any used message in a state X, then X can be constructed from $\mathbf{0}_X$ by a small–step algorithm A and some $\alpha \in \mathcal{A}$. If A is run on $\mathbf{0}_X, \beta$ for some $\beta \in \mathcal{B}$, we can produce a state X' in which k encrypts only zeros, like we did in Example 4.

Lemma 4. *Let X be a state with background BC_{CPA} and K a decryption key not occurring as a submessage of any used encryption in X. Then $X \xrightarrow{\text{CPA}} X'$ for some state X' with the same background reduct and the same accessibility of nonces and keys such that*

- *all keys and nonces are accessible with the same terms in both X and X';*
- *key K encrypts only zero strings in X'; and*
- *if encryption key k_1 encrypts decryption key K_2 or nonce n in X', then k_1 encrypts K_2 or n in X as well.*

Now we have everything we need to prove that acyclic states are reducible to normal form.

Lemma 5. *Let X be an acyclic state with background BC_{CPA} and accessible all exposed elements. Then X is IND-CPA reducible to its normal form.*

Proof. Enumerate inaccessible decryption keys such that encryption key k_j does not encrypt K_i if $i \leq j$. Since the state is acyclic, such numeration is possible.

We will reduce X in n steps to a state X_n such that 0 is the only used subject encrypted by an inaccessible encryption key. The proof is by induction on the enumeration of inaccessible decryption keys. Key K_1 is inaccessible and does not occur as a submessage of subject of any used encryption in X. By Lemma 4, then there is a state X_1 such that $X_0 \xrightarrow{\text{CPA}} X_1$, k_1 does not encrypt any decryption key in X_1 and encrypts in X_1 is a subrelation of encrypts in X. Hence, the enumeration of keys in X is good for X_1. Since key k_1 does not encrypts any decryption key in X_1, there is no key in X_1 that encrypts K_2 in X_1. But then K_2 satisfies the condition of Lemma 4 in X_1 and we can make another step of the induction.

In X_n, subject of every undecryptable encryption is zero. Thus X_n is in the normal form.

□

An example of a reduction of a (cyclic) state to its normal form is given in Example 4.

Since a normal form is a representative of its similarity class, we have:

Corollary 5. *Let X and Y be acyclic states with background BC_{CPA} and accessible all exposed elements. If $X \sim Y$ then $X \overset{\text{CPA}}{=} Y$.*

Theorem 5 (Soundness). *Let Π be an IND-CPA secure encryption scheme, Σ a pairing scheme, $\mathcal{N}$ a nonce generation algorithm, and X and Y acyclic states with background BC_{CPA}. If $X \sim Y$, then $[\![X]\!]_\eta$ and $[\![Y]\!]_\eta$ are indistinguishable by probabilistic polynomial time algorithms.*

Proof. We will assume that all exposed elements are accessible in both states. If a state contains exposed but inaccessible elements, replace it with a state obtained by undefining all foreground functions on such elements. The resulting state is clearly computationally indistinguishable from the original one, it provides the same information to the intruder. By Corollary 5, we have $X \overset{\text{CPA}}{=} Y$. Finally, by Lemma 3, $[\![X]\!]_\eta$ and $[\![Y]\!]_\eta$ are indistinguishable. □

5.2 Accessibility

If an element x is not accessible by a term in X, α for some state X with background BC_{CPA} and α whose codomain is in the reserve of the state, can we conclude that no PPT algorithm can output $[\![x]\!]_\eta$ when run on $[\![X]\!]_\eta$ with non-negligible probability? The similar theorem was proved for an Abadi–Rogaway language in [MW04b]. We will extend the soundness result of the previous subsection to accessibility here.

Lemma 6. *Let X be a state with background BC_{CPA} and $x \in X$ with non-empty support in X: $Sup_X(\{x\}) \neq \emptyset$. Then*

$$\Pr\left[\sigma \xleftarrow{\$} \mathcal{U} : \mathcal{A} = [\![x]\!]_{X,\eta,\sigma}\right]$$

is negligible for every PPT algorithm $\mathcal{A}$.

Intuitively, this means that a PPT algorithm cannot guess an independently created key, nonce or encryption if no data is provided to it.

Lemma 7. *Let Π be an IND-CCA secure encryption scheme and X, X' non-isomorphic states with background BC_{CPA} such that $X \xrightarrow{\text{K}} X'$ for IND-CCA contexts α and β. If some PPT algorithm $\mathcal{A}$ can produce $[\![x]\!]_{X,\eta,\sigma}$ with non-negligible probability when run on $[\![X]\!]_{\eta,\sigma}$, then*

- *decryption key K is not as a submessage of x in X (key $\mathsf{inv}_X(K)$ can occur as a submessage or as an encryption key);*
- *there is a term t such that $x = Val(t, \mathbf{0}_X, \alpha)$ and $\mathcal{A}$ can produce $[\![x']\!]_{X',\eta,\sigma}$ with non-negligible probability when run on $[\![X']\!]_{\eta,\sigma}$ for $x' = Val(t, \mathbf{0}_{X'}, \beta)$;*
- *x is accessible in X iff x' is accessible in X'.*

Proof. We argue by contradiction. Suppose that K is a submessage of x in X. All decryption keys are accessible in $\mathbf{0}_X, \alpha$ except K, and every encryption created by encryption oracle in α does not contain K in the subject. Hence we can use IND-CCA decryption oracle and decryption with accessible keys to retrieve $[\![K]\!]_{X,\eta,\sigma}$ from $[\![x]\!]_{X,\eta,\sigma}$. But then we can distinguish $[\![X]\!]_{\eta,\sigma}$ and $[\![X']\!]_{\eta,\sigma}$ with non-negligible probability, which is a contradiction by Lemma 3.

Since K can only occur in x as an encryption key, there is a term t such that $x = Val(t, \alpha)$. Suppose that $\mathcal{A}$ can produce $[\![x']\!]_{X',\eta,\sigma}$ with negligible probability only. Then

$$\Pr\left[\sigma \xleftarrow{\$} \mathcal{U} : [\![t]\!]_{\eta,\sigma} = \mathcal{A}([\![X]\!]_{\eta,\sigma})\right] - \Pr\left[\sigma \xleftarrow{\$} \mathcal{U} : [\![t]\!]_{\eta,\sigma} = \mathcal{A}([\![X']\!]_{\eta,\sigma})\right]$$

is non-negligible and can be used to distinguish states X and X', which is a contradiction.

The last part is a simple consequence of X and X' being indistinguishable. □

Lemma 8. *Let Π be an IND-CCA secure encryption scheme and X a state with background BC_{CPA} in the IND-CPA normal form. If x is not accessible in X, then $[\![x]\!]_{X,\eta,\sigma}$ is not accessible with non-negligible probability to* PPT *algorithms.*

Proof. If x is not accessible in X, then some inaccessible key K must occur as a submessage in x. Use IND-CCA decryption oracle and keys not used in X to retrieve it and break the IND-CCA security. □

Theorem 6. *Let Π be an IND-CCA secure encryption scheme and X a state reducible to its normal form. If $x \in X$ is not accessible in X to a small-step importing algorithm, then*

$$\Pr\left[\sigma \xleftarrow{\$} \mathcal{U} : \mathcal{A}([\![X]\!]_{\eta,\sigma}) = [\![x]\!]_{X,\eta,\sigma}\right]$$

is negligible for every PPT *algorithm $\mathcal{A}$.*

Proof. Let X_n be the normal form of X and

$$X \xrightarrow{K_1} X_1 \xrightarrow{K_2} X_2 \xrightarrow{K_3} \dots \xrightarrow{K_n} X_n$$

for some inaccessible decryption keys $K_1, \dots, K_n$. Let $x, x_1, x_2, \dots, x_n$ be elements from Lemma 7. Then x_n is inaccessible in X_n. By Lemma 8, $[\![x_n]\!]_{X_n,\eta,\sigma}$ is not accessible by PPT algorithms with non-negligible probability, which is a contradiction by Lemma 7.

6 Model-Based Testing of Protocols

In this section we will show how to encode ASM programs working over BC_{CPA} in Spec# and how to use SpecExplorer to explore all possible execution traces for a bounded number of roles and agents.

The interactive algorithms of [BG04a, BG04b] are implemented in AsmL and Spec#. SpecExplorer is a tool developed at Microsoft Research for exhaustive exploration of (finitized) state spaces of specifications written in AsmL or Spec#, in order to test an implementation for conformance and to generate unit tests.

We have found that it can be effectively used to explore state spaces of protocol adversary situations, given a finite number of roles ensuring that the state space is finite. Our analysis shows that this exploration also has direct computational significance.

```
class Coins {}

structure Message{
  public virtual int len(){ return 1; }
  case Nonce{
    private Coins c;
  }
  case Pair{
    public Message fst;
    public Message snd;
    public override int len(){ return fst.len() + snd.len(); }
  }
  case PrivateKey{
    private Coins c;
    public PublicKey inv(){ return PublicKey(this); }
  }
  case PublicKey{
    private PrivateKey sk;
  }
  case Encryption{
    public PublicKey pk;
    private Message subject;
    private Coins c;
    public Message decrypt(PrivateKey sk)
      require sk.inv() == pk;
    {
      return subject;
    }
    public bool sameKey(Encryption e){ return pk == e.pk; }
    public override int len(){ return subject.len() + 1; }
  }
  public PrivateKey key(){ return PrivateKey(new Coins()); }
  public Encryption encrypt(PublicKey pk, Message subject) {
    return Encryption(pk, subject, new Coins());
  }
  public Pair pair(Message f, Message s){ return Pair(f, s); }
}
```

Fig. 1. BC_{CPA} background encoding in Spec#

6.1 Encoding in Spec# and SpecExplorer

The original idea of modeling abstract properties of cryptographic primitives by an object–oriented programming language is from [RRS03]. An encoding of the BC_{CPA} background in Spec# is given in Figure 1. The encoding should be clear to a reader with some basic understanding of accessibility modifiers `private` and `public` in OO programming languages. A more elaborate discussion of the similar encoding in AsmL language can be found in [RRS03].

An honest role will be represented with a Spec# encoding of an ASM program operating over BC_{CPA} background, such as the one given in example 3. On the other hand, the intruder will not be represented explicitly in the model with a concrete program. We will use the exploration capabilities of SpecExplorer to explore all possible execution paths with a given set of honest roles. It is not very difficult to teach SpecExplorer to completely analyze a message created by an honest role, but we have a dramatically different situation when it comes to creating a message that would be accepted by a role, forcing it to make a step and possibly output a fresh message. The set of states of an honest role is closed under isomorphisms and therefore infinite. We will look into a very common class of protocols in which the set of messages that can be created by an intruder and accepted by an honest role is infinite, but representable with a finite set of messages. Every step that a role can make will produce a state isomorphic to one of the states obtained by running the role with one of the representative messages.

A role of a protocol exposes a very simple interface to the outside world. It analyzes an input message and, if certain conditions are satisfy, outputs a message. If conditions are not met, it typically hangs, not producing a new messages regardless of any future inputs. If A is an action with a message m given as input in a state X and an answer function α with only reserve elements in its codomain, then $\tau_A(X, m, \alpha)$ is a state

An action of such role is called *simple* if it checks the type of all submessages of an input message. This means that any encryption must be decrypted, any pair must be analyzed, and type of any nonce and key must be checked. A protocol is simple if all actions of its roles are simple.

Theorem 7. *Let A be a simple action and I an intruder with a finite set of messages accessible by ground terms. Then there is a finite set of messages M accessible to I in X, α such that for every message m' accessible to I in X, β there is $m \in M$ such that*

$$\tau_A(X, m, \alpha) \cong \tau_A(X, m', \beta)$$

Proof. If action A is simple, then atomic support of m' in X $Sup_X(m')$ is finite and bounded. It suffice to import $|Sup_X m'|$ fresh coins from the reserve of X and create all messages of a fixed submessage structure using freshly created coins and known messages. □

We use the above fact, together with theorems 1 and 6, to produce abstract representations of all non-negligible computational traces representable by the BC_{CPA} background for a bounded number of honest roles.

Fix a simple protocol P. Let k be a maximum number of coins in support of any message accepted by an action of an honest role in P. At the initialization phase, SpecExplorer creates a fixed number of honest agents and corrupted keys. In each subsequent step, SpecExplorer imports k fresh coins from the reserve, and creates all messages from fresh coins and already know messages that could potentially be accepted by some honest role. Each role is ran with each such message used as its input by SpecExplorer, thus producing a set of all reachable states in the model. The exact order in which states are explored is nondeterministic, although the tool allows different priorities to be assigned to states. A role accepting an input message, can possibly output a message. The output message gets analyzed by the tool, thus updating the internal memory of the intruder. At the end of each step, the protocol guarantees are checked in new states by the tool. If any of protocol guarantees is not satisfied, the exploration is aborted and a graph with explored states, including the one in which the guarantee is not fulfilled, is rendered by the tool. The trace that resulted with the bad state can be explored and studied using the tool.

One optimization of the exploring process can be achieved by a grouping of states and further exploration of a single state representative of a group. The exploration space can be dramatically reduced for an appropriate grouping, but an optimal grouping is not always easy to find. In our case, isomorphism seems like a good choice of grouping relation on states. Since SpecExplorer does not have a built-in option of grouping of isomorphic states, we use an ad–hoc coding of states resulting in a grouping relation finer than isomorphism, but still significantly reducing the exploration space.

Example 5 (Lowe's attack on Needham–Schroeder protocol). One example of a simple protocol in the above sense is the public–key variant of the Needham–Schroeder authentication protocol. The flaw found by Lowe is easily (re) discovered by SpecExplorer, usually in less than 100 explored states.

The model is initially in a state marked as `Initial` in Figure 2. The first step of initialization is performed by calling `CreateAgentFactory`, which creates an object capable of creating honest agents of the protocol. The next invocation of `CreateAgents(2,1)` creates two honest agents and one corrupted private key. The internal memory of the intruder is enriched with public keys of the honest agents and the private corrupted key. The resulting state is marked with `Agents Created`. The exploration process starts here. SpecExplorer now can create fresh roles of already created honest agents using `CreateInitiatorRole` and `CreateresponderRole`, or run already an created role using `RunRole`. The parameters for `RunRole` are picked up from the finite set of representative of messages using the Theorem 7.

The Lowe's attack on the protocol is found after creating one initiator and one responder role, and then calling `RunRole` four times with the appropriate parameters. In the resulting state, protocol guarantee is violated and the exploration process is terminated. The resulting state is clearly marked and the trace leading to the state is included in its description in the exploration graph in Figure 2.

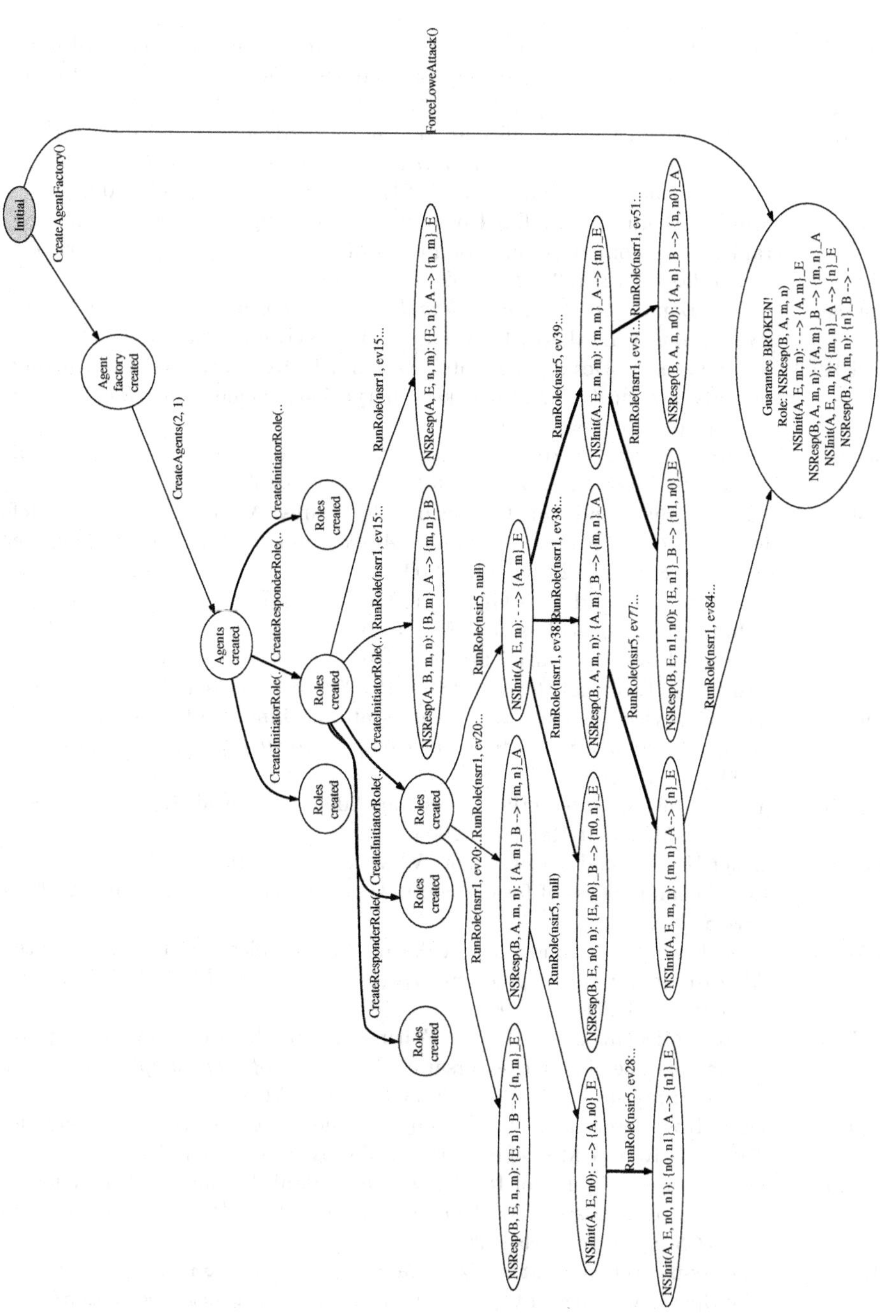

Fig. 2. SpecExplorer discovers Lowe's attack on the Needham–Schroeder protocol

References

[ABS05] Pedro Adão, Gergei Bana, and Andre Scedrov. Computational and information theoretic soundness and completeness of formal encryption. In *18th IEEE Computer Security Foundations Workshop – CSFW 2005*, 2005.

[AJ01] Martin Abadi and Jan Jürjens. Formal eavesdropping and its computational interpretation. In *Theoretical Aspects of Computer Software (4th International Symposium, TACS '01)*, volume 2215 of *LNCS*, 2001.

[AR02] Martin Abadi and Phillip Rogaway. Reconciling two views of cryptography (The computational soundness of formal encryption). *Journal of Cryptology*, 15(2):103–127, 2002.

[Ban04] Gergei Bana. *Soundness and Completeness of Formal Logics of Symmetric Encryption.* PhD thesis, University of Pennsylvania, 2004.

[BDPR98] M. Bellare, A. Desai, D. Pointcheval, and P. Rogaway. Relations among notions of security for public–key encryption schemes. In *CRYPTO '98*, volume 1462 of *LNCS*, 1998.

[BG00] Andreas Blass and Yuri Gurevich. Background, reserve, and Gandy machines. In *Proceedings of CSL '00*, volume 1862 of *LNCS*, 2000.

[BG03] Andreas Blass and Yuri Gurevich. Algortihms: A quest for absolute definitions. *Bulletin of the European Association for Theoretical Computer Science*, (81):195–225, October 2003.

[BG04a] Andreas Blass and Yuri Gurevich. Ordinary interactive small–step algorithms I. Technical Report MSR-TR-2004-16, Microsoft Research, 2004.

[BG04b] Andreas Blass and Yuri Gurevich. Ordinary interactive small–step algorithms II. Technical Report MSR-TR-2004-88, Microsoft Research, 2004.

[Gur00] Yuri Gurevich. Sequential abstract state machines capture sequential algorithms. *ACM Transactions on Computational Logic*, 1(1):77–111, July 2000.

[Gur05] Yuri Gurevich. Interactive algorithms 2005. Technical Report MSR-TR-2005-73, Microsoft Research, 2005.

[HG03] Omer Horvitz and Virgil Gligor. Weak key authenticity and the computational completeness of formal encryption. In *Crypto 2003*, volume 2729 of *LNCS*, 2003.

[MW04a] Daniele Micciancio and Bogdan Warinschi. Completeness theorems for the Abadi-Rogaway language of encrypted expressions. *Journal of Computer Security*, 12(1):99–130, 2004.

[MW04b] Daniele Micciancio and Bogdan Warinschi. Soundness of formal encryption in the presence of active adversaries. In *Theory of cryptography conference - Proceedings of TCC 2004*, volume 2951 of *LNCS*, 2004.

[RR05] Dean Rosenzweig and Davor Runje. Some things algorithms cannot do. Technical Report MSR-TR-2005-52, Microsoft Research, 2005.

[RRS03] Dean Rosenzweig, Davor Runje, and Neva Slani. Privacy, abstract encryption and protocols: an ASM model – Part I. In *ASM 2003*, volume 2589 of *LNCS*. Springer-Verlag, 2003.

[AsmL] The AsmL webpage. `http://research.microsoft.com/asml/`.

[Spec#] The Spec# webpage. `http://research.microsoft.com/specsharp/`.

[SpecExp] The SpecExplorer webpage. `http://research.microsoft.com/specexplorer/`.

A General Name Binding Mechanism*

Michele Boreale[1], Maria Grazia Buscemi[2], and Ugo Montanari[2]

[1] Dipartimento di Sistemi e Informatica, Università di Firenze, Italy
boreale@dsi.unifi.it
[2] Dipartimento di Informatica, Università di Pisa, Italy
{buscemi, ugo}@di.unipi.it

Abstract. We study fusion and binding mechanisms in name passing process calculi. To this purpose, we introduce the U-Calculus, a process calculus with no I/O polarities and a unique form of binding. The latter can be used both to control the scope of fusions and to handle new name generation. This is achieved by means of a simple form of typing: each bound name x is annotated with a set of *exceptions*, that is names that cannot be fused to x. The new calculus is proven to be more expressive than pi-calculus and Fusion calculus separately. In U-Calculus, the syntactic nesting of name binders has a semantic meaning, which cannot be overcome by the ordering of name extrusions at runtime. Thanks to this mixture of static and dynamic ordering of names, U-Calculus admits a form of labelled bisimulation which is a congruence. This property yields a substantial improvement with respect to previous proposals by the same authors aimed at unifying the above two languages. The additional expressiveness of U-Calculus is also explored by providing a uniform encoding of mixed guarded choice into the choice-free sub-calculus.

1 Introduction

Name binding is a key issue in many languages for the design of distributed and mobile systems based on message-passing. This is certainly the case for foundational calculi like pi-calculus [5,6] and Fusion [10], but the relevance of name binding extends also to languages like Biztalk [4] and Highwire [3], oriented towards web services. Fusion extends the pi-calculus by introducing *fusions*, i.e. name equivalences that, when applied onto a term, have the effect of a (possibly non-injective) name substitution. Fusions conveniently formalise, e.g., forwarders for objects that migrate among locations [2], or forms of pattern matching between pairs of messages [3].

While Fusion is presented in [10] as a generalisation of the pi-calculus, the authors prove in the paper [1] that no satisfactory semantic embedding exists of pi-calculus into Fusion. In particular, Fusion ignores the issue of name unicity. In pi-calculus, names declared through the restriction operator are unique, in the sense that they cannot be identified with any other name. In Fusion, the binder

* Research partially supported by IST FET Global projects *PROFUNDIS* IST-2001-33100 and *MIKADO* IST-2001-32222.

R. De Nicola and D. Sangiorgi (Eds.): TGC 2005, LNCS 3705, pp. 61–74, 2005.

(x) can be used to control the scope of fusions, but not to forbid them: names are like logical variables, i.e., unification always succeeds. In [1], we introduce D-Fusion, a calculus with two binders, ν and λ, which extend the binders of pi-calculus and Fusion. We show that D-Fusion is strictly more expressive than both pi-calculus and Fusion. In particular, we prove that both Fusion and pi-calculus can be uniformly mapped into D-Fusion, and exhibit an encoding of mixed guarded choice into the choice-free fragment of D-Fusion.

In D-Fusion, however, constraints on name fusions are totally determined by the extrusion ordering of names at runtime: the fact that a λ-name x will be fusable to a ν-name y depends on whether x will be extruded after y or before y. In other words, fusions cannot be constrained statically. As we explain below, this causes bisimilarity defined on the labelled transition system not to be a congruence. As a consequence, in D-Fusion one is forced to work with barbed congruence, which lacks adequate proof techniques.

In this paper we introduce the U-Calculus, a process calculus with no I/O polarities and a unique form of binding. In U-Calculus, the syntactic nesting of name binders has a semantic meaning, which cannot be overcome by the ordering of name extrusions at runtime. Thanks to this mixture of static and dynamic ordering of names, U-Calculus labelled bisimulation is a congruence.

To understand why a static ordering of names is useful, we can reason as follows. Assume that an agent has a free name x and a ν-bound name y. Names x and y cannot be fused in any reasonable semantics. For example, in open pi-calculus [13], one has $(\nu y)\,[x = y]P \sim \mathbf{0}$. This can be expressed by the following expansion law, which holds true because communication between the two prefixes is forbidden (here we use polarities for the sake of readability; $a\langle x\rangle$ is Fusion's free input, $\overline{a}\langle y\rangle$ is output, and $\sim$ is labelled bisimilarity):

$$P \stackrel{\triangle}{=} (\nu y)(a\langle x\rangle|\overline{a}\langle y\rangle) \;\sim\; (\nu y)(a\langle x\rangle.\overline{a}\langle y\rangle + \overline{a}\langle y\rangle.a\langle x\rangle) \stackrel{\triangle}{=} Q.$$

Now, suppose P and Q above are plugged into a context $(\lambda x)[\cdot]$. If $(\lambda x)P$ ν-extrudes y before λ-extruding x, fusion of x and y will be allowed. This must be the case, at least, if one keeps the traditional scope-extrusion law, which is common to Pi, Fusion and D-Fusion. In fact, scope extrusion allows the binders (λx) and (νy) in $(\lambda x)P$ to be freely swapped. This swapping makes the syntactic ordering of binders immaterial. So $(\lambda x)P$ is equivalent to $a(x)|(\nu y)\overline{a}\langle y\rangle$, where the bound input $a(x)$ is just the same as $(\lambda x)a\langle x\rangle$. In other words:

$$(\lambda x)P \;\sim\; (\lambda x)Q + \tau \not\sim (\lambda x)Q.$$

Thus, in D-Fusion, plugging an agent into a λ-context may trigger additional communication capabilities, making two agents in the λ-context not bisimilar, when the two original agents were so. Note that this is true even if we require that $\sim$ be closed under all substitutions, in sharp contrast with both open pi-calculus [13] and Fusion. In these calculi, the problem does not arise simply because free input and restriction do not coexist.

A static ordering of name binders solves the problem. In U-Calculus, the syntactic nesting $(\lambda x)(\nu y)$ forbids the fusion of the two names in any case. Operationally, when the extrusion of y takes place under (λx), name x is decorated with an *exception* y, yielding $(\lambda x : y)$. This indicates that the fusion between x and y will never be allowed, and so it holds that $(\lambda x)P \sim (\lambda x)Q$. Semantically, this fact has consequences on the scope extrusion laws. In particular, we have the following new swapping law:

$$(\lambda x)(\nu y)R \sim (\nu y)(\lambda x : y)R.$$

Incidentally, a simple generalisation of the exception types allows to operationally unify the mechanism of λ- and ν-binding. In fact, a ν-binder is just a λ-binder where *all* names free at the moment of extrusion are considered as exceptions. This is indicated by a new type ω, as in $(\lambda x : \omega)$. With this notation, ν and λ enjoy a uniform treatment. As a consequence, the U-Calculus achieves minimal syntax and operational rules.

The expressive power of the U-Calculus is essentially the same as D-Fusion's: also for the U-Calculus we can provide uniform mappings of both pi-calculus and Fusion, and a uniform encoding of mixed guarded choice into the choice-free sub-calculus. In our assesment of the expressive power we shall rely on barbed bisimilarity [12], when this is technically convenient.

The rest of the paper is organised as follows. In Section 2 we introduce the U-Calculus, its operational semantics and a notion of open bisimulation. In Section 3 we show that U-Calculus is strictly more expressive than both pi-calculus and Fusion. We further explore this expressiveness gap in Section 4, by encoding mixed guarded choice into the choice-free calculus. Section 5 contains a few concluding remarks.

2 The U-Calculus

Syntax. We consider a countable set of names $\mathcal{N}$ ranged over by $a, b, \ldots, u, v, \ldots, z$. We write $\widetilde{x}$ for a finite tuple $(x_1, \ldots, x_n)$ of names. The set $\mathcal{U}$ of U-Calculus *processes*, ranged over by $P, Q, \ldots$, is defined by the syntax:

$$P ::= \mathbf{0} \mid a\widetilde{v}.P \mid P|P \mid P+P \mid [x=y]P \mid !P \mid (\lambda x : T)\, P.$$

Types T are defined as:

$$T ::= N \mid \omega,$$

where $N \subseteq_{\mathit{fin}} \mathcal{N}$ and ω is a constant. The intended meaning of $(\lambda x : T)$ is that x cannot be fused with any name in T. In particular, ω stands for 'any name' free at the moment of extrusion, thus $(\lambda x : \omega)\, P$ corresponds to declaring x fresh. We will often abbreviate $(\lambda x : \omega)$ as (νx) and $(\lambda x : \emptyset)$ as (λx). By $(\lambda \widetilde{x} : \widetilde{T})$ we will denote $(\lambda x_1 : T_1) \cdots (\lambda x_n : T_n)$, where it is assumed that $x_i \in T_j$ implies $i < j$, for $i, j = 1, \cdots, n$. We will also adopt the convention that $(\lambda x : T)\, P \,|\, Q$ stands for $((\lambda x : T)\, P) \,|\, Q$.

The occurrences of x in $(\lambda x : T)\, P$ are *bound*, thus notions of *free names* and *bound names* of a process P arise as expected and are denoted by $\mathrm{fn}(P)$ and bn(P), respectively. The notion of *alpha-equivalence* also arises as expected. In the rest of the paper we will identify alpha-equivalent processes. A *context* $C[\cdot]$ is a process with a hole that can be filled with any process P, thus yielding a process $C[P]$.

Note that we consider one kind of prefix, thus ignoring polarities. However, a sub-calculus with polarities can be easily retrieved, as we will show later in this section.

Notation

- $T + T' \stackrel{\text{def}}{=} N \cup N'$ if $T = N$ and $T' = N'$, $T + T' \stackrel{\text{def}}{=} \omega$ if $T = \omega$ or $T' = \omega$. We abbreviate $T + \{y\}$ as $T + y$.
- $T - y \stackrel{\text{def}}{=} N \setminus \{y\}$ if $T = N$, $T - y \stackrel{\text{def}}{=} \omega$ if $T = \omega$.
- $T \sqcap N \stackrel{\text{def}}{=} N' \cap N$ if $T = N'$, $T \sqcap N \stackrel{\text{def}}{=} N$ if $T = \omega$.
- Predicate $y \,\mathcal{E}\, T$ is defined as follows:

$$y \,\mathcal{E}\, T \;\Leftrightarrow\; T = \omega \text{ or } (T = N \text{ and } y \in N)$$

The above notations are extended to tuples $\widetilde{T}$ as expected. For instance, $\widetilde{T} \sqcap N \stackrel{\text{def}}{=} T_1 \sqcap N, \cdots, T_n \sqcap N$, if $\widetilde{T} = T_1, \cdots, T_n$. For $\widetilde{x} = (x_1, \cdots, x_n)$, $\widetilde{T} = (T_1, \cdots, T_n)$, and $\widetilde{N} = (N_1, \cdots, N_n)$, by $\widetilde{x} : \widetilde{T} \sqcap \widetilde{N}$ we denote $x_1 : T_1 \sqcap N_1, \cdots, x_n : T_n \sqcap N_n$.

Operational Semantics. For R a binary relation over $\mathcal{N}$, let $R^\star$ denote the reflexive, symmetric and transitive closure of R with respect to $\mathcal{N}$. We use σ, σ' to range over substitutions, i.e. finite partial functions from $\mathcal{N}$ onto $\mathcal{N}$. The domain of σ is denoted by dom(σ). We denote by $t\sigma$ the result of applying σ onto a term t. Given a tuple of names $\widetilde{x}$, we define $\sigma_{|\widetilde{x}}$ as $\sigma \cap (\widetilde{x} \times \mathcal{N})$.

Below, we define fusions, that is, name equivalences. These arise as the result of equating two tuples of names in a synchronisation.

Definition 1 (fusions). *We let $\phi, \chi, \ldots$ range over* fusions, *that is total equivalence relations on $\mathcal{N}$ with only finitely many non-singleton equivalence classes. We let:*

- n(ϕ) *denote* $\{x : x\,\phi\,y \text{ for some } y \neq x\}$*;*
- τ *denote the identity fusion (thus,* n(τ) $= \emptyset$*);*
- ϕ_{-z} *denote* $(\phi - (\{z\} \times \mathcal{N} \cup \mathcal{N} \times \{z\}))^\star$*;*
- $\{\widetilde{x} = \widetilde{y}\}$ *denote* $\{(x_1, y_1), \ldots, (x_n, y_n)\}^\star$, *where* $\widetilde{x} = x_1, \ldots x_n$ *and* $\widetilde{y} = y_1, \ldots y_n$*;*
- $\phi[x]$ *denote the equivalence class of x in ϕ.*

Definition 2. *Let σ be a substitution. Then, σ is a* substitutive effect *of a fusion ϕ iff $\forall\, x, y : x\,\phi\,y \Leftrightarrow x\sigma = y\sigma$ and $\forall\, x, y : \sigma(x) = y \Rightarrow x\,\phi\,y$.*

We introduce below a concept of *distinction*, akin to [13]. The purpose of distinctions is to keep track of those name fusions that have to be forbidden.

Definition 3 (distinctions). *A* distinction D *is a tuple* $x_1 : T_1, x_2 : T_2, \ldots, x_n : T_n$*, written* $\widetilde{x} : \widetilde{T}$*, with* ω *not in* $\widetilde{T}$*, up to permutations and up to the law:*

$$\widetilde{x} : \widetilde{T}, w : T_1, w : T_2 = \widetilde{x} : \widetilde{T}, w : T_1 + T_2.$$

Let $D = \widetilde{x} : \widetilde{T}$ *and* $D' = \widetilde{x}' : \widetilde{T}'$ *be two distinctions. Then:*

- $D, D' \stackrel{\text{def}}{=} \widetilde{x}\widetilde{x}' : \widetilde{T}\widetilde{T}'$;
- $D \setminus z \stackrel{\text{def}}{=} (x_i : T_i - z)_{i:\, x_i \neq z}$;
- $D\sigma \stackrel{\text{def}}{=} \widetilde{x}\sigma : \widetilde{T}\sigma$.

We write $x\, D\, y$ *iff* $x \neq y$ *and* $x : T \in D$ *and* $y \;\mathcal{E}\; T$*, for some* T*. Given a substitution* σ *and a distinction* D*, we say that* σ respects D*, written* $\sigma \vdash D$*, if* $x\, D\, y$ *implies* $x\sigma \neq y\sigma$*.*

Definition 4 (structural congruence). *The structural congruence* $\equiv$ *is the least congruence on processes satisfying the abelian monoid laws for Summation and Composition (associativity, commutativity and* $\mathbf{0}$ *as identity) plus the following rules:*

$$\begin{array}{ll}
(\lambda x : T)\,(\lambda y : T' + x)\,P \equiv (\lambda y : T')\,(\lambda x : T + y)\,P & x \text{ not in } T' \\
(\lambda x : T)\,(\lambda y : T')\,P \equiv (\lambda y : T')\,(\lambda x : T)\,P & x \not\mathcal{E}\; T' \\
(\lambda x)\,(P + Q) \equiv (\lambda x)\,P \;+\; (\lambda x)\,Q & \\
(\lambda x : T)\,\mathbf{0} \equiv \mathbf{0} & \\
!P \equiv P \,|\, !P &
\end{array}$$

and the scope extrusion *law:*

$$(\lambda x : T)\,(P|Q) \equiv (\lambda x : T)\,P|Q \quad x \notin \text{fn}(Q) \text{ and } (T = \omega \text{ or } \omega \text{ does not occur in } Q).$$

Note that a special case of the first rule is: $(\lambda x)\,(\nu y)\,P \;\equiv\; (\nu y)\,(\lambda x : y)\,P$. The above structural congruence rules can be applied to reduce every pair of communicating subprocesses into a form where their ν-binders have been moved at top level. The side condition "ω does not occur in Q" prevents a λ-binder from 'capturing' ν-names out of its scope. For instance, according to the SOS rules presented below, a process $P = (\lambda x)\, ax \,|\, (\nu z)\, az$ can do a τ-transition. On the other side, extruding the scope of (λx) over $(\nu z)\, az$ would yield a process $P' = (\lambda x)\,(ax \,|\, (\nu z)\, az)$, which cannot do any synchronisation.

Definition 5 (labelled transition system). *The transition relation* $P \xrightarrow{\mu} Q$*, for* μ *a label of the form* $(\lambda\widetilde{y} : \widetilde{T})\, a\widetilde{v}$ (action) *or of the form* D, ϕ (effect) *is defined by the SOS rules in Table 1.*

Notation. In Table 1, we use the following abbreviation. We write $P > Q$ (and say that P *commits to* Q) if: $P = P_1 \,|\, P_2$, $P_1 \xrightarrow{(\lambda\widetilde{x}:\widetilde{T})\, a\widetilde{b}} P_1'$, $P_2 \xrightarrow{(\lambda\widetilde{y}:\widetilde{U})\, a\widetilde{c}} P_2'$, with ω not in $\widetilde{T}\widetilde{U}$, and $Q = (\lambda\widetilde{x}\widetilde{y} : \widetilde{T}\widetilde{U})\,(a\widetilde{b}.P_1' \,|\, a\widetilde{c}.P_2')$.

Some comments on the rules of Table 1 are in order. *Actions* occurring within the scope of a λ are governed by rules Pass and Open. Roughly, a name z that is declared with exceptions T' may get extruded (rule Open) or not (rule Pass) by an action occurring under the scope of its declaration $(\lambda z : T')$, depending on whether z occurs in the object part of the action. In the case of rule Pass, z is removed from the current set of exceptions $\widetilde{T}$. However, no distinction is lost, because the extruded names having z as an exception are added to T' (condition (1)). E.g.:

$$(\lambda z : a)\,(\lambda x : z)\,ax.P \xrightarrow{(\lambda x)\; ax} (\lambda z : \{a, x\})\,P.$$

Effects are similar to those found in Fusion, but here they also carry a set of exceptions represented by a distinction $\widetilde{x} : \widetilde{T}$. Effects are created as a result of a communication that unifies two tuples of names (rule Com), and propagated across parallel components, until a λ is encountered. The rule Pass$_f$ has a meaning similar to Pass. The rule Open$_f$ acts on a name z in the fusion: a substitutive effect $[{}^{w}/_{z}]$ is applied both to the transition label and to the target process, and z is removed from the fusion (the result is ϕ_{-z}). The side condition $\phi[z] \sqcap T'' = \emptyset$ forbids fusion of z with any name in its set of exceptions $(T' + \{T_j \,|\, z = x_j\})$, or having z as an exception $(\{x_i \,|\, z \;\mathcal{E}\; T_i\})$; in particular, the rule does not fire if $T' = \omega$, i.e. if z is declared to be new. Note that applying $[{}^{w}/_{z}]$ onto $(\widetilde{x}z : \widetilde{T}T')$ implicitly lets w inherit z's exceptions. For example:

$$(\lambda z : y)\,(\nu c)\,(cza.P|cww.\mathbf{0}) \xrightarrow{w:y,\,\{a=w\}} (\nu c)\,P[{}^{w}/_{z}]$$

while

$$(\lambda z : a)\,(\nu c)\,(cza.P|cww.\mathbf{0}) \not\rightarrow .$$

Here, z cannot be fused to w or to a, because a is in z's exceptions $(\phi[z] \sqcap T'' = \{a\})$. Note that in rule Com the labels in the premise have no binders because communication among processes with λ-binders is dealt by means of rule Commit. The absence of ν-binders in rule Commit is explained by the fact that, by the structural congruence, communicating processes can be reduced into a canonical form where the scope of ν-binders is extruded over parallel components.

Example 1.

1. The construct $(\lambda x)\,ax$ behaves as $a(x)$ in pi-calculus:

$$(\lambda x)\,ax.P \,|\, ay.\mathbf{0} \xrightarrow{\tau} P[{}^{y}/_{x}] \quad \text{and} \quad (\lambda x)\,ax.P \,|\, (\nu y)\,ay.\mathbf{0} \xrightarrow{\tau} (\nu y)\,P[{}^{y}/_{x}]$$

$$\text{but} \quad ax.P \,|\, (\lambda y : x)\,ay.\mathbf{0} \stackrel{\tau}{\not\rightarrow} \quad \text{and} \quad ax.P \,|\, (\nu y)\,ay.\mathbf{0} \stackrel{\tau}{\not\rightarrow}$$

Table 1. Actions and effects transitions in U-Calculus

(ACT) $a\widetilde{b}.P \xrightarrow{a\widetilde{b}} P$ (MATCH) $\dfrac{P \xrightarrow{\mu} Q}{[a=a]P \xrightarrow{\mu} Q}$ (SUM) $\dfrac{P \xrightarrow{\mu} Q}{P+R \xrightarrow{\mu} Q}$

(PASS) $\dfrac{P \xrightarrow{(\lambda\widetilde{x}:\widetilde{T})\,a\widetilde{b}} Q}{(\lambda z:T')\,P \xrightarrow{(\lambda\widetilde{x}:\widetilde{T}-z)\,a\widetilde{b}} (\lambda z:T'')\;Q}$ $z \notin \widetilde{b},\, \widetilde{x} \cup \{a\}$ and (1)

(OPEN) $\dfrac{P \xrightarrow{(\lambda\widetilde{x}:\widetilde{T})\,a\widetilde{b}} Q}{(\lambda z:T')\,P \xrightarrow{(\lambda z\widetilde{x}:T'\widetilde{T})\,a\widetilde{b}} Q}$ $z \in \widetilde{b} - \{a, \widetilde{x}\}$

(PASS_f) $\dfrac{P \xrightarrow{\widetilde{x}:\widetilde{T},\phi} Q}{(\lambda z:T')\,P \xrightarrow{(\widetilde{x}:\widetilde{T})\backslash z,\phi} (\lambda z:T'')\,Q}$ $z \notin \mathrm{n}(\phi)$ and (1)

(OPEN_f) $\dfrac{P \xrightarrow{\widetilde{x}:\widetilde{T},\phi} Q}{(\lambda z:T')\,P \xrightarrow{(\widetilde{x}z:\widetilde{T}T')[w/z],\phi_{-z}} Q[{}^{w}/_{z}]}$ $w\,\phi\,z,\; w \neq z,\; \phi[z] \sqcap T'' = \emptyset$ and (1)

(COM) $\dfrac{P_1 \xrightarrow{a\widetilde{b}} Q_1 \quad P_2 \xrightarrow{a\widetilde{c}} Q_2}{P_1|P_2 \xrightarrow{\{\widetilde{b}=\widetilde{c}\}} Q_1|Q_2}$ (COMMIT) $\dfrac{P|Q > A \xrightarrow{\widetilde{x}:\widetilde{T},\phi} R}{P|Q \xrightarrow{\widetilde{x}:\widetilde{T},\phi} R}$

(PAR) $\dfrac{P \xrightarrow{\mu} Q}{P|R \xrightarrow{\mu} Q|R}$ (STRUCT) $\dfrac{P \equiv P' \quad P' \xrightarrow{\mu} Q' \quad Q' \equiv Q}{P \xrightarrow{\mu} Q}$

(1) : Let $\widetilde{x} = x_1, \cdots, x_n$, and $\widetilde{T} = T_1, \cdots, T_n$ in

$T'' = T' + \Sigma\{x_i \mid z\;\mathcal{E}\;T_i\} + \{T_j \mid z = x_j\}$.

Symmetric rules for (SUM) and (PAR) are not shown. Usual conventions about freshness of bound names apply.

2. The two examples below show combined use of rules (COM), (OPEN_f) and (COMMIT):

$$(\lambda x:y)\,(axx.P \mid awz.\mathbf{0}) \xrightarrow{w:y,\{w=z\}} P[{}^{w}/_{x}].$$
$$(\nu y)\,axyz.P \mid (\lambda x':z)\,(\lambda y')\,ax'y'z'.Q \xrightarrow{x:z,\{z=z'\}} (\nu y)\,(P \mid Q)[{}^{x}/_{x'}][{}^{y}/_{y'}]$$

3. Nesting of binders is important, even on names in the same action:

$$(\nu y)\,(\lambda x)\,axy.\mathbf{0} \mid (\lambda u)\,auu \xrightarrow{\tau} \quad \text{while} \quad (\lambda x)\,(\nu y)\,axy.\mathbf{0} \mid (\lambda u)\,auu \not\xrightarrow{\tau}$$

Encoding I/O polarities We can encode polarities as follows:

$$\overline{a}\langle\widetilde{v}\rangle.P \triangleq (\nu x)\,(\lambda y)\,a\widetilde{v}xy.P \qquad a\langle\widetilde{v}\rangle.P \triangleq (\nu x)\,(\lambda y)\,a\widetilde{v}yx.P$$

for some chosen fresh x and y. The position of name x forbids fusions between actions with the same polarity and, hence, communication. For instance, the process $\overline{a}\langle\widetilde{v}\rangle.P|\overline{a}\langle\widetilde{u}\rangle.Q$ has no τ-transition, since the latter would force the fusion of two globally distinct names, which is forbidden by the operational rules. We denote by $\mathcal{U}^{\mathrm{p}}$, *polarised U-Calculus*, the subset of $\mathcal{U}$ in which every prefix can be interpreted as an input or output, in the above sense.

Open Bisimulation. Like in the case of Fusion, a 'natural' semantics of U-Calculus is required to be closed under substitutions. However, one should be careful in respecting exceptions raised by λ-extrusions. The following definition of *open bisimulation* relies on the notion of distinctions (Def. 3).

By $\{R_D\}_D$ we denote a set of process relations $\{R_D \mid D \text{ is a distinction}\}$. By $PR_{D'}Q$, with $D' = D \cdot (\nu\widetilde{x})\,,\ \widetilde{y} : \widetilde{T}$, we abbreviate $PR_{D''}Q$, with $D'' = D, x_1 : N_1, \cdots, x_k : N_k, \widetilde{y} : \widetilde{T}$ and $N_i = \mathrm{fn}(P, Q, D,) \cup \{x_1, \cdots, x_{i-1}\}$, with $i = 1, \cdots k$.

Definition 6 (open bisimulation). *A set $\mathcal{R} = \{R_D\}_D$ of process relations indexed by distinctions is an* indexed simulation *if for each D, whenever $P\ R_D\ Q$:*

– *if $P \xrightarrow{(\nu x)\,(\lambda\widetilde{y}:\widetilde{T})\,a\widetilde{z}} P'$ then $Q \xrightarrow{(\nu x)\,(\lambda\widetilde{y}:\widetilde{T})\,a\widetilde{z}} Q'$ and $P'\ R_{D'}\ Q'$, with*

$$D' = D \cdot (\nu\widetilde{x})\,,\ \widetilde{y} : \widetilde{T};$$

– *if $P \xrightarrow{\widetilde{x}:\widetilde{T},\phi} P'$, σ is a substitutive effect of ϕ and σ respects $D, \widetilde{x} : \widetilde{T}$ then $Q \xrightarrow{\widetilde{x}:\widetilde{T},\phi} Q'$ and $P'\sigma\ R_{D''}\ Q'\sigma$, with*

$$D'' = \big(D,\ \widetilde{x} : \widetilde{T}\,\big)\sigma.$$

$\mathcal{R}$ is an indexed bisimulation *if both $\mathcal{R} = \{R_D\}_D$ and $\mathcal{R}^{-1} = \{R_D^{-1}\}_D$ are indexed simulations.* Open bisimulation, *$\{\sim_D\}_D$, is the largest indexed bisimulation preserved by respectful substitutions, i.e.: for each σ and distinction D, if $P \sim_D Q$ and σ respects D then $P\sigma \sim_{D\sigma} Q\sigma$.*

We write $P \sim Q$ for $P \sim_\epsilon Q$, where ϵ is the empty distinction. In the following examples we shall write $\{\widetilde{x} = \widetilde{y}\}.P$ for $(\nu c)\,(c\widetilde{x}|c\widetilde{y}.P)$ (for a fresh name c).

Example 2.

1. $(\nu c)\,(\nu n)\,(\lambda x)\,(cx.P \mid cn.\mathbf{0}) \sim (\nu c)\,((\lambda x)\,cx.P \mid (\nu n)\,cn.\mathbf{0}) \sim (\nu c)\,(\nu n)\,\tau.P[{}^{n}\!/\!_{x}]$

   but $(\nu c)\,(\lambda x)\,(\nu n)\,(cx.P \mid cn.\mathbf{0}) \sim (\nu c)\,(\lambda x)\,(cx.P \mid (\nu n)\,cn.\mathbf{0}) \sim \mathbf{0}.$

2. An example of 'expansion' for parallel composition is as follows:

   $(\lambda y : T)\,ay.\mathbf{0}|ax.\mathbf{0}\ \sim\ (\lambda y : T)\,ay.ax.\mathbf{0}\ +\ ax.(\lambda y : T)\,ay.\mathbf{0} + \{x = y\}.\mathbf{0}\quad \text{if } x \not\mathcal{E}\ T,$

   while $(\lambda y : T)\,ay.\mathbf{0}|ax.\mathbf{0}\ \sim\ (\lambda y : T)\,ay.ax.\mathbf{0}\ +\ ax(\lambda y : T)\,ay.\mathbf{0}\quad \text{if } x\ \mathcal{E}\ T$

3. The static nesting of name binding is relevant:

$$(\nu y)\,(\lambda x)\,ay.ax.\{x = y\}.\mathbf{0} \not\sim (\lambda x)\,(\nu y)\,ay.ax.\{x = y\}.\mathbf{0}.$$

The above two processes extrude y and x in the same order. However, after the two extrusions, the process on the left-hand side can fuse the two names, while the other one cannot.

Theorem 1. *Let P and Q be two processes. Then:*

1. *$P \sim_{D,x:T\sqcap N} Q$ and $x \notin \mathrm{n}(D)$ imply $(\lambda x : T)\,P \sim_D (\lambda x : T)\,Q$, with $N = \mathrm{fn}(\,(\lambda x : T)\,P,\,(\lambda x : T)\,Q,\,D\,)$.*
2. *Prefix, parallel composition, sum, matching and replication operators preserve $\sim_D$.*

Example 3. Let $P \stackrel{\text{def}}{=} (\lambda y)\,ay.(\nu x)\,ax.\mathbf{0}$ and $Q \stackrel{\text{def}}{=} (\lambda y)\,ay.(\nu x)\,ax.\{x = y\}.Q'$. It holds that $P \sim Q$. Indeed, Q cannot fuse x and y, since ν-extruding x yields a distinction $x : y$. Suppose $R \stackrel{\text{def}}{=} (\lambda z)\,az$. It also holds that $P \,|\, R \sim Q \,|\, R$. Indeed, after synchronising $(\lambda z)\,az$ and $(\lambda y)\,ay$, $Q \,|\, R$ ν-extrudes x and then evolves, for instance, to $(\lambda z : x)\,\{x = z\}.Q'[z/y]$. Thus, the fusion $\{x = z\}$ cannot take place and $(\lambda z : x)\,\{x = z\}.Q'[z/y] \sim \mathbf{0}$.

3 Pi-Calculus and Fusion as Subcalculi of U-Calculus

The labelled transition systems of pi-calculus and Fusion are embedded into polarised U-calculus's, under the two obvious translations given below. Note that these translations are *uniform*, in the sense of [1]; in particular, no central coordinator is introduced in the translated processes.

Definition 7. *The translations $[\![\cdot]\!]_\pi : \Pi \to \mathcal{U}^{\mathrm{p}}$ and $[\![\cdot]\!]_f : \mathcal{F} \to \mathcal{U}^{\mathrm{p}}$ are defined by extending in the expected homomorphic way the following clauses, respectively:*

$$[\![\bar{a}\langle x\rangle.P]\!]_\pi = \bar{a}\langle x\rangle.[\![P]\!]_\pi \quad [\![a(x).P]\!]_\pi = (\lambda x)\ a\langle x\rangle.[\![P]\!]_\pi \quad [\![(\nu x)\,P]\!]_\pi = (\nu x)\,[\![P]\!]_\pi$$

$$[\![\bar{a}\langle x\rangle.P]\!]_f = \bar{a}\langle x\rangle.[\![P]\!]_f \qquad [\![a\langle x\rangle.P]\!]_f = a\langle x\rangle.[\![P]\!]_f \qquad [\![(x)P]\!]_f = (\lambda x)\ [\![P]\!]_f$$

Embedding in terms of labelled transition systems naturally lifts to behavioural equivalences. Here, we restrict our attention to equivalences based on barbed bisimulation.

Definition 8 (barbed bisimulation and barbed congruence). *We write $P \downarrow a$ if and only if there exist an action $\mu = ((\lambda\tilde{x} : \widetilde{T})\,, a\tilde{v})$ and a process Q such that $P \xrightarrow{\mu} Q$.*

A barbed bisimulation *is a symmetric binary relation $\mathcal{R}$ between processes such that $P\,\mathcal{R}\,Q$ implies:*

1. *whenever* $P \xrightarrow{\tau} P'$ *then* $Q \xrightarrow{\tau} Q'$ *and* $P' \mathcal{R} Q'$*;*
2. *for each name* a*, if* $P \downarrow a$ *then* $Q \downarrow a$*.*

P is barbed bisimilar to Q, written $P \stackrel{\cdot}{\sim} Q$, if $P\mathcal{R}Q$ for some barbed bisimulation $\mathcal{R}$.

Two processes P and Q are barbed congruent*, written $P \sim^b Q$, if for all contexts $C[\cdot]$, it holds that $C[P] \stackrel{\cdot}{\sim} C[Q]$.*

Let $\sim^\pi$ and $\sim^{\mathrm{f}}$ denote barbed congruence, respectively, over Π ([12]) and over $\mathcal{F}$ (see [14]). Also, let $\sim^{[\![\pi]\!]}$ and $\sim^{[\![\mathrm{f}]\!]}$ be the equivalences on $\mathcal{U}$ obtained by closing barbed bisimulation $\stackrel{\cdot}{\sim}$ only under translated pi- and Fusion-contexts, respectively (e.g., $P \sim^{[\![\pi]\!]} Q$ iff for each Π-context $C[\cdot]$, $[\![C]\!]_\pi[P] \stackrel{\cdot}{\sim} [\![C]\!]_\pi[Q]$).

Proposition 1.

1. *Let P and Q be two pi-calculus processes. $P \sim^\pi Q$ iff $[\![P]\!]_\pi \sim^{[\![\pi]\!]} [\![Q]\!]_\pi$.*

2. *Let P and Q be two Fusion processes. $P \sim^{\mathrm{f}} Q$ iff $[\![P]\!]_f \sim^{[\![\mathrm{f}]\!]} [\![Q]\!]_f$.*

Next, we now show that the U-calculus cannot be uniformly encoded into Π. The intuition is that, in U-calculus (like in D-Fusion [1]), the combined use of fusions and restrictions allows one to express a pattern matching atomically. This is not possible in Π. To show this fact, we restrict our attention to polarised U-calculus, $\mathcal{U}^{\mathrm{p}}$.

The reference semantics for Π is the late operational semantics. Given $P \in \Pi$ and a trace of U-calculus actions s, let us write $P \stackrel{\hat{s}}{\Longrightarrow}$ if $P \stackrel{s'}{\Longrightarrow}$ for some pi-actions trace s' that exhibits the same sequence of subject names as s, with the same polarities (e.g., $s = a\langle\widetilde{x}\rangle \cdot (\lambda\widetilde{y})\,\overline{b}\langle\widetilde{v}\rangle$ and $s' = a(\widetilde{z}) \cdot \overline{b}\langle\widetilde{w}\rangle$). The reference semantics for Π is again the late operational semantics.

Definition 9. *A translation $[\![\cdot]\!] : \mathcal{U}^{\mathrm{p}} \to \Pi$ is* uniform *if for each $P, Q \in \mathcal{U}^{\mathrm{p}}$:*

- *for each trace s, $P \stackrel{s}{\Longrightarrow}$ implies $[\![P]\!] \stackrel{\hat{s}}{\Longrightarrow}$;*
- *$[\![P|Q]\!] = [\![P]\!]|[\![Q]\!]$;*
- *for each y, $[\![(\nu y)\,P]\!] = (\nu y)\,[\![P]\!]$;*
- *for each substitution σ, $[\![P\sigma]\!] = [\![P]\!]\sigma$.*

Below, we denote by $\sim_{\mathcal{U}^{\mathrm{p}}}$ any fixed equivalence over $\mathcal{U}^{\mathrm{p}}$ contained in trace semantics (defined in the obvious way), and by $\sim_\Pi$ any fixed equivalence over Π contained in trace equivalence. Note that both barbed congruence over $\mathcal{U}^{\mathrm{p}}$, and open bisimulation are contained in trace equivalence.

Proposition 2. *There is no uniform translation $[\![\cdot]\!] : \mathcal{U}^{\mathrm{p}} \to \Pi$ such that $\forall\, P, Q \in \mathcal{U}^{\mathrm{p}}$:*

$$P \sim_{\mathcal{U}^{\mathrm{p}}} Q \Rightarrow [\![P]\!] \sim_\Pi [\![Q]\!].$$

PROOF: Suppose that there exists such a translation $[\![\cdot]\!]$. Let us consider the following two $\mathcal{U}^{\mathrm{p}}$-processes P and Q:

$$P = (\nu c, k, h)\,(c\langle k\rangle.\overline{a}.\mathbf{0}|c\langle h\rangle.\overline{b}.\mathbf{0}|\overline{c}\langle k\rangle.\mathbf{0}) \qquad Q = \tau.\overline{a}.\mathbf{0}.$$

It holds that $P \sim Q$ in $\mathcal{U}^{\mathrm{p}}$: the reason is that, in P, synchronisation between prefixes $c\langle h\rangle$ and $\overline{c}\langle k\rangle$, which carry different *restricted* names h and k, is forbidden (see rule $\textsc{Pass}_f$). Thus P can only make $c\langle k\rangle$ and $\overline{c}\langle k\rangle$ synchronise, and then perform $\overline{a}$. Thus, $P \sim_{\mathcal{U}^{\mathrm{p}}} Q$ holds too.

On the other hand, by Definition 9, for any uniform encoding $[\![\cdot]\!]$, c and $\overline{c}$ in $[\![P]\!]$ can synchronise and, thus, $[\![P]\!] \stackrel{\overline{b}}{\Longrightarrow}$, while $[\![Q]\!] \stackrel{\overline{b}}{\not\Longrightarrow}$ (because of $b \notin \mathrm{fn}(Q)$ and of the uniformity with respect to substitutions). Thus $[\![P]\!] \not\sim_{\Pi} [\![Q]\!]$. □

Of course, it is also true that the U-calculus cannot be uniformly encoded into $\mathcal{F}$, as this would imply the existence of a uniform fully abstract encoding from Π to $\mathcal{F}$, which does not exist (see [1]).

The conclusion is that there is some expressiveness gap between U-calculus on one side and Pi/Fusion on the other side, at least, as far as our simple notion of uniform encoding is concerned.

Remark. There cannot exist any encoding from D-Fusion to the U-calculus, or vice-versa, that is uniform in a sense extending Def. 9, in particular mapping λ to λ and ν to ν. The reason is that in D-Fusion, as mentioned, the order of λ's and ν's can be freely swapped, while in the U-calculus this requires changing the respective exceptions. More in detail, the equality $(\lambda x)\,(\nu n)\,\{x = n\}.\overline{c} \sim \mathbf{0}$ in the U-calculus would be mapped to $[\![(\lambda x)\,(\nu n)\,\{x = n\}.\overline{c}]\!] \sim_{\mathcal{DF}} [\![\mathbf{0}]\!]$ in D-Fusion (for $\sim_{\mathcal{DF}}$ included in trace equivalence). In D-Fusion, using commutativity of ν and λ, one would get $[\![(\nu n)\,(\lambda x)\,\{x = n\}.\overline{c}]\!] = [\![P]\!] \sim_{\mathcal{DF}} [\![\mathbf{0}]\!]$. But this equivalence does not hold true, since $P \stackrel{\overline{c}}{\Longrightarrow}$ implies by definition that $[\![P]\!] \stackrel{\overline{c}}{\Longrightarrow}$, while $[\![\mathbf{0}]\!] \stackrel{\overline{c}}{\not\Longrightarrow}$ (the latter follows by uniformity with respect to substitutions). This shows that the U-calculus cannot be uniformly encoded into D-Fusion. A similar argument applies to the other direction (that is, mapping D-Fusion to U-Calculus).

4 Encoding Guarded Choice

We show that in U-calculus, like in D-Fusion [1], the combined use of fusions and restrictions can still be used to uniformly encode guarded mixed choice *via* parallel composition. Practically, this guarantees that there is no significant loss of expressive power when moving from D-Fusion to U-calculus.

In the encoding, different branches of a guarded choice will be represented as concurrent processes. The encodings add pairs of extra names to the object part of each action: these extra names are used as 'side-channels' for atomic coordination among the different branches. Let us first look at a simple example.

Example 4. Consider the guarded choice $A = (\nu n)\,(\lambda x)\,a\langle xn\rangle.P + (\nu m)\,(\lambda x)\,a\langle xm\rangle.Q$. Its intended 'parallel' implementation is the process:

$$B = (\nu n)\,(\nu m)\,(\lambda x)\,\big(\, a\langle xn\rangle.P \,|\, a\langle xm\rangle.Q \,\big)$$

(here, $x, n, m \notin \mathrm{fn}(a, P, Q)$). Assume parallel contexts are constrained so that output actions on channel a must carry two identical names. In B, the parallel component that first consumes any such message, forces fusion of x either to n or to m, and consequently inhibits the other component, thus:

$$(\lambda u)\,\overline{a}\langle uu\rangle|B \xrightarrow{\tau}\sim (\nu n)\,(P\,|\,(\nu m)\,a\langle mn\rangle.Q) \quad\sim\quad P\,|(\nu n,m)\,a\langle mn\rangle.Q.$$

Under the mentioned assumption, $(\nu m,n)\,a\langle mn\rangle.Q$ should be 'equivalent' to $\mathbf{0}$, because there is no way of fusing m and n together. In other words, choice between P and Q has been resolved atomically. Note that this example exploits in a crucial way features of both Fusion (sharing of the variable x, in B) and of U-calculus (restricted input).

We generalise the above example by providing a fully abstract encoding of mixed guarded choice. For the sake of simplicity, we shall work here with barbed equivalence. We believe the results can also be stated in terms of labelled bisimilarity $\sim$, at the cost of breaking uniformity of the encoding (e.g. by introducing of 'firewalls' contexts which filter out output messages that disrupt the encoding, see [1]) .

As a source language we fix a sorted version of polyadic pi-calculus [5] with 'mixed' choice, Π^{mix}. In this language, prefixes and + are replaced by mixed summation, $\sum_{i\in I} a_i\,(\widetilde{x}_i).P_i + \sum_{j\in J} \overline{b_j}\langle\widetilde{v}_j\rangle.Q_j$. The target language is the fragment of polarised U-Calculus with no summation at all. The relevant clause is shown below, where $\widetilde{n} = (n_i)_{i\in I}$ and $\widetilde{m} = (m_j)_{j\in J}$ are two disjoint tuples of distinct names:

$$\begin{array}{l}[\![\sum_{i\in I} a_i\,(\widetilde{x}_i).P_i + \sum_{j\in J} \overline{b_j}\langle v_j\rangle.Q_j]\!]_{\mathrm{mix}} \quad = \\ (\nu\widetilde{n}\widetilde{m})\,((\lambda z,u)\,)\,(\,\Pi_{i\in I}(\lambda\widetilde{x}_i)\,a_i\langle\widetilde{x}_i z n_i uu\rangle.[\![P_i]\!]_{\mathrm{mix}} \;\mid\; \Pi_{j\in J}\overline{b_j}\langle\widetilde{v}_j uuzm_j\rangle.[\![Q_j]\!]_{\mathrm{mix}}\,).\end{array}$$

The encoding acts as a homomorphism over the remaining operators of Π^{mix}. Note that, differently from [1], the declaration of the λ-names is within the scope of the ν-names. Communication between two remote prefixes of opposite polarities causes all λ-names within the same choice to be fused to a single ν-name. This atomically inhibits the remaining prefixes. Note that the relative positions of ν-names correctly forbid communication between branches of opposite polarities within the same choice (no 'incestuous' communication, according to the terminology of [7]).

Below, $\sim^{\mathrm{mix}}$ denotes barbed congruence over Π^{mix}, and $\sim^{[\![\mathrm{mix}]\!]}$ the equivalence over the U-calculus obtained by closing barbed bisimulation under translated Π^{mix}-contexts, i.e.: $P \sim^{[\![\mathrm{mix}]\!]} Q$ iff for each Π^{mix}-context $C[\cdot]$, it holds $[\![C]\!]_{\mathrm{mix}}[P] \stackrel{\cdot}{\sim} [\![C]\!]_{\mathrm{mix}}[Q]$). Both equivalences are *reasonable* semantics in the sense of [9]. The proof of the following theorem is straightforward, given that there is a 1-to-1 correspondence between reductions and barbs of R and of $[\![R]\!]_{\mathrm{mix}}$, for any R, and given that the encoding is compositional, in particular, for any context $C[\cdot]$, it holds $[\![C]\!]_{\mathrm{mix}}[[\![P]\!]_{\mathrm{mix}}] = [\![C[P]]\!]_{\mathrm{mix}}$.

Theorem 2 (full abstraction for mixed choice). *Let $P,Q \in \Pi^{\mathrm{mix}}$. It holds that $P \sim^{\mathrm{mix}} Q$ if and only if $[\![P]\!]_{\mathrm{mix}} \sim^{[\![\mathrm{mix}]\!]} [\![Q]\!]_{\mathrm{mix}}$.*

In a pi-calculus setting, it is well-known that mixed choice cannot be encoded into the choice-free fragment, if one requires the encoding be uniform and preserve a reasonable semantics [8,9,7]. The theorem above shows that pi-calculus mixed choice *can* be implemented into the choice-free fragment of the U-calculus. The encoding is uniform, deadlock- and divergence-free, and preserves a reasonable semantics.

5 Conclusions

We have introduced U-Calculus, a process calculus with no I/O polarities and a unique binding, that can be used both to control the scope of fusions and new name generation. This is achieved by means of a simple form of typing that prevents a name x such that $x : T$ from being fused with any name in T.

We have proved that the U-Calculus is strictly more expressive than pi-calculus and Fusion calculus separately. Remarkably, thanks to the combination of static and dynamic ordering of names, the labelled bisimulation defined for the U-Calculus is a congruence. This property represents a substantial improvement with respect to D-Fusion.

We plan to extend the U-Calculus by generalising name fusions to substitutions over an arbitrary signature of terms. We believe that the extended calculus would be strictly more expressive that Logic Programming, the intuition being that restriction (creation of new fresh names) cannot be modelled in LP.

It would also be interesting to investigate whether the partition refinement algorithm proposed in [11] for checking open bisimilarity could be extended to U-Calculus.

References

1. M. Boreale, M. Buscemi, U. Montanari. D-Fusion: a Distinctive Fusion Calculus. In Proc. of APLAS'04, LNCS 3302, Springer-Verlag, 2004.
2. P. Gardner, C. Laneve, and L. Wischik. The fusion machine (extended abstract). In *Proc. of CONCUR '02*, LNCS 2421. Springer-Verlag, 2002.
3. L. G. Meredith, S. Bjorg, and D. Richter. Highwire Language Specification Version 1.0. Unpublished manuscript.
4. Microsoft Corp. Biztalk Server - `http://www.microsoft.com/biztalk`.
5. R. Milner. The Polyadic pi-Calculus: a Tutorial. Technical Report, Computer Science Dept., University of Edinburgh, 1991.
6. R. Milner, J. Parrow, and D. Walker. A calculus of mobile processes (parts I and II). *Information and Computation*, 100(1):1–77, 1992.
7. U. Nestmann and B. C. Pierce. Decoding choice encodings. *Information and Computation*, 163(1):1–59, 2000.
8. C. Palamidessi. Comparing the Expressive Power of the Synchronous and the Asynchronous pi-calculus. In *Conf. Rec. of POPL'97*, 1997.
9. C. Palamidessi. Comparing the Expressive Power of the Synchronous and the Asynchronous pi-calculus. *Mathematical Structures in Computer Science*, 13(5):685–719, 2003.

10. J. Parrow and B. Victor. The Fusion Calculus: Expressiveness and Symmetry in Mobile Processes. In *Proc. of LICS'98*. IEEE Computer Society Press, 1998.
11. M. Pistore and D. Sangiorgi. A Partition Refinement Algorithm for the Pi-Calculus. *Information and Computation*, 164(2): 264–321, 2001.
12. D. Sangiorgi. Expressing Mobility in Process Algebras: First-Order and Higher-Order Paradigms. PhD thesis, Department of Computer Science, University of Edinburgh, 1992.
13. D. Sangiorgi. A Theory of Bisimulation for the pi-Calculus. *Acta Informatica*, 33(1): 69-97, 1996.
14. B. Victor. The Fusion Calculus: Expressiveness and Symmetry in Mobile Processes. PhD thesis, Department of Computer Systems, Uppsala University, 1998.

Types for Security in a Mobile World *

Adriana B. Compagnoni[1] and Elsa L. Gunter[2]

[1] Department of Computer Science, Stevens Institute of Technology, Castle Point on Hudson, Hoboken, NJ 07030 USA
abc@cs.stevens.edu

[2] Department of Computer Science, University of Illinois, Urbana - Champaign, 201 N Goodwin Ave., Urbana, IL 61801-2302 USA
egunter@cs.uiuc.edu

Abstract. Our society is increasingly moving towards richer forms of information exchange where mobility of processes and devices plays a prominent role. This tendency has prompted the academic community to study the security problems arising from such mobile environments, and in particular, the security policies regulating who can access the information in question.

In this paper we propose a a mechanisms for specifying access privileges based on a combination of the identity of the user seeking access, its credentials, and the location from which he seeks it, within a reconfigurable nested structure.

We define $\mathbf{BACI_R}$, a boxed ambient calculus extended with a *Distributed Role-Based Access Control* mechanism where each ambient controls its own access policy. A process in $\mathbf{BACI_R}$ is associated with an owner and a set of activated roles that grant permissions for mobility and communication. The calculus includes primitives to activate and deactivate roles. The behavior of these primitives is determined by the process's owner, its current location and its currently activated roles. We consider two forms of security violations that our type system prevents: 1) attempting to move into an ambient without having the authorizing roles granting entry activated and 2) trying to use a communication port without having the roles required for access activated. We accomplish 1) and 2) by giving a static type system, an untyped transition semantics, and a typed transition semantics. We then show that a well-typed program never violates the dynamic security checks.

1 Introduction

The exchange of information by electronic means in a mobile environment has become part of everyday life, with cellphones, PDA's, and laptop computers accessing remote information and transmitting signals and data. An increasingly mobile workforce needs to be able to access corporate information while at work,

* This research was partially supported by the NSF Grant No. CCR-0220286 ITR:Secure Electronic Transactions and by US Army Research Office Grant number DAAAD19-01-1-0473.

R. De Nicola and D. Sangiorgi (Eds.): TGC 2005, LNCS 3705, pp. 75–97, 2005.

from home, and on the road. This tendency has prompted the academic community to study the security problems arising from this constantly escalating mobility.

The concept of Trust Management has been actively studied in the network security community since it was first introduced by Blaze, Feigenbaum, and Lacy in the paper *Decentralized Trust Management* [6]. According to their formulation, trust management addresses the question: *is this request, supported by these credentials, in compliance with this user's policy?* In [6], they identify three components of trust management: *security policies, security credentials*, and *trust relationships.* Security policies are local policies that an application trusts unconditionally, security credentials are assertions about objects by trusted third parties, and trust relationships are special cases of security policies.

One way to address Trust Management is by considering *Role-Based Access Control* (RBAC) [18,36,19], where a *role* is defined by a set of privileges. RBAC is a methodology for defining security policies and for giving privileges to users. However, it is not concerned with the authentication of users. Whether the user claiming to be Bob is indeed Bob is beyond the scope of Trust Management, and of this work. In an RBAC framework there are two special relations between roles, privileges, and users: one assigns privileges to roles, and the other one assigns users to roles. These two relations form part of the security policy.

Mobility adds a new dimension to RBAC, since the services available to a given user also depend on the location of the user, agreements between parties, and the technology underlying the connection. For example, without roaming agreements in place, a cell-phone may be rendered useless beyond the scope of its provider's network. Furthermore, whether a user's connection is wireless, wired, secure, or insecure also conditions the available services. For example, an administrator on an insecure wireless connection may be denied access to sensitive information.

In a distributed environment the policies regulating access control may be distributed among several parties, and each principal may only have partial knowledge of the overall security policy [29,30,27].

In a mobile environment, different domains will have different access policies and when users (and potentially programs) migrate from domain to domain they will be ruled by a combination of the access policies of their enclosing domain and remote server domains.

In this work we study RBAC based Trust Management. As we described earlier, RBAC is a method of regulating access of users to information and resources based on the activity they need to perform. Access is fundamentally controlled by roles. On one side, each user of a system is associated with a set of roles. On the other side, each role is associated with a set of permissions (access privileges to existing resources). Some roles may be mutually exclusive, and others may be deactivated leaving the user with only a subset of the full set of roles with which she is associated. Therefore, in simple RBAC, a user is granted an access privilege to a resource if one of her activated roles has that privilege. This factorization of access control simplifies the administration of the security policy by allowing the systems administrator to separately decide which resources a given role needs in order to successfully operate, and what roles to assign to each user. It also allows for the choice of authentication method to be handled separately. How to enrich RBAC by adding orderings and other forms of structure on the roles, and the privileges is an active area of research. They all share in common the separation of concerns given by the introduction of roles.

Role-based access control is currently a popular mechanism for governing the access to databases, files, executable programs and other computational resources. In networking there is another kind of access control that is done by packet filtering. A given router may be configured to drop all SMTP or HTTP packets denying access to certain services of a domain from outside that domain. Here, there is no notion of user and role, but only IP domain and packet type. However, it can be beneficial to have a finer-grain access control that is aware of roles and network domains. Consider the following example.

> The University of Wizbrau is equipped with intelligent buildings, and students carry their laptops with them to class. While in the classroom, students have only limited Internet access and they are not allowed to use e-mail, instant messenger, or visit general websites. However, these activities are allowed when done from the student lounge instead. Since the instructor of the course needs a greater access to resources than the students, those activities temporarily disabled to the students are available to the instructor. For example, during a lecture, the instructor may consult her e-mail to address a question raised by a student in an e-mail message.

The restrictions placed on users in this environment need to be sensitive to both the location of the user (classroom versus lounge) as well as the role (student versus instructor). Such fine-grained control is not readily handled by either packet filtering or RBAC.

In this paper we design a formal language featuring formal notions for resource, access, computation, communication, location and mobility. The starting point of our design is a mobile ambient calculus in the style of [14], where principals and locations are modeled by ambients.

1.1 Background on Ambient Calculi

In Cardelli and Gordon's Mobile Ambients (MA)[15], ambients represent nested computational environments containing data and live computation. In a nutshell, ambients are administrative units forming a dynamic hierarchy, where an ambient can move up and down the hierarchy by moving into a child or a parent ambient. Furthermore, a mobile ambient is a communicating entity that can exchange information with parents and children. Ambients are capable of moving under the influence of the process they enclose and can dissolve their perimeter with an *open* operation. Mobile Ambients provide a direct characterization of computational processes as well as computational devices.

Boxed Ambients (BA) [10] evolved from MA, by removing the ability of an ambient to dissolve its boundary. In BA, an ambient is a "box" that cannot be opened. This notion of closed ambient provides a complete encapsulation of the agents they contain. To enable the communication lost by disabling the open operation, ambients are equipped with communication channels to exchange information with adjacent ambients (parent and children ambients).

Both in MA and BA, ambient mobility is commanded by processes inside the ambient. The commands for mobility are called *capabilities*. The capabilities tell an ambient to open or move inside or outside another ambient. Unrestricted mobility, however, can lead to undesired *interferences* between two concurrent processes. Addressing this concern, control over capabilities was first introduced in Safe Ambients [25] and later used in New Boxed Ambients (NBA) [11] in the form of *co-capabilities*. A capability can be exercised only in the presence of a matching co-capability. Hence, in order to enter an ambient using the in capability, that ambient must contain a matching $\overline{\mathsf{in}}$ co-capability authorizing that access; similarly for exiting using the out capability.

BACI, a Boxed Ambients with Communication Interfaces [7], introduced the notion of *local views*. In this calculus, each ambient has an associated communication *port* and a *local view*. The communication port is used for sending and receiving messages to and from other ambients, and the local view represents the communication types that are used by the processes enclosed inside the ambient. **BACI** is flexible enough to allow an ambient to communicate with different parents using different types. However, this flexibility came with the price of a rather complex syntax and some run-time type checking required to guarantee type safety. **BACIv2** [20] further enhanced communication mechanisms and mobility control by introducing multiple communication ports, access control lists, and port hiding.

Motivated by our earlier work on **BACI** [7], we define a typed boxed ambient calculus called $\mathbf{BACI_R}$ extended with a *Distributed Role-Based Access Control* mechanism where each ambient controls its own access policy. Following the style of **BACI**, our new calculus distinguishes between names of ambients and names of communication ports. Ambients are used for mobility and ports are used for communication, either locally within a channel or between a parent and a child. This distinction is instrumental in defining our RBAC mechanism, since it provides for a finer grain in the security policy. Each ambient controls its own access policy by specifying which roles (or which porcesses with at least one of those roles activated) are allowed to enter it. Similarly, a port specifies its own access policy by specifying which roles can read from it and which roles can write to it.

A process in $\mathbf{BACI_R}$ is associated with an owner and a set of activated roles that grant permissions for mobility and communication. The calculus includes primitives to activate and deactivate roles. The behavior of these primitives is determined by the owner of the process and its current location and its currently activated roles. In order for a process to activate a role, the security policy has to allow the owner of the process to do so. Moreover, deactivating roles should should not remove the roles authorizing the process to be in its current location.

We consider two forms of *security violations* that our type system prevents: 1) attempting to move into an ambient without having the authorizing roles granting entry activated and 2) trying to use a communication port without having the roles required for access activated. We accomplish 1) and 2) by giving a static type system in Section 3, an untyped transition semantics, and a typed transition semantics in Section 4. We then show that a well-typed program never violates the dynamic security checks in Theorem 4.

2 Syntax of $\mathbf{BACI_R}$

Based on our earlier work on **BACI** [7], we define $\mathbf{BACI_R}$, a boxed ambient calculus with a Distributed Role-Based Access Control mechanism, where the location of an ambient conditions its privileges. The intuitive idea is that to accommodate security checking an ambient is associated with its owner and with a set of roles that are currently activated. This set of roles can be changed by activation and deactivation primitives. Whether a role can be activated or deactivated depends on the location of the ambient and its owner. This control is made explicit in the type system where the type of an ambient has a set of roles authorizing the entrance of ambients. Going back to the example, the professor can send mail because she can activate the FACULTY_MAIL, while the students can only activate the STUDENT_MAIL role, which is not enough to qualify to send mail in the classroom.

In order to define the syntax of $\mathbf{BACI_R}$ we use the following disjoint categories of identifiers:

User Names:	$u,\ v \in \mathit{Users}$
Roles:	$\mathsf{r} \in \mathit{Roles}$
Port Names:	$c,\ c' \in \mathcal{C}$
Ambient Names:	$n, m \in \mathit{Amb}$
Capability Variables:	$i \in \mathit{CapVar}$
Message Identifiers:	$x \in \mathit{Amb} \cup \mathit{CapVar}$

We assume a fixed set *Users* of users, a fixed set *Roles* of roles, and a fixed function *UserPolicy* associating each user and set of currently activated roles with a set of roles that may become activated. The syntax of $\mathbf{BACI_R}$ is presented in Table 1. *Processes* and *Messages* are the two main syntactic categories.

Messages, ranged over by M and N, include *message identifiers* and *capabilities.* Capabilities, ranged over by C, can be either the capabilities for entering and exiting an ambient, variables or a "path", which is a sequence of capabilities describing a mobility path. A special sort of capability is that of *quiet capability*, ranged over by Q, used for entry with no accompanying possibility of communication. These are used for mobility alone, and are the primary component of paths.

Processes, ranged over by P and R, are built from the constructors of *inactivity*, showing the end of a process; *parallel composition* of two processes;

Table 1. Syntax of $\mathbf{BACI_R}$

Quiet Capabilities:	
$Q ::= \mathsf{inQ}\ m$	quiet enter
$\mid \mathsf{outQ}\ m$	quiet exit
Capabilities:	
$C ::= Q$	quiet capability
$\mid \mathsf{in}\ m$	enter
$\mid \mathsf{out}\ m$	exit
$\mid Q.C$	path
$\mid i$	capability variable
Locations:	
$\eta ::= \uparrow c$	parent port γ
$\mid \downarrow c$	child port γ
$\mid \star$	local
Actions:	
$\pi ::= C(c)$	capability
$\mid S$	quiet co-capability
$\mid K(c)$	co-capability
$\mid \mathsf{activate}\langle \mathsf{r} \rangle$	activate a role
$\mid \mathsf{deactivate}\langle \mathsf{r} \rangle$	deactivate a role
$\mid (x_1, \ldots, x_k)^\eta$	input
$\mid \langle M_1, \ldots, M_k \rangle^\eta$	output
Quiet Co-Capabilities:	
$S \mid \overline{\mathsf{inQ}}$	allow quiet enter
$\mid \overline{\mathsf{outQ}}$	allow quiet exit
Co-Capabilities:	
$K \mid \overline{\mathsf{in}}\,(c)$	allow enter
$\mid \overline{\mathsf{out}}\,(c)$	allow exit
Messages:	
$M, N ::= x$	message identifier
$\mid C$	capability
Basic types	
$\tau ::= \mathsf{amb}(\rho_{in}, \sigma)$	ambient type
$\mid \mathsf{cap}(\rho_{in}, \sigma)$	capability
Communication types	
$\sigma ::= \mathsf{shh}$	no exchange
$\mid (\rho_r, \rho_w, \tau)$	exchange tuple
Processes:	
$P ::= \mathbf{0}$	nil process
$\mid P_1 \mid P_2$	composition
$\mid \boldsymbol{\nu}(n{:}\tau)P$	restriction
$\mid\ !P$	replication
$\mid \pi.P$	prefixing
$\mid m_u[P]@\rho$	ambient

replication, used for recursion; ambient name *restriction*; *prefixing*, where π is an operation that is followed by a continuation process P; and finally, a named *ambient* encapsulating a process, indexed by a user name u and a set of activated roles ρ.

An action or prefix π can be a *capability* ranged over by $C(c)$; a *co-capability*, ranged over by $K(c)$; and *quiet co-capability* ranged over by S, for granting permission to the matching capabilities; and *input* and *output* communication, indexed by a location η indicating whether the communication is local within the same ambient, with the parent ambient, or with a child ambient. Communication ports are established by one ambient entering or exiting another ambient. To request movement, we have the actions $\mathsf{in}\ m\,(c)$, $\mathsf{out}\ m\,(c)$, $\mathsf{inQ}\ m\,(c)$ and $\mathsf{outQ}\, m\,(c)$. The actions $\mathsf{in}\, m\,(c)$ and $\mathsf{out}\, m\,(c)$ request to enter to or exit to ambient m, establishing communication port c in the process. The actions $\mathsf{inQ}\ m\,(c)$ and $\mathsf{outQ}\ m(c)$ are similar but establish no actual communications port, and the typing rules enforce that the port c cannot subsequently be used for communication. The syntax $\mathsf{inQ}\ m$ and $\mathsf{outQ}\ m$ is allowed, but is an abbreviation for $\mathsf{inQ}\, m\,(c)$ and $\mathsf{outQ}\, m(c)$ respectively. It should be noted that we change the intention of $\mathsf{out}\, m$ from the usual of meaning a request to go out *from* m to a request to go out *to* m. For each action requesting the movement of an ambient to within another, there is a co-action enabling the ambient to enter: $\overline{\mathsf{in}}\, m(c)$, $\overline{\mathsf{out}}\, m(c)$, $\overline{\mathsf{inQ}}\, m$ and $\overline{\mathsf{outQ}}\, m$.

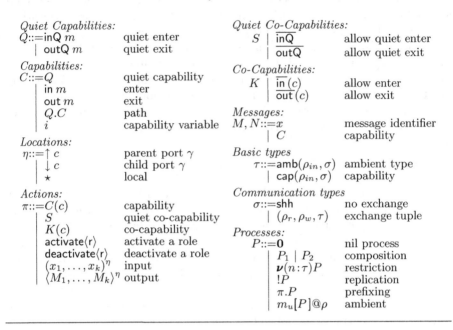

In addition to moving and communicating, there are two actions related to security: $\mathsf{activate}\langle \mathsf{r} \rangle$ for activating a user role r, and $\mathsf{deactivate}\langle \mathsf{r} \rangle$ for deactivating it. These control what privileges are available to the ambient at any given point during execution by modifying the set of activated roles ρ.

Table 2. Structural Congruence

$!P \equiv P \mid !P$	(Struct RepPar)
$\boldsymbol{\nu}(n{:}\tau)\boldsymbol{\nu}(m{:}\tau')P \equiv \boldsymbol{\nu}(m{:}\tau')\boldsymbol{\nu}(n{:}\tau)P$	(Struct Res Res)
$\boldsymbol{\nu}(n{:}\tau)(P \mid P_2) \equiv P \mid \boldsymbol{\nu}(n{:}\tau)P_2$, if $n \notin \mathrm{fn}(P)$	(Struct Res Par)
$\boldsymbol{\nu}(n{:}\tau)m_u[P]@\rho \equiv m_u[\boldsymbol{\nu}(n{:}\tau)P]@\rho$, if $n \neq m$	(Struct Res Amb)
$\mathsf{inQ}\, n\,.P \equiv \mathsf{inQ}\, n\,(c).P \equiv \mathsf{in}\, n\,(c).P$, if $c \notin \mathrm{fv}(P)$	(Struct InQ)
$\mathsf{outQ}\, n\,.P \equiv \mathsf{outQ}\, n\,(c).P \equiv \mathsf{out}\, n\,(c).P$, if $c \notin \mathrm{fv}(P)$	(Struct OutQ)
$\overline{\mathsf{in}}\,(c).P \equiv \overline{\mathsf{inQ}}\,(c).P$, if $c \notin \mathrm{fv}(P)$	(Struct Co-InQ)
$\overline{\mathsf{out}}\,(c).P \equiv \overline{\mathsf{outQ}}\,(c).P$, if $c \notin \mathrm{fv}(P)$	(Struct Co-OutQ)
$(Q.C).P \equiv Q(c).(C.P)$, where $c \notin \mathrm{fv}(P)$	(Struct Prefix)

We introduce the usual notion of process equivalence through the structural congruence generated by alpha conversion, associativity and commutativity of parallel composition with $\mathbf{0}$ for identity, and the rules given in Table 2. The rules for replication and restriction are fairly standard. We add a rule for allowing restriction to pass through an ambient, provided that ambient is the one whose name is being restricted. The third set of rules state that capabilities and co-capabilities that make no use of their associated communication port are equivalent to the corresponding quiet capabilities or co-capabilities. That is, a quiet capability is just a capability that doesn't communicate. The last rule tells us that to follow a path is the same as to follow it in pieces. This makes sense because ambients can only enter one other ambient at a time. In Section 4 we will see that the operational semantics respects process equivalence.

3 Types for Security

Attempting to enter an ambient without an authorizing role activated is a security violation. Trying to use a communication port without having activated at least one of the required roles to access the port is also a security violation. In this section we define a type system such that well-typed processes can compute without committing a security violation. The type of a process is a set of roles sufficient for it to compute without security violations. In particular, the type of an ambient name is the set of roles needed for mobility and communication.

The syntax of types can be found in Table 1. Basic types describe the kind of data to be communicated over a port. The communication type further includes the sets of roles ρ_r and ρ_w granting read and write access to a port. In Tables 3 to 8, let Γ be a mapping from message identifiers to basic types and from port names to communication types. The typing judgment for a process is of the form $\Gamma,\ \rho_{here},\ \rho_{deac}\, m,\ u \vdash P : \rho_{act}$, where Γ is a typing environment for free message identifiers and port names, ρ_{here} is the set of roles sufficient for authorizing the process to be in its current location (the entrance policy for ambient containing m), ρ_{deact} are the set of roles that the process may at any time in its computation safely deactivate, m is the assumed surrounding ambient, u is the current user, and ρ_{act} is the set of "currently active" roles. The judgments for the other syntactic categories are similar.

Table 3. Well-typed Quiet Capabilities

Quiet Enter:
$$\frac{\Gamma(m) = \mathsf{amb}(\rho_{in}, \sigma)}{\Gamma \vdash \mathsf{inQ}\ m\ : \rho_{in}}$$

Quiet Exit To:
$$\frac{\Gamma(m) = \mathsf{amb}(\rho_{in}, \sigma)}{\Gamma \vdash \mathsf{outQ}\ m\ : \rho_{in}}$$

Table 4. Well-typed Capabilities

Quiet Capability:
$$\frac{\Gamma \vdash Q : \rho_{in}}{\Gamma \vdash Q : (\rho_{in}, \mathsf{shh})}$$

Enter:
$$\frac{\Gamma(m) = \mathsf{amb}(\rho_{in}, \sigma)}{\Gamma \vdash \mathsf{in}\ m\ : (\rho_{in}, \sigma)}$$

Exit To:
$$\frac{\Gamma(m) = \mathsf{amb}(\rho_{in}, \sigma)}{\Gamma \vdash \mathsf{out}\ m\ : (\rho_{in}, \sigma)}$$

Path:
$$\frac{\Gamma \vdash Q : \rho_{in} \quad \Gamma, m \vdash C : (\rho_{in}, \sigma)}{\Gamma \vdash Q.C : (\rho_{in}, \sigma)}$$

Variable:
$$\frac{\Gamma(i) = \mathsf{cap}(\rho_{in}, \sigma)}{\Gamma \vdash i : (\rho_{in}, \sigma)}$$

An ambient name type $\mathsf{amb}(\rho_{in}, \sigma)$ has two arguments: a set of roles ρ_{in} indicating which roles are allowed to enter it, and the type σ of its communication port. The typing rules for quiet capabilities in Table 3 together with rule Quiet Capability in Table 4 reflect the fact that these capabilities allow mobility, while disabling communication. Therefore, the type of the communication port of the communication policy is shh. The only part we need to collect from the ambient type is the entrance policy ρ_{in}. However, in the general case for capabilities (Table 4), we need to learn the full security policy from the ambient type, i.e., the entrance policy ρ_{in} and the communication policy σ. It is worth noting that for a capability that is a path, i.e., a sequence of capabilities, the entrance security policy is required to be the same for all members in the path. See rule Path.

The type of a location (Table 5) is the read-write security policies for accessing the associated communication port, together with the security policy for the messages communicated through the port. For local communication, we use the

Table 5. Typing of Locations

Parent Port:	Child port:	Local:
$$\frac{\Gamma(c)=\sigma}{\Gamma,m\vdash\uparrow c:\sigma}$$	$$\frac{\Gamma(c)=\sigma}{\Gamma,m\vdash\downarrow c:\sigma}$$	$$\frac{\Gamma(m)=\mathsf{amb}(\rho_{in},(\rho_r,\rho_w,\tau))}{\Gamma,m\vdash\star:(\mathit{Roles},\mathit{Roles},\tau)}$$

Table 6. Well-typed Messages

Message Identifier:	Capability:
$$\frac{\Gamma(x)=\tau}{\Gamma,m\vdash x:\tau}$$	$$\frac{\Gamma\vdash C:(\rho_{in},\sigma)}{\Gamma\vdash C:\mathsf{cap}(\rho_{in},\sigma)}$$

ambient assumed as the surrounding ambient, and we want no restrictions on reading or writing. However, it is important that we maintain the restrictions on the types of data transmitted. We could violate the security policy if we omitted the type checks on messages locally communicated, because we potentially could send a capability with one security policy but receive it with a different one.

A message is either an ambient name or a capability, and thus its type is the security policy of the ambient or capability, appropriately labeled. See Table 6.

The rules for typing actions appear in Table 8. Actions are the basic unit of work in processes. They have the potential for changing the set of variables in scope, the current position and hence the current authorizing policy, and the set of activated roles. Thus the type of an action is a tuple of the revised typing environment, the revised authorizing policy, and the revised set of activated roles. Capabilities change the current position and hence the current authorizing policy, but co-capabilities do not. Capabilities and co-capabilities add a new port name and type to the typing environment. Unlike capabilities, co-capabilities do not incur any security checks. Inputting a message introduces a tuple of new message variables. Outputting a message does not change the typing environment.

The particular approach we have taken to handling local communications leads to allowing local communication only when at least one role has been activated for the process. See rules Input and Output. We can eliminate this requirement by removing the explicit rules for typing locations in Table 5, and replacing them by three rules for typing input actions and three rules for output actions. In this setting, we can then simply fail to check whether there is an active role among the roles for reading from or writing to a local port.

Activating a role adds the role to the set of currently active roles, provided the user of the process is allowed to activate that role, and deactivating a role removes it, provided the role is allowed to be deactivated and that removing

Table 7. Well-typed Actions

CAPABILITIES:

$$\frac{\Gamma \vdash C : (\rho_{in}, \sigma) \quad (\rho_{act} - \rho_{deact}) \cap \rho_{in} \neq \emptyset}{\Gamma,\ \rho_{here},\ \rho_{deact},\ \rho_{act},\ m,\ u \vdash C(c) : (\Gamma + \{c{:}\sigma\},\ \rho_{in},\ \rho_{act})}$$

CO-CAPABILITIES:

$$\frac{\Gamma(m) = \mathsf{amb}(\rho_{in}, \sigma)}{\Gamma,\ \rho_{here},\ \rho_{deact},\ \rho_{act},\ m,\ u \vdash K(c) : (\Gamma + \{c{:}\sigma\},\ \rho_{here},\ \rho_{act})}$$

QUIET CO-CAPABILITIES:

$$\frac{}{\Gamma,\ \rho_{here},\ \rho_{deact},\ \rho_{act},\ m,\ u \vdash S : (\Gamma, \rho_{here},\ \rho_{act})}$$

ACTIVATION:

$$\frac{\mathsf{r} \in \mathit{UserPolicy}(u, \rho_{act})}{\Gamma,\ \rho_{here},\ \rho_{deact},\ \rho_{act},\ m,\ u \vdash \mathsf{activate}\langle \mathsf{r} \rangle : (\Gamma,\ \rho_{here},\ \rho_{act} \cup \{\mathsf{r}\})}$$

DEACTIVATION:

$$\frac{r \notin \rho_{deact} \qquad (\rho - \{\mathsf{r}\} - \rho_{deact}) \cap \rho_{here} \neq \emptyset}{\Gamma,\ \rho_{here},\ \rho_{deact},\ \rho_{act},\ m,\ u \vdash \mathsf{deactivate}\langle \mathsf{r} \rangle : (\Gamma,\ \rho_{here},\ \rho_{act} - \{\mathsf{r}\})}$$

INPUT:

$$\frac{\Gamma, m \vdash \eta : (\rho_r, \rho_w, \tau) \quad (\rho_{act} - \rho_{deact}) \cap \rho_r \neq \emptyset}{\Gamma,\ \rho_{here},\ \rho_{deact},\ \rho_{act},\ m,\ u \vdash (x_1, \ldots, x_k)^\eta : (\Gamma + \Sigma_{i=1}^k \{x_i{:}\tau\},\ \rho_{here},\ \rho_{act})}$$

OUTPUT:

$$\frac{\Gamma, m \vdash \eta : (\rho_r, \rho_w, \tau) \quad \Gamma \vdash M_i : \tau \ \ i = 1, \ldots, k \quad (\rho_{act} - \rho_{deact}) \cap \rho_w \neq \emptyset}{\Gamma,\ \rho_{here},\ \rho_{deact},\ \rho_{act},\ m,\ u \vdash \langle M_1, \ldots, M_k \rangle^\eta : (\Gamma,\ \rho_{here},\ \rho_{act})}$$

it doesn't leave us without a way of satisfying the authorizing policy of our current position. With this last check and others of its kind, we always assume the roles that can be deactivated are. The reason for this is that with parallel composition, one process may type check based on needing certain roles, while a parallel process may have the ability to deactivate those roles.

The rules for typing processes appear in Table 8. Processes are the outermost level of syntax. The type for a process is a (any) set of roles, which if active at the start of the process, are sufficient to assure that the process will

Table 8. Well-typed Processes

NIL:

$$\frac{}{\Gamma,\, \rho_{here},\, \rho_{deact},\, m,\, u \vdash \mathbf{0} : \rho_{act}}$$

COMPOSITION:

$$\frac{\Gamma,\, \rho_{here},\, \rho_{deact},\, m,\, u \vdash P_1 : \rho_{act} \quad \Gamma,\, \rho_{here},\, \rho_{deact},\, m,\, u \vdash P_2 : \rho_{act}}{\Gamma,\, \rho_{here},\, \rho_{deact},\, m,\, u \vdash P_1 \mid P_2 : \rho_{act}}$$

RESTRICTION:

$$\frac{\Gamma + \{m' : \tau\},\, \rho_{here},\, \rho_{deact},\, m,\, u \vdash P : \rho_{act}}{\Gamma,\, \rho_{here},\, \rho_{deact},\, m,\, u \vdash \boldsymbol{\nu}(m' {:} \tau)P : \rho_{act}}$$

REPLICATION:

$$\frac{\Gamma,\, \rho_{here},\, \rho_{deact},\, m,\, u \vdash P : \rho_{act}}{\Gamma,\, \rho_{here},\, \rho_{deact},\, m,\, u \vdash !P : \rho_{act}}$$

PREFIXING:

$$\frac{\Gamma,\, \rho_{here},\, \rho_{deact},\, \rho_{act},\, m,\, u \vdash \pi : (\Gamma',\, \rho'_{here},\, \rho'_{act}) \qquad \Gamma',\, \rho'_{here},\, \rho_{deact},\, m,\, u \vdash P : \rho'_{act}}{\Gamma,\, \rho_{here},\, \rho_{deact},\, m,\, u \vdash \pi.P : \rho_{act}}$$

AMBIENT:

$$\frac{\Gamma(m') = \mathsf{amb}(\rho_{in}, \sigma) \qquad \Gamma,\, \rho_{in},\, \rho'_{deact},\, m,\, v \vdash P : \rho_m}{\Gamma,\, \rho_{here},\, \rho_{deact},\, m',\, u \vdash m_v[P]@\rho_m : \rho_{act}}$$

never attempt a security breach (*i.e.* an unauthorized entry, read, or write). The nil process ($\mathbf{0}$) types with any set of roles. The parallel composition of two processes types with a set of roles if both processes individually do. A process beginning with a restricted ambient name types with a given set of processes if the underlying process types with the same set of roles but using an extended environment with a binding for the restricted ambient name. The replication of a process types with a set of roles if the process to be replicated does. The most interesting cases are those of prefixes and ambients. For prefixes (PREFIXING in Table 8), we must type the action at the head to derive a new typing environment, new authorizing policy, and a new set of active roles, and then use the new environment, authorizing policy, and active role set to check the remaining process. This is because actions have the ability to expand the needed typing environment or alter the authorizing policy or the set of activated roles. If r is in ρ and the process begins by deactivating it, then the remainder of the process must be able to typecheck with a reduced set of activated roles. The typing for an ambient (AMBIENT in Table 8) throws away the surrounding ambient information and checks the ambient in isolation. Since an ambient may travel into other ambients with unknown active roles, an ambient must be secure relative to the context it carries with itself.

4 Operational Semantics

Our goal in defining the static type system given in Section 3 is to enable us to prove that if a process type checks with a given set of roles, then it will never attempt an action that it is not authorized to perform when executed in a state where all the roles in the set have previously been activated. To this end, we define two transition semantics for our language, one with dynamic security checks and one without. For the untyped semantics, we have a form of subject reduction. We also have that, if a process type checks, then it reduces to another process in the untyped transition system if and only if it reduces to that process in the typed transition system.

4.1 Untyped Transition Semantics

The untyped transition semantics is given in Tables 9 and 10. It is worth noting that almost all the reduction rules explicitly mention a context containing an ambient, except for the rule for Local communication.

The rules for ambient movement are the most complicated. For an ambient to move inside another, the first ambient must contain a process requesting entrance to the second, and the second ambient must have a process allowing the entrance. If these two conditions are met, then the request and permission are consumed and the resulting first ambient enters that resulting second ambient. All the rules for entrance are the same, except for the way the communication ports are handled. In general (ENTER, Table 9), when one ambient enters another a fresh port is created for the two ambients to share for communication. In the case (ENTER', Table 9) that a regular entrance request is permitted by only a quiet permission ($\overline{\mathsf{inQ}}$), the entrance still takes place, but the host ambient does not offer a port to be shared. The standard case on a quiet entrance request being granted by a quiet entrance permission (QUIET ENTER, Table 9) is similar to the previous case. We need to create a dummy port for the ambient requesting entrance, but there is no match with the other ambient, so no communication is possible. If an ambient requests a quiet entrance and it is granted by an ordinary entrance permission ($\overline{\mathsf{in}}$) (QUIET ENTER', Table 9), then strictly speaking they both create half of a port, but we prevent any communication by giving them two different fresh ports, neither of which will ever be usable.

An EXIT action is more complicated than an ENTER. We have three ambients nested in each other, m in n in p. The ambient m request to exit to p. The ambient p grants the request. The exit takes place so that now m and n are in parallel inside p. As m exits n, effectively entering p, there is the potential for establishing a communication port between m and p. In order to determine whether such a communication port really should be established, we consider the same cases as those for entrance and we handle them identically.

The rules for activation and deactivation cause the addition or deletion of the given role from the role set of the surrounding ambient. A message can be sent in one of three ways: locally, to a child, or to a parent. Communication is implemented by substitution of the values sent by one process for the variables

Table 9. Simple Transition System – Mobility

ENTER: $m_v[\mathsf{in}\, n\,(c).P_1 \mid P_2\,]@\rho_m \mid n_u[\overline{\mathsf{in}}\,(c').P_3 \mid P_4\,]@\rho_n \Rightarrow$
$n_u[m_v[P_1\{c := c''\} \mid P_2\,]@\rho_m \mid P_3\{c' := c''\} \mid P_4\,]@\rho_n$

for fresh variable c''

ENTER': $m_v[\mathsf{in}\, n\,(c).P_1 \mid P_2\,]@\rho_m \mid n_u[\overline{\mathsf{inQ}}\,.P_3 \mid P_4\,]@\rho_n \Rightarrow$
$n_u[m_v[P_1\{c := c'\} \mid P_2\,]@\rho_m \mid P_3 \mid P_4\,]@\rho_n$

for fresh variable c'

QUIET ENTER: $m_v[\mathsf{inQ}\, n\,(c).P_1 \mid P_2\,]@\rho_m \mid n_u[\overline{\mathsf{inQ}}\,.P_3 \mid P_4\,]@\rho_n \Rightarrow$
$n_u[m_v[P_1\{c := c'\} \mid P_2\,]@\rho_m \mid P_3 \mid P_4\,]@\rho_n$

for fresh variable c'

QUIET ENTER': $m_v[\mathsf{inQ}\, n\,(c).P_1 \mid P_2\,]@\rho_m \mid n_u[\overline{\mathsf{in}}\,(c')P_3 \mid .P_4\,]@\rho_n \Rightarrow$
$n_u[m_v[P_1\{c{:=}c''\} \mid P_2\,]@\rho_m \mid P_3\{c'{:=}c'''\} \mid P_4\,]@\rho_n$

for fresh distinct variables c'' and c'''

EXIT: $p_w[n_v[m_u[\mathsf{out}\, p\,(c).P_1 \mid P_2\,]@\rho_m \mid P_3\,]@\rho_n \mid \overline{\mathsf{out}}\,(c').P_4 \mid P_5\,]@\rho_p \Rightarrow$
$p_w[n_v[P_3\,]@\rho_n \mid m_u[P_1\{c{:=}c''\}]@\rho_m \mid P_4\{c'{:=}c''\} \mid P_5\,]@\rho_p$

for fresh variable c''

EXIT': $p_w[n_v[m_u[\mathsf{out}\, p\,(c).P_1 \mid P_2\,]@\rho_m \mid P_3\,]@\rho_n \mid \overline{\mathsf{outQ}}\,.P_4 \mid P_5\,]@\rho_p \Rightarrow$
$p_w[n_v[P_3\,]@\rho_n \mid m_u[P_1\{c{:=}c'\}]@\rho_m \mid P_4 \mid P_5\,]@\rho_p$

for fresh variable c'

QUIET EXIT: $p_w[n_v[m_u[\mathsf{outQ}\, p\,(c).P_1 \mid P_2\,]@\rho_m \mid P_3\,]@\rho_n \mid \overline{\mathsf{outQ}}\,.P_4 \mid P_5\,]@\rho_p \Rightarrow$
$p_w[n_v[P_3\,]@\rho_n \mid m_u[P_1\{c{:=}c'\}]@\rho_m \mid P_4 \mid P_5\,]@\rho_p$

for fresh variable c'

QUIET EXIT': $p_w[n_v[m_u[\mathsf{outQ}\, p\,(c).P_1 \mid P_2\,]@\rho_m \mid P_3\,]@\rho_n \mid \overline{\mathsf{out}}\,.(c')P_4 \mid P_5\,]@\rho_p \Rightarrow$
$p_w[n_v[P_3\,]@\rho_n \mid m_u[P_1\{c{:=}c''\}]@\rho_m \mid P_4\{c'{:=}c'''\} \mid P_5\,]@\rho_p$

for fresh distinct variables c'' and c'''

---

used to receive the values in another. It is worth noting that local communication is expressly not between ambients, but between ordinary processes. Recursion causes a copy of the body of the recursive process to be created and composed with the recursive process. In addition to the above rules for top-level reduction, there is a rule allowing us to descend through compositions, restrictions, and ambients to find a process capable of reducing. In particular, it is worth noting that an ambient within another ambient may keep computing, even while the outer ambient is blocked.

The untyped transition semantics respects process equivalence:

Table 10. Simple Transition System – Remaining Rules

ACTIVATE:	$m_u[(\mathsf{activate}\langle \mathsf{r}\rangle P) \mid R]@\rho \Rightarrow m_u[P \mid R]@(\rho \cup \{r\})$
DEACTIVATE:	$m_u[(\mathsf{deactivate}\langle \mathsf{r}\rangle P) \mid R]@\rho \Rightarrow m_u[P \mid R]@(\rho - \{r\})$
LOCAL:	$\langle M_1, \ldots, M_k\rangle^{\star}.\, P \mid (x_1, \ldots, x_k)^{\star}.\, R \Rightarrow P \mid R\{x_i := M_i \mid i = 1 \ldots k\}$
TO CHILD ($\downarrow$):	$m_u[\langle M_1, \ldots, M_k\rangle^{\downarrow c}.\, P_1 \mid n_v[(x_1, \ldots, x_k)^{\uparrow c}.P_2 \mid R_1]@\rho_n \mid R_2]@\rho_m \Rightarrow$ $m_u[P_1 \mid n_v[P_2\{x_i := M_i \vert i = 1 \ldots k\} \mid R_1]@\rho_n \mid R_2]@\rho_m$
TO PARENT ($\uparrow$):	$n_v[m_u[\langle M_1, \ldots, M_k\rangle^{\downarrow c}.P_1 \mid R_1]@\rho_m \mid (x_1, \ldots, x_k)^{\downarrow c}.\, P_2 \mid R_1]@\rho_n$ $\Rightarrow$ $n_v[m_u[P_1 \mid R_1]@\rho_m \mid P_2\{x_i := M_i \vert i = 1 \ldots k\} \mid R_2]@\rho_n$
RECURSION:	$!P \Rightarrow P \mid !P$
CONTEXT:	$\dfrac{P \Rightarrow R}{\mathbf{E}\{P\} \Rightarrow \mathbf{E}\{R\}}$

Evaluation Contexts: $\mathbf{E} ::= \{\cdot\} \mid \mathbf{E}|P \mid P|\mathbf{E} \mid \boldsymbol{\nu}(n{:}\tau)\mathbf{E} \mid m_u[\mathbf{E}]@\rho$

Theorem 1. *Let P_1, P_2, and P_3 be processes such that $P_1 \equiv P_2$ and $P_1 \Rightarrow P_3$. Then, there exists a process P_4 such that $P_2 \Rightarrow P_4$ and $P_3 \equiv P_4$.*

Theorem 2. *(Subject Reduction) Let P_1, P_2, and P_3 be processes, m and n be ambient names, u and v be users, ρ_{here}, ρ_{deact}, ρ_{act} and ρ'_{act}, be sets of roles, and let Γ be a mapping from message identifiers to basic types and port names to communication types. If Γ, ρ_{here}, ρ_{deact}, m, $u \vdash P_1 : \rho_{act}$ and $P_1 \Rightarrow P_2$, then Γ, ρ_{here}, ρ_{deact}, m, $u \vdash P_2 : \rho_{act}$. Moreover, if $m_u[P_1]@\rho_{act} \Rightarrow n_v[P_3]@\rho'_{act}$, then Γ, ρ_{here}, ρ_{deact}, n, $v \vdash P_3 : \rho'_{act}$, and $m = n$ and $u = v$.*

4.2 Typed Transition Semantics

In this subsection we introduce a transition semantics with runtime type checks (*e.g.* security checks). The rules of the semantics are found in Tables 11 – 15. In those tables, Γ is a mapping from message identifiers to basic types and port names to communication types (*i.e*, a typing environment), ρ_{here} is a set of roles, and τ is a basic type. As usual, the typing environment supplies us with the types for free ambient names and ports occurring in our process. The set of roles tells which roles are sufficient to authorize the process's current location. The basic type is the type of a message that can be locally communicated at top level. We do not need read and write policies, because there are no security checks on local communication. The typed reduction relation transforms a typing environment, a set of roles, a basic type and a process into a new typing environment, role set, basic type and process. If we ignore the typing environment, role set and basic type, including the premises concerning them, then we get the untyped system in the previous section.

Table 11. Roles

ACTIVATE:

$$\frac{r \in \mathit{UserPolicy}(u,\rho)}{(\Gamma, \rho_{here}, \tau) \rhd m_u[(\mathsf{activate}\langle \mathsf{r}\rangle P) \mid R]@\rho \longrightarrow (\Gamma, \rho_{here}, \tau) \rhd m_u[P \mid R]@(\rho \cup \{r\})}$$

DEACTIVATE:

$$\frac{(\rho - \{\mathsf{r}\}) \cap \rho_{here} \neq \emptyset}{(\Gamma, \rho_{here}, \tau) \rhd m_u[(\mathsf{deactivate}\langle \mathsf{r}\rangle P) \mid R]@\rho \longrightarrow (\Gamma, \rho_{here}, \tau) \rhd m_u[P \mid R]@(\rho - \{r\})}$$

The typing environment, role set and basic type are the extra information we need to carry around with us to do dynamic security checks.

Since the reductions on the processes are the same as in the untyped transition semantics, we will focus on the security checks and the transformations to the typing environment and basic type. Activation and deactivation are relative to an enclosing ambient and serve to change that ambient's set of active roles. For activation, we must check that the user of the ambient together with the currently active roles are allowed to activate the role. For deactivation, we need to check that deactivating the role will still leave some other role that is sufficient to authorize the ambient's current location.

When one ambient enters another, we need to know that the entering ambient has an appropriate role activated authorizing it to enter, and we need to establish a shared communication port sending and receiving messages of a type specified by the host ambient. The new communication port needs to be added to the typing environment. (See ENTER in Table 12.) When either the capability or co-capability involved in the move is quiet, then instead of the new port(s) receiving the basic type assigned by the host ambient, it is assigned the type shh. The location of the whole process hasn't changed, so ρ_{here} remains the same. The use of two distinct new ports in rules QUIET ENTER' (Table 12) and QUIET EXIT' (Table 13) is redundant. The assignment of shh to the type of the port is sufficient to assure that no communication takes place. We left the creation of distinct ports as a part of these rules to keep the connection with the untyped rules transparent. In general, the side conditions for the rules for exit are dual to those for enter.

There are three kinds of communication: local communication between top-level subprocesses, sending a message from a parent to a child and sending a message from a child to a parent. For local communication, we only need check that the type of the messages being sent are of the type specified for local communication (by τ), and that the number of messages sent is the same as those received. For trans-generational communication, in addition to checking the number of messages as before, we need to check that the writing ambient has write access to the port and the reading ambient has read access, and that the type of all messages sent is the type specified in the type of the port as given by the typing environment.

Table 12. Mobility – Enter

ENTER:

$$\frac{\Gamma(n) = \mathsf{amb}(\rho_{in}, \tau) \qquad \rho_m \cap \rho_{in} \neq \emptyset \qquad c'' \notin \mathbf{dom}(\Gamma).}{\begin{array}{c}(\Gamma, \rho_{here}, \tau) \rhd m_v[\mathsf{in}\; n\,(c).P_1 \mid P_2]@\rho_m \mid n_u[\overline{\mathsf{in}}\,(c').P_3 \mid P_4]@\rho_n \\ \longrightarrow \\ (\Gamma + (c'' : \tau), \rho_{here}, \tau) \rhd n_u[m_v[P_1\{c := c''\} \mid P_2]@\rho_m \mid P_3\{c' := c''\} \mid P_4]@\rho_n\end{array}}$$

ENTER':

$$\frac{\Gamma(n) = \mathsf{amb}(\rho_{in}, \tau) \qquad \rho_m \cap \rho_{in} \neq \emptyset \qquad c' \notin \mathbf{dom}(\Gamma).}{\begin{array}{c}(\Gamma, \rho_{here}, \tau) \rhd m_v[\mathsf{in}\; n\,(c).P_1 \mid P_2]@\rho_m \mid n_u[\overline{\mathsf{inQ}}.P_3 \mid P_4]@\rho_n \\ \longrightarrow \\ (\Gamma + (c' : \mathsf{shh}), \rho_{here}, \tau) \rhd n_u[m_v[P_1\{c := c'\} \mid P_2]@\rho_m \mid P_3 \mid P_4]@\rho_n\end{array}}$$

QUIET ENTER:

$$\frac{\Gamma(n) = \mathsf{amb}(\rho_{in}, \tau) \qquad \rho_m \cap \rho_{in} \neq \emptyset \qquad c' \notin \mathbf{dom}(\Gamma)}{\begin{array}{c}(\Gamma, \rho_{here}, \tau) \rhd m_v[\mathsf{inQ}\; n\,(c).P_1 \mid P_2]@\rho_m \mid n_u[\overline{\mathsf{inQ}}.P_3 \mid P_4]@\rho_n \\ \longrightarrow \\ (\Gamma + (c' : \mathsf{shh}), \rho_{here}, \tau) \rhd n_u[m_v[P_1\{c := c'\} \mid P_2]@\rho_m \mid P_3 \mid P_4]@\rho_n\end{array}}$$

QUIET ENTER':

$$\frac{\Gamma(n) = \mathsf{amb}(\rho_{in}, \tau) \qquad \rho_m \cap \rho_{in} \neq \emptyset \qquad c'', c''' \notin \mathbf{dom}(\Gamma)}{\begin{array}{c}(\Gamma, \rho_{here}, \tau) \rhd m_v[\mathsf{inQ}\; n\,(c).P_1 \mid P_2]@\rho_m \mid n_u[\overline{\mathsf{in}}\,(c').P_3 \mid P_4]@\rho_n \\ \longrightarrow \\ (\Gamma + (c'' : \mathsf{shh}) + (c''' : \mathsf{shh}), \rho_{here}, \tau) \rhd \\ n_u[m_v[P_1\{c := c''\} \mid P_2]@\rho_m \mid P_3\{c' := c'''\} \mid P_4]@\rho_n\end{array}}$$

The structural rules for our transition semantics tell us how and when we can descend through structures. None of the structural rules impose any security checks in and of themselves. The rules for recursion and composition use the same environment to security check the premises as they use in their conclusions. Restriction uses a type environment augmented by the type assignment for the restricted ambient name for reducing the body of the restriction. For descending through ambients, the typing environment is the same in the premise as in the conclusion, but here we need to change the type for the local communication to that of the basic type in the communication policy of the ambient, and we need to change the authorizing roles to the entrance policy of the outer ambient.

The next theorem gives us that the typed transition semantics is a refinement of the untyped transition semantics.

Theorem 3. *Let P and R be processes, Γ and Γ' be typing environments, ρ_{here} and ρ'_{here} be sets of roles, and τ and τ' be basic types. If $(\Gamma, \rho_{here}, \tau) \rhd P \longrightarrow (\Gamma', \rho'_{here}, \tau') \rhd R$, then $\rho_{here} = \rho'_{here}$, $\tau = \tau'$, $\Gamma \subseteq \Gamma'$, and $P \Rightarrow R$.*

Theorem 4 is the main result of the paper. It says that if a process type checks, then to evaluate it you can omit all runtime checks. A side-effect of this

Table 13. Mobility – Exit

EXIT:

$$\frac{\Gamma(p) = \mathsf{amb}(\rho_{in}, \tau) \qquad \rho_m \cap \rho_{in} \neq \emptyset \qquad c'' \notin \mathbf{dom}(\Gamma)}{\begin{array}{c}(\Gamma, \rho_{here}, \tau) \rhd p_w[n_v[m_u[\mathsf{out}\, p\,(c).P_1 \mid P_2\,]@\rho_m \mid P_3\,]@\rho_n \mid \overline{\mathsf{out}}.(c')P_4 \mid P_5\,]@\rho_p \\ \longrightarrow \\ (\Gamma + (c'':\tau), \rho_{here}, \tau) \rhd p_w[n_v[P_3\,]@\rho_n \mid m_u[P_1\{c{:=}c''\}]@\rho_m \mid P_4\{c'{:=}c''\} \mid P_5\,]@\rho_p\end{array}}$$

EXIT':

$$\frac{\Gamma(p) = \mathsf{amb}(\rho_{in}, \tau) \qquad \rho_m \cap \rho_{in} \neq \emptyset \qquad c' \notin \mathbf{dom}(\Gamma)}{\begin{array}{c}(\Gamma, \rho_{here}, \tau) \rhd p_w[n_v[m_u[\mathsf{out}\, p\,(c).P_1 \mid P_2\,]@\rho_m \mid P_3\,]@\rho_n \mid \overline{\mathsf{outQ}}.P_4 \mid P_5\,]@\rho_p \\ \longrightarrow \\ (\Gamma + (c':\mathsf{shh}), \rho_{here}, \tau) \rhd p_w[n_v[P_3\,]@\rho_n \mid m_u[P_1\{c{:=}c'\}]@\rho_m \mid P_4 \mid P_5\,]@\rho_p\end{array}}$$

QUIET EXIT:

$$\frac{\Gamma(p) = \mathsf{amb}(\rho_{in}, \tau) \qquad \rho_m \cap \rho_{in} \neq \emptyset \qquad c' \notin \mathbf{dom}(\Gamma)}{\begin{array}{c}(\Gamma, \rho_{here}, \tau) \rhd p_w[n_v[m_u[\mathsf{outQ}\, p\,(c).P_1 \mid P_2\,]@\rho_m \mid P_3\,]@\rho_n \mid \overline{\mathsf{outQ}}.P_4 \mid P_5\,]@\rho_p \\ \longrightarrow \\ (\Gamma + (c':\mathsf{shh}), \rho_{here}, \tau) \rhd p_w[n_v[P_3\,]@\rho_n \mid m_u[P_1\{c{:=}c'\}]@\rho_m \mid P_4 \mid P_5\,]@\rho_p\end{array}}$$

QUIET EXIT':

$$\frac{\Gamma(p) = \mathsf{amb}(\rho_{in}, \tau) \qquad \rho_m \cap \rho_{in} \neq \emptyset \qquad c'', c''' \notin \mathbf{dom}(\Gamma)}{\begin{array}{c}(\Gamma, \rho_{here}, \tau) \rhd p_w[n_v[m_u[\mathsf{outQ}\, p\,(c).P_1 \mid P_2\,]@\rho_m \mid P_3\,]@\rho_n \mid \overline{\mathsf{out}}\,(gv').P_4 \mid P_5\,]@\rho_p \\ \longrightarrow \\ (\Gamma + (c'':\mathsf{shh}) + (c''':\mathsf{shh}), \rho_{here}, \tau) \rhd \\ p_w[n_v[P_3\,]@\rho_n \mid m_u[P_1\{c{:=}c''\}]@\rho_m \mid P_4\{c'{:=}c'''\} \mid P_5\,]@\rho_p\end{array}}$$

is that if a process type checks, there is no runtime significance to activation and deactivation, and they could be removed after type-checking as an optimization.

Theorem 4. *Let P be a process that type checks with role set ρ using typing environment Γ, authorizing role set ρ_{here}, ambient m, and user u (e.g. Γ, ρ_{here}, ρ_{deact}, m, $u \vdash P : \rho_{act}$). If $P \Rightarrow R$ for some process R, then $(\Gamma, \rho_{in}, \tau) \rhd P \longrightarrow (\Gamma', \rho_{in}, \tau) \rhd R$ where $\Gamma(m) = \mathsf{amb}(\rho_{in}, (\rho_r, \rho_w, \tau))$ for some $\Gamma' \supseteq \Gamma$.*

Using Theorem 3 we can strengthen the conclusion of Theorem 4 to say that $P \Rightarrow R$ for some process R if and only if $(\Gamma, \rho_{in}, \tau) \rhd P \longrightarrow (\Gamma', \rho_{in}, \tau) \rhd R$.

The typed transitional semantics developed in this section was primarily introduced as a vehicle to formalize the benefit of static type checking. It is worth noting that this semantics is of value in its own right. The static rules are predicated on static access to the information as to which roles are granted access to which resources. With the typed transition semantics, we can still perform security checks even in a situation where the control policy is only known at runtime.

Table 14. Communication

LOCAL:

$$\frac{\Gamma \vdash M_i : \tau \quad i = 1, \dots, k}{\begin{array}{c}(\Gamma, \rho_{here}, \tau) \rhd \langle M_1, \dots, M_k \rangle^{\star}.P \mid (x_1, \dots, x_k)^{\star}.Q \\ \longrightarrow \\ (\Gamma, \rho_{here}, \tau) \rhd P \mid Q\{x_i := M_i \mid i = 1 \dots k\}\end{array}}$$

TO CHILD ($\downarrow$):

$$\frac{\Gamma(c) = (\rho_r, \rho_w, \tau') \quad \rho_m \cap \rho_w \neq \emptyset \quad \rho_n \cap \rho_r \neq \emptyset \quad \Gamma \vdash M_i : \tau' \quad i = 1, \dots, k}{\begin{array}{c}(\Gamma, \rho_{here}, \tau) \rhd m_u[\langle M_1, \dots, M_k \rangle^{\downarrow c}.P_1 \mid n_v[(x_1, \dots, x_k)^{\uparrow c}.P_2 \mid R_1]@\rho_n \mid R_2]@\rho_m \\ \longrightarrow \\ (\Gamma, \rho_{here}, \tau) \rhd m_u[P_1 \mid n_v[P_2\{x_i := M_i \mid i = 1 \dots k\} \mid R_1]@\rho_n \mid R_2]@\rho_m\end{array}}$$

TO PARENT ($\uparrow$):

$$\frac{\Gamma(c) = (\rho_r, \rho_w, \tau') \quad \rho_m \cap \rho_w \neq \emptyset \quad \rho_n \cap \rho_r \neq \emptyset \quad \Gamma \vdash M_i : \tau' \quad i = 1, \dots, k}{\begin{array}{c}(\Gamma, \rho_{here}, \tau) \rhd n_v[m_u[\langle M_1, \dots, M_k \rangle^{\downarrow c}.P_1 \mid R_1]@\rho_m \mid (x_1, \dots, x_k)^{\downarrow c}.P_2 \mid R_1]@\rho_n \\ \longrightarrow \\ (\Gamma, \rho_{here}, \tau) \rhd n_v[m_u[P_1 \mid R_1]@\rho_m \mid P_2\{x_i := M_i \mid i = 1 \dots k\} \mid R_2]@\rho_n\end{array}}$$

Table 15. Structural Rules

RECURSION:

$$\frac{}{(\Gamma, \rho_{here}, \tau) \rhd\, !P \longrightarrow (\Gamma, \rho_{here}, \tau) \rhd P \mid !P}$$

LEFT COMPOSTION:

$$\frac{(\Gamma, \rho_{here}, \tau) \rhd P_1 \longrightarrow (\Gamma, \rho_{here}, \tau) \rhd P_2}{(\Gamma, \rho_{here}, \tau) \rhd P_1 \mid R \longrightarrow (\Gamma, \rho_{here}, \tau) \rhd P_2 \mid R}$$

RIGHT COMPOSTION:

$$\frac{(\Gamma, \rho_{here}, \tau) \rhd P_1 \longrightarrow (\Gamma, \rho_{here}, \tau) \rhd P_2}{(\Gamma, \rho_{here}, \tau) \rhd R \mid P_1 \longrightarrow (\Gamma, \rho_{here}, \tau) \rhd R \mid P_2}$$

RESTRICTION:

$$\frac{(\Gamma + \{m : \tau\}, \rho_{here}, \tau) \rhd P \longrightarrow (\Gamma + \{m : \tau\}, \rho_{here}, \tau) \rhd R}{(\Gamma, \rho_{here}, \tau) \rhd \boldsymbol{\nu}(m{:}\tau)P \longrightarrow (\Gamma, \rho_{here}, \tau) \rhd \boldsymbol{\nu}(m{:}\tau)R}$$

AMBIENTS:

$$\frac{\begin{array}{c}\Gamma(m) = \mathsf{amb}(\rho_{in}, (\rho_r, \rho_w, \tau')) \\ (\Gamma, \rho_{in}, \tau') \rhd P \longrightarrow (\Gamma, \rho_{in}, \tau') \rhd R\end{array}}{(\Gamma, \rho_{here}, \tau) \rhd m_u[P]@\rho \longrightarrow (\Gamma, \rho_{here}, \tau) \rhd m_u[R]@\rho}$$

5 Related Work

For a variety of calculi for mobile and distributed systems that have emerged in the last years, access control was one of the primary concerns. The proposed access control mechanisms range from simple ones that use of co-actions [26,40,7] allowing or denying all access to a particular location (and the resources it contains) to more refined ones that use different aproaches: credentials to authorize the access [12], restricted groups [13,16], Mandatory Access Control mechanisms to constraint un-authorized access [9], and even "membranes" that specify security policies for controlling the access to a particular location [22].

The work most closely related to our study of RBAC for an ambient calculus is [8]. The authors define a distributed π-calculus (D-π) based on [23] with primitives to activate and deactivate roles. However, there is no notion of an individual privilege being disabled or enabled depending on the current location, and the domain topology is static: domains cannot move. In [24] Hennessy and Riely introduce a type system for a distributed version of the π-calculus for restricting the access of processes to resources based on the current location of the process. In this work, again the domain topology is static, and there is no direct connection to RBAC.

At the Symposium on Trustworthy Global Computing 2005 (TGC 2005), during his invited address, Matthew Hennessy presented a calculus for RBAC based on D-π. Unlike our system, his calculus has dependent types to avoid dynamic typechecks of the security policy.

The work of RBAC in [29,30] does not deal with the implementation of an RBAC mechanism in a given calculus as is the case in [8]. Instead they define a calculus to describe an RBAC security policy and how to answer queries to the security policy.

Various groups have developed methods for guaranteeing that specifications of RBAC systems are consistent. In [37], Schaad and Moffett discuss the application of formal methods for the development of specifications of a conflict-free role-based system. In [3] a formal language for the specification of role-based authorization constraints, including prohibition, is introduced. Bertino et al. [5] develop a logical framework for reasoning about access control models in general, including RBAC models.

6 Conclusions and Future Work

We defined $\mathbf{BACI_R}$, a boxed ambients calculus with Distributed Role-Based Access Control, where the privileges associated to processes change during computation and are determined by their location, their owners, the roles they have activated, and the security policy. The distributed nature of the RBAC mechanism comes from the fact that each ambient controls the security policy authorizing the entrance of ambients and each port specifies the security policy controlling the reading and writing privileges.

Our type system prevents two forms of security violations, those consisting of attempting to enter an ambient without proper authorization, and those consisting of trying to read or write from ports without the corresponding permissions. These security violations are controlled using roles, that can be dynamically activated and deactivated. The type system prevents security violating actions by those processes not vested with the required authorizing roles.

Our main contribution is the design of the first ambient calculus with a distributed RBAC mechanism where the location of a process conditions its mobility and its ability to communicate with other processes. Our main result in Theorem 4 shows that a well-typed program never violates the dynamic security checks.

Although the classroom example in the introduction is focused on Internet networking for a sense of location and communication, our Distributed RBAC mechanism should be applicable to other settings such as those arising from mobile telecommunications.

The area remains full of open and challenging problems. An interesting aspect to consider is the notion of trust in such a way that the access control policy governing the users' requests will further depend on whether the user is in a trusted or untrusted domain. Furthermore, RBAC can be enriched by placing order structures on roles (role hierarchies), constraints on roles such as mutual exclusion (no user may activate two given roles at the same time), combination of roles (two given roles have to be activated at the same time), and composition of roles (users having a given role are given another role). Defining type systems to address these richer notions of RBAC is the subject of our ongoing and future research.

Acknowledgments

We are grateful to Pablo Garralda, Healfdene Goguen, and Mariangiola Dezani for illuminating discussions and comments on earlier drafts. We also appreciate Kaijun Tan for introducing us to the idea of combining RBAC with calculi for concurrency.

References

1. Martin Abadi, Michael Burrows, Butler Lampson, and Gordon Plotkin. A calculus for access control in distributed system. *ACM Transactions on Programming Languages and Systems*, 15(4):706 – 734, sep 1993.
2. G.-J. Ahn and R. Sandhu. The RSL99 language for role-based separation of duty constraints. In *Proceedings of the 4th Workshop on Role-Based Access Control*, pages 43–54, 1999.
3. G. J. Ahn and R. Sandhu. Role-based authorization constraints specification. *ACM Transactions on Information and System Security*, 3(4):207–226, 2000.
4. Gail-Joon Ahn and Ravi Sandhu. Role-based authorization constraints specification. *ACM Trans. Inf. Syst. Secur.*, 3(4):207–226, 2000.
5. E. Bertino, B. Catania, E. Ferrari, and P. Perlasca. A logical framework for reasoning about access control models. In *Proc. of 6th SACMAT*, pages 41–52. ACM Press, 2001.

6. M. Blaze, J. Feigenbaum, and J. Lacy. Decentralized trust management. In *Proceedings of the 17th Symposium on Security and Privacy, IEEE Computer Society, Los Alamitos, 1996*, pages 164–173, 1996.
7. Eduardo Bonelli, Adriana Compagnoni, Mariangiola Dezani-Ciancaglini, and Pablo Garralda. Boxed Ambients with Communication Interfaces (BACI). In *Proceedings Of The 29th International Symposium On Mathematical Foundations Of Computer Science (MFCS 2004) Prague, Czech Republic, Europe. 22-27 August 2004*, volume 3153 of *Lecture Notes In Computer Science*, pages 119–148, August 2004.
8. C. Braghin, D. Gorla, and V. Sassone. A distributed calculus for role-based access control. In *Proceedings of 17th Computer Security Foundations Workshop (CSFW'04)*, pages 48–60. IEEE Computer Society, 2004.
9. Michele Bugliesi, Giuseppe Castagna, and Silvia Crafa. Reasoning about security in mobile ambients. In *CONCUR '01: Proceedings of the 12th International Conference on Concurrency Theory*, pages 102–120, London, UK, 2001. Springer-Verlag.
10. Michele Bugliesi, Giuseppe Castagna, and Silvia Crafa. Access Control for Mobile Agents: The Calculus of Boxed Ambients. *ACM Transactions on Programming Languages and Systems*, 26(1):57–124, 2004.
11. Michele Bugliesi, Silvia Crafa, Massimo Merro, and Vladimiro Sassone. Communication and Mobility Control in Boxed Ambients. To appear in *Information and Computation*. Extended and revised version of M. Bugliesi, S. Crafa, M. Merro, and V. Sassone. Communication Interference in Mobile Boxed Ambients. In FSTTCS'02, volume 2556 of LNCS, pages 71-84. Springer-Verlag, 2002.
12. Michele Bugliesi, Silvia Crafa, Massimo Merro, and Vladimiro Sassone. Communication interference in mobile boxed ambients. In *Proceedings of the 22nd Conference on Foundations of Software Technology and Theoretical Computer Science, FST&TCS 2002*, volume 2556 of *LNCS*, pages 71–84. Springer, 2002.
13. Luca Cardelli, Giorgio Ghelli, and Andrew D. Gordon. Ambient Groups and Mobility Types. In Jan van Leeuwen, Osamu Watanabe, Masami Hagiya, Peter D. Mosses, and Takayasu Ito, editors, *TCS'00*, volume 1872 of *Lecture Notes in Computer Science*, pages 333–347, Berlin, 2000. Springer-Verlag. Extended version to appear in Information and Computation, special issue on TCS'00.
14. Luca Cardelli and Andrew D. Gordon. Mobile ambients. In *Foundations of Software Science and Computation Structures: First International Conference, FOSSACS '98*. Springer-Verlag, Berlin Germany, 1998.
15. Luca Cardelli and Andrew D. Gordon. Mobile Ambients. *Theoretical Computer Science*, 240(1):177–213, 2000. Special Issue on Coordination, Daniel Le Métayer Editor.
16. Mario Coppo, Mariangiola Dezani-Ciancaglini, Elio Giovannetti, and Ivano Salvo. M3: Mobility Types for Mobile Processes in Mobile Ambients. In James Harland, editor, *CATS'03*, volume 78 of *ENTCS*. Elsevier, 2003.
17. R. Crook, D. Ince, and B. Nuseibeh. Towards an analytical role modelling framework for security requirements. In *Proc. of the 8 tn International Workshop on Requirements Engineering: Foundation for Software Quality*, pages 123–138, Essen, Germany, 2002.
18. D. Ferraiolo and R. Kuhn. Role-based access controls. In *15th NIST-NCSC National Computer Security Conference*, pages 554–563, 1992.
19. David F. Ferraiolo, Ravi Sandhu, Serban Gavrila, D. Richard Kuhn, and Ramaswamy Chandramouli. Proposed NIST standard for role-based access control. *ACM Trans. Inf. Syst. Secur.*, 4(3):224–274, 2001.

20. Pablo Garralda and Adriana Compagnoni. Splitting Mobility and Communication in Boxed Ambients. In Maribel Fernandez and Ian Mackie, editors, *International Workshop on Developements in Computational Models (DCM 2005)*, ENTCS. Elsevier, 2005.
21. Luigi Giuri and Pietro Iglio. A formal model for role-based access control with constraints. In *CSFW '96: Proceedings of the Ninth IEEE Computer Security Foundations Workshop*, page 136. IEEE Computer Society, 1996.
22. D. Gorla, M. Hennessy, , and V. Sassone. Security policies as membranes in systems for global computing. In *Foundations of Global Ubiquitous Computing, FGUC 2004*, ENTCS, 2004.
23. Matthew Hennessy, Massimo Merro, and Julian Rathke. Towards a behavioural theory of access and mobility control in distributed system (extended abstract). In Andrew D. Gordon, editor, *FOSSACS'03*, volume 2620 of *LNCS*, pages 282–299, Berlin, 2003. Springer-Verlag.
24. Matthew Hennessy and James Riely. Resource access control in systems of mobile agents. *Inf. Comput.*, 173(1):82–120, 2002.
25. Francesca Levi and Davide Sangiorgi. Controlling Interference in Ambients. *Transactions on Programming Languages and Systems*, 25(1):1–69, 2003.
26. Francesca Levi and Davide Sangiorgi. Mobile safe ambients. *Transactions on Programming Languages and Systems*, 25(1):1–69, 2003.
27. Ninghui Li, John C. Mitchell, and William H. Winsborough. Design of a role-based trust management framework. In *Proceedings of the 2002 IEEE Symposium on Security and Privacy*, pages 114–130. IEEE Computer Society Press, May 2002.
28. Ninghui Li and Mahesh V. Tripunitara. Security analysis in role-based access control. In *SACMAT '04: Proceedings of the ninth ACM symposium on Access control models and technologies*, pages 126–135. ACM Press, 2004.
29. Ninghui Li, William H. Winsborough, and John C. Mitchell. Distributed credential chain discovery in trust management: extended abstract. In *CCS '01: Proceedings of the 8th ACM conference on Computer and Communications Security*, pages 156–165. ACM Press, 2001.
30. Ninghui Li, William H. Winsborough, and John C. Mitchell. Beyond proof-of-compliance: Safety and availability analysis in trust management. In *SP '03: Proceedings of the 2003 IEEE Symposium on Security and Privacy*, page 123. IEEE Computer Society, 2003.
31. Imtiaz Mohammed and David M. Dilts. Design for dynamic user-role-based security. *Comput. Secur.*, 13(9):661–671, 1994.
32. Matunda Nyanchama and Sylvia L. Osborn. Access rights administration in role-based security systems. In *Proceedings of the IFIP WG11.3 Working Conference on Database Security VII*, pages 37–56. North-Holland, 1994.
33. R. S. Sandhu. The typed access control model. In *Proceedings of the IEEE Symposium on Research in Security and Privacy*, pages 122–136, 1992.
34. Ravi S. Sandhu. The typed access matrix model. In *SP '92: Proceedings of the 1992 IEEE Symposium on Security and Privacy*, page 122. IEEE Computer Society, 1992.
35. Ravi S. Sandhu. Lattice-based access control models. *IEEE Computer*, 26(11):9–19, 1993.
36. R.S. Sandhu, E.J. Coyne, H.L. Feinstein, and C.E. Youman. Role-based access control models. *IEEE Computer*, 29(2):38–47, 1996.

37. Andreas Schaad and Jonathan D. Moffett. A lightweight approach to specification and analysis of role-based access control extensions. In *SACMAT '02: Proceedings of the seventh ACM symposium on Access control models and technologies*, pages 13–22. ACM Press, 2002.
38. R. K. Thomas. Team-based access control (TMAC): a primitive for applying role-based access controls in collaborative environments. In *Proceedings of the second ACM workshop on Role-based access control*, pages 13–19, 1997.
39. R. K. Thomas and R. S. Sandhu. Task-based authorization controls (TBAC): A family of models for active and enterprise-oriented authorization management. In *Proceedings of the IFIP TC11 WG11.3 Eleventh International Conference on Database Securty XI: Status and Prospects*, pages 166–181, 1997.
40. Jan Vitek and Giuseppe Castagna. Seal: A framework for secure mobile computations. In Henri E. Bal, Boumediene Belkhouche, and Luca Cardelli, editors, *Internet Programming Languages*, volume 1686 of *Lecture Notes in Computer Science*, pages 47–77, Berlin, 1999. Springer-Verlag.
41. S. H. von Solms and Isak van der Merwe. The management of computer security profiles using a role-oriented approach. *Comput. Secur.*, 13(9):673–680, 1994.

History-Based Access Control for Distributed Processes

Francisco Martins[1] and Vasco Vasconcelos[2]

[1] Department of Mathematics, University of Azores, Portugal
[2] Department of Informatics, Faculty of Sciences, University of Lisbon, Portugal

Abstract. This paper presents a type system to control the migration of code between network nodes in a concurrent distributed framework, using the Dπ language. We express resource access policies as types and enforce policies via a type system. Types describe paths travelled by migrating code, enabling the control of history sensitive access to resources. Sites are logically organised in subnetworks that share the same security policies, statically specified by a network administrator. The type system guarantees that well-typed networks are exempt from security policy violations at runtime.

1 Introduction

The spreading of small, powerful portable machines like PDAs, cellular phones, and laptop computers, equipped with long lasting batteries and wireless communications, is promoting the integration of a broad range of services and encouraging the sharing of resources. Consequently, the protection of personal data and resources from abusive usage is a central concern for the global network participants. This paper proposes a discipline to control the security of resources in a mobile distributed environment.

Take, for example, a typical network architecture for an institution that exposes some services (*e.g.* SSH, HTTP, SMTP, and DNS) to an untrusted network, like the Internet, as described in Figure 1 (cf.[23]). The task of the network administrator is to find the correct balance between hiding and revealing the institution's services to the outside world. Some institutions, however, need to give permission to untrusted third parties, for example, to browse their web pages or to download information from their data server, while at the same time need to prevent valuable assets from being defrauded.

One common approach to tackle the problem is to separate the external untrusted network from the institution's network, using a firewall, and to split the inner network into three major areas, offering different levels of security to their components: an *internal network*, protected by an extra firewall, that is not exposed to the outside world at all; a *DMZ*—Demilitarised Zone—that houses servers which are visible to untrusted clients (a semi-protected area); and an *EDMZ*—Extended Demilitarised Zone—hosting internal servers that may be accessed from the DMZ, but not from the external network.

Clustering nodes that share the same security requirements (*e.g.* DMZ, EDMZ, and users subnet) seems a natural method to define security policies for a network. We propose a security model inspired on this notion of clusters (which we name *security groups*) each listing the necessary security requirements. Then, we use security groups as building blocks to set up security policies for larger networks, exploiting the policies already defined. Each group represents a kind of firewall that dictates the rules and

R. De Nicola and D. Sangiorgi (Eds.): TGC 2005, LNCS 3705, pp. 98–115, 2005.

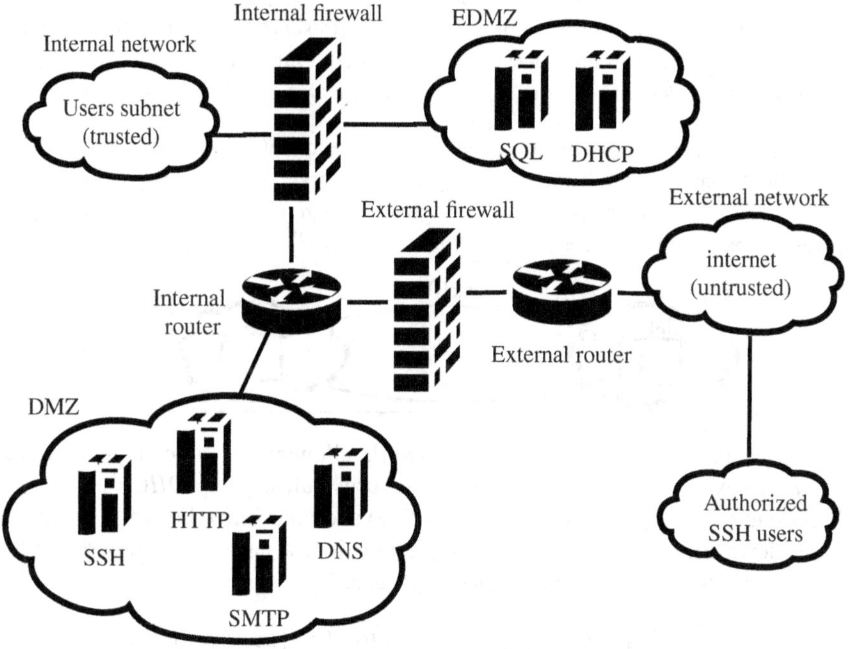

Fig. 1. A two-firewall tiered network architecture

supervises the migration of code that crosses its border. We conceive a model where sites may belong to more than one group and where groups form a hierarchical structure.

We choose Dπ [14, 15] as the underlying calculus and extend it with the notion of *security groups*, an enriched view of the groups Cardelli, Ghelli, and Gordon introduced for the ambient calculus [5–7], thus obtaining a flat computation model (that of Dπ), coupled with a hierarchical organisation from the point of view of security groups, promoting a layered specification of security. Our main motivation is to design a flexible security policy description language, while at the same time, statically guarantee the integrity of user-declared security policies.

Sites form a network of computational shells where processes compete for memory, CPU cycles, and other local resources. Communication is local; therefore, the interaction between sites must be programmed explicitly via code migration.

The group's security officer defines a set of rules enumerating what admissible migration paths are allowed to perform what actions. The *migration path*, path for short, is the sequence of groups a piece of code has travelled through, until reaching its current position. We classify actions as *resource usage actions*—the installRes and useRes control attributes describe reading and writing from local channels; *resource allocation actions*—the createRes, createSite, and createGroup attributes enumerate local channel, site, and group creation; *code migration actions* regulated through the tuning of forward control attribute; and finally *management actions*—the inherit attribute enables a group to inherit the policies specified for its parents.

In what follows we explain how to set up security policies using the example in Figure 1. As in most real life examples, we take a conservative approach to defining security: all actions are denied unless otherwise stated. Our simple method for writing security rules disables contradictory policies: granting and denying the same privilege.

Groups. The diagram below illustrates an interaction to obtain a valid IP address between a client named *data* from group *SQL* and a server named *kass*, belonging to group *DHCP*. The client runs the process goto $kass.askIP!\langle reply@data\rangle$, and the server replies back running process goto $data.reply!\langle IP\rangle$.

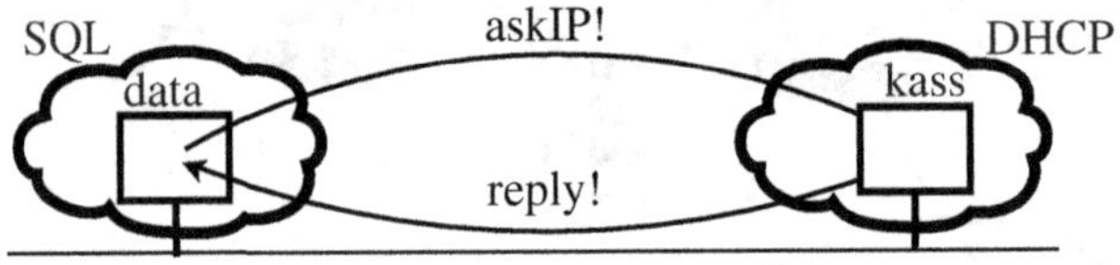

To establish the adequate policies for the network, allowing the code at site *data* and at site *kass* to execute without infringing the security rules, group *DHCP* must allow *SQL*'s code to use local resources (useRes policy) and vice-versa. For each group, we can write down these policies using a simple notation: a pair of sets describing the security policies for the group, and its parent groups.

$$SQL\colon (\{\mathsf{useRes}\colon DHCP\}, \_) \qquad\qquad DHCP\colon (\{\mathsf{useRes}\colon SQL\}, \_)$$

We omit the group hierarchy in group types, whenever it is not relevant for the example.

Subgroups. The notion of subgroups provides for a method to combine group policies. Consider now an IP query from a client *c1* in the *Users* internal network, as depicted in the following diagram.

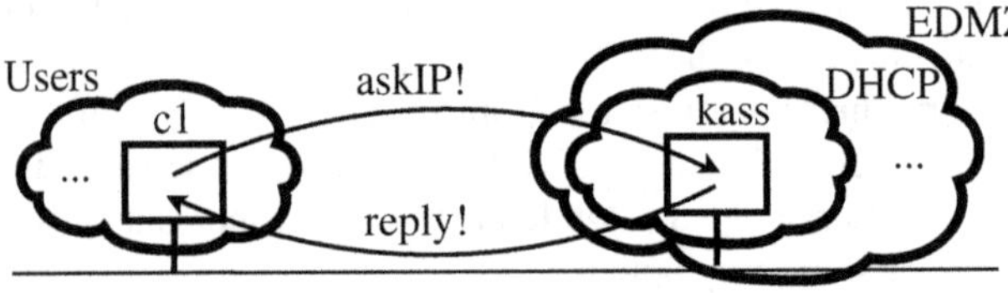

Group *EDMZ* must forward code from group *Users* and, furthermore, group *DHCP* must allow group *Users* to use local resources. The types for *EDMZ* and *DHCP* become

$$EDMZ\colon (\{\mathsf{forward}\colon Users\}, \_) \qquad DHCP\colon (\{\mathsf{useRes}\colon Users\}, \{EDMZ\})$$

Notice that group *DHCP* is now a subgroup of *EDMZ* (as specified in the second component of the type for *DHCP*), and that permission to use local resources is only specified at *DHCP*. The point is that each group specifies the policies for the sites that are directly under its control. When a site is under the control of a subgroup, the parent groups only concede the authority for code to cross their boundaries. The remaining policies are "delegated" to the groups where the sites directly belong to, thus avoiding the replication of policies at each group level.

Let us turn our attention to the response goto $c1.reply!\langle IP\rangle$ from site *kass*. Site *kass* is a member of group *DHCP*, which, in turn, is a subgroup of *EDMZ*. So, *kass* may be seen as a member of *DHCP* *or* as a member of *EDMZ*. Hence, group *Users* may specify security policies addressed specifically at group *DHCP* or at group *EDMZ*. Suppose that we want to express that group *Users* allows group *EDMZ* to install resources, but that only code from group *DHCP* may use resources. We could set up group *Users* policies as

$$\mathit{Users}\colon (\{\mathsf{useRes}\colon \mathit{DHCP}, \mathsf{installRes}\colon \mathit{EDMZ}\}, \_)$$

In addition, we may want to be more specific and enable the installation of resources only for group *DHCP* (thus denying code from sites belonging to group *SQL*). So, we could write

$$\mathit{Users}\colon (\{\mathsf{useRes}\colon \mathit{DHCP}, \mathsf{installRes}\colon \mathit{DHCP}\}, \_)$$

Policy inheritance. The inheritance of security policies helps in designing and maintaining policies for subgroups. The inheritance is twofold: (a) explicit, via keyword inherit, stating that a subgroup inherits the security policies of its direct parent groups; (b) implicit, adopting the identity of a parent group. Defining security policies for different levels on the grouping hierarchy prevents the enumeration of a myriad of leaf subgroups in the rules.

As an example, suppose all subgroups from group *EDMZ* allow subgroups from *DMZ* to use their resources. Furthermore, group *SQL* likewise consents the installation of resources from group *HTTP*.

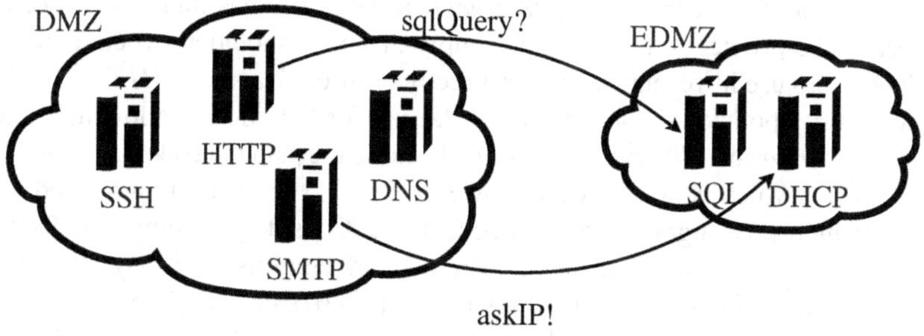

The security policy for *EDMZ*, *SQL*, and *DHCP* may then be written as

$$\mathit{EDMZ}\colon (\{\mathsf{forward}\colon \mathit{DMZ}, \mathsf{useRes}\colon \mathit{DMZ}\}, \_)$$
$$\mathit{SQL}\colon (\{\mathsf{inherit}, \mathsf{installRes}\colon \mathit{HTTP}\}, \{\mathit{EDMZ}\}) \quad \mathit{DHCP}\colon (\{\mathsf{inherit}\}), \{\mathit{EDMZ}\})$$

Notice that we write the policy for group *EDMZ* mentioning only group *DMZ*, thus implicitly conceding the privileges to all subgroups of *DMZ*; subgroups *SQL* and *DHCP* inherit explicitly common security policies from its parent *EDMZ*; moreover, group *SQL* specifically grants the installRes privilege to group *HTTP*.

Migration paths. In addition to indicate that a group may perform some action over the sites of a particular group, we may specify a *path* representing an acceptable sequence of groups that the code must pass through before entering the destination site. The path is specified using a regular expression.

Our last example addresses the granting of privileges when the code travels through sites from distinct groups. Consider an intruder browsing web pages that contain data sitting on some data server. We need to give rights to the intruder to view the web pages, but prevent him from gaining access to the data server, either directly from the Internet or via the web server. The network depicted below illustrates this situation

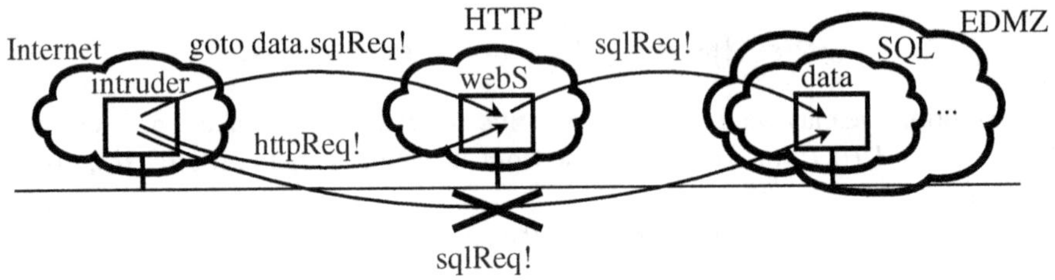

Suppose that the policies for groups *HTTP*, *EDMZ*, and *SQL* are

$$HTTP\colon (\{\mathsf{useRes}\colon Internet\}, \_) \qquad EDMZ\colon (\{\mathsf{forward}\colon HTTP\}, \_)$$
$$SQL\colon (\{\mathsf{useRes}\colon HTTP\}, \{EDMZ\})$$

Processes goto $webS.httpReq!\langle\diamond\rangle$ and goto $data.sqlReq!\langle\diamond\rangle$ do not violate the security rules, whereas goto $data.sqlReq!\langle\diamond\rangle$ launched by the intruder breaks the security rules at groups *EDMZ* (since *EDMZ* only forwards code from *HTTP* group) and *SQL* (since *SQL* only allows the use of resources from *HTTP*). What about process goto $webS$.goto $data.sqlReg!\langle\diamond\rangle$? A trusting relation must not be transitive: although group *HTTP* allows code from group *Internet* to use its resources, and group *SQL* allows *HTTP* the same privileges, that does not imply that *SQL* should allow code migrating from *Internet* to use its resources, either directly or through a site in *HTTP*.

The security policies set above for *EDMZ* and for *SQL* do not allow migration of code from *intruder* to *webS* and then to *data*, because the path the code travels is "*HTTP* after *Internet*", which is not allowed. However, it could be interesting to model a situation in which this migration path is acceptable. Consider the subgroup *SSHUsers* in *Internet* accessing to the *data* server. The network administrator may allow sites in group *SSH* to be used as proxies for sites in group *SSHUsers*, and allow code from an honest agent to migrate through *SSH* to use *SQL*'s resources. The types for *SSH*, *EDMZ*, and *SQL* groups would then become

$$SSH\colon (\{\mathsf{useRes}\colon SSHUsers\}, \_) \quad EDMZ\colon (\{\mathsf{forward}\colon SSH\; SSHUsers\}, \_)$$
$$SQL\colon (\{\mathsf{useRes}\colon SSH\; SSHUsers\}, \{EDMZ\})$$

Would the network administrator need to specify that all the code arriving through group *SSH* is welcome to use *SQL*'s resources, it might set *EDMZ* and *SQL* policies as

$$EDMZ\colon (\{\mathsf{forward}\colon SSH\bullet^\star\}, \_) \qquad SQL\colon (\{\mathsf{useRes}\colon SSH\bullet^\star\}, \{EDMZ\})$$

We use wildcard $\bullet$ to denote any site, and symbol * to represent a sequence of zero or more occurrences of an expression. Therefore, $SSH\bullet^\star$ means any migration path ending at group *SSH* that has passed through any sequence of sites (possible empty).

$v ::=$	*Values*	$n ::=$	*Names*
$a_{@}s$	located channel	a, b, c, x	channels
$\mid \diamond$	basic value	$\mid r, s, t, y$	sites
		$\mid f, g, h$	groups
$P, Q ::=$	*Processes*	$N, M ::=$	*Networks*
stop	termination	stop	termination
$\mid (\nu n{:}\ L_{@}s)\ P$	restriction	$\mid (\nu_{\tilde{t}} n{:}\ L)\ N$	restriction
$\mid P \mid Q$	composition	$\mid N \mid M$	composition
$\mid$ goto $s.P$	migration	$\mid \tilde{s}[P]$	site
$\mid a!\langle v\rangle$	output		
$\mid a?(v)\ P$	input	see Figure 12 for the syntax of types L	
$\mid a?^{*}(v)\ P$	replication		

Fig. 2. Syntax of Dπ

Other examples of simple path patterns are, for instance, code originated at group *SSH* as, $\bullet^{\star}$*SSH*, or code that passes through group *SSH* as, $\bullet^{\star}$*SSH*$\bullet^{\star}$.

Outline. The next section briefly introduces the Dπ syntax and its operational semantics. Section 3 introduces our approach to the checking of security policies and present the notion of runtime errors (via a tagged version of Dπ). Section 4 is devoted to the type assignment system and states the results we achieved. The last section presents the related work and states our conclusions.

2 Dπ Syntax and Operational Semantics

This section presents the syntax and the operational semantics of Dπ, mainly taken from Hennessy and Riely [15].

Syntax. The syntax of the calculus is defined in Figure 2. The main difference w.r.t. the original Dπ is the usage of groups, namely the new constructor to create groups, and the inclusion of the migration path in the syntax for sites. We consider a monadic version of the calculus where only located names can be passed around, since our main focus is the control of migration, not that of communication.

We briefly address the Dπ syntax; the interested reader should refer to [14, 15] for motivations and details. The calculus presents two main syntactic categories: processes and networks. At process level we find the usual asynchronous π-calculus constructs [2, 16]; processes are built from the inactive process, stop, and from the asynchronous output process, $a!\langle v\rangle$, using three constructs: name restriction, $(\nu n{:}\ T)\ P$, parallel composition, $P \mid Q$, and input, $a?(v)\ P$. We also include a form of replicated input, $a?^{*}(v)\ P$. Moreover, Dπ contains an operator that sends a process P to a specific location s: the goto $s.P$ process.

Networks are assembled from the inaction network, stop, and from processes running at specific named locations called sites, $s\tilde{t}[P]$, using name restriction, $(\nu_{\tilde{t}} n{:}\ T)\ N$,

$$1.\ (N \mid M) \mid M' \equiv N \mid (M \mid M') \qquad M \mid N \equiv N \mid M \qquad (N \mid \mathsf{stop}) \equiv N$$

$$2.\ (\boldsymbol{\nu}_{\tilde{t}}\, n\colon T)\ N \mid M \equiv (\boldsymbol{\nu}_{\tilde{t}}\, n\colon T)\ (N \mid M) \qquad \text{if } n \notin \mathrm{fn}(M)$$

$$(\boldsymbol{\nu}_{\tilde{r}}\, n\colon T)\ (\boldsymbol{\nu}_{\tilde{t}}\, m\colon T')\ N \equiv (\boldsymbol{\nu}_{\tilde{t}}\, m\colon T')\ (\boldsymbol{\nu}_{\tilde{r}}\, n\colon T)\ N \qquad i)$$

$$(\boldsymbol{\nu}_{\tilde{t}}\, n\colon L@s)\ s\tilde{t}[P] \equiv s\tilde{t}[(\boldsymbol{\nu} n\colon L)\ P] \qquad \text{if } n \text{ not in } s\tilde{t}$$

$$3.\ \tilde{s}[P] \mid \tilde{s}[Q] \equiv \tilde{s}[P \mid Q]$$

i) if m not in T and not in $\tilde{r}$, and n not in T' and not in $\tilde{t}$.

Fig. 3. Structural congruence

$$s\tilde{t}[a!\langle\diamond\rangle] \mid s\tilde{u}[a?(\diamond)\ P] \to s\tilde{u}[P] \qquad (\textsc{ComC}_1)$$

$$s\tilde{t}[a!\langle b@r\rangle] \mid s\tilde{u}[a?(x@y)\ P] \to s\tilde{u}[P\{r/y\}\{b/x\}] \qquad (\textsc{ComC}_2)$$

$$s\tilde{t}[a!\langle\diamond\rangle] \mid s\tilde{u}[a?^*(\diamond)\ P] \to s\tilde{u}[P] \mid s\tilde{u}[a?^*(\diamond)\ P] \qquad (\textsc{ComR}_1)$$

$$s\tilde{t}[a!\langle b@r\rangle] \mid s\tilde{u}[a?^*(x@y)\ P] \to s\tilde{u}[P\{r/y\}\{b/x\}] \mid s\tilde{u}[a?^*(x@y)\ P] \qquad (\textsc{ComR}_2)$$

$$\tilde{t}[\mathsf{goto}\ r.P] \to r\tilde{t}[P] \qquad \frac{N \to M}{(\boldsymbol{\nu}_{\tilde{t}}\, n\colon L@s)\ N \to (\boldsymbol{\nu}_{\tilde{t}}\, n\colon L@s)\ M} \qquad (\textsc{Mig}, \textsc{Res})$$

$$\frac{N \to N'}{N \mid M \to N' \mid M} \qquad \frac{N \equiv N' \quad N' \to M' \quad M' \equiv M}{N \to M} \qquad (\textsc{Par}, \textsc{Str})$$

Fig. 4. Reduction rules

and parallel composition, $N \mid M$. The site construct $s\tilde{t}[P]$ denotes a computational area named s, running process P. The (possibly empty) sequence of sites $\tilde{t}$ designates the sites P has visited before arriving at s. The top level syntax admits only sites where $\tilde{t}$ is the empty sequence. Network name restriction $(\boldsymbol{\nu}_{\tilde{t}}\, n\colon T)\ N$ records the sequence of sites $\tilde{t}$ visited by the process that has created name n.

Operational semantics. The binders of the calculus are the usual in π-calculi like languages: name n is bound in $(\boldsymbol{\nu} n\colon T)\ P$ and in $(\boldsymbol{\nu} n\colon T)\ N$, whereas x and y are both bound in $a?(x@y)\ P$. Networks are taken up to α-congruence in such a way that bound names are different from free names and from each other.

Operational semantics is defined on top of a *structural congruence relation*, $\equiv$, that is the least congruence relation closed under the rules defined in Figure 3. It follows closely the structural congruence relation introduced for Dπ. Notice that when extruding a name from process to network level (third rule of group two), we record the code journey leading to name creation, whereas restricting it to a site is only possible when the code running at the site followed the same migration path as that of name creation.

Reduction in Figure 4 is mainly taken from Dπ, except for obvious adjustments to incorporate groups and migration paths. When code migrates, rule Mig, we append the name of the source site to the migration path. Migration path information is fundamental to reason about security. We check the security policies considering the sites that migration code visits, since this information is important to express the trust between the destination group and the rest of the network.

$\mathcal{P}$ ::=	*Policies*	τ ::=	*Actions*	S ::=	*Paths*
$\{\pi_1, \ldots, \pi_n\}$		useRes	output	ε	empty path
		| installRes	input	| g	group
π ::=	*Security rules*	| createRes	ch. creation	| $\bullet$	any group
$\tau : S$	action rules	| createSite	site creation	| SS	concatenation
| inherit	inherit policies	| createGroup	group creation	| $S + S$	alternation
		| forward	code forward	| $S^\star$	kleene star

Fig. 5. Syntax for security policies

3 Security Policy

This section presents how we specify and verify security policies. To formalise the notion of runtime error, we develop a tagged version of the language introduced in the previous section.

Writing security policies. A security policy ($\mathcal{P}$) consists of a set of rules (π). Action rules ($\tau : S$) describe the set of admissible paths in the group hierarchy that code must visit before being able to perform the action the policy protects. Rule forward governs the migration of code. For code migration to succeed, there must be a path all along the group hierarchy that authorises the forwarding of the code to the destination site. The inherit allows a group to import the rules defined for its direct parents.

Actions τ correspond directly to the actions of the calculus: input and output actions are related with the installRes and useRes, respectively; channel, site, and group creation are associated with createRes, createSite, and createGroup actions.

A *path pattern* S is a regular expression. A group g stands for itself or for any group in its hierarchy; the symbol $\bullet$ is a wildcard representing any group. Concatenation, alternation, and Kleene closure possess the usual meaning.

Checking security policies. A *typing* Γ is a partial function of finite domain from names to types. The type for channels C represents the datatype channels may carry, the type for sites G is the set of groups that the site belongs to, and the type for groups is a pair $(\mathcal{P}, G)$ denoting the security policy and the parent groups of the group. For a complete discussion on types refer to Section 4. We write $\mathrm{dom}(\Gamma)$ for the domain of Γ. When $x \notin \mathrm{dom}(\Gamma)$, $\Gamma, x : T$ denotes the typing Γ' such that $\mathrm{dom}(\Gamma') = \mathrm{dom}(\Gamma) \cup \{x\}$, $\Gamma'(x) = T$ and $\Gamma'(y) = \Gamma(y)$ for $y \neq x$. One uses $\widetilde{s}$ and $\widetilde{g}$ to denote a possibly empty sequence of sites $s_1 \ldots s_n$ and of groups $g_1 \ldots g_n$.

Functions allows and canEnter, defined in Figures 7 and 8, perform security checking. Before outlining function allows, we give an overview of function matches defined in Figure 6. Formula $\widetilde{g}$ matches S means that a path $\widetilde{g}$ is an instance of path pattern S. The rules for most path constructs should be easy to understand and specify the matching for each path pattern constructor. Notice that ruleallows for a group to match any group in its hierarchy.

$$\frac{\Gamma, g \colon (\mathcal{P}, G) \vdash h \text{ matches } f \qquad h \in G}{\Gamma, g \colon (\mathcal{P}, G) \vdash g \text{ matches } f}$$

$$\frac{}{\Gamma \vdash \varepsilon \text{ matches } \varepsilon} \qquad \frac{}{\Gamma \vdash g \text{ matches } \bullet}$$

$$\frac{}{\Gamma \vdash g \text{ matches } g} \qquad \frac{\Gamma, g\colon (\mathcal{P}, \{h\} \cup G) \vdash h \text{ matches } f}{\Gamma, g\colon (\mathcal{P}, \{h\} \cup G) \vdash g \text{ matches } f}$$

$$\frac{\Gamma \vdash \widetilde{g} \text{ matches } S \qquad \Gamma \vdash \widetilde{g}' \text{ matches } S'}{\Gamma \vdash \widetilde{g}\widetilde{g}' \text{ matches } SS'}$$

$$\frac{}{\Gamma \vdash \varepsilon \text{ matches } S^\star} \qquad \frac{\Gamma \vdash \widetilde{g} \text{ matches } S \qquad \Gamma \vdash \widetilde{g}' \text{ matches } S^\star}{\Gamma \vdash \widetilde{g}\widetilde{g}' \text{ matches } S^\star}$$

$$\frac{\Gamma \vdash \widetilde{g} \text{ matches } S}{\Gamma \vdash \widetilde{g} \text{ matches } S + S'} \qquad \frac{\Gamma \vdash \widetilde{g} \text{ matches } S'}{\Gamma \vdash \widetilde{g} \text{ matches } S + S'}$$

Fig. 6. matches relation

Formula g allows $\widetilde{f}\colon \tau$ (Figure 7) says that group g grants privilege to perform action τ to code that has travelled along path $\widetilde{f}$; path $\widetilde{f}$ is matched against the path pattern associated with action τ using function matches. The createGroup action receives special treatment, since the creation of a group establishes a new node in the group hierarchy, and the groups above must accept its new member. Since a group may identify itself as any of its parents, the creation of a subgroup must collect the acceptance of the whole hierarchy. Forwarding code requires that at least one branch in the hierarchy grants the forward policy to the path the code travelled. When the inherit policy keyword is set for a group, the security policies for the direct parent groups are considered as a part of the security specification for the group.

Function canEnter (Figure 8) checks whether code that travels through a given path has permission to enter a target group. A formula $\widetilde{g}$ canEnter f means that group f accepts code that has travelled through path $\widetilde{g}$. This privilege is controlled using the forward policy. Code that went all along path $\widetilde{g}$ is able to enter the frontier of group f, if there exists a path through f's hierarchy granting, at each group in the path (except for the target group), the forward right to $\widetilde{g}$.

Tagged language. To precise the notion of runtime error, we are obliged to define a tagged version of the language introduced in Figure 2, since the exposed syntax does not express information about security policies (cf. [15]). In what follows, one presents the syntax and corresponding operational semantics for the tagged language.

Tagged syntax. We make explicit the policies for groups, by appending a typing Γ to the syntax of sites. In fact, this Γ contains enough information to type process P. The syntax for the tagged language is that of Figure 2, replacing the site construct by its tagged version $\widetilde{s}[P]_\Gamma$.

Tagged structural congruence. The rearrangements in the structural congruence relation for tagged networks, denoted by $\equiv_T$, are found in Figure 9 and, except for the

$$\frac{\Gamma(g) = (\mathcal{P} \cup \{\tau\colon S\}, G) \quad \Gamma \vdash \widetilde{f} \text{ matches } S \quad \tau \neq \mathsf{createGroup}}{\Gamma \vdash g \text{ allows } \widetilde{f}\colon \tau}$$

$$\frac{\Gamma(g) = (\mathcal{P} \cup \{\mathsf{createGroup}\colon S\}, G) \quad \Gamma \vdash \widetilde{f} \text{ matches } S \quad \forall h \in G \;\; \Gamma \vdash h \text{ allows } \widetilde{f}\colon \mathsf{createGroup}}{\Gamma \vdash g \text{ allows } \widetilde{f}\colon \mathsf{createGroup}}$$

$$\frac{\Gamma(g) = (\mathcal{P} \cup \{\mathsf{forward}\colon S\}, \emptyset) \quad \Gamma \vdash \widetilde{f} \text{ matches } S}{\Gamma \vdash g \text{ allows } \widetilde{f}\colon \mathsf{forward}}$$

$$\frac{\Gamma(g) = (\mathcal{P} \cup \{\mathsf{forward}\colon S\}, \{h\} \cup G) \quad \Gamma \vdash \widetilde{f} \text{ matches } S \quad \Gamma \vdash h \text{ allows } \widetilde{f}\colon \mathsf{forward}}{\Gamma \vdash g \text{ allows } \widetilde{f}\colon \mathsf{forward}}$$

$$\frac{\Gamma(g) = (\{\mathsf{inherit}\} \cup \mathcal{P}, \{h\} \cup G) \quad \Gamma \vdash h \text{ allows } \widetilde{f}\colon \tau}{\Gamma \vdash g \text{ allows } \widetilde{f}\colon \tau} \qquad \frac{}{\Gamma \vdash s \text{ allows } \varepsilon f\colon \tau}$$

$$\frac{\forall g \in G, f_1 \in F_1, \ldots f_n \in F_n,\ \Gamma \vdash g \text{ allows } \widetilde{f}\colon \tau}{\Gamma, s\colon G, r_1\colon F_1, \ldots, r_n\colon F_n \vdash s \text{ allows } \widetilde{r}\colon \tau}$$

Fig. 7. allows relation

$$\frac{\Gamma(f) = (\mathcal{P}, \emptyset)}{\Gamma \vdash \widetilde{g} \text{ canEnter } f} \qquad \frac{\Gamma(f) = (\mathcal{P}, \{h\} \cup G) \quad \Gamma \vdash h \text{ allows } \widetilde{g}\colon \mathsf{forward}}{\Gamma \vdash \widetilde{g} \text{ canEnter } f}$$

$$\frac{}{\Gamma \vdash \widetilde{g} \text{ canEnter } \varepsilon} \qquad \frac{\forall g_1 \in G_1, \ldots, g_n \in G_n, f \in F,\ \Gamma \vdash \widetilde{g} \text{ canEnter } f}{\Gamma, s_1\colon G_1, \ldots s_n\colon G_n, r\colon F \vdash \widetilde{s} \text{ canEnter } r}$$

Fig. 8. canEnter relation

displayed rules, the changes w.r.t. the original structural congruence relation only reflect the syntactic adjustments (and are omitted). As for scope extrusion (rule 2), the set of assumptions at the left-hand side of the congruence relation enlarges with the name declared at network level, announcing the creation of the name. Merging sites (rule 3) is only viable when tagged information agrees: it is not possible to merge sites governed by distinct security policies.

Tagged reduction. The tagged reduction relation, denoted by symbol $\rightarrow_T$, is obtained from the original reduction (Figure 4) by decorating sites with typing Γ. Function $\mathsf{tag}_\Gamma(N)$, Figure 10, takes an original network N and a typing Γ, and yields its tagged counterpart. Recall that security policies are expressed as types. Therefore, to obtain a tagged term we need to provide the missing security information. For the sake of simplicity, we often write a tagged term $\mathsf{tag}_\Gamma(N)$ as N_Γ.

Runtime errors. The unary relation, $\stackrel{err}{\longmapsto}$, partially defined in Figure 11, identifies processes that break some security policy during reduction.

The output (input) process fails, R-OUT (R-INP), if the site that sent the code, r, has no permission to use (install) resources. We omit the rule for replicated input, since it is similar to rule R-INP. For code migration, rule R-MIG states that a goto process incurs in a runtime error if it cannot enter the border of the groups where the target site resides. Notice the role of typing Γ (a placeholder for security policies), and the need

2. $(\nu_{\tilde{t}} n\colon L@s)\ \widetilde{st}[P]_{\Gamma,n\colon L@s} \equiv_T \widetilde{st}[(\nu n\colon L)\ P]_\Gamma$ if $n \notin \mathrm{dom}(\Gamma) \cup \{s\}$
3. $\widetilde{st}[P]_\Gamma \mid \widetilde{st}[Q]_\Gamma \equiv_T \widetilde{st}[P \mid Q]_\Gamma$

(plus rules in group 1. and the first two rules in group 2. from Figure 3)

Fig. 9. Tagged structural congruence

$$\begin{aligned}
\mathsf{tag}_\Gamma(\mathsf{stop}) &= \mathsf{stop}\\
\mathsf{tag}_\Gamma(N \mid M) &= \mathsf{tag}_\Gamma(N) \mid \mathsf{tag}_\Gamma(M)\\
\mathsf{tag}_\Gamma(\tilde{s}[P]) &= \tilde{s}[P]_\Gamma\\
\mathsf{tag}_\Gamma((\nu_{\tilde{t}} n\colon T)\ N) &= (\nu_{\tilde{t}} n\colon T)\ \mathsf{tag}_{\Gamma,n\colon T}(N)
\end{aligned}$$

Fig. 10. Tag function

to talk about the site where the code is, s, the sequence of sites visited by the code, $\tilde{r}$, and the site where the code is migrating to, t. Rule R-RESC$_1$ says that the channel creation operation fails if the current site does not allow the site that sent the code to create channels. Rule R-RESC$_2$ is similar. We omit the rules for creating sites and groups, since they are similar to rules R-RESC$_1$ and R-RESC$_2$, as well as the induction rules for name restriction, parallel composition, and structural congruence (cf. [15]).

4 Typing System

In this section we present two type systems (for the original and for the tagged languages) that check whether networks respect the security policies defined for groups, taking into account the path travelled by processes. The type systems are based on a subtyping relation *à la* Sangiorgi and Pierce [21], and are parametric on two functions that are used to check the security policies, namely, allows and canEnter functions.

Types. The syntax for types is depicted in Figure 12. We assign types to channels, to sites, and to groups. *Types* T may be local or global: *local types* L are used when creating names at a given site; *global* (or *located types*) $L@s$ are assigned to names when declared at network level. A name assignment $n\colon L@s$ means that name n has type L and was created at site s.

Name types L aggregate *channel types* C, *site type* $\mathcal{P}$, and *group types* $(\mathcal{P}, G)$. A channel type $\langle V\rangle^I$ traces the type V of the values communicated along the channel, as well as the channel usage I. The type for a site records the set of groups the site belongs to. Group types are a central notion in our work: it is at group level that we record information for security, namely, (a) the set of *security rules* $\mathcal{P}$ that govern the interaction with the network, and (b) the *set of the parent groups* G of the group.

Channels can carry other channels, as well as basic values, as described by *value types*, V. The *type for channel values* assumes the form $C@G$, where C is the type of the channels that can be carried, and G is the set of groups hosting the communicated channels. The subtype relation characterising *channel tags* I is introduced in Figure 13.

$s\widetilde{r}[a!\langle v\rangle]_\Gamma \overset{err}{\longmapsto}$	if $\Gamma \nvdash s$ allows $\widetilde{r}$: useRes	(R-OUT)
$s\widetilde{r}[a?(v)\ P]_\Gamma \overset{err}{\longmapsto}$	if $\Gamma \nvdash s$ allows $\widetilde{r}$: installRes	(R-INP)
$s\widetilde{r}[\text{goto } t.P]_\Gamma \overset{err}{\longmapsto}$	if $\Gamma \nvdash s\widetilde{r}$ canEnter t	(R-MIG)
$s\widetilde{r}[(\nu a\colon L)\ P]_\Gamma \overset{err}{\longmapsto}$	if $\Gamma \nvdash s$ allows $\widetilde{r}$: createRes	(R-RESC$_1$)
$(\nu_{\widetilde{r}}\, a\colon L@s)\ N \overset{err}{\longmapsto}$	if $\Gamma \nvdash s$ allows $\widetilde{r}$: createRes	(R-RESC$_2$)

Fig. 11. Runtime errors

$T ::=$	*Types*	$C ::=$	*Local channel types*	$V ::=$	*Value types*
L	local type	$\langle V\rangle^I$	local channel	$C@G$	channel
$\mid L@s$	global type			$\mid$ unit	basic type
$L ::=$	*Name types*	$I ::=$	*Tags*	G	*set of groups*
C	local channel	r	input		
$\mid G$	site type	$\mid$ w	output		
$\mid (\mathcal{P}, G)$	group type	$\mid$ rw	input/output		

Fig. 12. Syntax of types

Subtyping. The *subtyping relation*, <:, is defined as the least preorder relation on types that satisfies the rules in Figure 13, where channels are tagged according to their usage: input (r), output (w), and input/output (rw). We extend the subtyping relation to deal with types involving groups. The original intuitions remain unchanged, namely that the subtyping relation is covariant for inputs, contravariant for outputs, and invariant if the channels are used both for input and for output purposes. The subtyping rules are straightforward. Notice the set inclusion to handle groups in value subtyping and the last subtyping rule that relates located channels.

Typing the original language. Our type system checks each action performed by processes: either *input*, *output*, *restriction*, or *code migration*. We associate a policy with an action. Therefore, useRes, installRes, createRes, createSite, createGroup, and forward specify the security policies for *input*, *output*, *restriction*, and *code migration* actions. We do not check code running at its host site (code that is not in the continuation part of a goto process), since we assume that there is no need to grant specific privileges to code in such circumstances.

The type system, described in Figures 14–16, includes three kinds of judgements: (a) judgement $\vdash \Gamma$ asserts that Γ is a well-formed environment; (b) judgement $\Gamma \vdash_{s\tilde{t}} P$ means that process P is well typed under typing Γ, when running at site s, having travelled through the sequence of sites $\tilde{t}$; and (c) judgement $\Gamma \vdash N$ denotes that network N is well typed under typing Γ.

The typing rules in Figure 14 are intended solely to avoid group structures from being circular. Therefore, rule E-GROUP ensures that when we enlarge a typing with a new group definition, the parent groups of that new group are already in the typing.

$$\mathsf{unit} <: \mathsf{unit} \qquad \frac{C_1 <: C_2 \quad G_1 \subseteq G_2}{C_1 @ G_1 <: C_2 @ G_2} \qquad \textit{(Value subtyping)}$$

$$\frac{i = \mathsf{r}, \mathsf{rw} \quad V_1 <: V_2}{\langle V_1 \rangle^i <: \langle V_2 \rangle^{\mathsf{r}}} \qquad \frac{i = \mathsf{w}, \mathsf{rw} \quad V_2 <: V_1}{\langle V_1 \rangle^i <: \langle V_2 \rangle^{\mathsf{w}}} \qquad \frac{V_1 <: V_2 \quad V_2 <: V_1}{\langle V_1 \rangle^{\mathsf{rw}} <: \langle V_2 \rangle^{\mathsf{rw}}}$$

(Local channel subtyping)

$$\frac{C_1 <: C_2}{C_1 @ s <: C_2 @ s} \qquad \textit{(Global channel subtyping)}$$

Fig. 13. Subtyping relation

$$\text{(E-UNIT)} \quad \frac{}{\vdash \diamond : \mathsf{unit}} \qquad \text{(E-CHANNEL)} \quad \frac{\vdash \Gamma}{\vdash \Gamma, a : C @ r}$$

$$\text{(E-SITE)} \quad \frac{\vdash \Gamma}{\vdash \Gamma, s : G @ r} \qquad \text{(E-GROUP)} \quad \frac{\vdash \Gamma \quad G \subseteq \mathrm{dom}(\Gamma)}{\vdash \Gamma, g : (\mathcal{P}, G) @ r}$$

Fig. 14. Well-formed environments

As for processes (Figure 15), rule P-OUTB enforces that typing Γ is well formed, and that channel a, located at the site (s) where the process is running, is a write or a read-write channel and is capable of carrying unit values. Moreover, the host site s must permit that code that has travelled through site sequence $\widetilde{t}$ may use its resources. Rule P-OUTC is similar to NP-OUTB, but here channel a must be able to carry channels of the same type as b (located at the groups that site r is a member). To type an input process $a?(x@y)\ P$ using rule NP-INPC, channel a must be a read or a read-write channel. The continuation process P must be well typed in a typing augmented with x and y.

Notice that channel x is located at y and that y is defined as a site member of the groups that channel a can carry. Hence, we guarantee that the privileges for the actions involving x and y are correctly checked, since we verify policies against all groups in G. One requires that y must not appear (at all) in Γ. Notice that y may occur in the type of a free channel, and such networks should be ruled out, since we can not include the type of these channels in the typing (the type refers a name that is bound). Take $s[a?(x@y)$ goto $y.b!\langle\diamond\rangle]$ as an example. The type of channel b is $\langle \mathsf{unit} \rangle^I @ y$, which can not be part of Γ, since y is bound and b is free. Finally, we verify that the host site s concedes permission to use its resources to code that has travelled site sequence $\widetilde{t}$. Rules P-INPB and P-INPR are similar to rule P-INPC.

We split name restriction over three rules, P-RESS, P-RESC, and P-RESG, since there is a specific policy associated to each creation action.

To type code migration goto $r.P$ applying rule P-MIG, one types process P in the target site r, using path sequence $\widetilde{t}$, and verifies that code travelling path sequence $\widetilde{t}$ may reach its target r. Notice the use of function canEnter to check security upon code

$$\text{(P-OUTB)}\ \frac{\vdash \Gamma \quad \Gamma(a) <: \langle \mathsf{unit} \rangle^{\mathsf{w}}{}_{@s} \quad \Gamma \vdash s \ \mathsf{allows}\ \tilde{t}\colon \ \mathsf{useRes}}{\Gamma \vdash_{s\tilde{t}} a!\langle \diamond \rangle}$$

$$\text{(P-OUTC)}\ \frac{\vdash \Gamma \quad \Gamma(a) <: \langle C_{@}\Gamma(r) \rangle^{\mathsf{w}}{}_{@s} \quad \Gamma(b) = C_{@}r \quad \Gamma \vdash s \ \mathsf{allows}\ \tilde{t}\colon \ \mathsf{useRes}}{\Gamma \vdash_{s\tilde{t}} a!\langle b_{@}r \rangle}$$

$$\text{(P-INPB)}\ \frac{\Gamma \vdash_{s\tilde{t}} P \quad \Gamma(a) <: \langle \mathsf{unit} \rangle^{\mathsf{r}}{}_{@s} \quad \Gamma \vdash s \ \mathsf{allows}\ \tilde{t}\colon \ \mathsf{installRes}}{\Gamma \vdash_{s\tilde{t}} a?(\diamond)\ P}$$

$$\text{(P-INPC)}\ \frac{\Gamma, x\colon C_{@}y, y\colon G \vdash_{s\tilde{t}} P \quad \Gamma(a) <: \langle C_{@}G \rangle^{\mathsf{r}}{}_{@s} \quad y \text{ not in } \Gamma \quad \Gamma \vdash s \ \mathsf{allows}\ \tilde{t}\colon \ \mathsf{installRes}}{\Gamma \vdash_{s\tilde{t}} a?(x_{@}y)\ P}$$

$$\text{(P-INPR)}\ \frac{\Gamma \vdash_{\tilde{t}} a?(v)\ P}{\Gamma \vdash_{\tilde{t}} a?^{*}(v)\ P} \qquad \text{(P-PAR)}\ \frac{\Gamma \vdash_{\tilde{t}} P \quad \Gamma \vdash_{\tilde{t}} Q}{\Gamma \vdash_{\tilde{t}} P \mid Q} \qquad \text{(P-NIL)}\ \frac{\vdash \Gamma}{\Gamma \vdash_{\tilde{t}} \mathsf{stop}}$$

$$\text{(P-RESS)}\ \frac{\Gamma, r\colon G_{@}s \vdash_{s\tilde{t}} P \quad r \text{ not in } \Gamma \quad \Gamma \vdash s \ \mathsf{allows}\ \tilde{t}\colon \ \mathsf{createSite}}{\Gamma \vdash_{s\tilde{t}} (\nu r\colon G)\ P}$$

$$\text{(P-RESC)}\ \frac{\Gamma, a\colon C_{@}s \vdash_{s\tilde{t}} P \quad \Gamma \vdash s \ \mathsf{allows}\ \tilde{t}\colon \ \mathsf{createRes}}{\Gamma \vdash_{s\tilde{t}} (\nu a\colon C)\ P}$$

$$\text{(P-RESG)}\ \frac{\Gamma, g\colon (\mathcal{P}, G)_{@}s \vdash_{s\tilde{t}} P \quad g \text{ not in } \Gamma \quad \Gamma \vdash s \ \mathsf{allows}\ \tilde{t}\colon \ \mathsf{createGroup}}{\Gamma \vdash_{s\tilde{t}} (\nu g\colon (\mathcal{P}, G))\ P}$$

$$\text{(P-MIG)}\ \frac{\Gamma \vdash_{r\tilde{t}} P \quad \Gamma \vdash \tilde{t} \ \mathsf{canEnter}\ r}{\Gamma \vdash_{\tilde{t}} \mathsf{goto}\ r.P}$$

Fig. 15. Typing processes

migration. We must ensure that there exists a path through the group hierarchy that allows code to enter site r.

Figure 16 depicts the type system for networks. The rules are similar to those for processes, apart from rule N-SITE. To type a site $\Gamma \vdash s\tilde{t}[P]$, we type process P in site s, knowing that it has travelled the sequence of sites $\tilde{t}$.

The type system we present preserves typings during reduction.

Theorem 1 (Subject Reduction). *If $\Gamma \vdash N$ and $N \to M$, then $\Gamma \vdash M$.*

Typing the tagged language. The type system for the tagged language is obtained from that of the original language (Figures 14, 15, and 16) by just changing rule N-SITE. We use the symbol $\vdash_T$ when writing typing judgements for tagged networks and prefix typing rules with TN. To type tagged sites $s\tilde{t}[P]_\Gamma$, we propose the following typing rule.

$$\text{TN-SITE}\ \frac{\Gamma \vdash_{s\tilde{t}} P}{\Gamma \vdash_T s\tilde{t}[P]_\Gamma}$$

One types process P in site s, having travelled through site sequence $\tilde{t}$. The tagging information matches the typing for process P.

(N-SITE)
$$\frac{\Gamma \vdash_{s\tilde{t}} P}{\Gamma \vdash s\tilde{t}[P]}$$

(N-PAR)
$$\frac{\Gamma \vdash N \quad \Gamma \vdash M}{\Gamma \vdash N \mid M}$$

(N-RESC)
$$\frac{\Gamma, a\colon C@s \vdash N \quad \Gamma \vdash s \text{ allows } \tilde{t}\colon \text{createRes}}{\Gamma \vdash (\nu_{\tilde{t}} a\colon C@s)\ N}$$

(N-NIL)
$$\frac{\vdash \Gamma}{\Gamma \vdash \text{stop}}$$

(N-RESS)
$$\frac{\Gamma, r\colon G@s \vdash N \quad r \text{ not in } \Gamma \quad \Gamma \vdash s \text{ allows } \tilde{t}\colon \text{createSite}}{\Gamma \vdash (\nu_{\tilde{t}} r\colon G@s)\ N}$$

(N-RESG)
$$\frac{\Gamma, g\colon (\mathcal{P}, G)@s \vdash N \quad g \text{ not in } \Gamma \quad \Gamma \vdash s \text{ allows } \tilde{t}\colon \text{createGroup}}{\Gamma \vdash (\nu_{\tilde{t}} g\colon (\mathcal{P}, G)@s)\ N}$$

Fig. 16. Typing networks

Theorem 2 (Tagged subject reduction). *If $\Gamma \vdash_T N$ and $N \rightarrow_T M$, then $\Gamma \vdash_T M$.*

Type safety. There is an operational correspondence between the original and the tagged reduction relations. The following results ensure that types are preserved both by tagging function and by tagged reduction.

Theorem 3 (Tagging preserves types). *$\Gamma \vdash N$ if and only if $\Gamma \vdash_T N_\Gamma$.*

Theorem 4 (Operational correspondence between original and tagged languages). *Let $\Gamma \vdash N$. $N \rightarrow M$ if and only if $N_\Gamma \rightarrow_T M_\Gamma$.*

The type safety result states that well-typed networks do not incur in runtime errors.

Theorem 5 (Type safety). *If $\Gamma \vdash_T M$, then $M \overset{err}{\not\longmapsto}$.*

5 Conclusions and Related Work

Summary. We present an approach to express and control history-based access to resources using types. We use Dπ as the underlying calculus and, on top of it, define a hierarchical structure of security groups. The security model we propose is based on the notion of security group that delimits a region of the network with the same security requirements. Security groups may be understood as a firewall that dictates and supervises the sites under its control. We use a type system as the security mechanism to enforce that networks respect the security policies defined by groups and claim a type safety result.

Ongoing work comprise the refinement of the type system to enforce a fine grained control of resources' security and the study of how to change policies dynamically.

Related work. Refer to [3] for a general survey on concurrent mobile calculi, type systems, and security policies. As far as we known, our security model is the first to combine group policies with record history-based access to resources, and to use group hierarchies for helping the writing of new security rules and the reusing of existent ones.

Cardelli, Ghelli, and Gordon introduced the notion of groups for the Ambient calculus [5–7] to control the movement and the opening of ambients. They use groups to combine ambients in clusters, but specify the security properties for each ambient regardless the group the ambient belongs to. Instead, we use groups to specify security policies shared by the sites that compose each group.

Lhoussaine and Sassone [17] use dependent types as an alternative to groups. The type system is far more complex and the calculus does not facilitate the writing of policies.

The work on Dπ has proposed advanced type systems [14, 15] to control resource access. The control of policies is based on a subtype relation that permits the delivery of different types of the same channel to distinguished parties. Code mobility is controlled with the **mig** keyword. If a process "sees" the **mig** keyword as part of the type of a site, then it may migrate code to that site. The subtype relation, together with the capability to communicate site names, allows for a site to tailor the information (*e.g.* resource names, control keywords) that the target site is able to use. This approach spreads security annotations along the code and it makes difficult to understand what actions are really allowed to execute.

Martins and Ravara [18] presented a type system to control migration in $lsd\pi$ [22] with no site creation. The paper discusses an earlier stage of development of the current work, where there is no notion of groups, nor history-based access control to resources. The works of Abadi and Fournet [1] and of Edjlali, Anurag, and Vipin [11] present a practical application of history-based access control to resources. Both works are deeply committed with the frameworks they select to make their security experiments, namely, the Java language, and by this reason, are difficult to compare to the current work. Chothia and Stark [8] present a notion of *local areas* that resemble our group hierarchy, but they just use local areas to ensure that channels are used in the appropriate domain.

The decentralised label model of Myers and Liskov [20] uses the notions of *labels* and *principals* to control information flow. These are related with our idea of groups and policies. Labels, assigned to variables, define the information flow policy: the sequence of principals that can read information for each owner. Principals may *act* for other principals, thus forming a hierarchy similar to our group hierarchy. However, we assign policies to groups and manage other policies besides the read policy. Bugliesi, Colazzo, and Crafa [4] also work with groups to control information flow for the π-calculus. Channel types record the information carried by channels, as well as the path the channel travels. We use a similar mechanism to keep track of code mobility, but since we control code migration instead of information flow, the assignment of migration paths is to mobile threads rather than to channels.

Finally, KLAIM [9, 10, 12, 13] uses a capability type system to control operations on tuple spaces. The KLAIM approach uses a notion of security policies, which are declared at site level, but differs substantially from our approach in what concerns how policies are programmed and checked. One main distinction is the place where the security policies are defined: security policies in KLAIM talk about what operations a site may perform on other sites, whereas in our framework each security group talks about what actions it allows others to perform on it. From the administrator's point of view this looks more adequate. Recent type systems proposed for μKLAIM tackle the compilation of open systems, using a kind of partial compilation mechanism that marks parts of the processes that cannot be checked statically to be analysed at runtime.

Acknowledgements. The authors would like to acknowledge the financial support of the EU Global Computing project Mikado, contract IST–2001–32222, and thank Matthew Hennessey and António Ravara for fruitful discussions. The first author would like to thank Neva Slani for the endless suggestions and comments given on this work. We also wish to acknowledge the hospitality of the School of Cognitive and Computing Sciences, University of Sussex, during the academic year of 2002/2003.

References

1. M. Abadi and C. Fournet. Access control based on execution history. In *Proceedings of NDSSS'03*, pages 107–121, 2003.
2. G. Boudol. Asynchrony and the π-calculus. Rapport de Recherche 1702, INRIA Sophia-Antipolis, 1992.
3. G. Boudol, I. Castellani, F. Germain, and M. Lacoste. Models of distribution and mobility: State of the art. Mikado Deliverable D1.1.1, 2002.
4. M. Bugliesi, D. Colazzo, and S. Crafa. Type based discretionary access control. In *Proceedings of CONCUR'04*, volume 3170 of *LNCS*, pages 225–239. Springer-Verlag, 2004.
5. L. Cardelli, G. Ghelli, and A. Gordon. Mobility types for mobile ambients. In *Proceedings of ICALP'99*, volume 1644 of *LNCS*, pages 230–239. Springer-Verlag, 1999.
6. L. Cardelli, G. Ghelli, and A. Gordon. Ambient groups and mobility types. In *Proceedings of TCS'00*, volume 1872 of *LNCS*, pages 333–347. Springer-Verlag, 2000.
7. L. Cardelli and A. Gordon. Mobile ambients. *Theoretical Computer Science*, 240(1):177–213, 2000.
8. T. Chothia and I. Stark. A distributed pi-calculus with local areas of communication. In *ENTCS*, volume 41.
9. R. De Nicola, G. Ferrari, and R. Pugliese. KLAIM: a Kernel Language for Agents Interaction and mobility. *IEEE Trans. in Software Engineering*, 24(5):315–330, 1998.
10. R. De Nicola, G. Ferrari, R. Pugliese, and B. Veneri. Types for access control. *Theoretical Computer Science*, 240(1):215–254, 2000.
11. G. Edjlali, A. Anurag, and C. Vipin. History-based access-control for mobile code. In *Proceedings of CCS'98*.
12. D. Gorla and R. Pugliese. Resource access and mobility control with dynamic privileges acquisition. In *Proceedings of ICALP'03*, volume 2719 of *LNCS*, pages 119–132. Springer-Verlag, 2003.
13. D. Gorla and R. Pugliese. Controlling data movement in global computing applications. In *Proceedings of SAC'04*. ACM Press, 2004.
14. M. Hennessy, M. Merro, and J. Rathke. Towards a behavioural theory of access and mobility control in distributed systems. *Theoretical Computer Science*, 2003.
15. M. Hennessy and J. Riely. Resource access control in systems of mobile agents. *Journal of Information and Computation*, 173:82–120, 2002.
16. K. Honda and M. Tokoro. An object calculus for asynchronous communication. In *Proceedings of ECOOP'91*, volume 512 of *LNCS*, pages 133–147. Springer-Verlag, 1991.
17. C. Lhoussaine and V. Sassone. A dependently typed ambient calculus. In *Proceedings of ESOP'03*, LNCS. Springer-Verlag, 2003.

18. F. Martins and A. Ravara. Typing migration control in $lsd\pi$. In Andrei Sabelfield, editor, *Proceedings of FCS'04*. TUCS, 2004.
19. F. Martins and V. Vasconcelos. Controlling security policies in a distributed environment. DI/FCUL TR 04–01, 2004.
20. A. Myers and B. Liskov. Protecting privacy using the decentralized label model. *ACM Transactions on Software Engineering and Methodology*, 9(4):410–442, 2000.
21. B. Pierce and D. Sangiorgi. Typing and subtyping for mobile processes. *Mathematical Structures in Computer Science*, 6(5):409–454, 1996.
22. A. Ravara, A. Matos, V. Vasconcelos, and L. Lopes. Lexically scoping distribution: what you see is what you get. In *FGC: Foundations of Global Computing*, volume 85(1) of *ENTCS*.
23. E. Zwicky, S. Cooper, and D. Chapman. *Building Internet Firewalls, Second Edition*. OReilly & Associates, 2000.

Programming Cryptographic Protocols*

Joshua D. Guttman, Jonathan C. Herzog, John D. Ramsdell, and Brian T. Sniffen

The MITRE Corporation

Abstract. Cryptographic protocols are useful for trust engineering in distributed transactions. Transactions require specific degrees of confidentiality and agreement between the principals engaging in it. Moreover, trust management assertions may be attached to protocol actions, constraining the behavior of a principal to be compatible with its own trust policy. We embody these ideas in a cryptographic protocol programming language CPPL at the Dolev-Yao level of abstraction. A strand space semantics for CPPL shaped our compiler development, and allows a protocol designer to prove that a protocol is sound.

1 Introduction

In this paper, we describe the core of a cryptographic protocol programming language, CPPL, a domain specific language for expressing cryptographic protocols. It matches the level of abstraction of the Dolev-Yao model [15], in the sense that the programmer regards the cryptographic primitives as black boxes, and concentrates on the structural aspects of the protocol. CPPL allows the programmer to control protocol actions using trust constraints [23], so that an action such as transmitting a message will occur only when the indicated trust constraint is satisfied. We offer a semantics for CPPL in the style of structured operational semantics; this semantics identifies a set of *strands* [34] as the meaning of a role in a protocol. The semantics is useful for two reasons. First, it suggests a method by which the programmer may prove that a protocol meets its security goals [21]. Second, it clarifies issues of scope and binding, and therefore assisted us in implementing a correct compiler.

Trust Engineering. A domain specific language for cryptographic protocols raises the question, however, why programmers need to create new protocols. Although there could be several answers to this, one specific answer motivated our work on CPPL. When a programmer must implement a transaction in a distributed application, CPPL allows him to engineer a protocol to achieve the specific authentication and confidentiality goals needed by this transaction. This process—the process of shaping a transaction so that it can reflect the trust goals of its participants—we call *trust engineering.*

* Supported by the MITRE-Sponsored Research program. Authors' addresses: guttman, jherzog, ramsdell, bsniffen@mitre.org.

R. De Nicola and D. Sangiorgi (Eds.): TGC 2005, LNCS 3705, pp. 116–145, 2005.

Moreover, each participant must understand at exactly which step in the protocol they undertake a commitment, such as the commitment to pay for some goods. If a principal P makes several successive commitments in a protocol, then P should be able to decide before each of these steps whether it is willing to incur that commitment. If not, it may prefer to select some alternative, or it may need to abort the transaction. The content of the commitment will depend on the constituents of the messages in this execution, for instance the cost of the purchase or the principal to whom the money should be transferred.

Thus, it is not sufficient to have a few specific security protocols, such as TLS or SSH; instead, different combinations of confidentiality and agreement are required in different transactions. Although a transaction may be implemented using TLS or SSH as a lower level medium for confidentiality or entity authentication, a protocol design problem still persists, of ensuring the right degree of agreement and secrecy between the participants, and of identifying the trust and commitments required for each step in the protocol.

The protocol design problem is pervasive in electronic commerce, web services, and other aspects of distributed applications. CPPL is intended to express the core functionality that programmers will need, if they are to use cryptographic protocols as a central mechanism in trust engineering, and especially to connect trust management [25] and protocols [23].

An Example. Suppose that we would like to go into business, offering on-line stock quotes to a set of clients registered as customers. On a particular occasion, a client will request a collection of data D, possibly representing a market sector; we assume that the value D also contains a transaction identifier that the client can use to re-identify this request when billed. The client and server use a Needham-Schroeder-like protocol [32] to agree on a session key, and then the server delivers a real time stream of data containing stock quotes for sector D. In Figure 1, we see that the session key SK replaces the responder's nonce of the Needham-Schroeder protocol; we assume for now that each principal has the other's public encryption key. The server B wants to authenticate A to ensure that he can bill A for delivering this data. Conversely, the client A wants B to successfully authenticate its clients, so that A will not be charged for any service

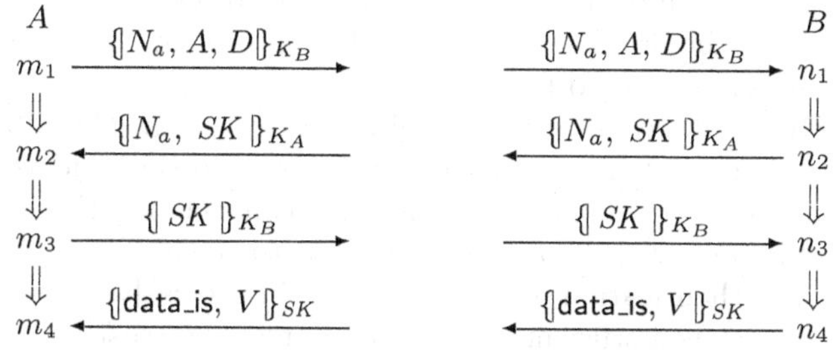

Fig. 1. NS Quote Protocol

consumed by other clients C. A also needs to authenticate B, and ensure that the session key is shared only with B. This allows A to infer—based on a trust decision about B—that the data is accurate, timely, and therefore suitable for business use.

In this protocol, A is committing himself to the request for D in sending the message on node m_1. B learns that A has made this request when the authenticating handshake completes, which occurs when B receives the third message on node n_3. When sending the message on node n_4, B is committing itself to the assertion that V is an accurate stream of values for the market sector D. B also must guarantee to itself that A will pay for the data D before transmitting it; this decision may depend on databases of subscribers, accounts in arrears, and similar facts.

Structure of the paper. In Section 2, we summarize the main ideas of the language, describing its core syntax and informal semantics in Section 3. A strand-based semantics for individual local protocol runs in given in structured operational semantics format in Section 4, and the global execution semantics in terms of bundles is in Section 5. The strand space methods for proving results about protocols are adapted to this context in Section 6. Our stock quote service example is described in detail in Section 7.

2 Main Ideas of CPPL

CPPL is intended to provide only the minimal expressiveness necessary for protocol design, which calls for three fundamental ingredients. First, a protocol run must respond to choices made by its peer, as encoded in different formats of message that could be received from the peer. Second, the principal on behalf of whom the protocol is executing must be able to dictate choices reflecting its trust management policy [2,7,17,23], using the choices to determine whether messages are sent, and if so of what format. Finally, CPPL provides a mechanism to encapsulate behaviors into subprotocols, so that design may be modularized. The interface to a subprotocol shows what data values must be supplied to it and what values will be returned back on successful termination. The interface also shows what *properties* the callee assumes about the input parameters, and what properties it will guarantee to its caller about values resulting from successful termination. These—branching on messages received, consulting a trust management theory before transmission, and subprotocols—are the three main forms of expressiveness offered by CPPL.

We also rely on three libraries. The first is a cryptographic library, which is used to format messages, to encrypt and decrypt, to sign and verify, and to hash. The second is a communications library. It connects to other principals on the network and manages network level channels to them. These channels need not achieve any authentication or confidentiality in themselves [15].

The third library is a trust management engine. The trust management engine allows us to integrate the protocol behavior with access control in a trust management logic [2,5,28], giving an open-ended way to control when to abort a run, and to control the choice between one subprotocol and another. The trust management engine is free to determine the formulas expressing trust constraints. However, CPPL determines the set of values that may appear as individual constants in these formulas. These values are nonces, keys, and other values that we regard as texts; texts include addresses and names. The trust management engine maintains a theory, a set of formulas in the trust management logic. The theory is used to infer that trust constraints are satisfied; a theory may be augmented with new formulas as a protocol execution proceeds.

We associate a formula with each message transmission or reception. The formula associated with a message transmission is a *guarantee* that the sender must assert in order to transmit the message. The formula associated with a message reception is an *assumption* that the recipient is allowed to *rely* on. It says that some other principal has previously guaranteed something. A protocol is *sound* if in every execution, whenever one principal P relies on P' having said a formula ϕ, then there was previously an event at which P' transmitted a message as part of this protocol, and the guarantee formula on that transmission implies ϕ.

In the NS Quote protocol shown in Figure 1, on node m_1 the client guarantees that it is requesting the value of D from B. We represent this with the formula $\mathsf{requests}(A, B, D)$. At the end of the authentication phase, in node n_3, B has ascertains that this has occurred, and relies on the formula A says $\mathsf{requests}(A, B, D)$. Knowing that A has made this request presumably helps B be sure of being paid. On node n_4, B guarantees $\mathsf{will\_pay}(A, D)$ and $\mathsf{curr\_val}(D, V)$. The first part is intended to protect B itself, since B wants not to transmit the value V without an expectation of being paid. The second part is intended to protect A, that is, to ensure that A receives correct information. There is one other guarantee in this protocol. It guards node n_2, stipulating $\mathsf{owns}(A, K_A)$, i.e. that the value used to encrypt the second message is in fact the public key of A.

The same rely/guarantee idea shapes our treatment of subprotocols. A local message, sent by the calling protocol, starts a subprotocol run. Hence, the caller makes a guarantee on which the callee can rely. When the subprotocol run terminates normally, the callee sends a message back to its caller; the callee now makes a guarantee on which the caller can rely for the remainder of its run. Thus, a subprotocol call is a mechanism for the caller to discover the information guaranteed when the callee terminates successfully.

The Run-Time Environment. The language is organized around a specific view of protocol behavior. In this view, as a principal executes a single local run of a protocol, it builds up an *environment* that binds identifiers to values encountered. Some of these values are given by the caller as values of parameters when the protocol is initiated; some are chosen randomly; some are received as ingredients in incoming messages; and some are chosen to satisfy trust management requirements. These bindings are commitments, never to be updated; once a value has been bound to an identifier, future occurrences of that identifier must match the value or else execution of this run aborts. In particular, when a known value (such as SK) is expected in an incoming message (such as the message received on n_3), any other value will prevent execution of this run from continuing.

The environment at the end of a run records everything learnt during execution. A selection of this information is returned to the caller.

Related Work. Despite the large amount of work on protocol *analysis*, the predominant method for *designing* and *implementing* a new protocol currently consists of a prolonged period of discussion among experts, accompanied by careful hand-crafted implementations of successive draft versions of the protocol. The recent reworking of the IP Security Protocols including the Internet Key Exchange [24] for instance, involved a complex and important cluster of protocols.

Languages for cryptographic protocols, such as spi calculus [4,3,14,8], have been primarily tools for analysis rather than programming languages.

There has been limited work on compilation for cryptographic protocols, with [33,31,13] as relevant examples. We add a more rigorous model of protocol behavior, centered around the environment mentioned above. We provide clear interfaces to communications services and the cryptographic library. We stress a model for the choices made by principals, depending on a trust management interpretation of protocols and on an explicit pattern-matching treatment of message reception. A semantics ties our input language to the strand space model [21]. This semantics motivates the structure of our compiler; moreover, a designer can use it to verify that a new protocol meets its confidentiality and authentication goals. Alternatively one could translate CPPL into spi or the applied pi calculus [4,3], allowing other verification methods [18,1].

3 The CPPL Core Language

We describe here not the user-level syntax for CPPL, but a simplified syntax, which we call the CPPL *core language*. It provides information at the right locations to make the semantics easy to express, and likewise to direct the compiler. Users write programs in a different surface syntax, illustrated in Section 7.

The syntax of the CPPL core language is presented in Figure 2. The CPPL core language has procedure declarations and seven types of code statements. Programming language identifiers are indicated by x and y, and message tags by r. When used to concatenate message patterns, the comma operator is right associative, and tagging binds less tightly than comma. The language has syntax for guarantees and relies—by convention we write guarantees as Φ and relies as Ψ—which are finite lists of trust management formulas. We use finite lists, which we interpret conjunctively. Formulas in relies and guarantees may contain, in addition to logical variables and CPPL values, also CPPL identifiers. If bound in the environment at runtime, a CPPL identifier will be replaced in Φ, Ψ by the value to which it is bound; if not yet bound, it serves as a query variable that will be bound as a consequence of a trust management call. Logical variables in a trust management formula, if they occur, are interpreted implicitly universally.

$$
\begin{array}{rl}
p \rightarrow & \text{proc } p\ (x^*)\ \Psi\ c \\
c \rightarrow & \text{return } \Phi\ x^* \\
| & \text{let } x = \text{new in } c \\
| & \text{let } x = \text{accept in } c \\
| & \text{let } x = \text{channel } y \text{ in } c \\
| & (sb^*) \mid (x\ rb^*) \mid (cb^*) \\
sb \rightarrow & \text{send } \Phi\ x\ m\ c \\
rb \rightarrow & \text{recv } m\ \Psi\ c \\
cb \rightarrow & \text{call } \Phi\ p\ (x^*)\ (y^*)\ \Psi\ c \\
m \rightarrow & x \quad | \quad m, m' \quad | \quad r\, m \\
| & (m) \quad | \quad [\, m\,]\, x \quad | \quad \{\, m\, \}\, x
\end{array}
$$

Fig. 2. CPPL Core Language

A procedure declaration specifies the name p of the procedure, a list (x^*) of formal parameters, and a list of preconditions Ψ involving the formal parameters. The body of the procedure is a code statement c. A code statement may be: a return instruction, which specifies a list of postconditions Φ and return parameters (x^*); a let-statement; or a list of send branches, receive branches, or call branches. An identifier x is either a lowercase identifier `id`, or else an identifier with typing information `id:type`. We write $\mathsf{ide}(X)$ for the set of identifiers used in the phrase X.

A well-formed code statement c with two return statements at different locations must have the same postconditions Φ and return parameters x^*. Our translation from the user-level syntax to the core language ensures this.

NS Quote Example in CPPL. To illustrate the CPPL core language, we will return to the NS Quote example. We first focus on the protocol actions, leading to the behavior shown in Figure 3. We replace the trust management annotations with underscores to focus attention on the channels, new values, and messages. The server's parameters are its own name and public encryption key. It waits to accept an incoming connection, which the communication layer delivers as the bidirectional channel `chan`. It reads a message off this channel, which binds `na` to a nonce, and `a` and `d` to texts interpreted as a name and the desired data.

```
proc server (b:text, kb:key) _
  let chan = accept in
  (chan recv {na:nonce, a:text, d:text} kb _
    let sk:symkey = new in
    (send _ chan {na, sk, b} ka
      (chan recv {sk} kb _
        (send _ chan {Data_is v} sk
          return _))))
```

Fig. 3. The NS Quote Server's Behavior

The server generates a fresh session key sk, which is transmitted and received back in different encrypted forms to accomplish the authentication test of a's identity. Finally, the current value is returned encrypted with the session key sk, tagged with Data_is to make its interpretation unambiguous.

We now insert the trust management information in italicized form in Figure 4. The procedure relies on the assumption that kb is really the public key that

```
proc server (b:text, kb:key) [owns(b, kb)]
  let chan = accept in
  (chan recv {na:nonce, a:text, d:text} kb [true]
    let sk:symkey = new in
    (send [owns(a, ka)] chan {na, sk, b} ka
      (chan recv {sk} kb [says_requests(a, a, b, d)]
        (send [will_pay(a, d); curr_val(d, na, v:text)]
              chan {Data_is v} sk
          return [supplied(a, na, d, v)]))))
```

Fig. 4. The NS Quote Server, with Trust Formulas

b owns, and states this assumption in its procedure header. The caller must arrange to start the server with values satisfying this assumption. The server learns nothing from the first message; it is encrypted using b's public key, and could have been prepared by an adversary as well as a regular principal. The transmission of sk is guarded by a guarantee that a owns the public encryption key ka. We regard this as a query against a deductive database. As a consequence, either ka becomes bound to a suitable value, or the query fails, aborting execution of this run. Presumably, the server has a database of keys for all of its subscribers. After the next message is received, b has authenticated the peer a, and relies on a having said that a is requesting the data d from b. We use the predicate says_requests(A, A', B, D) to mean that A says requests(A', B, D). This has the advantage of fitting the "says" locution into Datalog [10], our implementation's trust management logic, at least when only atomic formulas rather than compound formulas are said. It places a burden however on a principal—the server in this case—to include rules in its theory to allow requests(A, B, D) to be inferred from says_requests(A, A', B, D) for suitable values of the variables.

If b convinces itself that a will pay, and that the current value is v, then the value can be sent. The return parameters may be used by the caller for accounting and billing, with the guarantee that this data was supplied. We will extend the example in Section 7 to illustrate branching and subprotocols.

Informal execution semantics. To explain how procedures execute, we first introduce an auxiliary notion: *guaranteeing* formulas Φ in a runtime environment. This means to ask the runtime trust management system to attempt to ascertain the formulas Φ. Identifiers in Φ already bound in the runtime environment are instantiated to the associated values. Identifiers not yet bound in the runtime environment are instantiated by the trust management system, if possible, to values that make the formulas Φ true. The runtime environment extended with these new bindings is the result of successfully guaranteeing Φ. If the runtime trust management system fails to establish an instance of Φ the guarantee fails.

To execute a **return** statement, we attempt to guarantee the formulas Φ. If successful, we select from the resulting environment the values of each of the return parameters x^*; these values are returned to the caller. If the attempt to guarantee Φ fails, execution terminates abnormally, and the caller is informed of the failure. The caller receives no parameter values in case of failure.

To execute a list of **send branches**, the runtime trust management system selects a branch within which it can successfully guarantee the formulas Φ. The message pattern m specified on this branch, instantiated using the values in the resulting extended runtime environment, is then transmitted. Execution proceeds with the code c embedded within this send branch in the extended environment. If the runtime trust management system fails to guarantee the formulas Φ on any send branch, then execution terminates abnormally, and the caller is informed of the failure.

To execute a list of **receive branches** with identifier x, the runtime environment is consulted for the value bound to x. This value should be a channel. When a message is received over this channel, the message is matched against the patterns m within the receive branches. In a successful match, the message must agree with the runtime environment for identifiers in m that are already associated with a value. Other identifiers in m will be bound to the values observed in the incoming message, yielding an extended runtime environment. If at least one receive branch has a successful match, one such branch is selected. The formulas Ψ are instantiated using the extended runtime environment, and supplied to the runtime trust management system as additional premises. Execution proceeds with the code c embedded within this send branch in the extended environment. If no receive branch has a successful match, then execution terminates abnormally, and the caller is informed of the failure.

To execute a list of **call branches**, the system treats the call branches as sends followed by receives. That is, the the runtime trust management system selects a branch, within which it can successfully guarantee the formulas Φ. It calls the associated subprotocol procedure p with the parameters x^* instantiated using the values in the resulting extended runtime environment. This procedure may return normally, in which case it supplies values for the parameters y^*; execution continues with the embedded statement c, using the extended runtime environment. The instances of the formulas Ψ are supplied to the runtime trust management system as additional premises during execution of c. If p does not return normally, then execution may continue with a different call branch; execution proceeds in the original environment, without any extension from the abnormally terminated call branch.

Local nature of this description. This execution semantics is local in the sense that it describes what one principal P does. This involves deciding what values to bind to identifiers; what messages to send; how to process a message that is received; and how to select a procedure to call as a subprotocol. It says nothing about how messages are routed on a network; nothing about what another principal P' does with messages received from P; nothing about how another principal P' created the messages that P receives. Likewise, it describes only the execution of one procedure. It says nothing about the behavior of a subprotocol invoked in a call branch. In essence, the execution semantics describes only a single principal executing a single run of a single procedure. Thus, it is natural to describe any single run by a strand. We describe how to do this in Section 4, and then describe what global executions are possible in Section 5.

4 Local Semantics

We give the semantics of CPPL procedures and code statements by describing the *strands* describing their possible behavior. Each strand specifies a sequence of transmissions and receptions that is possible for a principal executing this CPPL phrase faithfully.

Term Algebra. Each transmission or reception is a term in a free algebra A. The atomic terms are texts, nonces, and keys, denoted below as a. A compound term in A is either a concatenation $g,\ h$, a tagged message $\mathsf{tagname}\ g$, or the result of a cryptographic operation. In this section and the next, we will write the results of all cryptographic operations involving a plaintext g and an atomic key K in the form $\{\!|g|\!\}_K$. However, CPPL has syntax to distinguish symmetric and asymmetric operations, and to distinguish encryptions from signatures.

A direction is a value with polarity $+$ or $-$, which we use to indicate transmission and reception respectively. A directed term is a pair (d, t) where d is a direction and $t \in \mathsf{A}$.

Strand Spaces. A *strand space* Σ is a set equipped with a trace mapping tr such that $S \in \Sigma$ implies $\mathsf{tr}(S)$ is a finite sequence of directed terms. We regard finite sequences such as $\mathsf{tr}(S)$ as (1-based) finite partial functions defined on an initial segment of the positive integers. Σ is typically defined to be the union of a set of *regular* strands, representing the behaviors compatible with a protocol being studied, and a set of *penetrator* strands, representing behaviors within the capability of an adversary. Our standard adversary model is formalized in the Appendix as Definition 9.

Σ is an *annotated strand space* if in addition Σ is equipped with pair of functions γ, ρ, such that for all $S \in \Sigma$ and all positive integers i, if $\mathsf{tr}(S)(i)$ has positive [respectively, negative] direction, then $\gamma(S)(i)$ [respectively, $\rho(S)(i)$] is a finite list of formulas. The formulas in the range of γ and ρ are called guarantee formulas and rely formulas respectively. We do not stipulate the logic to which the formulas belong, as the logic is an implementation-specific choice, which in our implementation is Datalog. The formulas are of interest only when $S \in \Sigma$ is regular; penetrator strands never make an enforceable commitment, and never rely on assertions of other principals. Thus, if S is a penetrator strand, then $\gamma(S)(i) = []$ and $\rho(S)(i) = []$ whenever they are defined.

Σ is a *strand space with uniqueness assumptions* if Σ is equipped with an operation Υ such that, for each $S \in \Sigma$, $\Upsilon(S)$ is a set of atoms that occur in $\mathsf{tr}(S)$; these are values that are uniquely originating in bundles of interest.

To give the semantics for a set of CPPL procedures, we define an annotated strand space with uniqueness assumptions. We give the semantics in the form of a Structured Operational Semantics. The primary judgments are of the form $\sigma; \Gamma \vdash c : s, \upsilon$. Here σ is a runtime environment, meaning a finite function mapping identifiers to values; Γ is a set of formulas serving as a theory; c is the code to be executed; and s, υ describes a strand. In this description, s describes the messages and associated formulated, while υ is a set of atoms containing the values assumed to have been freshly chosen. The judgment $\sigma; \Gamma \vdash c : s, \upsilon$ says that s, υ is one possible behavior that can result if c is executed in environment σ, when the principal holds theory Γ. A typical rule shows that a larger piece of code c_1 can unleash a strand of length $n+1$, assuming that a code statement c_0 embedded within c_1 can unleash a strand of length n. The behavior of c_0 describes everything after the first event of some behavior of c_1.

We describe strands $S \in \Sigma$ by grouping $\mathsf{tr}, \gamma, \rho$ together:

Definition 1 (Strand Descriptions). *Let s be a finite sequence of pairs, where the first element in each pair is a directed term $\pm t$ and the second element in each pair is a list of formulas. A sequence of length 1 $\langle(\pm t\,,\ \Phi)\rangle$ describes a strand $S \in \Sigma$ iff the length of S is 1, $\mathsf{tr}(S)(1) = \pm t$; if its direction is $+$, then $\gamma(S)(1) = \Phi$; if its direction is $-$, then $\rho(S)(1) = \Phi$.*

Sequence $(-t\,,\ \Psi) \Rightarrow s_0$ describes S if for some $S_0 \in \Sigma$, s_0 describes S_0 and

1. *$\mathsf{tr}(S)(1) = -t$ and $\rho(S)(1) = \Psi$;*
2. *$\mathsf{tr}(S)(i+1) = \mathsf{tr}(S_0)(i)$, $\gamma(S)(i+1) = \gamma(S_0)(i)$, and $\rho(S)(i+1) = \rho(S_0)(i)$, where in each equation, the left hand side is defined just in case the right hand side is.*

Similarly, $(+t\,,\ \Phi) \Rightarrow s$ describes S if for some $S_0 \in \Sigma$, s_0 describes S_0 and

1. *$\mathsf{tr}(S)(1) = +t$ and $\gamma(S)(1) = \Phi$; and*
2. *$\mathsf{tr}(S)(i+1) = \mathsf{tr}(S_0)(i)$, $\gamma(S)(i+1) = \gamma(S_0)(i)$, and $\rho(S)(i+1) = \rho(S_0)(i)$, where in each equation, the left hand side is defined just in case the right hand side is.*

A strand space for a set of procedures $p_1, \ldots p_n$ is a Σ containing strands described by all the s, υ for which, for some σ, Γ, c, we have $\sigma; \Gamma \vdash p_i : s, \upsilon$.

Since σ, σ' are finite partial functions mapping identifiers to values, we write $\sigma \oplus \sigma'$ to mean their disjoint union. That is, if $\sigma \oplus \sigma'$ is defined, then σ, σ' have disjoint domains, and $\sigma \oplus \sigma'$ maps x to a if either σ maps x to a or σ' does.

We use two auxiliary judgments. First, we use the judgment $\Gamma \longrightarrow \phi$ to mean that the formula ϕ is a logical consequence of the formulas Γ. We do not provide inference rules for $\Gamma \longrightarrow \phi$ here; they are inherited from the underlying logic, e.g. Datalog in our implementation. Second, we use the judgment $\Gamma \Vdash \Phi$ to record the successive derivation of the formulas in the list Φ. The values instantiating identifiers appearing free in $\Phi = [\phi_1, \ldots, \phi_n]$ may be chosen left-to-right, in the sense that an implementation may commit to some binding $x \mapsto a$ when x appears free in ϕ_1, even though some later formula ϕ_j may be jointly satisfiable with ϕ_1 only if some other binding $x \mapsto b$ had been chosen. That is, an implementation may get stuck and cause a strand to fail, even when a more farsighted choice of bindings would have made success possible.

SEQUENTIAL DERIVATION

$$\frac{\sigma_1 = \sigma \oplus \sigma' \qquad \mathsf{dom}(\sigma') \subseteq \mathsf{ide}(\phi_1) \qquad \Gamma \longrightarrow \phi_1\,\sigma \qquad \Gamma \Vdash \Phi\,\sigma_1}{\Gamma \Vdash [\phi_1; \Phi]\,\sigma_1}$$

VACUOUS DERIVATION

$$\Gamma \Vdash [\,]$$

Fig. 5. Sequential derivation and instantiation

Structured Operational Semantics. The semantics of procedure p is given by describing its behavior when it is invoked. In this semantics, a procedure is invoked when it receives a message with a call tag, its own principal identity, an activation identifier a, and a vector of atoms, one for each parameter declared by the procedure (Invocation in Figure 6). The initial environment σ_{orig} maps the principal identifier pr to the executing principal's identity.

INVOCATION

$$\frac{\sigma_1 = \sigma_{orig} \oplus \sigma' \qquad \mathsf{dom}(\sigma') \subseteq \mathsf{ide}(pr,\ n,\ ai,\ x^*) \qquad \sigma_1; \Gamma_0, (\Psi\,\sigma) \vdash\ c : s, v}{\sigma_{orig}; \Gamma_0 \vdash\ \texttt{proc}\ n\ \Psi\ x^*\ c : (-\mathsf{call}\ pr,\ n,\ ai,\ x^*\,\sigma_1\,,\ \Psi\,\sigma_1) \Rightarrow s, v}$$

Fig. 6. Procedure Semantics

The procedure semantics show the principal and activation identifier being bound to pr, ai, but this binding is hidden from programmers. In CPPL programs, there is nothing special about the identifiers `pr` and `ai`.

A run of a procedure may conclude by signaling a failure. It does so by sending a message with a fail tag, its principal identifier, and the activation identifier ai. The code c causing a failure may be an empty list of send branches `()`, or a return statement return $\Phi\ x^*$ whose formulas Φ cannot be guaranteed. It may also be a channel name together with an empty list of receive branches (x), or else a name that is not bound to a channel, followed by zero or more receive branches, or else any receive statement that the implementation considers to have timed out. A successful run of a procedure concludes by returning its results, or by invoking a subprotocol by means of a tail recursive call. In this semantics, to return, the strand sends a message with a ret tag, the activation identifier ai, and an atom for each variable named in the return statement (Return, Tail call in Figure 7). The activation identifier ai is used to ensure results are delivered

FAIL

$$\sigma; \Gamma \vdash \ c : \langle(+\mathsf{fail}\; ai\, \sigma\;,\; \mathsf{true})\rangle, \emptyset$$

RETURN

$$\frac{\sigma_1 = \sigma \oplus \sigma' \qquad \mathsf{dom}(\sigma') \subseteq \mathsf{ide}(\Phi) \qquad \Gamma \Vdash \Phi\, \sigma_1}{\sigma; \Gamma \vdash \ \mathtt{return}\ \Phi\ x^*\ : \langle(+\mathsf{ret}\,(ai,\ x^*)\,\sigma_1\;,\; \Phi\,\sigma_1)\rangle, \emptyset}$$

TAIL CALL

$$\frac{\sigma_1 = \sigma \oplus \sigma' \qquad \mathsf{dom}(\sigma') \subseteq \mathsf{ide}(\Phi) \qquad \Gamma \Vdash \Phi\, \sigma_1}{\begin{array}{l}\sigma; \Gamma \vdash \ (\mathtt{call}\ \Phi\ n\ x^*\ y^*\ \Psi\ \mathtt{return}\ \Psi\ y^*\ cb^*)\ : \\ \qquad \langle(+(\mathsf{call}\, pr,\ n,\ ai,\ x^*)\,\sigma_1\;,\; \Phi\,\sigma_1)\rangle, \emptyset\end{array}}$$

Fig. 7. Success and Failure Semantics

to the proper caller. To do so, the caller uses a uniquely originating atom, noted in the semantics by adding it to the set of atoms associated with the calling strand (see Figure 11). The "let new" statement generates a nonce or session key, also a uniquely originating atom (Let new in Figure 8). The "let channel" and "let accept" statements also bind the variable x to a value, in this case a channel created by the runtime system. We omit formalizing them. In all of the "let" statements, we require the let-bound identifier not to have been bound previously. In this way we preserve the principle that the environment may be extended with new bindings, but the value bound to any identifier never changes.

LET NEW

$$\frac{a \notin v \qquad \sigma_1 = \sigma \oplus (x \mapsto a) \qquad \sigma_1; \Gamma \vdash \ c : s, v}{\sigma; \Gamma \vdash \ \mathtt{let}\ x = \ \mathtt{new}\ \mathtt{in}\ c : s, v \cup \{a\}}$$

Fig. 8. Let new semantics

The semantics of sending and receiving have much in common. A send branch adds an event—consisting of the sent message paired with the guarantee guarding the send—to the front of any behavior of the following statement (Figure 9). If a send statement has a number of branches, the semantics is non-deterministic, taking the union of the behaviors possible for the send branches, together with a failure if all branches are refused (Figure 7). For a group of rules, σ' assigns values to identifiers occurring free in Φ, i.e. $\mathsf{dom}(\sigma') \subseteq \mathsf{ide}(\Phi)$. This group contains the successful Send rule with its guarantee, as well as the Return rule and the Tail call rule in Figure 7.

The semantics of a receive statement has the opposite sign (Figure 10). Moreover, in a group of rules, σ' assigns values to identifiers occurring free in the message pattern m, i.e. $\mathsf{dom}(\sigma') \subseteq \mathsf{ide}(x,\ m)$. This group includes the successful Receive rule, as well as procedure invocation in Figure 6, where the pattern m is $pr,\ n,\ ai,\ x^*$.

The semantics of subprotocol call is a combination of a transmission to the callee and a message reception from it (Figure 11). A call may start a subpro-

Send with guarantee

$$\frac{\sigma_1 = \sigma \oplus \sigma' \qquad \mathsf{dom}(\sigma') \subseteq \mathsf{ide}(\Phi) \qquad \Gamma \Vdash \Phi\,\sigma_1 \qquad \sigma_1; \Gamma \vdash \ c : s, \upsilon}{\sigma; \Gamma \vdash \ \texttt{(send}\ \Phi\ x\ m\ c\ sb^*\texttt{)} : (+\mathsf{msg}\,(x,\ m)\,\sigma_1\,,\ \Phi\,\sigma_1) \Rightarrow s, \upsilon}$$

Send alternative

$$\frac{\sigma; \Gamma \vdash \ \texttt{(}sb^*\texttt{)} : s, \upsilon}{\sigma; \Gamma \vdash \ \texttt{(send}\ \Phi\ x\ m\ c\ sb^*\texttt{)} : s, \upsilon}$$

Fig. 9. Semantics of send

Receive and rely

$$\frac{\sigma_1 = \sigma \oplus \sigma' \qquad \mathsf{dom}(\sigma') \subseteq \mathsf{ide}(m) \qquad \sigma_1; \Gamma, \Psi\,\sigma_1 \vdash \ c : s, \upsilon}{\sigma; \Gamma \vdash \ \texttt{(}x\ \texttt{recv}\ m\ \Psi\ c\ rb^*\texttt{)} : (-\mathsf{msg}\,(x,\ m)\,\sigma_1\,,\ \Psi\,\sigma_1) \Rightarrow s, \upsilon}$$

Receive alternative

$$\frac{\sigma; \Gamma \vdash \ \texttt{(}x\ rb^*\texttt{)} : s, \upsilon}{\sigma; \Gamma \vdash \ \texttt{(}x\ \texttt{recv}\ m\ \Psi\ c\ rb^*\texttt{)} : s, \upsilon}$$

Fig. 10. Semantics of receive

Call and rely

$$\frac{\begin{array}{c}\sigma_1 = \sigma \oplus \sigma' \qquad \mathsf{dom}(\sigma') \subseteq \mathsf{ide}(\Phi) \\ \Gamma \Vdash \Phi\,\sigma_1 \qquad \sigma_2 = \sigma_1 \oplus \sigma'' \qquad \mathsf{dom}(\sigma'') \subseteq \mathsf{ide}(y^*) \qquad \sigma_2; \Gamma, \Psi\,\sigma_2 \vdash \ c : s, \upsilon\end{array}}{\begin{array}{l}\sigma; \Gamma \vdash \ \texttt{(call}\ \Phi\ n\ x^*\ y^*\ \Psi\ c\ cb^*\texttt{)} : \\ \quad (+\mathsf{call}\,pr,\ n,\ ai,\ x^*\,\sigma_1\,,\ \Phi\,\sigma_1) \Rightarrow (-(\mathsf{ret}\,ai,\ y^*\,\sigma'')\,,\ \Psi\,\sigma_2) \Rightarrow s, \upsilon \cup \{ai\}\end{array}}$$

Callee fails

$$\frac{\sigma_1 = \sigma \oplus \sigma' \qquad \mathsf{dom}(\sigma') \subseteq \mathsf{ide}(\Phi) \qquad \Gamma \Vdash \Phi\,\sigma_1 \qquad \sigma; \Gamma \vdash \ \texttt{(}cb^*\texttt{)} : s, \upsilon}{\begin{array}{l}\sigma; \Gamma \vdash \ \texttt{(call}\ \Phi\ n\ x^*\ y^*\ \Psi\ c\ cb^*\texttt{)} : \\ \quad (+(\mathsf{call}\,pr,\ n,\ ai,\ x^*\,\sigma_1)\,,\ \Phi\,\sigma_1) \Rightarrow (-\mathsf{fail}\,ai\,,\ \mathsf{true}) \Rightarrow s, \upsilon \cup \{ai\}\end{array}}$$

Call alternative

$$\frac{\sigma; \Gamma \vdash \ \texttt{(}cb^*\texttt{)} : s, \upsilon}{\sigma; \Gamma \vdash \ \texttt{(call}\ \Phi\ p\ x^*\ y^*\ \Psi\ c\ cb^*\texttt{)} : s, \upsilon}$$

Fig. 11. Call Semantics

tocol that eventually fails, in which case execution has not committed to this branch; execution may continue with the next call branch and the unextended environment σ.

In the "Call and rely" production, σ' assigns values to identifiers occurring in Φ, i.e. $\mathsf{dom}(\sigma') \subseteq \mathsf{ide}(\Phi)$, while σ'' assigns values to identifiers occurring free in the pattern $\mathsf{ret}\,ai,\ y^*$, i.e. $\mathsf{dom}(\sigma'') \subseteq \mathsf{ide}(ai,\ y^*) = y^*$. Our implementation assumes that all of the identifiers y^* will be unbound in σ_1, and issues an error message otherwise, but an implementation could allow some of these identifiers already to be bound, in which case the values received in these positions would have to match the values already bound to the identifiers in σ_1.

Definition 2. *If* $\delta = proc\ n\ \Phi\ x^*\ c$ *is a* CPPL *procedure declaration, then* $[\![\delta]\!]\sigma\Gamma$ *is the set of* s, υ *such that*

$$\sigma; \Gamma \vdash \ \delta : s, \upsilon$$

is derivable using the inference rules in this section and the rules for the underlying logic's consequence relation $\longrightarrow$.

Given CPPL *procedures* $\delta_1, \ldots, \delta_n$, *let*

$$\Delta = \bigcup_{\delta_i, \sigma, \Gamma} [\![\delta_i]\!]\sigma\Gamma.$$

Σ, *an annotated strand space with uniqueness assumptions,* models *the procedures* $\delta_1, \ldots, \delta_n$ *if every* $S \in \Sigma$ *is described by some* s *with* $s, \Upsilon(S) \in \Delta$, *and for every* $s, \upsilon \in \Delta$, s *describes at least one* $S \in \Sigma$ *with* $\Upsilon(S) = \upsilon$.

Parametric Strands. The structured operational semantics that we have just given clarifies the relations between the code being executed, the runtime environment, the theory in force, and the actions taken. However, there is another kind of regularity in the behavior of CPPL programs. This is the fact that the infinite number of strands described by the semantics are in fact all instances of a finite number of genuinely different strands. They are simply instantiated with infinitely many different values.

Any execution of the return statement `return` $\Phi\ x^*$ unleashes either a strand of the form

$$\langle (+\mathsf{ret}\,(ai,\ x^*)\,\sigma\,,\ \Phi\sigma)\rangle, \emptyset$$

or one of the form $\langle (+\mathsf{fail}\ ai\,\sigma\,,\ \mathsf{true})\rangle, \emptyset$. If we let σ_0 be an assignment that maps each identifier in this code statement to a value of the appropriate type, then every assignment σ in these two forms may be written as $\sigma_0 \circ \alpha$ for some replacement α. That is, every strand of the forms shown is an instance of the strands for the specific value $\sigma = \sigma_0$. Similarly, any strand unleashed from `let` $x =$ `new in` c will be of the form $s, \upsilon \cup \{a\}$ for some $a \notin \upsilon$ where s, υ is a strand unleashed from c.

Send and receive branches are roughly tagged unions. The strands that may be unleashed by the send branches `(`sb^*`)` are, in addition to a failure, all strands that may be unleashed by the code embedded within the send branches, each prefixed with a single positive message pattern. For receive branches, the prefixed pattern is negative. However, our nondeterministic semantics does not require the "tagging" initial patterns to be disjoint. Call branches are slightly more complex, since there is the uncommitted behavior of a call and a failure, preceding invocation of another branch.

We refer to this informally presented finite set of strands as $\mathcal{S}$. Suppose in a procedure δ the *nesting depth* d is the number of nested parentheses introduced by send, receive, and call statements. Let the *branching factor* k be the maximum number of send branches, receive branches, and call branches in any one statement.

Proposition 1. *Suppose the depth of a procedure δ is d and its branching factor is k. There is a set $\mathcal{S}(\delta)$ of strands with cardinality $|\mathcal{S}(\delta)| \leq k^d$ such that, for every strand s, υ, if $s, \upsilon \in [\![\delta]\!]\sigma\Gamma$, then $s, \upsilon = (s_0, \upsilon_0) \cdot \alpha$ for some α and some $s_0, \upsilon_0 \in \mathcal{S}(\delta)$.*

If $s, \upsilon = (s_0, \upsilon_0) \cdot \alpha$ for some α and some $s_0, \upsilon_0 \in \mathcal{S}(\delta)$, then for some σ, Γ, $s, \upsilon \in [\![\delta]\!]\sigma\Gamma$. If $s_0, \upsilon_0 \in \mathcal{S}(\delta)$, then $\mathsf{length}(s_0) \leq (2kd) + 2$.

Typically, k and d are small, and the cardinality of $\mathcal{S}(\delta)$ is far less than k^d. Although a finite set of procedures δ_i yields a finite set $\bigcup \mathcal{S}(\delta_i)$, there are nevertheless infinitely many global executions associated with the δ_i; indeed, natural questions such as secrecy are not uniformly decidable [16], although important classes are decidable [6,22].

We assume that for every replacement α, $\Gamma \longrightarrow \phi$ implies $\Gamma \cdot \alpha \longrightarrow \phi \cdot \alpha$, this being a defining property of a consequence relation for logics with replacements.

Proposition 2. *For every procedure δ, and replacement α, the judgment*

$$\sigma; \Gamma \vdash\ \delta : s, \upsilon \quad \textit{implies} \quad \sigma \cdot \alpha; \Gamma \cdot \alpha \vdash\ \delta : (s, \upsilon) \cdot \alpha.$$

Proof. Each rule is invariant under applying a replacement α.

5 Global Semantics

In order to model subprotocol call and return, and other local or inherently secure interactions, we enrich the notion of a direction. Directions will distinguish transmission from reception as before. However, a direction may additionally specify that the peer at the other end of a message transmission arrow is regular. It may also specify, in the case of message transmission, that the message will definitely be delivered.

Definition 3. *A* direction *d is a value with the following properties: (1) the* polarity *of d is one of the symbols $+, -$, indicating transmission and reception respectively; (2) the* partner *of d is one of the symbols* regular *and* any*; and (3) the delivery* confidence *of d is one of the symbols* guaranteed *and* maybe.

We write directions in the form $+^c_p$ and $-^c_p$. The subscript p indicates whether the partner is regular (r) or any (a). The superscript c indicates whether the delivery confidence is guaranteed (g) or maybe (m). When the partner is any, we generally omit the subscript. When the delivery confidence is maybe, we generally omit the superscript. We say that a node is *negative* when its polarity is $-$, and that it is positive when its polarity is $+$. The delivery confidence is of interest only when a node is positive; the recipient of a message knows that it has been received. With this amplification of the notion of direction, we preserve the definitions of strand space from the beginning of Section 4.

Strands are either *penetrator strands*, taking the forms shown in Definition 9 from Appendix A, or else substitution instances of a finite number of *roles* of a given protocol. When a protocol is defined by a finite number of CPPL declarations $\delta_1, \ldots, \delta_n$, then these roles are the members of $\bigcup \mathcal{S}(\delta_i)$ as in Proposition 1. We call the instances of the roles *regular strands.*

Transmission that preserves confidentiality is a special kind of message transmission; these nodes have direction d with positive polarity and regular partner. Reception that ensures authenticity is (dually) a special kind of message reception; these nodes have direction d with negative polarity and regular partner. If a communication arrow $n \rightarrow n'$ ensures both confidentiality and authentication, then the directions of n and n' both have regular partner. Purely local communication such as subprotocol call or return is of this kind.

We write Conf for the set of nodes n of the form $+^c_r$ and Auth for the set of nodes n of the form $-^c_r$ (where c may be either g or m).

The set $\mathcal{N}$ of all nodes forms a directed graph $\langle \mathcal{N}, (\rightarrow \cup \Rightarrow) \rangle$ together with both sets of edges $n_1 \rightarrow n_2$ for communication and $n_1 \Rightarrow n_2$ for succession on the same strand (Definition 8). The content of the annotations comes from an enriched notion of bundle, in which message transmission arrows $n_1 \rightarrow n_2$ behave as indicated by the properties of the directions of the two nodes.

Definition 4. *Let $\mathcal{B} = \langle \mathcal{N}_\mathcal{B}, (\rightarrow_\mathcal{B} \cup \Rightarrow_\mathcal{B}) \rangle$ be a finite acyclic subgraph of $\langle \mathcal{N}, (\rightarrow \cup \Rightarrow) \rangle$. $\mathcal{B}$ is a* bundle with secure communication *or* sc-bundle *if:*

1. *If $n_2 \in \mathcal{N}_\mathcal{B}$ is negative, then there is a unique n_1 such that $n_1 \rightarrow_\mathcal{B} n_2$.*
2. *If $n_2 \in \mathcal{N}_\mathcal{B}$ and $n_1 \Rightarrow n_2$ then $n_1 \Rightarrow_\mathcal{B} n_2$.*
3. *If $n' \in$ Auth and $n \rightarrow_\mathcal{B} n'$, then n is regular. If $n \in$ Conf and $n \rightarrow_\mathcal{B} n'$, then n' is regular; if moreover $n \rightarrow_\mathcal{B} n''$, then $n' = n''$.*
4. *If $n_1 \in \mathcal{N}_\mathcal{B}$ is positive with delivery confidence* guaranteed, *then there is a n_2 such that $n_1 \rightarrow_\mathcal{B} n_2$.*

$n \preceq_\mathcal{B} n'$ if some sequence of zero or more arrows $\rightarrow_\mathcal{B}, \Rightarrow_\mathcal{B}$ lead from n to n'.

An sc-bundle $\mathcal{B}$ does not assume secure communication if every node n occurring in it has partner *any* and delivery confidence *maybe.* Thus, the bundles in the sense of earlier work such as [21] are a special case of sc-bundles.

Proposition 3. *If $\mathcal{B}$ is an sc-bundle, $\preceq_\mathcal{B}$ is a finite partial order. Every non-empty subset of the nodes in $\mathcal{B}$ has $\preceq_\mathcal{B}$-minimal members.*

Secure Communication within CPPL. We represent the strands in the CPPL semantics as strands with secure communication as a function of the tags in the terms. In particular, if a term is of one of the forms $\pm$call t, $\pm$ret t, or $\pm$fail t, then we regard the direction as being $\pm^g_r$. That is, the partner is assumed regular, and the delivery is assumed to be guaranteed. If a term is of the form $\pm$msg t, then we regard the direction as being $\pm^m_a$. As a consequence, any sc-bundle formed from CPPL strands will provide authentication, confidentiality, and guarantee of delivery for the local mechanism of subprotocol invocation and termination. No assumption is made for the messages dispatched and received in ordinary protocol transmission and reception events.

In this, we follow the Dolev-Yao model for protocol messages over the network, but we assume that each individual participant has a secure platform on which to run her CPPL procedures. Secure communication in the sense of Definition 4 can also be used to represent communication through a secure transport medium such as the tunnels provided by TLS and IPsec, thus providing a strand space variant to the methods of Broadfoot and Lowe [9]. We will now develop a method—encapsulated in Propositions 4–6 and the finite semantics $\mathcal{S}(\delta)$—to prove security properties for the procedure definitions of a protocol.

6 Reasoning About the Global Semantics

Occurrences and Sets. We view each term as an abstract syntax tree, in which atoms are leaves and internal nodes are either *tagged messages*, *concatenations*, or else *encryptions*. A branch through the tree *traverses a key child* if the branch traverses an encryption $\{|t|\}_K$ and then traverses the second child (the key) labeled K.

An *occurrence* of t_0 in t is a branch within the tree for t that ends at a node labeled t_0 without traversing a key child. A *use* of K in t (for encryption) is a branch within the tree for t that ends at a node labeled K and that has traversed a key child. We say that t_0 is a *subterm* of t (written $t_0 \sqsubset t$; see Definition 8, Clause 1) if there is an occurrence of t_0 within t. When S is a set of terms, t_0 *occurs only within* S in t if, in the abstract syntax tree of t, every occurrence of t_0 traverses a node labeled with some $t_1 \in S$ (properly) before reaching t_0. Term t_0 *occurs outside* S in t if $t_0 \sqsubset t$ but t_0 does not occur only within S in t.

A term t *originates* at node n_1 if n_1 is positive, $t \sqsubset \mathrm{term}(n_1)$, and $n_0 \Rightarrow^+ n_1$ implies $t \not\sqsubset \mathrm{term}(n_0)$. It *originates uniquely* in a set N of nodes if there is exactly one $n \in N$ at which it originates. It is *non-originating* in N if there is no $n \in N$ at which it originates.

Definition 5 (Safety). *Let $\mathcal{B}$ be an sc-bundle. $a \in \mathsf{Safe\_ind}_0(\mathcal{B})$ if a originates nowhere in $\mathcal{B}$. $a \in \mathsf{Safe\_ind}_{i+1}(\mathcal{B})$ if either (1) $a \in \mathsf{Safe\_ind}_i(\mathcal{B})$ or else*

(2) a originates uniquely on a regular node $n_0 \in \mathcal{B}$ and, for every positive regular node $n \in \mathcal{B}$ such that $a \sqsubset term(n)$, the following holds: Either $n \in \mathsf{Conf}$ or else a occurs only within S in $term(n)$, where

$$S = \{ \{|h|\}_{K_0} : K_0^{-1} \in \mathsf{Safe\_ind}_i(\mathcal{B}) \}.$$

$a \in \mathsf{Safe\_ind}(\mathcal{B})$ if there exists an i such that $a \in \mathsf{Safe\_ind}_i(\mathcal{B})$.

Proposition 4 (Safety ensures secrecy). *If $a \in \mathsf{Safe\_ind}(\mathcal{B})$ and there exists $n \in \mathcal{B}$ such that $term(n) = a$, then n is regular.*

Proofs of this proposition and the others in this section will appear elsewhere.

Definition 6 (Export Protection). *A set S of terms provides* export protection *for $\mathcal{B}$ if for every $t \in S$, t is of the form $\{|h|\}_K$ where $K^{-1} \in \mathsf{Safe\_ind}(\mathcal{B})$.*

When C is a set of terms, we also write $\mathsf{Conf}(C)$ for the set of nodes $n \in \mathsf{Conf}$ such that term$(n) \in C$. The outgoing authentication test allows us to infer that there is a *regular* strand including $m_0 \Rightarrow^+ m_1$ as in Figure 12.

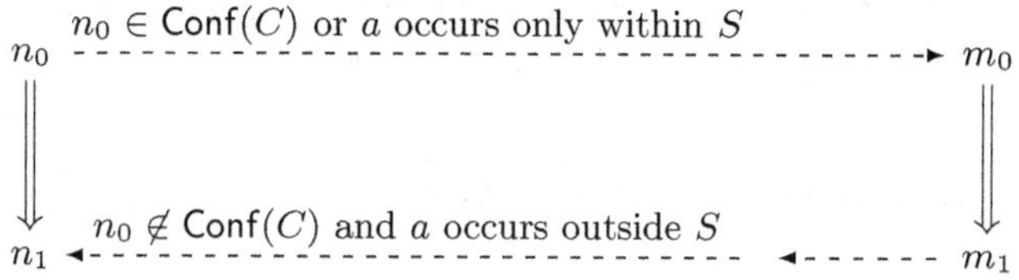

Fig. 12. The Outgoing Authentication Test

Proposition 5 (Outgoing Authentication Test). *Let $\mathcal{B}$ be an sc-bundle with regular nodes $n_0, n_1 \in \mathcal{B}$; let S be a set of terms providing export protection for $\mathcal{B}$; and let C be a set of terms. Suppose that (1) a originates uniquely at n_0 and either $n_0 \in \mathsf{Conf}(C)$ or else a occurs only within S in term(n_0); and (2) $n_1 \notin \mathsf{Conf}(C)$ and a occurs outside S in term(n_1).*

There exists a regular $m_0 \Rightarrow^+ m_1$ such that (1) m_0 is the earliest occurrence of a on its strand s; (2) m_1 is the earliest node on s such that $m_1 \notin \mathsf{Conf}(C)$ and a occurs outside S in term(m_1); (3) m_1 is positive, and m_0 is negative unless $m_0 = n_0$. Moreover, $n_0 \preceq_{\mathcal{B}} m_0 \Rightarrow^+ m_1 \preceq_{\mathcal{B}} n_1$; $a \sqsubset$ term(m_0); and for all $m \preceq_{\mathcal{B}} m_0$, either $n_0 \in \mathsf{Conf}(C)$ or a occurs only within S in m.

Proposition 6 (Incoming Authentication Test). *Suppose $n_1 \in \mathcal{B}$ is negative. (1) If $t \sqsubset$ term(n_1) and $t = \{\!|h|\!\}_K$ for $K \in \mathsf{Safe\_ind}(\mathcal{B})$, then there exists a positive regular $m_1 \prec n_1$ such that t originates at m_1. (2) If $n_1 \in \mathsf{Auth}$, then there exists a unique positive regular $m_1 \to n_1$. Moreover in either case:*

Solicited Incoming Test. *If $a \sqsubset t$ originates uniquely on $n_0 \neq m_1$, then $n_0 \preceq m_0 \Rightarrow^+ m_1 \prec n_1$.*

Propositions 4–6 suffice to prove the main authentication and secrecy properties of protocols. In our context, we want particularly to establish *soundness*, i.e. that in every execution, one principal's relies are supported by earlier guarantees by other principals [23]. We write $\mathsf{prin}(m)$ to refer to the regular principal acting on a node m, which we assume is some conventionally chosen parameter to the regular strand that m lies on. If m lies on a penetrator strand, then $\mathsf{prin}(m)$ is undefined. We also write P says ϕ, subject to the understanding that this will be encoded suitably into the implemented logic.

Definition 7. Soundness. *Bundle $\mathcal{B}$* supports *a negative node $n \in \mathcal{B}$ iff $\rho(n)$ is a logical consequence of the set of formulas $\{\mathsf{prin}(m)$ says $\gamma(m)\colon m \prec_{\mathcal{B}} n\}$.*

Let Π be an annotated protocol, and let $\mathbb{B}$ be a set of sc-bundles over Π. Π is sound for $\mathbb{B}$ *if, for all $\mathcal{B} \in \mathbb{B}$, for every negative $n \in \mathcal{B}$, $\mathcal{B}$ supports n.*

In practice, we use the authentication test theorems to prove the existence of nodes m such that the formulas $\mathsf{prin}(m)$ says $\gamma(m)$ imply $\rho(n)$. Since only positive regular nodes m help to support $\rho(n)$, if we cannot prove the existence of positive regular nodes m of a protocol preceding a negative node n, then the rely formula on n must be trivial, i.e. a consequence of the empty set of formulas. In particular if the message received on n could have been generated without help by the adversary, then $\rho(n) = [\,]$, i.e. it is vacuously true.

7 Example: Protocol-Based Access

We will now return to the NS Quote Protocol given at the beginning of the paper in Figure 1. In it, an initiator A requests on-line stock quotes from a responder B, and B delivers them if it can determine that A is a registered subscriber. We prove first that it is unsound, hardly surprising as it is based on the (broken) Needham-Schroeder protocol.

Proposition 7. *NSQ is unsound; there is a bundle $\mathcal{B}$ in which the public keys of A and B are non-originating, and the nonces N_a, N_b are uniquely originating, but in which node n_4 is unsupported.*

Proof. In Figure 13, $\rho(n_4) = A$ says $\mathsf{requests}(A, B, D)$, while by contrast $\gamma(m_1) = \mathsf{requests}(A, M, D')$.

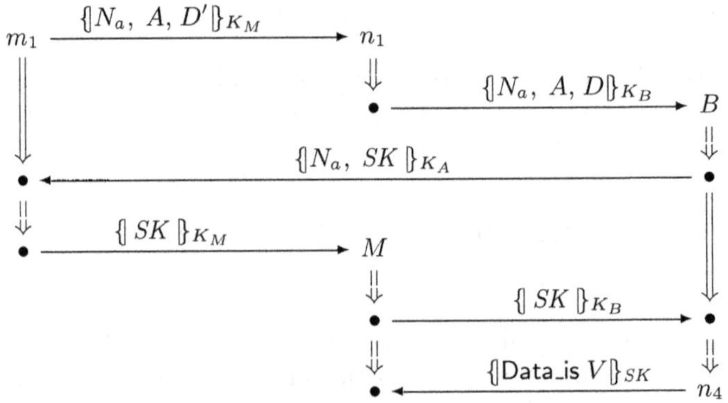

Fig. 13. Counterexample to NS Quote Soundness

A Corrected Protocol. To correct the protocol, and also enrich its functionality, we revise our example protocol to take the form in Figure 14. In this version of the protocol, we add B's name to the message sent from node n_2, as suggested by Lowe [29] when he discovered the attack we showed in Figure 13. We also add a decision, made by the server B. It chooses in nodes n_4 and n_4' between two levels of service. Corporate users may pay dear, but they receive prompt delivery of precise data at a premium price; individual users may pay much more cheaply to receive information that is delayed a few minutes and rounded from thirty-seconds of a point to the nearest eighth of point. The resulting protocol is the same except at the last step, where different tags distinguish the two types of outcome (Figure 14). There are three steps we will take to implement this

$$
\begin{array}{ccc}
A & & B \\
m_1 & \xrightarrow{\quad \{\!|N_a,\, A,\, D|\!\}_{K_B} \quad} & \quad \xrightarrow{\quad \{\!|N_a,\, A,\, D|\!\}_{K_B} \quad} & n_1 \\
m_2 & \xleftarrow{\quad \{\!|N_a,\, SK,\, B|\!\}_{K_A} \quad} & \quad \xleftarrow{\quad \{\!|N_a,\, SK,\, B|\!\}_{K_A} \quad} & n_2 \\
m_3 & \xrightarrow{\quad \{\!|\, SK\, |\!\}_{K_B} \quad} & \quad \xrightarrow{\quad \{\!|\, SK\, |\!\}_{K_B} \quad} & n_3 \\
m_4 & \xleftarrow{\quad \{\!|\text{Dear } V|\!\}_{SK} \quad} & \quad \xleftarrow{\quad \{\!|\text{Dear } V|\!\}_{SK} \quad} & n_4 \\
\cdots & & & \cdots \\
m_4' & \xleftarrow{\quad \{\!|\text{Cheap } V|\!\}_{SK} \quad} & \quad \xleftarrow{\quad \{\!|\text{Cheap } V|\!\}_{SK} \quad} & n_4'
\end{array}
$$

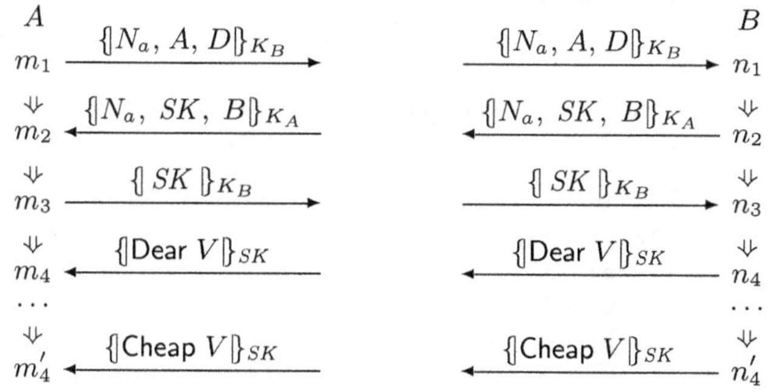

Fig. 14. NSL Quote Protocol with Choice

example. First, we will program the message flow, namely the portion of the CPPL implementation that manipulates communication channels, generates nonces and session keys, and sends and receives messages. Second, we will integrate the trust management semantics for each of the messages. The final step is to specify procedure headers, thereby providing a way to link behaviors together by calling subprotocols. In this example, the benefit is to allow flexibility in retrieval of certified public keys. However, the general ability to encapsulate subprotocols in an informative way appears to us to be one of the major strengths of the CPPL integration of trust management and protocols.

Message Behavior. The client generates a nonce, opens a channel to the server, and then expects to engage in two round trips of sending a message and receiving a reply (Figure 15). The **return** statements here do not carry the parameters and final guarantee, because those will be declared instead in the procedure header. We omit the trust management formulas for now, leaving only underscores in their place.

The server (Figure 16) waits to accept an incoming connection. It then receives a message off that channel, authenticates the claimed sender via a message round trip, and delivers data of one quality or the other, tagged with either Dear or Cheap.

Trust Management Annotations. For readability, we italicize the trust management formulas. The client (Figure 17) guarantees that it is requesting the information in its first outgoing message, and relies on the server having guaranteed the information in its last incoming message, at one of the two possible levels of service.

```
let chan = connect(b_addr) in
let na = new nonce in
  send _ chan {na, a, d} kb
  receive chan {na, k, b} ka _
  send _ chan {k} kb
  receive chan cases
    {Dear v} k _  return
  | {Cheap v} k _ return
end
```

Fig. 15. Client Behavior in NSL Quote

```
let chan = accept in
  receive chan {na, a, d} kb _
  let k = new symkey in
    send _ chan {na, k, b} ka
    receive chan {k} kb _
    send cases
      _ chan {Dear v} k  return
    | _ chan {Cheap v} k return
end
```

Fig. 16. Server Behavior in NSL Quote

```
let chan = connect(b_addr) in
let na = new nonce in
  send [requests(a,b,d)] chan {na, a, d} kb
  receive chan {na, k, b} ka []
  send [] chan {k} kb
  receive chan cases
    {Dear v} k [says_curr_val(b, d, v)]    return
  | {Cheap v} k [says_approx_val(b, d, v)] return
end
```

Fig. 17. Client Trust Management, NSL Quote

The server's trust management behavior is described in Figure 18. The rely formula on the server's first receive statement is empty, i.e. an empty list `[]` meaning *true*, as is required because the adversary may have prepared the message `{na, a, d} kb`. Before the final transmission, the server chooses between the two branches in the send statement according to a trust management formula, guaranteeing payment for the information transmitted, and retrieving a current value for v. If B can establish that A will pay for the high quality data it selects the first branch. If B can establish only that A will pay for the low quality data, it selects the second branch. If B cannot establish even that, for instance because A is not yet a subscriber, then B must fail in this protocol run, terminating abnormally without sending either of these messages, and without returning information to its caller. For either class of service, part of determining whether A will pay for the data is determining whether he has requested it. A crucial authentication service provided by the protocol is to justify B in relying on this conclusion when B receives message three, illustrating the value of protocol soundness. B has one other guarantee in this version of the protocol; he guarantees `owns(a,ka)` asserting that the purported peer in this run is the owner of the public encryption key to be used in this run. This is the first occurrence of the identifier `ka`, reflecting the fact that the guarantee is a query, in the manner of logic programming; it binds the new identifier `ka` to some value k for which the trust management engine can establish that the principal bound to `a` owns k as public encryption key.

Procedure Headers. We encapsulate the behavior of CPPL procedures using headers. The header gives the name of the procedure, the parameters with which it should be called, the parameters that it will return, and two formulas. The first, the *rely* statement, declares the condition under which this procedure may properly be called. It is a relation on the parameters to the call. The caller must guarantee at least this strong a condition before calling the procedure with actual parameters. The second statement is the procedure's *guarantee.* This is a relation on the procedure's input and output parameters, and it defines what the caller has learned by means of the procedure call. The guarantee need only hold on successful termination; failure returns no parameters and guarantees no formula. The server's guarantee *supplied(a, q, d, v)* informs its caller that data has been supplied to a client, so that the client may be billed. The identifier `q` is one of the return parameters; the participants use it to interpret the quality of the information returned in `v`. The identifier `q` occurs only in the return guarantee, and the trust management engine selects a suitable value for it immediately before a successful return. It uses the rules in Figure 20 as an ingredient in selecting its value.The client must additionally use its trust in `b` for this type of data, inferring `curr_val(d, V)` from `says_curr_val(b, d, V)`, and inferring `approx_val(d, V)` from `says_approx_val(b, d, V)`.

```
let chan = accept in
  receive chan {na, a, d} kb []
  let k = new symkey in
    send [owns(a, ka)] chan {na, k, b} ka
    receive chan {k} kb [says_requests(a, a, b, d)]
    send cases
      [will_pay_dear(a, d); curr_val(d, v)] chan {Dear v} k
      return
    | [will_pay_cheap(a, d); approx_val(d, v)] chan {Cheap v} k
      return
end
```

Fig. 18. Server Trust Management, NSL Quote

```
client (a, ka, b, kb, b_addr, d) (na, q, v)
    rely [owns(a, ka); owns(b, kb); at(b, b_addr)]
    guarantee [val(d, q, v)]
  statement, see Figure 17
end

server (b:text, kb) (a, q, d, v)
    rely [owns(b, kb)]
    guarantee [supplied(a, q, d, v)]
  statement, see Figure 18
end
```

Fig. 19. Client and Server Procedure Headers in NSL Quote

```
val(D, "high quality", V) :-
  curr_val(D, V).

val(D, "low quality", V) :-
  approx_val(D, V).
```

Fig. 20. Axioms Governing Quality for NSL Quote

Subprotocols. An advantage of connecting procedures with their trust management pre- and post-conditions in this way is that it leads to attractive notions of subprotocol and of call. We illustrate subprotocols here (Figure 21) by incorporating an optional subprotocol for certificate retrieval when the server B does not have a certificate for the client in its local certificate database. Possibly B would like to increase its clientele; an independent service certifies customers, and delivers the certificates for a fee. B attempts to retrieve the client's public key from its local store; if that succeeds, it calls the `null_protocol`, which does nothing. If the local retrieval fails, it consults the certification service via the `get_public_key` protocol. This protocol may be implemented separately, as the only constraint that the programmer requires is that it should satisfy the interface given in its header. We summarize the protocol's correctness in a soundness assertion. We state it here without being precise about the unique origination and non-origination assumptions that define the set $\mathbb{B}$ of bundles with respect to which soundness holds.

Proposition 8. *The set of* CPPL *procedures displayed in Figures 17–21 is sound for bundles in which the private decryption keys are uncompromised and the newly generated values are uniquely originating.*

Using the disjoint encryption result for protocol composition [20], the soundness of the main protocol depends only on a simple property of the certificate retrieval subprotocol, beyond what is declared in its header.

```
maybe_get_public_key (a:text) (ka:verkey)
    guarantee [owns(a, ka)]
  call cases
    [owns(a, ka)]
      null_protocol () () []
    return
  | [cert_auth(c:text); owns(c, kc:verkey); at(c, c_addr:text)]
      get_public_key (a, c, kc, c_addr) (ka)
      [owns(a, ka)]
    return
end

null_protocol () () return end

get_public_key (a:text, c:text, kc, c_addr) (ka:verkey)
    rely [owns(c, kc); at(c, c_addr)]
    guarantee [owns(a, ka)]
  ... statement ...
end
```

Fig. 21. Subprotocols for Certificate Retrieval

8 The Current CPPL Implementation

We have developed two successive CPPL implementations. The second generation compiler was written after the structured operational semantics presented here in Section 4, and benefited from the concise specification. In both cases, we used OCaml [27] as the implementation language, and the compilers translate a CPPL source file into OCaml. When parsing a source file, the compiler generates an abstract syntax tree modeled after the core syntax given in Figure 2. In particular, it replicates the return parameter list and the guarantee formula in the header for a procedure at each `return` statement within that procedure. Each CPPL procedure is translated into an OCaml procedure that takes a number of CPPL values as arguments and returns a tuple of results.

A full CPPL program is constructed from at least two source files. The first is a CPPL source file used to specify the CPPL procedures. The other is an OCaml source file that defines the main routine invoked when the program is started. This routine generates the principal's theory from a sequence of Datalog [10] formulas, and generates additional Datalog facts by opening a keystore containing public keys. Code generated from both files is linked against three libraries needed at runtime. One is a communications library. It provides the channel abstraction, including code to open channels to specified addresses and to await an incoming connection. Second, the cryptographic library controls the formatting of messages as bitstrings, and provides abstractions of keys and operations for encryption, decryption, hashing, signatures, and verification. Because of the well-defined interfaces, alternative libraries can easily be substituted; we have developed one cryptographic library based on Leroy's Cryptokit [26] and another that provides access to a Trusted Platform Module [35,36], if the latter is available on the underlying hardware.

The third main runtime library is our Datalog [10] trust management engine. Datalog is a declarative logic language in which each formula is a function-free Horn clause, and every variable in the head of a clause must appear in the body of the clause. Our implementation uses the tabled logic programming algorithm described in [11,12]. All queries terminate because of Datalog's syntactic restrictions, and because the implementation maintains a table of intermediate results.

One of the main jobs of the compiler is to translate the message patterns contained in the CPPL source program into executable code. For a message pattern in a receive statement, the generated code must parse incoming messages. The compiler emits code containing calls to the interface procedures exported by the cryptographic library. The emitted code must raise an exception if the incoming message is not of the right form, or if an identifier in the pattern is already bound, and the incoming message contains a different value in that position from the value bound in the runtime environment. For message patterns in transmission statements, the generated code must use the cryptographic library to assemble a suitable concrete message, which is then handed to the communications library for transmission through a channel. When asymmetric cryptography is used in message transmission or reception, the code may require the cryptographic library to use a private key held only in its own keystore. For instance, when the NSL Quote server B parses the message `{na, a, d}kb`, `kb` is bound in the runtime environment. However, parsing succeeds only if the cryptographic library possesses a private decryption key K_B^{-1} inverse to the value K_B bound to `kb`. The private decryption key is not mentioned in CPPL source programs, and it is the obligation of the cryptographic library together with the main routine to ensure that suitable private keys are available. The semantic productions for Send and Receive in Figures 9 and 10 are optimistic, since they do not indicate that these keys may be missing. The Receive production also does not explicitly say that the environment is extended only from values contained as subterms of an incoming message, not from values used only as encryption keys.

A number of different demonstration-sized protocols have been implemented in CPPL, suggesting solutions to different information security problems. Alternative protocols allow adapting the solutions to differing trust relations among the principals.

9 Conclusion

Three central ideas have shaped our approach to CPPL. First, cryptographic protocols are a coordination mechanism between principals. The purpose of a cryptographic protocol is to ensure that principals which have successfully completed their strands are sure to agree on certain values [37,30]. In this view, an authentication property is an assertion about parameters matching between separate strands. "Entity authentication" means agreeing specifically on the parameters naming the principals; "message authentication" for a message t requires agreement on all of the atomic values contained in t. These and other variants of agreement may be proved uniformly using the authentication test theorems (Propositions 4–6). In the case of an annotated protocol, in which nodes are associated with rely and guarantee formulas, an agreement on values also ensures a corresponding degree of agreement between the principals on assertions; we summarize this in the notion of soundness (Definition 7). Many protocols must also establish recency, by ensuring that an event in each local run occurs between two events of each other local run [19]. Recency comes for free from the outgoing test and the solicited incoming test. A cryptographic protocol thus coordinates values, assertions, and time across different strands.

Our second motivating idea was that trust decisions at run time may control a principal's protocol behavior. Each message transmission is associated with a *commitment* that the principal makes if it transmits the message. If the principal cannot derive the trust constraint for a message, then the principal does not send the message. This provides a mechanism for selecting between branches of execution, namely to choose a branch with a derivable guarantee. If there is no such branch, then the principal stops and aborts this protocol run.

Our third central idea was a semantic idea. We gave the semantics for a single protocol procedure as a finite number of parametric strands, each of bounded length. Each regular strand determines a sequence of messages that may have been sent and received by the time the run is complete; these messages are parametrized by the values (keys, nonces, names, prices, etc.) selected in this run. The instances of the parametric strands are determined by the structured operational semantics presented in Section 4. A global execution is a *bundle.* This says that it is a number of regular strands, possibly together with penetrator strands, that are linked together in a causally well founded way (Section 5). A regular (non-penetrator) strand in a bundle represents a sequence of transmissions and receptions enacted by one principal while executing a single session of a single protocol role or subprotocol role. The bundle may use *secure communication,* allowing it to model subprotocol call and return as local, secure message transmissions. In Section 6 we developed useful techniques for determining whether all bundles for a particular set of protocols and subprotocols satisfy security goals.

Future Work. Various areas remain for future work. For instance, our method carefully separates the protocol properties that are used to prove soundness, but not represented in a logic, from the trust management decisions that are logically represented. The advantage of this procedure is that there is a clear boundary between operational reasoning about protocol behavior and logical reasoning within trust theories. However, there is also a disadvantage, since reasoning involving both protocol behavior and its trust consequences is not easily integrated. As an example, if a principal is deciding whether to accept a new protocol, it would be desirable to deduce its acceptability from an explicit policy. We also need a better way to represent the imperative effects that may be the result of a protocol execution, for instance, a bank transferring money from buyer to seller at the end of an electronic commerce transaction. Finally, the current data model of CPPL is extremely impoverished, and an improved language would allow processing of structured data to be integrated with protocol actions and trust decisions.

References

1. Martín Abadi, Bruno Blanchet, and Cédric Fournet. Just Fast Keying in the pi calculus. In David Schmidt, editor, *Programming Languages and Systems: ESOP 2004 Proceedings*, number 2986 in LNCS, pages 340–354. Springer Verlag, January 2004.
2. Martín Abadi, Michael Burrows, Butler Lampson, and Gordon D. Plotkin. A calculus for access control in distributed systems. *ACM Transactions on Programming Languages and Systems*, 15(4):706–34, September 1993.
3. Martín Abadi and Cédric Fournet. Mobile values, new names, and secure communication. In *28th ACM Symposium on Principles of Programming Languages (POPL '01)*, pages 104–115, January 2001.
4. Martín Abadi and Andrew D. Gordon. A calculus for cryptographic protocols: The spi calculus. *Information and Computation*, 148(1):1–70, January 1999.
5. Andrew W. Appel and Edward W. Felten. Proof-carrying authentication. In *6th ACM Conference on Computer and Communications Security*, November 1999.
6. Bruno Blanchet and Andreas Podelski. Verification of cryptographic protocols: Tagging enforces termination. In Andrew D. Gordon, editor, *Foundations of Software Science and Computation Structures*, number 2620 in LNCS, pages 136–152. Springer, April 2003.
7. Matt Blaze, Joan Feigenbaum, and Jack Lacy. Distributed trust management. In *Proceedings, 1996 IEEE Symposium on Security and Privacy*, pages 164–173, May 1997.
8. Michele Boreale. Symbolic trace analysis of cryptographic protocols. In *ICALP*, 2001.
9. Philippa Broadfoot and Gavin Lowe. On distributed security transactions that use secure transport protocols. In *Proceedings, 16th Computer Security Foundations Workshop*, pages 63–73. IEEE CS Press, 2003.
10. Stefano Ceri, Georg Gottlob, and Letizia Tanca. What you always wanted to know about datalog (and never dared to ask). *IEEE Transactions of Knowledge and Data Engineering*, 1(1), 1989.
11. W. Chen, T. Swift, and D. S. Warren. Efficient top-down computation of queries under the well-founded semantics. *J. Logic Prog.*, 24(3):161–199, 1995.
12. W. Chen and D. S. Warren. Tabled evaluation with delaying for general logic programs. *J. ACM*, 43(1):20–74, 1996.
13. Federico Crazzolara and Giuseppe Milicia. Developing security protocols in χ-spaces. In *Proceedings, 7th Nordic Workshop on Secure IT Systems*, Karlstad, Sweden, November 2002.
14. Federico Crazzolara and Glynn Winskel. Composing strand spaces. In *Proceedings, Foundations of Software Technology and Theoretical Computer Science*, number 2556 in LNCS, pages 97–108, Kanpur, December 2002. Springer Verlag.
15. Daniel Dolev and Andrew Yao. On the security of public-key protocols. *IEEE Transactions on Information Theory*, 29:198–208, 1983.

16. Nancy Durgin, Patrick Lincoln, John Mitchell, and Andre Scedrov. Multiset rewriting and the complexity of bounded security protocols. *Journal of Computer Security*, 12(2):247–311, 2004. Initial version appeared in *Workshop on Formal Methods and Security Protocols*, 1999.
17. Cédric Fournet, Andrew Gordon, and Sergei Maffeis. A type discipline for authorization policies. In Mooly Sagiv, editor, *European Symposium on Programming*, volume 3444 of *LNCS*, pages 141–156. Springer Verlag, 2005.
18. Andrew D. Gordon and Alan Jeffrey. Types and effects for asymmetric cryptographic protocols. In *Proceedings, 15th Computer Security Foundations Workshop*. IEEE Computer Society Press, June 2002.
19. Joshua D. Guttman. Key compromise and the authentication tests. *Electronic Notes in Theoretical Computer Science*, 47, 2001. Editor, M. Mislove. URL `http://www.elsevier.nl/locate/entcs/volume47.html`, 21 pages.
20. Joshua D. Guttman and F. Javier Thayer. Protocol independence through disjoint encryption. In *Proceedings, 13th Computer Security Foundations Workshop*. IEEE Computer Society Press, July 2000.
21. Joshua D. Guttman and F. Javier Thayer. Authentication tests and the structure of bundles. *Theoretical Computer Science*, 283(2):333–380, June 2002.
22. Joshua D. Guttman and F. Javier Thayer. The sizes of skeletons: Decidable cryptographic protocol authentication and secrecy goals. MTR 05B09 Revision 1, The MITRE Corporation, March 2005.
23. Joshua D. Guttman, F. Javier Thayer, Jay A. Carlson, Jonathan C. Herzog, John D. Ramsdell, and Brian T. Sniffen. Trust management in strand spaces: A rely-guarantee method. In David Schmidt, editor, *Programming Languages and Systems: 13th European Symposium on Programming*, number 2986 in LNCS, pages 325–339. Springer, 2004.
24. Charlie Kaufman, ed. Internet key exchange (IKEv2) protocol. Internet Draft, September 2004. Available at `http://www.ietf.org/internet-drafts/draft-ietf-ipsec-ikev2-17.txt`.
25. Butler Lampson, Martín Abadi, Michael Burrows, and Edward Wobber. Authentication in distributed systems: Theory and practice. *ACM Transactions on Computer Systems*, 10(4):265–310, November 1992.
26. Xavier Leroy. Cryptokit. Sofwtare available via `http://pauillac.inria.fr/~xleroy/software.html`, April 2005. Version 1.3.
27. Xavier Leroy, Damien Doligez, Jacques Garrigue, Didier Rémy, and Jérôme Vouillon. *The Objective Caml System*. INRIA, `http://caml.inria.fr/`, 2000. Version 3.00.
28. Ninghui Li, John C. Mitchell, and William H. Winsborough. Design of a role-based trust management framework. In *Proceedings, 2002 IEEE Symposium on Security and Privacy*, pages 114–130. May, IEEE Computer Society Press, 2002.
29. Gavin Lowe. An attack on the Needham-Schroeder public key authentication protocol. *Information Processing Letters*, 56(3):131–136, November 1995.
30. Gavin Lowe. A hierarchy of authentication specifications. In *10th Computer Security Foundations Workshop Proceedings*, pages 31–43. IEEE Computer Society Press, 1997.
31. Jonathan Millen and Frederic Muller. Cryptographic protocol generation from CAPSL. Technical Report SRI-CSL-01-07, SRI International, December 2001.
32. Roger Needham and Michael Schroeder. Using encryption for authentication in large networks of computers. *Communications of the ACM*, 21(12), December 1978.

33. Adrian Perrig and Dawn Xiaodong Song. A first step toward the automatic generation of security protocols. In *Network and Distributed System Security Symposium*. Internet Society, February 2000.

34. F. Javier Thayer, Jonathan C. Herzog, and Joshua D. Guttman. Strand spaces: Proving security protocols correct. *Journal of Computer Security*, 7(2/3):191–230, 1999.

35. Trusted Computing Group, `https://www.trustedcomputinggroup.org/downloads/TCG_1_0_Architecture_Ov%erview.pdf`. *TCG Specification Architecture Overview*, revision 1.2 edition, April 2004.

36. Trusted Computing Group, `https://www.trustedcomputinggroup.org/downloads/specifications/mainP1DP%_rev85.zip`. *TPM Main: Part I Design Principles*, specification version 1.2, revision 85 edition, February 2005.

37. T. Y. C. Woo and S. S. Lam. Authentication for distributed systems. *Computer*, 25(1):39–52, January 1992.

A Additional Strand Notions

Definition 8. *Fix a strand space Σ:*

1. *The subterm relation $\sqsubset$ is the smallest reflexive, transitive relation such that $t \sqsubset \{\!|g|\!\}_K$ if $t \sqsubset g$, and $t \sqsubset g,\ h$ if either $a \sqsubset g$ or $a \sqsubset h$.*
   (Hence, for $K \in \mathsf{K}$, we have $K \sqsubset \{\!|g|\!\}_K$ only if $K \sqsubset g$ already.)
2. *A* node *is a pair $\langle s, i\rangle$, with $s \in \Sigma$ and i an integer satisfying $1 \leq i \leq \mathsf{length}(tr(s))$. We often write $s \downarrow i$ for $\langle s, i\rangle$. The set of nodes is $\mathcal{N}$. The* directed term *of $s \downarrow i$ is $\mathsf{tr}(s)(i)$.*
3. *There is an edge $n_1 \rightarrow n_2$ iff $term(n_1) = +t$ or $+_c\, t$ and $term(n_2) = -t$ or $-_a\, t$ for $t \in \mathsf{A}$. $n_1 \Rightarrow n_2$ means $n_1 = s \downarrow i$ and $n_2 = s \downarrow i+1 \in \mathcal{N}$.*
   $n_1 \Rightarrow^* n_2$ (respectively, $n_1 \Rightarrow^+ n_2$) means that $n_1 = s \downarrow i$ and $n_2 = s \downarrow j \in \mathcal{N}$ for some s and $j \geq i$ (respectively, $j > i$).
4. *Suppose I is a set of terms. The node $n \in \mathcal{N}$ is an* entry point *for I iff $term(n) = +t$ for some $t \in I$, and whenever $n' \Rightarrow^+ n$, $term(n') \notin I$. t* originates *on $n \in \mathcal{N}$ iff n is an entry point for $I = \{t' : t \sqsubset t'\}$.*
5. *An term t is* uniquely originating *in $S \subset \mathcal{N}$ iff there is a unique $n \in S$ such that t originates on n, and* non-originating *if there is no such $n \in S$.*

If a term t originates uniquely in a suitable set of nodes, then it plays the role of a nonce or session key. If it is non-originating, it can serve as a long-term shared symmetric key or a private asymmetric key.

Definition 9. *A* penetrator strand *is a strand s such that $\mathsf{tr}(s)$ is one of the following:*

M_t: $\langle +t \rangle$ *where* $t \in$*text*
K_K: $\langle +K \rangle$ *where* $K \in \mathsf{K}_{\mathcal{P}}$
$\mathsf{C}_{g,h}$: $\langle -g,\ -h,\ +g,\ h \rangle$
$\mathsf{S}_{g,h}$: $\langle -g,\ h,\ +g,\ +h \rangle$
$\mathsf{E}_{h,K}$: $\langle -K,\ -h,\ +\{\!|h|\!\}_K \rangle$
$\mathsf{D}_{h,K}$: $\langle -K^{-1},\ -\{\!|h|\!\}_K,\ +h \rangle$
$\mathsf{V}_{h,K}$: $\langle -[\![\, h \,]\!]_K,\ +h \rangle$
$\mathsf{A}_{h,K}$: $\langle -K^{-1},\ -h,\ +[\![\, h \,]\!]_K \rangle$
H_h: $\langle -h,\ +\mathsf{hash}(h) \rangle$
TC_h: $\langle -h,\ +\mathsf{tag\ h} \rangle$
TS_h: $\langle -\mathsf{tag\ h},\ +h \rangle$

A node is a penetrator node *if it lies on a penetrator strand, and otherwise it is a* regular *node.*

A Framework for Analyzing Probabilistic Protocols and Its Application to the Partial Secrets Exchange*

Konstantinos Chatzikokolakis and Catuscia Palamidessi

LIX, École Polytechnique, 91128 Palaiseau, France
{kostas, catuscia}@lix.polytechnique.fr

Abstract. We propose a probabilistic variant of the pi-calculus as a framework to specify randomized security protocols and their intended properties. In order to express an verify the correctness of the protocols, we develop a probabilistic version of the testing semantics. We then illustrate these concepts on an extended example: the Partial Secret Exchange, a protocol which uses a randomized primitive, the Oblivious Transfer, to achieve fairness of information exchange between two parties.

1 Introduction

Probabilistic security protocols involve *probabilistic choices* and are used for many purposes including signing contracts, sending certified email and protecting the anonymity of communication agents. Some probabilistic protocols rely on specific random primitives such as the *Oblivious Transfer* ([1]). There are various examples in this category, notably the contract signing protocol in [2] and the privacy-preserving auction protocol in [3].

A large effort has been dedicated to the formal verification of security protocols, and several approaches based on process-calculi techniques have been proposed. However, in the particular case of probabilistic protocols, they have been analyzed mainly by using model checking methods, while only few attempts of applying process calculi techniques have been made. One proposal of this kind is [4], which defines a probabilistic version of the noninterference property, and uses a probabilistic variant of CCS and of bisimulation to analyze protocols wrt this property.

In this paper we present a framework for analyzing probabilistic security protocols using the π_{prob}-calculus, a probabilistic extension of the π-calculus inspired by the work in [5]. In order to express security properties in this calculus, we extend the notion of testing equivalence ([6]) to the probabilistic setting. We propose a preorder based on the probability of passing a certain class of tests: a process P is considered smaller than a process Q if, for each test, the probability

* Supported by the Project Rossignol of the ACI Sécurité Informatique (Ministère de la recherche et nouvelles technologies)

R. De Nicola and D. Sangiorgi (Eds.): TGC 2005, LNCS 3705, pp. 146–162, 2005.

of passing the test is smaller for P than for Q. Following the lines of [7], a test can be seen as an adversary who interacts with an agent in order to break some security property. In order to verify a security property, then, we can create a specification which satisfies the property and show that the protocol is smaller than the specification with respect to the testing preorder. If this holds, then the adversary has smaller probability of succeeding with the protocol than with the specification, so the protocol is correct with respect to the intended property.

We illustrate the framework with an extended example of fair exchange protocol, where the property to verify is fairness. In this kind of protocol two agents, A and B, want to exchange information simultaneously, namely each of them is willing to send its secrets only if he receives the ones of the other party. We consider the Partial Secrets Exchange protocol (PSE, [2]) which uses the Oblivious Transfer as its main primitive. An important characteristic of the fair exchange protocols is that the adversary is in fact one of the agents and not an external party. As a consequence the behavior of A will be different when B behaves normally from the case in which B is trying to cheat. After encoding the protocol in the π_{prob}-calculus, we give a specification which models the behavior of A in case he is being cheated (the non-cheating case is straightforward). We then express fairness by means of a testing relation between the protocol and the specification and we prove that it holds.

The rest of the paper is organized as follows: in the next section we introduce π_{prob}, our variant of the probabilistic π-calculus. We present its semantics and propose a notion of probabilistic testing preorder. In Section 3 we illustrate the Oblivious Transfer primitive, the Partial Secrets Exchange protocol (PSE), and their encoding in the π_{prob}-calculus. In Section 4 we specify the fairness property and we prove the correctness of PSE. In Section 5 we discuss related work, notably the analysis of the PSE protocol using probabilistic model checking. Finally, Section 6 concludes and presents some ideas for future work.

For reasons of space, the proofs have been removed from the main text. They can be found in the report version of this paper ([8]).

2 A Probabilistic Variant of π-Calculus

In this section we define a probabilistic process calculus suitable for implementing security protocols. This calculus, which will be referred as the π_{prob}-calculus, is a probabilistic extension of the π-calculus, similar to the probabilistic asynchronous π-calculus presented in [5].

A common feature of π_{prob} and the calculus in [5] is that there is a distinction between probabilistic and deterministic behavior. The former, represented by the choice operator, is associated with the random choices performed by the process itself. The latter, represented by the parallel operator, is related to the decisions of an external scheduler.

The π_{prob}-calculus differs from the calculus in [5] in that it allows only blind (probabilistic) choices. This simplifies considerably semantics and reasoning, while the calculus remains rich enough to model probabilistic security protocols. Furthermore, the π_{prob}-calculus contains some extra constructs, like output prefix and pair splitting, that are useful to express the protocols we have considered.

We could also add certain cryptographic primitives like the shared-key encryption of the spi-calculus, however this is not necessary for the protocols considered in this paper.

2.1 Syntax

Let x, y range over a countable set of variables and n, m over a countable set of *channel names*. The terms and processes of the π_{prob}-calculus are defined by the following grammar:

$M, N ::=$	**terms**	$P, Q ::=$	**processes**
x	variable	$\overline{M}N.P$	output
$\mid n$	name	$\mid M(x).P$	input
$\mid \langle M, N\rangle$	pair	$\mid P \mid Q$	composition
		$\mid \sum_i p_i P_i$	prob. choice
		$\mid \nu n P$	restriction
		$\mid !P$	replication
		$\mid [M \text{ is } N]P$	match
		$\mid \text{let } \langle x, y\rangle = M \text{ in } P$	pair splitting
		$\mid 0$	nil

The distinction between variables and channel names does not exist in the original π-calculus but simplifies the treatment of some relations.

2.2 Probabilistic Automata

The semantics of π_{prob} is based on Probabilistic Automata, which were introduced in [9]. We briefly recall here the main notions, simplified and adapted for our needs.

A *discrete probabilistic space* is a pair (X, pb) where X is a set and pb a function $pb : X \mapsto (0, 1]$ s.t. $\sum_{x \in X} pb(x) = 1$. Given a set Y we define the set of all probabilistic spaces on Y:

$$Prob(Y) = \{(X, pb) \mid X \subseteq Y \text{ and } (X, pb) \text{ is a discrete probabilistic space}\}$$

Let S be a set of states and A a set of actions. A *probabilistic automaton* is a triple $(S, \mathcal{T}, s_0)$ where $s_0 \in S$ (initial state) and $\mathcal{T} \subseteq S \times Prob(A \times S)$. The elements of $\mathcal{T}$ are called *transition groups* or *steps*. The idea is that the choice between transition groups is made non-deterministically by an external scheduler while the choice of a transition within a group is made probabilistically by the process itself.[1]

Given a probabilistic automaton $M = (\mathcal{S}, \mathcal{T}, s_0)$ we define $tree(M)$ as the tree obtained by unfolding the transition system. The root n_0 of $tree(M)$ is labeled by s_0 and if n is a node labeled by s then for each $(s, (X, pb)) \in \mathcal{T}$ and each $(\mu, s') \in X$ there is a node n' labeled by s' and an arc from n to n' labeled by μ and $pb(\mu, s')$.

A *scheduler* ζ is a function which solves the nondeterminism by selecting, at each moment of the computation, a transition group among the ones allowed at the current state. The *execution tree* of an automaton M under a scheduler ζ, denoted by $etree(M, \zeta)$ is the tree obtained from $tree(M)$ by pruning all the arcs corresponding to transitions in groups not selected by ζ.

2.3 Semantics of π_{prob}

The operational semantics of the π_{prob}-calculus is given by means of probabilistic automata defined inductively on the basis of the syntax. In order to simplify the notation, we write

$$s\ \{\xrightarrow[p_i]{\mu_i} s_i \mid i \in I\}$$

iff $(s, (\{(\mu_i, s_i) \mid i \in I\}, pb)) \in \mathcal{T}$ and $\forall i \in I : p_i = pb(\mu_i, s_i)$, where I is an index set. When I is not relevant we will use the notation $s\ \{\xrightarrow[p_i]{\mu_i} s_i\}_i$.

The transitions of the automaton associated to a process are defined by the rules in Figure 1.

The behavior of the choice operator is defined by the SUM rule. The transition to every member of the sum is possible with a τ action (blind choice). Note that all transitions belong to the same group which means that the choice is not controlled by the scheduler but is made by the process itself. IN and OUT are self-explanatory. The RES rules model restriction on channel n: actions on that channel are not allowed by the restricted process. Note that we have two rules for the sake of clarity: for the transition groups which contain only τ actions there is no need to check the channel name. PAR models interleaving, in which each process maintains its transition groups. COM models communication by handshaking. Since input/output transitions are always alone in their group, this rule is rather simple and very similar to the non-probabilistic case. CLOSE is similar to COM but works together with OPEN in order to implement scope extrusion, that is the transfer of a new channel name between processes. Finally CONG states that equivalent processes perform the same actions. The *structural equivalence* $\equiv$ used in CONG is defined as follows:

[1] For π_{prob} we actually need only a subset of P.A., namely we can restrict to the case in which the second composant of a transition is either a singleton (a probabilistic distribution which is 1 on exactly one pair label-state) or it is a distribution which is positive only on τ labels. This restricted class of automata is similar (although not identical) to the so-called *simple probabilistic automata*.

$$\text{IN} \quad m(x).P \, \{\xrightarrow[1]{m(x)} P\} \qquad\qquad \text{OUT} \quad \overline{m}M.P \, \{\xrightarrow[1]{\overline{m}M} P\}$$

$$\text{SUM} \quad \textstyle\sum_i p_i P_i \, \{\xrightarrow[p_i]{\tau} P_i\}_i \qquad\qquad \text{OPEN} \quad \frac{P \, \{\xrightarrow[1]{\overline{m}n} P'\}}{\nu n P \, \{\xrightarrow[1]{\overline{m}(n)} P'\}} \quad m \neq n$$

$$\text{RES1} \quad \frac{P \, \{\xrightarrow[1]{\mu} P'\}}{\nu n P \, \{\xrightarrow[1]{\mu} \nu n P'\}} \quad {\scriptstyle \mu \neq \tau, \; n \notin nm(\mu)} \qquad\qquad \text{RES2} \quad \frac{P \, \{\xrightarrow[p_i]{\tau} P_i\}_i}{\nu n P \, \{\xrightarrow[p_i]{\tau} \nu n P_i\}_i}$$

$$\text{COM} \quad \frac{P \, \{\xrightarrow[1]{\overline{m}M} P'\} \qquad Q \, \{\xrightarrow[1]{m(x)} Q'\}}{P \mid Q \, \{\xrightarrow[1]{\tau} P' \mid Q'[M/x]\}} \qquad\qquad \text{PAR} \quad \frac{P \, \{\xrightarrow[p_i]{\mu_i} P_i\}_i}{P \mid Q \, \{\xrightarrow[p_i]{\mu_i} P_i \mid Q\}_i} \quad \forall i \; fn(\mu_i) \cap bn(Q) = \emptyset$$

$$\text{CLOSE} \quad \frac{P \, \{\xrightarrow[1]{\overline{m}(n)} P'\} \qquad Q \, \{\xrightarrow[1]{m(x)} Q'\}}{P \mid Q \, \{\xrightarrow[1]{\tau} \nu n(P' \mid Q'[n/x])\}} \qquad\qquad \text{CONG} \quad \frac{P \equiv P' \quad P' \, \{\xrightarrow[p_i]{\mu_i} Q'_i\}_i \quad \forall i. Q'_i \equiv Q_i}{P \, \{\xrightarrow[p_i]{\mu_i} Q_i\}_i}$$

Fig. 1. The late-instantiation semantics of the π_{prob}-calculus. The functions *fn*,*bn* and *nm* give the free, bound and total names of their argument respectively.

$$\begin{array}{llr} (\alpha\text{-renaming}) & P \equiv Q \quad \text{iff } P \equiv_\alpha Q & P \mid Q \equiv Q \mid P \\ & P \mid 0 \equiv P & !P \equiv P \mid !P \\ \multicolumn{2}{l}{\text{let } \langle x, y\rangle = \langle M, N\rangle \text{ in } P \equiv P[M/x][N/y]} & [M \text{ is } M]P \equiv P \end{array}$$

In the following sections we define some relations between π_{prob} processes which will help us expressing some properties of probabilistic protocols and reasoning about them. We will also examine some properties of these relations.

2.4 Testing Relations Between π_{prob} Processes

Testing is a well-known method of comparing processes, resulting in equivalences weaker than the ones of the bisimulation family. The idea, proposed by De Nicola and Hennessy ([6]), is that two processes are equivalent if they both pass the same set of tests. A *test* is a process running in parallel with the one being tested and which can perform a distinguished action ω that represents success. This idea is very useful for the analysis of security protocols, as suggested in [7], since a test can be seen as an adversary who interferes with a communication agent and declares his success with an ω action. Then two processes are testing equivalent if they are vulnerable to the same attacks.

In the probabilistic setting there are different approaches for defining testing equivalence. For example [10] proposes a probabilistic extension of testing equivalence which considers the ability of each process to pass a test with non-zero probability (may testing) or probability one (must testing). However, when analyzing security protocols we are not only interested in the ability of passing a test, but also in the exact probability of success. Thus our definition resembles more the one of [11] and the result is no longer an equivalence but a preorder.

We start by defining the probability of a set of executions. Given a probabilistic automaton M and a scheduler ζ, an *execution fragment* ξ is a path (finite or infinite) from the root of $etree(M, \zeta)$. The probability of an execution fragment $\xi = n_0 \xrightarrow[p_0]{\mu_0} n_1 \xrightarrow[p_1]{\mu_1} n_2 \xrightarrow[p_2]{\mu_2} \ldots$ is defined as $pb(\xi) = \prod_i p_i$. An *execution* is a maximal execution fragment. The set of all executions of M under ζ is denoted by $exec(M, \zeta)$.

Given an execution fragment ξ, a *cone* with prefix ξ is defined as $C_\xi = \{\xi' \in exec(M, \zeta) \mid \xi \leq \xi'\}$ where $\leq$ is the prefix relation. We define $pb(C_\xi) = pb(\xi)$. Let $\{C_i\}_{i \in I}$ be a countable set of disjoint cones. We define $pb(\bigcup_{i \in I} C_i) = \sum_{i \in I} pb(C_i)$. We can show that this probability is well defined, that is two different sets of disjoint cones with the same union give the same probability.

A *test* O is a π_{prob}-calculus process able to perform a distinguished action ω. An *interaction* between O and a process P is a sequence of τ transitions starting from $P|O$. In order to allow only τ actions we define $\nu P = \nu n_1 \ldots \nu n_k P$, where $n_1, \ldots, n_k$ are all the free names in P. Then an interaction between P and O is an element of $exec(\nu(P|O), \zeta)^2$:

$$\nu(P|O) = Q_0 \xrightarrow[p_0]{\tau} Q_1 \xrightarrow[p_1]{\tau} Q_2 \xrightarrow[p_2]{\tau} \ldots$$

An interaction ξ is *successful* if $Q_i \xrightarrow[p]{\omega}$ for some i. Let $sexec(\nu(P|O), \zeta) = \{\xi \in exec(\nu(P|O), \zeta) \mid \xi \text{ is successful}\}$. This set can be obtained as a countable union of disjoint cones ([5]), so the probability of a successful execution can be defined as $pb(sexec(\nu(P|O), \zeta))$.

We now define the upper and lower probability for P to pass O.

Definition 1. *Let P be a process and O a test. We define*

$$P\lceil O\rceil = \sup\{pb(sexec(\nu(P \mid O), \zeta)) \mid \zeta \textit{ is a scheduler}\}$$
$$P\lfloor O\rfloor = \inf\{pb(sexec(\nu(P \mid O), \zeta)) \mid \zeta \textit{ is a scheduler}\}$$

Then we define the testing preorders for π_{prob}-processes.

Definition 2. *Let P, Q be processes. We define must and may-testing preorders as follows:*

$$P \sqsubseteq_{may} Q \quad \textit{iff for all tests } O : P\lceil O\rceil \leq Q\lceil O\rceil$$
$$P \sqsubseteq_{must} Q \quad \textit{iff for all tests } O : P\lfloor O\rfloor \leq Q\lfloor O\rfloor$$

In this paper we will only use may-testing to express safety properties of security protocols, so we will write just $\sqsubseteq$ for $\sqsubseteq_{\mathbf{may}}$.

As we will see in the following sections, an agent in the PSE protocol behaves differently when his partner deviates from the protocol in an attempt to cheat. In order to model this behavior we introduce a *conditional testing preorder*, which is exactly the same as may-testing except that it only considers tests that satisfy a certain condition.

2 With a slight abuse of notation we will sometimes use a process to denote its corresponding probabilistic automaton.

Definition 3. *Let P, Q be processes. We define the conditional may-testing preorder as follows:*

$$P \sqsubseteq^{\phi} Q \quad \textit{iff for all tests } O : \phi(O) \Rightarrow P\lceil O\rceil \leq Q\lceil O\rceil$$

where $\phi(O)$ is a condition on O.

Finally we define a useful preorder between pairs of processes:

Definition 4. *Let P_1, P_2, Q_1, Q_2 be processes. We define the relation $\sqsubseteq_p$ between pairs of processes as follows*

$$(P_1, P_2) \sqsubseteq_p (Q_1, Q_2) \quad \textit{iff} \quad P_1 +_p P_2 \sqsubseteq Q_1 +_p Q_2$$

where $P_1 +_p P_2$ stands for $\sum_{i=1}^{2} p_i P_i$ with $p_1 = p$ and $p_2 = 1 - p$.

2.5 Properties of Testing Preorders

In this section we examine some properties of the previously defined relations. We present only the corresponding lemmas, all proofs can be found in [8].

The following lemma is very useful for reasoning about the upper probability of passing a test. It crucially relies on the fact that in π_{prob} probabilistic choices are blind.

Lemma 1. *Let P, Q be π_{prob} processes and $p \in [0, 1]$. Then for all tests O*

$$P +_p Q\lceil O\rceil = pP\lceil O\rceil + (1 - p)Q\lceil O\rceil$$

A *context* C is a process containing a "hole". We will denote by $C[P]$ the process obtained by replacing the hole in C by P. A preorder is a *precongruence* if it is closed under any context. May-testing is not a precongruence on arbitrary processes since for $P = [x \text{ is } y]P', Q = [x \text{ is } z]Q', C = n(x).[\,]$, we have $P \sqsubseteq Q$ but $C[P] \sqsubseteq C[Q]$ does not hold for all P', Q'. However all previous relations become precongruences if we restrict to closed processes.

Definition 5. *A process is called* closed *if it contains no free variables.*

Remark 1. Because of the distinction between variables and channel names, a closed process can still have free channel names and therefore be able to communicate with the environment.

Lemma 2. *$\sqsubseteq$ is a precongruence on closed processes.*

The following lemma states that all probabilistic choices can be made in the begging of the execution.

Lemma 3. *Let P, Q be π_{prob} processes and $p \in [0, 1]$. Then for all contexts C:*

$$C[P +_p Q] \simeq C[P] +_p C[Q]$$

where $\simeq$ is the equivalence induced by $\sqsubseteq$.

Finally, the following corollary is a consequence of lemmas 2 and 3.

Corollary 1. *$\sqsubseteq_p$ is a precongruence on closed processes, that is for all contexts C and all closed processes P_1, P_2, Q_1, Q_2*

$$(P_1, P_2) \sqsubseteq_p (Q_1, Q_2) \Rightarrow (C[P_1], C[P_2]) \sqsubseteq_p (C[Q_1], C[Q_2])$$

3 Probabilistic Security Protocols

In this section we discuss probabilistic security protocols based on the Oblivious Transfer and we show how to model them using the π_{prob}-calculus.

3.1 1-out-of-2 Oblivious Transfer

The Oblivious Transfer is a primitive operation used in various probabilistic security protocols. In this particular version a sender A sends exactly one of the messages M_1, M_2 to a receiver B. The latter receives i and M_i where i is 1 or 2, each with probability 1/2. Moreover A should get no information about which message was received by B. More precisely the protocol $\mathrm{OT}^1_2(A, B, M_1, M_2)$ should satisfy the following conditions:

1. If A executes $\mathrm{OT}^1_2(A, B, M_1, M_2)$ properly then B receives exactly one message, $(1, M_1)$ or $(2, M_2)$, each with probability 1/2.
2. After the execution of $\mathrm{OT}^1_2(A, B, M_1, M_2)$, if it is properly executed, for A the probability that B got M_i remains 1/2.
3. If A deviates from the protocol, in order to increase his probability of learning what B received, then B can detect his attempt with probability at least 1/2.

It is worth noting that in the literature the reception of the index i by B is often not mentioned, at least not explicitly ([2]). However, omitting the index can lead to possible attacks. Consider the case where A executes (properly) $\mathrm{OT}^1_2(M_1, M_1)$. Then B will receive M_1 with probability one, but he cannot distinguish it from the case where he receives M_1 as a result of $\mathrm{OT}^1_2(M_1, M_2)$. So A is forcing B to receive M_1. We will see that, in the case of the PSE protocol, A could exploit this situation in order to get an unfair advantage. Note that the condition 3 does not apply to this situation since this cannot be considered as a deviation from the Oblivious Transfer. A generic implementation of the Oblivious Transfer could not detect such behavior since A executes OT properly, the problem lies only in the data being transfered.

Using the indexes, however, solves the problem since B will receive $(2, M_1)$ with probability one half. This is distinguishable from any outcome of $\mathrm{OT}^1_2(M_1, M_1)$ so, in the case of PSE, B could detect that he's being cheated. Implementations of the Oblivious Transfer do provide the index information, even though sometimes it is not mentioned ([2]). In other formulations of the OT the receiver can actually select which message he wants to receive, so this problem is irrelevant.

Encoding in the π_{prob}-calculus. The Oblivious Transfer can be implemented in the π_{prob}-calculus, using the probabilistic choice operator. In order to make it impossible to cheat, a server process is used to coordinate the transfer. The processes of the sender and the server are the following:

$$\mathrm{OT}^1_2(m_1, m_2, c_{as}) \triangleq \overline{c_{as}} m_1 . \overline{c_{as}} m_2 . 0$$

$$S(c_{as}, c_{sb}) \triangleq c_{as}(m_1) . c_{as}(m_2) . (\overline{c_{bs}}\langle 1, m_1\rangle +_{0.5} \overline{c_{bs}}\langle 2, m_2\rangle)$$

```
PSE (A, B, {a_i}_i, {b_i}_i) {
    for i = 1 to n do
        OT½(A,B, a_i, a_{i+n})
        OT½(B, A, b_i, b_{i+n})
    next
    for j = 1 to m do
        for i = 1 to 2n do
            A sends jth bit of a_i to B
        for i = 1 to 2n do
            B sends jth bit of b_i to B
    next
}
```

Fig. 2. Partial Secrets Exchange protocol

where m_1, m_2 are the names to be sent. c_{as} is a channel private to A and S and c_{sb} a channel private to B and S. Each agent communicates only with the server and not directly with the other agent. B receives the message from the server (which should be in parallel with A and B) by making an input action on c_{sb}.

It is easy to see that these processes correctly implement the Oblivious Transfer. The only requirement is that A should not contain c_{sb}, so that he can only communicate with B through the server.

3.2 Partial Secrets Exchange Protocol

This protocol is the core of three probabilistic protocols for contract signing, certified email and coin tossing, all presented in [2]. It involves two agents, each having $2n$ secrets split in pairs, $(a_1, a_{n+1}), \ldots, (a_n, a_{2n})$ for A and $(b_1, b_{n+1}), \ldots,$ (b_n, b_{2n}) for B. Each secret consists of m bits. The purpose is to exchange a single pair of secrets under the constraint that, if at a specific time B has one of A's pairs, then with high probability A should also have one of B's pairs and vice versa.

The protocol, displayed in figure 2, consists of two parts. During the first A and B exchange their pairs of secrets using OT^1_2. After this step A knows exactly one half of each of B's pairs and vice versa. During the second part, all secrets are exchanged bit per bit. Half of the bits received are already known from the first step, so both agents can check whether they are valid. Obviously, if both A and B execute the protocol properly then all secrets are revealed.

The problem arises when B tries to cheat and sends incorrectly some of his secrets. In this case it can be proved that with high probability some of the tests of A will fail causing A to stop the execution of the protocol and avoid revealing his secrets. The idea is that, in order for B to cheat, he must send at least one half of each of his pairs incorrectly. However he cannot know which of the two halves is already received by A during the first part of the protocol. So a pair sent incorrectly will have only one half probability of being accepted by A, leading to a total 2^{-n} probability of success.

Now imagine, as discussed in section 3.1, that B executes $\mathrm{OT}^1_2(B, A, b_i, b_i)$, thus forcing A to receive b_i. Now, in the second part, he can send all $\{b_{i+n} \mid 1 \leq i \leq n\}$ incorrectly without failing any test. Moreover A cannot detect this situation. If indexes are available A will receive $(2, b_{i+n})$ with probability one half and since he knows that b_{i+n} is not the second half of the corresponding pair he will stop the protocol.

Encoding in the π_{prob}-calculus. In this paragraph we present an encoding of the PSE protocol in the π_{prob}-calculus. Before giving the corresponding process there are two points worth discussing.

- The secrets exchanged by PSE should be *recognizable*, which means that agent A cannot compute B's secrets, but he can recognize them when he receives them. Of course a secret can be recognized only as a whole, no single bit can be recognized by itself. To implement this feature we allow B's secrets to appear in A's process, as if A knew them. However we allow a secret to appear only as a whole (not decomposed) and only inside a test construct, which means that it can only be used to recognize another message.
- In our analysis we need to detect the fact that an agent sends a specific bit in a certain position of a specific message. Thus, in the implementation of PSE, each parameter a_{ij} (resp. b_{ij}) is considered to take values from the domain $\{0_{ij}, 1_{ij}\}$, where 0_{ij} (resp. 1_{ij}) is a public channel but different for each i, j.

  Note that having secrets composed by public bits can lead to guessing attacks by non-deterministic adversaries. Many analysis tools for security protocols, such as the spi-calculus, do not allow the decomposition of secrets to avoid such guesses. In our analysis, however, we express the correctness of a protocol as the equivalence with a properly constructed specification. This only proves that the protocol will not *reveal* any secrets and is not related with the adversary's ability of *guessing* the secrets without interfering with any partner (of course, this is known to happen with very small probability). Such attacks will apply to both the protocol and the specification.

The encoding for the general case of n pairs and m bits per message is displayed in figure 3. We denote by a_i (resp. b_i) the i-th secret of A (resp. B) and by a_{ij} (resp. b_{ij}) the j-th bit of a_i (resp. b_i). r_i is the i-th message received by Oblivious Transfer and k_i is the corresponding index.

The first part consists of the first 4 lines of the process definition. In this part A sends his pairs using OT^1_2, receives the ones of B and decomposes them. To check the received messages A starts a loop of n steps, each of whom is guarded by an input action on q_i for synchronization. During the i-th step, r_i is tested against b_i or b_{i+n} depending on the outcome of the OT, that is on the value of k_i. The qs_i channels are used to send the values to test to the $TestOT$ sub-process.[3]

The second part consists of a loop of m steps, each of whom is guarded by an input action on s_j. During each step the j-th bit of each secret is sent

[3] Note that we use the syntax $c(\langle x1, \ldots, xn \rangle).P$ for $c(x).\mathrm{let}\ \langle x_1, \ldots, x_n \rangle = x$ in P.

$$
\begin{aligned}
&A(\{a_{ij}\}_{i=1..2n,j=1..m}, \{b_i\}_{i=1..2n}) \triangleq \\
&\quad \textstyle\prod_{i=1}^{n} \mathrm{OT}^{1}_{2}(\langle a_{i1}, \ldots, a_{im}\rangle, \langle a_{(i+n)1}, \ldots, a_{(i+n)m}\rangle, c_{as_i}) \mid \\
&\quad c_{sa_1}(\langle k_1, r_1\rangle).\text{let } \langle r_{11}, \ldots, r_{1m}\rangle = r_1 \text{ in } \ldots c_{sa_n}(\langle k_n, r_n\rangle).\text{let } \langle r_{n1}, \ldots, r_{nm}\rangle = r_n \text{ in} \\
&\quad \nu q_1 \ldots \nu q_{n+1}(\overline{q_1} \star \mid \textstyle\prod_{i=1}^{n} q_i(x).\nu qs_i(\overline{qs_i}\langle k_i, r_i\rangle \mid \mathit{TestOT}(i)) \mid \\
&\qquad q_{n+1}(x).\nu s_1 \ldots \nu s_{m+1}(\overline{s_1} \star \mid \\
&\qquad \textstyle\prod_{j=1}^{m} s_j(x).\overline{c_p} a_{1j}. \ldots \overline{c_p} a_{(2n)j}.c_p(d_{1j}). \ldots c_p(d_{(2n)j}). \\
&\qquad\quad \nu t_1 \ldots \nu t_{n+1}(\overline{t_1} \star \mid \\
&\qquad\qquad \textstyle\prod_{i=1}^{n} t_i(x).\nu ts_i(\overline{ts_i}\langle k_i, r_{ij}, d_{ij}, d_{(i+n)j}\rangle \mid \mathit{Test}(i,j)) \mid \\
&\qquad\quad t_{n+1}(x).\overline{s_{j+1}}\star) \mid \\
&\qquad s_{m+1}(x).\overline{c_p}ok))
\end{aligned}
$$

$$
\begin{aligned}
&\mathit{TestOT}(i) \triangleq qs_i(\langle k, w\rangle).([k \text{ is } 1][w \text{ is } b_i]\overline{q_{i+1}} \star \mid [k \text{ is } 2][w \text{ is } b_{i+n}]\overline{q_{i+1}}\star) \\
&\mathit{Test}(i,j) \triangleq ts_i(\langle k, w, x, y\rangle).([k \text{ is } 1][w \text{ is } x]\overline{t_{i+1}} \star \mid [k \text{ is } 2][w \text{ is } y]\overline{t_{i+1}}\star)
\end{aligned}
$$

Fig. 3. Encoding of PSE protocol

and the corresponding bits of B are received in d_{ij}. Then there is nested loop of n tests controlled by the input actions on t_i. Each test, performed by the Test subprocess, ensures that B's bits are valid. $\mathit{Test}(i,j)$ checks the j-th bit of the i-th pair. The bit received during the first part, namely r_{ij}, is compared to d_{ij} or $d_{(i+n)j}$ depending on k_i. If the bit is valid, an output action on t_{i+j} is performed to continue to the next test. Again, the ts_i channels are used to send the necessary values to the Test sub-process.

Finally, an instance of the protocol is an agent A put in parallel with servers for all oblivious transfers:

$$
I \triangleq A(\{a_{ij}\}_{i=1..2n,j=1..m}, \{b_i\}_{i=1..2n}) \mid \prod_{i=1}^{n}(S(c_{as_i}, c_{sb_i}) \mid S(c_{bs_i}, c_{sa_i}))
$$

4 Verification of Security Properties

A well known method for expressing and proving security properties using process calculi is by means of *specifications*. A specification P_{spec} of a protocol P is a process which is simple enough in order to prove (or accept) that it models the correct behavior of the protocol. Then the correctness of P is implied by $P \simeq P_{spec}$ where $\simeq$ is a testing equivalence. The idea is that, if there exists an attack for P, this attack can be modeled by a test O which performs the attack and outputs ω if it succeeds. Then P should pass the test and since $P \simeq P_{spec}$, P_{spec} should also pass it, which is a contradiction (no attack exists for P_{spec}).

However, in case of probabilistic protocols, attacks do exist but only succeed with a very small probability. So examining only the ability of passing a test is not sufficient since the fact that P_{spec} has an attack is no longer contradictory. Instead we will use a specification which can be shown to have very small probability of been attacked and we will express the correctness of P as $P \sqsubseteq P_{spec}$ where $\sqsubseteq$ is the testing preorder defined in section 2.4. Then an attack of high probability for P should be applicable with at least the same probability for P_{spec} which is contradictory.

4.1 A Specification for PSE

Let us recall the fairness property for the PSE protocol.

> If B receives one of A's pairs then with high probability A should also be able to receive one of B's pairs.

First of all we must point out two important differences between this type of protocols and the traditional cryptographic ones.

- In traditional protocols both A and B are considered honest. The purpose of the protocol is to ensure that no outside adversary can access the messages being transfered.
  On the other hand, in PSE the adversary is B himself, who might try to deviate from the protocol in order to get A's secrets without revealing his own ones.
- In traditional protocols the secrets must remain secret all the time. A and B always perform the same actions and always want to communicate with each other.
  On the other hand in PSE A shows different behavior when B is honest than in case of an attempt to cheat. A is willing to reveal his secrets, only when B wants the same too.

A specification of a protocol shows the correct behavior of the agents. Since A's behavior depends on B it makes sense to have different specifications depending on B's behavior. Since the case where B is honest is trivial, we are considering the case where B tries to deviate from the protocol. That is B will try to send some of his bits incorrectly. Moreover the behavior of A depends on which these bits are. If B stays honest for the first half bits then A will do the same.

It order to model B's intention to cheat, we will use a function $h : \{1..n\} \mapsto \{1..m\}$ that shows on which bit B is going to cheat for each pair. So $h(3) = 4$ means that B is going to send the 4th bit of (at least) one of the 3rd pair's secrets incorrectly. We consider "cheating" to be a deviation from the protocol in a way that leads to a violation of fairness. Thus, in order for B to cheat h must be defined on its whole domain. The goal is to exchange just one pair, if at least one pair is sent correctly by B then fairness is not violated.

The specification is displayed in figure 4. As already discussed, it depends on B's cheating behavior, that is on the function h. The specification resembles a lot the protocol, with two major differences:

$$
\begin{array}{l}
A_{spec}(\{a_{ij}\}_{i=1..2n,j=1..m}, h) \triangleq \\
\quad \prod_{i=1}^{n} \mathrm{OT}_2^1(\langle a_{i1}, \dots, a_{im}\rangle, \langle a_{(i+n)1}, \dots, a_{(i+n)m}\rangle, c_{as_i}) \mid \\
\quad c_{sa_1}(x) \dots c_{sa_n}(x). \\
\quad \nu q_1 \dots \nu q_{n+1}(\overline{q_1} \star \mid \prod_{i=1}^{n} q_i(x).\nu qs_i(\overline{qs_i}\langle k_i, r_i\rangle \mid TestOT_{spec}(i)) \mid \\
\quad\quad q_{n+1}(x).\nu s_1 \dots \nu s_{m+1}(\overline{s_1} \star \mid \\
\quad\quad \prod_{j=1}^{m} s_j(x).\overline{c_p} a_{1j}. \dots \overline{c_p} a_{(2n)j}.c_p(x). \dots c_p(x). \\
\quad\quad\quad \nu t_1 \dots \nu t_{n+1}(\overline{t_1} \star \mid \\
\quad\quad\quad\quad \prod_{i=1}^{n} t_i(x).\nu ts_i(\overline{ts_i}\langle k_i, r_{ij}, d_{ij}, d_{(i+n)j}\rangle \mid Test_{spec}(i,j,h)) \mid \\
\quad\quad\quad t_{n+1}(x).\overline{s_{j+1}}\star) \mid \\
\quad\quad s_{m+1}(x).\overline{c_p} ok))
\end{array}
$$

$$
TestOT_{spec}(i) \triangleq qs_i(x).\overline{q_{i+1}}\star
$$

$$
Test_{spec}(i,j,h) \triangleq \begin{cases} ts_i(x).(\overline{t_{i+1}}\star +_{0.5} 0) & \text{if } h(i) = j \\ ts_i(x).\overline{t_{i+1}}\star & \text{otherwise} \end{cases}
$$

Fig. 4. Specification for the PSE protocol

1. The specification does not use any of its input (all input variables are replaced by x to point out this fact). Moreover b_i's are no longer used (thus they are removed from the parameter list).
2. The specification does not test the received bits. In the first part, $TestOT_{spec}$ accepts all messages. In the second, $Test_{spec}$ accepts all bits, except those on which B is known to cheat, which are accepted only with probability one half.

As a consequence the specification is much simpler than the protocol. As we will show in the next section, if h is total then A will make n choices and the probability of succeeding in all of them will be negligible.

4.2 Proving the Correctness of PSE

Correctness of the specification. First we show that the specification is indeed a proper specification for PSE with respect to fairness, in case B tries to cheat. Let l be the maximum number of bits that B is willing to reveal for its secrets. So B's cheating behavior will be described by a function h, such that $h(i) \leq l+1$ for all $i \in \{1..n\}$. This is by definition of PSE, otherwise B would reveal $l+1$ bits of at least one pair of secrets and one pair is enough for A.

As we already discussed A_{spec} does not depend on its input. Moreover it is deterministic, that is only one transition is possible at any moment, except from $Test_{spec}(i,j,h)$ for $h(i) = j$ where the process stalls with probability one half. Since $h(i) \leq l+1, \forall i \in \{1..n\}$, all n of these tests will appear in the first $l+1$ steps of the second part of the protocol. If A fails in even one test then he stalls, so the total probability of advancing to step $l+2$ and reveal its $l+2$ pair is 2^{-n}.

This means that A_{spec} satisfies fairness. If B at some point of the protocol has l bits of one of A's pairs, then with probability at least $1 - 2^{-n}$ A will have $l-1$ bits of at least one of B's pairs. If $l = m$ (B has a whole pair) then A should have at least $m - 1$ bits and the last bit can be easily computed by trying both 0 and 1. In other words B cannot gain an advantage of more than one bit with probability greater than 2^{-n}.

Relation between A and A_{spec}. Having proved the correctness of the specification with respect to fairness, it remains to show its relation with the original protocol. Proving $A \sqsubseteq A_{spec}$ means to prove that if A is vulnerable with high probability to an attack O, then A_{spec} will be also vulnerable with at least the same probability. Since we know that the probability of a successful attack for A_{spec} is very small, we can conclude that an attack on A is very unlikely.

Note however that A_{spec} models the behavior of A only in case of an attack described by the function h. So $A \sqsubseteq A_{spec}$ cannot hold in general since A will pass with greater probability a test which models an honest agent. Thus, we need to use the conditional may-testing defined in section 2.4.

An instance of the specification is a process A_{spec} put in parallel with servers for all oblivious transfers:

$$I_{spec}(h) \triangleq A_{spec}(\{a_{ij}\}_{i=1..2n,j=1..m}, h) \mid \prod_{i=1}^{n}(S(c_{as_i}, c_{sb_i}) \mid S(c_{bs_i}, c_{sa_i}))$$

Let H be the set of all total functions $h : \{1..n\} \mapsto \{1..m\}$. PSE will be considered correct wrt fairness if:

$$\begin{aligned}
&\forall h \in H : I \sqsubseteq^{\phi_h} I_{spec}(h) \\
&\text{where } \phi_h(O) = \mathit{true} \text{ iff } \forall i \in \{1..n\} : \\
&\qquad O \text{ does not contain both } b_{ih(i)} \text{ and } b_{(i+n)h(i)}
\end{aligned}$$

The condition ϕ_h ensures that the test will try to cheat on the $h(i)$-th bit of each pair i. The idea is that in order to cheat, an intruder should refuse to send at least one bit of each message. It can be proved that $\sqsubseteq^{\phi_h}$, for the specific condition ϕ_h described above, is a precongrunce on closed processes wrt the contexts that satisfy ϕ_h. More details can be found in [8].

We can now state the correctness of PSE, as defined above.

Theorem 1. *PSE is correct with respect to fairness.*

5 Related Work

Security protocols have been extensively studied during the last decade and many formal methods have been proposed for their analysis. However, the vast majority of these methods refer to non-deterministic protocols and are not suitable for the probabilistic setting, since they do not allow to model random choices. One exception is the work of Aldini and Gorrieri ([4]), where they use a probabilistic process algebra to analyze fairness in a non-reputation protocol. Their work is close to ours in spirit, although technically it is quite different. In particular, we base our analysis on a notion of testing while theirs is based on a notion of bisimulation.

With respect to the application, the results the most related to ours come from Norman and Schmatikov ([12], [13]), who use probabilistic model checking to study fairness in two probabilistic protocols, including the Partial Exchange Protocol. In particular, in [13] they model the PSE using Prism, a probabilistic model checker. Their treatment however is very different from ours: their model describes only the "correct" behavior for both A and B, as specified by the protocol. B's ability to cheat is limited to prematurely stopping the execution, so attacks in which B deviates completely from the protocol are not taken into account. Having a simplified model is important in model checking since it helps overcoming the search state explosion problem, thus making the verification feasible.

The results in [13] show that with probability one B can gain a one bit advantage, that is he can get all m bits of a pair of A by revealing only $m-1$ bits of his. This is achieved simply by stopping the execution after receiving the last bit from A. Moreover a method of overcoming the problem is proposed, which gives this advantage to A or B, each with probability one half. Is is worth noting that this is a very weak form of attack and could be considered as negligible, since A can compute the last bit very easily by trying both 0 and 1. Besides a one bit advantage will always exist in contract signing protocols, simply because synchronous communication is not feasible.

In our approach, by modeling an adversary as an arbitrary π_{prob} process we allow him to perform a vast range of attacks including sending messages, performing calculations, monitoring public channels etc. Our analysis shows not only that a one bit attack is possible, but more important that no attack to obtain an advantage of two or more bits exists with non-negligible probability. Moreover our method has the advantage of being easily extendible. For example, treating more sessions, even an infinite number of ones, can be done by putting many copies of the processes in parallel.

Of course, the major advantage of the model checking approach, with respect to ours, is that it can be totally automated.

6 Conclusion

In this paper we examined a method to analyze probabilistic security protocols using process calculi. The main tool for this analysis is the π_{prob}-calculus, a probabilistic variant of the π-calculus. The probabilistic choice, provided by π_{prob}, allowed us to encode the Partial Exchange Protocol, a probabilistic protocol based on the Oblivious Transfer. In order to prove the correctness of this protocol, we defined various preorders between π_{prob} processes and examined their properties. Then we presented a properly constructed specification and showed that it is stronger than the original protocol, thus proving that the possibility of success for any attack is very small.

Our results show that process calculi techniques can be successfully applied to security protocol analysis. There are various advantages of this approach. First of all the use of process calculi allows the use of various tools from the corresponding theory. The proofs obtained are general, covering every possible adversary and are not instance-based as in model checking techniques. Moreover process calculi allow the analysis of a protocol in a more complex environment, having for example many agents and multiple simultaneous instances of a protocol. It is worth noting that many attacks of well known protocols only appear in such situations.

In [14] an algorithm for deciding may-testing is presented, for fully probabilistic automata. We believe that this result can be extended to the probabilistic automata defined in section 1.2, giving the ability of automatically proving the correctness of probabilistic security protocols.

References

1. Rabin, M.: How to exchange secrets by oblivious transfer. Technical Memo TR-81, Aiken Computation Laboratory, Harvard University (1981)
2. Even, S., Goldreich, O., Lempel, A.: A randomized protocol for signing contracts. Commun. ACM **28** (1985) 637–647
3. Naor, M., Pinkas, B., Sumner, R.: Privacy preserving auctions and mechanism design. In: Proceedings of the 1st ACM conference on Electronic commerce, ACM Press (1999) 129–139
4. Aldini, A., Gorrieri, R.: Security analysis of a probabilistic non-repudiation protocol. In Hermanns, H., Segala, R., eds.: Process Algebra and Probabilist Methods. Performance Modeling and Verification: Second Joint International Workshop PAPM-PROBMIV 2002, Copenhagen, Denmark, July 25–26, 2002. Proceedings. Volume 2399 of Lecture Notes in Computer Science., Heidelberg, Springer-Verlag (2002) 17
5. Herescu, O.M., Palamidessi, C.: Probabilistic asynchronous π-calculus. In Tiuryn, J., ed.: Proceedings of FOSSACS 2000 (Part of ETAPS 2000). Lecture Notes in Computer Science, Springer-Verlag (2000) 146–160
6. Nicola, R.D., Hennessy, M.C.B.: Testing equivalences for processes. Theoretical Computer Science **34** (1984) 83–133
7. Abadi, M., Gordon, A.: A calculus for cryptographic protocols: The spi calculus. Information and Computation **148** (1999) 1–70
8. Chatzikokolakis, K., Palamidessi, C.: A framework for analyzing probabilistic protocols and its application to the partial secrets exchange. Report version, available at http://www.lix.polytechnique.fr/ catuscia/papers/PartialSecrets/report.pdf (2005)
9. Segala, R., Lynch, N.: Probabilistic simulations for probabilistic processes. Nordic Journal of Computing **2** (1995) 250–273
10. Palamidessi, C., Herescu, O.M.: A randomized encoding of the pi-calculus with mixed choice. In: Proceedings of the *2nd IFIP International Conference on Theoretical Computer Science*. (2002) 537–549
11. Jonsson, B., Larsen, K.G., Yi, W.: Probabilistic extensions of process algebras. Handbook of Process Algebras (2001)

12. Norman, G., Shmatikov, V.: Analysis of probabilistic contract signing. In Abdallah, A., Ryan, P., Schneider, S., eds.: Proc. BCS-FACS Formal Aspects of Security (FASec'02). Volume 2629 of LNCS., Springer (2003) 81–96
13. Norman, G., Shmatikov, V.: Analysis of probabilistic contract signing. Formal Aspects of Computing (to appear) (2005)
14. Christoff, L., Christoff, I.: Efficient algorithms for verification of equivalences for probabilistic processes. In Larsen, Skou, eds.: Proc. Workshop on Computer Aided Verification. Volume 575 of LNCS., Springer Verlag (1991)

A Formal Semantics for Protocol Narrations

Sébastien Briais* and Uwe Nestmann

School of Computer and Communication Sciences,
EPFL, Switzerland

Abstract. Protocol narrations are an informal means to describe, in an idealistic manner, the functioning of cryptographic protocols as a single intended sequence of cryptographic message exchanges among the protocol's participants. Protocol narrations have also been informally "turned into" a number of formal protocol descriptions, e.g., using the spi-calculus. In this paper, we propose a direct formal operational semantics for protocol narrations that fixes a particular and, as we argue, well-motivated interpretation on how the involved protocol participants are supposed to execute. Based on this semantics, we explain and formally justify a natural and precise translation of narrations into spi-calculus.

1 Introduction

The setting. In the cryptographic protocol literature, protocols are usually expressed as *narrations* (see for example [CJ97, MvOV96]). A protocol narration is a simple sequence of message exchanges between the different participating principals and can be interpreted as the intended trace of the ideal execution of the protocol. The protocol in Table 1 is a typical example of this style. The two principals A and B are both connected to the server S who shares secret keys k_{AS} and k_{BS} with each of them. The protocol tells the story (narration) where A wants to establish a secret connection (a shared key) with B via the common server S: first, A should contact S, S generates the fresh key intended for A and B and passes it on to A; then, A contacts B directly, at the same time delivering the fresh key. The name t is used as a time-stamp required to prevent from replay attacks; earlier version of the protocol were flawed in this respect.

$$
\begin{array}{l}
A \leadsto S : (A\,.\,B) \\
S \leadsto A : \{((B\,.\,(k_{AB}\,.\,t))\,.\,\{(A\,.\,(k_{AB}\,.\,t))\}_{k_{BS}})\}_{k_{AS}} \\
A \leadsto B : \{(A\,.\,(k_{AB}\,.\,t))\}_{k_{BS}}
\end{array}
$$

Table 1. Denning-Sacco protocol

While much of the literature is concerned with stating and proving a security property of protocols like this one, we are more interested in the bare operational content of the description technique of narrations.

Our own motivation for the interest in a formal semantics for narrations is that we had implemented a "straightforward" translator [Gen03] from protocol narrations into the spi-calculus, which is a pi-calculus extended with encryption

* Supported by the Swiss National Science Foundation, grant No. 21-65180.1

R. De Nicola and D. Sangiorgi (Eds.): TGC 2005, LNCS 3705, pp. 163–181, 2005.

primitives [AG99]. Then, we were looking for a way to formally prove our translator correct and had the problem that there was no formal intended semantics to compare to. This lacking semantics is what we provide within this paper. Indeed, it turns out that the attempt to properly formalize narrations brings one already much closer to spi-like executable descriptions, but there are a number of insightful observations along the way, on which we report here as well.

The challenge. Despite being rather intuitive, the description technique of protocol narrations contains lots of implicit concepts. Looking for a formal semantics, these need to be rendered explicit. For example, Abadi [Aba00] pointed out that "informal protocol narrations" need to be complemented with explanations of some either implicitly assumed facts or additional information to remove ambiguities. He raised four tasks that need to be pursued:

1. One should make explicit what is known (public, private) before a protocol run, and what is to be generated freshly during a protocol run.
2. One should make explicit which checks the individual principals are expected to carry out on the reception of messages.
3. Principals act concurrently, in contrast to the apparently sequential idealized execution of a run according to a narration.
4. Concurrency occurs also at the level of different protocol sessions, which may happen to be executed simultaneously while sharing principals across.

(Interestingly, Abadi used these requirements to motivate the use of the spi-calculus as a description technique for "formal protocol narrations".)

The first item above should be clear: data is missing otherwise. To this aim, narrations usually come with a bit of explanation in natural language on the spirit of the protocol and on the assumptions made. Essentially, these assumptions consist of expliciting the *pieces of data* known in advance by the agents[1] and those that are to be *freshly generated* during the course of a protocol run.

The second item above results from the too high level of abstraction of message exchanges, noted as $A \leadsto B{:}M$. There are a number of problems connected to the fact that message M is usually transmitted from A to B by passing through an asynchronous insecure network where a potential intruder can interfere [DY83]. Thus, once B receives some message, it may be just the expected one according to the protocol, but it may also be an intended message received at the wrong moment and, worse, it may even be an unintended message forged by some malicious attacker. So, B needs to perform some informative checks. But precisely which ones? For example, when B receives M it must first check in how far, at this very moment, it "understands" M (with respect to possible encryptions). Then, if B acquires new knowledge by this analysis, it must ensure that this new knowledge is consistent with its previously acquired knowledge. Some careful analysis is due, requiring a suitable representation of knowledge.

The third item above looks innocent at first, but once the non-atomic passage of messages through the network is properly taken into account, some surprising

[1] We use the terms principal and agent interchangeably.

effects arise due to parts of *later* message exchanges (referring to the order of exchanges in a narration) possibly occurring before *earlier* message exchanges have completed or even started.

The fourth item above is again intuitively straightforward, but the description technique of narrations completely ignores the problem.

Our approach. In this paper, we present solutions to the first three items, leaving the fourth for future work (see Section 6). Concerning the first item, we simply add a declaration part to narrations (§2). Here, we are no different from competing approaches (see the paragraph on Related work). On item two, we propose to compile exchanges of the form $A \rightsquigarrow B{:}M$ into three separate syntactic parts (§3):

(i) A *asynchronously* sends M towards B,
(ii) B receives some message (intended to be M), and
(iii) finally B checks that the message it just received indeed has the expected properties (associated with M, from the point of view of B).

With respect to the required checks, our approach is to automatically generate the maximum of checks derivable from the static information of protocol narrations. We call the resulting refined notion of narrations *executable*, because it will allow us to formalize an operational semantics of narrations, which was not possible with an atomic, or synchronous, interpretation of message exchanges.

Concerning the third item, we profit from the above decomposition of message transmission and introduce a natural structural equivalence relation on executable narrations that allows us to bring any of the (con-)currently enabled actions to top-level. On this basis, we provide a labeled transition semantics (§4).

Finally, we rewrite executable narrations within the spi-calculus, which is then only a minor, albeit insightful, remaining step (§5). We then establish a straightforward formal operational correspondence between the two semantics.

Impact. Our paper targets at two different audiences.

To the cryptographic protocol audience, we offer a high-level bridge to the low-level (process calculus motivated) semantics of protocol narrations. However, it is our primary intention to accomplish this undertaking such that a reader does not need to be proficient in spi-calculus or its relatives. Thus, we propose—for an only slightly refined narration syntax—a formal semantics in which we cast in high-level narration terms the behavior of a corresponding low-level spi-calculus semantics. Analysis techniques can now be built on top of this direct semantics.

To the process calculus audience, mainly as a by-product, we offer a gentle systematic way to comprehend and formally justify spi-calculus representations corresponding to protocol narrations. In particular, the uniform generation of "checks-on-reception" was lacking in earlier translations. In this sense, our formal description can also be seen as an abstract formulation of our compiler [Gen03].

Related work and future work are deferred to the concluding section (§6).

Table 2. Protocol narrations

$M, N ::= a \mid A \mid \{M\}_N \mid (M \,.\, N)$	(messages $\boldsymbol{M}$)
$T ::= A \rightsquigarrow B{:}M$	(exchanges)
$L ::= \epsilon \mid T; L$	(narrations)
$D ::= A$ **knows** $M \mid A$ **generates** $n \mid$ **private** k	(declarations)
$P ::= D; P \mid L$	(protocol narrations $\boldsymbol{D}$)

2 Extending Protocol Narrations

Like in the competing approaches on the representation of protocol narrations, we extend narrations with a header that declares the initial knowledge of each agent, the names generated by them and also the names that are assumed to be initially only known by the system (this last point permits to simulate for example a first pass where shared keys have been distributed among some agents).

Hence, an extended protocol narration is composed of two parts: a sequence of *declarations* followed by the *narration* itself. The agents are picked among a countably infinite set $\boldsymbol{A}$ of *agent names* ranged over by $A, B, C, \ldots, S, \ldots$ and the messages are built upon a countably infinite set $\boldsymbol{N}$ of *names* ranged over by $a, b, c, \ldots, k, l, m, n, \ldots$. For sake of simplicity, we assume that $\boldsymbol{A} \cap \boldsymbol{N} = \emptyset$.

For simplicity, we consider here only the possibility to concatenate messages (denoted by $(M \,.\, N)$ for M and N) or to encrypt them under a shared-key cryptosystem ($\{M\}_N$ is the encryption of message M with shared-key N). It is straightforward to extend the following formal development to a richer message language (using ideas of [Bri04, BBN04]). We implicitly assume that all agents involved in the protocol know each other; this can be generalized by explicit declarations. The syntax of messages and protocol narrations is given in Table 2.

The meaning of **private** k is that k is a name which is initially only available for the agents involved in the protocol. Typically, it is useful to simulate that an agent A and a server S initially share a secret key k_{AS}. The meaning of A **knows** M is simply that initially, agent A knows the piece of data M. Finally the meaning of A **generates** n is that A will generate a fresh name n (typically a nonce). For the sake of clarity, we enforce fresh generated names to be declared explicitly. Table 3 shows the Denning-Sacco protocol using our framework.

Table 3. Denning-Sacco protocol, with formal declarations

private k_{AS}; **private** k_{BS};
A **knows** k_{AS}; A **knows** t; B **knows** k_{BS}; B **knows** t;
S **knows** k_{AS}; S **knows** k_{BS}; S **knows** t; S **generates** k_{AB};
$A \rightsquigarrow S{:}(A \,.\, B)$;
$S \rightsquigarrow A{:}\{((B \,.\, (k_{AB} \,.\, t)) \,.\, \{(A \,.\, (k_{AB} \,.\, t))\}_{k_{BS}})\}_{k_{AS}}$;
$A \rightsquigarrow B{:}\{(A \,.\, (k_{AB} \,.\, t))\}_{k_{BS}}; \epsilon$

It often happens in cryptographic protocols that a secret is shared by several participants. For this reason, we propose to introduce as a macro the construct

$$A_1, \ldots, A_n \ \textbf{share}\ k$$

which is intended to mean that the agents $A_1, \ldots, A_n$ share the secret name k. This macro is simply expanded into:

$$\textbf{private}\ k; A_1\ \textbf{knows}\ k; \ldots; A_n\ \textbf{knows}\ k$$

To ease the writing of formal declarations, one can also imagine to introduce the shortcut $A_1, \ldots, A_n$ **knows** M to mean A_1 **knows** $M; \ldots; A_n$ **knows** M.

3 Compiling Protocol Narrations

Target syntax. As motivated in the Introduction, *executable narrations* (set $\boldsymbol{X}$, as defined in Table 4) are to be more explicit about the behavior of individual agents. Instead of atomic exchanges of the form $A \rightsquigarrow B{:}M$ as used in the standard narrations of Table 2, we observe four more fine-grained basic actions (nonterminal I in Table 4): emission $A{:}B!E$, reception $B{:}?x$, and checking $B{:}\phi$, which are explicitly attached to some principal, and scoping νk, which is reminiscent of the spi-calculus and represents the creation and scope of private names. Scoping is decoupled from principals, allowing us to use a single construct for names that are **private** and **generated** according to the declarations of §2.

In interacting systems, when an agent receives a message, it binds it to a fresh variable for reference in subsequent processing. For this purpose, we introduce a well-founded totally ordered countably infinite set $x, y, z, \ldots$ of *variables* $\boldsymbol{V}$ that we assume to be disjoint from $\boldsymbol{A} \cup \boldsymbol{N}$. An agent can operate in different ways on a message: (1) as with the previous standard narrations, it can concatenate two messages or encrypt one message with another (the key); (2) it can project a message onto its parts using $\pi_1(E)$ or $\pi_2(E)$ (if E "represents" a pair of two messages) or decrypt it using $\mathrm{D}_F(E)$ (if it knows the key "represented by" F that was used to encrypt the message "represented by" E). Since an agent does not only handle messages but also variables, we introduce the notion of message *expressions* ($\boldsymbol{E}$), including the above further operations. The process of finding out whether some expression indeed "represents" some

Table 4. Syntax of executable narrations

$E, F ::= a \mid A \mid \{E\}_F \mid (E\,.\,F)$		(expressions $\boldsymbol{E}$)
$\quad\quad \mid x \mid \mathrm{D}_F(E) \mid \pi_1(E) \mid \pi_2(E)$		
$\phi, \psi ::= tt \mid [E{=}F] \mid [E{:}\boldsymbol{M}] \mid \phi \wedge \phi$		(formulae $\boldsymbol{F}$)
$I ::= \nu k \mid A{:}B!E \mid A{:}?x \mid A{:}\phi$		(simple action)
$X ::= \epsilon \mid I; X$		(executable narrations $\boldsymbol{X}$)

particular message, will be formalized later on using the *evaluation function* in Table 10.

Formulae ϕ on received messages are described by (conjunctions of) two kinds of checks: *equality tests* $[E{=}F]$ on expressions denote the comparison of two bit-streams of E and F; *well-formedness tests* $[E:\boldsymbol{M}]$ denote the verification of whether the projections and decryptions contained in E are likely to succeed.

Table 4 lists the syntax of expressions, formulae and executable narrations. In the following, we will omit the trailing $;\epsilon$ of a non-empty executable narration. Moreover, we overload the operator ; to also concatenate narrations.

Definition 1. *Let* $M \in \boldsymbol{M}$, $E \in \boldsymbol{E}$, $\phi \in \boldsymbol{F}$, $x \in \boldsymbol{V}$. *We let* $\mathrm{n}(M)$, $\mathrm{n}(E)$, *and* $\mathrm{n}(\phi)$ *denote the set of names occurring in* M, E, *and* ϕ, *respectively. Similarly, we let* $\mathrm{v}(E)$ *and* $\mathrm{v}(\phi)$ *denote the set of variables occurring in* E *and* ϕ. $E\{^M/_x\}$ *and* $\phi\{^M/_x\}$ *denote the substitution of* M *for* x *in* E *and* ϕ, *respectively.*

Knowledge representation. As motivated in the Introduction, the central point of the actual behavior of protocols is to find out which checks are to be performed. We further motivated that such checks need to be based on (1) the narration code, which statically spells out the intended message to be received, and (2) the current knowledge at the moment of reception, which imposes constraints on how much the recipient can dynamically learn from the received message and on what other information the newly acquired knowledge must be consistent with.

Instead of accumulating only the dynamically acquired messages (stored in variables x) we propose to tightly connect the (according to the narration) statically intended messages M with the dynamically received actual messages x. For this, we simply use pairs (M, x). Since consistency checks will then (have to) operate on such pairs, we need to generalize this representation of principal's knowledge to finite subsets of $\boldsymbol{M} \times \boldsymbol{E}$. The underlying idea is that a pair (M, E) means that the expression E is supposed to be equal (or: has to evaluate) to M.

The following definition introduces knowledge sets, and also some traditionally employed operations on them: *synthesis* reflects the closure of knowledge sets using message constructors; *analysis* reflects the exhaustive recursive decomposition of knowledge pairs as enabled by the currently available knowledge.

Definition 2 (Knowledge). Knowledge sets $K \in \boldsymbol{K}$ *are finite subsets of* $\boldsymbol{M} \times \boldsymbol{E}$.

The set of names occurring in K *is denoted by* $\mathrm{n}(K)$.

Table 5. Synthesis

$$\text{SYN-PAIR}\ \frac{(M,E) \in \mathcal{S}(K) \qquad (N,F) \in \mathcal{S}(K)}{((M\,.\,N),(E\,.\,F)) \in \mathcal{S}(K)}$$

$$\text{SYN-ENC}\ \frac{(M,E) \in \mathcal{S}(K) \qquad (N,F) \in \mathcal{S}(K)}{(\{M\}_N,\{E\}_F) \in \mathcal{S}(K)}$$

Table 6. Analysis

$$\text{ANA-INI}\ \frac{(M, E) \in K}{(M, E) \in \mathcal{A}_0(K)}$$

$$\text{ANA-FST}\ \frac{((M \,.\, N), E) \in \mathcal{A}_n(K)}{(M, \pi_1(E)) \in \mathcal{A}_{n+1}(K)} \qquad \text{ANA-SND}\ \frac{((M \,.\, N), E) \in \mathcal{A}_n(K)}{(N, \pi_2(E)) \in \mathcal{A}_{n+1}(K)}$$

$$\text{ANA-DEC}\ \frac{(\{M\}_N, E) \in \mathcal{A}_n(K) \qquad (N, F) \in \mathcal{S}(\mathcal{A}_n(K))}{(M, \mathrm{D}_F(E)) \in \mathcal{A}_{n+1}(K)}$$

$$\text{ANA-DEC-REC}\ \frac{(\{M\}_N, E) \in \mathcal{A}_n(K) \qquad (N, F) \notin \mathcal{S}(\mathcal{A}_n(K))}{(\{M\}_N, E) \in \mathcal{A}_{n+1}(K)}$$

$$\text{ANA-NAM-REC}\ \frac{(M, E) \in \mathcal{A}_n(K) \qquad M \in \boldsymbol{N} \cup \boldsymbol{A}}{(M, E) \in \mathcal{A}_{n+1}(K)}$$

The synthesis $\mathcal{S}(K)$ *of* K *is the smallest subset of* $\boldsymbol{M} \times \boldsymbol{E}$ *containing* K *and satisfying the* SYN*-rules in Table 5.*

The analysis $\mathcal{A}(K)$ *of* K *is* $\bigcup_{n \in \mathbb{N}} \mathcal{A}_n(K)$ *where the sets* $\mathcal{A}_i(K)$ *are the smallest sets satisfying the* ANA*-rules in Table 6.*

Our definition of analysis refines the usual approach reminiscent of Paulson [Pau98]. Instead of directly defining a "flat" analysis set, we had to define a finitely stratified hierarchy $(\mathcal{A}_n(K))_{n \in \mathbb{N}}$. Essentially, the index n of an analysis set $\mathcal{A}_n(K)$ approximates the number of proper deconstruction steps that were needed in order to derive its knowledge items (see the rules ANA-INI, ANA-FST, ANA-SND, and ANA-DEC). In contrast to the standard approach, corresponding to $\mathcal{A}_n(K) \subseteq \mathcal{A}_{n+1}(K)$, here only certain items—not all of them—may be be propagated from analysis level n to $n{+}1$ without proper deconstruction step.

As the following example shows, with the notion of knowledge of this paper the simple rule $\mathcal{A}_n(K) \subseteq \mathcal{A}_{n+1}(K)$ would allow us to possibly analyse the same message several times, in different ways, which would indeed be harmful. Assume that we remove the rules ANA-DEC-REC and ANA-NAM-REC as well as the indices of analysis sets in Table 6 (which amounts to admitting $\mathcal{A}_n(K) \subseteq \mathcal{A}_{n+1}(K)$). If we now analyze the knowledge set $K = \{(k, k), (\{k\}_k, x)\}$ according to this "standard" approach then we would first get the pair $(k, \mathrm{D}_k(x))$, then the pair $(k, \mathrm{D}_{\mathrm{D}_k(x)}(x))$, then $(k, \mathrm{D}_{\mathrm{D}_{\mathrm{D}_k(x)}(x)}(x))$, etc. The resulting analysis set $\mathcal{A}(K)$ would be of infinite size, and thus not even be a knowledge set[2], which counters the goal of providing a finite representation of the knowledge of participants.

Instead, we control the propagation from analysis level n to $n{+}1$ by the rules ANA-NAM-REC and ANA-DEC-REC. Knowledge items (M, E) can only be

[2] In contrast, the "standard" analysis of the corresponding (i.e., projected onto the static component) knowledge set $K_1 = \{k, \{k\}_k\}$ simply yields $\mathcal{A}(K_1) = \{k, \{k\}_k\}$.

propagated to the next level of the analysis if M is not analysable (i.e., deconstructible) with the knowledge of the same level: either M is a pure name (possibly an agent name) or M can *not* be decrypted with knowledge from the same analysis level. Note that when computing the sequence $(\mathcal{A}_n(K))_{n\in\mathbb{N}}$, the rules ANA-FST, ANA-SND and ANA-DEC strictly decrease the size of the messages, so they can only be applied a finite number of times. Thus, it is obvious that the sequence $(\mathcal{A}_n(K))_{n\in\mathbb{N}}$ converges and thus $\mathcal{A}(K)$ is finite.

Generating checks. The above knowledge representation allows us to generate the checks required on message reception in a justified manner. Recall that these checks must verify (1) in how far the expectations of the recipient on the received message (as expressed statically in the narration) are matched according to the recipient's current knowledge, and (2) in how far the gained knowledge is consistent with previously acquired knowledge.

Thus, obviously necessary checks are due to the *type* of messages: if an expression shall correspond to a pair then it better allows for projections; if an expression shall correspond to an encrypted piece of data, then it better allows for decryption with the appropriate (corresponding) key—but only if it is known.

Less obviously required checks result from the following observation. Since a message (identifier) M may occur more than once in a protocol narration it may happen that, in some knowledge set, M is related to two different expressions E_1 and E_2. As M was precisely used in protocol narrations to indicate the *very same* piece of data, such a knowledge set can only be considered consistent if E_1 and E_2 indeed evaluate to the same message. Let us assume, as it is customary, that agents dispose of some meaningful initial knowledge (usually of the form (M, M) with M representing some initially known key or participant name). Then, the consistency check for repeated occurrences of data implicitly may take care of testing, e.g., whether some received datum was sent by the expected agent.

To formalize these requirements, we generate consistency formulae.

Definition 3 (Consistency formula). *Let K be a knowledge set. Its* consistency formula *$\Phi(K)$ is defined as follows:*

$$\begin{aligned}\Phi(K) \stackrel{\text{def}}{=} \quad & \textstyle\bigwedge_{((M\,.\,N),E)\in K} \left([\pi_1(E):\boldsymbol{M}] \wedge [\pi_2(E):\boldsymbol{M}]\right) \\ \wedge & \textstyle\bigwedge_{(\{M\}_N,E)\in K \,\wedge\, (N,F)\in\mathcal{S}(K)} \left[\mathrm{D}_F(E):\boldsymbol{M}\right] \\ \wedge & \textstyle\bigwedge_{(M,E_i)\in K \,\wedge\, (M,E_j)\in K \,\wedge\, E_i\neq E_j} \left[E_i = E_j\right]\end{aligned}$$

The third conjunction clause actually may include some of the checks produced in the other conjunction clauses. Since our main goal was to capture all possible checks in a uniform manner, we accept this redundancy.

Usually, knowledge sets can often be simplified without loss of information by reducing complex elements to their parts. In our case, we can further simplify due to the occurrence of duplicated elements; there is no loss of information once the consistency formula of Definition 3 remembers the duplication.

Definition 4 (Irreducibles). *Let K be a knowledge set. We define the set of* irreducibles $\mathcal{I}(K)$ *as follows:*

$$\mathcal{I}(K) \stackrel{\text{def}}{=} \mathcal{A}(K) \setminus \left(\begin{array}{l} \{((M\,.\,N), E) \in \mathcal{A}(K)\} \\ \cup \{(\{M\}_N, E) \in \mathcal{A}(K) \mid \exists F \in \boldsymbol{E} : (N, F) \in \mathcal{S}(\mathcal{A}(K))\} \end{array} \right)$$

Let $\sim$ denote the equivalence relation on $\boldsymbol{M} \times \boldsymbol{E}$ induced by $(M, E) \sim (N, F) \iff M = N$. We let rep$(K)$ *denote the result of deterministically selecting*[3] *one representative element for each equivalence class induced by $\sim$ on K.*

Example 1. *To see all the previous definitions in action, we consider the initial knowledge $K_0 = \{(A, A), (B, B), (S, S), (k_{AS}, k_{AS}), (t, t)\}$ of agent A of the Denning-Sacco protocol given Table 3.*

(For the sake of readability, we sometimes write $M \bullet E$ for (M, E).)

We now consider $K \stackrel{\text{def}}{=} K_0 \cup \{(\{((B\,.\,(k_{AB}\,.\,t))\,.\,\{(A\,.\,(k_{AB}\,.\,t))\}_{k_{BS}})\}_{k_{AS}}, x_1)\}$.

$$\text{We have } \mathcal{A}(K) = K \cup \left\{ \begin{array}{r} ((B\,.\,(k_{AB}\,.\,t))\,.\,\{(A\,.\,(k_{AB}\,.\,t))\}_{k_{BS}}) \bullet \mathrm{D}_{k_{AS}}(x_1) \\ (B\,.\,(k_{AB}\,.\,t)) \bullet \pi_1(\mathrm{D}_{k_{AS}}(x_1)) \\ \{(A\,.\,(k_{AB}\,.\,t))\}_{k_{BS}} \bullet \pi_2(\mathrm{D}_{k_{AS}}(x_1)) \\ B \bullet \pi_1(\pi_1(\mathrm{D}_{k_{AS}}(x_1))) \\ (k_{AB}\,.\,t) \bullet \pi_2(\pi_1(\mathrm{D}_{k_{AS}}(x_1))) \\ k_{AB} \bullet \pi_1(\pi_2(\pi_1(\mathrm{D}_{k_{AS}}(x_1)))) \\ t \bullet \pi_2(\pi_2(\pi_1(\mathrm{D}_{k_{AS}}(x_1)))) \end{array} \right\}.$$

$$\begin{array}{rl} \Phi(\mathcal{A}(K)) = & [\mathrm{D}_{k_{AS}}(x_1) : \boldsymbol{M}] \\ \wedge & [\pi_1(\mathrm{D}_{k_{AS}}(x_1)) : \boldsymbol{M}] \wedge [\pi_2(\mathrm{D}_{k_{AS}}(x_1)) : \boldsymbol{M}] \\ \wedge & [\pi_1(\pi_1(\mathrm{D}_{k_{AS}}(x_1))) : \boldsymbol{M}] \wedge [\pi_2(\pi_1(\mathrm{D}_{k_{AS}}(x_1))) : \boldsymbol{M}] \\ \wedge & [\pi_1(\pi_2(\pi_1(\mathrm{D}_{k_{AS}}(x_1)))) : \boldsymbol{M}] \wedge [\pi_2(\pi_2(\pi_1(\mathrm{D}_{k_{AS}}(x_1)))) : \boldsymbol{M}] \\ \wedge & [\pi_1(\pi_1(\mathrm{D}_{k_{AS}}(x_1))) = B] \wedge [\pi_2(\pi_2(\pi_1(\mathrm{D}_{k_{AS}}(x_1)))) = t] \end{array}$$

$$\text{And finally, } \mathrm{rep}(\mathcal{I}(K)) = K_0 \cup \left\{ \begin{array}{c} \{(A\,.\,(k_{AB}\,.\,t))\}_{k_{BS}} \bullet \pi_2(\mathrm{D}_{k_{AS}}(x_1)) \\ k_{AB} \bullet \pi_1(\pi_2(\pi_1(\mathrm{D}_{k_{AS}}(x_1)))) \end{array} \right\}.$$

Here, rep$(\mathcal{I}(K))$ *includes (t, t) instead of $(t, \pi_2(\pi_2(\pi_1(\mathrm{D}_{k_{AS}}(x_1)))))$ and (B, B) instead of $(B, \pi_1(\pi_1(\mathrm{D}_{k_{AS}}(x_1))))$.*

The compilation. We now have set up all the required ingredients to compile an extended protocol narration into an executable protocol narration.

Definition 5 (Compilation). *The translation $\mathcal{X}[\![\cdot]\!]^{(\upsilon,\varpi,\kappa,\nu)} : \boldsymbol{D} \to \boldsymbol{X}$ is defined inductively in Table 7, where $\upsilon \subset \boldsymbol{V}$ (current set of used variables), $\varpi \subset \boldsymbol{N}$ (current set of private names), $\kappa : \boldsymbol{A} \to \boldsymbol{K}$ (partial mapping from agents to their current knowledge), and $\nu : \boldsymbol{A} \to \boldsymbol{N}$ (partial mapping from agents to their current set of generated names).*

[3] Choose a well-founded total order for expressions and select the smallest expression.

Let $P \in \boldsymbol{D}$ *be a protocol narration. Let* $\boldsymbol{A}_P$ *denote the set of agent names appearing in* P. *Then,* $\mathcal{X}[\![P]\!]^{(\emptyset,\emptyset,\kappa_P,\emptyset)}$ *denotes the* compilation of P, *where the* initial knowledge κ_P *is defined by* $\kappa_P(A) := \{(B,B) \mid B \in \boldsymbol{A}_P\}$ *for all* $A \in \boldsymbol{A}_P$.

P *is called* well-formed *iff its compilation is defined.*

For simplicity, the compilation assumes that all agents initially know each other, as expressed in the initial knowledge set κ_P. Checks-on-reception are deduced from the individual knowledge set of a receiver. To avoid to perform the same checks again and again, the compilation keeps the knowledge sets of κ in reduced form, i.e., $\kappa(A) = \text{rep}(\mathcal{I}(\kappa(A)))$. To update $\text{f} \in \{\kappa, \upsilon\}$, we note $\text{f}\,[x \leftarrow y]$ with $\text{f}\,[x \leftarrow y]\,(x) = y$ and $\text{f}\,[x \leftarrow y]\,(z) = \text{f}(z)$ for $z \neq x$.

The compilation of **private** k and A **generates** n checks in both cases that the local (or generated) name is fresh, but differs with respect to the addition of the fresh name to the knowledge sets of agents: whereas A **generates** n increases the knowledge of A, the name k of **private** k is not added to any knowledge; this task is deferred to explicit A **knows** k clauses for the intended A.

The compilation of $A \rightsquigarrow B{:}M$ checks that M can be synthesized by A, picks a new variable x and adds the pair (M, x) to the knowledge of B.[4] The consistency formula $\Phi(\mathcal{A}(K'_B))$ of the analysis of this updated knowledge K'_B defines the checks ϕ to be performed by B at runtime. Note that this must be done on the non-reduced version. In fact, it is just the consistency check that allows us then to continue with the knowledge in reduced form.

Example 2. *Let DS be the Denning-Sacco protocol presented Table 3.*

We have $\kappa_{DS} : \boldsymbol{A} \rightarrow \boldsymbol{K}$

$$\begin{aligned} A &\mapsto \{(A,A),(B,B),(S,S)\}\\ B &\mapsto \{(A,A),(B,B),(S,S)\}\\ S &\mapsto \{(A,A),(B,B),(S,S)\}\end{aligned}$$

DS is well-formed and its compilation is

$\mathcal{X}[\![DS]\!]^{(\emptyset,\emptyset,\kappa_{DS},\emptyset)} =$

$$\begin{array}{lr} \nu k_{AS}; \nu k_{BS}; \nu k_{AB}; & \\ A{:}S!(A\,.\,B); & S{:}?x_0;\ S{:}\phi_0;\\ S{:}A!\{((B\,.\,(k_{AB}\,.\,t))\,.\,\{(A\,.\,(k_{AB}\,.\,t))\}_{k_{BS}})\}_{k_{AS}}; & A{:}?x_1;\ A{:}\phi_1;\\ A{:}B!\pi_2(\mathrm{D}_{k_{AS}}(x_1)); & B{:}?x_2;\ B{:}\phi_2 \end{array}$$

where $\phi_0 \stackrel{\text{def}}{=} [\pi_1(x_0) : \boldsymbol{M}] \wedge [\pi_2(x_0) : \boldsymbol{M}] \wedge [\pi_1(x_0) = A] \wedge [\pi_2(x_0) = B]$

$\phi_1 \stackrel{\text{def}}{=} \Phi(\mathcal{A}(K))$ *where* K *has been defined in Example 1*

$$\begin{aligned}\phi_2 \stackrel{\text{def}}{=}\ & [\mathrm{D}_{k_{BS}}(x_2) : \boldsymbol{M}]\\ \wedge\ & [\pi_1(\mathrm{D}_{k_{BS}}(x_2)) : \boldsymbol{M}] \wedge [\pi_2(\mathrm{D}_{k_{BS}}(x_2)) : \boldsymbol{M}]\\ \wedge\ & [\pi_1(\pi_2(\mathrm{D}_{k_{BS}}(x_2))) : \boldsymbol{M}] \wedge [\pi_2(\pi_2(\mathrm{D}_{k_{BS}}(x_2))) : \boldsymbol{M}]\\ \wedge\ & [\pi_1(\mathrm{D}_{k_{BS}}(x_2)) = A] \wedge [\pi_2(\pi_2(\mathrm{D}_{k_{BS}}(x_2))) = t]\end{aligned}$$

---

[4] Usually, narrations are defined such that the sender A is supposed to statically know the precise name B of the intended receiver. In a dynamic scenario, the compilation would need to check that B is synthesizable by A.

Table 7. Definition of $\mathcal{X}[\![\cdot]\!]^{\cdot}$

$$\mathcal{X}[\![\epsilon]\!]^{(\upsilon,\varpi,\kappa,\nu)} \stackrel{\text{def}}{=} \epsilon$$

$$\mathcal{X}[\![A \textbf{ knows } M; P]\!]^{(\upsilon,\varpi,\kappa,\nu)} \stackrel{\text{def}}{=} \mathcal{X}[\![P]\!]^{(\upsilon,\varpi,\kappa',\nu)} \quad \text{if } \mathrm{n}(M) \cap \bigcup_{A \in \boldsymbol{A}} \nu(A) = \emptyset$$
$$\text{where } K'_A \stackrel{\text{def}}{=} \kappa(A) \cup \{(M,M)\}$$
$$\text{and } \kappa' \stackrel{\text{def}}{=} \kappa\,[A \leftarrow \mathrm{rep}(\mathcal{I}(K'_A))]$$

$$\mathcal{X}[\![\textbf{private } k; P]\!]^{(\upsilon,\varpi,\kappa,\nu)} \stackrel{\text{def}}{=} \nu k; \mathcal{X}[\![P]\!]^{(\upsilon,\varpi\cup\{k\},\kappa,\nu)}$$
$$\text{if } k \notin \varpi \cup \bigcup_{A \in \boldsymbol{A}} (\mathrm{n}(\kappa(A)) \cup \nu(A))$$

$$\mathcal{X}[\![A \textbf{ generates } n; P]\!]^{(\upsilon,\varpi,\kappa,\nu)} \stackrel{\text{def}}{=} \nu n; \mathcal{X}[\![P]\!]^{(\upsilon,\varpi,\kappa',\nu')}$$
$$\text{if } n \notin \varpi \cup \bigcup_{A \in \boldsymbol{A}} (\mathrm{n}(\kappa(A)) \cup \nu(A))$$
$$\text{where } K'_A \stackrel{\text{def}}{=} \kappa(A) \cup \{(n,n)\}$$
$$\text{and } \kappa' \stackrel{\text{def}}{=} \kappa\,[A \leftarrow \mathrm{rep}(\mathcal{I}(K'_A))]$$
$$\text{and } \nu' \stackrel{\text{def}}{=} \nu\,[A \leftarrow \nu(A) \cup \{n\}]$$

$$\mathcal{X}[\![A \rightsquigarrow B{:}M; P]\!]^{(\upsilon,\varpi,\kappa,\nu)} \stackrel{\text{def}}{=} A{:}B!E \;;\; B{:}?x \;;\; B{:}\phi \;;\; \mathcal{X}[\![P]\!]^{(\upsilon\cup\{x\},\varpi,\kappa',\nu)}$$
$$\text{if } A \neq B \text{ and } (M,E) \in \mathcal{S}(\kappa(A))$$
$$\text{where } x \stackrel{\text{def}}{=} \min(\boldsymbol{V} \setminus \upsilon)$$
$$\text{and } K'_B \stackrel{\text{def}}{=} \kappa(B) \cup \{(M,x)\}$$
$$\text{and } \kappa' \stackrel{\text{def}}{=} \kappa\,[B \leftarrow \mathrm{rep}(\mathcal{I}(K'_B))]$$
$$\text{and } \phi \stackrel{\text{def}}{=} \Phi(\mathcal{A}(K'_B))$$

In the last example, the obtained formulae apparently contain some redundant checks. As usual, two formulae ϕ and ψ may be considered equivalent if for all substitutions $\sigma : \boldsymbol{V} \to \boldsymbol{M}$, we have $[\![\phi\sigma]\!] = [\![\psi\sigma]\!]$. Then, for example, ϕ_2 is equivalent to ϕ'_2 where:

$$\phi'_2 \stackrel{\text{def}}{=} [\pi_1(\mathrm{D}_{k_{BS}}(x_2)) = A] \wedge [\pi_2(\pi_2(\mathrm{D}_{k_{BS}}(x_2))) = t]$$

Formulae like ϕ_2 are to be generated automatically, and it seems mandatory to also provide automatic simplification to remove redundant checks. However, in general, it is not obvious to define an intuitive notion of *minimality* for formulae. For example, $\phi = [E_1 = F_1] \wedge [E_2 = F_2]$ and $\psi = [(E_1 \,.\, E_2) = (F_1 \,.\, F_2)]$ are equivalent; which one should be qualified as simpler? An even more interesting case is $\phi = [E = F] \wedge [G{:}\boldsymbol{M}]$ and $\psi = [\pi_1((E \,.\, G)) = F]$, which indicates that there is a trade-off between the bare number of conjoints and their size.

4 Executing Protocol Narrations

In this section, we propose an operational semantics for narrations. It proceeds in a traditional syntax-directed manner by analyzing the current top-level construct in order to see what to execute next. Since narrations contain some implicit

Table 8. Substitution

$$\epsilon\{^{M}/_{x}\}_{@A} \stackrel{\text{def}}{=} \epsilon$$

$$(A'{:}B!E;X)\{^{M}/_{x}\}_{@A} \stackrel{\text{def}}{=} \begin{cases} A'{:}B!E;X\{^{M}/_{x}\}_{@A} & \text{if } A' \neq A \\ A{:}B!E\{^{M}/_{x}\};X\{^{M}/_{x}\}_{@A} & \text{otherwise} \end{cases}$$

$$(A'{:}?y;X)\{^{M}/_{x}\}_{@A} \stackrel{\text{def}}{=} \begin{cases} A'{:}?y;X\{^{M}/_{x}\}_{@A} & \text{if } A' \neq A \\ A{:}?y;X\{^{M}/_{x}\}_{@A} & \text{if } A = A' \text{ and } y \neq x \\ A{:}?x;X & \text{otherwise} \end{cases}$$

$$(A'{:}\phi;X)\{^{M}/_{x}\}_{@A} \stackrel{\text{def}}{=} \begin{cases} A'{:}\phi;X\{^{M}/_{x}\}_{@A} & \text{if } A' \neq A \\ A{:}\phi\{^{M}/_{x}\};X\{^{M}/_{x}\}_{@A} & \text{otherwise} \end{cases}$$

$$(\nu n;X)\{^{M}/_{x}\}_{@A} \stackrel{\text{def}}{=} \nu n;X\{^{M}/_{x}\}_{@A}$$

concurrency among principals, we introduce a structural reordering relation to shuffle concurrently enabled actions to the top level. The actual execution of steps further needs to take care of the evaluation of messages to be sent, and also to prevent from name clashes that are possible due to the presence of binders.

Binders and α-conversion. Our language of executable narrations contains two sort of binders: one for names and one for variables.

The first binder is introduced by the construction νn. If $X = \nu n;X'$, then n is bound in X (i.e. the free occurrences of n in X' refers to this binder). As the identity of n is not important, we identify X with $\nu n';X'\{^{n'}/_{n}\}$ where n' is a name that is not free in X and $X'\{^{n'}/_{n}\}$ is X' where all the free occurrences of n has been replaced with n'. X and $\nu n';X'\{^{n'}/_{n}\}$ are called α-equivalent. In the following, we identify α-equivalent executable narrations. Now, for an executable narration X, we can define the usual *bound names* $\text{bn}(X)$, *free names* $\text{fn}(X)$ of X and, moreover, if $n, n' \in \boldsymbol{N}$, $X\{^{n'}/_{n}\}$, the substitution of n' for n in X.

The second binder is the one introduced by the construction $A{:}?x$. If $X = A{:}?x;X'$, then x is bound in the actions of X' concerning A: indeed, if further in the executable narration, B refers to x, the x is not the same as the one used by A. Since variables will typically be substituted with messages, we do not need α-conversion on variables but we need to define a new kind of *local substitution*: if X is an executable narration, $x \in \boldsymbol{V}$, $M \in \boldsymbol{M}$ with $\text{n}(M) \cap \text{bn}(X) = \emptyset$ (which can be assured by choosing a suitable α-equivalent version of X), and $A \in \boldsymbol{A}$, we define in Table 8 the substitution $X\{^{M}/_{x}\}_{@A}$ of M for x in X on A.

Reordering. Protocol narrations are sequences of actions. However, the sequential character is not always causally motivated. Instead, the order of two consecutive actions carried out by *different* principals can always be swapped, because —after our split of message exchanges in the compilation process of Section 3— they are *independent*. The same holds for the consecutive occurrence of an action and a scope, unless the scope's name occurs in the action. Formally, we manifest the swapping of independent actions in a structural congruence relation.

Table 9. Reordering

$$\cong\text{-S-S}\ \frac{A \neq C}{A{:}B!E;C{:}D!F \cong C{:}D!F;A{:}B!E} \qquad \cong\text{-S-C}\ \frac{A \neq C}{A{:}B!E;C{:}\phi \cong C{:}\phi;A{:}B!E}$$

$$\cong\text{-S-R}\ \frac{A \neq C}{A{:}B!E;C{:}?x \cong C{:}?x;A{:}B!E} \qquad \cong\text{-R-C}\ \frac{A \neq C}{A{:}?x;C{:}\phi \cong C{:}\phi;A{:}?x}$$

$$\cong\text{-R-R}\ \frac{A \neq C}{A{:}?x;C{:}?y \cong C{:}?y;A{:}?x} \qquad \cong\text{-C-C}\ \frac{A \neq C}{A{:}\phi;C{:}\psi \cong C{:}\psi;A{:}\phi}$$

$$\cong\text{-S-N}\ \frac{n \notin \mathrm{n}(E)}{A{:}B!E;\nu n \cong \nu n;A{:}B!E} \qquad \cong\text{-C-N}\ \frac{n \notin \mathrm{n}(\phi)}{A{:}\phi;\nu n \cong \nu n;A{:}\phi}$$

$$\cong\text{-R-N}\ \frac{}{A{:}?x;\nu n \cong \nu n;A{:}?x} \qquad \cong\text{-N-N}\ \frac{}{\nu n;\nu m \cong \nu m;\nu n}$$

Definition 6. *The* reordering $\cong \subseteq \boldsymbol{X} \times \boldsymbol{X}$ *is the least equivalence relation satisfying the rules given in Table 9, and closed under contexts of the form* $X\,;[\cdot]\,;X'$.

We define $\cong_\alpha$ *to be the union of* $\cong$ *and* α*-equivalence.*

Given a particular message exchange $A{\leadsto}B{:}M$, it may possibly seem surprising at first that the reordering relation allows the respective reception action $B{:}?x$ to occur *before* its associated emission action $A{:}B!M$. Clearly, the received message cannot be the intended one. Such a behavior must be dealt with carefully, e.g., by rejecting unintended messages, but its existence cannot be avoided; it is a matter of fact in concurrent systems that exchange messages asynchronously.

Evaluation of expressions and formulae. Table 10 shows how to evaluate expressions and formulae. The definitions are straightforward and offer no surprises, except for allowing the observation that $[E : \boldsymbol{M}]$ is just a macro for $[E{=}E]$.

Labeled transitions. We define a straightforward labeled semantics of executable narrations, in style influenced by semantics for the spi-calculus, in Table 11.

Our semantics relates two executable narrations with a transition $\xrightarrow{A:\beta}$ where $A \in \boldsymbol{A}$ and β is either an input action $?M$ where $M \in \boldsymbol{M}$ or a bound output action $(\nu\tilde{n})\,B!M$ where $\tilde{n}$ is a (possibly empty) list of pairwise distinct names $n_1 \cdots n_k$ (that are bound in the remainder), $B \in \boldsymbol{A}$ and $M \in \boldsymbol{M}$. If $k = 0$ (i.e. $\tilde{n}$ is empty), we will simply write $B!M$. Note that there is no internal action in our formal semantics of narrations. We might also have introduced a rule like

$$\textsc{Com}\ \frac{X \xrightarrow{A:(\nu\tilde{n})\,B!M} X' \qquad X' \xrightarrow{B:?M} X''}{X \xrightarrow{\tau} \nu\tilde{n};X''}$$

but we tend to insist on the fact that every communication necessarily passes through the network, while such a rule Com would allow to avoid this.

Table 10. Evaluation of expressions (can fail, in particular if $\mathrm{v}(E) \neq \emptyset$) and formulae

Definition of $[\![\cdot]\!] : \boldsymbol{E} \to \{\bot\} \cup \boldsymbol{M}$	
$[\![E]\!] \stackrel{\text{def}}{=} E$	if $E \in \boldsymbol{N} \cup \boldsymbol{A}$
$[\![(E\,.\,F)]\!] \stackrel{\text{def}}{=} (M\,.\,N)$	if $[\![E]\!] = M \in \boldsymbol{M}$ and $[\![F]\!] = N \in \boldsymbol{M}$
$[\![\pi_1(E)]\!] \stackrel{\text{def}}{=} M$	if $[\![E]\!] = (M\,.\,N) \in \boldsymbol{M}$
$[\![\pi_2(E)]\!] \stackrel{\text{def}}{=} N$	if $[\![E]\!] = (M\,.\,N) \in \boldsymbol{M}$
$[\![\{E\}_F]\!] \stackrel{\text{def}}{=} \{M\}_N$	if $[\![E]\!] = M \in \boldsymbol{M}$ and $[\![F]\!] = N \in \boldsymbol{M}$
$[\![\mathrm{D}_F(E)]\!] \stackrel{\text{def}}{=} M$	if $[\![E]\!] = \{M\}_N \in \boldsymbol{M}$ and $[\![F]\!] = N \in \boldsymbol{M}$
$[\![E]\!] \stackrel{\text{def}}{=} \bot$	in all other cases
Definition of $[\![\cdot]\!] : \boldsymbol{F} \to \{\mathbf{true}, \mathbf{false}\}$	
$[\![tt]\!] \stackrel{\text{def}}{=} \mathbf{true}$	
$[\![\phi \wedge \psi]\!] \stackrel{\text{def}}{=} [\![\phi]\!]$ and $[\![\psi]\!]$	
$[\![[E{=}F]]\!] \stackrel{\text{def}}{=} \mathbf{true}$	if $[\![E]\!] = [\![F]\!] = M \in \boldsymbol{M}$
$[\![[E{:}\boldsymbol{M}]]\!] \stackrel{\text{def}}{=} \mathbf{true}$	if $[\![E]\!] = M \in \boldsymbol{M}$
$[\![\phi]\!] \stackrel{\text{def}}{=} \mathbf{false}$	in all other cases

Table 11. Labeled semantics of executable narrations

$$\textsc{Send}\ \frac{[\![E]\!] = M \in \boldsymbol{M}}{A{:}B!E;X \xrightarrow{A:B!M} X} \qquad \textsc{Receive}\ \frac{}{A{:}?x;X \xrightarrow{A:?M} X\{^{M}/_{x}\}_{@A}}\ M \in \boldsymbol{M}$$

$$\textsc{Check}\ \frac{X \xrightarrow{A:\beta} X'}{A{:}\phi;X \xrightarrow{A:\beta} X'}\ [\![\phi]\!] = \mathbf{true} \qquad \textsc{Open}\ \frac{X \xrightarrow{A:(\nu\tilde{n})\,B!M} X'}{\nu z;X \xrightarrow{A:(\nu z\tilde{n})\,B!M} X'}\ z \in \mathrm{n}(M) \setminus \{\tilde{n}\}$$

$$\textsc{Rearrange}\ \frac{X \cong_\alpha X' \qquad X' \xrightarrow{A:\beta} X''}{X \xrightarrow{A:\beta} X''}$$

5 Rewriting Protocol Narrations ... into Spi-Calculus

The spi-calculus is a process calculus that was designed in order to study cryptographic protocols. In this section, we show that executable narrations closely correspond to terms in a quite restricted fragment of the spi-calculus.

Syntax. We use a finite spi-calculus without choice, generated as P by:

$$P ::= \mathbf{0} \mid E(x).P \mid \overline{E}\langle F\rangle.P \mid P \,|\, Q \mid (\nu n)\,P \mid \phi P$$

We use the same syntactic categories (names, agent names) as for narrations.

Table 12. Labeled semantics of spi-calculus

$$\textsc{Input}\ \frac{[\![E]\!] = A \in \boldsymbol{A} \qquad M \in \boldsymbol{M}}{E(x).P \xrightarrow{A\,M} P\{^M/_x\}} \qquad \textsc{Output}\ \frac{[\![E]\!] = A \in \boldsymbol{A} \qquad [\![F]\!] = M \in \boldsymbol{M}}{\overline{E}\langle F\rangle.P \xrightarrow{\overline{A}\,M} P}$$

$$\textsc{Open}\ \frac{P \xrightarrow{(\nu\tilde{n})\,\overline{A}\,M} P'}{(\nu z)\,P \xrightarrow{(\nu z\tilde{n})\,\overline{A}\,M} P'}\ z \in \mathrm{n}(M) \setminus \tilde{n} \qquad \textsc{Res}\ \frac{P \xrightarrow{\mu} P'}{(\nu n)\,P \xrightarrow{\mu} (\nu n)\,P'}\ n \notin \mathrm{fn}(\mu)$$

$$\textsc{Guard}\ \frac{P \xrightarrow{\mu} P'}{\phi P \xrightarrow{\mu} P'}\ [\![\phi]\!] = \mathbf{true} \qquad \textsc{Par}\ \frac{P \xrightarrow{\mu} P'}{P \,|\, Q \xrightarrow{\mu} P' \,|\, Q}\ \mathrm{bn}(\mu) \cap \mathrm{fn}(Q) = \emptyset$$

$$\textsc{Struct}\ \frac{P \equiv P' \qquad P' \xrightarrow{\mu} P''}{P \xrightarrow{\mu} P''}$$

In process $E(x).P$, the variable x is bound in P and in the process $(\nu n)\,P$, the name n is bound in P. For a process P, we denote its set of free names $\mathrm{fn}(P)$, bound names $\mathrm{bn}(P)$, free variables $\mathrm{fv}(P)$ and bound variables $\mathrm{bv}(P)$.

Semantics. Table 12 shows a labeled semantics for the spi-calculus. It relies on the definition of structural congruence $\equiv$ defined as the least congruence satisfying:

- $\forall P, Q, R : (P \,|\, Q) \,|\, R \equiv P \,|\, (Q \,|\, R)$
- $\forall P, Q : P \,|\, Q \equiv Q \,|\, P$
- $\forall P : P \,|\, \mathbf{0} \equiv P$
- $\forall P, Q, n : (\nu n)\,P \,|\, Q \equiv (\nu n)\,(P \,|\, Q)$ if $n \notin \mathrm{fn}(Q)$
- $\forall P, Q : P \equiv Q$ if P and Q are α-equivalent

Communication can only occur on agent names. Moreover, since it is syntactically not possible to hide an agent name from outside, we do not consider internal communications. Transitions are thus of two kinds: either an input action $A\,M$ or a bound output action $(\nu\tilde{n})\,\overline{A}\,M$ where in both cases $A \in \boldsymbol{A}$ and $M \in \boldsymbol{M}$, $\tilde{n}$ being a (possibly empty) list of pairwise distinct names that are binding occurrences in M.

Executable narrations in spi-calculus. As the reader might have noticed, the executable narrations as of §3 and the spi-calculus above are similar. Thus, we may now provide a straightforward translation of executable narrations into the spi-calculus and easily show that the semantics is preserved. The main idea is that the implicit concurrency structure of narrations as encoded with explicit agent names is projected out ($X\!\upharpoonright_A$ of Definition 7) and explicitly represented using the parallel composition operator of the spi-calculus. Any intended sequential occurrence of actions, namely those actions that are associated to the same agent, is preserved by using the prefix operator of the spi-calculus. The private names are then simply put as a top-level restricted around the parallel composition.

Table 13. Definition of $\mathcal{A}(\cdot)$, $R(\cdot)$, and $\cdot\restriction$.

$$\begin{aligned}
\mathcal{A}(\epsilon) &\stackrel{\text{def}}{=} \emptyset \\
\mathcal{A}(A{:}B!E;X) &\stackrel{\text{def}}{=} \{A\} \cup \mathcal{A}(X) \\
\mathcal{A}(A{:}?x;X) &\stackrel{\text{def}}{=} \{A\} \cup \mathcal{A}(X) \\
\mathcal{A}(A{:}\phi;X) &\stackrel{\text{def}}{=} \{A\} \cup \mathcal{A}(X) \\
\mathcal{A}(\nu n;X) &\stackrel{\text{def}}{=} \mathcal{A}(X)
\end{aligned}$$

$$\begin{aligned}
R(\epsilon) &\stackrel{\text{def}}{=} \emptyset \\
R(A{:}B!E;X) &\stackrel{\text{def}}{=} R(X) \\
R(A{:}?x;X) &\stackrel{\text{def}}{=} R(X) \\
R(A{:}\phi;X) &\stackrel{\text{def}}{=} R(X) \\
R(\nu n;X) &\stackrel{\text{def}}{=} \{n\} \cup R(X)
\end{aligned}$$

$$\begin{aligned}
\epsilon\restriction_A &\stackrel{\text{def}}{=} \mathbf{0} \\
(A'{:}B!E;X)\restriction_A &\stackrel{\text{def}}{=} \begin{cases} \overline{B}\langle E\rangle.X\restriction_A & \text{if } A' = A \\ X\restriction_A & \text{otherwise} \end{cases} \\
(A'{:}?x;X)\restriction_A &\stackrel{\text{def}}{=} \begin{cases} A(x).X\restriction_A & \text{if } A' = A \\ X\restriction_A & \text{otherwise} \end{cases} \\
(A'{:}\phi;X)\restriction_A &\stackrel{\text{def}}{=} \begin{cases} \phi X\restriction_A & \text{if } A' = A \\ X\restriction_A & \text{otherwise} \end{cases} \\
(\nu n;X)\restriction_A &\stackrel{\text{def}}{=} X\restriction_A
\end{aligned}$$

Definition 7 (Translation). *Let $X \in \boldsymbol{X}$ be an executable narration.*

1. *$\mathcal{A}(X)$ (Table 13) defines the set of agents acting in X.*
2. *$R(X)$ (Table 13) defines the set of fresh restricted names of X.*
3. *$X\restriction_A$ (Table 13) defines the spi projection of X on $A \in \boldsymbol{A}$.*
4. *The translation $\mathcal{T}[\![X]\!]$ of X into spi-calculus is defined by:*

$$\mathcal{T}[\![X]\!] \stackrel{\text{def}}{=} (\nu n)_{n \in R(X)} \prod\nolimits_{A \in \mathcal{A}(X)} X\restriction_A$$

where $(\nu n)_{n \in I}$ and $\prod_{n \in I}$ denote n-ary restriction and composition.

5. *$\mathcal{T}[\![A{:}?M]\!] \stackrel{\text{def}}{=} A\,M$ and $\mathcal{T}[\![A{:}(\nu\tilde{n})\,B!M]\!] \stackrel{\text{def}}{=} (\nu\tilde{n})\,\overline{B}\,M$ map transition labels.*

The following theorem concludes that the operational semantics of executable narrations and their spi-calculus translations precisely coincide up to $\equiv$.

Theorem 1. *Let $X \in \boldsymbol{X}$ be an executable narration.*

1. *If $X \xrightarrow{A:\beta} X'$ then $\mathcal{T}[\![X]\!] \xrightarrow{\mathcal{T}[\![A:\beta]\!]} P'$ with $P' \equiv \mathcal{T}[\![X']\!]$.*
2. *If $\mathcal{T}[\![X]\!] \xrightarrow{\mu} P'$ then there exists $A \in \boldsymbol{A}$, X' and β such that $X \xrightarrow{A:\beta} X'$, $P' \equiv \mathcal{T}[\![X']\!]$ and $\mu = \mathcal{T}[\![A{:}\beta]\!]$.*

6 Conclusions

Contributions. In summary, we stepwise enhance protocol narrations in order to build up enough structure such that a well-motivated formalization of their semantics becomes possible. The main technical contribution is the proposal of the automatic generation of "checks-on-reception", together with a suitable representation of the principals' knowledge on which the generation depends.

In summary, if one wants to reformulate informal protocol narrations within a calculus like the spi-calculus, then we propose the following method:

1. Extend the narration, as shown in §2, by a declaration part making precise the origin of and initial knowledge about the involved data (names). This step requires human interaction, because ambiguities need to be resolved.
2. Compile the resulting narration, as shown in §3, into an executable narration. This step can now be done automatically.
3. Extract the implicit concurrency, as shown just above. Again, automatically.

It is worthwhile pointing out that our approach does not bother the protocol designer to come up with suitable or sufficient checks-on-reception, because they are generated automatically. Our approach does not even require the designer to actually look at these generated checks at all.

Tool support. We have implemented the previous developments in OCaml, including the syntactic sugar mentioned at the end of Section 2. Due to the big size of the formulae generated, we have studied possible simplifications for them. To this end, we have implemented naive ideas such as removing duplicated atoms, or removing atoms like $[E:\boldsymbol{M}]$ when E is a message or when it appears as a subexpression of the remaining formula. We also perform some rewriting inside formulae, which apparently gives good result in practice.

We have also investigated extension of the work of this paper towards richer message languages (i.e. with public/private key, hashing). It appears that simplifying formulae becomes even more of a necessity.

Related work. Sumii et. al. [STY05] propose a formal semantics of narrations by translation into spi-calculus. The paper is written in Japanese, so it remains unclear to us how they treat the problem of checks-on-reception. In any case, our intention was to provide a formal semantics that does *not require* an underlying (too) general process calculus, so our approach is still substantially different.

The work of Bodei et. al. [BBD+03] is also similar to ours, although still quite different. Like us, they present a refinement of protocol narrations, but the respective checks-on-reception appear only informally. Like us, they split message exchanges into three parts, albeit different to ours. A formal semantics is then only provided after "rewriting", again informally, refined narrations into terms of their process calculus LySa. In the above paper (the only that we are aware of), the system underlying their "systematic expansion" is not unambiguously explained, while our expansion is fully automatic and generates a maximum number of checks. Finally, their approach aims at static analysis techniques, while we ultimately target at dynamic analysis in the form of bisimulation checks [BBN04] in the full spi-calculus (LySa is channel-free).

In other related approaches, narrations are reformulated or translated using Casper [Low98], HLPSL2IF [BMV03], CAPSL [Mil], CASRUL [JRV00], or (s)pi-calculus [AG99, Bla03]. They have in common that they do not easily help to understand how the gap between the rather informal narrations and the target formalism is bridged. A compiler can itself be interpreted as giving semantics to narrations, but usually the translation process is not well explained or otherwise justified, in particular regarding the treatment of checks-on-reception. Moreover, our interest was to try to formalize the semantics at the level of narrations rather than by translation into some reasonably unrelated target formalism.

A subtle, but interesting difference between our work and Casper [Low98] is their modified message syntax using a construction `M % v`, meaning that the recipient of `M` should *not* try to decrypt `M`. We think this construct was added because of Casper's rather strict policy to *require*, unless the % is used, to be able to fully decrypt all messages (and possibly provide a warning in case this fails). Our (arguably more flexible) policy is instead to require agents to always *just try* to decrypt messages as far as their current knowledge permits, so we implicitly let agents accept messages even if they cannot (yet) fully decrypt them.

Future work. Here, we do not tackle the fourth task listed by Abadi [Aba00] on how to get to a formalization of concurrent sessions on the basis of protocol narrations. The main problem is that *principals* may play different *roles* in concurrent sessions such that the lookup of their respective keys needs to be dealt with dynamically. The usual convenient confusion of the two concepts of principal and role is no longer appropriate, so we propose to non-trivially extend the narration notation rather than providing a suboptimal semantics to an inappropriate notation. Note that this confusion also rules out the naïve modeling of concurrent sessions by the bare unbounded replication within spi-calculus. Some inspiration from the work of Cremers and Mauw [CM05] may help us here.

Furthermore, we intend to develop reasoning techniques for protocol narrations via an *environment-sensitive* extension of our semantics that could be used to define and study meaningful behavioral equivalences.

References

[Aba00] M. Abadi. Security Protocols and their Properties. In *Foundations of Secure Computation*, pages 39–60. NATO ASI, IOS Press, 2000.

[AG99] M. Abadi and A. D. Gordon. A Calculus for Cryptographic Protocols: The Spi Calculus. *Information and Computation*, 148(1):1–70, 1999.

[BBD+03] C. Bodei, M. Buchholtz, P. Degano, F. Nielson and H. Nielson. Automatic validation of protocol narration. In *Proceedings of 16th IEEE Computer Security Foundations Workshop (CSFW 16)*, pages 126–140, 2003.

[BBN04] J. Borgström, S. Briais and U. Nestmann. Symbolic Bisimulation in the Spi Calculus. In *Proceedings of CONCUR 2004*, volume 3170 of *LNCS*, pages 161–176. Springer, Sept. 2004.

[Bla03] B. Blanchet. Automatic Verification of Cryptographic Protocols: A Logic Programming Approach. In *Proceedings of Principles and Practice of Declarative Programming (PPDP'03)*. ACM, 2003.

[BMV03] D. Basin, S. Mödersheim and L. Viganò. An On-The-Fly Model-Checker for Security Protocol Analysis. In *Proceedings of ESORICS'03*, LNCS 2808, pages 253–270. Springer-Verlag, Heidelberg, 2003.

[Bri04] S. Briais. Formal proofs about hedges using the Coq proof assistant, 2004. `http://lamp.epfl.ch/~{}sbriais/spi/hedges/hedge.html`.

[CJ97] J. A. Clark and J. L. Jacob. A survey of authentication protocol literature. Technical Report 1.0, University of York, 1997.

[CM05] C. Cremers and S. Mauw. Operational Semantics of Security Protocols. In *Scenarios: Models, Algorithms and Tools (Dagstuhl 03371 Post-Seminar Proceedings)*, volume 3466 of *LNCS*, 2005.

[DY83] D. Dolev and A. C. Yao. On the security of public key protocols. *IEEE Transactions on Information Theory*, IT-29(12):198–208, Mar. 1983.

[Gen03] C. Gensoul. *Spyer — un compilateur de protocoles cryptographiques.* Semester Project Report, EPFL, July 2003.

[JRV00] F. Jacquemard, M. Rusinowitch and L. Vigneron. Compiling and Verifying Security Protocols. In *Logic for Programming and Automated Reasoning*, volume 1955 of *LNCS*, pages 131–160. Springer-Verlag, November 2000.

[Low98] G. Lowe. Casper: A Compiler for the Analysis of Security Protocols. *Journal of Computer Security*, 6:53–84, 1998.

[Mil] J. K. Millen. CAPSL: Common Authentication Protocol Specification Language. http://www.csl.sri.com/users/millen/capsl/.

[MvOV96] A. J. Menezes, P. C. van Oorschot and S. A. Vanstone. *Handbook of Applied Cryptography*. CRC Press, 1996.

[Pau98] L. C. Paulson. The Inductive Approach to Verifying Cryptographic Protocols. *Journal of Computer Security*, 6(1-2):85–128, 1998.

[STY05] E. Sumii, H. Tatsuzawa and A. Yonezawa. Translating Security Protocols from Informal Notation into Spi Calculus. *IPSJ Transactions on Programming*, 45, 2005. Written in Japanese, abstract in English. To appear.

webπ at Work

Cosimo Laneve and Gianluigi Zavattaro

Dipartimento di Scienze dell'Informazione, Università di Bologna,
Mura A.Zamboni 7, I-40127 Bologna, Italy
{laneve, zavattar}@cs.unibo.it

Abstract. webπ is a recent process calculus that has been inspired by the emerging Web Services technologies. In this paper we explore the expressivity of webπ by discussing two case studies. The first case study is about the formal semantics of the transactional construct of BPEL – the scope construct. The second case study is about a standard pattern of Web Services composition – the *speculative parallelism* – that allows several alternative activities to start; only the first one that completes is taken into account while the other ones are aborted.

1 Introduction

Web Services technologies are emerging mechanisms for describing the services available on the web, as well as their interfaces and the protocols for locating and invoking such services. A challenging issue in this area is the definition of languages and tools for composing services. In fact it is often the case to define new services out of finer-grained subtasks that are likely available as Web Services. As a consequence, several proposals for service composition have been recently devised – the so called *Web Services orchestration and choreography languages*. Among the others we recall XLANG [9], WSFL [8], BPEL [1], and WS-CDL [6].

Long-running transactions are used in most of the Web Services orchestration and choreography languages as basic mechanisms for composing services. These transactions – that we will call *web transactions* – usually do not grant any isolation or atomicity property. As regards isolation, it requires that different activities have the same effect whether they are executed in sequence or in parallel. This is usually enforced by locking the resources used by each activity until the transaction commits. In the context of Web Services, the processes involved in a transaction may belong to different companies, and there is no chance to lock resources of other companies. Additionally, commercial transactions usually last long periods of time, even months, and it is not feasible and not reasonable to block resources so long. For similar reasons, it is not adequate supplying a perfect rollback in the context of Web Services composition. As a matter of facts, in Web Services orchestration and choreography languages, the transaction isolation is delegated to explicit protocols realized through messages; whilst the roll-back mechanisms are defined by ad-hoc programs.

Even if web transactions are attracting a great interest, the Web Services community has not reached a common agreement on a unique notion of this form

R. De Nicola and D. Sangiorgi (Eds.): TGC 2005, LNCS 3705, pp. 182–194, 2005.

of transaction. Additionally, the semantics that is usually defined is informal and requires a mathematical analysis. Exceptions we are aware of rely on specific proposals: the work [5] that is mainly inspired by `XLANG`, the calculus of Butler and Ferreira [4] is inspired by `BPBeans`, the πt-calculus [2] considers `BizTalk`, the work [3] deals with short-lived transactions in `BizTalk`.

A different approach has been recently taken in [7], where a process calculus is explicitly designed for modelling web transactions. This calculus, called webπ, is independent of the different proposals and allows to grab the key concepts. Three major aspects are considered in webπ: interruptible processes, failure handlers that are activated when the main process is interrupted, and time. Time has been considered because it is fundamental for dealing with the typical latency of web activities or with message losses. The above three aspects are analyzed in a model consisting of a network of locations that contain processes. In this model time proceeds asynchronously at the network level, while it is constrained by the *local urgency* property inside a location. Local urgency entails the fact that process reductions in a location cannot be delayed to favour idle steps. Said otherwise, local urgency means that the time may elapse in a location either because the process inside progresses or because no progress is possible. We refer to [7] for a discussion about the model of webπ, and its extensional semantics – the *timed bisimilarity.*

The aim of this paper is to explore the expressivity of webπ in two non-trivial case studies inspired by the Web Services technology. The first case study is about the formal semantics of `BPEL`. This language, being the conjoint effort of three major information technology companies, is becoming the standard *de facto* for Web Service orchestration. Defining its formal semantics is therefore a valuable task. In this paper we focus on the unique transactional mechanism in `BPEL` – the `scope` construct – and we define its semantics by means of webπ. The `scope` construct is used to associate a failure handler, a compensation handler, and an event handler to a so-called primary activity. The failure handler is executed if a fault condition occurs during the execution of the primary activity. The compensation handler, on the other hand, is activated if the execution of the primary activity is required to be undone after it has provisionally committed. Finally, the event handler is executed if the primary activity is still under execution and a specific message or allarm is triggered. In this paper we only define the formal semantics of fault and compensation handlers that are used for error handling.

The second case study is about a prototypical pattern of service composition – the so-called *speculative parallelism.* This pattern generalizes the request-response pattern between a client and a server, to cases in which the response can be produced by more than one server. In these cases, the client sends the request to all the possible (alternative) servers. The accepted response is the first one that is received, the other responses are deleted. The non-trivial issue of speculative parallelism is the synchronization of the winner server (the one producing the accepted response) with the communications of failure to the other servers. We model the pattern of speculative parallelism in webπ, together with a number of erroneous patterns that manifest subtle misbehaviours.

The paper is structured as follows. In Section 2 we recall the syntax ans semantics of webπ. In Section 3 we discuss the first case study while in Section 4 we discuss the second one. We conclude in Section 5.

2 The Calculus webπ

In this Section we recall the syntax of webπ and informally describe its semantics.

The syntax uses a countable set of *names*, ranged over by $x, y, z, u, \cdots$. Tuples of names are written $\widetilde{u}$. The syntax of webπ includes machines and processes.

M ::=	**(machines)**	P ::=	**(processes)**
$\mathbf{0}$	(nil)	$\mathbf{0}$	(nil)
$\mid [\, P \,]_{\widetilde{x}}$	(location)	$\mid \overline{x}\,\widetilde{u}$	(message)
$\mid (x)\mathsf{M}$	(machine restriction)	$\mid x(\widetilde{u}).P$	(input)
$\mid \mathsf{M} \mid \mathsf{M}$	(network)	$\mid (x)P$	(restriction)
		$\mid P \mid P$	(parallel composition)
		$\mid !x(\widetilde{u}).P$	(replicated input)
		$\mid \langle\!| P \,;\, P |\!\rangle_x^n$	(transaction)

A location $[\, P \,]_{\widetilde{x}}$ is a uniprocessor machine; the names $\widetilde{x}$ indicate that the location is responsible for accepting messages on such names. Locations possess their own clock that is not synchronized with the clock of other locations (time progresses asynchronously between different locations). Namely, if M and N are locations, and M evolves in M' then also $\mathsf{M} \mid \mathsf{N}$ evolves in $\mathsf{M}' \mid \mathsf{N}$ (the clock of N remains unchanged).

Processes extend the asynchronous π-calculus with *transactions* $\langle\!| P \,;\, Q |\!\rangle_x^n$, where P and Q are the *body* and the *compensation*, respectively, n indicates the deadline, and x is the name of the transaction. The body of a transaction executes either until termination or until the transaction fails. On failure, the compensation is activated. A transaction may fail in two different ways, either explicitly (when the abort message $\overline{x}$ is consumed, where x is the name of the transaction to be aborted) or implicitly (when the deadline is reached). The deadline may be reached either because of computational steps of the body or because of computational steps of processes in parallel in the same location.

The model of time of webπ is such that, within a location, operations cannot be delayed in favour of idle operations – this property is called *local urgency*. For example, consider two processes running on the same location: a printer process of a warning message with a timeout and an idle process waiting for an external event. Local urgency means that, if the external event doesn't occur, then the printer process cannot be delayed. Said otherwise, the time elapses in a location either because the process inside progresses or because no progress is possible.

In webπ networks names always index a unique location. The *location names* used in a network are denoted with $\mathtt{ln}(\mathsf{M})$. Formally, let $\mathtt{ln}(\mathsf{M})$ be defined as $\mathtt{ln}(\mathbf{0}) = \emptyset$, $\mathtt{ln}([\, P \,]_{\widetilde{x}}) = \widetilde{x}$, $\mathtt{ln}((x)\mathsf{M}) = \mathtt{ln}(\mathsf{M}) \setminus \{x\}$, and $\mathtt{ln}(\mathsf{M} \mid \mathsf{N}) = \mathtt{ln}(\mathsf{M}) \cup$

$\mathtt{ln}(\mathsf{N})$. Networks $\mathsf{M} \mid \mathsf{N}$ are constrained to satisfy the property $\mathtt{ln}(\mathsf{M}) \cap \mathtt{ln}(\mathsf{N}) = \emptyset$. This constraint permits to deliver messages to the unique machine in the network that is responsible for accepting that message. However it is also possible to consume messages in the same machine in which they have been produced as it will be made clear by the formal definition below.

The input $x(\widetilde{u}).P$, restriction $(x)P$, replicated input $!x(\widetilde{u}).P$, and machine restriction $(x)\mathsf{M}$ are binders of names $\widetilde{u}$, x, and $\widetilde{u}$, and x, respectively. The scope of these binders are the processes P and the machine M. We use the standard notions of α-equivalence, *free* and *bound names* of processes, and machines, noted $\mathtt{fn}(P)$, $\mathtt{bn}(P)$, $\mathtt{fn}(\mathsf{M})$, $\mathtt{bn}(\mathsf{M})$, respectively. In particular,

- $\mathtt{fn}(\langle\!| P \; ; \; Q |\!\rangle^n_x) = \mathtt{fn}(P) \cup \mathtt{fn}(Q) \cup \{x\}$ and α-equivalence equates $(x)(\langle\!| P \; ; \; Q |\!\rangle^n_x)$ with $(z)(\langle\!| P\{^z/_x\} \; ; \; Q\{^z/_x\} |\!\rangle^n_z)$ provided $z \notin \mathtt{fn}(\langle\!| P \; ; \; Q |\!\rangle^n_x)$;
- $\mathtt{fn}([\, P \,]_{\widetilde{x}}) = \widetilde{x} \cup \mathtt{fn}(P)$.

Following the tradition of π-calculus, the semantics of webπ is defined in terms of a reduction relations that relies on a structural congruence that equates all terms one never wants to distinguish.

Definition 1. *The* structural congruence $\equiv$ *is the least congruence closed with respect to α-renaming, satisfying the abelian monoid laws for parallel (associativity, commutativity and* $\mathbf{0}$ *as identity), and the following axioms:*

for processes:

1. *the scope laws:*

$$\begin{array}{rcl} (u)\mathbf{0} \equiv \mathbf{0}, & & (u)(v)P \equiv (v)(u)P, \\ P \mid (u)Q \equiv (u)(P \mid Q)\,, & & \text{if } u \notin \mathtt{fn}(P) \\ \langle\!| (z)P \; ; \; Q |\!\rangle^n_x \equiv (z)\langle\!| P \; ; \; Q |\!\rangle^n_x\,, & & \text{if } z \notin \{x\} \cup \mathtt{fn}(Q) \\ \langle\!| P \; ; \; (z)Q |\!\rangle^0_x \equiv (z)\langle\!| P \; ; \; Q |\!\rangle^0_x\,, & & \text{if } z \notin \{x\} \cup \mathtt{fn}(P) \end{array}$$

2. *the repetition law:*

$$!x(\widetilde{u}).P \equiv x(\widetilde{u}).P \mid !x(\widetilde{u}).P$$

3. *the transaction laws:*

$$\begin{array}{c} \langle\!| \mathbf{0} \; ; \; Q |\!\rangle^n_x \equiv \mathbf{0} \\ \langle\!| \langle\!| P \; ; \; Q |\!\rangle^n_y \mid R \; ; \; R' |\!\rangle^m_x \equiv \langle\!| P \; ; \; Q |\!\rangle^n_y \mid \langle\!| R \; ; \; R' |\!\rangle^m_x \end{array}$$

4. *the floating laws:*

$$\begin{array}{c} \langle\!| \overline{z}\,\widetilde{u} \mid P \; ; \; Q |\!\rangle^n_x \equiv \overline{z}\,\widetilde{u} \mid \langle\!| P \; ; \; Q |\!\rangle^n_x \\ \langle\!| y(\widetilde{v}).P \mid P' \; ; \; \overline{z}\,\widetilde{u} \mid Q |\!\rangle^0_x \equiv \overline{z}\,\widetilde{u} \mid \langle\!| y(\widetilde{v}).P \mid P' \; ; \; Q |\!\rangle^0_x \end{array}$$

for machines:

1. *the machine scope laws:*

$$\begin{array}{rcl} (u)\mathbf{0} \equiv \mathbf{0}, & & (x)(z)\mathsf{M} \equiv (z)(x)\mathsf{M}, \\ \mathsf{M} \mid (x)\mathsf{N} \equiv (x)(\mathsf{M} \mid \mathsf{N})\,, & & \text{if } x \notin \mathtt{fn}(\mathsf{M}) \\ [\,(x)P\,]_{\widetilde{z}} \equiv (x)\,[\,P\,]_{\widetilde{z}x}\,, & & \text{if } x \notin \widetilde{z} \end{array}$$

2. the lifting law:

$$[P]_{\widetilde{x}} \equiv [Q]_{\widetilde{x}}\,, \qquad \textit{if } P \equiv Q$$

The dynamic behaviour of processes and machines is defined by the reduction relation. The operation of decreasing by 1 the time stamps of active transactions on the same machine is modelled by the *time stepper function*. The definitions of this function and another auxiliary function are in order:

input predicate $\mathtt{inp}(P)$**:** this predicate verifies whether a process contains an input that is not underneath a transaction. It is the least relations such that:

$$\begin{array}{ll} \mathtt{inp}(x(\widetilde{u}).P) & \\ \mathtt{inp}((x)P) & \text{if } \mathtt{inp}(P) \\ \mathtt{inp}(P\,|\,Q) & \text{if } \mathtt{inp}(P) \text{ or } \mathtt{inp}(Q) \\ \mathtt{inp}(!x(\widetilde{u}).P) & \end{array}$$

time stepper function $\phi(P)$**:** this function decreases the time stamps by 1. For the missing cases, $\phi(P) = P$.

$$\begin{array}{rcl} \phi((x)P) &=& (x)\phi(P) \\ \phi(P\,|\,Q) &=& \phi(P)\,|\,\phi(Q) \\ \phi(\langle\!| P\,;\,R |\!\rangle^0_x) &=& \begin{cases} \langle\!| \phi(P)\,;\,\phi(R) |\!\rangle^0_x & \text{if } \mathtt{inp}(P) \\ \langle\!| \phi(P)\,;\,R |\!\rangle^0_x & \text{otherwise} \end{cases} \\ \phi(\langle\!| P\,;\,R |\!\rangle^{n+1}_x) &=& \langle\!| \phi(P)\,;\,R |\!\rangle^n_x \end{array}$$

We are finally in place for defining the reduction relation.

Definition 2. *The* reduction relation $\rightarrow$ *is the least relation satisfying the reductions:*

for processes:

$$\text{(COM)}\quad \overline{x}\,\widetilde{v}\,|\,x(\widetilde{u}).P \;\rightarrow\; P\{\widetilde{v}/\widetilde{u}\}$$

$$\text{(FAIL)}\quad \overline{x}\;|\;\langle\!| z(\widetilde{u}).P\,|\,Q\,;\,R |\!\rangle^{n+1}_x \;\rightarrow\; \langle\!| z(\widetilde{u}).P\,|\,\phi(Q)\,;\,R |\!\rangle^0_x$$

and closed under $\equiv$, (x)-*, and the rules:*

$$\frac{P \rightarrow Q}{P\,|\,R \rightarrow Q\,|\,\phi(R)} \qquad \frac{P \rightarrow Q}{\langle\!| P\,;\,R |\!\rangle^{n+1}_x \rightarrow \langle\!| Q\,;\,R |\!\rangle^n_x} \qquad \frac{P \rightarrow Q}{\langle\!| y(\widetilde{v}).R\,|\,R'\,;\,P |\!\rangle^0_x \rightarrow \langle\!| y(\widetilde{v}).R\,|\,\phi(R')\,;\,Q |\!\rangle^0_x}$$

for machines:

$$\text{(INTRA)}\ \frac{P \rightarrow Q}{[P]_{\widetilde{x}} \rightarrow [Q]_{\widetilde{x}}} \qquad \text{(TIME)}\ \frac{P \not\rightarrow}{[P]_{\widetilde{x}} \rightarrow [\phi(P)]_{\widetilde{x}}} \qquad \text{(DELIV)}\ [\overline{x}\,\widetilde{v}\,|\,P]_{\widetilde{z}}\,|\,[Q]_{\widetilde{y}x} \rightarrow [P]_{\widetilde{z}}\,|\,[\overline{x}\,\widetilde{v}\,|\,Q]_{\widetilde{y}x}$$

and closed under $\equiv$, (x)-*, and parallel composition.*

It is worth noting that a message can be either consumed in the machine where it has been produced, see rule (COM), or in the machine responsible for managing the channel on which the message was sent, see rule (DELIV).

We illustrate the semantics by discussing few examples. The process

$$\overline{z} \mid \overline{x} \mid \langle\!| x().\mathbf{0} \; ; \; \overline{y} |\!\rangle_z^n$$

has the following two computations ($n > 0$):

$$\overline{z} \mid \overline{x} \mid \langle\!| x().\mathbf{0} \; ; \; \overline{y} |\!\rangle_z^n \;\rightarrow\; \overline{z} \mid \langle\!| \mathbf{0} \; ; \; \overline{y} |\!\rangle_z^{n-1}$$

$$\overline{z} \mid \overline{x} \mid \langle\!| x().\mathbf{0} \; ; \; \overline{y} |\!\rangle_z^n \;\rightarrow\; \overline{x} \mid \langle\!| x().\mathbf{0} \; ; \; \overline{y} |\!\rangle_z^0$$

Transactions with time stamps equal to 0 are *terminated.* There are two kinds of terminated transactions: (a) the *committed transactions*, such as $\langle\!| \mathbf{0} \; ; \; \overline{y} |\!\rangle_z^{n-1}$ that is (structurally) equivalent to $\langle\!| \mathbf{0} \; ; \; \overline{y} |\!\rangle_z^0$, whose bodies do not contain input-guarded processes, and (b) the *failed transactions*, such as $\langle\!| x().\mathbf{0} \; ; \; \overline{y} |\!\rangle_z^0$, whose body contains input-guarded processes. The input operations in the body of failed transactions can no longer be executed: the transaction is actually failed because it has not completed its tasks. In committed transactions the compensation handler is no more considered. This is reflected in the first computation by the fact that the message $\overline{y}$ cannot be produced. This message is syntactically part of the process but it cannot be consumed. In failed transactions the compensation process becomes active. This is made clear in the second computation, where the message $\overline{z}$ explicitly abort the transaction thus making the time stamp equal to 0. After abortion, the message $\overline{x}$ cannot be consumed.

The process $\overline{x} \mid \langle\!| x().\mathbf{0} \; ; \; \overline{u} |\!\rangle_z^1 \mid \langle\!| x().\mathbf{0} \; ; \; \overline{v} |\!\rangle_{z'}^1$ evolves as follows

$$\overline{x} \mid \langle\!| x().\mathbf{0} \; ; \; \overline{u} |\!\rangle_z^1 \mid \langle\!| x().\mathbf{0} \; ; \; \overline{v} |\!\rangle_{z'}^1 \quad\rightarrow\quad \langle\!| \mathbf{0} \; ; \; \overline{u} |\!\rangle_z^0 \mid \langle\!| x().\mathbf{0} \; ; \; \overline{v} |\!\rangle_{z'}^0$$

(and in a similar way, but consuming the input of z' instead of the input of z). This reduction shows the progress of time in a location: a computational step of a process makes the time elapse of one unit. This is manifested by decreasing the time stamps of every transaction in parallel (in the previous case, of $\langle\!| x().\mathbf{0} \; ; \; \overline{v} |\!\rangle_{z'}^1$). We note that the transaction $\langle\!| \mathbf{0} \; ; \; \overline{u} |\!\rangle_z^0$ is completed, therefore the message $\overline{u}$ is never emitted. On the contrary, $\langle\!| x().\mathbf{0} \; ; \; \overline{v} |\!\rangle_{z'}^0$ is failed, thus $\overline{v}$ is emitted.

In webπ, the delivery of one message to its receptor machine is modeled by the computation step $[\, \overline{x}\widetilde{w} \mid P \,]_{\widetilde{y}} \mid [\, Q \,]_{\widetilde{z}x} \;\rightarrow\; [\, P \,]_{\widetilde{y}} \mid [\, \overline{x}\widetilde{w} \mid Q \,]_{\widetilde{z}x}$. Asynchrony between machines may give rise to unpredictable delays in communication. This latency could make timed transaction fail. Consider, for instance, the machine (trailing $\mathbf{0}$ are omitted)

$$[\, \langle\!| \overline{x} \mid y() \; ; \; \overline{z} |\!\rangle_x^n \,]_y \mid [\, x().\overline{y} \,]_x$$

where the leftmost location sends the message $\overline{x}$ to the rightmost one and waits for the answer $\overline{y}$. Due to asynchrony between machines, the following computation is possible (let $m < n$ and $n < m + m'$):

$$
\begin{aligned}
[\, \langle\!| \overline{x} \mid y() \,;\, \overline{z} \,|\!\rangle^{n}_{x} \,]_{y} \mid [\, x().\overline{y} \,]_{x} \;\rightarrow^{m}\; & [\, \overline{x} \mid \langle\!| y() \,;\, \overline{z} \,|\!\rangle^{n-m}_{x} \,]_{y} \mid [\, x().\overline{y} \,]_{x} \\
\rightarrow\; & [\, \langle\!| y() \,;\, \overline{z} \,|\!\rangle^{n-m}_{x} \,]_{y} \mid [\, \overline{x} \mid x().\overline{y} \,]_{x} \\
\rightarrow\; & [\, \langle\!| y() \,;\, \overline{z} \,|\!\rangle^{n-m}_{x} \,]_{y} \mid [\, \overline{y} \,]_{x} \\
\rightarrow^{m'}\; & [\, \langle\!| y() \,;\, \overline{z} \,|\!\rangle^{0}_{x} \,]_{y} \mid [\, \overline{y} \,]_{x} \\
\rightarrow\; & [\, \overline{y} \mid \langle\!| y() \,;\, \overline{z} \,|\!\rangle^{0}_{x} \,]_{y} \mid [\, \mathbf{0} \,]_{x}
\end{aligned}
$$

where $\rightarrow^{k}$ is used to denote the effect of k subsequent reductions. In the final state the message $\overline{y}$ cannot be consumed by the transaction $\langle\!| y() \,;\, \overline{z} \,|\!\rangle^{0}_{x}$ as the time stamp is 0.

A usual source of failure in networks is the loss of messages. Such failures have not been explicitly considered in webπ because they are modelled by indefinitely delaying messages.

3 The Scope Construct in BPEL

The first case study we discuss is the modelling of the the `scope` construct of BPEL. This construct defines transactional activities by associating a failure handler and a compensation handler to a primary activity. The `scope` construct in BPEL also specifies an event handler. In our simplified modeling we only consider fault and compensation handlers used to deal with exceptional bahaviours.

The failure handler is activated in case a fault condition occurs during the execution of the primary activity. The compensation handler is executed in case the execution of the primary activity is required to be undone after is has provisionally committed. In fact, the primary activity could be part of a more complex task that fails, thus requiring to cancel those subactivities that provisionally completed.

In this section we consider only the timeless transactions of webπ as we are mainly interested in the flow of control in the execution of fault and compensation handlers, independently of the time constraints that can be associated to the execution of the primary activity within a BPEL `scope`. Indeed, a timeout can be associated to a `scope` using an event handler (the third form of handler that we do not model) that is triggered by a timed allarm.

We denote the `scope` construct with $\mathtt{scope}_x(P \,;\, F \,;\, C)$, where P is the primary activity, F is the failure handler, and C is the compensation handler. The name x is used to signal either the occurrence of a failure during the execution of the primary activity, or the external request of compensation. We assume that P, F, and C are asynchronous π-calculus processes.

Before discussing the webπ semantics of `scope`, we present a prototypal example about scopes. Consider a travel organization service that requires to orchestrate an hotel and a flight reservation service. We first define the last two services, then we show how to orchestrate them using the `scope` construct.

The hotel reservation service is (abstractly) modeled as follows:

$$
\begin{aligned}
\mathsf{HOTEL} = [\; & !res_h(arr, dep, conf_h).(id_h)(\overline{conf_h}\,\langle id_h\rangle \mid \overline{id_h}\,) \\
& \mid\; !cancel_h(id_h).id_h() \\
]&_{res_h, cancel_h}
\end{aligned}
$$

The service receives reservation requests indicating the arrival date *arr*, the departure date *dep*, and a channel to be used for communicating the reservation confirmation $conf_h$. Each reservation has a unique identifier id_h, which is communicated through the reservation confirmation channel $conf_h$. The service keeps track of the reservation by producing an internal message $\overline{id_h}$. In case of cancellation, this message is consumed. This occurs when the name id_h is received back through the channel $cancel_h$.

The flight registration service is modeled similarly, with the unique difference that the reservation could fail. Let $P \oplus Q$ be the process $(x)(\overline{x} \mid x().P \mid x().Q)$, assuming that $x \notin \mathtt{fv}(P) \cup \mathtt{fv}(Q)$.

$$\begin{aligned} \mathsf{FLIGHT} = [\ & !res_f(arr, dep, conf_h, t).\quad ((id_f)(\overline{conf_f}\langle id_f\rangle \mid \overline{id_f}\ ) \oplus \overline{t}\ ) \\ & \mid\ !cancel_f(id_f).id_f() \\ ]&_{res_f, cancel_f} \end{aligned}$$

The flight reservation request, besides the arrival and departure dates and the confirmation channel, carries a fourth name t used in case of reservation failure. After the reservation request is received, the service internally choose either to accept or reject it; in case of failure, a message on the channel t is produced.

We are now in place for programming an orchestrator – the travel organization service – that combines the above services:

$$\begin{aligned} \mathsf{TRVL}\ = &\ (conf_h, conf_f, store_h, store_f, t) \\ & [\quad \mathtt{scope}_t(\ \overline{res_h}\langle arr, dep, conf_h\rangle \\ & \qquad\qquad \mid conf_h(id_h).(\ \overline{store_h}\langle id_h\rangle\ \mid \overline{res_f}\langle arr, dep, conf_f, t\rangle \\ & \qquad\qquad\qquad \mid conf_f(id_f).\overline{store_f}\langle id_f\rangle\ ) \\ & \quad ;\ store_h(id_h).\overline{cancel_h}\langle id_h\rangle \\ & \quad ;\ store_h(id_h).\overline{cancel_h}\langle id_h\rangle \mid store_f(id_f).\overline{cancel_f}\langle id_f\rangle\quad) \\ &]_{conf_h, conf_f, t} \end{aligned}$$

The travel service uses two local channels $store_h$ and $store_f$ to store the identifiers of the hotel and flight reservations, respectively. The *primary activity* first sends a request to the hotel reservation service, then to the flight reservation service. The *failure* handler manages those cases in which the flight reservation does not succeed; in these cases the hotel reservation is cancelled. The *compensation* handler, on the other hand, manages those cases (that we do not model explicitly) in which the travellers decides to cancel its travel after it has been fully reserved; in this case both the hotel and the flight reservations are cancelled.

The whole reservation system is modeled as the parallel composition of the three services described above:

$$\mathsf{HOTEL} \mid \mathsf{FLIGHT} \mid \mathsf{TRVL}$$

The semantics of scope is defined by the following function $[\![\cdot]\!]$ translating the term $\mathtt{scope}_x(P\ ;\ F\ ;\ C)$ for any name x and asynchronous π-calculus processes P, F, and C. Let $z_f, z_c \notin \{x\} \cup \mathtt{fn}(P \mid F \mid C)$.

$$\begin{aligned} [\![\mathtt{scope}_x(P\ ;\ F\ ;\ C)]\!] = &\ (z_c, z_f) \\ & \langle\!|\, \overline{z_f} \mid (y)([\![P]\!]_y \mid y().z_f().(\overline{z_c} \mid (v)v()))\ ;\ z_f().F \mid z_c().C\, |\!\rangle_x \end{aligned}$$

The webπ process associated to scope is a timeless transaction having the same name x. The body of this transaction cannot commit because of the ending process $(v)v()$ that is deadlocked. The channels z_f and z_c are used to indicate whether the failure or the compensation handler should be activated in case the transaction is aborted. In particular, the message $\overline{z_f}$ activates the failure handler, while $\overline{z_c}$ activates the compensation handler. The message $\overline{z_f}$ is present during the execution of the primary activity. If the primary activity completes, the message $\overline{z_f}$ is replaced by $\overline{z_c}$. In order to detect the completion of the primary activity P we use a continuation passing style.

Let $[\![P]\!]_y$ be the function that executes P and produces $\overline{y}$ when P terminates. Let also assume that y, y', y'' are always fresh names:

$$\begin{array}{rcl} [\![\mathbf{0}]\!]_y & = & \overline{y} \\ [\![\overline{x}\,\widetilde{u}]\!]_y & = & \overline{x}\,\widetilde{u} \,|\, \overline{y} \\ [\![x(\widetilde{u}).P]\!]_y & = & x(\widetilde{u}).[\![P]\!]_y \\ [\![(x)P]\!]_y & = & (x)[\![P]\!]_y \\ [\![P \,|\, Q]\!]_y & = & (y', y'')([\![P]\!]_{y'} \,|\, [\![Q]\!]_{y''} \,|\, y'().y''().\overline{y}) \\ [\![!x(\widetilde{u}).P]\!]_y & = & !x(\widetilde{u}).[\![P]\!]_y \end{array}$$

The definition of $[\![P]\!]_y$ is standard; we comment only the rule dealing with the parallel composition $P \,|\, Q$. Two new names y' and y'' are used to communicate the completion of the two processes P and Q, respectively. When both $\overline{y'}$ and $\overline{y''}$ are produced, the overall process completes (thus $\overline{y}$ is produced).

4 Speculative Parallelism

The second case study is about a special pattern of client-services interaction: the so-called *speculative parallelism*. Speculative parallelism is used by a client that engages (in parallel) request-response interactions with several services in such a way that if one of the services completes – the *winner* –, the remaining services – the *losers* – are abandoned.

Before discussing a formal representation of speculative parallelism, we consider a simpler case of request-response protocol between one client and one service. The protocol is modelled in webπ using the following network:

$$\begin{array}{rcl} \mathsf{RP} & = & [\ \langle\!|\, \overline{req}\,.resp().(\overline{ack} \,|\, \overline{success}) \ ; \ \overline{fail} \,|\, \overline{nack} \,|\!\rangle_t^n \ ]_{resp} \\ & | & [\ req().(\overline{resp} \,|\, ack().\overline{done} \,|\, nack().\overline{abort}\,) \ ]_{req,ack,nack} \end{array}$$

The client (the machine on the first line) sends a request $\overline{req}$ to the service (the machine on the second line) and blocks waiting for the response message $\overline{resp}$. If the response arrives in due time (i.e. before the timeout n expires), the client produces the message $\overline{success}$; otherwise, it produces the message $\overline{fail}$. The service produces the message $\overline{done}$ in the case the request-response interaction succeeds, $\overline{abort}$ otherwise. This is achieved by letting the client to produce $\overline{ack}$ (respectively, $\overline{nack}$) when it succeeds (respectively, fails).

Informally, the request-response protocol is correct if it satisfies the following property: *every partial computation may be completed in such a way that both the client and the service communicate their final state; moreover, the final states of the client and the service are consistent.* The transliteration of this property in the network RP is: "every computation may be completed in such a way that the client emits $\overline{success}$ or $\overline{fail}$, while the service emits $\overline{done}$ or $\overline{abort}$; additionally, $\overline{success}$ and $\overline{abort}$ cannot be both produced, as well as $\overline{fail}$ and $\overline{done}$".

To be more formal, let $\mathsf{M} \downarrow x$, read M *has barb* x, be the predicate defined by

$$\mathsf{M} \downarrow x \quad \text{if and only if} \quad \mathsf{M} \equiv (\widetilde{y})(\,[\,\overline{x}\,\widetilde{w} \mid P\,]_{\widetilde{z}} \mid \mathsf{N}) \text{ for some } \widetilde{y}, \widetilde{w}, P, \widetilde{z}, \mathsf{N}$$

The following auxiliary notations are also used:

$$\begin{array}{ll} \mathsf{M} \downarrow \langle x_1 \ldots x_n \rangle & \text{if } \mathsf{M} \downarrow x_i \text{ for } i \in 1 \ldots n \\ \mathsf{M} \not\downarrow \langle x_1 \ldots x_n \rangle & \text{if } \mathsf{M} \downarrow \langle x_1 \ldots x_n \rangle \text{ does not hold} \\ \mathsf{M} \Downarrow \langle x_1 \ldots x_n \rangle & \text{if } \mathsf{M} \rightarrow^* \mathsf{M}' \text{ for some } \mathsf{M}' \text{ and } \mathsf{M}' \downarrow \langle x_1 \ldots x_n \rangle \end{array}$$

where $\rightarrow^*$ denotes the reflexive and transitive closure of the reduction relation $\rightarrow$ defined for machines. Then the correctness property may be rewritten as follows: for every machine M such that $\mathsf{RP} \rightarrow^* \mathsf{M}$, the following two conditions hold:

- $\mathsf{M} \Downarrow \langle success, done \rangle$ or $\mathsf{M} \Downarrow \langle fail, abort \rangle$,
- $\mathsf{M} \not\Downarrow \langle fail, done \rangle$ and $\mathsf{M} \not\Downarrow \langle success, abort \rangle$.

It is not difficult to verify that RP is a correct request-response protocol.

We now move to the more general case of speculative parallelism. For simplicity, we consider the case of one client and two services; the generalization to more than two services is trivial. Let the client send in parallel two requests to two different services. If at least one response reaches the client in due time, that service is completed and the other one must be aborted. If no response arrives before the time-out expires, both services must be aborted.

The first machine we discuss is a direct adaptation of RP:

$$\begin{array}{rl} \mathsf{SP1} = & [\,(f)(\;f().\overline{fail} \\ & \quad\quad \mid \langle\!|\, \overline{req1} \mid resp1().(\overline{ack1} \mid \overline{success} \mid \overline{t2}\,)\;;\; \overline{f} \mid \overline{nack1}\,|\!\rangle_{t1}^{n} \\ & \quad\quad \mid \langle\!|\, \overline{req2} \mid resp2().(\overline{ack2} \mid \overline{success} \mid \overline{t1}\,)\;;\; \overline{f} \mid \overline{nack2}\,|\!\rangle_{t2}^{n}\;) \\ &]_{resp1,resp2} \\ & \mid \quad [\,req1().(\overline{resp1} \mid ack1().\overline{done1} \mid nack1().\overline{abort1}\,)\,]_{req1,ack1,nack1} \\ & \mid \quad [\,req2().(\overline{resp2} \mid ack2().\overline{done2} \mid nack2().\overline{abort2}\,)\,]_{req2,ack2,nack2} \end{array}$$

The locations in the last two lines are the two services. They behave in much the same way as the service in RP (the difference is that we use the indexes 1 and 2 to separate them). The client performs two transactions similar to the one performed by the client in RP. Each transaction engages an interaction with the corresponding service. The difference with RP is that, in case of success of one transaction, the other transaction is aborted explicitly (using the message $\overline{t1}$ or $\overline{t2}$). The local name f is used to implement failure. This is necessary in order to avoid that two instances of $\overline{fail}$ are produced when, e.g., the time-out expires. In this last case both the transactions fail and the two compensations are activated.

To analyse the correctness of SP1, we generalize to two services the above property. Let SP1 be correct if the following property holds: *for every machine* M *such that* SP1 $\rightarrow^*$ M, *the following two conditions hold:*

- M $\Downarrow \langle success, done1, abort2\rangle$ *or* M $\Downarrow \langle success, abort1, done2\rangle$ *or* M $\Downarrow \langle fail, abort1, abort2\rangle$,
- M $\not\Downarrow \langle done1, done2\rangle$ *and* M $\not\Downarrow \langle fail, done1, abort2\rangle$ *and* M $\not\Downarrow \langle fail, abort1, done2\rangle$ *and* M $\not\Downarrow \langle success, abort1, abort2\rangle$.

We notice that SP1 is incorrect because it may happen that both transactions commit. This occurs if both messages $\overline{resp1}$ and $\overline{resp2}$ reach the client when the time stamp is $n' > 1$. For instance, consider the computation

$$\begin{array}{rl}
\mathsf{SP1} \;\rightarrow^* [& \overline{resp1} \mid \overline{resp2} \\
& \mid (f)(\; f().\overline{fail} \\
& \qquad\qquad \mid \langle\!|\, resp1().(\overline{ack1} \mid \overline{success} \mid \overline{t2}\,) \;;\; \overline{f} \mid \overline{nack1} \,|\!\rangle^{n'}_{t1} \\
& \qquad\qquad \mid \langle\!|\, resp2().(\overline{ack2} \mid \overline{success} \mid \overline{t1}\,) \;;\; \overline{f} \mid \overline{nack2} \,|\!\rangle^{n'}_{t2}\;) \\
&]_{resp1,resp2} \\
& \mid \quad [\, ack1().\overline{done1} \mid nack1().\overline{abort1}\;]_{req1,ack1,nack1} \\
& \mid \quad [\, ack2().\overline{done2} \mid nack2().\overline{abort2}\;]_{req2,ack2,nack2}
\end{array}$$

It is easy to verify that this computation may be completed yielding a machine M such that M $\downarrow \langle done1, done2\rangle$. This contradicts the second condition of the previous property.

This problem may be avoided by enclosing the two transactions in an outermost transaction that is responsible to check that at most one transaction succeeds. This solution is implemented by the machine SP2.

$$\begin{array}{rl}
\mathsf{SP2} \;=\; [\,(r, a1, a2)\,\langle\!| & \langle\!|\,\overline{req1} \mid resp1().(\overline{r}\,\langle t2, a1\rangle \mid a1().\overline{ack1}\,) \;;\; \overline{nack1} \,|\!\rangle_{t1} \\
& \mid \langle\!|\,\overline{req2} \mid resp2().(\overline{r}\,\langle t1, a2\rangle \mid a2().\overline{ack2}\,) \;;\; \overline{nack2} \,|\!\rangle_{t2} \\
& \mid r(u,v).(\overline{u} \mid \overline{v} \mid \overline{success}\,) \\
& ;\; \overline{t1} \mid \overline{t2} \mid \overline{fail} \quad |\!\rangle^{n}_{t} \\
]_{resp1,resp2} & \\
\mid \quad [\, req1().(\overline{resp1} \mid ack1().\overline{done1} \mid nack1().\overline{abort1}\,)\,]_{req1,ack1,nack1} & \\
\mid \quad [\, req2().(\overline{resp2} \mid ack2().\overline{done2} \mid nack2().\overline{abort2}\,)\,]_{req2,ack2,nack2} &
\end{array}$$

This machine is correct. The formal proof of this result is not reported, as it is a tedious analysis of the possible computations. We report an informal discussion of the basic idea underlying the implementation.

The request-response interactions with the services are realized by the transactions $t1$ and $t2$, which are inside a transaction t that is responsible for deciding the winner and the loser. The transactions $t1$ and $t2$ send a request to the corresponding service and wait for the answer. On reception of the answer, $t1$ and $t2$ communicate their end on the private channel r. The message carries two names: the first one is the name of the opposite transaction while the second one is the name of an input where the transaction body is waiting for an acknowledgement. When the t-transaction receives these two names, they are used to cancel the loser and to acknowledge the winner. Both $t1$ and $t2$ have an associated compensation process that may cancel the task itself. The compensation process of t simply invokes the compensations of $t1$ and $t2$.

As regards time, the time stamp n is associated to the transaction t, while $t1$ and $t2$ are timeless. It is worth noting that, if $t1$ and $t2$ where timed, the protocol turns out to be incorrect. In fact, the time-outs of $t1$ and $t2$ may expire after the transaction t has received a message on the channel r, but before the winner transaction is notified. To clarify this circumstance, let $\mathsf{SP2}'$ be the machine $\mathsf{SP2}$ where the time stamp n is also associated to the transactions $t1$ and $t2$. It is possible to obtain

$$\begin{array}{lll}
\mathsf{SP2}' \to^* & [\,(r, a1, a2)\, \langle\!| & \langle\!| a1().\overline{ack1}\ ;\ \overline{nack1}\, |\!\rangle^0_{t1} \\
& & \mid \langle\!| \overline{req2} \mid resp2().(\overline{r}\,\langle t1, a2\rangle \mid a2().\overline{ack2}\,)\ ;\ \overline{nack2}\, |\!\rangle^0_{t2} \\
& & \mid \overline{t2} \mid \overline{a1} \mid \overline{success} \\
& & ;\ \overline{t1} \mid \overline{t2} \mid \overline{fail} \quad |\!\rangle^0_t \\
&]_{resp1,resp2} & \\
& \mid\quad [\,ack1().\overline{done1} \mid nack1().\overline{abort1}\,]_{req1,ack1,nack1} & \\
& \mid\quad [\,req2().(\overline{resp2} \mid ack2().\overline{done2} \mid nack2().\overline{abort2}\,)\,]_{req2,ack2,nack2} &
\end{array}$$

The reader may verify that this computation may be extended reaching a machine M such that $\mathsf{M} \downarrow \langle success, abort1, abort2\rangle$ thus contradicting the second condition of the property formalized above.

5 Conclusion

We have explored the expressivity of webπ for modeling and reasoning about typical mechanisms of Web Services orchestration and composition. In particular, two case studies have been considered, one inspired by the orchestration language BPEL and another one based on the pattern of services combination known as speculative parallism.

In the next future we intend to consider a more significant fragment of BPEL, in particular the so-called event handlers, as well as composition mechanisms of other emerging languages such as WS-CDL. We also intend to model and compare a whole class of patterns of composition for services. In this respect, the library of patterns described in [10] will be taken as the main source of inspiration for the protocols to be considered.

References

1. T. Andrews and et.al. Business process execution language for web services. Version 1.1. Specification, BEA Systems, IBM Corp., Microsoft Corp., SAP AG, Siebel Systems, 2003.
2. L. Bocchi, C. Laneve, and G. Zavattaro. A calculus for long running transactions. In *FMOODS'03, Proceedings of the 6th IFIP International Conference on Formal Methods for Open Object-based Distributed Systems*, volume 2884 of *LNCS*, pages 124–138. Springer-Verlag, 2003.

3. R. Bruni, C. Laneve, and U. Montanari. Orchestrating transactions in join calculus. In *CONCUR 2002: Proceedings of the 13th International Conference on Concurrency Theory*, volume 2421 of *LNCS*, pages 321–337. Springer Verlag, 2002.
4. M. Butler and C. Ferreira. An operational semantics for stac, a language for modelling long-running business transactions. In *COORDINATION'04, Proceedings of the 6th International Conference on Coordination Models and Languages*, volume 2949 of *LNCS*, pages 87–104. Springer-Verlag, 2004.
5. M. Butler, T. Hoare, and C. Ferreira. A trace semantics for long-running transactions. In Proceedings of 25 Years of CSP, London, 2004.
6. N. Kavantzas, G. Olsson, J. Mischkinsky, and M. Chapman. Web services choreography description languages. W3C Web Services Choreography Working Group, 2003.
7. C. Laneve and G. Zavattaro. Foundations of web transactions. In *FOSSACS 2005: Proceedings of Foundations of Software Science and Computation Structure*, volume to appear of *LNCS*. Springer Verlag, 2005.
8. F. Leymann. Web services flow language (wsfl 1.0). Technical report, IBM Software Group, 2001.
9. S. Thatte. XLANG: Web services for business process design. Microsoft Corporation, 2001.
10. M. van der Aalst, A. ter Hofstede, B. Kiepuszewski, and A. Barros. Workflow patterns. *Distributed and Parallel Databases*, 14(3):5–51, 2003.

Concurrency Among Strangers

Programming in E as Plan Coordination

Mark S. Miller[1,2], E. Dean Tribble, and Jonathan Shapiro[1]

[1] Johns Hopkins University
[2] Hewlett Packard Laboratories

Abstract. Programmers write programs, expressing plans for machines to execute. When composed so that they may cooperate, plans may instead interfere with each other in unanticipated ways. *Plan coordination* is the art of simultaneously enabling plans to cooperate, while avoiding hazards of destructive plan interference. For sequential computation within a single machine, object programming supports plan coordination well. For concurrent computation, this paper shows how hard it is to use locking to prevent plans from interfering without also destroying their ability to cooperate.

In Internet-scale computing, machines proceed concurrently, interact across barriers of large latencies and partial failure, and encounter each other's misbehavior. Each dimension presents new plan coordination challenges. This paper explains how the E language addresses these joint challenges by changing only a few concepts of conventional sequential object programming. Several projects are adapting these insights to existing platforms.

1 Introduction

The fundamental constraint we face as programmers is complexity. It might seem that we could successfully formulate plans only for systems we can understand. Instead, every day, programmers successfully contribute code towards working systems too complex for anyone to understand *as a whole*. We make use of modularity and abstraction mechanisms to construct systems whose component plans we can understand piecemeal, and whose compositions we can understand without fully understanding each plan being composed.

> Programmers are not to be measured by their ingenuity and their logic but by the completeness of their case analysis.
>
> —Alan Perlis

In the human world, when you plan for yourself, you make assumptions about future situations in which your plan will unfold. Occasionally, someone else's plan may interfere with yours, invalidating the assumptions on which your plan is based. To plan successfully, you need some sense of which assumptions are usually safe from such disruption. You do not need to anticipate every possible

R. De Nicola and D. Sangiorgi (Eds.): TGC 2005, LNCS 3705, pp. 195–229, 2005.

contingency, however. If someone does something you did not expect, you will probably be better able to figure out how to cope at that time anyway.

To formulate plans for machines to execute, programmers must also make assumptions. When separately formulated plans are composed, conflicting assumptions can cause the run-time situation to become *inconsistent* with a given plan's assumptions, leading it awry. By dividing the state of a computational system into separately encapsulated objects, and by giving objects limited access to each other, we limit outside interference and extend the range of assumptions our programs may safely rely upon.[1] Beyond these assumptions, correct programs must handle all relevant contingencies. By abstraction, we limit one object's need for knowledge of others, reducing the number of cases which are relevant. However, even under sequential and benign conditions, the remaining case analysis can still be quite painful.

Under concurrency, an object's own plans may destructively interfere with each other. In distributed programming, asynchrony and partial failure limit an object's local knowledge of relevant facts, increasing the number of relevant cases it must consider. In secure programming, we carefully distinguish those objects whose good behavior we rely on from those we don't, but we seek to cooperate with both. Confidentiality further constrains local knowledge; deceit and malice are further sources of possible plan interference. Each of these dimensions threatens an explosion of new cases we must consider. To succeed, we must find ways of reducing the size of the resulting case analysis.

Previous papers have focused on E's support for limited trust within the constraints of distributed systems [MMF00, MYS03, MS03, MTS04]. This paper focuses on E's support for concurrent and distributed programming within the constraints of limited trust.

2 Overview

Throughout this paper, we do not seek universal solutions to coordination problems, but rather, abstraction mechanisms adequate to craft diverse solutions adapted to the needs of many applications. We illustrate many of our points with a simple example, a "statusHolder" object implementing the listener pattern.

The Sequential StatusHolder introduces the statusHolder and examines its hazards in a sequential environment.

Why Not Shared-state Concurrency shows several attempts at a conventionally thread-safe statusHolder in Java and the ways each suffers from plan interference.

A Taste of E shows a statusHolder written in E and explains E's eventual-send operator in the context of a single thread of control.

[1] This view of encapsulation and composition parallels Hayek's explanation of how property rights protect human plans from interference and how trade brings about their cooperative alignment [vH45]. See [MD88, TM02] for more.

Communicating Event-Loops explains how the statusHolder handles concurrency and distribution under benign conditions.

Protection from Misbehavior examines how the plans coordinated by our statusHolder are and are not vulnerable to each other.

Promise Pipelining introduces promises for the results of eventually-sent messages, and shows how pipelining helps programs tolerate latency and how broken promise contagion lets programs handle eventually-thrown exceptions.

Partial Failure shows how statusHolder's clients can regain access following a partition or crash and explains the issues involved in regaining distributed consistency.

The When-Catch Expression explains how to turn data-flow back into control-flow.

From Objects to Actors and Back Again presents a brief history of E's concurrency control.

Related Work discusses other systems with similar goals, as well as current projects adapting these insights to existing platforms.

Discussion and Conclusions summarizes current status, what remains to be done, and lessons learned.

3 The Sequential StatusHolder

Throughout the paper, we will examine different forms of the listener pattern [Eng97]. The code below is representative of the basic sequential listener pattern.[2] In it, a statusHolder object is used to coordinate a changing status between *publishers* and *subscribers*. A subscriber can ask for the current status of a statusHolder by calling `getStatus`, or can subscribe to receive notifications when the status changes by calling `addListener` with a listener object. A publisher changes the status in a statusHolder by calling `setStatus` with the new value. This in turn will call `statusChanged` on all subscribed listeners. In this way, publishers can communicate status updates to subscribers without knowing of each individual subscriber.

We can use this pattern to coordinate several loosely coupled plans. For example, in a simple application, a bank account manager publishes an account balance to an analysis spreadsheet and a financial application. Deposits and withdrawals cause a new balance to be published. The spreadsheet adds a listener that will update the display to show the current balance. The finance application adds a listener to begin trading activities when the balance falls below some threshold. Although these clients interact cooperatively, they know very little about each other.

[2] The listener pattern [Eng97] is similar to the observer pattern [GHJV94]. However, the analysis which follows would be quite different if we were starting from the observer pattern.

```
public class StatusHolder {
    private Object myStatus;
    private final ArrayList<Listener> myListeners
                        = new ArrayList();

    public StatusHolder(Object status) {
        myStatus = status;
    }
    public void addListener(Listener newListener) {
        myListeners.add(newListener);
    }
    public Object getStatus() {
        return myStatus;
    }
    public void setStatus(Object newStatus) {
        myStatus = newStatus;
        for (Listener listener: myListeners) {
            listener.statusChanged(newStatus);
        }
    }
}
```

Even under sequential and benign conditions, this pattern creates plan interference hazards.

Aborting the wrong plan: If a listener throws an exception, this prevents some other listeners from being notified of the new status and possibly aborts the publisher's plan. In the above example, the spreadsheet's inability to display the new balance should not impact either the finance application or the bank account manager.

Nested subscription: The actions of a listener could cause a new listener to be subscribed. For example, to bring a lowered balance back up, the finance application might initiate a stock trade operation, which adds its own listener. Whether that new listener sees the current event, fails to see the current event, or fails to be subscribed depends on minor details of the listener implementation.

Nested publication: Similarly, a listener may cause a publisher to publish a new status, possibly unknowingly due to aliasing. For example, during an update, the invocation of `setStatus` notifies the finance application, which deposits money into the account. A new update to the balance is published and an inner invocation of `setStatus` notifies all listeners of the new balance. After that inner invocation returns, the outer invocation of `setStatus` continues notifying listeners of the older, pre-deposit balance. Some of the listeners would receive the notifications *out of order*. As a result, the spreadsheet might leave the display showing the wrong balance, or worse, the finance application might initiate transactions based on incorrect information.

The nested publication hazard is especially striking because it reveals that problems typically associated with concurrency may arise even in a simple sequential example. This is why we draw attention to *plans*, rather than programs or processes. The statusHolder, by running each subscriber's plan during a step of a publisher's plan, has provoked plan interference: these largely independent plans now interact in surprising ways, creating numerous new cases that are difficult to identify, prevent, or test. Although these hazards are real, experience suggests that programmers can usually find ways to avoid them in sequential programs under benign conditions.

4 Why Not Shared-State Concurrency

With genuine concurrency, interacting plans unfold in parallel. To manipulate state and preserve consistency, a plan needs to ensure others are not manipulating that same state at the same time. This section explores the plan coordination problem in the context of the conventional shared-state concurrency-control paradigm [VH04], also known as shared-memory multi-threading. We present several attempts at a conventionally *thread-safe* statusHolder—searching for one that prevents its clients from interfering without preventing them from cooperating.

In the absence of real-time concerns, we can analyze concurrency without thinking about genuine parallelism. Instead, we can model the effects of concurrency as the non-deterministic interleaving of atomic units of operation. We can roughly characterize a concurrency-control paradigm with the answers to two questions:

Serializability: What are the coarsest-grain units of operation, such that we can account for all visible effects of concurrency as equivalent to some fully ordered interleaving of these units [IBM68]? For shared-state concurrency, this unit is generally no larger than a memory access, instruction, or system call—which is often finer than the "primitives" provided by our programming languages [Boe05]. For databases, this unit is the transaction.

Mutual exclusion: What mechanisms can eliminate the possibility of some interleavings, so as to preclude the hazards associated with them? For shared-state concurrency, the two dominant answers are monitors [Hoa74, BH93] and rendezvous [Hoa78]. For distributed programming, many systems restrict the orders in which messages may be delivered [BJ87, Ami95, Lam98].

Java is loosely in the monitor tradition. Ada, Concurrent ML, and the synchronous π-calculus are loosely in the rendezvous tradition. With minor adjustments, the following comments apply to both.

4.1 Preserving Consistency

If we place our sequential statusHolder into a concurrent environment, publishers or subscribers may call it from different threads. The resulting interleaving of

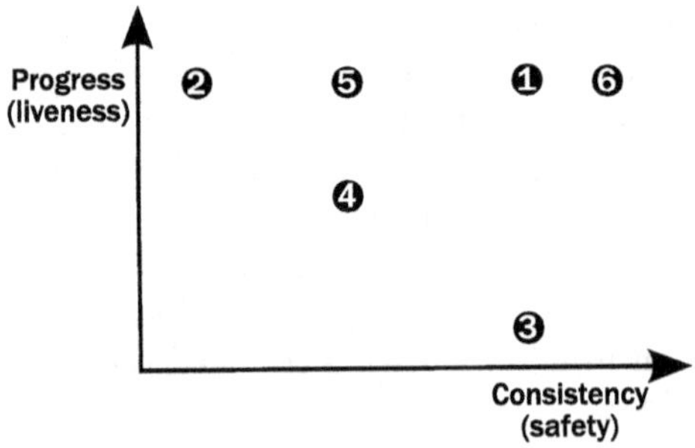

Fig. 1. A correct program must both remain consistent and continue to make progress. The sequence above represents our search for a statusHolder which supports both well: (1) The sequential statusHolder. (2) The sequential statusHolder in a concurrent environment. (3) The fully synchronized statusHolder. (4) Placing the for-loop outside the synchronized block. (5) Spawning a new thread per listener notification. (6) Using communicating event-loops.

operations might, for example, mutate the `myListeners` list while the for-loop is in progress.

Adding the "`synchronized`" keyword to all methods of the above code causes it to resemble a monitor. This fully synchronized statusHolder eliminates exactly those cases where multiple plans interleave within the statusHolder. It is as good at preserving its own consistency as our original sequential statusHolder was.

However, it is generally recommended that Java programmers avoid this fully synchronized pattern because it is prone to deadlock [Eng97]. Although each listener is called from some publisher's thread, its purpose may be to contribute to a plan unfolding in its subscriber's thread. To defend itself against such concurrent entry, the objects at this boundary may themselves be synchronized. If a `statusChanged` notification gets blocked here, waiting on that subscriber's thread, it blocks the statusHolder, as well as any other objects whose locks are held by that publisher's thread. If the subscriber's thread is itself waiting on one of these objects, we have a classic deadly embrace.

Although we have eliminated interleavings that lead to inconsistency, some of the interleavings we eliminated were necessary to make progress.

4.2 Avoiding Deadlock

To avoid this problem, [Eng97] recommends changing the `setStatus` method to clone the listeners list within the synchronized block, and then to exit the block before entering the for-loop, as shown by the code below. This pattern avoids holding a lock during notification and thus avoids the obvious deadlock described above between a publisher and a subscriber. It does not avoid the underlying hazard, however, because the publisher may hold other locks.

```
public void setStatus(Object newStatus) {
    ArrayList<Listener> listeners;
    synchronized (this) {
        myStatus = newStatus;
        listeners = (ArrayList<Listener>)myListeners.clone();
    }
    for (Listener listener: listeners) {
        listener.statusChanged(newStatus);
    }
}
```

For example, if the account manager holds a lock on the bank account during a withdrawal, a deposit attempt by the finance application thread may result in an equivalent deadlock, with the account manager waiting for the notification of the finance application to complete, and the finance application waiting for the account to unlock. The result is that all the associated objects are locked and other subscribers will never hear about this update. Thus, the underlying hazard remains.

In this approach, some interleavings needed for progress are still eliminated, and as we will see, some newly-allowed interleavings lead to inconsistency.

4.3 Race Conditions

The approach above has a consistency hazard: if `setStatus` is called from two threads, the order in which they update `myStatus` will be the order they enter the synchronized block above. However, the for-loop notifying listeners of a later status may race ahead of one that will notify them of an earlier status. As a result, even a single subscriber may see updates out of order, so the spreadsheet may leave the display showing the wrong balance, even in the absence of any nested publication.

It is possible to adjust for these remaining problems. The style recommended for some rendezvous-based languages, like Concurrent ML and the π-calculus, corresponds to spawning a separate thread to perform each notification. This avoids using the producer's thread to notify the subscribers and thus avoids the deadlock hazard—it allows all interleavings needed for progress. However, this style still suffers from the same race condition hazards and so still fails to eliminate the right interleavings. We could compensate for this by adding a counter to the statusHolder and to the notification API, and by modifying the logic of all listeners to reorder notifications. But a formerly trivial pattern has now exploded into a case-analysis minefield. Actual systems contain thousands of patterns more complex than the statusHolder. Some of these will suffer from less obvious minefields.

> This is "Multi-Threaded Hell". As your application evolves, or as different programmers encounter the sporadic and non-reproducible corruption or deadlock bugs, they will add or remove locks around different

> data structures, causing your code base to veer back and forth . . . , erring first on the side of more deadlocking, and then on the side of more corruption. This kind of thrashing is bad for the quality of the code, bad for the forward progress of the project, and bad for morale.
>
> —An experience report from the development of Mojo Nation [WO01]

5 A Taste of E

Before revisiting the issues above, let's first use this example to briefly explain E as a sequential object language. (For a more complete explanation of E, see [Sti04].) Here is the same statusHolder as defined in E.

```
def makeStatusHolder(var myStatus) {
    def myListeners := [].diverge()
    def statusHolder {
        to addListener(newListener) {
            myListeners.push(newListener)
        }
        to getStatus() { return myStatus }
        to setStatus(newStatus) {
            myStatus := newStatus
            for listener in myListeners {
                listener.statusChanged(newStatus)
            }
        }
    }
    return statusHolder
}
```

E has no classes. Instead, the expression beginning with "`def statusHolder`" is an object definition expression. It creates a new object with the enclosed method definitions and binds the new `statusHolder` variable to this object. An invocation, such as "`statusHolder.setStatus(33)`", causes a message to be delivered to an object. When an object receives a message, it reacts according to the code of its matching method. As with Smalltalk [GR83] or Actors [HBS73], all values are objects, and all computation proceeds only by delivering messages to objects.

From a λ-calculus perspective, an object definition expression is a lambda expression, in which the (implicit) parameter is bound to the incoming message and the body selects a method to run according to the message. The delivery of a message to an object is the application of an object-as-closure to a message-as-argument. An object's behavior is indeed a function of the message it is applied to. This view of objects goes back to Smalltalk-72 [GK76] and Actors, and is hinted at earlier in [Hoa65]. Also see [SS04].

Unlike a class definition, an object definition does not declare its instance variables. Instead, the instance variables of an object are simply the variables used freely within the object definition (which therefore must be defined in some lexically enclosing scope). The instance variables of statusHolder are `myStatus` and `myListeners`. Variables are unassignable by default; the "`var`" keyword defines `myStatus` as an assignable variable. Square brackets evaluate to an immutable list containing the values of the subexpressions (the empty-list in the example). Lists respond to the "`diverge()`" message by returning a new mutable list whose initial contents are a snapshot of the diverged list. Thus, `myListeners` is initialized to a new, empty, mutable list, which acts much like an `ArrayList`.

E provides syntactic shorthands to use objects that define a "`run`" method as if they were functions. The syntax for `makeStatusHolder` is a shorthand for defining an object with a single "`run`" method. It expands to:

```
def makeStatusHolder {
    to run(var myStatus) { ...
```

The corresponding function call syntax, "`makeStatusHolder(44)`", is shorthand which expands to "`makeStatusHolder.run(44)`". Each time `makeStatusHolder` is called, it defines and returns a new statusHolder.

5.1 Two Ways to Postpone Plans

The E code for statusHolder above retains the simplicity and hazards of the sequential Java version. To address these hazards requires examining the underlying issues. When the statusHolder—or any agent—is executing plan X and discovers the need to engage in plan Y, in a sequential system, it has two simple alternatives of when to do Y:

Immediately: Put X aside, work on Y until complete, then go back to X.
Eventually: Put Y on a "to-do" list and work on it after X is complete.

The "immediate" option corresponds to conventional, sequential call-return control flow (or strict applicative-order evaluation), and is represented by the "`.`" or *immediate-call* operator, which delivers the message immediately. Above, statusHolder's `addListener` method tells `myListeners` to push the `newListener` *immediately*. When `addListener` proceeds past this point, it may assume that all side effects it requested are done.

For the statusHolder example, all of the sequential hazards (e.g., Nested Publication) and many of the concurrent hazards (deadlock) occur because the `statusChanged` method is also invoked immediately: the publisher's plan is set aside to pursue the listener's plan (which might then abort, change the state further, etc.).

The "eventual" option corresponds to the human notion of a "to-do" list: the item is queued for later execution. E provides direct support for this asynchronous messaging option, represented by the "`<-`" or *eventual-send* operator. Using eventual-send, the `setStatus` method can ensure that each listener will be notified of the changed status in such a way that it does not interfere with the statusHolder's current plan. To accomplish this in E, the `setStatus` method becomes:

```
to setStatus(newStatus) {
    myStatus := newStatus
    for listener in myListeners {
        listener <- statusChanged(newStatus)
    }
}
```

As a result of using eventual-send above, all of the sequential hazards are addressed. Errors, new subscriptions, and additional status changes caused by listeners will all take place after all notifications for a published event have been scheduled. Publishers' plans and subscribers' plans are temporally isolated—so these plans may unfold with fewer unintended interactions. For example, it can no longer matter whether `myStatus` is assigned before or after the for-loop.

5.2 Simple E Execution

This section describes how temporal isolation is achieved within a single thread of control. The next section describes how it is achieved in the face of concurrency and distribution.

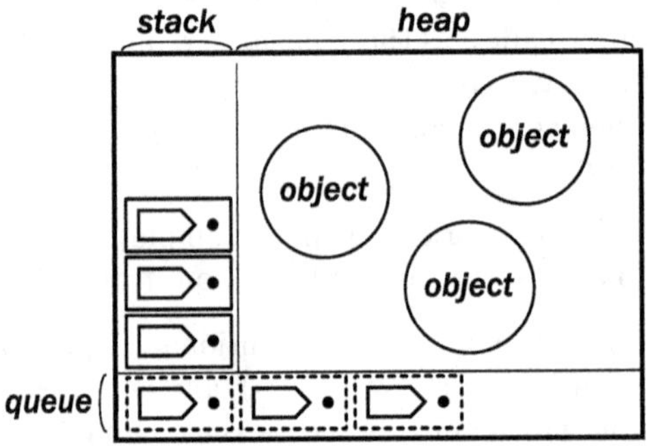

Fig. 2. An E vat consists of a heap of objects and a thread of control. The stack and queue together record the postponed plans the thread needs to process. An immediate-call pushes a new frame on top of the stack, representing the delivery of a message (*arrow*) to a target object (*dot*). An eventual-send enqueues a new pending delivery on the right end of the queue. The thread proceeds from top to bottom and then from left to right.

In E, an eventual-send creates and queues a *pending delivery*, which represents the eventual delivery of a particular message to a particular object. Within a single thread of control, E has both a normal execution stack for immediate call-return and a queue containing all the pending deliveries. Execution proceeds by taking a pending-delivery from the queue, delivering its message to its object, and processing all the resulting immediate-calls in conventional call-return order. This is called a *turn*. When a pending delivery completes, the next one is dequeued, and so forth. This is the classic event-loop model, in which all of the events are pending deliveries. Because each event's turn runs to completion before the next is serviced, they are temporally isolated.

Additional mechanisms to process results and exceptions from eventual-sends will be discussed in further sections below.

The combination of a stack, a pending delivery queue, and the heap of objects they operate on is called a *vat*, illustrated in Figure 2.[3] Each E object lives in exactly one vat and a vat may host many objects. Each vat lives on one machine at a time and a machine may host many vats. The vat is also the minimum unit of persistence, migration, partial failure, resource control, and defense from denial of service. We will return to some of these topics below.

6 Communicating Event-Loops

We now consider the case where our account (including account manager and its statusHolder) runs in VatA on one machine, and our spreadsheet (including its listener) runs in VatS on another machine.

In E, we distinguish several reference-states. A direct reference between two objects in the same vat is a *near reference*.[4] As we have seen, near references carry both immediate-calls and eventual-sends. Only *eventual references* may cross vat boundaries, so the spreadsheet holds an eventual reference to the statusHolder, which in turns holds an eventual reference to the spreadsheet's listener. Eventual references are first class—they can be passed as arguments, returned as results, and stored in data structures, just like near references. However, eventual references carry only eventual-sends, not immediate-calls—an immediate-call on an eventual reference throws an exception. Our statusHolder is compatible with this constraint, since it stores, retrieves, and eventual-sends to its listeners, but never immediate-calls them. Figure 3 shows what happens when a message is sent between vats.

When the statusHolder in VatA performs an eventual-send of the `statusChanged` message to the spreadsheet's listener in VatS, VatA creates a pending delivery as before, recording the need to deliver this message to this listener. Pending deliveries need to be queued on the pending delivery queue of the vat hosting the object that will receive the message—in this case, VatS. VatA serializes (marshals) the pending delivery onto an encrypted, order-preserving byte stream read by VatS. Should it ever arrive at VatS, VatS will unserialize it and queue it on its own pending delivery queue.

Since each vat runs concurrently with all other vats, turns in different vats no longer have actual temporal isolation. If VatS is otherwise idle, it may service this delivery, notifying the spreadhseet's listener of the new balance, while the original turn is still in progress in VatA. But so what? These two turns can

[3] Figures 2–5 were created by Ka-Ping Yee with input from the e-lang community.

[4] For brevity, we generally do not distinguish a near reference from the object it designates.

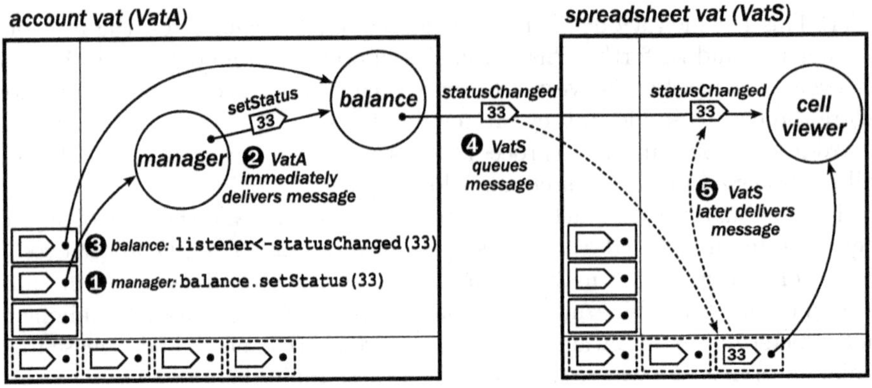

Fig. 3. If the account manager and the spreadsheet are in separate vats, when the account manager (1) tells the statusHolder that represents its balance to immediately update, this (2) transfers control to the statusHolder, which (3) notes that its listeners should eventually be notified. The message is (4) sent to the spreadsheet's vat, which queues it on arrival and eventually (5) delivers it to the listener, which updates the display of the spreadsheet cell.

only execute simultaneously when they are in different vats. In this case, the spreadsheet cannot affect the account manager's turn-in-progress. Because only eventual references span between vats, the spreadsheet can only affect VatA by eventual-sending to objects hosted by VatA. This cannot affect any turn already in progress in VatA—VatA only queues the pending delivery, and will service it sometime after the current turn and turns for previously queued pending deliveries, complete.

Only near references provide one object synchronous access to another. Therefore an object has synchronous access to state only within its own vat. Taken together, these rules guarantee that a running turn—a sequential call-return program—has mutually exclusive access to everything to which it has synchronous access. In the absence of real-time concerns, this provides all the isolation that was achieved by temporal isolation in the single-threaded case.

The net effect is that a turn is E's unit of operation. We can faithfully account for the visible effects of concurrency without any interleaving of the steps within a turn. Any actual multi-vat computation is equivalent to some fully ordered interleaving of turns.[5] Because E has no explicit locking constructs, computation

[5] An E turn may never terminate, which is hard to account for within this simple model of serializability. There are formal models of asynchronous systems that can account for non-terminating events [CL85]. Within the scope of this paper, we can safely ignore this issue.

The actual E system does provide synchronous file I/O operations. When these files are local, prompt, and private to the vat accessing them, this does not violate turn isolation, but since files may be remote, non-prompt, or shared, the availability of these synchronous I/O operations does violate the E model.

within a turn can never block—it can only run, to completion or forever. A vat as a whole is either processing pending deliveries, or is idle when there are no pending deliveries to service. Because computation never blocks, it cannot deadlock. Other lost progress hazards are discussed in the section on "Datalock" below.

As with database transactions, the length of an E turn is not predetermined. It is a tradeoff left for the developer to decide. How the object graph is carved up into vats and how computation is carved up into turns will determine which interleaving cases are eliminated, and which must be handled explicitly by the programmer. For example, when the spreadsheet was co-located with the statusHolder, it could immediate-call both `getStatus` and `addListener` in order to ensure that the spreadsheet's cell sees exactly the updates to an initial valid state. But when it can only eventual-send these messages, they may arrive at the statusHolder interleaved with other messages. To relieve potentially remote clients of this burden, the statusHolder should send an initial notification to newly subscribed listeners:

```
to addListener(newListener) {
    myListeners.push(newListener)
    newListener <- statusChanged(myStatus)
}
```

6.1 Issues with Event-Loops

This architecture imposes some strong constraints on programming (e.g., no threads or coroutines), which can impede certain useful patterns of plan cooperation. In particular, recursive algorithms, such as recursive-descent parsers, must a) happen entirely within a single turn, b) be redesigned (e.g., as a table-driven parser), or c) if it needs external non-prompt input (e.g., a stream from the user), be run in a dedicated vat. E programs have used each of these approaches.

Thread-based coordination patterns can typically be adapted to vat granularity. For example, rather than adding the complexity of a priority queue for pending deliveries, different vats would simply run at different processor priorities. For example, if a user-interaction vat *could* proceed (has pending deliveries in its queue), it should; a helper "background" vat (e.g., spelling check) should consume processor resources only if no user-directed action could proceed. A divide-and-conquer approach for multi-processing could run a vat on each processor and divide the problem among them. The event-loop approach is unsuitable for problems that cannot easily be adapted to a message-passing hardware architecture, such as fluid dynamics computation.

7 Protection from Misbehavior

When using a language that supports shared-state concurrency, one can choose to avoid it and adopt the event-loop style instead. Indeed, several Java libraries, such as AWT, were initially designed to be thread-safe, and were then redesigned around event-loops. Using event-loops, one can easily write a Java class equivalent to our `makeStatusHolder`. If one can so easily choose to avoid shared-state concurrency, does E actually need to prohibit it?

E uses the event-loop approach to simplify the task of preserving consistency while maintaining progress. Preserving consistency stays simple for the statusHolder only if it executes in at most one thread at a time. As we discussed previously, the possibility of multiple threads would necessitate complex locking. If one of its clients *could* create a new thread and call it, then the simple version of the statusHolder could not preserve consistency (i.e., it would need to perform the complex locking mentioned in the previous section).

In the extreme case, one object may actively intend to disrupt the plans of another. This leads us to examine plan coordination in the presence of malicious behavior. The topic is of interest both because large and distributed systems in practice need to handle potentially malicious components, and because analysis of the malicious case can help uncover hazards that are already present in the non-malicious case.

7.1 Defensive Correctness

If a user browsing a webserver were able to cause incorrect pages to be displayed to other users, we would likely consider it a bug in the webserver—we expect it to remain correct regardless of the client's behavior. We call this property *defensive correctness*: a program P is defensively correct if it remains correct despite arbitrary behavior on the part of its clients. Before this definition can be useful, we need to pin down what we mean by "arbitrary" behavior.

When we say that a program P is correct, this normally means that we have a specification in mind, and that P behaves according to that specification. There are some implicit caveats in that assertion. For example, P cannot behave at all unless it is run on a machine; if the machine operates incorrectly, P on that machine may behave in ways that deviate from its specification. We do not consider this to be a bug in P, because P's correctness implicitly depends on the machine's correctness. If P's correctness depends on another component R's correctness, we will say that P *relies upon* R. For example, a typical webserver relies on the underlying machine and on operating system features such as files and sockets. We will refer to the set of all elements on which P relies as P's *reliance set.*[6]

We define Q's *authority* as the set of effects Q could cause. With regard to P's correctness, Q's *relevant authority* is bounded by the assumption that everything in P's reliance set is correct, since P was defined under this assumption.

[6] The set of all things that P relies on is similar in concept to P's "Trusted Computing Base" or TCB. "Rely" articulates the objective situation (P is vulnerable to R), and so avoids confusions engendered by the word "trust".

While the focus in this paper is on correctness, a similar "reliance" analysis could be applied to other program properties, such as promptness [Har85].

For example, if a user could cause a webserver to show the wrong page to other browsers by replacing a file through an operating system exploit, then the underlying operating system would be incorrect, not the webserver. We say that P *protects against* Q if P remains correct despite any of the effects in Q's relevant authority, that is, despite any possible actions by Q, assuming the correctness of P's reliance set.

Now we can speak more precisely about defensive correctness. The "arbitrary behavior" mentioned earlier is the combined relevant authority of an object's clients. P is *defensively correct* if it protects against all of its clients. The focus is on *clients* in particular in order to enable the composition of correct components into larger correct systems. If P relies on R, then P also relies on all of R's other clients *unless* R is defensively correct. If R does not protect against its other clients, P cannot prevent them from interfering with its own plan, which makes it infeasible for P to ensure its own correctness. By not relying on its clients, R enables them to avoid relying on each other.

This explains why it is important for E to forbid the spawning of threads. As we saw earlier, it can be very difficult to write programs in which threads protect against each other. Removing threads eliminates a key obstacle to defensive correctness.

Correctness can be divided into consistency (safety) and progress (liveness). An object that is vulnerable to denial-of-service by its clients may nevertheless be *defensively consistent.* Given that all the objects it relies on themselves remain consistent, a defensively consistent object will never give incorrect service to well-behaved clients, but it may be prevented from giving them any service. While a defensively correct object is invulnerable to its clients, a defensively consistent object is merely incorruptible by its clients.

Different security properties are feasible at different granularities. Some conventional operating systems attempt to provide support for protecting users from each other's misbehavior. But because programs are normally run with their user's full authority, all software run under the same account is mutually reliant: since each is granted the authority to corrupt the others via underlying components on which they all rely, they cannot usefully protect against such "friendly fire".[7] Some operating system designs [DH65] support process-granularity defensive consistency. Others, by providing principled controls over computational resource rights [Har85, SSF99], can also protect against denial of service. Among machines distributed over today's Internet, cryptographic protocols help support defensive consistency, but defensive correctness remains infeasible.

In most programming languages, all objects in the same process are mutually reliant. A secure language is one which supports some useful form of protections within a process. Among objects in the same vat, E supports defensive consistency: Any object may go into an infinite loop, thereby preventing the progress of all other objects within their vat. Therefore, within E's architecture, defensive correctness *within* a vat is impossible. With respect to progress, all objects within

[7] See [SKYM04] for an unconventional way to use conventional OSes to provide greater security.

the same vat are mutually reliant. In many situations, defensive consistency is adequate—a potential adversary often has more to gain from corruption than denial of service. This is especially so in iterated relationships, since corruption may misdirect plans but go undetected, while loss of progress is quite noticeable.

7.2 Principle of Least Authority (POLA)

Our statusHolder itself is now defensively consistent, but is it a good abstraction for the account manager to rely on to build its own defensively consistent plans? In our example scenario, we have been assuming that the account manager acts only as a publisher and that the finance application and spreadsheet act only as subscribers. However either subscriber *could* invoke the `setStatus` method. If the finance application calls `setStatus` with a bogus balance, the spreadsheet will dutifully render it.

This is a problem of access control. The statusHolder, by bundling two kinds of authority into one object, encouraged patterns where both kinds of authority were provided to objects that only needed one. This can be addressed by grouping these methods into separate objects, each of which represents a sensible bundle of authority.

```
def makeStatusPair(var myStatus) {
    def myListeners := [].diverge()
    def statusGetter {
        to addListener(newListener) {
            myListeners.push(newListener)
            newListener <- statusChanged(myStatus)
        }
        to getStatus() { return myStatus }
    }
    def statusSetter {
        to setStatus(newStatus) {
            myStatus := newStatus
            for listener in myListeners {
                listener <- statusChanged(newStatus)
            }
        }
    }
    return [statusGetter, statusSetter]
}
```

Now the account manager can make use of `makeStatusPair` as follows:

```
def [sGetter, sSetter] := makeStatusPair(33)
```

The call to `makeStatusPair` on the right side makes four objects—an object representing the `myStatus` variable, a mutable `myListeners` list, a `statusGetter`, and a `statusSetter`. The last two each share access to the first two. The call to `makeStatusPair` returns a list holding these last two objects. The left side pattern-matches this list, binding `sGetter` to the new `statusGetter`, and binding `sSetter` to the new `statusSetter`.

The account manager can now keep the new `statusSetter` for itself and give the spreadsheet and the finance application access only to the new `statusGetter`. More generally, we may now describe publishers as those with access to `statusSetter` and subscribers as those with access to `statusGetter`. The account manager can now provide consistent balance reports to its clients because it has denied them the possibility of corrupting this service.

As with concurrency control, the key to access control is to allow the possibilities needed for cooperation, while limiting the possibilities that would allow for plan interference. We wish to provide objects the authority needed to carry out their proper duties—publishers gotta publish—but little more. This is known as *POLA*, the *Principle of Least Authority* (See [MS03] for the relationship between POLA and the Principle of Least Privilege [SS75]). By not granting its subscribers the authority to publish a bogus balance, the account manager no longer needs to worry about what would happen if they did. This discipline helps us compose plans so as to allow well-intentioned plans to successfully cooperate, while minimizing the kinds of plan interference they must defend against.

7.3 A Taste of E Across a Network

E's computational model extends across the network. An eventual reference in a vat can refer to an object in a vat on another machine; eventual-sends to that reference are sent across an encrypted, authenticated link and posted as pending deliveries for the target object on the remote vat.

E's network protocol, Pluribus, actually runs between vats, not between machines. Therefore, we can ignore the distinction between vats and machines without loss of generality. An incorrect machine is, from our perspective, simply a set of incorrect vats; i.e., vats that do not implement the language and/or protocol correctly. The design of Pluribus is beyond the scope of this document, but a few words are in order.

Pluribus enforces characteristics of the E computational model, such as reference integrity, so that E programs can rely on those properties between vats and therefore between machines. Even if a remote vat runs its objects in an unsafe language like C++, other vats could still view it from a correctness point of view as a set of (possibly incorrect) objects written in E. From the perspective of other vats, the objects in the remote vat could collude and act arbitrarily within the union of the authorities granted to any of them, but they cannot feasibly[8] manufacture new authorities. Thus, if an object relies on another object in a remote vat, then it also relies on that remote vat (because the remote object relies on that vat).

[8] Pluribus relies on the standard cryptographic assumptions that large random numbers are not feasibly guessable, and that well-accepted algorithms are immune to feasible cryptanalysis.

8 Promise Pipelining

The eventual-send examples so far were carefully selected to be evaluated only for their effects, with no use made of the value of these expressions. This section discusses the handling of return results and exceptions produced by eventual-sends.

8.1 Promises

As discussed previously, eventual-sends queue a pending delivery and complete immediately. The return value from an eventual-send operation is called a *promise* for the eventual result. The promise is not a near reference for the result of the eventual-send because the eventual-send cannot have happened yet (i.e., it will happen in a later turn). Instead, the promise is an eventual-reference for the result. A pending delivery, in addition to the message and reference to the target object, includes a *resolver* for the promise, which provides the right to choose what the promise designates. When the turn spawned by the eventual-send completes, its vat reports the outcome to the resolver, *resolving* the promise so that the promise eventually becomes a reference designating that outcome, called the *resolution.*

Once resolved, the promise is equivalent to its resolution. Thus, if it resolves to an eventual-reference for an object in another vat, then the promise becomes that eventual reference. If it resolves to an object that can be passed by copy between vats, then it becomes a near-reference to that object.

Because the promise starts out as an eventual reference, messages can be eventually-sent to it even *before* it is resolved. Messages sent to the promise cannot be delivered until the promise is resolved, so they are buffered in FIFO order within the promise. Once the promise is resolved, these messages are forwarded, in order, to its resolution.

8.2 Pipelining

Since an object can eventual-send to the promises resulting from previous eventual-sends, functional composition is straightforward. If object *L* in VatL executes

```
def r3 := x <- a() <- c(y <- b())
```

or equivalently

```
def r1 := x <- a()
def r2 := y <- b()
def r3 := r1 <- c(r2)
```

and `x` and `y` are on VatR, then all three requests are serialized and streamed out to VatR immediately and the turn in VatL continues without blocking. By contrast, in a conventional RPC system, the calling thread would only proceed after multiple network round trips.

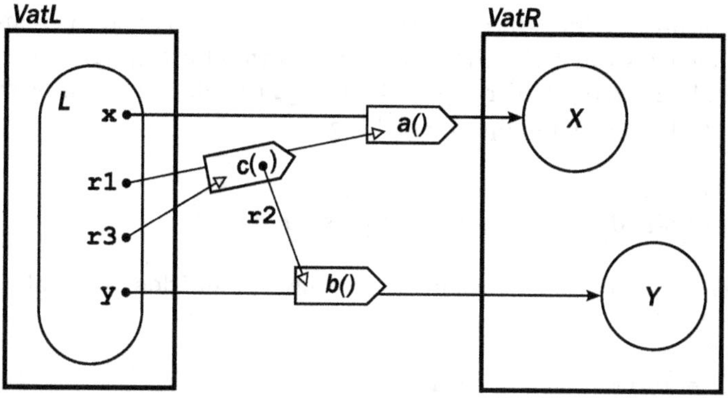

Fig. 4. The three messages in `def r3 := x <- a() <- c(y <- b())` are streamed out together, with no round trip. Each message box "rides" on the reference it is sent on. References `x` and `y` are shown with solid arrowheads, indicating that their target is known. The others are *promises*, whose open arrowhead represents their *resolvers*, which provide the right to choose their promises' value.

Figure 4 depicts an unresolved reference as an arrow stretching between its promise-end, the tail held by `r1`, and its resolver, the open arrowhead within the pending delivery sent to VatR. Messages sent on a reference always flow towards its destination and so "move" as close to the arrowhead as possible. While the pending delivery for `a()` is in transit to VatR, so is the resolver for `r1`, so we send the `c(r2)` message there as well. As VatR unserializes these three requests, it queues the first two in its local to-do list, since their target is known and local. It sends the third, `c(r2)`, on a local promise that will be resolved by the outcome of `a()`, carrying as an argument a local promise for the outcome of `b()`.

If the resolution of `r1` is local to VatR, then as soon as `a()` is done, `c(r2)` is immediately queued on VatR's to-do list and may well be serviced before VatL learns of `r1`'s resolution. If `r1` is on VatL, then `c(r2)` is streamed back towards VatL just behind the message informing VatL of `r1`'s resolution. If `r1` is on yet a third vat, then `c(r2)` is forwarded to that vat.

Across geographic distances, latency is already the dominant performance consideration. As hardware improves, processing will become faster and cheaper, buffers larger, and bandwidth greater, with limits still many orders of magnitude away. But latency will remain limited by the speed of light. Pipes between fixed endpoints can be made wider but not shorter. Promise pipelining reduces the impact of latency on remote communication. Performance analysis of this type of protocol can be found in Bogle's "Batched Futures" [BL94]; the promise pipelining protocol is approximately a symmetric generalization of it.

8.3 Datalock

Promise chaining allows some plans, like `c(r2)`, to be postponed pending the resolution of previous plans. We introduce other ways to postpone plans below.

Using the primitives introduced so far, however, it is possible to create circular data dependencies which, like deadlock, are a form of lost-progress bug. We call this kind of bug, *datalock*. For example, the `epimenides` function below returns a promise for the boolean opposite of `flag`.

```
var flag := true
def epimenides() { return flag <- not() }
```

If `flag` were assigned to the result of invoking `epimenides` eventually, datalock would occur.

```
flag := epimenides <- run()
```

In the current turn, a pending-delivery of `epimenides <- run()` is queued, and a promise for its result is immediately assigned to `flag`. In a later turn when `epimenides` is invoked, it eventual-sends a message to the promise in `flag`, and then resolves the `flag` promise to the new promise for the `not()` sent to that *same* `flag` promise. The datalock is created, not because a promise is resolved to another promise (which is acceptable and common), but because computing the eventual resolution of `flag` requires already knowing it.

Although the E model trades one form of lost-progress bug for another, it is still more reliable. As above, datalock bugs primarily represent circular dependencies in the computation, which manifest reproducibly like normal program bugs. This avoids the significant non-determinism, non-reproducibility, and resulting debugging difficulty of deadlock bugs. Anecdotally, in many years of programming in E and E-like languages and a body of experience spread over perhaps 60 programmers and two substantial distributed systems, we know of only two datalock bugs. Perhaps others went undetected, but these projects did not spend the agonizing time chasing deadlock bugs that projects of their nature normally must spend. Further analysis is needed to understand why datalock bugs seem to be so rare.

8.4 Explicit Promises

Besides the implicit creation of promise-resolver pairs by eventual-sending, E provides a primitive to create these pairs explicitly. In the following code

```
def [p, r] := Ref.promise()
```

`p` and `r` are bound to the promise and resolver of a new promise/resolver pair. Explicit promise creation gives us yet greater flexibility to postpone plans until other conditions occur. The promise, `p`, can be handed out and used just as any other eventual reference. All messages eventually-sent to `p` are queued in the promise. An object with access to `r` can wait until some condition occurs before resolving `p` and allowing these pending messages to proceed, as a later example will demonstrate.

8.5 Broken Promise Contagion

Because eventual-sends are executed in a later turn, an exception raised by one can no longer signal an exception and abort the plan of its "caller". Instead, the vat executing the turn for the eventual send catches any exception that terminates that turn and *breaks* the promise by resolving the promise to a *broken reference* containing that exception. Any immediate-call or eventual-send to a broken reference breaks the result with the broken reference's exception. Specifically, an immediate-call to a broken reference would throw the exception, terminating control flow. An eventual-send to a broken reference would break the eventual-send's promise with the broken reference's exception. As with the original exception, this would not terminate control flow, but does affect plans dependent on the resulting value.

E's split between control-flow exceptions and data-flow exceptions was inspired by signaling and non-signaling NaNs in floating point. Like non-signaling NaNs, broken promise contagion does not hinder pipelining. Following sections discuss how additional sources of failure in distributed systems cause broken references, and how E handles them while preserving defensive consistency.

9 Partial Failure

Not all exceptional conditions are caused by program behavior. Networks suffer outages, partitioning one part of the network from another. Machines fail: sometimes in a transient fashion, rolling back to a previous stable state; sometimes permanently, making the objects they host forever inaccessible. From a machine not able to reach a remote object, it is generally impossible to tell which failure is occurring or which messages were lost.

Distributed programs need to be able to react to these conditions so that surviving components can continue to provide valuable and correct—though possibly degraded—service while other components are inaccessible. If these components may change state while out of contact, they must recover distributed consistency when they reconnect. There is no single best strategy for maintaining consistency in the face of partitions and merges; the appropriate strategy will depend on the semantics of the components. A general purpose framework should provide simple mechanisms adequate to express a great variety of strategies. Group membership and similar systems provide one form of such a general framework, with strengths and weaknesses in comparison with E. Here, we explain E's framework. We provide a brief comparison with mechanisms like group membership in the "Related Work" section below.

E's support for partial failure starts by extending the semantics of our reference states. Figure 5 shows the full state transition diagram among these states.

We have added the possibility of a vat-crossing reference—a remote promise or a far reference—getting broken by a partition. A partition between a pair of

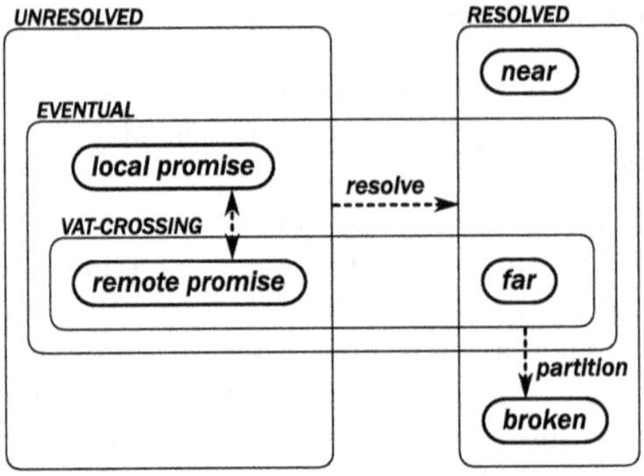

Fig. 5. A resolved reference's target is known. Near references are resolved and local; they carry both immediate-calls and eventual-sends. Promises and vat-crossing references are eventual; they carry only eventual-sends. Broken references carry neither. Promises may *resolve* to near, far or broken. *Partition* may break vat-crossing references.

vats eventually breaks all references that cross between these vats, creating eventual common knowledge of the loss of connection. A partition simultaneously breaks all references crossing in a given direction between two vats. The sender of messages that were still in transit cannot know which were actually received and which were lost. Later messages will only be delivered by a reference if all earlier messages sent on that same reference were already delivered. This fail-stop FIFO delivery order relieves the sender from needing to wait for earlier messages to be acknowledged before sending later dependent messages.[9]

On our state-transition diagram (a Harel statechart), we see that "near" and "broken" are terminal states. Even after a partition heals, all references broken by that partition stay broken.

In our listener example, if a partition separates the account's vat from the spreadsheet's vat, the statusHolder's reference to the spreadsheet's listener will eventually be broken with a partition-exception. Of the `statusChanged` messages sent by the statusHolder, this reference will deliver them reliably in FIFO order until it fails. Once it fails to deliver a message, it will never deliver any further messages and will eventually become visibly broken.

An essential consequence of these semantics is that defensive consistency is preserved across partition and reconnect. A defensively consistent program that makes no provisions for partition remains defensively consistent. In the earlier statusHolder example, `statusChanged` notifications sent to broken listener references (e.g., broken because the connection to its subscriber vat was severed) are harmlessly discarded.

[9] The message delivery order E enforces is stronger than FIFO and weaker than Causal [TMK+87], but FIFO is adequate for all points we make in this paper.

9.1 Handling Failure

To explicitly manage failure of a reference, an object registers a handler to be eventually notified when that reference becomes broken. For the statusHolder to clean up broken listener references, it must register a handler on each one.

```
to addListener(newListener) {
    myListeners.push(newListener)
    newListener <- statusChanged(myStatus)
    def handler() { remove(myListeners, newListener) }
    newListener <- __whenBroken(handler)
}
```

The `__whenBroken` message is one of a handful of universally understood messages that all objects respond to by default.[10] Of these, the following messages are for interacting with a reference itself, as distinct from interacting only with the object designated by a reference.

`__whenBroken(`*`handler`*`)` When sent on a reference, this message registers its argument, `handler`, to be notified when this reference breaks.

`__whenMoreResolved(`*`handler`*`)` When sent on a reference, this message is normally used so that one can react when the reference is first resolved. We explain this in the later "When-Catch" section below.

`__reactToLostClient(`*`exception`*`)` When a vat-crossing reference breaks, it sends this message to its target object, to notify it that some of its clients may no longer be able to reach it.

Near references and local promises make no special case for these messages—they merely deliver them to their targets. Objects by default respond to a `__whenBroken` message by ignoring it, because they are not broken. So, in our single-vat scenario, when all these references are near, the additional code above has no effect. A broken reference, on the other hand, responds by eventual-sending a notification to the handler, as if by the following code:

```
to __whenBroken(handler) { handler <- run() }
```

When a local promise gets broken, all its messages are forwarded to the broken reference; when the `__whenBroken` message arrives, the broken reference will notify the handler.

A vat-crossing reference notifies these handlers if it becomes broken, whether by partition or resolution. In order to be able to send these notifications during partition, a vat-crossing reference registers the handler argument of a `__whenBroken` message at the tail end of the reference, *within the sending vat.* If the sending vat is told that one of these references has resolved, it re-sends equivalent `__whenBroken` messages to this resolution. If the sending vat decides that a partition has occurred (perhaps because the internal keep-alive timeout

[10] In Java, the methods defined in `java.lang.Object` are similarly universal.

has been exceeded), it breaks all outgoing references and notifies all registered handlers.

For all the reasons previously explained, the handler behavior built into E's references only eventual-sends notifications to handlers. Until the above handler reacts, the statusHolder will continue to harmlessly use the broken reference to the spreadsheet's listener. Contingency concerns can thus be handled separately from normal operation.

But what of the spreadsheet? We have ensured that it will receive `statusChanged` notifications in order, and that it will not miss any in the middle of a sequence. But, during a partition, its display may become arbitrarily stale. Technically, this introduces no new consistency hazards because the data may be stale anyway due to notification latencies. Nonetheless, the spreadsheet may wish to provide a visual indication that the displayed value may now be more stale than usual, since it is now out of contact with the authoritative source. To make this convenient, when a reference is broken by partition, it eventual-sends a `__reactToLostClient` message to its target, notifying it that at least one of its clients may no longer be able to send messages to it. By default, objects ignore `__reactToLostClient` messages. The spreadsheet could override the default behavior:

```
to __reactToLostClient(exception) { ...update display... }
```

Thus, when a vat-crossing reference is severed by partition, notifications are eventually-sent to handlers at both ends of the reference. This explains how connectivity is safely severed by partition and how objects on either side can react if they wish. Objects also need to regain connectivity following a partition. For this purpose, we introduce *offline capabilities.*

9.2 Offline Capabilities

An offline capability in E has two forms: a "captp://..." URI string and an encapsulated `SturdyRef` object. Both contain the same information: the fingerprint of the public key of the vat hosting its target object, a list of TCP/IP location hints to seed the search for a vat that can authenticate against this fingerprint, and a so-called *swiss-number*, a large unguessable random number which the hosting vat associates with the target [Clo04a]. Like the popular myth of how Swiss bank account numbers work, one demonstrates knowledge of this secret to gain access to the object it designates. Like an object reference, if you do not know an unguessable secret, you can only come to know it if someone who knows it and can talk to you chooses to tell it to you. An offline capability is a form of "password capability"—it contains the cryptographic information needed both to authenticate the target and to authorize access to the target [Don76].

Both forms of offline capability are pass-by-copy and can be passed between vats even when the vat of the target object is inaccessible. Offline capabilities do not directly convey messages to their target. To establish or reestablish access to the target, one makes a new reference from an offline capability. Doing so initiates a new attempt to connect to the target vat and immediately returns a promise for the resulting inter-vat reference. If the connection attempt fails, this promise is eventually broken.

Typically, most inter-vat connectivity is only by references. When these break, applications on either end should not try to recover the detailed state of all the plans in progress between these vats. Instead, they should typically spawn a new fresh structure from the small number of offline capabilities from which this complex structure was originally spawned. As part of this respawning process, the two sides may need to explicitly reconcile in order to reestablish distributed consistency.

In our listener example, the statusHolder should not hold offline capabilities to listeners and should not try to reconnect to them. This would put the burden on the wrong party. A better design would have a listener hold an offline capability to the statusHolder. The listener's `__reactToLostClient` method would be enhanced to attempt to reconnect to the statusHolder and to resubscribe the listener on the promise for the reconnected statusHolder.

But perhaps the spreadsheet application originally encountered this statusHolder by navigating from an earlier object representing a collection of accounts, creating and subscribing a spreadsheet cell for each. While the vats were out of contact, not only may this statusHolder have changed, the collection may have changed so that this statusHolder is no longer relevant. In this case, a better design would be for the spreadsheet to maintain an offline capability only to the collection as a whole. When reconciling, it should navigate afresh, in order to find the statusHolders to which it should now subscribe.

The separation of references from offline capabilities encourages programming patterns that separate reconciliation concerns from normal operations.

9.3 Persistence

For an object that is designated only by references, the hosting vat can tell when it is no longer reachable and can garbage-collect it.[11] Once one makes an offline capability to a given object, its hosting vat can no longer determine when it is unreachable. Instead, this vat must retain the association between this object and its swiss-number until its obligation to honor this offline capability expires.

The operations for making an offline capability provide three options for ending this obligation: It can expire at a chosen future date, giving the association a *time-to-live.* It can expire when explicitly cancelled, making the association *revocable.* And it can expire when the hosting vat crashes, making the association *transient.* Here, we examine only this last option. An association which is not transient is *durable.*

A vat can be either ephemeral or persistent. An ephemeral vat exists only until it terminates or crashes; so for these, the last option above is irrelevant. A persistent vat periodically *checkpoints*, saving its persistent state to non-volatile

[11] E's distributed garbage collection protocol does not currently collect unreachable inter-vat references cycles. See [Bej96] for a GC algorithm able to collect such cycles among mutually suspicious machines.

storage. A vat checkpoints only between turns when its stack is empty. A crash terminates a vat-incarnation, rolling it back to its last checkpoint. Reviving the vat from checkpoint creates a new incarnation of the same vat. A persistent vat lives through a sequence of incarnations. With the possibility of crash admitted into E's computational model, we can allow programs to cause crashes, so they can preemptively terminate a vat or abort an incarnation.

The persistent state of a vat is determined by traversal from persistent roots. This state includes the vat's public/private key pair, so later incarnations can authenticate. It also includes all unexpired durable swiss-number associations and state reached by traversal from there. As this traversal proceeds, when it reaches an offline capability, the offline capability itself is saved but is not traversed to its target. When the traversal reaches a vat-crossing reference, a broken reference is saved instead and the reference is again not traversed. Should this vat be revived from this checkpoint, old vat-crossing references will be revived as broken references. A crash partitions a vat from all others. Following a revival, only offline capabilities in either direction enable it to become reconnected.

10 The When-Catch Expression

The `__whenMoreResolved` message can be used to be register for notification when a reference resolves. Typically this message is used indrectly through the "when-catch" syntax. A when-catch expression takes a promise, a "when" block to execute if the promise resolves to a value, and a "catch" block to execute if the promise is broken. This is illustrated by the following example.

```
def asyncAnd(answers) {
    var countDown := answers.size()
    if (countDown == 0) { return true }
    def [result, resolver] := Ref.promise()
    for answer in answers {
        when (answer) -> {
            if (answer) {
                countDown -= 1
                if (countDown == 0) {
                    resolver.resolve(true)
                }
            } else {
                resolver.resolve(false)
            }
        } catch exception {
            resolver.smash(exception)
        }
    }
    return result
}
```

The asyncAnd takes a list of promises for booleans. It immediately returns a reference representing the conjunction, which must eventually be true if all elements of the list become true, or false or broken if any of them become false or broken. Using when-catch, asyncAnd can test these as they become available, so it can report a result as soon as it has enough information.

If the list is empty, the conjunction is true right away. Otherwise, countDown remembers how many true answers are needed before asyncAnd can conclude that the conjunction is true. The "when-catch" expression is used to register a handler on each reference in the list. The behavior of the handler is expressed in two parts: the block after the "->" handles the normal case, and the catch-clause handles the exceptional case. Once answer resolves, if it is near or far, the normal-case code is run. If it is broken, the catch-clause is run. Here, if the normal case runs, answer is expected to be a boolean. By using a "when-catch", the if is postponed until asyncAnd has gathered enough information to know which way it should branch.

Once asyncAnd registers all these handlers, it immediately returns result, a promise for the conjunction of these answers. If they all resolve to true, asyncAnd *reveals* that the result is true, i.e., it eventually resolves the already-returned promise to true. If it is notified that any resolve to false, asyncAnd reveals false immediately. If any resolve to broken, asyncAnd reveals a reference broken by the same exception. Asking a resolver to resolve an already-resolved promise has no effect, so if one of the answers is false and another is broken, the above asyncAnd code may reveal either false or broken, depending on which handler happens to be notified first.

The following snippet illustrates using asyncAnd and when-catch to combine independent validity checks in a toy application to resells goods from a supplier.

```
def allOk := asyncAnd([inventory <- isAvailable(partNo),
                       creditBureau <- verifyCredit(buyerData),
                       shipper <- canDeliver(...)])
when (allOk) -> {
    if (allOk) {
        def receipt := supplier <- buy(partNo, payment)
        when (receipt) -> {
```

Promise-chaining postpones plans efficiently by data-flow; the "when-catch" postpones plans until the data needed for control-flow is available.

11 From Objects to Actors and Back Again

Here we present a brief history of E's concurrency-control architecture. In this section, the term "we" indicates that one or both of this paper's first two authors participated in a project involving other people. All implied credit should be understood as shared with these others.

Objects. The nature of computation provided within a single von Neumann machine is quite different than the nature of computation provided by networks of such machines. Distributed programs must deal with both. To reduce cases, it would seem attractive to create an abstraction layer that can make these seem more similar. Distributed Shared Memory systems try to make the network seem more like a von Neumann machine. Object-oriented programming started by trying to make a single computer seem more like a network.

> ... Smalltalk is a recursion on the notion of computer itself. Instead of dividing "computer stuff" into things each less strong than the whole—like data structures, procedures, and functions which are the usual paraphernalia of programming languages—each Smalltalk object is a recursion on the entire possibilities of the computer. Thus its semantics are a bit like having thousands and thousands of computers all hooked together by a very fast network.
>
> —Alan Kay [Kay93]

Smalltalk imported only the aspects of networks that made it easier to program a single machine—its purpose was not to achieve network transparency. Problems that could be avoided within a single machine—like inherent asynchrony, large latencies, and partial failures—were avoided. The sequential subset of E has much in common with the early Smalltalk: Smalltalk's object references are like E's near references and Smalltalk's message passing is like E's immediate-call operator.

Actors. Inspired by the early Smalltalk, Hewitt created the Actors paradigm [HBS73], whose goals include full network transparency within all the constraints imposed by decentralization and mutual suspicion [Hew85]. Although the stated goals require the handling of partial failure, the actual Actors model assumes this issue away and instead guarantees that all sent messages are eventually delivered. The asynchronous-only subset of E is an Actors language: Actors' references are like E's eventual references, and Actors' message passing is much like E's eventual-send operator. Actors provide both data-flow postponement of plans by futures (like E's promises without pipelining or contagion) and control-flow postponement by continuations (similar in effect to E's when-catch).

The price of this uniformity is that all programs had to work in the face of network problems. There was only one case to solve, but it was the hard case.

Vulcan. Inspired by Shapiro and Takeuchi [ST83], the Vulcan project [KTMB87] merged aspects of Actors and concurrent logic/constraint programming [Sha83, Sar93]. The pleasant properties of concurrent logic variables (much like futures or promises) taught us to emphasize data-flow postponement and de-emphasize control-flow postponement.

Vulcan was built on a concurrent logic base, and inherited from it the so-called "merge problem" [SM87] absent from pure Actors languages: Clients can only share access to a stateful object by explicit pre-arrangement, so the equivalent of object references were not usefully first-class. To address this problem, we created the "Channels" abstraction, which also provides useful ordering properties [TMK+87].

Joule. The Joule language [TMHK95] is a capability-secure, massively-concurrent, distributed language that is one of the primary precursors to E. Joule merges insights from the Vulcan project with the remaining virtues of Actors. Joule channels are similar to E's promises generalized to provide multicasting. Joule tanks are the unit of separate failure, persistence, migration, and resource management, and inspired E vats. E vats further define the unit of sequentiality; E's event-loop approach achieves much of Joule's power with a more familiar and easy to use computational model. Joule's resource management is based on abstractions from KeyKOS [Har85]. E vats do not yet address this issue.

Promise pipelining in Udanax Gold. This was a pre-web hypertext system with a rich interaction protocol between clients and servers. To deal with network latencies, in the 1989 timeframe, we independently reinvented an asymmetric form of promise pipelining as part of our protocol design [Mil92]. This was the first attempt to adapt Joule channels to an object-based client-server environment (it did not support peer-to-peer).

Original-E. The language now known as Original-E was the result of adding the concepts from Joule to the sequential, capability-secure subset of Java. Original-E was the first to successfully mix sequential immediate-call programming with asynchronous eventual-send programming. Original-E cryptographically secured the Joule-like network extension—something that had been planned for but not actually realized in prior systems. Electric Communities created Original-E, and used it to build Habitats—a graphical, decentralized, secure, social virtual reality system.

From Original-E to E. In Original-E, the co-existence of sequential and asynchronous programming was still rough. E brought the invention of the distinct reference states and the transitions among them explained in this paper. With these rules, E bridges the gap between the network-as-metaphor view of the early Smalltalk and the network-transparency ambitions of Actors. In E, the local case is strictly easier than the network case, so the guarantees provided by near references are a strict superset of the guarantees provided by other reference states. When programming for known-local objects, a programmer can do it the easy way. Otherwise, the programmer must address the inherent problems of networks. Once the programmer has done so, the same code will painlessly also handle the local case without requiring any further case analysis.

12 Related Work

Promises and Batched Futures at MIT. The promise pipelining technique was first invented by Liskov and Shrira [LS88]. These ideas were then significantly improved by Bogle [BL94]. Like the Udanax Gold system mentioned above, these are asymmetric client-server systems. In other ways, the techniques used in Bogle's protocol resembles quite closely some of the techniques used in E's protocol.

Group Membership. There is an extensive body of work on group membership systems [BJ87, Ami95] and (broadly speaking) similar systems such as Paxos [Lam98]. These systems provide a different form of general-purpose framework for dealing with partial failure: they support closer approximations of common knowledge than does E, but at the price of weaker support for defensive consistency and scalability. These frameworks better support the tightly-coupled composition of separate plan-strands into a virtual single overall plan. E's mechanisms better support the loosely-coupled composition of networks of independent but cooperative plans.

For example, when a set of distributed components form an application that provides a single logical service to all their collective clients, and when multiple separated components may each change state while out of contact with the others, we have a *partition-aware application* [OBDMS98, SM03], providing a form of fault-tolerant replication. The clients of such an application see a close approximation of a single stateful object that is highly available under partition. Some mechanisms like group membership shine at supporting this model under mutually reliant and even Byzantine conditions [CL02].

E itself provides nothing comparable. The patterns of fault-tolerant replication we have built to date are all forms of primary-copy replication, with a single stationary authoritative host. E supports these patterns quite well, and they compose well with simple E objects that are unaware they are interacting with a replica. An area of future research is to see how well partition-aware applications can be programmed in E and how well they can compose with others.

Croquet and TeaTime. The Croquet project has many of the same goals as the Habitats project referred to above: to create a graphical, decentralized, secure, user-extensible, social virtual reality system spread across mutually suspicious machines. Regarding E, the salient differences are that Croquet is built on Smalltalk extended onto the network by TeaTime, which is based on Namos [Ree78] and Paxos [Lam98], in order to replicate state among multiple authoritative hosts. Unlike Habitats, Croquet is user-extensible, but is not yet secure. It will be interesting to see how they alter Paxos to work between mutually suspicious machines.

12.1 Work Influenced by E's Concurrency Control

The Web-Calculus. The Web-Calculus [Clo04b] brings to web URLs the following simultaneous properties:

- The cryptographic capability properties of E's offline capabilities—both authenticating the target and authorizing access to it.
- Promise pipelining of eventually-POSTed requests with results.
- The properties recommended by the REST model of web programming [Fie00]. REST attributes the success of the web largely to certain loose-coupling properties of "http://..." URLs, which are well beyond the scope of this paper. See [Fie00, Clo04b] for more.

As a language-neutral protocol compatible and composable with existing web standards, the Web-Calculus is well-positioned to achieve widespread adoption. We expect to build a bridge between E's references and Web-Calculus URLs.

Oz-E. Like Vulcan, the Oz language [VH04] descends from both Actors and concurrent logic/constraint programming. Unlike these parents, Oz supports shared-state concurrency, though Oz programming practice discourages its use. Oz-E [SV05a] is a capability-based successor to Oz designed to support both local and distributed defensive consistency. For the reasons explained in the "Defensive Correctness" section above, Oz-E suppresses Oz's shared-state concurrency.

Twisted Python. This is a library and a set of conventions for distributed programming in Python, based on E's model of communicating event-loops, promise pipelining, and cryptographic capability security [Lef].

13 Discussion and Conclusions

Electric Communities open-sourced E in 1998. Since then, a lively open source community has continued development of E at http://www.erights.org/. Seven companies and two universities have used E—to teach secure and distributed programming, to rapidly prototype distributed architectures, and to build several distributed systems.

Despite these successful trials, we do not yet consider E ready for production use—the current E implementation is a slow interpreter written in Java. Two compiler-based implementations are in progress: Kevin Reid is building an E on Common Lisp [Rei05], and Dean Tribble is building an E on Squeak (an open-source Smalltalk). Several of E's libraries, currently implemented in Java, are being rewritten in E to help port E onto other language platforms. Separately, Fred Spiessens continues to make progress on formalizing the reasoning about *authority* on which E's security is based [SV05b].

Throughout, our engineering premise is that lambda abstraction and object programming, by their impressive plan coordination successes in the small, have the seeds for coordinating plans in the large. As Alan Kay has urged [Kay98], our emphasis is less on the objects and more on the interstitial fabric which connects them: the dynamic reference graph carrying the messages by which their plans interact.

Encapsulation separates objects so their plans can avoid disrupting each other's assumptions. Objects compose plans by message passing while respecting each other's separation. However, when client objects request service from provider objects, their continued proper functioning is often vulnerable to their provider's misbehavior. When providers are also vulnerable to their clients, corruption is potentially contagious over the reachable graph in both directions, severely limiting the scale of systems we can compose.

Reduced vulnerability helps contain corruption. In this paper, we draw attention to a specific composable standard of robustness: when a provider is *defensively consistent*, none of its clients can corrupt it or cause it to give incorrect service to any of its well-behaved clients, thus protecting its clients from each other. When a system is composed of defensively consistent abstractions, to a good approximation, corruption is contagious only upstream. (Further vulnerability reduction beyond this standard is, of course, valuable and often needed.)

Under shared-state concurrency—conventional multi-threading—we have shown by example that defensive consistency is unreasonably difficult. We have explained how an alternate concurrency-control discipline, communicating event-loops, supports creating defensively consistent objects in the face of concurrency and distribution. Our enhanced reference graph consists of references in different states, where their message delivery abilities depends on their state. Only *eventual references* convey messages between event-loops, and deliver messages only in separately scheduled turns, providing temporal separation of plans. *Promises* pipeline messages towards their likely destinations, compensating for latency. *Broken references* safely abstract partition, and *offline capabilities* abstract the ability to reconnect.

We have used small examples in this paper to illustrate principles with which several projects have built large robust distributed systems.

Acknowledgements

For various helpful suggestions, we thank Darius Bacon, Dan Bornstein, John Corbett, Bill Frantz, Ian Grigg, Jim Hopwood, Piotr Kaminski, Alan Karp, Matej Kosik, Jon Leonard, Kevin Reid, Michael Sperber, Fred Spiessens, Terry Stanley, Marc Stiegler, Bill Tulloh, Bryce "Zooko" Wilcox-O'Hearn, Steve Witham, and the e-lang and cap-talk communities. We thank Terry Stanley for suggesting the listener pattern and purchase-order examples.

We are especially grateful to Ka-Ping Yee and David Hopwood for a wide variety of assistance. They reviewed numerous drafts, contributed extensive and deep technical feedback, clarifying rephrasings, crisp illustrations, and moral support.

References

[Ami95] Yair Amir. *Replication Using Group Communication Over a Partitioned Network*. PhD thesis, 1995.

[Bej96] Arturo Bejar. The Electric Communities distributed garbage collector, 1996.
`http://www.crockford.com/ec/dgc.html`.

[BH93] Per Brinch Hansen. Monitors and concurrent Pascal: a personal history. In *HOPL-II: The second ACM SIGPLAN conference on History of programming languages*, pages 1–35, New York, NY, USA, 1993. ACM Press.

[BJ87] Ken Birman and T. Joseph. Exploiting virtual synchrony in distributed systems. In *SOSP '87: Proceedings of the eleventh ACM Symposium on Operating systems principles*, pages 123–138, New York, NY, USA, 1987. ACM Press.

[BL94] Phillip Bogle and Barbara Liskov. Reducing cross domain call overhead using batched futures. In *OOPSLA '94: Proceedings of the ninth annual conference on Object-oriented programming systems, language, and applications*, pages 341–354, New York, NY, USA, 1994. ACM Press.

[Boe05] Hans-J. Boehm. Threads cannot be implemented as a library. *SIGPLAN Not.*, 40(6):261–268, 2005.

[CL85] K. Mani Chandy and Leslie Lamport. Distributed snapshots: determining global states of distributed systems. *ACM Trans. Comput. Syst.*, 3(1):63–75, 1985.

[CL02] Miguel Castro and Barbara Liskov. Practical byzantine fault tolerance and proactive recovery. *ACM Trans. Comput. Syst.*, 20(4):398–461, 2002.

[Clo04a] Tyler Close. Waterken YURL, 2004. `www.waterken.com/dev/YURL/httpsy/`.

[Clo04b] Tyler Close. web-calculus, 2004. `www.waterken.com/dev/Web/`.

[DH65] J. B. Dennis and E. C. Van Horn. Programming semantics for multiprogrammed computations. Technical Report MIT/LCS/TR-23, M.I.T. Laboratory for Computer Science, 1965.

[Don76] Jed Donnelley. A Distributed Capability Computing System, 1976.

[Eng97] Robert Englander. *Developing Java Beans.* O'Reilly & Associates, Inc., 981 Chestnut Street, Newton, MA 02164, USA, 1997.

[Fie00] Roy Thomas Fielding. *Architectural styles and the design of network-based software architectures.* PhD thesis, 2000. Chair-Richard N. Taylor.

[GHJV94] Erich Gamma, Richard Helm, Ralph Johnon, and John Vlissides. *Design Patterns, elements of reusable object-oriented software.* Addison Wesley, 1994.

[GK76] Adele Goldberg and Alan C. Kay. Smalltalk-72 instruction manual. March 1976. Xerox Palo Alto Research Center.

[GR83] Adele Goldberg and David Robson. *Smalltalk-80: The Language and Its Implementation.* Addison-Wesley, Reading, MA, 1983.

[Har85] Norman Hardy. KeyKOS architecture. *SIGOPS Oper. Syst. Rev.*, 19(4):8–25, 1985.

[HBS73] Carl Hewitt, Peter Bishop, and Richard Steiger. A universal modular ACTOR formalism for artificial intelligence. In Nils J. Nilsson, editor, *Proceedings of the 3rd International Joint Conference on Artificial Intelligence*, pages 235–245, Standford, CA, August 1973. William Kaufmann.

[Hew85] Carl Hewitt. The challenge of open systems: current logic programming methods may be insufficient for developing the intelligent systems of the future. *BYTE*, 10(4):223–242, 1985.

[Hoa65] C.A.R Hoare. Record handling, in Algol Bulletin 21.3.6, 1965.

[Hoa74] C. A. R. Hoare. Monitors: an operating system structuring concept. *Commun. ACM*, 17(10):549–557, 1974.

[Hoa78] C. A. R. Hoare. Communicating sequential processes. *Commun. ACM*, 21(8):666–677, 1978.

[IBM68] IBM Corporation. *IBM System/360 Principles of Operation.* IBM Corporation, San Jose, CA, USA, eighth edition, 1968.

[Kay93] Alan C. Kay. The early history of Smalltalk. *SIGPLAN not.*, 28(3):69–95, 1993.

[Kay98] Alan Kay. prototypes vs classes, 1998. `lists.squeakfoundation.org/pipermail/-squeak-dev/1998-October/017019.html`.

[KTMB87] Kenneth M. Kahn, Eric Dean Tribble, Mark S. Miller, and Daniel G. Bobrow. Vulcan: Logical concurrent objects. In *Research Directions in Object-Oriented Programming*, pages 75–112. 1987.

[Lam98] Leslie Lamport. The part-time parliament. *ACM Trans. Comput. Syst.*, 16(2):133–169, 1998.

[Lef] Glyph Lefkowitz. Generalization of deferred execution in Python. `python.org/pycon/papers/deferex/`.

[LS88] Barbara Liskov and Lubia Shrira. Promises: linguistic support for efficient asynchronous procedure calls in distributed systems. In *PLDI '88: Proceedings of the ACM SIGPLAN 1988 conference on Programming Language design and Implementation*, pages 260–267, New York, NY, USA, 1988. ACM Press.

[MD88] Mark Miller and K. Eric Drexler. Markets and computation: Agoric open systems. In Bernardo Huberman, editor, *The Ecology of Computation*, pages 133–176. North-Holland, 1988.

[Mil92] Mark S. Miller. Transcript of talk: The promise system, 1992. `sunless-sea.net/Transcripts/promise.html`.

[MMF00] Mark S. Miller, Chip Morningstar, and Bill Frantz. Capability-based financial instruments. In *Financial Cryptography*, pages 349–378, 2000.

[MS03] Mark S. Miller and Jonathan S. Shapiro. Paradigm Regained: Abstraction mechanisms for access control. In *ASIAN*, pages 224–242, 2003.

[MTS04] Mark S. Miller, Bill Tulloh, and Jonathan S. Shapiro. The Structure of Authority: Why security is not a separable concern. In *MOZ*, pages 2–20, 2004.

[MYS03] Mark S. Miller, Ka-Ping Yee, and Jonathan Shapiro. Capability Myths Demolished, 2003.

[OBDMS98] Özalp Babaoğlu, Renzo Davoli, Alberto Montresor, and Roberto Segala. System support for partition-aware network applications. *SIGOPS Oper. Syst. Rev.*, 32(1):41–56, 1998.

[Ree78] David Patrick Reed. Naming and synchronization in a decentralized computer system., January 01 1978.

[Rei05] Kevin Reid. E on Common Lisp, 2005. `homepage.mac.com/kpreid/elang/e-on-cl/`.

[Sar93] Vijay A. Saraswat. *Concurrent Constraint Programming.* MIT Press, Cambridge, MA, 1993.

[Sha83] Ehud Shapiro. A subset of Concurrent Prolog and its interpreter. Technical Report TR-003, Institute for New Generation Computer Technology (ICOT), January 1983.

[SKYM04] Marc Stiegler, Alan H. Karp, Ka-Ping Yee, and Mark S. Miller. Polaris: Virus safe computing for Windows XP. Technical Report HPL-2004-221, Hewlett Packard Laboratories, 2004.

[SM87] E. Shapiro and C. Mierowsky. Fair, biased, and self-balancing merge operators: Their specification and implementation in Concurrent Prolog. In Ehud Shapiro, editor, *Concurrent Prolog: Collected Papers (Volume I)*, pages 392–413. MIT Press, London, 1987.

[SM03] Jeremy Sussman and Keith Marzullo. The bancomat problem: an example of resource allocation in a partitionable asynchronous system. *Theor. Comput. Sci.*, 291(1):103–131, 2003.

[SS75] Jerome H. Saltzer and Michael D. Schroeder. The protection of information in computer system. *Proceedings of the IEEE*, 63(9):1278–1308, 1975.

[SS04] Paritosh Shroff and Scott F. Smith. Type inference for first-class messages with match-functions, 2004.

[SSF99] Jonathan S. Shapiro, Jonathan M. Smith, and David J. Farber. EROS: a fast capability system. In *SOSP '99: Proceedings of the seventeenth ACM symposium on Operating systems principles*, pages 170–185, New York, NY, USA, 1999. ACM Press.

[ST83] Ehud Y. Shapiro and Akikazu Takeuchi. Object oriented programming in concurrent prolog. *New Generation Comput.*, 1(1):25–48, 1983.

[Sti04] Marc Stiegler. The E language in a walnut, 2004. `www.skyhunter.com/marcs/ewalnut.html`.

[SV05a] Fred Spiessens and Peter Van Roy. The Oz-E project: Design guidelines for a secure multiparadigm programming language. In *Multiparadigm Programming in Mozart/Oz: Extended Proceedings of the Second International Conference MOZ 2004*, volume 3389 of *Lecture Notes in Computer Science*. Springer-Verlag, 2005.

[SV05b] Fred Spiessens and Peter Van Roy. A practical formal model for safety analysis in Capability-Based systems, 2005. To be published in Lecture Notes in Computer Science (Springer-Verlag). Presentation available at `www.info.ucl.ac.be/people/fsp/auredsysfinal.mov`.

[TM02] Bill Tulloh and Mark S. Miller. Institutions as abstraction boundaries. In Jack High, editor, *Social Learning: Essays in Honor of Don Lavoie*. 2002.

[TMHK95] E. Dean Tribble, Mark S. Miller, Norm Hardy, and David Krieger. Joule: Distributed application foundations. Technical Report ADd03.4P, Agorics Inc., Los Altos, December 1995. `www.agorics.com/Library/joule.html`.

[TMK+87] Eric Dean Tribble, Mark S. Miller, Kenneth M. Kahn, Daniel G. Bobrow, Curtis Abbott, and Ehud Y. Shapiro. Channels: A generalization of streams. In *ICLP*, pages 839–857, 1987.

[vH45] Friedrich von Hayek. The uses of knowledge in society. *American Economic Review*, 35:519–530, September 1945.

[VH04] Peter Van Roy and Seif Haridi. *Concepts, Techniques, and Models of Computer Programming*. MIT Press, March 2004.

[WO01] Bryce "Zooko" Wilcox-O'Hearn. Deadlock-free, 2001. `www.eros-os.org/pipermail/e-lang/2001-July/005410.html`.

Links to on-line versions of many of these references are available at `http://www.erights.org/talks/promises/paper/references.html`.

The Modelling and Analysis of OceanStore Elements Using the CSP Dependability Library

William Simmonds and Tim Hawkins

Trusted Information Management, QinetiQ, Malvern, UK
{W.Simmonds, T.Hawkins}@eris.QinetiQ.com

Abstract. This paper reports on work undertaken for the FORWARD project on the formal verification of distributed data replication mechanisms using CSP and the CSP model checker FDR.

The *Dependability Library* is an evolving CSP framework and tool suite for aiding in the design, modelling and verification of fault-tolerant distributed systems; *OceanStore* is an architecture for a global-scale, persistent, distributed storage mechanism. In this paper, we describe the application of the Dependability Library to two algorithms used by OceanStore; some correctness results are obtained for these algorithms for small static networks.

CSP structural induction is a technique for enabling correctness results of algorithms to be proved for arbitrary large networks. Assumptiom-Commitment is a form of specification in which the specified behaviour of a system is split into the behaviour assumed of the system's environment and the behaviour the system commits to as a result of that behaviour. We discuss ways in which the Dependability Library is affording support for these important techniques, and how they can be applied to extend the correctness results for the OceanStore algorithms to larger networks.

A software demonstrator of the OceanStore models using the new Dependability Library IDE will be made available on the Forward project website at `www.forward-project.org.uk`.

1 Introduction

1.1 Context

This document reports the second of the four groups of studies constituting Workpackage 5 of the FORWARD[2] project aimed at establishing basic mechanisms for assuring quality of service in ad-hoc networks, a core component of Next Wave, future ubiquitous computing, environments. The first two studies address black-and-white questions of "correctness"; the first of these focussed on routing, whilst this document focuses on distributed data replication.

Industry has traditionally employed simulation and testing in its verification of computer systems. Whilst these approaches are proven to identify errors/bugs, they are not exhaustive; unless you have simulated every situation, or tested every configuration, you simply cannot be sure that your system will always

R. De Nicola and D. Sangiorgi (Eds.): TGC 2005, LNCS 3705, pp. 230–247, 2005.

behave correctly. In contrast, formal verification techniques can offer exhaustive analysis (equivalent to 100% coverage testing of system states) which has often not only led to the discovery of errors previously undetected, but also, in the absence of errors, provides a guarantee of correctness. The formal verification of systems of realistic size and complexity in itself requires the help of computers. We have chosen to use CSP and the accompanying model checker FDR to enable formal verification of distributed data replication-based systems.

1.2 Replication and Quality of Service

Replication is a fundamental technique, well established in computer hardware, distributed databases and distributed file systems design etc. Network replication involves the storing of multiple copies of data objects in distributed locations throughout the network. Access to data are satisfied by copies stored nearby, thus saving the need to route requests all the way back to the original source. This results in four significant benefits: reduced access latency, reduced bandwidth consumption, server load balancing, and improved data availability/redundancy.

From a quality-of service perspective, there is an important distinction between caching and replication. Caches have relatively small storage capacity, and therefore have to evict old objects to make room for new ones; caches cannot therefore provide any guarantees of data persistence. Replication, on the other hand, represents a service commitment to keep a persistent copy of the object.

A distributed data replication system should thus provide a means of data storage that is guaranteed to a high degree of certainty to be resilient to loss or destruction of individual servers. Information stored on the system must be highly *durable.* Also, archiving of information should be automatic and reliable.

1.3 CSP/FDR and the Dependability Library

CSP is a process algebra which is useful for describing systems that interact by communication. A system is modelled as a *process* (itself possibly constructed from a collection of processes) that interacts with its environment by means of atomic *events.* Communication is synchronous; an event takes place precisely when both the process and the environment agree on its occurrence. The syntax of CSP provides a variety of operators for modelling processes, and the associated algebra provides rewrite laws. The shared-parallel operator, $\underset{X}{\parallel}$, is referred to in several places in this document[1].

The three main CSP semantic models - traces (T), failures (F) and failures-divergences (FD) - facilitate the capture of a wide range of process behaviours. The theory of refinement in CSP allows correctness conditions to be encoded as refinement checks between processes in the different semantic models. If process P refines process Q, written $Q \sqsubseteq_M P$, then all possible behaviours of P must also

[1] If P and Q are CSP processes and X a set of communicate-able events shared by those processes, then $P \underset{X}{\parallel} Q$ is P in parallel with Q constrained so that an event in X can only occur when both P and Q are willing to perform it.

be possible behaviours of Q (although Q may admit many other behaviours). Therefore, P is a correct, and more deterministic, implementation of Q. This notion of refinement holds for all three of the semantic models (T,F,FD), where the possible behaviours of processes are interpreted in terms of the semantic model, M, under consideration.

CSP_M [14] is a machine-readable dialect of CSP, it is the combination of a rich data language, based on functional programming, and the CSP algebra. FDR [1] is a commercially available CSP_M model checker, it can be used to check not only refinement but also determinism, deadlock-freedom and livelock-freedom of processes written in CSP_M.

The Dependability Library is a CSP_M framework for helping in the design, modelling and verification of fault-tolerant distributed systems. In the Dependability Library, a system is described through a diagrammatic representation of its network topology - the nodes of the system and communications links - together with descriptions of the behaviours of the individual leaf processes, which may be specified using a simple state-machine language. The resultant model of the system can then be automatically translated to a compile-able CSP model which may be machine-checked using against a specifaction of the system using FDR. The main style of specification adopted by the Dependability Library is assumption-commitment.

The Dependability Library allows one to specify the replication of components in a system, amongst other things . Replication is an important means of achieving greater dependability - the more nodes in the system, the more tolerant the system can be made to the failure of some of those nodes. An example of the use of replication is OceanStore, where data may be replicated over a number of nodes.

1.4 OceanStore

The use of the Dependability Library is illustrated through an analysis of elements of OceanStore [8]. OceanStore is an architecture for a global-scale, persistent, distributed storage mechanism, designed by a team at the University of California, Berkeley.

1.5 Related Work

Diagrammatic representation of CSP processes is not new - see Yong and Butler's formalisation of UML State Diagrams in CSP [12] .

Davies and Chricthon [5] have used CSP to provide a formal behavioural semantics for models and model components expressed in a subset of UML.

Circus is a Z/CSP based specification/modelling language developed by Woodcock et. al. [16].

There are many other examples of successful front-ends to CSP, including Lowe's Casper [10], a security protocol analysis tool.

CSP specification in the assumption-commitment style has been studied by Roscoe (unpublished) and Kay and Reed [7] amongst others.

The novelty of our work perhaps lies not so much in the individual components of the Dependability Library, rather it is in the bringing together of various important modelling and specification techniques in one coherent framework.

1.6 Structure of Document

In Section 2 we give an overview of the Dependability Library. In Section 3 we give an overview of OceanStore and describe our modelling of OceanStore's data location and routing algorithms within the Dependability Library framework, for a limited topology. In Section 4.2 we discuss the potential for CSP structural induction support within the Dependability Library and its application to OceanStore. In Section 5 we make our conclusions.

2 The Dependability Library

2.1 Introduction

The Dependability Library is a tool suite for aiding in the design, modelling and verification of dependable distributed systems.

In our experience it has tended to be the case that modelling efforts in this problem domain have delivered highly bespoke models, tailored to the specific processing and communications topologies of the systems under scrutiny. The bespoke nature of the models is a problem particularly when it comes to using them to compare the relative dependability of systems - objective comparisons are only possible when a common basis is used for characterising dependability.

Another concern of the authors is the time and effort typically involved in the modelling process. Even experienced modellers can take months to model modest systems, and it tends to be that a large part of the modelling effort is concerned with making an already faithful model amenable to analysis – the need to reduce state space is a constant concern in the model-checking community.

From the above considerations and others, a wish list of objectives was drawn up for our modelling framework, as follows.

1. It should be a generic framework for modelling distributed systems.
2. It should de-skill the modelling process to a significant degree, in part by allowing easy re-use of existing models.
3. It should provide a common basis for objectively comparing the dependability of systems through modelling.
4. It should address the scalability problem in a generic, re-usable way.
5. It should provide an environment that can incorporate (and promote) new modelling techniques and theory.

The Dependability Library currently comprises: (i) a library of generic scripts; (ii) a graphical design notation for specifying the topology of the system - i.e. the nodes and the communications mediums linking the nodes; (iii) a simple state-machine language used for describing the behaviour of leaf node processes;

(iv) translators from the graphical network design notation and state-machine language to the target modelling languages; (v) templates for various dependability mechanisms; (vi) models of commonly used processes; (vii) notional support for the specification of system properties based on the assumption-commitment paradigm.

The Dependability Library is underpinned by concepts and theory mainly formulated in the CSP process algebra.

A major Java-based Integrated Development Environment (IDE), *ModelWorks*, is being written for the Dependability Library.

Below, we describe selected elements of the Dependability Library used in the OceanStore modelling sufficient to report on that work and the use of structural induction to extend the results.

Systems, Nodes and Connectors. In the Dependability Library, systems are represented graphically by connected finite graphs. Each *node* of a graph is connected to at least one other node by an arrow. We refer to arrows as *connectors.*

We adopted a graphical terminology for the Dependability Library, to avoid implying overly-restricted applicability. In the Dependability Library, a node may be anything that can be viewed as providing a stand-alone *service* to the rest of its *environment* via a well-defined *interface*, e.g. a 'process', 'machine' or 'sub-system'. Likewise, a connector could be viewed as a physical layer 'communications medium' or as a network layer 'link', depending on the attributes associated with it.

Communications Model. The Dependability Library encourages a distinction between inter-node and intra-node communications. The natural choice of communications model for inter-node communication in distributed systems is *message-passing*, as opposed to the *shared variable.* All inter-node communications are achieved by passing messages along connectors. The Library provides generic models of these connectors, as parameterised CSP_M processes. The user chooses the parameters for these connector processes from a predefined set of availability and security attributes – e.g. *timed/untimed*, *ordered/unordered* and *authenticated/unauthenticated.*

Graphical Network Topology Notation and Process Description Languages. The Library allows designers to describe the system through a family of modelling notations. These were devised specifically for systems designers and programmers, rather than formal methods experts. They are intended for use by people unfamiliar with formal modelling languages. There are two types of notation, described below.

The first type of notation is a *graphical network topology notation* for describing the system's communications topology and fault contexts. Nodes of the system and the communications infrastructure linking the nodes are described through diagrams (actually connected graphs) drawn from a formal, pre-defined 'palette' of shapes. These diagrams can be annotated by text specifying, among other things, the attributes of the communications mediums, the names of the processes running on individual nodes and the types of failure (if any) to which each node is susceptible. The palette includes shapes representing *atomic nodes*, *user interfaces*, *N-replicated nodes*, *transient nodes* and *subsystems*[2]. It also includes 'lightning strike' boxes for specifying the fault context of nodes; this is done by simply drawing lightning strike boxes that cite the types of failure, and connecting them to the fail-prone nodes.

Figure 3 of Section 3 depicts a small OceanStore network drawn according to the Dependability Library's graphical notation.

The second type of notation are *process description languages*. These can be used to specify the *de-facto* 'normal' processing of leaf nodes with respect to the messages received from the rest of the system. Currently, the Dependability Library provides a state machine language DL-SML as the primary language for describing the way nodes process information, but CSP can also be used provided certain modelling conventions used by the library are adhered to. [3]

Translation to Target Modelling Languages and Compilation. In the Dependability Library, a system is described through a diagrammatic representation of its network topology in the prescribed graphical notation together with descriptions of its leaf node processes, possibly written in the process description language DL-SML.

The diagram of the network topology is annotated with various text such as node identifiers and descriptions of the nature of the communications link. For example, in figure 3 the three nodes are named $NodeQuery\_N1$, $NodeQuery\_N2$ and $NodeQuery\_N3$. Also in that figure, my_medium, is used to define the attributes of the communications links.

A translator is provided that will take as input the network diagram and outputs a representation of that diagram as a CSP module. A second translator takes as input the individual leaf node process descriptions and maps them to CSP processes. These outputs are in turn passed as parameters to a generic CSP script that returns a compile-able CSP process of the system as a whole. So, in particular, the user is freed from modelling the communications infrastructure of a system in the target modelling language – invariably a major part of the modelling of any distributed system.

2.2 Assumption-Commitment

The problem of scalability is essentially the problem of producing models of systems with state-space small enough to be amenable to analysis by automatic checkers - such as FDR - it is an ever present concern in the model-checking community.

CSP model-checking is refinement-based, that is checks are of the form:

---

[2] Using the subsystem shape, designers may import diagrammatically previously defined systems as subsystems in a new system design. This encourages a modular approach to the design and verification of systems.

[3] Other languages will be supported in due course.

$$Spec \sqsubseteq System \tag{1}$$

where *Spec* is a property being verified of a system *System*. In our problem domain, *System* may be a large distributed system composed of smaller subsystems and indivisible nodes. Here, for a check such as (1) to be scalable, we need to be able to reason compositionally about *System* and *Spec*. To this end we are developing what appears to be a novel approach based on *assumption-commitment* style reasoning. Rely-Guarantee/Assumption-Commitment theory appears in many forms in the literature, the theory is attributed independantly to Jones [6] and Misra-Chandy [11]. Of particular interest to us are the CSP formulations of A.W. Roscoe (unpublished) and Kay and Reed [7]. Our approach, very briefly, goes as follows.

Each individual component (node), *Component*, in a system design is specified by its own assumption and commitment expressed as CSP processes. We can then express as a CSP refinement check that *Component* commits to the behaviour *Commitment* under the assumption that its environment behaves as *Assumption*:

$$Commitment \sqsubseteq Component \parallel Assumption \tag{2}$$

where $\parallel$ is the shared-parallel operator.[4] This check, plus a number of side-conditions, again expressed as CSP refinements, can be checked by FDR. Assuming each component's assumption-commitment holds, then our theory gives us an assumption-commitment on the system as a whole, this being a function of the individual assumption-commitments of the system's individual components. In a bit more detail, this compositional reasoning goes as follows.

Suppose systems Sys_1 and Sys_2 are being composed to form *Sys* as a parallel composition of Sys_1 and Sys_2 (often with the interface events hidden):

$$Sys = Sys_1 \parallel Sys_2 \tag{3}$$

Suppose also Sys_1 and Sys_2 satisfy the individual assumption-commitment properties:

$$Com_1 \sqsubseteq_M Sys_1 \parallel Ass_1 \tag{4}$$

$$Com_2 \sqsubseteq_M Sys_2 \parallel Ass_2 \tag{5}$$

Then the Dependability Library IDE will automatically produce a candidate *Com* and *Ass* for *Sys* as a function of $Com_1, Ass_1, Com_2, Ass_2$. It will also produces a number of side conditions in terms of refinement checks to ascertain: (i) whether *Com* and *Ass* are 'useful' in the sense that $Com \sqsubseteq_M Sys \parallel Ass$; (ii) whether the assumptions are 'enforceable' in a strict technical sense.[5]

[4] The more traditional formulation of refinement check, (1), is a special case of (2) in which no assumption is made of the environment.

[5] The side conditions, among other things, assert that the assumptions of each component are satisfied by the commitments of its environment. Non-interference is also tested for, the 'enforceability' notion being a strong form of non-interference.

The side condition refinement tests involve relatively small processes involving combinations of the Com_i and Sys_i. So, to infer that $Com \sqsubseteq_M Sys \parallel Ass$, we need only verify a number of automatically produced smaller refinement tests, none of which refer to Sys. So, it is fair to anticipate that the well-known scaling advantages of assumption-commitment reasoning can be realised by the Dependability Library to some extent at least.

The compositional assumption-commitment theory outlined above is intended to be published fully in a separate paper.

3 A Case Study: OceanStore

3.1 Overview of OceanStore

OceanStore [8] is an architecture for a global-scale, persistent, distributed storage mechanism, designed by a team at the Computer Science department at the University of California, Berkeley.

OceanStore was designed with two principal goals in mind. The first of these is that it can be constructed from an entirely untrusted infrastructure, and that it is therefore resilient to server crashes and information leakage to third parties. In order that such an infrastructure can be used without data being compromised, all data is protected through redundancy and cryptographic techniques. The second goal is that OceanStore supports *nomadic data*, i.e. data that is allowed to flow freely. In a system as large as OceanStore, locality of data is of extreme importance; therefore, a stated aim is that data may be cached *anywhere, anytime.*

The elements of OceanStore that we have modelled using the Dependability Library are related to data location and routing. The mechanism that performs these processes is fairly sophisticated, as a result of the fact that objects in the OceanStore are free to reside at *any* of the servers. The mechanism used is a two-tiered approach, with a fast probabilistic algorithm [13], backed up by a slower, reliable hierarchical method. The reason for this is that objects that are accessed frequently are likely to be located near to where they are being used. The probabilistic algorithm may route to objects rapidly if they reside nearby, but if this method fails, a large-scale hierarchical data structure locates objects wherever they are in the OceanStore.

The focus of our attention so far has been the probabilistic data location and routing algorithm; this is described in the next Section.

3.2 Probabilistic Data Location and Routing

In order to perform the probabilistic data location and routing algorithm, each server must maintain a set of neighbours. A server associates with each neighbour a probability of finding each object in the system through that neighbour. This association is maintained efficiently (and in constant space) using an *attenuated Bloom filter*, a data structure based on a *Bloom filter* [3]. To locate an object, the attenuated Bloom filters are inspected according to the query algorithm, as described later in this Section.

Bloom Filters. Bloom filters are an efficient, lossy way of describing sets. A Bloom filter is a vector of bits, of width w. It is associated with a number of independent hash functions, each of which maps to the range $[0,w\text{-}1]$. To represent a set of elements as a Bloom filter, each element is hashed, and the bits of the vector that correspond to the results are set.

To determine whether a set represented by a Bloom filter contains a particular element, that element is hashed and the corresponding bits in the filter are examined. If any of those bits in the filter are not set, the set definitely does not contain the element. However, if all of the bits are set, the set *may* contain the element; but there is a non-zero probability that it does not. This case is called a false positive. Figure 1 shows a sample Bloom filter.

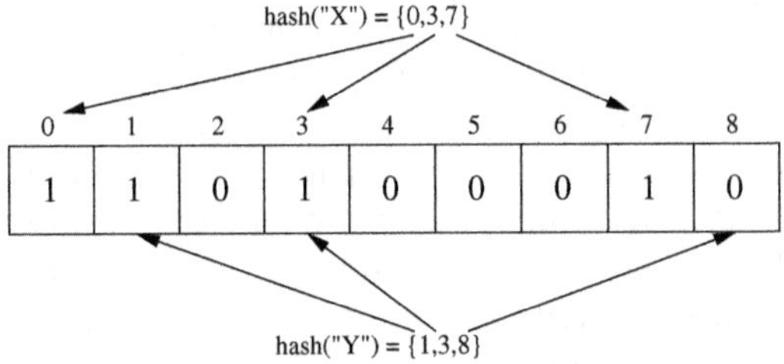

Fig. 1. A Bloom filter associated with three hash functions. The set represented by this Bloom filter probably contains "X", because bits 0, 3 and 7 are all true. However, it definitely does not contain "Y", because bit 8 is false.

Attenuated Bloom Filters. An attenuated Bloom filter of depth d is an array of d normal Bloom filters. In the probabilistic algorithm, each neighbour link is associated with an attenuated Bloom filter. The first filter in the array summarises objects stored at that neighbour, while the ith filter in the array is the merging of all Bloom filters for all nodes i hops along any path starting at that link. Figure 2 represents a network of four nodes, and shows the attenuated Bloom filter that Node A would associate with Node B in this network. For example, both "W" and "Z" are two hops away from Node A through Node B, so the second level of filter F contains true values at all bits in the union of those objects' hash values (0, 2, 3, 5, 7).

The Update Algorithm. For servers to have a chance of locating data stored in the local network, the attenuated Bloom filters stored at each node must be kept up-to-date. Each time a new piece of data is added to a server, it is possible that the Bloom filter representing the set of data items it stores will change as well. This change must be propagated to them in some manner; the method used is the *update algorithm.*

An update proceeds as follows. Every server in the system stores both an attenuated Bloom filter for each outgoing link, and a copy of its neighbour's

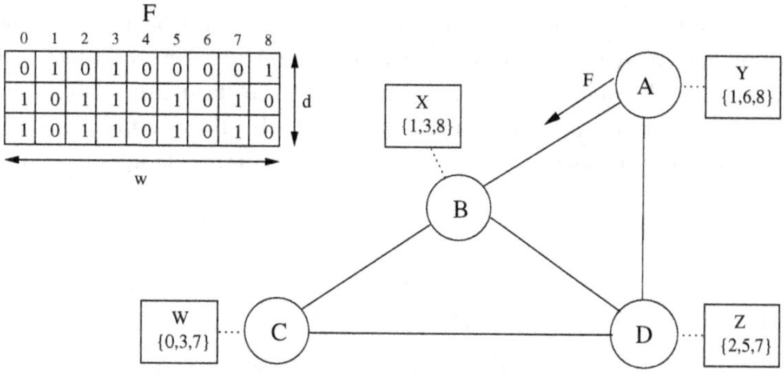

Fig. 2. A network of four nodes. F is the attenuated Bloom filter associated with the link A → B.

view of the reverse direction. When a new piece of data is stored, the server calculates the changed bits in its own filter and in each filter its neighbours maintain of it. It then sends these bits out to each neighbour. On receiving such a message, each neighbour attenuates the bits one level and calculates the changes they will make in each of its own neighbours' filters. These changes are then sent out as well. The update continues to be propagated until the last level of a receiving node's attenuated Bloom filters is reached.

The Query Algorithm. To perform a location query, the querying node examines the first level of the attenuated Bloom filter associated with each of its neighbour links. If any of the filters matches, it is likely that the desired data item is located at one of the corresponding neighbours, and the query is forwarded to the nearest one. If no match is found, the querying node examines the second level of each attenuated Bloom filter, and if there is a match, forwards the query to the nearest matching neighbour. In this case, it is not the immediate neighbour who is likely to possess the data, but one of its neighbours, and so the algorithm proceeds as before, with the current node examining its own stored attenuated Bloom filters.

A filter of depth d by definition stores information only about servers d hops from the current server. For this reason, there is no incentive to propagate a query for more than d hops. When such circumstances arise, the normal action is to give up and defer to the deterministic algorithm.

3.3 Modelling the System

In order to keep the state space of our model of the probabilistic algorithm to manageable levels, we split it into two submodels, the first being a model of the update algorithm, and the second a model of the query algorithm. We describe our modelling of the query algorithm only.

The graph for a fully connected network of three nodes performing the Query algorithm is shown in Figure 3. This graph shows the nodes connected by bidirectional links, with each node having a user input and output. One of the nodes also has an environmental input and output, which allows communication with other networks. The names of the input and output transitions of each node are also shown.

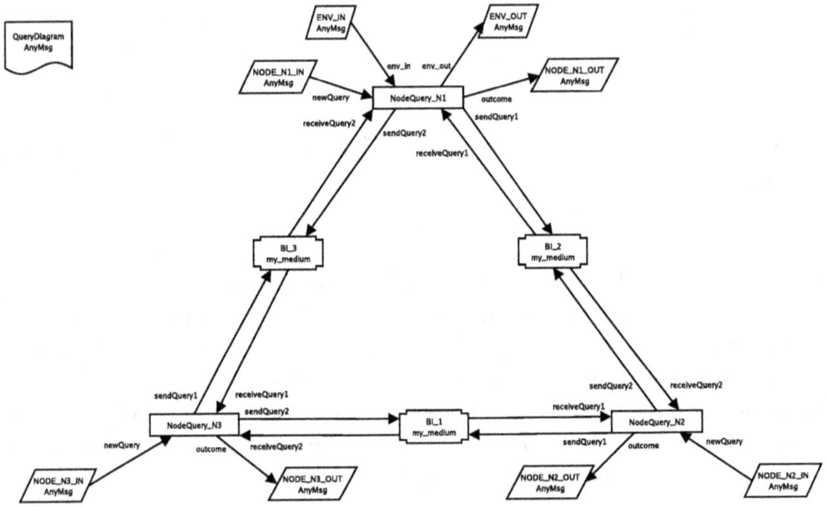

Fig. 3. Network graph for query algorithm

The graph of figure 3 was automatically translated to a representative CSP module. There remained to specify the behaviour of the leaf nodes performing the Query algorithm, this behaviour was specified in the state-machine language DL-SML and the state-machines translated automatically into CSP. We omit the full code for the state-machines here in favour of a brief outline, below.

In our model, each node has two hash functions, and an initial set of data; these will be defined after the state-machine specification has been translated into CSP, when instantiations are made of the resultant process. Each node also has a set of neighbour/attenuated Bloom filter pairs, which are initially 'populated' in accord with various distributions of the data on the network. The nodes maintain a number of other variables, mainly buffers storing, for example, the next Query to be forwarded.

The first event defined in our state-machine specification is `newQuery`, which is a user-input transition - this represents queries from the node's local user as to the wherabouts of some data item.

The second and third events are `sendQuery` and `receiveQuery`, one for each neighbouring node. These represent the sending to and receiving of Queries from neighbouring nodes. A node receives a query, examines it as explained in 3.2, and may forward it to a neighbour.

The third event is the `outcome` event. This is an output to the local user that is used to declare that a Query concerning some data item, x, was received by the node and that the data item resides on that node.

Following translation of the state-machine description into CSP, three instantiations of it are made, one corresponding to each node in the network; the hash functions and the names of data present at each node are specified at this point. A function is also defined that associates the state-machine transitions with the labels on the edges of the network graph.

The state-machine translations together with the CSP module representing the network graph were passed to a generic CSP function called *graph2csp*. This returned a compile-able CSP process of the whole 3-node network, *Query Diagram*. *QueryDiagram* was machine-checked using FDR for 'success of Queries' as described in the next section.

3.4 Specifying Success of Queries

Our 'successful Query' refinement tests were quite standard assumption-commitment style tests of the following form:

$$Com \sqsubseteq_{FD} (QueryDiagram \parallel Ass) \setminus HideSet \tag{6}$$

where *QueryDiagram* is the model of the complete system and *Com*, *Ass* and *HideSet* are as follows.

COM is a CSP process indicating that a successful query occurs (after which we generally do not care what happens).

HideSet is used to hide all events other than those indicating *all* possible results of a Query (successful or not).

Ass is a CSP process that was used to restrict the behaviour of the environment of any particular node being queried. The restriction had to ensure 'fairness' conditions to some degree in that: (a) the query had a chance of being processed, i.e. other queries did not always take precedence; (b) that the commmunications links behaved reliably during the course of the query, if, that is, they were not intrinsically defined as being reliable through the *my_medium* attribute.

In all cases the semantic model was failures-divergences in order to ensure that some outcome (successful or not) was eventually declared.

The strongest assumption we made was that only one query was allowed to take place. In that case, *Com*, *HideSet* and *Ass* were as follows.

Com stated that some node, *nodeId'*, would (correctly) declare that the particular data item x resided on that node:

$$Com = out!outcome!nodeId'!x.true \rightarrow STOP \tag{7}$$

Ass stated that node *nodeId* would receive the initial Query as to the whereabouts of the data item x, no other queries were permitted to take place:

$$Ass = in!newQuery!nodeId!x \rightarrow STOP \tag{8}$$

HideSet was used to hide all events except the initial *newQuery* referred to in 8 and the possible Query *outcome* events, successful or not.

3.5 Results for Networks of Fixed Size

The checks we performed on our model is that the query algorithm will always terminate, i.e. the events that indicate that the query has propagated to a node on which the queried data item resides will always be performed for given initial distributions of data. All the checks were refinement tests of the form 6. In each case, the test was under a relatively strong assumption, *Ass*, as outlined in 3.4.

The checks were performed on a number of different versions of the model, including all arrangements of three pieces of data over a three node network up to symmetry. The check passed for each version of the model on which it was performed, indicating that the query is guaranteed to terminate for this network topology under the given assumptions.

4 Appying CSP Structural Induction to OceanStore

4.1 Rationale

The OceanStore Query modelling reported on in 3 was restricted in a number of ways. First, it involved a static, relatively small three-node loop topology, whereas, in reality, OceanStore is likely to be used on much larger, possibly global-scale networks with dynamic topologies. Second, it was under strong assumptions. Third, there was high abstraction of Hash functions and the Bloom Filter depth was very shallow.

There are various ways to mitigate, to some extent, all of the above limitations, but arguably the most pressing is the size of the networks. Ideally, we would like to extend our results to much larger (arbitrary large) networks, and *structural induction* is one means to achieve this.

4.2 CSP Structural Induction

Many authors have demonstrated that structural induction is a method which can be successfully used in the analysis of distributed systems [9,15]. CSP structural induction is a compositional[6] technique for verifying certain properties of arbitrary large systems by verifying only a finite number of *base* and *step* cases. There follows a digest of the description of CSP structural induction be found in [4].

For structural induction to be applicable, we must be able to reason that any single usage of the service is a *network invariant* - meaning that the specification of the property is the same for all (sufficiently large) networks.

---

6 "'Composition' in the strict CSP sense of composing implementation and specification processes from a number of simpler sub-processes" [4].

Suppose we want to show that a property *Spec* (the network invariant) holds of some network no matter how large the network. Let Sys_i, $i \in I$ be a finite set of network models and suppose that the following hold for some CSP operator $\circ$ and all $i \in I$:

$$Spec \sqsubseteq Sys_i \tag{9}$$

$$Spec \sqsubseteq Spec \circ Sys_i \tag{10}$$

then it would follow that:

$$Spec \sqsubseteq Sys_{i_1} \circ Sys_{i_2} \circ \ldots \circ Sys_{i_n} \tag{11}$$

for any i_j from I. I.e., *Spec* holds for any system composed from an arbitrary number of the systems Sys_i using the operator $\circ$. Usually $\circ$ is piping ($[left \leftrightarrow right]$), shared parallel ($\|$), or, less commonly, interleaving ($|||$). The equations (9) are called the *base cases*, and the equations (10) are called the *step cases.*

4.3 The Challenges of CSP Structural Induction Proofs

CSP structural induction proofs require a high degree of expertise to formulate correctly. In 4.4-4.6, below, we discuss the potential for Dependability Library support for structural induction proofs. We consider, in turn, the three most challenging aspects of a structural induction proof, i.e.: (i) deriving Sys_i suitable for base and step case statements; (ii) the correct formulation of those statements from a given set of Sys_i and a *Spec*; (iii) the formulation of a suitable *Spec*.

Our support is intended to be generic, but we will refer often to the Ocean Store Update and Query algorithms - we want the support to be applicable to those algorithms at least.

4.4 Formulating Suitable Sys_i

The Sys_i of equations (9) and (10) of Section 4.2 are inextricably linked to the invariant property, represented by *Spec*, that we want to prove holds of our systems. The Sys_i are 'building blocks' from which one may construct more complex system topologies. In general, the onus is on the modeller to identify the 'building blocks' sufficient to construct her network, but we could reasonably provide a library of such 'building blocks', represented in our graphical notation, sufficient, for example, to build some of the more commonly studied networks - e.g. arbitrary large binary trees, loops or star networks, and, perhaps, more complex networks formed by 'gluing together' networks of those three types.

Let us consider, by way of example, the OceanStore Update algorithm running on a loop network. Let d be the depth of the Bloom filter. An important invariant property that we would like to prove is that, for sufficiently large loops, i.e. loops of more than $1+2d$ nodes, precisely $1+2d$ nodes declare a *doneUpdate* following an *Update* request[7]. This would be our *Spec* process.

Regarding the Sys_i. We note first that nodes have to distinguish between their two neighbours in order to process an Update correctly. For algorithms with this characteristic, we should expect Sys_i of at least three nodes in order to demonstrate that the invariant holds in the base cases, (9).

There are many ways of inductively constructing arbitrary large loops, the following is probably the best known construction. There is a single Sys_i, Sys_1, consisting of one node with an *input* and *output* channel. The Sys_1 are then glued together by piping the output of one node into the input channel of another to form a chain. The chain is closed at any point to form a closed loop.

However, in the above construction information flows around the loop is uni-directional - which is not the case for the Update algorithm. Below, we describe a new, more general loop construction, using a Sys_1 and a Sys_2 each of three nodes, giving bi-directional information flow around the loop. Informally, Sys_1 is used to form parallel chains of nodes of arbitrary length by adding a new 'link', while Sys_2 is used to 'glue' the two ends of the chains together to form a loop.

Figure 4 depicts a number of Sys_1s being composed using piping. The graphic has been much simplified by omitting all the connector-process shapes and all channel (arrow) labels. The rectangles represent individual nodes each running the same algorithm, P. P has the characteristic that it only need distinguish between the host node and between its host's neighbours, each node has been carefully allocated an identifier $\in \{1 \ldots 3\}$ sufficient for it to make these distinctions. The dotted lines indicate the interfaces between the Sys_1s.

Figure 5 depicts a Sys_1 composed with (i.e. piped to) a Sys_2, thereby 'closing' one end of the loop.

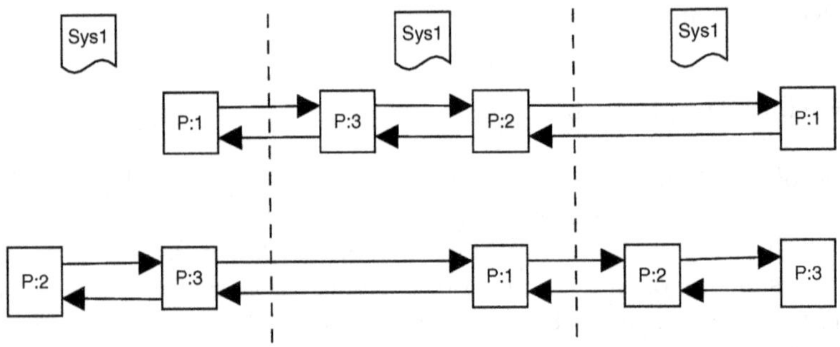

Fig. 4. Using a Sys_1 to add another link onto the right side of two parallel chains

[7] An Update request propagates to the d nodes either side of the node that received the request.

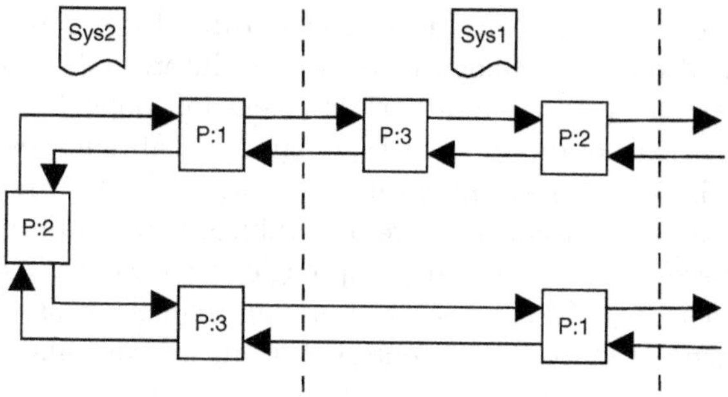

Fig. 5. Using Sys_2 to close the left ends of two parallel chains

As mentioned above, care must be taken allocating the node identifiers - even for this simple loop topology where nodes only have to distinguish between their neighbours. In general, the construction of suitable Sys_i, including the allocation of appropriate identifiers and channels, becomes increasingly difficult as the number of nodes that need to be distinguished increases. Thus it would be of considerable help to structural induction proofs if we could provide a library of Sys_is with identifiers already allocated and arrows correspondingly labelled. These graphically described Sys_is would not refer to the processes being run in the system beyond placeholder process name tags ('P' in the case of Sys_1 and Sys_2). Neither would they refer to the semantics of the messages being communicated between nodes. Rather, they would be generic templates describing the basic building blocks sufficient to build particular arbitrary large networks which, by construction, would be amenable to structural induction proofs.

4.5 Formulating Base and Step Cases

For the loop-topologies constructed using Sys_1 and Sys_2 of Section 4.4, there is one base case and two step cases as follows. The base case is:

$$Spec \sqsubseteq Sys_2 \tag{12}$$

and the step cases are:

$$Spec \sqsubseteq Sys_2[left \leftrightarrow right]Spec \tag{13}$$

and

$$Spec \sqsubseteq Sys_1[left \leftrightarrow right]Spec \tag{14}$$

In the above, *left* is a channel coming from a Sys_i's environment to the Sys_i, while *right* is a channel from a Sys_i to its environment. With reference to figures 4 and 5 the *left* channel will be a single channel demultiplexed from the channels crossing into the Sys_i through a dotted line. The *right* channel is a single channel multiplexed to the channels going out from the Sys_i through a dotted line.

As we can see from the above, the exact nature of the base and step statements will depend on the topologies that we are interested in. The single base case and two step cases stated above are sufficient for loops, but other combinations could give rise to quite different topologies, possibly not even connected.

Suppose we have an invariant property, represented by *Spec*, plus a given set of Sys_i. It would be useful to have a graphical convention for representing the different classes of arbitrary large topologies that we wanted to form from the building block Sys_i. Then the corresponding refinement assertions could be automatically generated from that representation, the Sys_i and the *Spec*.

4.6 Formulating a Suitable *Spec*

The derivation of a *Spec* suitable for a structural induction proof can be a very tricky business. The *Spec* appears on both sides of the step cases, (13) and (14), it has to account for the behaviour of *every* node on an input from inside its parent Sys_i and from outside that part of the system. Accounting for so much behaviour usually results in a complex, quite chaotic *Spec* process. We are experimenting with an alternative approach in which the Sys_i are put in parallel with assumption-commitment style assumption processes, Ass_i, that constrain the inputs to the Sys_i (i.e. wherever the Sys_i appear in the base and step cases, they would be replaced by $Sys_i \parallel Ass_i$), thereby allowing for a far simpler *Spec* process. This is arguably a more natural approach, as the Sys_i in the context of both base and step cases represent parts of a system otherwise unconstrained by their natural environment (that being the rest of the system).

5 Conclusions

In this report we described the Dependability Library, an evolving framework that de-skills and makes more generic the modelling and analysis of dependable distributed systems. We illustrated the use of this framework in analysing OceanStore's probabilistic data location algorithm. Some simple correctness properties were formally verified using FDR for a particular network of finite size. It was shown that queries propagated according to the probabilistic query algorithm are, under certain specified conditions, guaranteed to be resolved successfully.

We discussed the difficulties inherent in generalising model-checked verifications to models of realistically (arbitrary) large systems, and the accompanying problem of scalability. We outlined plans for addressing those problems to some extent through the provision of structural induction support within the Dependability Library.

Acknowledgements

The authors would like to thank Sadie Creese for her help and encouragement in the preparation of this document, also Nick Moffat - who is the main author of the assumption-commitment approach described in this document.

References

1. Formal Systems (Europe) Limited, FDR User Manual and Tutorial. `http://www.fsel.com/`.
2. FORWARD - A Future Of Reliable Wireless Ad-hoc networks of Roaming Devices. `http://www.forward-project.org.uk/`.
3. B. H. Bloom. Space/time trade-offs in hash coding with allowable errors. Communications of the ACM, 13(7):422–426, 1970.
4. Sadie Creese. *Data independent induction: CSP Model Checking of Arbitrary Sized Networks*, 2001. D.Phil. Thesis, University of Oxford.
5. Jim Davies and Charles Crichton. *Concurrency and Refinement in the Unified Modelling Langauge*, 2002. Electronic Notes in Theoretical Computer Science 70 No. 3.
6. C.B. Jones. Tentative steps towards a development method for interfering programs. In *ACM Transactions on Programming Languages and Systems 5(4):596-619*. ACM, 1983.
7. Andrew Kay and Joy N. Reed. A rely and guarantee method for timed csp: A specification and design of a telephone exchange. In *IEEE Transactions in Software Engineering 19(6): 625-639*. IEEE, 1993.
8. John Kubiatowicz, David Bindel, Yan Chen, Patrick Eaton, Dennis Geels, Ramakrishna Gummadi, Sean Rhea, Hakim Weatherspoon, Westly Weimer, Christopher Wells, and Ben Zhao. Oceanstore: An architecture for global-scale persistent storage. In *Proceedings of ACM ASPLOS*. ACM, November 2000.
9. R.P. Kurshan and K. McMillan. A structural induction theorem for processes. In *Proceedings of the 8th Symposium on Principles of Distributed Computation*. Edmonton, 1989.
10. G. Lowe. Casper: A compiler for the analysis of security protocols. In *10th IEEE Computer Security Foundations Workshop*, 1997.
11. J. Misra and K. Mani Chandy. Proofs of networks of processes. In *IEEE Transactions in Software Engineering 7(4): 417-426*. IEEE, 1981.
12. Michael Butler Muan Yong Ng. Towards formalizing uml state diagrams in csp. In *sefm, vol. 00, no. , p. 138-147, First 2003*. IEEE, 2003.
13. Sean C. Rhea and John Kubiatowicz. Probabilistic location and routing. In *Proceedings of INFOCOM 2002*, 2002.
14. A. W. Roscoe. *The Theory and Practice of Concurrency*. Prentice Hall, 1997.
15. P. Wolper and V. Lovinfosse. Verifying properties of large sets of processes with network invariants (extended abstract). In *Proceedings of the International Workshop on Automatic Verification Methods for Finite State Machines*. LNCS 407, 1989.
16. J. C. P. Woodcock and A. L. C. Cavalcanti. The semantics of circus - a concurrent language for refinement. In *ZB 2002 - The 2nd International Z and B conference*, 2002.

A Practical Formal Model for Safety Analysis in Capability-Based Systems

Fred Spiessens and Peter Van Roy

Université catholique de Louvain,
Louvain-la-Neuve, Belgium
{fsp, pvr}@info.ucl.ac.be

Abstract. We present a formal system that models programmable abstractions for access control. Composite abstractions and patterns of arbitrary complexity are modeled as a configuration of communicating subjects. The subjects in the model can express behavior that corresponds to how information and authority are propagated in capability systems.

The formalism is designed to be useful for analyzing how information and authority are confined in arbitrary configurations, but it will also be useful in the reverse sense, to calculate the necessary restrictions in a subject's behavior when a global confinement policy is given.

We introduce a subclass of these systems we call "saturated", that can provide safe and tractable approximations for the safety properties in arbitrary configurations of collaborating entities.

1 Introduction

Since Harrisson, Ruzzo, and Ullman (HRU) showed in 1976 [HRU76] that safety properties are generally intractable, two approaches have been explored to calculate a safe approximation for safety properties. The first one is to keep on using Turing Complete models and to deal with the intractability by limiting the resources allocated to the safety checker. The checker will "give up" after exhausting the given resources, and report the possibility of a safety breach without proof. Such an approach can for instance be implemented in the SPIN model checker [Hol97]. This allows the user of the model checker to iteratively increase the precision (depth) of the calculation.

A second approach builds tractability into the model: instead of calculating a finite approximation of a possibly intractable safety property, it tries to calculate the exact value of the corresponding tractable safety property in an approximate model. Take-Grant systems [BS79] are an example of this approach, in which the safety properties are tractable [LS77, FB96]. This is the approach we take in this paper. Because checking tractable models can take arbitrary many resources too, we will take care that the approximation can be easily adapted: coarsening the model in some regions to make it simpler while refining it in other regions to gain precision.

Regardless of the approach taken, model checking involves the translation from a real world situation to a configuration in the formalism, and from the

R. De Nicola and D. Sangiorgi (Eds.): TGC 2005, LNCS 3705, pp. 248–278, 2005.

calculated safety properties to conclusions that can be applied to the actual problem. Both translations should be well understood by the user of the model checker and should be explicit and well documented.

To ensure that the formalism is practical and useful to software engineers, we aimed for these translations to be easily described in terms of programming and design properties. We want our formalism to be useful at all levels of abstraction, during all stages of the software building process. The precision of modeling can be iteratively adapted. The resulting formal system forms a suitable base for the implementation of a dedicated model checker.

We developed Authority Reduction Systems via a series of consecutive refinements starting from Take-Grant systems [BS79]. The structure of this paper coarsely reflects this history. We first give an introduction to capability based security in Section 2. As a running example, we describe in Section 3 a simple pattern of authority delegation and revocation, called the Caretaker [MS03]. We will use this pattern as a touch stone for the expressive power of our formalism.

From studying capabilities [DH65] in general, and especially from the clarifications about capability based security recently provided by Miller and Shapiro [MS03], we concluded that modeling *collaborative behavior* is crucial when modeling capabilities accurately. When propagating authority from one subject to another, the authority reducing behavior of the subjects involved should be taken into account.

We explain in Section 4 that this collaborative aspect is underdeveloped in classical Take-Grant configurations, where only two kinds of subject behavior are considered: active vs. passive. We then describe three consecutive steps to refine this formalism. We present every step in its own section: Sections 5 to 7. Every consecutive refinement will build upon the previous one: avoiding its drawbacks and adding expressive power where necessary while keeping the safety properties tractable.

As a first step, we model collaborative behavior in Section 5 by annotating every subject with a set of properties. Each property describes three orthogonal aspects of collaborative behavior:

- the possibility of *initiating* a collaboration (invoking behavior) vs. *responding* (being invoked)
- the possibility of exchanging *capabilities* vs. *data* (information)
- the possibility of providing something during the collaboration (the emitting subject or *emitter*) vs. accepting something (the collecting subject or *collector*).

These three orthogonal aspects result in eight distinctive properties (e.g. possibly *initiate* the *emitting* of *data*), the combination of which allowed us to model 256 different types of behavior, including both types that are available in Take-Grant systems. While the resulting formalism had gained considerable expressiveness, it soon became clear that to model many relevant problems and patterns further refinement would be required.

We tried several approaches to make behavior compositional (to build arbitrarily complex subject behavior from configurations of simple subjects), and we present the most important one in Section 6. This is step two in our effort to gain expressive power. The approach is well fit to model composite entities like components and modules. However, this step did not completely meet our "practicality" requirement at the finest grained level. The collaborative behavior of smaller entities like objects or procedures is often *not* structured as a configuration of collaborating sub-entities with simpler collaborative behavior. Our model had to allow us to express more refined behavior *directly*.

In Section 7 (step three) we show how to express a subject's behavior in terms of its relations to other subjects it has access to. We think this approach will provide a practical way to model security related problems in software engineering. Variables in the scope of procedures or objects often *do* correspond to relations with other program entities.

The behavior can now express how *future relations* will be decided too, concerning subjects that will be acquired through collaboration. This is relevant in practice since it can be deduced from static analysis how entities acquired via invocation will be treated: some will be stored into a variable with limited scope, some will be used as arguments in consecutive invocations, and some will be invoked. We are not trying to accurately model relations between subjects for its own sake however. We just want to model a more precise approximation of an entity's collaborative behavior by taking (part of) its relations into account.

We discuss similar use of predicates and logic programming in other research work on security (Section 8) and give an overview of what remains to be done in Section 9.

A streaming video presentation on the contents of this paper is available [SV05b].

2 Capability Security and Capability Secure Languages

The security concept we call a *capability* was introduced by Dennis and Van Horn [DH65] in 1965. The concept is very simple: make designation unforgeable and combine it with authority, then you have a capability. If you are able to reference an entity (or a resource), you are allowed to use it. On first sight this can seem a very weak and discretional policy, but a quick exploration of the consequences will correct this impression.

We have to define the concept of *authority* first. Authority is the influence a program entity can have on other program entities and on the "system" in general. Part of this influence can be through the redistribution of information (data), and part of it can be about redistributing authority itself amongst the program entities. Potential authority is the whole of effects a subject could possibly induce if it would use its capabilities to the largest possible extent. Actual authority is the part of Potential Authority that is actually used by the entity. Actual authority takes the known restrictions in an entity's collaborative behavior into account. We use the term *Authority Reduction* to indicate the difference between a entity's potential authority and its actual authority.

In capability systems, all authority is carried via capabilities and capabilities can be distributed in four ways:

By Initial Conditions: We start reasoning from a given configuration in which some entities have access to some other entities. Since access is via references and all references are unforgeable capabilities, all entities are only referred to by (via, as) capabilities.

By Parenthood: An entity can create another entity, and by the act of creation get access to the created entity.

By Endowment: The created entity is endowed with (part of) the parent's authority. The parent decides which part.

By Invocation: Alice can introduce Bob to Carol by invoking Carol with Bob as an argument, but only if Alice has access to Bob and to Carol. This mechanism is sometimes referred to as "granting". If on the other hand Carol has access to Alice and Alice to Bob, then Carol can invoke Alice, and Alice can return Bob as the result of the invocation. This is sometimes referred to as "taking".

Ambient authority is all authority that can be acquired in any other way. Capability systems completely avoid ambient authority. Invocation is the most important (and potentially dangerous) way of authority propagation. Keep in mind though, that both the invoker and the invoked entity have control. The principle is also called object-capabilities, because the encapsulation of authority resembles the encapsulation of data, and the control that can be exerted by the invoked entity resembles the invocation of a method. Instead of setting up an access control policy separated from the functionality of a program, the programmer controls capability propagation by carefully controlling what entities will invoke what other entities and what will be the input and output arguments. This is not always a simple task, but a well designed capability secure programming language can help [SV05a].

Let us see how capabilities score on the security checklist compiled by Salzer and Schroeder [HS73]:

Least Authority: This is the principle of least authority (POLA) at which capabilities excel. No ambient authority is provided and no authority is ever granted implicitly. Instead of granting coarse grained privileges or rights, capabilities are created to *fit almost exactly* the least authority an entity needs. Even if the right to use and pass a capability is eternal and absolute, one-shot authority, temporal authority, revocable or conditional authority can all be programmed into a capability.

Simplicity of Mechanism: No other mechanisms than referencing and invocation are necessary to propagate and control authority. The mechanism to enforce the capability rules (at the base of every programmed policy) is simple and universal, and limits the way how capabilities can be distributed, and how data can be overtly distributed. That makes the reference monitor so simple that it will usually be a part of the language runtime.

Complete Mediation: Because of the necessity for collaboration when exerting or propagating authority, the actual authority provided by the invocation can be very dynamic and can change with every invocation. Without the need for managing the validity or expiration of a capability, the invoked entity can completely control the actual authority it provides, based on the circumstances it can observe and on what it can learn from the arguments it is invoked with.

Least Common Mechanism: Another property at which capabilities excel: the authority provided by every capability is programmed and can react to what it can observe of its environment (local state, parameters, etc.). Of course, invocations of the same procedure or method share the static part of their behavior (by having the same code) but to have capabilities share their authority policies beyond this obvious lower bound would actually be hard to accomplish, and because of the scalability of the design, there is certainly no need to do so.

Tamper Resistance: This burden is on the language designers. They have to make sure that no holes exist through which ambient authority becomes available. If done well, capabilities can even prevent confused deputy attacks. A deputy is an entity to which its clients have to delegate authority to enable it to perform a service on their behalf. A confused deputy is a deputy that does not know the difference between its own authority and the authority delegated by the client, so that it can be lured into using its own authority on behalf of a faking client. As explained in [Har89, SV05a], capabilities can easily avoid that vulnerability.

Scalability: Since references are necessary anyway, combining them with authority does not in the least affect scalability, even as the authority is managed at the finest grained level.

But there are drawbacks too:

Ease of Use: Instead of carelessly giving out access to unknown entities, the programmer has to consider very carefully what the least authority is he should provide. Giving less will introduce bugs, giving more will introduce unnecessary vulnerabilities. This is certainly *not an easy task*. Therefore a real capability secure programming language should have no mechanisms that make this task even harder [SV05a]. But since capabilities are the only mechanism that can actually prevent confused deputy attacks [Har89], the task becomes feasible at last. It would seem that actually enforcing a security policy (not just being able to declare it) is never an easy task indeed.

Open Design: Attackers should be allowed to inspect the code base in which they will inject their malicious entity. They then have the same weapons as the programmer to search for security holes. That means that the programmer's weapons should be nearly perfect, but they definitely are not, as code analysis is a hard task, even in well designed capability languages. This topic reveals the *need for tool-supported formal safety analysis*. This is the main rationale for our contribution in this paper: to provide a simple but powerful and practical formal model for authority propagation that can be the basis for such a tool.

Orthogonality of Concerns: The security policy is completely entangled with the functionality, programmed together into the same methods and procedures. In “The Structure of Authority: Why Security is Not a Separable Concern” [MTS05] Miller, Tulloh, and Shapiro explain the deeper reasons for this intrinsic entanglement of concerns. It remains to be investigated whether this unavoidable burden can somehow be relieved.

3 A Running Example: The Caretaker Pattern

Throughout this paper we will refer to a pattern of capability propagation and revocation, called the Caretaker. The pattern is useful and used in practice when programming revocable authority in capability secure language [MSC+01]. Consider a configuration of five subjects, having access to each other as indicated by the arrows (first part of Figure 1). As usual in a capability system, access and right-of-invocation are combined.

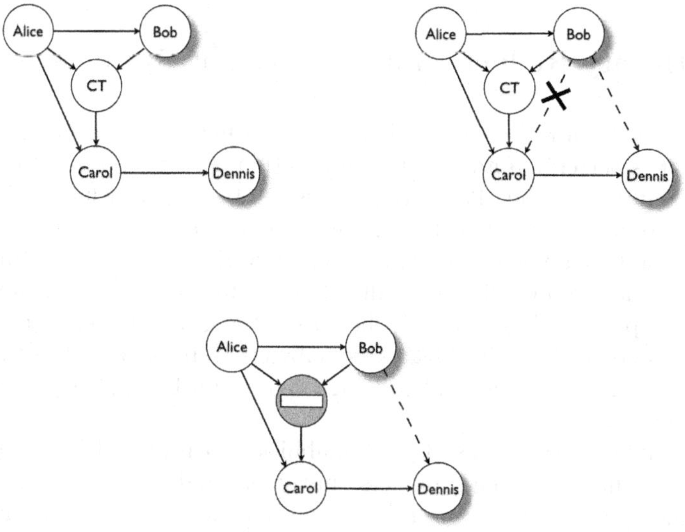

Fig. 1. The Caretaker in different stages

Alice wanted to give Bob revocable authority to use Carol, and therefore created a Caretaker entity (CT) that will proxy for Carol, and provided CT to Bob. Dennis depicts some authority Carol does not mind sharing with Bob. Bob and Dennis are subjects of which we do not model any knowledge about their behavior, and therefore have to assume that they might use all authority they have. We indicate “unknown” subjects with a shadow, and access that *could possibly* be gained via collaboration with a dashed arrow. The second part of Figure 1 shows what access is expected to be propagated by collaboration (dashed arrow), and what access should be impossible (dashed arrow with cross).

Alice can instruct CT to stop being a proxy for Carol, thereby becoming opaque to authority propagation (the stop sign in the last part of the figure), and depriving Bob of the authority to further use Carol. The reason for this revocation could be that Alice got hold of some secret she wants to share with Carol, but not with Bob.

The question now is: can we prevent that Bob gets direct accesss to Carol, – and thereby irrevocable authority to invoke Carol – and if so, who's cooperation is needed to prevent this, and what other authority propagation should these behavior restrictions prevent?

It will be a touchstone for the formal systems we describe in this paper, to see how well they can express the necessary behavior restrictions Alice, Carol, and CT have to respect. Since we aim for a *practical* formalism, an important criterion will be how well the modeled abstraction resembles actual code. This resemblance is crucial because we want to provide (semi-automated) support for safely and accurately modeling the authority propagation that is going on at runtime, using static analysis and abstract interpretation.

4 Authority Reduction in Take-Grant Systems

In this section we introduce a slightly modified form of the Take-Grant systems of [BS79] that is better adapted to our presentation but that retains the properties of the original formalism. This formalism is the basis from which we will evolve Authority Reduction Systems in Sections 5, 6, and 7.

Take-Grant systems are configurations of subjects propagating information and capabilities, represented in a directed graph of nodes with labeled arcs. Rights are represented by labels on the arcs in the graph. Capabilities are represented by these labeled arcs. The nodes (subjects) represent entities that can use capabilities (outgoing arcs) and to which rights can be applied(incoming arcs) via capabilities.

Some entities will not use their capabilities to propagate information and capabilities. These are called "objects" in the original paper [BS79], but we will refer to them as "passive subjects". We will indicate the subjects that need to be active by a bold circle.

Capabilities can have (any combination of) four rights:

`Take` enables a user (Alice) to "take" any capability from the subject (Bob) at the end of the Take-arc. Graphically it means that (a subset of) the arcs originating at Bob are duplicated and given an origin at Alice, and labeled with a subset of the original rights. (Figure 2 left)

`Grant` enables a user (Bob) to propagate any capability it has, towards the subject (Alice) at the end of the Grant-arc. (including the very Grant capability to Alice, used by Bob). Graphically it means that (a subset of) the arcs orig-

Fig. 2. Rights Propagation via `Take` (left) and `Grant` (right)

inating at Bob are duplicated and are given an origin at Alice, and labeled with a subset of the original rights. (Figure 2 right)

`Read` enables a user to read information from the subject at the end of the Read-arc. (Figure 3 left)

`Write` enables a user to write any information it has, to the subject at the end of the Write-arc. (Figure 3 right)

Fig. 3. Data propagation resulting in De-Facto authority

Whereas `Take` and `Grant` enable the propagation of capabilities (Figure 2), `Read` and `Write` enable the propagation of information (Figure 3). The arrows in bold indicate which capabilities are used to propagate authority or data. A dashed arrow indicates a new capability that became available through propagation by using the bold-arrow capabilities. Dotted arrows labeled `R` represent the closure of information propagation in the graph.

The dotted arcs are labeled with *de facto authority*, as opposed to the labels of normal arcs that indicate *de jure authority* (by right). De facto read authority (`R`) can always be replaced by de facto write authority (`W`) in the reverse direction (not shown in Figure 3).

Remark that passive subjects can enable the propagation of both data and authority by allowing active subjects to use them as a communication channel. Therefore, when two subgraphs should be authority-separated (kept from influencing each other), they can be connected only via paths that have at least two consecutive passive subjects.

Besides taking, granting, reading and writing, an active subject can also:

Create new subjects that initially have no capabilities, and to whom the parent can have all capabilities.

Drop its capabilities totally or partially. When the last capability towards a subject is dropped, the arc itself is removed. As all propagation in take-grant systems only depends on the presence of rights and capabilities – never on the absence of a right or a capability – dropping rights or capabilities cannot lead to more propagation. This means that when calculating safety properties (limits of propagation) there is no need to consider the possible dropping of rights or capabilities.

Algorithms to check safety properties are proposed in [LS77] and [FB96]. The tractability is due to the fact that a single generation of created subjects (one newly created subject for every subject in the initial graph) is enough to enable maximum propagation of capabilities and data.

4.1 Discussion

The Caretaker Touchstone: Let us investigate the expressive power of Take-Grant systems when we model the caretaker pattern of Section 3. It turns out that, to make sure that Bob cannot get a capability to Carol, we must *not* give him either a take- or a grant-capability to CT. A take-capability would immediately result in Bob taking all capabilities from CT. Since CT has to us his capabilities to Carol, it can only be an active subject. If Bob can grant CT access to Bob himself, CT will inevitably grant Carol to Bob. CT's active but restricted behavior as a proxy cannot accurately be expressed.

The Caretaker pattern, when modeled *directly and in a straightforward way* in the Take-Grant formalism, can only be used to provide revocable *read/write* authority to Bob. Can we find a solution by modeling CT as a subgraph of subjects, some of them being passive? This is possible, at the cost of losing any resemblance to a simple implementation of a proxy.

Authority Reduction: Only passive subjects can model authority reduction. They model programmed entities that do not (or cannot) exert *any* of their rights. A subject that actively uses its read rights but only passively assists in the propagation of its take and grant capabilities can only be modeled as an active subject, a safe but generally too coarse approximation.

On the other hand, passive subjects are often too transparent for authority and allow active subjects to use them as a capability channel. A file reference in a capability secure language only provides authority to store and retrieve *data*, not capabilities. Modeling it as a passive subject will be as if it could also store authority, again a very coarse approach. Passive subjects are well fit to model state that is shared between active subjects, but that is not generally useful in capability languages that support some form of concurrency: the practice of (secure) concurrent programming strongly deprecates the use of shared state concurrency [SV05a, VH04, Rei03].

Conceptually the most important drawback of Take-Grant systems to model object-capabilities is their inability to model the dynamics of collaboration. A "Take" right represents static and eternal authority to acquire all capabilities from a the subject the right points to. The behavior of an entity that always refrains from using a certain capability cannot be modeled by simply removing that capability, because then the model would ignore the fact that the unused capability could still be propagated and be used by another subject. In a capability secure program, entities have to collaborate to propagate data and authority. The invoking entity can offer or request authority but the invoked entity's behavior will decide when and what authority it will return. The only real "right" available in capability systems is the right to use the capabilities that you have. Taking, granting, reading and writing are the *possible effects* (authority) of exerting that right. The decision to actually exert a right is up to the invoking entity, but the effect of the right exertion is largely decided by the invoked entity.

We are not the first to notice this lack of modeling power, as can be inferred from a comment in one of the original papers on Take-Grant systems. In [BS79] Bishop and Snyder mention that Ruzzo suggested them *to use "two place" rules, i.e. two vertices connected by an edge, that describe the circumstances under which a "token" (corresponding to the information) can be moved along from one vertex to another.* The authors give the idea the benefit of doubt, as it could lead to an alternative way of modeling de facto transfer that has *an appealing technical simplicity*, but do not pursue the question any further.

5 Static Authority Reduction Systems

In this section we propose a way to statically model a safe approximation to an entity's readiness to collaborate with other entities. We find 3 orthogonal dimensions in the role an entity plays is collaboration:

1. invoking or being invoked
2. emitting or collecting
3. propagating capabilities or data

For a collaboration between two subjects to succeed, one subject should invoke the other, either one should emit and the other should collect, and both should be compatible in their modus of propagation (data or capabilities). We assume that all entities differentiate data from capabilities.

The possibility of invoking will be indicated with the prefix `i`, the possibility of responding with the prefix `r`. Emitting capabilities will be indicated with `G` (grant), emitting data with `W` (write). Collecting capabilities will be indicated with `T` (take), collecting data with `R` (read). This gives us eight independent properties of an entity's collaborative behavior to model, as presented in table 1

Instead of considering four rights to define the type of authority a capability carries, we will now have only one: *access*. This is the irrevocable and eternal right to invoke the entity designated by the capability. Access is also a necessary condition for emitting: one can only emit what one has access to. The potential authority carried by a capability depends on the collaborative behavior of the entity designated by it. The actual authority also depends on the collaborative behavior of the owner of the capability.

Table 1. Eight independent aspects of subject behavior

		capabilities	data
invoker	collecting	iT	iR
	emitting	iG	iW
responder	collecting	rT	rR
	emitting	rG	rW

Table 2. Take-Grant authority from collaboration

Invoker	Responder	Actual Authority	Comments
iT	rG	Take	Invoker might try to collect capabilities, responder might emit them when being invoked
iG	rT	Grant	Invoker might try to emit capabilities, responder might collect them when being invoked
iR	rW	Read	Invoker might try to collect data, responder might emit data when being invoked
iW	rR	Write	Invoker might try to emit data, responder might collect data when being invoked

The new model can also be seen as Take-Grant systems in which the static "rights" are replaced by static authority. Instead of propagating different kinds of rights, only *access* is propagated directly. Indirectly, authority can be propagated too, because the propagation of access will usually give rise to new authority. The authority is static in the sense that the behavior of each of the two collaborating subjects is a static approximation of the behavior of the respective entities they model. Table 2 shows in what case the authority that corresponds to the four former rights can be generated by collaboration, given that the invoker has access to the responder.

Just like subjects in Take-Grant systems can drop their rights and capabilities, a subject will be able to drop access to another subject in Static Authority Reduction Systems. However, just like in Take-Grant systems, this possibility will not be taken into account when calculating safety properties. A future extension, shortly discussed in Section 9, will allow us to explicitly model dropping access, for reasons of additional expressive power.

Subject Creation: Parenthood and Endowment: Like in Take-Grant systems, a subject can only be created by a parent. By *parenthood*, the parent will be the only subject that has access to its child right after the creation. Because the child's cooperation is needed for further propagation of access to it, we have to model *endowment* explicitly. A child could very well be unwilling to accept any authority its clients want to grant to it, but upon creation the parent can always "impose" part of its access to the child. In that way, endowment is not very different from imposing initial conditions on an access graph of communicating entities.

This "imposing" of information and authority is only possible by endowment, and can be an indication to the child that its authority came from its parent. However, this kind of discriminative knowledge will become useful only in Section 7, when subjects will be able to decide their behavior based on what they can observe from their environment.

5.1 Authority Reduction

The eight independent collaborative aspects of behavior allow us to model entities as one of 2^8 different types of subjects. Table 3 shows 15 of these 256 subject types, including both that were available in Take-Grant Systems.

Take-Grant systems have only two types of subjects but they have four independent rights and therefore $2 \times 2^4 = 32$ types of capabilities. We can therefore claim a gain in expressive power by a factor $256 \div 32 = 8$ compared to Take-Grant systems. More importantly, by modeling collaboration explicitly, we have a substantial gain in practical applicability to model capability oriented code.

A simple example that illustrates the need for this expressive power is presented in [MS03], where the authors explain that capabilities obviously *can* implement the $*$-property, contrary to the claim made by Boebert [Boe84] in 1984 and supported by Kain and Landwehr [KL87] in 1987. The authors have to resort to an example in E-language source code to make their claim. The data diodes from table 3 can easily be used to model this code in a Static Au-

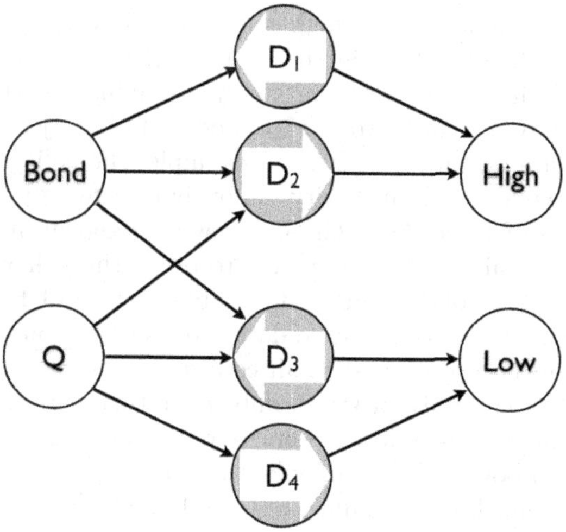

Subjects	Type	Approximated by aspects
Bond, Q, High, Low	unknown	{iT, iG, iR, iW, rT, rG, rR, rW}
D2, D4	data diode forward	{rR,iW}
D1, D2	data diode backward	{iR,rW}

Fig. 4. The $*$-property expressed with Static Authority Reduction

Table 3. Subject types as subsets of behavior aspects: some examples

Behavior aspects	Take-Grant subject type	Used to model
{iT,iG,iR,iW, rT,rG,rR,rW}	active	Unknown behavior, approximated by maximal collaboration
{rT,rG,rR,rW}	passive	Non-invoking behavior (shared store) approximated by maximal responder behavior
{iT,iG,iR,iW}	-	Non-invokable behavior, approximated by maximal invoker behavior
{iT,iG,rT,rG}	-	Data opacity (capability filter)
{iR,iW,rR,rW}	-	Capability opacity (data filter)
{rT,rR,iG,iW}	-	Broadcaster in forward direction
{iT,iR,rG,rW}	-	Broadcaster in backward direction
{iG,iW,rG,rW}	-	Source (emits only)
{iT,iR,rT,rR}	-	Drain (collects only)
{rR,iW}	-	Data diode in forward direction
{iR,rW}	-	Data diode in backward direction
{rR,rW}	-	Data store (file, shared data-only store)
{rW}	-	Data source (read only file)
{rR}	-	Data drain (write only file)
{}	-	No Behavior (unforgeable token, name)

thority Reduction configuration, and to prove their claim on an abstract level. (Figure 4)

The $*$-property stipulates that high confidential information should not leak to low clearance subjects. Bond in the example (Figure 4) is a high clearance subject and should have read/write authority to the high confidentiality subject High, but read-only authority to low confidentiality subject Low: *no writing down*. For low clearance subjects (Q in the example) the policy means *no reading up*. Q should have read/write authority to Low but write-only authority to High. Since the behavior of Bond, Q, High, and Low is unknown, it is safe to assume that they are potential conspirators trying to break the policy.

The fact that this policy holds in the configuration of Figure 4 can easily be derived from the restrictions on de data diodes D_1 through D_4. First of all, no capabilities can be propagated as all connections are to/from data filtering devices. Q has 3 capabilities, of which only D_3 returns information. Given the direction of this diode, this information can only come from Low. Only D_4 can give information to Low, and D_4 can only get its information from Q. This closes the circle: only Q and Low can influence Q and Low.

5.2 Precautions When Modeling Behavior

The proof is nice but there is another important reason why the formal approach is preferable. All assumptions are made explicit now, and we can deduce the requirements for the real code that implements D_1 through D_4. Most important:

D_2 and D_3 should be carefully implemented to avoid that they enable one of their clients (Bond) to signal to the other (Q). If Q can observe Bond's usage of D_2 or D_3, then Bond can modulate that usage to signal to Q. The formal approach reveals that special care should be taken when implementing D_2 and D_3, whereas D_1 or D_4 need no such special attention.

The fact that some extra analysis is needed here stems from the fact that the model only expresses knowledge about what a subject will *not* do. The aspects {`rR,iW`} of the forwarding data diodes mean they *could possibly* forward data, but *certainly do nothing else.* This negative knowledge is necessary to calculate safety properties. But when the actual behavior of a subject is observable, the uncertainty about the actual behavior in the model can hide an overt data communication channel.

Every subject that is invokable (modeled with at least one `r`-prefixed aspect) should also carry the {`rW rR`} aspects, unless extra precautions are taken not to be influenced by invocations (`rR`) and not to leak information during invocation (`rW`). Throwing exceptions is but one obvious example of observable behavior that should not be overlooked when modeling and entity's behavior as a set of collaborative behavior aspects.

Conversely, subjects with at least one `i`-prefixed aspect, modeling uncertainty about an entity's invoking behavior, should be augmented with {`iW iR`}, unless extra precautions are taken not to influence the responder (`iW`) and not to be influenced by what can be learned from (trying) actual invocations (`iR`).

The precaution is even more important in Take-Grant systems. Because they use explicit take-grant rights to model what *could* happen, every right *from* an active subject should be accompanied by `Read` and `Write` rights, and so should every right *to* a passive subject. This observation further diminishes the practical use of Take-Grant systems for actual safety analysis.

5.3 Saturation

Until now, we considered the propagation of authority and data via collaboration, but not yet via parenthood and endowment. When investigating propagation by parenthood and endowment, we realized that it has no influence on the safety properties, if some simple conditions are met.

Definition (Saturation): We call a configuration *saturated* when parenthood and endowment do *not* lead to extra propagation of authority or data amongst the subjects in the original access graph. Definition 6 in the appendix provides the formal definition of saturation.

Theorem: The maximal propagation of authority and access is not influenced by the effects of parenthood and endowment, if the following conditions are met:

1. The parent has access to itself before creating the child.
2. The child's behavior aspects are a subset of the parent's behavior aspects.

The proof of this theorem is by induction on the propagation steps, and is provided in an appendix (Theorem 1).

Take for example an *unknown* subject that has access to itself. By creating maximally endowed offspring subjects with maximal collaborative behavior (also of type *unknown*), it can introduce extra paths in the access graph, to propagate authority and data. These extra paths cannot add to the propagation of authority amongst the original subjects however, because for every propagation from one original subject to another one, that involves the offspring, there will be an equally valid propagation path that involves only the parent subject.

Corollary: This result allows us to model subject creation *implicitly*, by modeling entities that can create offspring as follows:
1. give the subject modeling the parent entity access to itself
2. add to the subject's behavior aspects the union of the behavior aspects of all its possible offspring (for all generations).

This is a very practical way of approximating the unbounded creation of new entities. In some pure object oriented languages every object can have access to itself by default anyway.

The above theorem has a nice consequence for unknown (untrusted) subjects. By giving all unknown subjects self-access, the effects of subject creation by unknown subjects on the propagation of authority and data is completely taken into account.

When the analysis of data and authority propagation is still too coarse grained, the last resort is to start from a more elaborate initial configuration, that includes some of the created subjects.

5.4 The Caretaker Touchstone

As shown in Section 5.1, Static Authority Reduction Systems can model a simple implementation of the $*$-property better than Take-Grant systems, but what about our comparison standard, the caretaker pattern? For ease of reasoning, Figure 5 shows the caretaker pattern in a simplified version.

Again, there is no way that Bob can get direct access to Dennis without also getting direct access to Carol. To understand what is wrong, let us first consider CT's behavior aspects that would allow him to *emit* Dennis to Bob, and see if one of them is safe:

`rG`: When emitting as a responder, CT would immediately emit Carol to Bob.
`iG`: When emitting as an invoker, CT should not get access to Bob, because then he would actively grant Carol to Bob.

This means that CT cannot *emit* Dennis to Bob without also emitting Carol to Bob. Since CT is not able to emit Dennis to Bob in a safe way, Carol has to do the emitting of Dennis to Bob. To enable that, CT should propagate Bob to Carol, and that is impossible without CT itself getting access to Bob. Therefore CT needs `rT` behavior, allowing Bob to grant himself to CT. Then Carol should

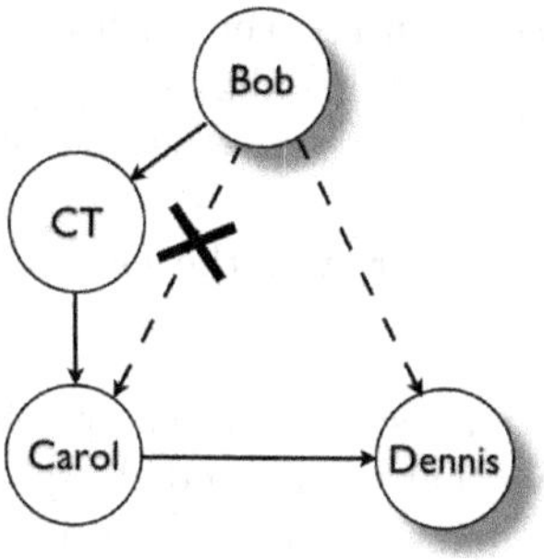

Fig. 5. The caretaker pattern: a simplified version of Figure 1

"take" Bob from CT, but that is impossible because CT would need `rG` behavior to enable this collaboration (see above).

Although we have gained some necessary expressiveness compared to Take-Grant systems (Section 5.1), it would seem we still need more. In Static Authority Reduction Systems as presented here, a subject can neither:

- differentiate its behavior towards different subjects it has access to, nor
- differentiate its behavior towards subjects it has collected actively (as invoker) vs. passively (as responder).

Section 7 will provide a solution for both problems, but we will first investigate the problem of differentiating behavior in Section 6, and see how far we can get with that.

6 Extensions for More Expressiveness

The research work for this section directly followed from our frustrating inability to model a suitable forwarding CT object in the caretaker pattern. We approach the problem pragmatically and introduce an extra set of behavior aspects, to express the fact that a subject is willing to propagate a capability without necessarily also emitting to or collecting from the subject designated by that capability.

We thus add the possibility to express that an entity only passes capabilities, without using them, either forward (collecting as a responder, and emitting as an invoker) or backward (collecting as an invoker, and emitting as a responder).

The rationale is simple and sound: it was the data diodes that allowed us to model the ∗-property in a practical way. We will also have *capability* diodes by modeling the *will-pass-but-not-use* behavior towards collected capabilities. This corresponds directly to the possible behavior of a pure proxy entity like CT in the caretaker pattern.

The extra behavior aspects are presented with a ∼ prefix, to indicate:

∼`G` : collecting capabilities as a responder, with the sole intent to emit them as an invoker. (Forward capability diode)

~T : collecting capabilities as an invoker, with the sole intent to emit them as a responder. (Backward capability diode)

~W : collecting data as a responder, with the sole intent to emit it as an invoker. (Forward data diode)

~R : collecting data as an invoker, with the sole intent to emit it as a responder. (Backward data diode)

Equipped with these extra aspects, we show some new and useful types of subjects in Table 4. Observe that the extended aspects are no longer completely orthogonal to the standard ones: ~G is automatically implied by subjects that already have the aspects {rT,iG}, ~T is automatically implied by subjects that already have the aspects {iT,rG}, and similar for ~R and ~W.

The converse is not true however: neither for capability diodes nor for data diodes. The difference is in what will happen to data (authority) that was not collected, but available from initial conditions or endowment. The standard data diodes from table 3 will emit this data, while the ones from table 4 will not (unless of course the same data is re-collected).

Table 4. Subject types with extended behavior aspects: some examples

Aspects	Implied	Used to model
{iT,iG,iR,iW, rT,rG,rR,rW}	{~T,~G,~R,~W}	Unknown behavior, approximated by maximal collaboration
{iT,iG,rT,rG, ~R,~W}	{~T,~G}	Secret data keeper, will not reveal any data provided by initial conditions or endowment
{iR,iW,rR,rW, ~T,~G}	{~R,~W}	Authority keeper, will not reveal any capability provided by initial conditions or endowment
{iR,iW,rR,rW}	{~R,~W}	Capability opacity (data filter)
{~R,~W}	-	Data relay (direction sensitive two-way data filter)
{rT,rR,iG,iW}	{~G,~W}	Forward broadcaster, will forward to all capabilities is collects
{~G,~W}	-	Forward diode, will forward only to capabilities acquired via initial conditions or endowment
{iT,iR,rG,rW}	{~T,~R}	Standard backward broadcaster, reveals its initial capabilities and data
{~T,~R}	-	Backward broadcaster, does not reveal its initial capabilities or data
{rR,iW}	{~W}	Standard data diode in forward direction
{~W}		Data diode in forward direction
{iR,rW}	{~R}	Standard data diode in backward direction
{~R}		Data diode in backward direction

Conclusions: Experiments with these extensions revealed two major results:

1. **Caretaker:** We can now model a working caretaker formalism without resorting to composed subjects. Figure 6 shows the caretaker configuration

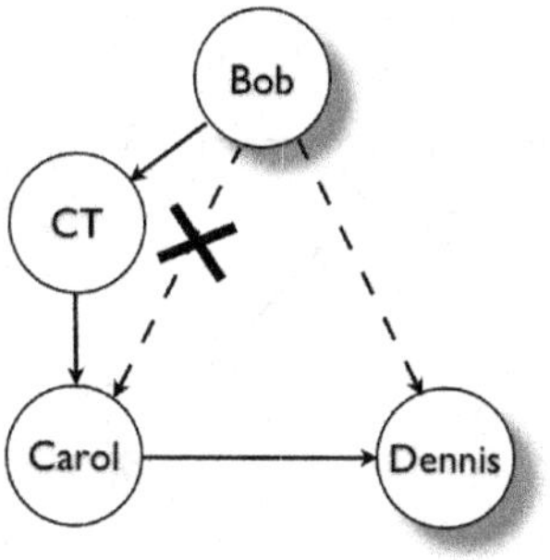

Subjects	Aspects	Comment
Bob and Dennis	{iT,iG,iR,iW,rT,rG,rR,rW	Unknown behavior
CT	{∼T,∼G,∼R,∼W}	Direction sensitive 2-way relay
Carol	{iT,rT,∼T,∼G,iR,rR,iW,rW}	Do not emit what is not collected.

Fig. 6. Behavior of the subjects in the caretaker

with the behavior restrictions of Carol and CT in the table at the bottom. Alice is out of the picture, but she can have all behavior aspects except iG, to make sure that she does not introduce Carol to Bob herself. All subjects are assumed to have self-access. Carol will possibly emit Dennis but never herself, because she only submits what she can collect. The possibility that Bob can get access Dennis is therefore not disabled, while the possibility that Bob can get access to Carol is.

2. **Differentiation via Composite Systems:** When complex subjects are composed from simple subjects, the composed subjects can now differentiate their behavior towards different subjects they have access to. This is illustrated in Figure 7.

The figure shows a composite subject Bob that differentiates its influence propagation policy towards the two distinct subjects it has access to: Carol and Dave. If Alice grants a capability, Bob will make sure that it is passed to Carol, but not to Dave. Alice is allowed to write information to Dave, but not to pass capabilities to him. Here is an overview of what kinds of things Bob can guarantee, on condition that Dave is not connected via any other paths to Alice, Bob, or Carol. The reader is encouraged to verify the statements.

- Dave will never have access to Alice, Bob (any part of Bob), or Carol
- Carol and Alice will never have direct access to Dave, but they might influence him.
- Carol can only have access to Bob if Alice cooperates. (e.g: Alice grants B_1 to Carol)

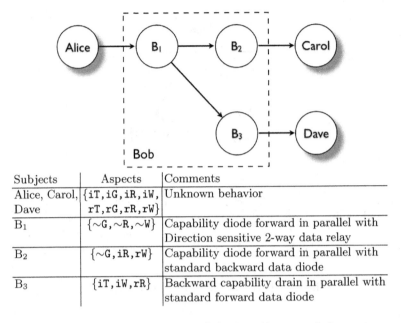

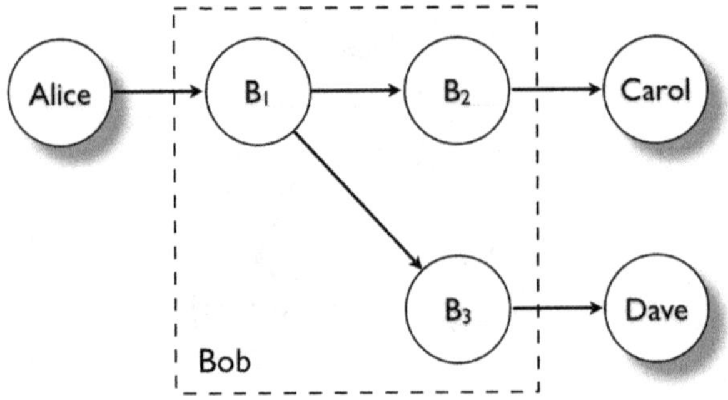

Subjects	Aspects	Comments
Alice, Carol, Dave	{iT,iG,iR,iW, rT,rG,rR,rW}	Unknown behavior
B_1	{∼G,∼R,∼W}	Capability diode forward in parallel with Direction sensitive 2-way data relay
B_2	{∼G,iR,rW}	Capability diode forward in parallel with standard backward data diode
B_3	{iT,iW,rR}	Backward capability drain in parallel with standard forward data diode

Fig. 7. Differentiating composite behavior using extended aspects

- Carol can only influence Dave if Alice cooperates. (e.g.: Alice grants herself to Carol and then passes all influence from Carol via Bob to Dave). Without Alice's cooperation, Bob will not leak information from Carol to Dave.
- Dave can influence (a part of) Bob (B_3) by allowing Bob to take access to whatever subject Dave might have access to, but this access will stay confined to Bob's B_3 part, and never influence Alice or Carol. Bob will treat all subjects he takes from Dave the same way as he treats Dave: accessed via B_3.

The possibility to let composite subjects model abstractions in programming constructs is explained in [MS03]. Composite Authority Reduction Systems are an important step towards the formalization of that idea.

7 Conditional Collaboration

When modeling the propagation of authority and influence, we are now able to express twelve aspects of a subject's behavior. Without resorting to composite subjects, we still cannot model a restriction in Alice's behavior towards Bob without at the same time restricting her possibilities to collaborate with Alice. For Alice, the fact that she cannot return herself when being revoked, means that she also cannot return Dennis or any other capability she might have accepted from the Caretaker. Because attempts to solve this problem in Section 6 complicated the modeling by introducing more aspects, some of which were no longer independent, we now focus on modeling conditional behavior.

Knowledge: A subject can (only) base its behavior on knowledge about its environment. This knowledge can be built into the subject's behavior (default, endowed knowledge), or it can become available through collaboration (deduction from experience). The availability of knowledge that can *cause* collaboration should never be underestimated and should be approximated from above. For safe approximation we need not directly model knowledge that can *prevent* collaboration, just as we do not need to consider subjects deliberately dropping access. Non-collaboration conditions should not be overestimated and are therefore only expressed by the absence of corresponding collaboration conditions.

Knowledge is positive and eternal in our model, but it can grow. A subject can react to changes in its environment by learning more, not by forgetting previous knowledge. Conditional collaboration will wait (possibly forever) until the subject can know the truth of the condition, before being activated.

Monotonic Evolution: We now have three monotonically changing conditions, depicted in Figure 8. New knowledge can increase a subject's readiness to collaborate and successful collaboration (propagation of information and access) can provide new access to data and capabilities, and can provide new knowledge about the subject's environment.

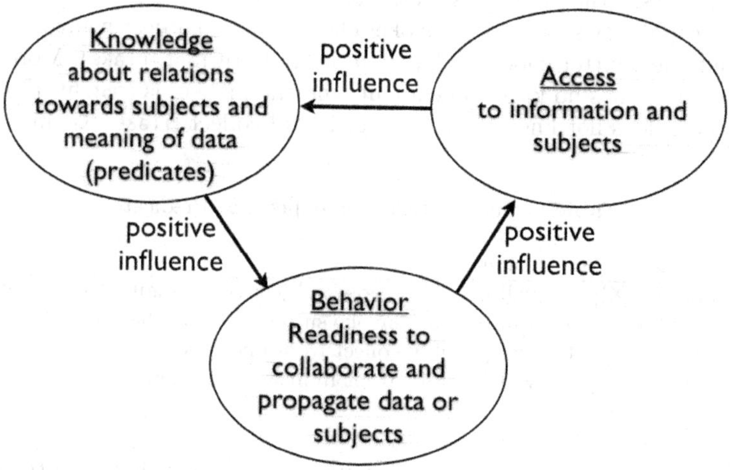

Fig. 8. A subject's monotonic view on the world

By forcing monotonic evolution of knowledge and access we inherit the rich semantics of Concurrent Constraint Programming (CPP) [Sar93] and the expressiveness that comes with it. A conditional collaboration is an *ask* operation, waiting in its own thread until the condition is either entailed or disentailed by the constraint store. We also use CCP to implement a model checker that simply mimics the monotonic evolution of knowledge by *telling* initial conditions and subject behavior to the store, and waiting until the store has reached a global fix-point.

Because we want this to be feasible in a finite amount of time, to keep the system tractable, we allow only a finite number of initial conditions, a finite quantity of discrete knowledge, and a finite upper limit to propagation of access and data in any configuration. This is not a real restriction, in fact it brings an important advantage when controlling the precision of the model: not only can infinite precision be arbitrarily approximated with unbounded finite precision, but this refinement can be applied selectively to specific areas in the model.

Returning to the caretaker pattern, we can now express that Alice could give Bob access to the Caretaker but not to anything else. Alice's "emitting-invoking" behavior will read: I will invoke X and emit Y to it if X is Bob and Y is the caretaker. This rule states a *sufficient* condition for Alice to grant Y to X. The "but to nothing else" part is modeled by the *absence* of any rule that states that another condition can enable Alice to emit something to Bob.

A subject's knowledge about its environment will be expressed as a set of n-ary predicates representing relations between the subject and a tuple of subjects and/or data. Subject behavior is a set of universally quantified implications (Horn clauses), the condition of which (the body of the Horn clause) is a conjunction of predicates representing knowledge.

Behavioral aspects are expressed as predicates too and are listed in Table 5. The arguments of the predicates show what can be decided by collaborating subjects in a capability system: the invoker chooses what subject it invokes (iGrant, iTake) but the emitter chooses what item it emits (iGrant, rTake). Moreover the invoked subject has no knowledge about who the invoker is (rGrant, rTake), and the collector does not know what subject it will collect (iTake, rGrant).

Table 5. Subject Behavior Aspects as Predicates

predicate	arity	comments
iGrant(S, X)	2	will possibly invoke subject S and emit item X to it
iTake(S)	1	will possibly invoke subject S and collect from it
rGrant()	0	will possibly collect from invokers
rTake(X)	1	will possibly grant item X to invokers

The effects of successful collaboration will become available to the collaborating subjects as read-only predicates, listed in Table 6. Notice that the propagated item (the parameter of the invocation) becomes known to the collector (iTook, rGranted), but the invoker (S) remains unknown to the invoked subject.

Besides the predefined predicates listed in Tables 5 and 6, subjects can use other predicates to express their knowledge. As an example, Table 7 shows the Caretaker's behavior as a set of Horn clauses. When the condition is always true

Table 6. Effects of Collaboration as Predicates

predicate	arity	comments
iGranted(S, X)	2	succeeded in invoking subject S and emitting item X to it
iTook(S, X)	2	succeeded in invoking subject S and collecting item X from it
rGranted(X)	1	succeeded in being invoked and collecting item X from the invoker
rTaken(X)	1	succeeded in being invoked and emitting item X to the invoker

Table 7. The Caretaker's Proxy Behavior as a set of Horn Clauses

iGrant(S, X)	:- proxyFor(S) ∧ relayForward(X)
iTake(S)	:- proxyFor(S)
rGrant()	
rTake(X)	:- relayBackward(X)
relayForward(X)	:- **rGranted**(X)
relayBackward(X)	:- **iTook**(_, X)
proxyFor(carol)	

it is not shown and the Horn clause is shortened to a fact. Predefined predicates are put in bold, variables are in uppercase and constants are in lowercase.

The Caretaker is a proxy and will invoke only the subject(s) it is a proxy for (iGrant, iTake). Items granted to the Caretaker by its invokers will be accepted and forwarded to the proxy (rGrant, iGrant, relayForward). To invokers that collect items from it, the Caretaker will emit the items it can collect from (invoking) its proxy (iTake, rTake, relayBackward). Upon initialization, the Caretaker will be told that it is a proxy for Carol. In the definition of relayBackward, the subject is not relevant and replaced by "_" . Note that in this simple case, the use of relayForward(X) and relayBackward(X) could have easily been replaced by their definitions.

Implicit Subject Creation: When the behavior of a configuration of subjects does not depend on knowledge about the identity of a subject, the capability rules provide an easy way to take the creation of arbitrary many subjects into account. We are confident that the approach taken in Section 5.3 (safe approximation in saturated systems), can be applied to the dynamic Authority Reductions systems explained in this section. A formal proof of this assumption is future work.

8 Related Work

Another invited talk presented at the TGC'05 workshop by Joshua Guttman, [Jos] showed us how in their work the authors model a dialog between two parties that accumulate monotonically growing knowledge, and we realized that in their setting, the accumulated knowledge can result in less cooperation as well as in more cooperation. A "simplistic" way to model protocols would have involved temporal logic to constrain the order between the events. The fact that they were able to avoid this, gave us hope that there could be a way for us to model a conditional *decrease* in collaborative behavior without resorting to non-monotonic modeling techniques such as (default) timed concurrent constraint programming [SJG95] or temporal concurrent constraint programming[NPV02].

Shortly after we found a solution for this problem. We will simply model two CT subjects: one exhibiting the CT behavior before the revocation and one that will be created as soon as the revocation conditions apply, to exhibit the post-revocation behavior of CT. To model the uncertainty about the actual time of the revocation, the creation of the second one will not disable the first one. In the future we will simply require that all authority and information between Carol and Bob flows only through the pre-revocation-CT subject. That way we will be able to analyze successive "states" of a subject without loosing monotonicity and tractability in our model.

Another approach to security analysis that is also based on an expressive model for the specifications of security-critical systems can be found in Jan Jürjen's work on Secure Systems Development with UML [JÖ5]. His work extends UML by using the built-in extension features (stereotypes, tagged values, and constraints), for expressing security-related properties. This approach is similar to Authority Reduction Systems in the sense that it also models software (specifications) and then reasons on safety properties in the model. Reasoning in secure UML is done in first order logic.

9 Ongoing and Future Work

The formalized presentation of the Authority Reduction Systems presented in Sections 5 and 6 are presented in the Appendix. We are currently working on the formalization of the concepts introduced in Section 7. In the appendix we provide a proof for the saturation theorem of Section 5. Most of the reasoning in this proof can be applied to the Authority Reduction Systems of Sections 6 and 7 as well. We will give a similar formal proof for these system in a dedicated technical report.

The safety properties is currently express constraints on the the eventual *effects* of authority propagation. It is better to reason about the *flow* of authority. Recent work on graph reachability constraints [QVD05] enables us to impose safety properties expressed as constraints in graphs that are derived from the access graph. The arcs in these derived graphs will indicate the flow of a specific kind of authority or information. We will then be able to express a more precise safety property for the caretaker pattern: "Carol's authority should be *reachable* for Bob only via the caretaker".

To further enhance the expressive power of Authority Reduction Systems, we plan to add the possibility to explicitly and conditionally create new subjects. Because we want the safety properties to remain tractable, we will use the technique of approximation by saturation (Section 5.3) after a given number of creations.

We have build a model checker for the models discussed in SectionstaticArs, and we are currently extending this tool to include the formalism of Section dynamic. The latter tool is not only be useful to check the safety properties in a given configuration of collaborating subjects, but also to calculate the maximal permissive behavior of any subject in the configuration, given a set of global safety properties that have to be guaranteed. Using this tool, we will investigate patterns of capability based collaboration (capability patterns) to discover the limitations of their use. We anticipate that later versions of this tool will also allow us to discover new and useful capability patterns.

Acknowledgments

This work was partially funded by the EVERGROW project in the sixth Framework Programme of the European Union under contract number 001935, and partly by the MILOS project of the Walloon Region of Belgium under convention 114856. We thank Yves Jaradin for reviewing the formal definitions and proofs in the appendix, Raphaël Collet and Yves Jaradin for discussing the formal aspects of the model, and Boriss Mejias for reviewing our drafts. We thank Mark Miller for his assistance on issues of capability-based security and on the flaws in the existing capability formalisms. Only the authors are responsible for any remaining errors.

References

[Boe84] W. E. Boebert. On the inability of an unmodified capability machine to enforce the *-property. In *Proceedings of 7th DoD/NBS Computer Security Conference*, pages 45–54, September 1984. http://zesty.ca/capmyths/boebert.html.

[BS79] Matt Bishop and Lawrence Snyder. The transfer of information and authority in a protection system. In *Proceedings of the seventh ACM symposium on Operating systems principles*, pages 45–54. ACM Press, 1979.

[DH65] J. B. Dennis and E. C. Van Horn. Programming semantics for multiprogrammed computations. Technical Report MIT/LCS/TR-23, M.I.T. Laboratory for Computer Science, 1965.

[FB96] Jeremy Frank and Matt Bishop. Extending the take-grant protection system, December 1996. Available at: `http://citeseer.ist.psu.edu/frank96extending.html`.

[Har89] Norm Hardy. The confused deputy. *ACM SIGOPS Oper. Syst. Rev*, 22(4):36–38, 1989. `http://www.cap-lore.com/CapTheory/ConfusedDeputy.html`.

[Hol97] Gerard J. Holzmann. The model checker spin. *IEEE Trans. Softw. Eng.*, 23(5):279–295, 1997.

[HRU76] Michael A. Harrison, Walter L. Ruzzo, and Jeffrey D. Ullman. Protection in operating systems. *Commun. ACM*, 19(8):461–471, 1976.

[HS73] Jerome H.Salzer and Michael D. Schroeder. The protection of information in computer systems. In *Fourth ACM Symposium on Operating System Principles*, March 1973.

[Jö05] Jan Jürjens. *Secure Systems Development with UML*. Springer, Berlin, June 2005.

[Jos] Joshua D. Guttman and Jonathan C. Herzog and John D. Ramsdell and Brian T. Sniffen. Programming cryptographic protocols. Technical report, The MITRE Corporation. Availalbe at `http://www.ccs.neu.edu/home/guttman/`.

[KL87] Richard Y. Kain and Carl E. Landwehr. On access checking in capability-based systems. *IEEE Trans. Softw. Eng.*, 13(2):202–207, 1987.

[LS77] R. J. Lipton and L. Snyder. A linear time algorithm for deciding subject security. *J. ACM*, 24(3):455–464, 1977.

[MS03] Mark S. Miller and Jonathan Shapiro. Paradigm regained: Abstraction mechanisms for access control. In *8th Asian Computing Science Conference (ASIAN03)*, pages 224–242, December 2003.

[MSC+01] Mark Miller, Marc Stiegler, Tyler Close, Bill Frantz, Ka-Ping Yee, Chip Morningstar, Jonathan Shapiro, Norm Hardy, E. Dean Tribble, Doug Barnes, Dan Bornstien, Bryce Wilcox-O'Hearn, Terry Stanley, Kevin Reid, and Darius Bacon. E: Open source distributed capabilities, 2001. Available at `http://www.erights.org`.

[MTS05] Mark S. Miller, Bill Tulloh, and Jonathan S. Shapiro. The structure of authority: Why security is not a separable concern. In *Multiparadigm Programming in Mozart/Oz: Proceedings of MOZ 2004*, volume 3389 of *Lecture Notes in Computer Science*. Springer-Verlag, 2005.

[NPV02] Mogens Nielsen, Catuscia Palamidessi, and Frank D. Valencia. Temporal concurrent constraint programming: denotation, logic and applications. *Nordic J. of Computing*, 9(2):145–188, 2002.

[QVD05] Luis Quesada, Peter Van Roy, and Yves Deville. The reachability propagator. Research Report INFO-2005-07, Université catholique de Louvain, Louvain-la-Neuve, Belgium, 2005.

[Rei03] Stefan Reich. Escape from mutlithreaded hell. concurrency in the language "e", March 2003. Presentation available at: `http://www.drjava.de/e-presentation/html-english/img0.html`.

[Sar93] Vijay A. Saraswat. *Concurrent Constraint Programming*. MIT Press, Cambridge, MA, 1993.

[SJG95] Vijay A. Saraswat, Radha Jagadeesan, and Vineet Gupta. Default timed concurrent constraint programming. In *POPL '95: Proceedings of the 22nd ACM SIGPLAN-SIGACT symposium on Principles of programming languages*, pages 272–285, New York, NY, USA, 1995. ACM Press.

[SMRS04] Fred Spiessens, Mark Miller, Peter Van Roy, and Jonathan Shapiro. Authority Reduction in Protection Systems. Available at: `http://www.info.ucl.ac.be/people/fsp/ARS.pdf`, 2004.

[SV05a] Fred Spiessens and Peter Van Roy. The Oz-E project: Design guidelines for a secure multiparadigm programming language. In *Multiparadigm Programming in Mozart/Oz: Extended Proceedings of the Second International Conference MOZ 2004*, volume 3389 of *Lecture Notes in Computer Science*. Springer-Verlag, 2005.

[SV05b] Fred Spiessens and Peter Van Roy. A practical formal model for safety analysis in Capability-Based systems, 2005. To be published in Lecture Notes in Computer Science (Springer-Verlag). Available at `http://www.info.ucl.ac.be/people/fsp/tgc/tgc05fs.pdf`. Presentation available at `http://www.info.ucl.ac.be/people/fsp/auredsysfinal.mov`.

[VH04] Peter Van Roy and Seif Haridi. *Concepts, Techniques, and Models of Computer Programming.* MIT Press, March 2004.

Appendix

Formal Authority Reduction Systems

In this appendix we give the formal definition of Authority Reduction Systems (ARS) based on transformations of labeled digraphs. The transformation rules will correspond to capability rules for propagation of data and authority, described in Section 2. The formalism is derived from the more general formal systems we described in [SMRS04]. It corresponds to the Static Authority Reduction Systems introduced in Section 5. We will provide a subclass of "Saturated" Authority Reduction Systems, in which the safety problems of finite configuration are decidable, and show how the safety properties in every ARS can be safely approximated by a corresponding ARS in this class. This will proof the claims of Section 5.3.

We will then show how the formal model can be extended with the extra behavior aspects described in Section 6, and how that affects the theorem on saturation, and its proof. The formal model corresponding to Section 7 will be described in future work.

Definitions

Let *Aspects* be the set $\{\mathtt{iT}, \mathtt{iG}, \mathtt{iR}, \mathtt{iW}, \mathtt{rT}, \mathtt{rG}, \mathtt{rR}, \mathtt{rW}\}$ of behavior aspects.

Definition 1 (Authority Reduction Systems).
An ARS is a tuple $(\mathbf{S}, \mathbf{B}, \mathbf{P})$ *such that:*

- $\mathbf{S}$ *is a countably infinite set of subjects*
- $\mathbf{B}$ *is a behavior function :* $\mathbf{S} \to 2^{Aspects}$
- $\mathbf{P}$ *is a parenthood function :* $\mathbf{S} \to \mathbf{S} : \mathbf{P}^n(x) = x \iff \mathbf{P}(x) = x$

Definition 2 (Authority Reduction Configuration ARC).
Let $A = (\mathbf{S}, \mathbf{B}, \mathbf{P})$ *be an ARS.*
An ARC is a tuple (S, E, A) *such that:*

- $S \subseteq \mathbf{S}$ *contains the subjects of the configuration*
- $E \subseteq S \times S$ *represents the access relation between them*

Given an ARC $C = (S, E, A)$*, we will indicate its components:*
$S_C = S$;
$E_C = E$;
$A_C = A$.

Informally, an ARC is an access graph between subjects of an ARS.

Definition 3 ($\vdash$ **and** $\vdash^*$**).**
Let $A = (\mathbf{S}, \mathbf{B}, \mathbf{P})$ *be an ARS.*
Let $C_1 = (S_1, E_1, A)$ *be an ARC,*
Let $C_2 = (S_2, E_2, A)$ *be an ARC with* $S_1 \subseteq S_2$
$C_1 \vdash C_2 \iff$ *one of the following conditions applies:*

$create(p, c, \Delta)$: $\exists p, c \in S_2, \exists \Delta \subseteq \{c\} \times S_1$
$S_2 = S_1 \cup \{c\} \wedge P(c) = p$ *(creation of c by p)*
$E_2 = E_1 \cup \{(p, c)\} \cup \Delta$ *(parenthood)*
$\forall (c, x) \in \Delta : (p, x) \in E_1$ *(endowment)*
$grant(x, a, b)$: $S_2 = S_1 \wedge \exists a, b \in S_1 : E_2 = E_1 \cup \{(a, b)\} \wedge \texttt{rT} \in \mathbf{B}(a)$
and $\exists x \in S_1 : \texttt{iG} \in \mathbf{B}(x) \wedge \{(x, a), (x, b)\} \subseteq E_1$ *(x grants b to a)*
$take(a, x, b)$: $S_2 = S_1 \wedge \exists a, b \in S_1 : E_2 = E_1 \cup \{(a, b)\} \wedge \texttt{iT} \in \mathbf{B}(a)$
and $\exists x \in S_1 : \texttt{rG} \in \mathbf{B}(x) \wedge \{(a, x), (x, b)\} \subseteq E_1$ *(a takes b from x)*

From this we derive the following definitions:

$\vdash^*$: *is the reflexive and transitive closure of* $\vdash$
$\vdash^n$: $C \vdash^0 C$ *and* $C \vdash^n C' \iff C \vdash^{n-1} C'' \wedge C'' \vdash C'$

Definition 4 (The predicate couldGetAccess(C,x,y)).
Let $C = (S, E, A)$ *be an ARC, let* $x, y \in S$
$couldGetAccess(C, x, y) \iff \exists C' : C \vdash^* C' \wedge (x, y) \in E_{C'}$

Definition 5 (The predicate couldGetInfo(C,x,y)).
Let $A = (\mathbf{S}, \mathbf{B}, \mathbf{P})$ *be an ARS*
Let $C = (S, E, A)$ *be an ARC, let* $x, y \in S$
$couldGetInfo(C, x, y) \iff$ *one of the following conditions applies:*

1. $x = y$
2. $\texttt{iR} \in \mathbf{B}(x) \wedge \texttt{rW} \in \mathbf{B}(y) \wedge (x, y) \in E_C$ *(x reads from y in C)*
3. $\texttt{rR} \in \mathbf{B}(x) \wedge \texttt{iW} \in \mathbf{B}(y) \wedge (y, x) \in E_C$ *(y writes to x in C)*
4. $\exists C' : C \vdash^* C' \wedge \exists z \in S_{C'} : couldGetInfo(C', z, y) \wedge couldGetInfo(C', x, z)$

Lemma 1 (The effect of adding access to the graph).
Let $A = (\mathbf{S}, \mathbf{B}, \mathbf{P})$ *be an ARS*
Let C *and* C' *be ARCs over* A *with* $E_C \subseteq E_{C'}$ *and* $S_C = S_{C'}$
Let $x, y \in S_C$
$couldGetAccess(C, x, y) \Rightarrow couldGetAccess(C', x, y)$
$couldGetInfo(C, x, y) \Rightarrow couldGetInfo(C', x, y)$

Proof. We will prove that every derivation $\vdash^*$ from C is also applicable from C' and that the second derivation results in more (or equal) access in the graph. We prove that every step in the derivation respects these invariants:

- More (or equal) access in the graph and the same behavior of the subjects, does not prevent a step to be applicable

- More (or equal) access in the graph and the same behavior of the subjects before the step, will result in more (or equal) access in the graph and the same behavior of the subjects after the step.

Both requirements follow directly from inspection of the preconditions and the postconditions of the possible steps in Definition 3. Since the initial configuration C has more (or equal) access than C' and the same behavior as C', the lemma follows from the definitions of couldGetAccess() (Definition 4) and couldGetInfo() (Definition 5).

Lemma 2 (The influence of more collaborative behavior).
Let $A = (\mathbf{S}, \mathbf{B}, \mathbf{P})$ *be an ARS*
Let $A^+ = (\mathbf{S}, \mathbf{B}^+, \mathbf{P})$ *be an ARS with* $\forall x \in \mathbf{S} : \mathbf{B}(x) \subseteq \mathbf{B}^+(x)$
Let $C = (S, E, A)$ *and* $C' = (S, E, A^+)$ *be ARCs*
Let $x, y \in S$
$couldGetAccess(C, x, y) \Rightarrow couldGetAccess(C', x, y)$
$couldGetInfo(C, x, y) \Rightarrow couldGetInfo(C', x, y)$

Proof. The proof has the same structure as the proof of Lemma 1. We will prove that every derivation $\vdash^*$ from C is also applicable from C' and that the second derivation can result in the same access in the graph, while the subjects in the graph resulting from the second derivation will obviously still have more collaborative behavior. We prove that every step in the derivation respects these invariants:

- More (or equal) behavior and equal access does not prevent a step from being applicable
- More (or equal) behavior and equal access before the step, will result in more (or equal) behavior and equal access after the step.

Both requirements follow directly from inspection of the preconditions and the postconditions of the possible steps in Definition 3. Since C has the same access as C' and more (or equal) behavior than C, the lemma now follows from the definitions of couldGetAccess() (Definition 4) and couldGetInfo() (Definition 5).

Definition 6 (Saturation).
Let $A = (\mathbf{S}, \mathbf{B}, \mathbf{P})$ *be an ARS*
Let $A_0 = (\mathbf{S}, \mathbf{B}, \mathbf{I})$ *be the ARS derived from A by replacing* $\mathbf{P}$ *by the identity function on* $\mathbf{S}$ *(no creation is possible)*
Let $C = (S, E, A)$ *and* $C_0 = (S, E, A_0)$ *be ARCs,*
C *is saturated* $\iff \forall x, y \in S$ *both the following conditions apply:*

1. $couldGetAccess(C, x, y) \Rightarrow couldGetAccess(C_0, x, y)$
2. $couldGetInfo(C, x, y) \Rightarrow couldGetInfo(C_0, x, y)$

Corollary 1 (Calculating safety properties in a Saturated ARC). *Since by definition, every step in* A_0 *is also a step in* A*, the converse implications of definition 6 also hold. This means that in a saturated ARC* C*, the safety properties :*

$$\neg couldGetAccess(C, x, y)$$
$$\neg couldGetInfo(C, x, y)$$

can be calculated without considering creation steps.

Theorem 1 (Safely approximating safety properties via saturation). *This theorem is the formal version of the theorem in Section 5.3.*
Let $A = (\mathbf{S}, \mathbf{B}, \mathbf{P})$ *be an ARS*
Let $C = (S, E, A)$ *be an ARC,*
Define the following:

$$\mathbf{B}^+ : \mathbf{S} \to 2^{Aspects} : \mathbf{B}^+(x) = \bigcup_{c \in S : \exists n \in \mathbb{N} : \mathbf{P}^n(c) = x} \mathbf{B}(c) \quad (1)$$

$$E^+ = E \cup \{(x, x) | x \in S \wedge \exists c \in \mathbf{S} \setminus S, n \in \mathbb{N}_0 : \mathbf{P}^n(c) = x\} \quad (2)$$

Let $A^+ = (\mathbf{S}, \mathbf{B}^+, \mathbf{P})$
Let $C^+ = (S, E^+, A^+)$

1. C^+ *is saturated*
2. *The safety properties in* C *are safely approximated in* C^+.

Proof (part 1). Let P_S be the parenthood function $\mathbf{P}$ of A^+, applied zero or more times, up to the first element in S :

$P_S(x) = P^k(x)$ with $k = \min_{i \in \mathbb{N}, \mathbf{P}^i(x) \in S} i$ if such a k exists,
$P_S(x) = x$ otherwise
From this definition it can be easily deduced that :

$$\forall C, D : C \vdash^* D : P_S(S_D) = S_C \quad (3)$$

$$\forall x \in \mathbf{S} : \mathbf{B}^+(P_S(x)) \supseteq \mathbf{B}^+(x) \quad (4)$$

First we proof that $couldGetAccess(C^+, x, y) \Rightarrow couldGetAccess(C_0^+, x, y)$ with $C_0^+ = (S, E^+, A_0^+)$ and $A_0^+ = (\mathbf{S}, \mathbf{B}^+, \mathbf{I})$.

We will first prove by induction that for any $C^{+'}$ such that $C^+ \vdash^* C^{+'}$, there exists a $C_0^{+'}$ such that $C_0^+ \vdash^* C_0^{+'}$ and $\forall x, y \in \mathbf{S} : (x, y) \in E_{C^{+'}} \Rightarrow (P_S(x), P_S(y)) \in E_{C_0^{+'}}$.

The base case is true because from the definition of C^+ and C_0^+ follows immediately that $E^+ \subseteq E_0^+$.

For the induction case, let's suppose that $C^+ \vdash^* C^{+''}$, $C^{+''} \vdash C^{+'}$ and there exists a $C_0^{+''}$ such that $\forall x, y \in \mathbf{S} : (x, y) \in E_{C^{+''}} \Rightarrow (P_S(x), P_S(y)) \in E_{C_0^{+''}}$.

We conclude by analysis of the $\vdash$ relation between $C^{+''}$ and $C^{+'}$.

For a step $take(a, x, b)$ (resp. $grant(x, a, b)$), there exists a $C_0^{+'}$ derived from $C_0^{+''}$ by a step $take(P_S(a), P_S(x), P_S(b))$ (resp. $grant(P_S(x), P_S(a), P_S(b))$). The access pre-conditions apply because of the induction hypothesis. The behavior conditions apply because of (4). The conclusion follows from Definition 3.

For a creation step $create(p, c, \Delta)$, we can take $C_0^{+\prime} = C_0^{+\prime\prime}$. For the newly created parent-child access $p \to c$ (parenthood): $P_S(c) = P_S(p) \in S$ and so from (2): $(P_S(p), P_S(c)) \in E_{C^{+\prime}}$ already (and thus also $(P_S(p), P_S(c)) \in E_{C_0^{+\prime}}$ by induction). The preconditions for creating access via endowment indicate that if access $(c, x) \in \Delta$ is created then $(p, x) \in E_{C^{+\prime\prime}}$ should already have been available. From the induction hypothesis, $(P_S(p), P_S(x)) \in E_{C_0^{+\prime\prime}}$ and since $P_S(c) = P_S(p)$ it follows that $(P_S(p), P_S(c)) \in E_{C_0^{+\prime\prime}}$ already.

Now we proof that $couldGetInfo(C^+, x, y) \Rightarrow couldGetInfo(C_0^+, x, y)$ with $C_0^+ = (S, E^+, A_0^+)$ and $A_0^+ = (\mathbf{S}, \mathbf{B}^+, \mathbf{I})$.
$\forall x \in S : P_S(x) = x$; so $\mathtt{iR} \in \mathbf{B}^+(x) \Rightarrow \mathtt{iR} \in \mathbf{B}_0^+(P_S(x))$
The same goes for iW, rR, and rW.

We conclude by induction on the number of intermediate z in the definition of $couldGetConf$ (Definition 5), replacing any subject x by $P_S(x)$, the access conditions are satisfied by the first part of this proof.

Proof (part 2). We have to prove that:
$\neg couldGetAccess(C^+, x, y) \Rightarrow \neg couldGetAccess(C, x, y)$
$\neg couldGetInfo(C+, x, y) \Rightarrow \neg couldGetInfo(C, x, y)$
As $E^+ \supseteq E$, and $\forall x \in \mathbf{S} : \mathbf{B}^+(x) \supseteq \mathbf{B}(x)$, this follows immediately from Lemmas 1 and 2.

Corollary 2 (Tractability). *Safety properties in ARCs with a finite set of subjects can be tractably and safely approximated in a corresponding saturated ARC, by :*

- *giving the subjects that can create offspring self-access, and*
- *adding to their behavior aspects the behavior aspects of all their potential offspring*

Proof. It is trivial to show that in a finite ARC, only a finite number of $grant(x, a, b)$-rules and $take(a, x, b)$-rules can be applicable that have an actual effect on the access graph (adding *non pre-existing* access from a to b). The maximum number of possible access arcs in the graphs also being finite, the corollary follows from Theorem 1. Notice that from the monotonicity of these steps, it can even be deduced that actual order of the chosen steps is not influencing the final result (confluency).

Definition 7 (Extensions).
Let $Aspects^{\sim} = Aspects \cup \{\sim T, \sim G, \sim R, \sim W\}$

Exentended ARS : *is an ARS as defined in Definition 1, except for using* $Aspects^{\sim}$ *instead of Aspects.*
Extended ARC : *is an ARC as defined in Definition 2, but over an extended ARS*

Extended Step $\vdash^{\sim}$ **:** *a step as defined in Definition 3, with the following additional possibilities:*

grantFar(x, Ω, a, b) **:** $S_2 = S_1, \wedge \exists a, b \in S_1 : E_2 = E_1 \cup \{(a, b)\} \wedge rT \in \mathbf{B}(a)$ *and* Ω *is a finite series of length* $k \geq 1$ *of elements in* S *such that and* $\forall i \in \mathbf{N} : 1 \leq i < k : (\Omega_i, \Omega_{i+1}) \in E_1$ *and* $(\Omega_k, a) \in E_1$ *and* $\forall i \in \mathbf{N} : 1 \leq i \leq k :\sim G \in \mathbf{B}(\Omega_i)$ $\exists x \in S : \{(x, \Omega_1), (x, b)\} \subseteq E_1 \wedge iG \in \mathbf{B}(x)$ *(x grants b to a via a series of forwarding relays between x and a)*

takeFar(a, Ω, x, b) **:** $S_2 = S_1, \wedge \exists a, b \in S_1 : E_2 = E_1 \cup \{(a, b)\} \wedge iT \in \mathbf{B}(a)$ *and* Ω *is a finite series of length* $k \geq 1$ *of elements in* S *such that and* $\forall i \in \mathbf{N} : 1 \leq i < k : (\Omega_i, \Omega_{i+1}) \in E_1$ *and* $(a, \Omega_1) \in E_1$ *and* $\forall i \in \mathbf{N} : 1 \leq i \leq k :\sim T \in \mathbf{B}(\Omega_i)$ $\exists x \in S : \{(\Omega_k, x), (x, b)\} \subseteq E_1 \wedge rG \in \mathbf{B}(x)$ *(x grants b to a via a series of forwarding relays between x and a)*

Extended Safety Properties : *Extended versions of couldGetAccess() and couldGetInfo() :*

couldGetAccess(C, x, y) **:** *completely similar to Definition 4*

couldGetInfo(C, x, y) **:** *as defined in Definition 5, but with 2 extra possibilities:*

readFar(x,y) : $iR \in \mathbf{B}(x) \wedge rW \in \mathbf{B}(y)$ *and* $\exists$ *a finite series* Ω *with length* $k \geq 1$ *of elements in* S *such that :* $\forall i : 1 \leq i < k : (\Omega_i, \Omega_{i+1}) \in E$ *and* $\forall i : 1 \leq i \leq k :\sim R \in \mathbf{B}(\Omega_i)$*and* $\in E$ *and* $\{(x, \Omega_1), (\Omega_k, y)\} \subseteq E$ *(x reads from y in C via a series of backwards data relays)*

writeFar(x,y) : $rR \in \mathbf{B}(x) \wedge iW \in \mathbf{B}(y)$ *and* $\exists$ *a finite series* Ω *with length* $k \geq 1$ *of elements in* S *such that :* $\forall i : 1 \leq i < k : (\Omega_i, \Omega_{i+1}) \in E$ *and* $\forall i : 1 \leq i \leq k :\sim W \in \mathbf{B}(\Omega_i)$*and* $\in E$ *and* $\{(y, \Omega_1), (\Omega_k, x)\} \subseteq E$ *(y writes to x in C via a series of forward data relays)*

Extended Saturation : *completely similar to Defintion 6.*

A theorem similar to Theorem 1 for extended ARS and extended saturation can be proven in a similar way. We plan to publish this theorem and its proof in a dedicated technical report.

Mixin Modules for Dynamic Rebinding*

Davide Ancona, Sonia Fagorzi, and Elena Zucca

DISI - Università di Genova,
Via Dodecaneso, 35, 16146 Genova (Italy)
{davide, fagorzi, zucca}@disi.unige.it

Abstract. *Dynamic rebinding* is the ability of changing the definitions of names at execution time. While dynamic rebinding is clearly useful in practice, and increasingly needed in modern systems, most programming languages provide only limited and ad-hoc mechanisms, and no adequate semantic understanding currently exists.

Here, we provide a simple and powerful mechanism for dynamic rebinding by means of a calculus $CMS^{\ell,v}$ of *mixin modules* (mutually recursive modules allowing redefinition of components) where, differently from the traditional approach, module operations can be performed after selecting and executing a module component: in this way, execution can refer to *virtual* components, which can be rebound when module operators are executed. In particular, in our calculus module operations are performed on demand, when execution would otherwise get stuck.

We provide a sound type system, which ensures that execution never tries to access module components which cannot become available, and show how the calculus can be used to encode a variety of real-world dynamic rebinding mechanisms.

1 Introduction

In the last years considerable effort has been invested in developing kernel module/fragment calculi [12,7,23,21,7,19] providing foundations for flexible manipulation and combination of software components. In particular, a simple unifying notion emerged from this research stream is that of *mixin module* [11,3], that is, a module which allows late (re)definition of components. In a mixin module components are either defined inside the module (exported) or *deferred* (imported), that is, to be provided later by means of combination with other modules (notably, in a mutually recursive way by a symmetric sum operator). Moreover, some defined components can be *virtual*, that is, can be later modified as an effect of combination with other modules (notably, by an overriding operator), so that all their internal references are dynamically rebound to the new definition. The possibility of defining virtual components is a generalization to an arbitrary context of software composition of a key idea of the object-oriented

* Partially supported by Dynamic Assembly, Reconfiguration and Type-checking - EC project IST-2001-33477, APPSEM II - Thematic network IST-2001-38957i, and MIUR EOS - Extensible Object Systems.

R. De Nicola and D. Sangiorgi (Eds.): TGC 2005, LNCS 3705, pp. 279–298, 2005.

approach, that is, the ability of writing code fragments (classes in this case) where components (methods) are simultaneously ready to be used and available to be modified (*open-closed* property).

Calculi supporting mixin modules, such as the Calculus of Module Systems (shortly *CMS*) developed by two of the authors[7], can be used to encode and compare on a formal basis a large variety of existing mechanisms for software composition, including parameterized modules like ML functors, overriding, extra-linguistic mechanisms like those provided by a linker. However, these calculi are based on a *static* view of software manipulation, hence fail in many ways to be adequate to model modern software systems, which become increasingly dynamic. For instance, programming environments such as those of Java and C# support dynamic linking, and we can expect in the future more and more forms of *reconfiguration* interleaved with standard *execution* steps; when values of computations are marshaled from a running program and moved elsewhere, some of their identifiers may need to be dynamically rebound; systems which provide uninterrupted service must be dynamically updated.

All these situations could be hardly represented in, e.g., *CMS*, even though the notion of virtual component, allowing the same name to be bound to different definitions during successive steps of configuration of a software system, seems to exactly correspond to rebinding. This is due to the fact that in *CMS* and similar calculi all module operators must be performed *before* starting execution of a program, that is, evaluation of a module component. Hence, virtual components can be usefully employed to rebind the same name to different definitions, and thus reuse in different ways the same module in different contexts, but this rebinding is *static* in the sense that only closed modules (that is, with no deferred or virtual components) can be actually used at execution time.

Here, we are able to obtain a simple and powerful calculus for dynamic rebinding from *CMS* by developing the following simple key ideas.

- Components of open modules can be selected and executed, keeping their module context. In this way, execution of module operators can be interleaved with *program execution*, that is, execution of a module component in the context of the components offered by the module. We already introduced this idea in CMS^{ℓ} [6], where in particular we adopted a lazy strategy which performs reconfiguration steps (execution of module operators) only if necessary, that is, when program execution would otherwise gets stuck (since a not yet available component is needed.)
- Program execution refers to not only *local*, but also *virtual* components, that is, components which are associated with a definition which is directly available to the executing program and can also be redefined by performing module operators. This conceptually simple extension greatly enhances the expressive power. Indeed, in CMS^{ℓ}, reconfiguration steps can either be performed or not depending on which components program execution needs, but when a component is bound to a definition this binding can no longer be changed. On the contrary, in $CMS^{\ell v}$ execution can refer to components which can be redefined when module operators are executed.

Another important novelty w.r.t. CMS^{ℓ} is that $CMS^{\ell,v}$ keeps the full expressive power of higher-order features of *CMS*. This allows to express interaction of execution at different levels (e.g., modules with module components, triggering of a local module simplification inside program execution, and so on).

In Section 2 and Section 3 we formally define the calculus. In Section 4 we show how the calculus can be used to model real-world dynamic rebinding requirements. In Section 5 we provide a sound type system, which ensures that execution will never try to access module components which cannot become available. Section 6 collects the technical results (limited to the claims), and finally Section 7 contains concluding remarks and directions for further work.

2 Syntax

Notations We denote by $A \stackrel{fin}{\rightarrow} B$ the set of partial functions f from A into $B = \mathsf{cod}f$ with finite domain $\mathsf{dom}(f) \subseteq A$. For I set of indexes, $a_i \in A$, $b_i \in B$, for $i \in I$, we denote by $a_i : b_i{}^{i \in I}$ the partial function f s.t. $\mathsf{dom}(f) = \{a_i \mid i \in I\}$, $f(a_i) = b_i$ for $i \in I$. We will use the following operators on partial functions: f, g is the union of two functions with disjoint domain; $f \mid g$ means that f, g are *compatible*, that is, s.t. $f(a) = g(a)$ for all $a \in \mathsf{dom}(f) \cap \mathsf{dom}(g)$; $f \cup g$ is the union of two compatible functions; $\circ$ is the composition of functions; $f\backslash_A$ is the restriction of f to the domain $\mathsf{dom}(f) \setminus A$; we write $f\backslash_a$ instead of $f\backslash_{\{a\}}$.

The syntax of $CMS^{\ell,v}$ is given in Fig.1.

$e \in \mathsf{Exp}$	$::=$		**expression**
	$\ldots$		core operators
	$\mid\ x$		variable
	$\mid\ [\iota; o; \rho]$	$(\mathsf{dom}(\iota) \cap \mathsf{dom}(\rho) = \emptyset)$	basic module
	$\mid\ [\iota; o; \rho \mid e]$	$(\mathsf{dom}(\iota) \cap \mathsf{dom}(\rho) = \emptyset)$	basic configuration
	$\mid\ e_1 + e_2$		sum
	$\mid\ \mathsf{freeze}_X e$		freeze
	$\mid\ e \backslash X$		delete
	$\mid\ e \downarrow X$		run
	$\mid\ e \uparrow$		result
$\iota : \mathsf{Var} \stackrel{fin}{\rightarrow} \mathsf{Name}$			**input** assignment
$o : \mathsf{Name} \stackrel{fin}{\rightarrow} \mathsf{Exp}$			**output** assignment
$\rho : \mathsf{Var} \stackrel{fin}{\rightarrow} \mathsf{Exp}$			**local** assignment

Fig. 1. Syntax

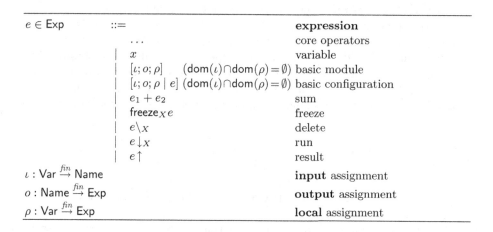

We assume an infinite set Name of *names* X, and an infinite set Var of *variables* x. Names are used to refer to a module from the outside (hence they are used by module operators), while variables are used to refer to a (basic) module from a program executing in the context of the components offered by this module. This distinction between names and variables is standard in module calculi and, besides the methodological motivation explained above, has technical motivations as well, such as allowing α-conversion for variables while preserving external interfaces (see, e.g., [7] for an extended discussion of this point).

As *CMS* and CMS^{ℓ}, $CMS^{\ell,v}$ is a parametric and stratified calculus, which can be instantiated over different core calculi. However, while in *CMS* [7] this dependence on the core level is represented in a more rigorous way by using explicit substitutions, here we adopt for simplicity a less formal approach where we assume module expressions to be merged with expressions of the core calculus (that is, the dots in the syntax correspond to core productions). In the examples we assume that core expressions include integers with the usual operations.

Basic modules are as in *CMS* and consist of three parts: the *input assignment* ι, which is a mapping from variables into *input names*, the *output assignment* o, which is a mapping from *output names* into expressions, and the *local assignment* ρ, which is a mapping from *local variables* into expressions. Input names are called *virtual* if they are output names as well, *deferred* otherwise; variables in the domain of ι are called either virtual or deferred depending on the associated name. A basic configuration is a pair $[\iota; o; \rho \mid e]$, consisting of a basic module and an expression, called *program*.

Both basic modules and basic configurations are well-formed only if the sets of deferred and virtual variables and that of local variables are disjoint.

Operators *sum*, *freeze* and *delete* are a simplified version of *CMS* module operators, and provide primitive ways to manipulate and combine software fragments. *Modules* can be constructed by applying these operators on top of basic modules, and *configurations* can be constructed by applying these operators on top of basic modules and at least one basic configuration (actually, exactly one in well-behaving terms, see in the sequel, hence we can correctly talk of *the* program running inside a configuration). Operator $\_\downarrow\_$ allows to obtain a basic configuration from a (basic) module, by starting the execution of a module component. Operator $\_\uparrow$ extracts from a configuration the (final result of) the program. Operators will be explained more in detail when introducing reduction rules.

3 Semantics

In this section we give the semantics of the calculus. Reduction rules are given in Fig. 2 and Fig. 3.

By definition, the one step reduction relation $\longrightarrow$ is the relation over well-formed terms inductively defined by the rules. For sake of clarity, we write also some side conditions which are redundant since implied by the fact that terms must be well-formed.

The semantics is given by using evaluation contexts (to control the evaluation order) and redexes (reducible expressions), following the approach of Felleisen and Friedman [18]. Rule ($\mathcal{E}$) is the usual contextual closure, where evaluation contexts $\mathcal{E}$ include a non specified set of core evaluation contexts,

Evaluation contexts

$\mathcal{E} ::= \square \mid \ldots \mid [\iota; o; \rho \mid \mathcal{E}] \mid \mathcal{E} + e \mid \mathcal{E} \backslash_X \mid \mathsf{freeze}_X \mathcal{E} \mid \mathcal{E}{\downarrow_X} \mid \mathcal{E}{\uparrow}$
$\quad \mid [\iota; o; \rho] + \mathcal{E} \mid [\iota; o; \rho \mid \mathcal{E}[x]] + \mathcal{E} \ (x \in \mathsf{dom}(\iota) \wedge \iota(x) \notin \mathsf{dom}(o))$

Contextual closure and core execution

$$(\mathcal{E})\ \frac{r \longrightarrow e}{\mathcal{E}[r] \longrightarrow \mathcal{E}[e]}$$

... (rules for core operators)

Module simplification

$$(\text{m-sum})\ \frac{}{[\iota_1; o_1; \rho_1] + [\iota_2; o_2; \rho_2] \longrightarrow [\iota_1, \iota_2; o_1, o_2; \rho_1, \rho_2]} \quad \begin{array}{l} \mathsf{dom}(\iota_1, \rho_1) \cap \mathsf{FV}([\iota_2; o_2; \rho_2]) = \emptyset \\ \mathsf{dom}(\iota_2, \rho_2) \cap \mathsf{FV}([\iota_1; o_1; \rho_1]) = \emptyset \\ \mathsf{dom}(\iota_1, \rho_1) \cap \mathsf{dom}(\iota_2, \rho_2) = \emptyset \\ \mathsf{dom}(o_1) \cap \mathsf{dom}(o_2) = \emptyset \end{array}$$

$$(\text{m-freeze})\ \frac{}{\mathsf{freeze}_X [\iota; o; \rho] \longrightarrow \left[\iota\backslash_F; o; \rho, x : o(X)^{x \in F}\right]} \quad \begin{array}{l} F = \{x \mid \iota(x) = X\} \\ F \neq \emptyset \Rightarrow X \in \mathsf{dom}(o) \end{array}$$

$$(\text{m-del})\ \frac{}{[\iota; o; \rho] \backslash_X \longrightarrow [\iota; o\backslash_X; \rho]} \quad X \in \mathsf{dom}(o)$$

Variable resolution and reconfiguration

$$(\text{local})\ \frac{}{[\iota; o; \rho \mid \mathcal{E}[x]] \longrightarrow [\iota; o; \rho \mid \mathcal{E}\{\rho(x)\}]} \quad \begin{array}{l} x \notin \mathsf{HB}(\mathcal{E}) \\ x \in \mathsf{dom}(\rho) \end{array}$$

$$(\text{virtual})\ \frac{}{[\iota; o; \rho \mid \mathcal{E}[x]] \longrightarrow [\iota; o; \rho \mid \mathcal{E}\{o(\iota(x))\}]} \quad \begin{array}{l} x \notin \mathsf{HB}(\mathcal{E}) \\ x \in \mathsf{dom}(\iota) \wedge \iota(x) \in \mathsf{dom}(o) \end{array}$$

$$(\text{sum})\ \frac{}{[\iota_1; o_1; \rho_1 \mid \mathcal{E}[x]] + [\iota_2; o_2; \rho_2] \longrightarrow [\iota_1, \iota_2; o_1, o_2; \rho_1, \rho_2 \mid \mathcal{E}[x]]} \quad \begin{array}{l} x \notin \mathsf{HB}(\mathcal{E}) \\ x \in \mathsf{dom}(\iota_1) \wedge \iota_1(x) \notin \mathsf{dom}(o_1) \\ \mathsf{dom}(\iota_1, \rho_1) \cap \mathsf{FV}([\iota_2; o_2; \rho_2]) = \emptyset \\ \mathsf{dom}(\iota_2,\rho_2) \cap \mathsf{FV}([\iota_1; o_1; \rho_1 \mid \mathcal{E}[x]]) = \emptyset \\ \mathsf{dom}(\iota_1, \rho_1) \cap \mathsf{dom}(\iota_2, \rho_2) = \emptyset \\ \mathsf{dom}(o_1) \cap \mathsf{dom}(o_2) = \emptyset \end{array}$$

$$(\text{freeze})\ \frac{}{\mathsf{freeze}_X [\iota; o; \rho \mid \mathcal{E}[x]] \longrightarrow \left[\iota\backslash_F; o; \rho, x : o(X)^{x \in F} \mid \mathcal{E}[x]\right]} \quad \begin{array}{l} x \notin \mathsf{HB}(\mathcal{E}) \\ x \in \mathsf{dom}(\iota) \wedge \iota(x) \notin \mathsf{dom}(o) \\ F = \{x \mid \iota(x) = X\} \\ F \neq \emptyset \Rightarrow X \in \mathsf{dom}(o) \end{array}$$

$$(\text{del})\ \frac{}{[\iota; o; \rho \mid \mathcal{E}[x]] \backslash_X \longrightarrow [\iota; o\backslash_X; \rho \mid \mathcal{E}[x]]} \quad \begin{array}{l} x \notin \mathsf{HB}(\mathcal{E}) \wedge x \in \mathsf{dom}(\iota) \wedge \iota(x) \notin \mathsf{dom}(o) \\ X \in \mathsf{dom}(o) \end{array}$$

Fig. 2. Reduction rules

and the metavariable r ranges over redexes, that is, the left-hand sides of the consequence in (instantiations of) the other rules, called *computational*. We denote by $\mathcal{E}[e]$ the expression obtained by replacing by e the hole in context $\mathcal{E}$. *Reconfiguration contexts* $\mathcal{R}$ are special contexts used in rule (res-extract) and (res-var), as explained below.

The evaluation context $[x : X, \iota; o; \rho \mid \mathcal{E}[x]] + \mathcal{E}$ expresses the fact that in the sum of a configuration with a module the evaluation of the right-hand-side argument is only triggered when the configuration is fully reduced and the running

Table 1. Free variables and hole binders

$e \in \mathsf{Exp}$	$\mathsf{FV}(e)$
$\ldots$	free variables for core operators
x	$\{x\}$
$[\iota; o; \rho]$	$\mathsf{FV}(o) \cup \mathsf{FV}(\rho) \setminus \mathsf{dom}(\iota, \rho)$
$[\iota; o; \rho \mid e]$	$(\mathsf{FV}(o) \cup \mathsf{FV}(\rho) \cup \mathsf{FV}(e)) \setminus \mathsf{dom}(\iota, \rho)$
$e_1 + e_2$	$\mathsf{FV}(e_1) \cup \mathsf{FV}(e_2)$
$e \setminus_X \mid \mathsf{freeze}_X e \mid e{\downarrow}_X \mid e{\uparrow}$	$\mathsf{FV}(e)$
$f : A \stackrel{fin}{\rightarrow} \mathsf{Exp}$	$\cup\{\mathsf{FV}(f(a)) \mid a \in \mathsf{dom}(f)\}$
$\mathcal{E}$	$\mathsf{HB}(\mathcal{E})$
$\square$	$\emptyset$
$[\iota; o; \rho \mid \mathcal{E}]$	$\mathsf{dom}(\iota, \rho) \cup \mathsf{HB}(\mathcal{E})$
$\mathcal{E} + e \mid \mathcal{E} \setminus_X \mid \mathsf{freeze}_X \mathcal{E} \mid \mathcal{E}{\downarrow}_X \mid \mathcal{E}{\uparrow}$	$\mathsf{HB}(\mathcal{E})$

program still needs reconfiguration steps to proceed (indeed, in this case the module needs to be reduced in order sum to be performed.)
We assume that computational rules for the core operators are provided.

Module simplification. Simplification rules for sum, freeze and delete on modules are exactly as in *CMS*. We give here a brief description, referring to [7] for more detailed comments.

Sum. The sum operation has the effect of gluing together two modules. The first two side conditions avoid undesired captures of free variables. Free variables of expressions are defined in Table 1, assuming that their definitions on core terms are provided. Since the reduction is defined only over well-formed terms, the deferred and local variables of one module must be disjoint from those of the other (second side condition). These side conditions can always be satisfied by an appropriate α-conversion. For the same reason of well-formedness, the output names of the two modules must be disjoint (last side condition)[1]; however, in this case the reduction gets stuck since this conflict cannot be resolved by an α-conversion.

Freeze. The freeze operator removes the name X appearing as index from the input names. All the virtual variables mapped by ι into it are *frozen*, that is, become local, and take as defining expression the current definition of X in the output assignment. Hence, this definition must exist in case there is at least one variable mapped into X (side-condition); otherwise, the freeze operator has simply no effect. The name of the operator refers to the fact that, once a component has been frozen, other components will permanently refer to its current definition, even in case the component is updated from outside (by delete and then sum, see below).

[1] Note that, since ι goes "backwards", that is, from variables into names, the fact that ι_1, ι_2 must be well-formed does not prevent to share input names, but only to share deferred variables, what can be avoided by α-conversion.

Delete. The delete operator removes an output name (which must be present in the module) with the associated definition.

Note that these three operators provide complementary capabilities for changing the status of a variable x in a basic module, as follows:

- A deferred variable can become virtual as an effect of the sum operator (if x is mapped by ι into an input name X, and X is an output name in the other argument of the sum).
- A virtual variable can become local as an effect of the freeze operator (if x is mapped into the name X appearing as index).
- A virtual variable can become deferred as an effect of the delete operator (if x is mapped into the name X appearing as index).

Local variables are not visible from outside a basic module (or basic configuration), hence cannot change their status.

Variable resolution and reconfiguration. Rules (local) and (virtual) model the situation where program execution needs a variable which is either local or virtual, hence has a corresponding definition, in the enclosing basic configuration.

In both cases, program execution can proceed by replacing the variable by its defining expression.

Here and in the following rules, the side condition $x \notin \mathsf{HB}(\mathcal{E})$ expresses the fact that the occurrence of the variable x in the position denoted by the hole of the context $\mathcal{E}$ is free (that is, not captured by any binder around the hole). Hole binders are defined in Table 1 (we assume their definitions on core terms are provided). Finally, we denote by $\mathcal{E}\{e\}$ the capture avoiding substitution, with the expression e, of the hole $\Box$ in context $\mathcal{E}$.

These two rules, together with rules for core operators and contextual closure, model standard program execution (that is, execution which does not trigger reconfiguration steps), as illustrated by the following example.[2]

$$[x : X; X : 1; y : 2 \mid x + y] \stackrel{\text{(virtual)}}{\longrightarrow} [x : X; X : 1; y : 2 \mid 1 + y] \stackrel{\text{(local)}}{\longrightarrow}$$
$$[x : X; X : 1; y : 2 \mid 1 + 2] \stackrel{\text{(core)}}{\longrightarrow} [x : X; X : 1; y : 2 \mid 3]$$

Note that, since a program can be in turn a configuration, variable resolution can take place at an outer configuration level:

$$[x : X; X : 1; y : 2 \mid [;;\mid x + y]] \stackrel{\text{(virtual)}}{\longrightarrow} [x : X; X : 1; y : 2 \mid [;;\mid 1 + y]] \stackrel{\text{(local)}}{\longrightarrow}$$
$$[x : X; X : 1; y : 2 \mid [;;\mid 1 + 2]] \stackrel{\text{(core)}}{\longrightarrow} [x : X; X : 1; y : 2 \mid [;;\mid 3]]$$

The side condition $x \notin \mathsf{HB}(\mathcal{E})$ ensures that a variable which is bound at an inner configuration level cannot be resolved at an outer level:

---

[2] In examples we label reduction steps with the applied computational rule. We label with (core) reduction steps where we apply core computational rules.

$$[x:X;X:1;y:2 \mid [x:Z;Z:5;\mid x+y]] \xrightarrow{\text{(virtual)}}$$
$$[x:X;X:1;y:2 \mid [x:X;X:5;\mid 5+y]]$$

$$[x:X;X:1;y:2 \mid [x:X;X:5;\mid x+y]] \not\longrightarrow$$
$$[x:X;X:1;y:2 \mid [x:X;X:5;\mid 1+y]]$$

where $\not\longrightarrow$ denotes a not allowed reduction step.
The fact that substitution is capture avoiding prevents variables from outer levels to be captured at an inner level:

$$[x:X;X:y+1;y:2 \mid [;;y:3 \mid x]] \xrightarrow{\text{(virtual)}} [x:X;X:z+1;z:2 \mid [;;y:3 \mid z+1]]$$
$$[x:X;X:y+1;y:2 \mid [;;y:3 \mid x]] \not\longrightarrow [x:X;X:y+1;y:2 \mid [;;y:3 \mid y+1]]$$

A different choice, allowing variables to "migrate" into inner levels, would correspond to a form of dynamic binding for variables.

The following three rules model the situation where program execution needs a variable which is deferred, that is, is bound in the current basic module but has no corresponding definition. In this case, a *reconfiguration* step is triggered: more precisely, the innermost enclosing module operator is performed.

As combined effect of the rules illustrated until now, execution proceeds by standard execution steps until a deferred variable is encountered; in this case, reconfiguration steps are performed (from the innermost to the outermost module operator) until the variable becomes virtual and rule (virtual) can be applied, as illustrated below.

$$[x:X;;y:2 \mid x+y] + [;X:1;] \xrightarrow{\text{(sum)}} [x:X;X:1;y:2 \mid x+y] \xrightarrow{\text{(virtual)}}$$
$$[x:X;X:1;y:2 \mid 1+2] \xrightarrow{\text{(core)}} [x:X;X:1;y:2 \mid 3]$$

As happens for variable resolution, also reconfiguration steps can take place at an outer configuration level if the needed variable is not bound yet.

Note that, whereas sum of two modules and sum of a configuration with a module (conventionally taken in this order) are handled by rule (m-sum) and (sum), respectively, there is no rule for sum of two configurations which, hence, gets stuck (and will be rejected by the type system). This corresponds to the fact that we are considering a sequential calculus, in which there is only one executing program at a given configuration level.

Run and result. Rules in Fig.3 deal with introduction and elimination of a configuration level, respectively. In rule (run), the operator $\downarrow$ constructs an initial configuration by taking as program an output component of a basic module.

$$[x:X;X:1,Z:x+y;y:2]\downarrow_Z \xrightarrow{\text{(run)}} [x:X;X:1,Z:x+y;y:2 \mid x+y] \xrightarrow{\text{(virtual)}} \ldots$$

The following two rules deal with the operator $\uparrow$, which extracts the program from a configuration level. Formally, a configuration level for a program e is

Values and reconfiguration contexts

$v \in \mathsf{Val} ::= \ldots \mid [\iota; o; \rho] \mid \mathcal{R}[\iota; o; \rho \mid v]$
$\mathcal{R} \quad ::= \Box \mid \mathcal{R} + e \mid \mathcal{R} \setminus_X \mid \mathsf{freeze}_X \mathcal{R}$

Run and result

$$\text{(run)}\ \frac{}{[\iota; o; \rho] \downarrow X \longrightarrow [\iota; o; \rho \mid o(X)]}\ X \in \mathsf{dom}(o)$$

$$\text{(res-extract)}\ \frac{}{(\mathcal{R}[\iota; o; \rho \mid v]) \uparrow \longrightarrow v}\ \mathsf{FV}(v) \cap (\mathsf{dom}(\iota, \rho)) = \emptyset$$

$$\text{(res-var)}\ \frac{\mathcal{R}[\iota; o; \rho \mid x] \longrightarrow \mathcal{R}'[\iota'; o'; \rho' \mid e]}{(\mathcal{R}[\iota; o; \rho \mid v[x]]) \uparrow \longrightarrow (\mathcal{R}'[\iota'; o'; \rho' \mid v\{e\}]) \uparrow}\ x \in \mathsf{dom}(\iota, \rho)$$

Fig. 3. Reduction rules (cont)

modeled by an expression of the form $\mathcal{R}[\iota; o; \rho \mid e]$ where $\mathcal{R}$ is a context consisting only of reconfiguration operators.

Rule (res-extract) allows to extract the program from a configuration level if it is a value which contains no variables bound at this level. Note that remaining reconfiguration operators are simply ignored, since they can no longer have any effect on the result of the computation. This is illustrated by the following example, where we assume to have lambda-abstractions in the core calculus.

$$[;;y:2 \mid ([;;x:1 \mid \lambda z.1+y] + [;Z:0;]) \uparrow] \stackrel{\text{(res-extract)}}{\longrightarrow}$$
$$[;;y:2 \mid \lambda z.1+y]$$

If the program is a value still containing some variables bound at the current configuration level, these variables must be resolved before extracting the value. This is handled by rule (res-var), where we write $v[x]$ to denote a value which contains a free occurrence of x, and, analogously to the notation used for evaluation contexts, $v\{e\}$ to denote the expression obtained by replacing this occurrence by e. The effect we want to obtain is that the action needed to solve variable x is triggered (x is replaced by its definition if it is either local or virtual, and the innermost module operator in $\mathcal{R}$ is performed if x is deferred). For sake of brevity, we write just one compact rule instead of five rules analogous to those which handle resolution of a variable x in a program which is not a value (hence can be decomposed as $\mathcal{E}[x]$), that is, (local), (virtual), (sum), (freeze) and (del). In order to have a deterministic reduction strategy, we assume some arbitrary rule for selecting one among all the occurences of variables in $\mathsf{dom}(\iota, \rho)$[3], that is, for decomposing a value containing free variables in $\mathsf{dom}(\iota, \rho)$ as $v[x]$.
The effect of rule (res-var) is illustrated by the following example.

[3] For instance, the leftmost innermost occurrence.

$$[;;y:2 \mid ([;;x:1 \mid \lambda z.x+y] + [;Z:0;]) \uparrow] \uparrow \xrightarrow{\text{(res-var)}}$$
$$[;;y:2 \mid ([;;x:1 \mid \lambda z.1+y] + [;Z:0;]) \uparrow] \uparrow \xrightarrow{\text{(res-extract)}}$$
$$[;;y:2 \mid \lambda z.1+y] \uparrow \xrightarrow{\text{(res-var)}}$$
$$[;;y:2 \mid \lambda z.1+2] \uparrow \xrightarrow{\text{(res-extract)}}$$
$$\lambda z.1+2$$

Relation with CMS and CMS^{ℓ}. Apart from the selection operator, *CMS* corresponds to the subset of the calculus obtained by only taking basic modules, module operators (sum, reduct and freeze) and corresponding rules (m-sum), (m-reduct) and (m-freeze). Selection can be simulated by using the run and result operator (see Section 4.1). CMS^{ℓ}corresponds to the subset obtained by taking basic modules and module operators, basic configurations and the run operator in a non higher-order setting (that is, components of modules and configurations can only be core terms), hence there is no result operator. Moreover, no access to virtual variables is supported (formally, there is no rule (virtual)). This leads to a confluent calculus under the hypothesis that the core calculus is confluent as well; in the calculus presented in this paper, instead, since definition of components may change by performing module operators, there are potentially different results depending on the time when module operators is performed. Hence, it is important to fix (and to assume at the core level as well) a deterministic strategy.

4 Expressive Power of the Calculus

In this section we show that $CMS^{\ell,v}$ is much more expressive than *CMS* and CMS^{ℓ}, and illustrate how it could serve as a formal basis for modeling some interesting mechanisms like marshaling and dynamic software update.

4.1 Module Selection

Module selection [13,23,21,7] allows the users to execute module components from the outside. Conventionally, this operation is permitted only for closed modules in order to avoid scope extrusion of variables which would lead to dynamic errors. For instance, in the ML-like module systems, selection is allowed for structures but not for functors. In *CMS* selection takes the usual syntactic form $e.X$, where e is a module expression and X is a component name. The corresponding reduction rule can be applied only when e is a basic mixin module $[\iota; o; \rho]$ where ι is empty (hence, the module is closed), and X is in the domain of o. If so, the corresponding expression $o(X)$ is extracted out of the module, and all variables in the domain of ρ possibly occurring free in $o(X)$ are replaced, following the usual unfolding semantics for mutually recursive declarations.

CMS selection can be encoded as a derived operation in $CMS^{\ell,v}$ by means of the $\_\downarrow_X$ and $\_\uparrow$ operators.

Consider for instance, the *CMS* expression $[;X : x; x : 1].X$, where we select an output component from a basic module. This expression can be encoded in $CMS^{\ell v}$ as $[;X : x; x : 1] \downarrow_X \uparrow$, which in one step reduces to the basic configuration $[;X : x; x : 1 \mid x] \uparrow$. In this way, the defining expression of the selected component can be executed within the context offered by other definitions inside the module and extracted only when it does no longer depends on them. In contrast to *CMS*, this semantics definition, besides being more perspicuous (no unfolding is needed), allows selection of open modules. For example, the expression $[y : Y; Z : y, X : x; x : 1].X$ is stuck in *CMS*, while here reduces to the expected value 1.

4.2 Static and Dynamic Rebinding of Virtual Components

The *CMS* calculus supports redefinition of virtual components, a feature analogous to method overriding in object-oriented languages. To see this, let us consider a simple example written in a hypothetical module language with virtual components, whose semantics can be easily expressed in terms of $CMS^{\ell v}$.

```
M1 = module {
 virtual X=1;
 virtual Y=X+1;
}
```

Here `X` and `Y` are the names of the two externally visible components of `M1`. The semantics of `M1` is given by translation into the following basic module:

$$M_1 = [x : X, y : Y; X : 1, Y : x + 1;]$$

As already explained in the previous section, the two components X and Y cannot be selected in *CMS* as they are, but in order to do that, they first need to be frozen with the $\mathsf{freeze}_{\_}$ operator which permanently binds their values to the corresponding variables x and y (which become local).

$$\mathsf{freeze}_X \mathsf{freeze}_Y [x : X, y : Y; X : 1, Y : x + 1;] \longrightarrow [;X : 1, Y : x + 1; x : 1, y : x+1]$$

Then, X and Y can be selected obtaining respectively 1 and 2, as expected.

However, before being frozen, virtual components can be redefined by means of the overriding operator, which can be expressed as a combination of the delete and sum operators at the lower level. For instance, the expression

```
M2 = M1 <- module {virtual X=2;}
```

translates into the lower level expression

$$M_2 = M_1 \setminus_X + [x : X; X : 2;]$$

which reduces to $[x : X, x' : X, y : Y; X : 2, Y : x + 1;]$.

After freezing, if we select Y, then we get 3 rather than 2; hence, the modification of the virtual component X has affected Y as well, whose definition depends on X. In other words, the variable x associated with X has been *rebound*. However, in *CMS* such a rebinding is always *static* rather than *dynamic*, in the sense that it can never happen that a variable of a module is rebound during the execution of a component of the same module.

In fact, in *CMS* the module operators model static configuration of software fragments (as the conventional static linking), whereas selection corresponds to execution, and there is no way to interleave configuration and execution phases for a given module. In CMS^{ℓ} linking can take place at execution time, but the program cannot use virtual components. Hence a needed component must be linked in order to be available, and then there is no way to change its definition. In contrast, $CMS^{\ell,v}$ supports *dynamic* rebinding of virtual components. This is possible because execution and configuration phases can be interleaved, and the program can use virtual components.

For instance, consider the following expression (in the higher level language):

```
result(module { E=X+Y+X; virtual X=1; } with main E <-
       module { virtual X=2; virtual Y=X+1; })
```

where the left hand side of the overriding operator `<-` is a configuration whose program is the non virtual (that is, frozen) component `E`, the right hand side lazily overrides the configuration, and **`result`** is the higher level syntax for the operator $\_\uparrow$. By considering the corresponding translation at the lower level, the reader may verify that the first occurrence of `X` in the definition of `E` reduces to 1, whereas the second to 2, and that the overall expression reduces to 6.

$$[x : X, y : Y; X : 1, E : x + y + x;] \downarrow_E \backslash_X + [x : X, y : Y; X : 2, Y : x + 1;] \uparrow$$

4.3 Dynamic Rebinding for Marshaling and Update

Since $CMS^{\ell,v}$ supports dynamic rebinding, it provides a natural formal basis for modeling marshaling and update.

Consider again an example in our hypothetical higher level language:

```
M3 = module {
  virtual X=1;
          Y=2;
          Z=3;
}
with main marshal X+Y+X+Z rebind Y;
```

In the definition of the main expression of `M3`, the expression to be marshaled depends on three different components, already defined in the scope of the main; however, when marshaling an expression e, the user may specify a list of components which have to be rebound when e will be eventually unmarshaled. In this specific case, for correctly unmarshaling the value returned by the execution of `M3`, a new definition for `Y` must be provided, whereas for `X`, `Z` this is left to choice, as in the following example:

```
M2=unmarshal result(M3) bind Y:4,X:5,Z:6;
```

We can now show how the marshal and unmarshal expressions above could be translated into the lower level calculus $CMS^{\ell,v}$. For marshaling we have:

$$e_3 = \mathsf{marshal}([x : X, y : Y; X : 1, Z : z; z : 3 \mid x + y + x + z])$$

The translation is based on the following basic idea: the expression e to be marshaled is packaged with a basic module into a configuration $[\iota; o; \rho \mid e']$, where e' is a suitable translation of e, and $[\iota; o; \rho]$ is obtained from the current context by making deferred all components which have to be rebound. Then, the marshal constructor can be applied to the resulting configuration.[4]
In the running example, the module corresponding to the current context of the `main` expression is

$$[x : X; X : 1, Y : y, Z : z; y : 2, z : 3]$$

However, since `Y` must be rebound, its definition is removed and its variable becomes deferred.

For unmarshaling, the corresponding lower level expression is:

$$e_2 = (\mathsf{unmarshal}(e_3)\backslash_X \backslash_Z + [; Y : 4, X : 5, Z : 6;])\uparrow$$

where $[; Y : 4, X : 5, Z : 6;]$ is obtained from the binding specified by the unmarshal operator. Since e_3 is closed, $\mathsf{unmarshal}(e_3)$ reduces to $[x : X, y : Y; X : 1, Z : z; z : 3 \mid x + y + x + z]$. Therefore e_2 reduces to

$$([x : X, y : Y; X : 1, Z : z; z : 3 \mid x + y + x + z]\backslash_X \backslash_Z + [; Y : 4, X : 5, Z : 6;])\uparrow$$

Now, in the expression $x + y + x + z$, the first occurrence of x is bound to 1; then, since y is needed, the delete and sum operators are performed, hence y is bound to 4, and the value of X is overriden, hence the second occurrence of x is bound to 5. Finally, z is bound to 3 (the overriding of Z has no effect).

The example illustrates that the representation of marshaled values as $CMS^{\ell,v}$ configurations allows to code in a natural way different requirements for unmarshaling. If there is an explicit `rebind` directive in marshaling, as for `Y`, then `Y` must be provided since it is undefined (deferred) in the marshaled expression. If there is no `rebind` directive, as for `X` and `Z`, then the latest available versions of `X` and `Z` can be provided in order to update the marshaled code in case it contains obsolete versions. However, while the update of `X` (which is virtual) might be reflected into a rebinding of some occurrence of `X` inside the unmarshaled expression, the update of `Z` (which is frozen) has no effects on the evaluation of the inner expression; this is an import feature which provides a protection mechanism against unwanted software update. Finally, note that the update of `X` is lazy (only the second occurrence of x is updated).

[4] The constructor marshal and the corresponding destructor unmarshal must be introduced in the lower level calculus for distinguishing between marshaled and ordinary values.

We have shown above just some simple examples; the definition of a worked out higher-level language based on $CMS^{\ell,v}$ with marshaling and unmarshaling operators, including more convenient and practical mechanisms for obtaining the configuration to be packaged with the marshaled expression, as the **mark** operator in [10], remains an important subject of further work. However, we believe the examples above are enough to give the flavour of how marshaling mechanisms (where the expression to be marshaled needs to be packaged together with some of the currently available bindings, and needs to be abstracted w.r.t. the components that have to be rebound) could be expressed in a natural way by the notions of basic module (abstractions plus bindings) and configuration (expression packaged with a basic module) provided by $CMS^{\ell,v}$.

5 Type System

In this section we present a type system for $CMS^{\ell,v}$ which prevents reduction from getting stuck.

Types have the following form:

$$\begin{array}{lll} \tau \in \mathsf{Type} & ::= c\tau \mid [\pi^\iota; \pi^o; \tau^\bullet] \\ \tau^\bullet \in \mathsf{Type}^\bullet & ::= \tau \mid \bullet \end{array}$$

Core types are ranged over by $c\tau$. Module types are as in *CMS*, that is, pairs $[\pi^\iota; \pi^o; \bullet]$ where $\pi^\iota, \pi^o : \mathsf{Name} \xrightarrow{fin} \mathsf{Type}$ are the *input* and *output signature*, respectively. Configuration types have the form $[\pi^\iota; \pi^o; \tau]$: the first two components have the same meaning as for module types, whereas τ is the type of the program running in the configuration.

Fig.4 gives the typing rules for deriving judgments of the form $\Gamma \vdash e : \tau$, meaning "e is a well-formed expression of type τ in the environment Γ", where $\Gamma : \mathsf{Var} \xrightarrow{fin} \mathsf{Type}$.

The definition of the type system is parametric in the typing rules for the core level.

In rule (m-basic) and (basic), $\_[\_]$ denotes environment updating. In the side-condition of these rules, we check that virtual names have the same types in the input and the output signatures (recall that the notation $f|g$ means that f and g agree on the common domain).

The (sum) typing rules allow sharing of input components having the same name and type, while preventing output components from being shared (recall that $f_1 \cup f_2$ denotes the union of two compatible partial functions, while f_1, f_2 denotes the union of two maps with disjoint domain). Moreover, we check that names that will become virtual performing the sum will have the same types in both the (resulting) input and the output signatures.

In rule (basic) and (res) the judgment $\vdash \tau \diamond$ means "τ is a closed type". A closed type is either a core or module type, or a configuration type with no deferred components, as formally defined in Fig.5.

Intuitively, (ground) terms of closed types are those which can be safely used in isolation, since they do not depend on any missing variable or component.

... (rules for core operators)

$$\text{(m-basic)}\ \frac{\begin{array}{c}\{\Gamma[\Gamma^\iota,\Gamma^\rho] \vdash o(X) : \pi^o(X) \mid X \in \mathsf{dom}(o)\} \\ \{\Gamma[\Gamma^\iota,\Gamma^\rho] \vdash \rho(x) : \Gamma^\rho(x) \mid x \in \mathsf{dom}(\rho)\}\end{array}}{\Gamma \vdash [\iota; o; \rho] : [\pi^\iota; \pi^o; \bullet]} \quad \begin{array}{l}\mathsf{dom}(\pi^\iota) = \mathsf{img}(\iota) \\ \mathsf{dom}(\pi^o) = \mathsf{dom}(o) \\ \Gamma^\iota = \pi^\iota \circ \iota \\ \mathsf{dom}(\Gamma^\rho) = \mathsf{dom}(\rho) \\ \pi^\iota | \pi^o\end{array}$$

$$\text{(basic)}\ \frac{\begin{array}{l}\{\Gamma[\Gamma^\iota,\Gamma^\rho] \vdash o(X) : \pi^o(X) \mid X \in \mathsf{dom}(o)\} \\ \{\Gamma[\Gamma^\iota,\Gamma^\rho] \vdash \rho(x) : \Gamma^\rho(x) \mid x \in \mathsf{dom}(\rho)\} \quad \Gamma[\Gamma^\iota,\Gamma^\rho] \vdash e : \tau\end{array}}{\Gamma \vdash [\iota; o; \rho \mid e] : [\pi^\iota; \pi^o; \tau]} \quad \begin{array}{l}\mathsf{dom}(\pi^\iota) = \mathsf{img}(\iota) \\ \mathsf{dom}(\pi^o) = \mathsf{dom}(o) \\ \Gamma^\iota = \pi^\iota \circ \iota \\ \mathsf{dom}(\Gamma^\rho) = \mathsf{dom}(\rho) \\ \pi^\iota | \pi^o \text{ and } \vdash \tau \diamond\end{array}$$

$$\text{(sum)}\ \frac{\begin{array}{c}\Gamma \vdash e_1 : [\pi^\iota{}_1;\ \pi^o{}_1;\ \tau^\bullet] \\ \Gamma \vdash e_2 : [\pi^\iota{}_2;\ \pi^o{}_2;\ \bullet]\end{array}}{\Gamma \vdash e_1 + e_2 : [\pi^\iota{}_1 \cup \pi^\iota{}_2;\ \pi^o{}_1, \pi^o{}_2;\ \tau^\bullet]} \quad \pi^\iota{}_1 \cup \pi^\iota{}_2 | \pi^o{}_1, \pi^o{}_2$$

$$\text{(del)}\ \frac{\Gamma \vdash e : [\pi^\iota;\ \pi^o;\ \tau^\bullet]}{\Gamma \vdash e\backslash_X : [\pi^\iota;\ \pi^o\backslash_X;\ \tau^\bullet]} \quad X \in \mathsf{dom}(\pi^o)$$

$$\text{(freeze)}\ \frac{\Gamma \vdash e : [\pi^\iota;\ \pi^o;\ \tau^\bullet]}{\Gamma \vdash \mathsf{freeze}_X e : [\pi^\iota{}_2\backslash_X;\ \pi^o;\ \tau^\bullet]} \quad X \in \mathsf{dom}(\pi^\iota) \Rightarrow X \in \mathsf{dom}(\pi^o)$$

$$\text{(run)}\ \frac{\Gamma \vdash e : [\pi^\iota;\ \pi^o;\ \bullet]}{\Gamma \vdash e{\downarrow_X} : [\pi^\iota;\ \pi^o;\ \pi^o(X)]} \quad \vdash \pi^o(X) \diamond$$

$$\text{(res)}\ \frac{\Gamma \vdash e : [\pi^\iota;\ \pi^o;\ \tau]}{\Gamma \vdash e{\uparrow} : \tau} \quad \vdash [\pi^\iota;\ \pi^o;\ \tau] \diamond$$

Fig. 4. Typing rules

$$\frac{}{\vdash c\tau \diamond} \qquad \frac{}{\vdash [\pi^\iota;\ \pi^o;\ \bullet] \diamond} \qquad \frac{}{\vdash [\pi^\iota;\ \pi^o;\ \tau] \diamond}\ \pi^\iota \subseteq \pi^o$$

Fig. 5. Closed types

Formally, we state the progress property only on these terms. The reason for requiring that the program in a basic configuration and the argument of a result operator are of closed type is that in both cases the term is inserted in a context where no more reconfiguration operators are applied, hence, in case it is a configuration term whose program needs a deferred variable, this will never be provided. For instance, the term $[y : Y;; \mid y]$ is a well-typed term of (non-closed) type, which can be for instance inserted in the context $\Box + [; Y : 0;]$ giving a safe term which reduces to the value $[y : Y; Y : 0; \mid 0]$. However, the terms of the form $[\iota; o; \rho \mid [y : Y;; \mid y]]$ and the term $[y : Y;; \mid y] \uparrow$ are ill-formed since they give a stuck computation in whichever context they are inserted, since there is no way to provide component Y to the program.

6 Results

In this section we illustrate the properties of the type system of $CMS^{\ell,v}$. For space limitations, all proof have been omitted, together with the results on the determinacy of the reduction relation; however, they are available in an extended version of this paper.[5]

In general, all the results we state hold under the assumption that (roughly speaking) they are verified at the core level as well. This assumption is formally detailed for each case.

The type system guarantees that the reduction relation does not get stuck on ground terms of closed type (progress property) and preserves types (subject reduction property).

In order to prove these results, we need the following lemmas, which can be proved by induction on the typing rules under the assumption that, for each core typing rule, if the property holds for the premises, then it holds for the consequence as well.

Lemma 1 (Weakening). *If $\Gamma \vdash e : \tau$ and $\Gamma \subseteq \Gamma'$, then $\Gamma' \vdash e : \tau$.*

Lemma 2 (Strengthening). *If $\Gamma \vdash e : \tau$, $\Gamma' \subseteq \Gamma$, and $\mathsf{FV}(e) \subseteq \mathsf{dom}(\Gamma')$, then $\Gamma' \vdash e : \tau$.*

Lemma 3 (Substitution). *If $\Gamma \vdash \mathcal{E}[x] : \tau$, $\Gamma(x) = \tau_x$ and $\Gamma \vdash e : \tau_x$, then $\Gamma \vdash \mathcal{E}\{e\} : \tau$.*

Lemma 4 (Canonical Forms). *Given $v \in \mathsf{Val}$,*

- *if $\Gamma \vdash v : c\tau$, then v is a core value;*
- *if $\Gamma \vdash v : [\pi^\iota; \pi^o; \bullet]$, then v has the form $[\iota; o; \rho]$;*
- *if $\Gamma \vdash v : [\pi^\iota; \pi^o; \tau]$, then v has the form $\mathcal{R}[\iota; o; \rho \mid v']$, and $\Gamma[\Gamma^\iota][\Gamma^\rho] \vdash v' : \tau$, with $\mathsf{dom}(\Gamma^\iota) = \mathsf{dom}(\iota)$ and $\mathsf{dom}(\Gamma^\rho) = \mathsf{dom}(\rho)$.*

In the standard formulation, soundness of a type system is shown by separately proving subject reduction and progress property. Subject reduction (preservation of type under reduction) holds for all well-typed terms, whereas progress only holds for terms which can be seen as "executable", that is, can be safely reduced in isolation. Usually, executable terms correspond to ground terms, that is, terms without free variables. Terms with free variables represent open code fragments, which cannot be safely reduced, but are still well-typed since they can be safely used as subterms of an executable program.

In $CMS^{\ell,v}$, the progress property holds on terms that are not only ground, but also of a closed type, that is, a type with no deferred components. However, terms of non-closed types are still well typed, since they can be inserted inside contexts providing all needed components.

Theorem 1 (Subject Reduction). *If $\Gamma \vdash e : \tau$ and $e \longrightarrow e'$, then $\Gamma \vdash e' : \tau$ under the assumption that, for each core reduction rule, if the property holds for the premises, then it holds for the consequence as well.*

[5] `ftp://ftp.disi.unige.it/pub/person/AnconaD/MMDRlong.pdf`

The progress property follows as a corollary of a *generalized progress* property, which states that a well-typed term can get stuck for two reasons: either it contains some free variable (in which case, intuitively, execution could proceed by replacing this variable) or it is a basic configuration whose program needs a deferred component which is not available (in which case, intuitively, execution could proceed by providing this component.)

Theorem 2. *If $\Gamma \vdash e : \tau$, then one of the following cases holds*

- $e \in \mathsf{Val}$
- $e \longrightarrow e'$, *for some* $e' \in \mathsf{Exp}$,
- $e = \mathcal{E}[x]$, $x \notin \mathsf{HB}(\mathcal{E})$, $x \in \mathsf{dom}(\Gamma)$,
- $e = [\iota; o; \rho \mid \mathcal{E}[x]]$, *with* $x \notin \mathsf{HB}(\mathcal{E}), x \in \mathsf{dom}(\iota)$ *and* $\iota(x) \notin \mathsf{dom}(o)$
under the assumption that, for each core typing rule, if the property holds for the premises, then it holds for the consequence as well.

Corollary 1 (Progress). *If* $\emptyset \vdash e : \tau$ *and* $\vdash \tau \diamond$, *then either* $e \in \mathsf{Val}$ *or* $e \longrightarrow e'$, *for some* $e' \in \mathsf{Exp}$.

7 Conclusion

We have presented a module calculus $CMS^{\ell,v}$ which allows to express in a natural way rebinding through the notion of *virtual component*, and to make this rebinding dynamic by allowing standard program execution to be interleaved with reconfiguration steps. We have illustrated the expressive power of the calculus and provided a sound type system.

This work is part a stream of research [4,6,5,16] whose aim is the development of foundational calculi providing an abstract framework for dynamic software reconfiguration. In particular, the possibility of extending module calculi with selection on open modules, interleaving of component evaluation with reconfiguration steps and a lazy strategy has been firstly explored in [6]. As already explained, the calculus presented in this paper contains two key novelties.

First, $CMS^{\ell,v}$ allows the executing program to use *virtual* variables; this provides a natural mechanism for rebinding, which greatly enhances the expressive power. Indeed, execution can refer to components whose definition may change by performing module operators, leading potentially to different results depending on the time when module operators is performed, that is, before or after accessing a virtual variable. This is avoided here by taking a deterministic strategy which performs substitution of local/virtual variables and resolution (by reconfiguration steps) of deferred variables only on demand.

Then, higher-order configurations, together with the run and result operators, allow to express interaction of execution at different levels (e.g., modules with module or configuration components, starting a local configuration level inside program execution, a scoping mechanism for nested variable resolution and triggering of reconfiguration steps).

In [5] we have investigated how to increase flexibility in a different direction, that is, by allowing a limited form of swapping between module operators. Finally, Fagorzi's thesis [16] provides a comprehensive presentation of most part of this work, and, moreover, the definition of a pure[6] reconfiguration calculus called R, in two versions which either allow or not to use virtual variables. This calculus is confluent in the non-virtual version, and a comparative discussion on different possible type systems is also given.

On the theoretical side, the ideas presented in this paper look similar to those at the basis of literature on laziness in functional calculi (see, e.g., [8]) and dynamic binding. In particular, some recent work on dynamic rebinding [10] presents a call-by-value λ-calculus which delays instantiation of identifiers, in such a way that computations can use the most recent versions of rebound definitions. It is well-known that record-based calculi can provide an alternative computational paradigm where λ-calculus can be encoded [1,7]. In our work, we are firstly exploring laziness (obtained by delaying record composition after selection) in this alternative paradigm. The advantages offered by the record-based paradigm are a natural syntactic representation of a scope (a record, or basic module in the terminology of this paper) and a built-in mechanism for rebinding (by deleting and then adding record component) without any need of introducing imperative features at the core level.

Hence, a very interesting subject of further work is a formal comparison with laziness obtained by delaying application in functional calculi. A preliminary attempt in this direction is in [17], where we outline a call-by-need strategy for R(in the non-virtual version) which smoothly generalizes the approach in [8] where an expression is evaluated the first time it is needed and only once.

On a more applicative side, though the area of unanticipated software evolution continues attracting large interest, with its foundations studied in, e.g., [22], there is a little amount of work going toward the development of abstract models for dynamic linking and updating. Apart from the wide literature concerning concrete dynamic linking mechanisms in existing programming environments [14,15], we mention [9], which presents a simple calculus modeling dynamic software updating, where modules are just records, many versions of the same module may coexist and update is modeled by an external transition which can be enforced by an `update` primitive in code, [2], where dynamic linking is studied as the programming language counterpart of the axiom of choice, and the module system defined in [20], where static linking, dynamic linking and cross-computation communication are all defined in a uniform framework.

Further work includes, as already mentioned, a deeper investigation of the relation with lazy lambda-calculi, and the further development of the techniques for encoding dynamic rebinding, marshaling and update outlined in Sect.4. The expressive power of lazy module calculi should also be analyzed by showing which kind of real-world reconfiguration mechanisms can be modeled and which kind require a richer model. Finally, an important issue is the integration with

---

[6] That is, with no fixed strategy.

mobility aspects, that is, the design of calculi for reconfiguration where, roughly speaking, code to be used for reconfiguring the running program can migrate from a different process.

References

1. M. Abadi and L. Cardelli. *A Theory of Objects*. Monographs in Computer Science. Springer, 1996.
2. Martin Abadi, Goerges Gonthier, and Benjamin Werner. Choice in dynamic linking. In *FOSSACS'04 - Foundations of Software Science and Computation Structures 2004*, Lecture Notes in Computer Science, pages 12–26. Springer, 2004.
3. D. Ancona, C. Anderson, F. Damiani, S. Drossopoulou, P. Giannini, and E. Zucca. A type preserving translation of Fickle into Java. *Electonical Notes in Theoretical Computer Science*, 62, 2002.
4. D. Ancona, S. Fagorzi, and E. Zucca. A calculus for dynamic linking. In C. Blundo and C. Laneve, editors, *Italian Conf. on Theoretical Computer Science 2003*, number 2841 in Lecture Notes in Computer Science, pages 284–301, 2003.
5. D. Ancona, S. Fagorzi, and E. Zucca. A calculus for dynamic reconfiguration with low priority linking. *Electonical Notes in Theoretical Computer Science*, 2004. In WOOD'04: Workshop on Object-Oriented Developments. To appear.
6. D. Ancona, S. Fagorzi, and E. Zucca. A calculus with lazy module operators. In Jean-Jacques Levy, Ernst W. Mayr, and John C. Mitchell, editors, *TCS 2004 (IFIP Int. Conf. on Theoretical Computer Science)*, pages 423–436. Kluwer Academic Publishers, 2004.
7. D. Ancona and E. Zucca. A calculus of module systems. *Journ. of Functional Programming*, 12(2):91–132, 2002.
8. Z. M. Ariola and M.Felleisen. The call-by-need lambda calculus. *Journ. of Functional Programming*, 7(3):265–301, 1997.
9. G. Bierman, M. Hicks, P. Sewell, and G. Stoyle. Formalizing dynamic software updating (Extended Abstract). In *USE'03 - the Second International Workshop on Unanticipated Software Evolution*, 2003.
10. G. Bierman, M. Hicks, P. Sewell, G. Stoyle, and K. Wansbrough. Dynamic rebinding for marshalling and update, with destruct-time λ. In C. Runciman and O. Shivers, editors, *Intl. Conf. on Functional Programming 2003*, pages 99–110. ACM Press, 2004.
11. G. Bracha. *The Programming Language JIGSAW: Mixins, Modularity and Multiple Inheritance*. PhD thesis, Department of Comp. Sci., Univ. of Utah, 1992.
12. L. Cardelli. Program fragments, linking, and modularization. In *ACM Symp. on Principles of Programming Languages 1997*, pages 266–277. ACM Press, 1997.
13. L. Cardelli and X. Leroy. Abstract types and the dot notation. Technical Report 56, DEC SRC, 1990.
14. S. Drossopoulou. Towards an abstract model of Java dynamic linking and verfication. In R. Harper, editor, *TIC'00 - Third Workshop on Types in Compilation (Selected Papers)*, volume 2071 of *Lecture Notes in Computer Science*, pages 53–84. Springer, 2001.
15. S. Drossopoulou, G. Lagorio, and S. Eisenbach. Flexible models for dynamic linking. In Pierpaolo Degano, editor, *ESOP 2003 - European Symposium on Programming 2003*, pages 38–53, April 2003.

16. S. Fagorzi. *Module Calculi for Dynamic Reconfiguration.* PhD thesis, Dipartimento di Informatica e Scienze dell'Informazione, Università di Genova, 2005.
17. S. Fagorzi and E. Zucca. A calculus for reconfiguration. In *DCM 2005 - International Workshop on Developments in Computational Models*, July 2005. To appear.
18. Matthias Felleisen and Daniel P. Friedman. Control operators, the SECD-machine, and the lambda-calculus. In *3rd Working Conference on the Formal Description of Programming Concepts*, pages 193–219, Ebberup, Denmark, August 1986.
19. T. Hirschowitz and X. Leroy. Mixin modules in a call-by-value setting. In D. Le Métayer, editor, *ESOP 2002 - European Symposium on Programming 2002*, number 2305 in Lecture Notes in Computer Science, pages 6–20. Springer, 2002.
20. Y. D. Liu and S. F. Smith. Modules with interfaces for dynamic linking and communication. In M. Odersky, editor, *ECOOP'04 - Object-Oriented Programming*, number 3086 in Lecture Notes in Computer Science, pages 414–439. Springer, 2004.
21. E. Machkasova and F.A. Turbak. A calculus for link-time compilation. In *ESOP 2000 - European Symposium on Programming 2000*, number 1782 in Lecture Notes in Computer Science, pages 260–274. Springer, 2000.
22. Tom Mens and Guenther Kniesel. Workshop on foundations of unanticipated software evolution. ETAPS 2004, http://joint.org/fuse2004/, 2004.
23. J. B. Wells and R. Vestergaard. Confluent equational reasoning for linking with first-class primitive modules. In *ESOP 2000 - European Symposium on Programming 2000*, number 1782 in Lecture Notes in Computer Science, pages 412–428. Springer, 2000.

A Distributed Object-Oriented Language with Session Types*

Mariangiola Dezani-Ciancaglini[1], Nobuko Yoshida[2], Alexander Ahern[2], and Sophia Drossopoulou[2]

[1] Dipartimento di Informatica, Università di Torino
[2] Department of Computing, Imperial College London

Abstract. In the age of the world-wide web and mobile computing, programming communication-centric software is essential. Thus, programmers and program designers are exposed to new levels of complexity, such as ensuring the correct composition of communication behaviours and guaranteeing deadlock-freedom of their protocols.

This paper proposes the language $\mathcal{L}_{doos}$, a simple distributed object-oriented language augmented with session communication primitives and types. $\mathcal{L}_{doos}$ provides a flexible object-oriented programming style for structural interaction protocols by prescribing channel usages within signatures of distributed classes.

We develop a typing system for $\mathcal{L}_{doos}$ and prove its soundness with respect to the operational semantics. We also show that in a well-typed $\mathcal{L}_{doos}$ program, there will never be a connection error, a communication error, nor an incorrect completion between server-client interactions. These results demonstrate that a consistent integration of object-oriented language features and session types can statically check the consistent composition of communication protocols.

1 Introduction

In distributed systems, physically separated (and potentially mobile) computational entities cooperate or compete by passing code and data to one another. Existing theoretical foundations, which have been successful in sequential programming (as structured programming [9] and type disciplines for programming languages [23]) require non-trivial extensions for the distributed setting. Several new issues arise in this setting, including how to structure communication-based software, how to guarantee security concerns such as confidentiality and integrity, and how to identify correct behaviour of concurrent programs so that we can safely discuss (for example) optimisation of distributed software.

The scenario we are considering in the present paper is a set of users at different locations interacting by means of *object-oriented* code. Distributed objects are one of the most popular programming paradigms in today's computing environments [20], naturally extending the sequential message-passing-oriented paradigm of objects. In current

* Work partially supported by the Royal Society, by EU within the FET - Global Computing initiative, project DART IST-2001-33477, and by EPSRC Advanced Fellowship (GR/T03208/01) and EPSRC GR/R33465/02, GR/S55538/01 and GR/T04724/01.

R. De Nicola and D. Sangiorgi (Eds.): TGC 2005, LNCS 3705, pp. 299–318, 2005.

practice, however, code is often written in terms of bare socket-based communications [21]; it consists of isolated method invocations and returns, and there is no way to ascertain that the code conforms to the intended structure of interaction.

Therefore, the quest for frameworks to enable the expression of *structured interaction*, and for ways to assure the safety of the resulting *interaction protocols* based on that structure, are concerns of paramount importance.

Session types, first introduced in [15], can specify protocols of communication by describing the sequence and types of entities read on a channel. For example, the session type !**int**.!**int**.?**bool**.**end** expresses that two **int**-values will be sent, then a **bool**-value is expected as an input, and finally that the protocol is completed. Thus, session types provide a natural way to specify the communication behaviour of a piece of software, and allow verification that several pieces of software are safely composed.

Session types have been widely used to describe protocols in different settings, *i.e.* for π-calculus-based formalisms [4, 5, 13, 15, 17, 25], for CORBA [26], for a λ-calculus with side-effects [14], for a multi-threaded functional language [27], and recently, for a W3C standard description language for web services called Choreography Description Language (CDL) [29]. To our knowledge, the integration of session types into an object-oriented language (even a small, core calculus, as in [3, 10, 18]) has not been attempted so far.

In the present paper we argue that a seamless integration of class-based object-oriented programming and session types is possible, and that the resulting combination offers a powerful framework for writing safe, structured distributed applications with a formal foundation. We substantiate our proposal through the language $\mathcal{L}_{doos}$, a *Distributed Object-Oriented language with Session types*.

By extending class and method signatures to include the types of sessions, we achieved a clean integration of session types into the class based, object-oriented paradigm. Through a combination of remote method invocation (RMI), a standard distributed primitive in objects, session-based distributed primitives [17, 25] and linear interactions [16, 19], we obtained a flexible high-level programming style for remote communication. We also found that the functionality of branching and selection constructs in session types [4, 5, 13–15, 17, 25–27] can be compensated by methods, a natural notion of branching in objects. Subtyping on the branching types [13, 26] is, then, formalised through a standard inheritance mechanism.

Although we did not include branching and selection constructs in $\mathcal{L}_{doos}$, we did include a more specialized construction: conditional and iterative session types. For example, the conditional session type !**int**.!⟨?**char**, !**float**⟩.!**int**.**end** expresses that an integer will be sent followed by a boolean. If this boolean is true, then a character will be received, otherwise a float will be sent. Finally, an integer will be sent and the session will complete. Similarly, the iterative session type !**int**.!⟨?**char**.!**float**⟩*.!**int**.**end** expresses that an integer will be sent followed by a boolean. If this boolean is true, then a character will be received, and then a float will be sent, and the process will iterate until a false is sent. An integer will then be sent, and the session will complete. Such types allow us to express protocols that require conditionals or repetition on *the same channel*.

To focus on the introduction of session types, $\mathcal{L}_{doos}$ does not include language features such as exceptions [2], synchronisation, serialisation [1], class (down)loading [1, 11], code or agent mobility [1, 7, 28], polymorphism [6, 18, 27], recursive types [26] or correspondence assertions [4, 5]. We believe that the inclusion of such features into $\mathcal{L}_{doos}$ is possible, albeit not necessarily trivial.

A key point for the safety of session communication is channel linearity. To check linearity by typing in an imperative object-oriented setting where object fields can contain channels requires sophisticated types, see for example [12]. In $\mathcal{L}_{doos}$ channel linearity as in [4, 5, 13–15, 17, 25, 27] comes from creating a private fresh channel name every time a session starts. Typing then ensures that all communication in the current session uses this new channel, and that after the session is completed there are no further occurrences of this channel. In this way we also avoid the need to deal with opening and closing operations on channels [27].

Apart from guaranteeing that all communications have the expected types (soundness), our type system guarantees that in a a well-typed $\mathcal{L}_{doos}$ program, there will never be a connection error (*i.e.* request and accept on same channel will have the same type), nor a communication error (*i.e.* never two simultaneous send or receive on same channel), nor an incorrect completion between server-client interactions (*i.e.* after a session started, it will complete on each of the participants, unless there is an exception, or divergence, or an unsuccessful attempt to start a further session). Thus, the type system can statically check the consistent composition of communication protocols.

The soundness of our system is weaker than that of all systems of session types for π-calculus processes [4, 5, 13, 15, 17, 25]. In fact all these systems assure a perfect pairing between processes willing to communicate. This is obtained simply by checking the compatibility of type environments before putting processes in parallel. Our system instead, following the approach of [14, 27], only ensures that a communication will safely evolve *after starting*: there is no guarantee that processes ready to start a session will ever find a companion. It is not difficult to add to our system a compatibility check between environments to ensure the stronger soundness discussed above, but we chose to avoid it since our aim is to model an open distributed system where new processes can appear at run time, and so no global assumption on safety liveness can be guaranteed.

In the remainder, Section 2 illustrates the basic ideas of $\mathcal{L}_{doos}$ through an example. Section 3 defines the syntax of the language. Section 4 presents the operational semantics. Section 5 illustrates the typing system. Section 6 is devoted to basic theorems on type safety and communication safety. Section 7 concludes.

A preliminary version of this paper is [8].

2 Example

The following example demonstrates some of the features of $\mathcal{L}_{doos}$.[1] It describes a situation where a seller employs an agent to sell some item to some buyer for the best price possible:

[1] Note that in order to write our example more naturally we use several constructs which are not part of our minimum language $\mathcal{L}_{doos}$, *i.e.* types float and void, methods without parameters, local variables, and conditionals, which can easily be added to $\mathcal{L}_{doos}$.

The agent begins negotiations by asking the seller both the price and by the minimum price. Then the agent sends the price to the buyer. The buyer, upon receipt of this price, makes an offer which he sends to the agent. The agent calculates whether the offer exceeds the minimum price and notifies the seller and the buyer accordingly. If the offer does not exceed the minimum price then the agent invites the seller to lower his minimum price and the negotiation iterates. Note however that the agent may now communicate with a different buyer, but will continue communicating with the same seller.

The example consists of classes Agent, Buyer, and Seller, each of which we shall now discuss separately:

```
class Agent extends Object {
  float price, minPrice;      // seller's asking and minimum price
  float offer;                // the offer made by the buyer

   bool tryToSell () c1: !float.?float.!bool.end {
        // connect with a buyer
        request c1 : !float.?float.!bool.end {
             c1.send(price); offer := c1.receive; c1.send(offer<minPrice);
             return( offer <minPrice ); } }

  void mediate() c2: ?float.?float.!⟨?float⟩*.end {
        // connect with a seller
        request c2 ?float.?float.!⟨?float⟩*.end {
            price := c2.receive; minPrice := c2.receive;
             c2.sendWhile ( tryToSell() )
                  // if the value of tryToSell () is true
                  { minPrice := c2.receive; }    }}
}
```

The class Agent represents the agent, with fields price to store the asking price, and minPrice to store the minimum price. The signature of the method tryToSell contains the type of the channel c1, *i.e.* **!float.?float.!bool.end**, thus indicating that c1 will send one **float** value, will then receive a **float** value, and then send a **bool** value.

Indeed, in the body of this method, the agent asks for a connection with a buyer through a channel c1 by the statement **request** c1 ..., which must be matched by a statement **accept** c1 ... at another node in the network.

In general, **accept** u s{e} represents the creation of a new server-side socket as in the java.net.ServerSocket class. Here u can be either a public channel name c (as in line 6 of class Buyer) or a variable x whose value is a public channel name c. In both cases the name c is analogous to the port used to instantiate the ServerSocket, which is the port on which the server will listen for connections. Execution proceeds when another node in the network contains a statement **request** u′s{e′} where u′ is either the name c or a variable whose value is c. The statement **request** is similar to the creation of a new client-side socket from the java.net.Socket class. Here the name c can be thought of as corresponding to the hostname and port number of the server socket. When these match, execution continues and a new private channel is created to connect the two nodes. Execution of e and e′ proceeds concurrently, with all occurrences of u in e and all occurrences of u′ in e′ replaced by the name of the just created channel. So both public channel names and channel variables play the role of placeholders in session bodies, since they are replaced by restricted and fresh channel names.

In the method tryToSell, after the connection has been established, *i.e.* in the body of the **request** c1 ..., the agent sends the asking price (c1.**send**(price)), then receives the buyer offer along the same channel (offer := c1.**receive**). Lastly he compares the offer with the minimum price and then decides on behalf of the buyer whether the offer was successful, and tells the buyer through c1 (c1.**send**(offer < minPrice)).

The signature of the method mediate contains the type of channel c2, *i.e.* c2 : ?**float**.?**float**.!⟨?**float**⟩*.**end**, which is an *iterative* session type, and which indicates that c2 will receive two **float**s and then send a **bool**; it that boolean is true, it will iterate, otherwise it will be the end of the session. The body of method mediate asks for a connection through channel c2, receives the asking and the minimum price along that channel, and then attempts a sale using method tryToSell (which returns a boolean). It sends the value of tryToSell along channel c2 to the seller; if the value is true, then it iterates, by receiving a new asking price along channel c2.

```
class Buyer extends Object {
    float price;  //  seller's asking price
    float offer;  //  offer made by the buyer

    void buy() c1: !float.?float.!bool.end {
        accept c1 !float.?float.!bool.end {
        // connect with an agent
            price := c1.receive; offer :=....;    c1.send(offer);
            if c1.receive then .... else ... }  }
}
```

The class Buyer represents the buyer, with fields price, offer, with the obvious meaning. In the method buy, the buyer connects with some agent, receives the asking price, calculates his offer and send it. He then receives a boolean indicating whether the seller's agent accepted the bid, and proceeds with appropriate actions. The signature of the method buy contains the type of the channel c1, *i.e.* !**float**.?**float**.!**bool**.**end**. Notice that this type describes the session from the viewpoint of the Agent, which is dual to that of the Buyer.

The class Seller represents the seller, with fields price and minPrice for the asking and the minimum price. The type of the channel c2 in method sell is the same that in mediate in Agent.

The method sell starts by calculating the asking and minimum prices. After the connection on channel c2 is established, the seller sends the asking and minimum prices along the newly created channel. It then receives a boolean value indicating whether the negotiations need to continue. If so, then the seller will proceed with the body of the **receiveWhile** ... statement, and will calculate a new minimum price and send it on the same channel to the agent. This process is repeated until the seller receives false, *i.e.* until no more negotiations are required.

Our example demonstrates session types and in particular the use of branching and iterative session types to express repetition and conditional execution over the same channel. [2]

```
class Seller {
  float price ,minPrice;      // asking price and minimum price

  void sell ( ) c2: ?float.?float .! ⟨?float⟩*.end {
      price := ... ; minPrice:= ... ;
      // connect to an agent
      accept c2 ?float.?float .! ⟨?float⟩*.end {
          c2.send(price); c2.send(minPrice);
          c2.receiveWhile
            // if the value received is true, then
            { minPrice:= ... ; c2.send(minPrice); } }   }
}
```

The present example can be seen as a simplified object-oriented version of the Auctioneer example in [4]; the main difference is that the type system of [4] using correspondence assertions can detect bad behaviours which are type correct in our system.

Our type system guarantees the consistent composition of communication protocols of the various participants. Thus, it guarantees that:

- All communications have the expected types, *e.g.* in the method buy, in line 8 the expression c1.**receive** will return a **float**, while in line 9 the same expression will return a **bool**.
- There will never be a connection error, *e.g.* when line 13 of method mediate establishes a connection, it will only be with a channel of the appropriate type.
- There will never be a a communication error, *e.g.* when line 14 of method mediate performs c2.receive, there will not be a simultaneous **receive** on channel c2.
- There will never be an incorrect completion between server-client interactions, *e.g.* once the session in line 13 of mediate started, it will complete in each of the participants, unless there is an exception, or divergence. In particular notice that all iterations in line 15 will be successful.

3 A Distributed Object Oriented Language with Sessions

User syntax. We distinguish *user syntax*, for programs at a local node, and *runtime syntax*, which occurs only at runtime as intermediate forms. We introduce the user syntax in Fig. 3. It is an extension of FJ [18], MJ [3] and DJ [1] (while omitting the new distributed primitives introduced in [1]), augmented with primitives for session communication [5, 15, 17, 27].

[2] In earlier work [8] we had shown sessions as first class values, (*e.g.* objects containing session channels), assigning session values to session variables, session types carrying session types, and nesting of sessions. However these constructs are not sufficient to enforce repeated execution on the *same* channel.

(type)	$\mathsf{t} ::= C \mid \textbf{bool} \mid \mathsf{s}$
(direction)	$\dagger ::= \; ! \mid ?$
(part of session)	$\pi ::= \; \varepsilon \mid \dagger\mathsf{t} \mid \dagger\langle\pi,\pi\rangle \mid \dagger\langle\pi\rangle^{*} \mid \pi.\pi$
(session)	$\mathsf{s} ::= \; \pi.\textbf{end}$
(meth sig)	$\mathit{methSig} ::= \mathsf{t}\ \mathsf{m}\ (\mathsf{t})\ \Sigma$
(class sig)	$\mathsf{CSig} ::= \emptyset \mid \mathsf{CSig}, \textbf{class}\ C\ \textbf{extends}\ C\ \{\mathit{field}^{*}\ \mathit{methSig}^{*}\}$
(session env)	$\Sigma ::= \emptyset \mid \Sigma, \mathsf{c} : \mathsf{s}$
(class table)	$\mathsf{CT} ::= \emptyset \mid \mathsf{CT}, \mathit{class}$
(class)	$\mathit{class} ::= \textbf{class}\ C\ \textbf{extends}\ C\ \{\mathit{field}^{*}\ \mathit{meth}^{*}\}$
(field)	$\mathit{field} ::= \mathsf{f}\,\mathsf{t}$
(method)	$\mathit{meth} ::= \mathsf{t}\ \mathsf{m}\ (\mathsf{t}\ \mathsf{x})\ \Sigma\ \{\mathsf{e}\}$
(expression)	$\mathsf{e} ::= \mathsf{x} \mid \mathsf{v} \mid \mathsf{this} \mid \mathsf{true} \mid \mathsf{false}$
	$\mid \mathsf{e};\mathsf{e} \mid \textbf{new}\ C \mid \mathsf{x} := \mathsf{e} \mid \mathsf{e.f} := \mathsf{e} \mid \mathsf{e.f} \mid \mathsf{e.m(e)}$
	$\mid \mathsf{u}.\textbf{receive} \mid \mathsf{u}.\textbf{send}(\mathsf{e})$
	$\mid \mathsf{u}.\textbf{receiveIf}\{\mathsf{e}\}\{\mathsf{e}\} \mid \mathsf{u}.\textbf{sendIf}(\mathsf{e})\{\mathsf{e}\}\{\mathsf{e}\}$
	$\mid \mathsf{u}.\textbf{receiveWhile}\{\mathsf{e}\} \mid \mathsf{u}.\textbf{sendWhile}(\mathsf{e})\{\mathsf{e}\}$
	$\mid \textbf{request}\ \mathsf{u}\ \mathsf{s}\{\mathsf{e}\} \mid \textbf{accept}\ \mathsf{u}\ \mathsf{s}\{\mathsf{e}\}$
(identifier)	$\mathsf{u} ::= \mathsf{c} \mid \mathsf{x}$
(value)	$\mathsf{v} ::= \mathsf{null} \mid \mathsf{c}$

Fig. 1. User Syntax

The metavariable t ranges over types for channels and expressions, C ranges over class names, s ranges over session types. ? means *input*, while ! means *output*, and † ranges over $\{!,?\}$, while **end** indicates the end of the session.

The metavariable π describes *parts* of a session. The *conditional* session part $!\langle\pi_1,\pi_2\rangle$ sends a boolean value and proceeds with π_1 if the value is true, or π_2 if the value is false. Similarly $?\langle\pi_1,\pi_2\rangle$ receives a boolean value and proceeds with π_1 if the value is true, π_2 if it is false. The *iterative* session part $!\langle\pi_1\rangle^*$ sends a boolean value and if that value is true, continues with π_1, *iterating*. If the value sent is false, this session part finishes. The meaning of $?\langle\pi_1\rangle^*$ is similar. Note that, the closing of a session, **end**, cannot appear within a conditional or iterative session part. This supports the design principle that sessions have to be closed at the level where they were opened; in other words, the responsibility of closing a session stays with the party that opened it.

To prescribe the channel usage in a method, we introduce *session environments*, Σ, which map channels to session types. Method declarations have the shape

$$\mathsf{t}\,\mathsf{m}\ (\mathsf{t}\mathsf{x})\ \Sigma\ \{\mathsf{e}\}$$

which is standard, except for the addition of Σ.

A *Class signature*, CSig, denotes a class's interface [1]; it contains the types of fields, its superclass name and method signatures. This provides a lightweight mech-

$$
\begin{array}{lll}
\text{(type)} & \mathsf{t} ::= \ldots \mid \textbf{chan}\,(\mathsf{t}) \\
\text{(identifier)} & \mathsf{u} ::= \ldots \mid \mathsf{o} \\
\text{(value)} & \mathsf{v} ::= \ldots \mid \mathsf{o} \\
\text{(expression)} & \mathsf{e} ::= \ldots \mid \mathsf{NullExc} \\
\text{(thread)} & P ::= \mathsf{e} \mid P|P \\
\text{(store)} & \sigma ::= \emptyset \mid \sigma{\cdot}[x \mapsto \mathsf{v}] \mid \sigma{\cdot}[\mathsf{o} \mapsto (C, \vec{\mathsf{f}} : \vec{\mathsf{v}})] \\
\text{(network)} & N ::= \mathbf{0} \mid l[P, \sigma, \mathrm{CT}] \mid N \| N \mid (\nu \mathsf{u} : \mathsf{t}) N
\end{array}
$$

Fig. 2. Runtime Syntax

anism for determining the type of remote methods. We assume that CSig is available globally (this does not restrict generality, since in standard implementations uniqueness of each class is maintained through its digital signature). In contrast, class tables (containing method bodies) are maintained on a per-location basis.

The syntax of expressions, e, e′, is standard except for the four pairs of communication primitives. The first two lines express standard syntax, *i.e.* parameter, value, the receiver this, the literals true and false, sequence of expressions, object creation, assignment to parameters or fields, field access and method call. The next four lines describe the four communication pairs.

The first pair is for exchange of values or channels: u **.receive** receives a value or a channel via u, while u **.send** (e) first evaluates the expression e, then sends its result via u.

The second pair is for *conditional* communication: u **.receiveIf**{e}{e′} receives a value via u, and if it is true continues with e, otherwise with e′. The expression u **.sendIf** (e){e′}{e″} first evaluates the boolean expression e, then sends its result via u and if the result was true continues with e′, otherwise with e″.

The third pair is for *iterative* communication: u **.receiveWhile**{e} receives a value via u, and if it is true continues with e and iterates, otherwise ends. The expression u **.sendWhile** (e){e′} first evaluates the boolean expression e, then sends its result via u and if the result was true continues with e′ and iterates, otherwise ends.

The last pair is for establishing connections: **request** u s{e} is for use by clients, and **accept** u s{e} for use by servers. The channel u denotes a shared interaction point which is used for creating new channels. In both **request** ... s{e}, and **accept** ... s{e}, the term {e} (called *session body*) denotes the block of (a sequence of) expressions in which the new channel is created at the beginning, and discarded at the end; the session s prescribes the communication protocol, which is opened by **request** or **accept**.

Runtime Syntax. The runtime syntax in Fig. 3 extends the user syntax and represents a distributed state of multiple sites communicating with each other. The syntax uses *location names* $l, m, \ldots$ which can be thought of as IP addresses in a network.

Metavariable t is extended with *runtime channel types*, denoting the channel types used only for method invocations. Identifiers, u, and values, v, are extended to allow for object identifiers o, o′, ..., which denote references to instances of classes. We shall frequently write "o-id" for brevity, and we shall call o and c *names*. We extend expressions with NullExc, denoting a null-pointer error. *Threads* are ranged over by P, P', where $P \,|\, P'$ says that P and P' are running in parallel.

A store σ contains local variables and objects, and $\mathsf{f} : \mathsf{v}$ is short-hand for a sequence $\mathsf{f}_1 : \mathsf{v}_1; \ldots; \mathsf{f}_n : \mathsf{v}_n$. We apply similar abbreviations to other sequences [1, 18]. Sequences contain no duplicate names.

Networks, written N, comprise zero or more located configurations executing in parallel. We use $\mathbf{0}$ to denote the empty network, $l[P, \sigma, \mathtt{CT}]$ to denote the thread P executing at location l with store σ and class table CT, $N_1 \parallel N_2$ is the parallel composition of two networks, and $(\nu \mathsf{u} : \mathsf{t})N$ makes the identifier u local to N.

The binding is standard and we use $\mathsf{fn}(\mathsf{e})/\mathsf{fv}(\mathsf{e})$ to denote a set of free names/variables. We say that a class name C occurs *free* in a expression e if e contains **new** C: the function $\mathsf{fcl}(\mathsf{e})$ returns the set of free class names of e.

4 Operational Semantics

This section presents the operational semantics of $\mathcal{L}_{doos}$, which extends the standard small step call-by-value reduction of [1, 3, 23]. The reduction relation is given modulo the standard structural equivalence rules of the π-calculus [22], written $\equiv$. We define *multi-step* reduction as: $\twoheadrightarrow \stackrel{\text{def}}{=} (\longrightarrow \cup \equiv)^*$. We only discuss the more interesting rules. We start by listing the evaluation contexts.

$$E ::= [\,] \mid E.\mathsf{f} \mid E;\mathsf{e} \mid \mathsf{x} := E \mid E.\mathsf{f} := \mathsf{e} \mid \mathsf{o}.\mathsf{f} := E \mid E.\mathsf{m}(\mathsf{e}) \mid \mathsf{o}.\mathsf{m}(E) \mid \mathsf{c}.\mathbf{send}(E) \\ \mid \mathsf{u}.\mathbf{sendIf}(E)\{\mathsf{e}\}\{\mathsf{e}\} \mid \mathsf{u}.\mathbf{sendWhile}(E)\{\mathsf{e}\}$$

Notice that **request** $E\,\mathsf{s}\{\mathsf{e}\}$, and **accept** $E\,\mathsf{s}\{\mathsf{e}\}$, are not evaluation contexts.[3] Neither are **request** $\mathsf{u}\,\mathsf{s}\{E\}$, **accept** $\mathsf{u}\,\mathsf{s}\{E\}$, $\mathsf{u}.\mathbf{sendIf}(\mathsf{e})\{E\}\{\mathsf{e}\}$, $\mathsf{u}.\mathbf{sendIf}(\mathsf{e})\{\mathsf{e}\}\{E\}$, $\mathsf{u}.\mathbf{sendWhile}(\mathsf{e})\{E\}$, $\mathsf{u}.\mathbf{receiveIf}\{E\}\{\mathsf{e}\}$, $\mathsf{u}.\mathbf{receiveIf}\{\mathsf{e}\}\{E\}$, or $\mathsf{u}.\mathbf{receiveWhile}\{E\}$ evaluation contexts, because they would allow session bodies to run before the start of the session, or parts of a conditional or iterative session to run before determining which conditional branch should be selected, or whether the iteration should continue.

Local Expressions. The rules for execution of expressions which correspond to the sequential part of the language are standard [3, 10, 18]. Only the local store is modified, and the rules involve only the local store and the local class table. In Fig. 4 we give the rules for object creation and method invocation.

Allocation of new objects, described by **RC-New**, explicitly restricts identifiers, thus representing "freshness" or "uniqueness" of the address in the store. The function $\mathsf{fields}(C)$ examines the class signature and returns the field declarations for C.

---

[3] Namely, if **request** $E\,\mathsf{s}\{\mathsf{e}\}$ were an evaluation context, it would replace the name of a channel in E without replacing it in e. For example, then, for some session type s, and some state σ_1, where $\sigma_1(\mathsf{x}) = \mathsf{c}$, and applying also rule **RN-ReqAcc**, we would have:
$\ldots\mathbf{request}\,\mathsf{x}\;\;\mathsf{s}\{\mathsf{x}.\mathbf{receive}\}\ldots\sigma_1\ldots \parallel \ldots\mathbf{accept}\,\mathsf{c}\,\mathsf{s}\{\mathsf{c}.\mathbf{send}(3)\}\ldots\sigma_2\ldots \;\longrightarrow$
$\ldots\mathbf{request}\,\mathsf{c}\;\;\mathsf{s}\{\mathsf{x}.\mathbf{receive}\}\ldots\sigma_1\ldots \parallel \ldots\mathbf{accept}\,\mathsf{c}\,\mathsf{s}\{\mathsf{c}.\mathbf{send}(3)\}\ldots\sigma_2\ldots \;\longrightarrow$
$(\nu \mathsf{c}' : \mathsf{s})(\ldots x.\mathbf{receive}\ldots\sigma_1\ldots \parallel \ldots\mathsf{c}'.\mathbf{send}(3)\ldots\sigma_2\ldots)$, and execution would be stuck.
For similar reasons, **accept** $E\,\mathsf{s}\{\mathsf{e}\}$ is not a context.

RC-New

$$\frac{\mathsf{fields}(C) = \vec{\mathtt{f}}\vec{\mathtt{t}}}{\textbf{new}\ C, \sigma, \mathtt{CT} \longrightarrow (\nu\mathtt{o}:C)(\mathtt{o}, \sigma\cdot[\mathtt{o} \mapsto (C, \vec{\mathtt{f}}:\vec{\mathtt{null}})], \mathtt{CT})}\ C \in \mathsf{dom}(\mathtt{CT})$$

RC-LocMeth

$$\frac{\sigma(\mathtt{o}) = (C, \ldots) \quad \mathsf{mbody}(\mathtt{m}, C, \mathtt{CT}) = (\mathtt{x}, \mathtt{e}) \quad \mathsf{mtype}(\mathtt{m}, C) = \mathtt{t} \to \mathtt{t}'}{\mathtt{o.m(v)}, \sigma, \mathtt{CT} \longrightarrow (\nu\mathtt{x}:\mathtt{t})(\mathtt{e}[\mathtt{o}/\mathtt{this}], \sigma\cdot[\mathtt{x} \mapsto \mathtt{v}], \mathtt{CT})}$$

Fig. 3. Expression Reduction

The method invocation rule is **RC-LocMeth**; the function $\mathsf{mbody}(\mathtt{m}, C, \mathtt{CT})$ looks up m in the local class table, and returns a pair consisting of the method code and the formal parameter name. The function $\mathsf{mtype}(\mathtt{m}, C)$ looks up m in the global class signature and returns the type of the method [18]. The receiver o replaces `this` in the method body and a new store entry x is allocated for the formal parameter v.

Communication. $\mathcal{L}_{doos}$ has two kinds of communication rules: those for *remote method and field invocation*, and those for *session communication*, which are inspired by π-calculus rules [22]. Fig. 4 defines reduction for remote method and field invocation; the first three rules are for congruence, the fourth rule is structural.

Rule **RN-Fld** allows reading at location l_1 a field of an object stored at a *different location*, l_2. Similarly, **RN-FldAss** allows the code in location l_1 to assign a value to a field stored in a different location, l_2.

Rule **RN-RemMeth** describes remote method call; location l_1 executes a method call where the receiver is an object stored in a different location l_2: a new runtime private channel c, shared between l_1 and l_2, is created; after that, at l_2 the method call is executed by rule **RC-LocMeth**; the result v is then safely sent back from l_2 to l_1 via this new private channel c by **RN-CommMeth**; since c is only used once (*i.e.* it is a linear channel in the sense of [1, 16, 19]), it is finally discarded.

Session Communication. The main session communication rules are formalised in Fig. 4. Rule **RN-ReqAcc** describes opening of sessions: if location l_1 requires a session on $\mathtt{u}_1$ and location l_2 accepts a session on $\mathtt{u}_2$ and the values of $\mathtt{u}_1$ and $\mathtt{u}_2$ are the same channel name, then, a new private channel c is created and $\mathtt{u}_1$ and $\mathtt{u}_2$ are replaced by c in the session bodies in the standard way noting that

$$\textbf{request}\ \mathtt{u's\{e\}[c/u]} = \textbf{request}\ \mathtt{u's\{e[c/u]\}}$$
$$\textbf{accept}\ \mathtt{u's\{e\}[c/u]} = \textbf{accept}\ \mathtt{u's\{e[c/u]\}}$$

but importantly

$$\textbf{request}\ \mathtt{u\,s\{e\}[c/u]} = \textbf{request}\ \mathtt{u\,s\{e\}}$$
$$\textbf{accept}\ \mathtt{u\,s\{e\}[c/u]} = \textbf{accept}\ \mathtt{u\,s\{e\}}$$

RN-Conf
$$\frac{P,\sigma,\mathtt{CT} \longrightarrow (\nu\vec{\mathtt{u}}:\vec{\mathtt{t}})(P',\sigma',\mathtt{CT})}{l[P,\sigma,\mathtt{CT}] \longrightarrow (\nu\vec{\mathtt{u}}:\vec{\mathtt{t}})(l[P',\sigma',\mathtt{CT}])}$$

RN-Par
$$\frac{N \longrightarrow N'}{N \,\|\, N_0 \longrightarrow N' \,\|\, N_0}$$

RN-Res
$$\frac{N \longrightarrow N'}{(\nu\mathtt{u}:\mathtt{t})N \longrightarrow (\nu\mathtt{u}:\mathtt{t})N'}$$

RN-Str
$$\frac{N \equiv N_0 \longrightarrow N_0' \equiv N'}{N \longrightarrow N'}$$

RN-Fld
$$l_1\,[E[\mathtt{o}.\mathtt{f_i}]\,|\,P,\sigma_1,\mathtt{CT}_1]\,\|\,l_2\,[Q,\sigma_2,\mathtt{CT}_2] \longrightarrow l_1\,[E[\mathtt{v_i}]\,|\,P,\sigma_1,\mathtt{CT}_1]\,\|\,l_2\,[Q,\sigma_2,\mathtt{CT}_2]$$
$$\sigma_2(\mathtt{o}) = (C,\vec{\mathtt{f}}:\vec{\mathtt{v}})$$

RN-FldAss
$$l_1\,[E[\mathtt{o}.\mathtt{f}:=\mathtt{v}]\,|\,P,\sigma_1,\mathtt{CT}_1]\,\|\,l_2\,[Q,\sigma_2,\mathtt{CT}_2] \longrightarrow l_1\,[E[\mathtt{v}]\,|\,P,\sigma_1,\mathtt{CT}_1]\,\|\,l_2\,[Q,\sigma_2',\mathtt{CT}_2]$$
$$\mathtt{o} \in \mathsf{dom_o}(\sigma_2) \quad \sigma_2{}' = \sigma_2\,[\mathtt{o} \mapsto \sigma_2(\mathtt{o})[\mathtt{f} \mapsto \mathtt{v}]]$$

RN-RemMeth
$$l_1\,[E[\mathtt{o}.\mathtt{m}(\mathtt{v})]\,|\,P,\sigma_1,\mathtt{CT}_1]\,\|\,l_2\,[Q,\sigma_2,\mathtt{CT}_2]$$
$$\longrightarrow$$
$$(\nu\mathtt{c}:\mathbf{chan}(\mathtt{t}))(l_1\,[E[\mathtt{c}.\mathbf{receive}]\,|\,P,\sigma_1,\mathtt{CT}_1]\,\|\,l_2\,[\mathtt{c}.\mathbf{send}(\mathtt{o}.\mathtt{m}(\mathtt{v}))\,|\,Q,\sigma_2,\mathtt{CT}_2])$$
$$\sigma_2(\mathtt{o}) = (C,\ldots) \quad \mathsf{mtype}(\mathtt{m},C) = \mathtt{t}' \rightarrow \mathtt{t} \qquad \mathtt{c}\ \text{fresh}$$

RN-CommMeth
$$(\nu\mathtt{c}:\mathbf{chan}(\mathtt{t}))(l_1\,[E_1[\mathtt{c}.\mathbf{send}(\mathtt{v})]\,|\,Q_1,\sigma_1,\mathtt{CT}_1]\,\|\,l_2\,[E_2[\mathtt{c}.\mathbf{receive}]\,|\,Q_2,\sigma_2,\mathtt{CT}_2])$$
$$\longrightarrow$$
$$l_1\,[E_1[\mathtt{null}]\,|\,Q_1,\sigma_1,\mathtt{CT}_1]\,\|\,l_2\,[E_2[\mathtt{v}]\,|\,Q_2,\sigma_2,\mathtt{CT}_2]$$

Fig. 4. Network Communication

i.e. substitutions of synchronisation channel names cannot move inside nested sessions synchronising on the same name. The freshness of $\mathtt{c}$ guarantees privacy and linearity of the session communication between l_1 and l_2. Notice that stores associate values with variables, so if $\mathtt{u}_1$ is a variable of type $\mathtt{s}$ then $\sigma_1(\mathtt{u}_1)$ will be a channel name, and similarly for $\mathtt{u}_2$.

Rule **RN-CommSess** formalises the session communication where sent value $\mathtt{v}$ has the type $\mathtt{t}$; after a series of applications of this rule, the session completes and the channel $\mathtt{c}$ has type **end**.

In rules **RN-CommSessIf-true** and **RN-CommSessIf-false** first a boolean is exchanged, and then according to the value of this boolean the execution proceeds with the first or the second branches.

Rule **RN-CommSessWhile** simply expresses the iteration by means of the conditional.

RN-ReqAcc

$$l_1\,[E_1[\mathbf{request}\ \mathsf{u}_1\ \mathsf{s}\{\mathsf{e}_1\}] \mid Q_1, \sigma_1, \mathrm{CT}_1] \parallel l_2\,[E_2[\mathbf{accept}\ \mathsf{u}_2\ \mathsf{s}\{\mathsf{e}_2\}] \mid Q_2, \sigma_2, \mathrm{CT}_2]$$
$$\longrightarrow$$
$$(\nu\mathsf{c}:\mathsf{s})(l_1\,[E_1[\mathsf{e}_1[\mathsf{c}/\mathsf{u}_1] \mid Q_1], \sigma_1, \mathrm{CT}_1] \parallel l_2\,[E_2[\mathsf{e}_2[\mathsf{c}/\mathsf{u}_2]] \mid Q_2, \sigma_2, \mathrm{CT}_2]) \quad \mathsf{c}\ \text{fresh}$$

u_1 and u_2 are the same channel name or $\sigma_1(\mathsf{u}_1) = \mathsf{u}_2$ or $\mathsf{u}_1 = \sigma_2(\mathsf{u}_2)$ or $\sigma_1(\mathsf{u}_1) = \sigma_2(\mathsf{u}_2)$

RN-CommSess

$$(\nu\mathsf{c}:\dagger\mathsf{t}.\mathsf{s})(l_1\,[E_1[\mathsf{c}.\mathbf{send}(\mathsf{v})] \mid Q_1, \sigma_1, \mathrm{CT}_1] \parallel l_2\,[E_2[\mathsf{c}.\mathbf{receive}] \mid Q_2, \sigma_2, \mathrm{CT}_2])$$
$$\longrightarrow$$
$$(\nu\mathsf{c}:\mathsf{s})(l_1\,[E_1[\mathsf{null}] \mid Q_1, \sigma_1, \mathrm{CT}_1] \parallel l_2\,[E_2[\mathsf{v}] \mid Q_2, \sigma_2, \mathrm{CT}_2])$$

RN-CommSessIf-true

$$(\nu\mathsf{c}:\dagger\langle\pi_1, \pi_2\rangle.\mathsf{s})$$
$$(l_1\,[E_1[\mathsf{c}.\mathbf{sendIf}(\mathsf{true})\{\mathsf{e}_1\}\{\mathsf{e}_2\}] \mid Q_1, \sigma_1, \mathrm{CT}_1] \parallel l_2\,[E_2[\mathsf{c}.\mathbf{receiveIf}\{\mathsf{e}_3\}\{\mathsf{e}_4\}] \mid Q_2, \sigma_2, \mathrm{CT}_2])$$
$$\longrightarrow$$
$$(\nu\mathsf{c}:\pi_1.\mathsf{s})(l_1\,[E_1[\mathsf{e}_1] \mid Q_1, \sigma_1, \mathrm{CT}_1] \parallel l_2\,[E_2[\mathsf{e}_3] \mid Q_2, \sigma_2, \mathrm{CT}_2])$$

RN-CommSessIf-false

$$(\nu\mathsf{c}:\dagger\langle\pi_1, \pi_2\rangle.\mathsf{s})$$
$$(l_1\,[E_1[\mathsf{c}.\mathbf{sendIf}(\mathsf{false})\{\mathsf{e}_1\}\{\mathsf{e}_2\}] \mid Q_1, \sigma_1, \mathrm{CT}_1] \parallel l_2\,[E_2[\mathsf{c}.\mathbf{receiveIf}\{\mathsf{e}_3\}\{\mathsf{e}_4\}] \mid Q_2, \sigma_2, \mathrm{CT}_2])$$
$$\longrightarrow$$
$$(\nu\mathsf{c}:\pi_2.\mathsf{s})(l_1\,[E_1[\mathsf{e}_2] \mid Q_1, \sigma_1, \mathrm{CT}_1] \parallel l_2\,[E_2[\mathsf{e}_4] \mid Q_2, \sigma_2, \mathrm{CT}_2])$$

RN-CommSessWhile

$$(\nu\mathsf{c}:\dagger\langle\pi\rangle^*.\mathsf{s})$$
$$(l_1\,[E_1[\mathsf{c}.\mathbf{sendWhile}(\mathsf{e})\{\mathsf{e}_1\}] \mid Q_1, \sigma_1, \mathrm{CT}_1] \parallel l_2\,[E_2[\mathsf{c}.\mathbf{receiveWhile}\{\mathsf{e}_2\}] \mid Q_2, \sigma_2, \mathrm{CT}_2])$$
$$\longrightarrow$$
$$(\nu\mathsf{c}:\dagger\langle\pi.\dagger\langle\pi\rangle^*, \varepsilon\rangle.\mathsf{s})(l_1\,[E_1[\mathsf{c}.\mathbf{sendIf}(\mathsf{e})\{\mathsf{e}_1;\mathsf{c}.\mathbf{sendWhile}(\mathsf{e})\{\mathsf{e}_1\}\}\{\mathsf{null}\}] \mid Q_1, \sigma_1, \mathrm{CT}_1] \parallel$$
$$l_2\,[E_2[\mathsf{c}.\mathbf{receiveIf}\{\mathsf{e}_2;\mathsf{c}.\mathbf{receiveWhile}\{\mathsf{e}_2\}\}\{\mathsf{null}\}] \mid Q_2, \sigma_2, \mathrm{CT}_2])$$

Fig. 5. Session Communication

5 Session Types and Typing System

The type system of $\mathcal{L}_{doos}$ has three kinds of typing judgments. The judgments for threads and nets are standard, they just tell us that under certain assumptions on the types of variables, o-ids, `this` and channels, the thread and respectively the net is well-formed. So the judgments have the shape:

$$\Gamma \vdash P : \mathbf{thread} \quad \text{and} \quad \Gamma \vdash N : \mathbf{net}$$

where the environment Γ is defined by:

$$\Gamma := \emptyset \mid \Gamma, \mathsf{x}:\mathsf{t} \mid \Gamma, \mathsf{o}:C \mid \Gamma, \mathsf{this}:C \mid \Gamma, \mathsf{c}:\mathsf{s} \mid \Gamma, \mathsf{c}:\mathbf{chan}(\mathsf{t})$$

When typing expressions we need to take into account how session types are "consumed", *i.e.* when an input or an output communication prescribed by a session type takes place through **receive** or **send** instruction. For this reason we add session environments to both sides of typing judgments, giving them the shape

$$\Gamma;\Sigma \vdash \mathtt{e} : \mathtt{t};\Sigma'$$

where Γ is the environment, $\mathtt{t}$ is the type of $\mathtt{e}$, Σ and Σ' give the session types of channels before and after the evaluation of $\mathtt{e}$. We call them the *pre* and *post session environment* respectively.

Notice that since **request** and **accept** instructions contain the session types of the connecting channels and method declarations contain the session environment (i.e. the session types of the used channels), we could avoid global assumptions on session types of channel names. The cost would be a run time check that the session types in request and accept coincide before starting sessions.

In the following subsections we will discuss the more interesting rules. We only mention here that there is a standard subtyping (denoted by <:), which we assume causes no cycle as in [3, 18], and which is judged on the class signature.

Well-formed class tables. Methods, classes and class tables are well-formed with respect to an environment which must contain all session environments of methods. This is prescribed by the rule checking that a method is ok:

M-ok

$$\frac{\Sigma, \mathtt{this} : C, \mathtt{x} : \mathtt{t}_1; \emptyset \vdash \mathtt{e} : \mathtt{t}; \emptyset}{\Gamma, \mathtt{this} : C \vdash \mathtt{t}_2\,\mathtt{m}(\mathtt{t}_1\,\mathtt{x})\Sigma\{\mathtt{e}\} : \mathtt{ok\ in}\ C} \quad \begin{array}{l} \Sigma \subseteq \Gamma \\ \mathsf{mtype}(\mathtt{m}, C) = \mathtt{t}_1 \to \mathtt{t}_2 \\ \mathtt{t} <: \mathtt{t}_2 \end{array}$$

The environment Γ is propagated in the rules for checking well-formedness of classes and class tables.

Notice that both the pre and the post session environments for typing the method body are empty. This ensures that all send and receive instructions are inside sessions as we will see in discussing thread and network typing.

Expression typing. The rule for typing expression composition illustrates a first use of session environments:

TE-Seq

$$\frac{\Gamma;\Sigma \vdash \mathtt{e} : \mathtt{t};\Sigma' \qquad \Gamma;\Sigma' \vdash \mathtt{e}' : \mathtt{t}';\Sigma''}{\Gamma;\Sigma \vdash \mathtt{e};\mathtt{e}' : \mathtt{t}';\Sigma''}$$

The post session environment Σ' of $\mathtt{e}$ typing is used as pre session environment for typing $\mathtt{e}'$. The typing rule for method calls:

TE-Meth

$$\frac{\Gamma;\Sigma \vdash \mathtt{e} : C;\Sigma' \qquad \Gamma;\Sigma' \vdash \mathtt{e}' : \mathtt{t}';\Sigma''}{\Gamma;\Sigma \vdash \mathtt{e.m}(\mathtt{e}') : \mathtt{t};\Sigma''} \quad \begin{array}{l} \mathsf{msignature}(\mathtt{m}, C) \subseteq \Gamma \\ \mathsf{mtype}(\mathtt{m}, C) = \mathtt{t}'' \to \mathtt{t} \\ \mathtt{t}' <: \mathtt{t}'' \end{array}$$

demands that the method signature of m in C (determined by the method signature look-up function $\mathsf{msignature}(\mathsf{m}, C)$) is contained in the environment Γ. Further, the session environments of e and e' must agree as in rule **TE-Seq**. Finally the type of e' should conform to the method type returned by the look-up function $\mathsf{mtype}(\mathsf{m}, C)$.

Session typing. The importance of the session environments in expression typing is made clear by the rules for typing **send** and **receive**:

TE-SessSend

$$\frac{\Gamma;\Sigma \vdash \mathsf{e} : \mathsf{t};\Sigma', \mathsf{c} : !\mathsf{t}.\mathsf{s}}{\Gamma;\Sigma \vdash \mathsf{c}.\mathbf{send}(\mathsf{e}) : \mathit{Object};\Sigma', \mathsf{c} : \mathsf{s}}$$

TE-SessReceive

$$\frac{}{\Gamma;\Sigma, \mathsf{c} : ?\mathsf{t}.\mathsf{s} \vdash \mathsf{c}.\mathbf{receive} : \mathsf{t};\Sigma, \mathsf{c} : \mathsf{s}}$$

The key observation is that in both cases the typing consumes exactly the output or the input type that heads the session type of the current channel c. The typing of **send** also takes into account that the typing of e can modify the session environment.

The typing rules for opening sessions are:

TE-Req

$$\frac{\Gamma, \mathsf{u} : \mathsf{s};\Sigma, \mathsf{c} : \mathsf{s} \vdash \mathsf{e}[\mathsf{c}/\mathsf{u}] : \mathsf{t};\Sigma', \mathsf{c} : \mathbf{end} \quad \mathsf{c} \notin \mathsf{fn}(\mathsf{e}) \quad \mathsf{c} \notin \mathsf{dom}(\Gamma)}{\Gamma, \mathsf{u} : \mathsf{s};\Sigma \vdash \mathbf{request}\ \mathsf{u}\ \mathsf{s}\{\mathsf{e}\} : \mathsf{t};\Sigma'}$$

TE-Acc

$$\frac{\Gamma, \mathsf{u} : \mathsf{s};\Sigma, \mathsf{c} : \overline{\mathsf{s}} \vdash \mathsf{e}[\mathsf{c}/\mathsf{u}] : \mathsf{t};\Sigma', \mathsf{c} : \mathbf{end} \quad \mathsf{c} \notin \mathsf{fn}(\mathsf{e}) \quad \mathsf{c} \notin \mathsf{dom}(\Gamma)}{\Gamma, \mathsf{u} : \mathsf{s};\Sigma \vdash \mathbf{accept}\ \mathsf{u}\ \mathsf{s}\{\mathsf{e}\} : \mathsf{t};\Sigma'}$$

where $\overline{\mathsf{s}}$ denotes the *dual* session type of s defined inductively by $\overline{\mathbf{end}} = \mathbf{end}$, $\overline{!\mathsf{t}.\mathsf{s}} = ?\mathsf{t}.\overline{\mathsf{s}}$, $\overline{?\mathsf{t}.\mathsf{s}} = !\mathsf{t}.\overline{\mathsf{s}}$, and the substitution $[\mathsf{c}/\mathsf{u}]$ obeys the same conditions as given in Section 4.[4]

The key point is that these rules ensure *linear* use of runtime session channels; for every new session, there should be exactly one receiver waiting to receive from c, and one sender waiting to send on c. This is guaranteed by replacing the opening channel u in e by a fresh channel c. The type **end** of c in the post session environment of typing e ensures that the session is completed after evaluation of e. Notice that c does not appear in the conclusion.

The remaining rules give types for conditional and iterative session types. Note that within iterations depending on the value received/sent on a channel c, rules **TE-SessRecWhile** and **TE-SessSendWhile** forbid communication on any other open channel except for c; *e.g.* for $\mathsf{c}.\mathbf{sendWhile}(\mathsf{e}')\{\mathsf{e}\}$ and $\mathsf{c}.\mathbf{receiveWhile}\{\mathsf{e}\}$, the typing rules require for any communication $\mathsf{c}'.\mathbf{receive}$ or $\mathsf{c}'.\mathbf{send}(...)$ within e that $\mathsf{c}=\mathsf{c}'$, or that the communication is enclosed within an inner **accept** $\mathsf{c}'\mathsf{s}\{...\}$ or **request** $\mathsf{c}'\mathsf{s}\{...\}$. This constraint is clearly necessary in order to get soundness of communications (Theorem 3).

[4] Notice that the name of the channel, u, is replaced by a fresh channel name, c. This is so, because, a) u may be a variable, but Σ contains only constant channels, and b) it allows us to type nested session openings of the same name, *e.g.* **request** $\mathsf{c}\,\mathsf{s}\{...$**request** $\mathsf{c}\,\mathsf{s}\{...\}...\}$.

TE-SessRecIf

$$\frac{\Gamma;\Sigma,\mathsf{c}:\pi_1.\mathsf{s}\vdash \mathsf{e}_1:\mathsf{t};\Sigma',\mathsf{c}:\mathsf{s} \qquad \Gamma;\Sigma,\mathsf{c}:\pi_2.\mathsf{s}\vdash \mathsf{e}_2:\mathsf{t};\Sigma',\mathsf{c}:\mathsf{s}}{\Gamma;\Sigma,\mathsf{c}:?\langle\pi_1,\pi_2\rangle.\mathsf{s}\vdash \mathsf{c}.\mathbf{receiveIf}\{\mathsf{e}_1\}\{\mathsf{e}_2\}:\mathsf{t};\Sigma',\mathsf{c}:\mathsf{s}}$$

TE-SessSendIf

$$\frac{\Gamma;\Sigma\vdash \mathsf{e}:\mathbf{bool};\Sigma \qquad \Gamma;\Sigma,\mathsf{c}:\pi_1.\mathsf{s}\vdash \mathsf{e}_1:\mathsf{t};\Sigma',\mathsf{c}:\mathsf{s} \qquad \Gamma;\Sigma,\mathsf{c}:\pi_2.\mathsf{s}\vdash \mathsf{e}_2:\mathsf{t};\Sigma',\mathsf{c}:\mathsf{s}}{\Gamma;\Sigma,\mathsf{c}:!\langle\pi_1,\pi_2\rangle.\mathsf{s}\vdash \mathsf{c}.\mathbf{sendIf}(\mathsf{e})\{\mathsf{e}_1\}\{\mathsf{e}_2\}:\mathsf{t};\Sigma',\mathsf{c}:\mathsf{s}}$$

TE-SessRecWhile

$$\frac{\Gamma;\Sigma,\mathsf{c}:\pi.\mathsf{s}\vdash \mathsf{e}:\mathsf{t};\Sigma,\mathsf{c}:\mathsf{s}}{\Gamma;\Sigma,\mathsf{c}:?\langle\pi\rangle^*.\mathsf{s}\vdash \mathsf{c}.\mathbf{receiveWhile}\{\mathsf{e}\}:\mathsf{t};\Sigma,\mathsf{c}:\mathsf{s}}$$

TE-SessSendWhile

$$\frac{\Gamma;\Sigma\vdash \mathsf{e}:\mathbf{bool};\Sigma \qquad \Gamma;\Sigma,\mathsf{c}:\pi.\mathsf{s}\vdash \mathsf{e}':\mathsf{t};\Sigma,\mathsf{c}:\mathsf{s}}{\Gamma;\Sigma,\mathsf{c}:!\langle\pi\rangle^*.\mathsf{s}\vdash \mathsf{c}.\mathbf{sendWhile}(\mathsf{e})\{\mathsf{e}'\}:\mathsf{t};\Sigma,\mathsf{c}:\mathsf{s}}$$

Thread and Network typing. Rule **TT-Start** promotes expressions to threads; all channels of the post session environment should be completed (*i.e.* be typed by **end**) and all sessions in the pre session environment should conform to the environment.

TT-Start

$$\frac{\Gamma;\{\mathsf{c}_i:\mathsf{s}_i \mid i\in I\}\vdash \mathsf{e}:\mathsf{t};\{\mathsf{c}_i:\mathbf{end}\mid i\in I\} \quad \forall i\in I.\mathsf{c}_i:\mathsf{s}_i\in\Gamma\vee \mathsf{c}_i:\overline{\mathsf{s}_i}\in\Gamma}{\Gamma\vdash \mathsf{e}:\mathbf{thread}}$$

Notice that when all send and receive operations are inside sessions, both the pre and the post session environments for typing e can be empty.

Rule **TN-Conf** states that a location is a well-typed network in an environment if its thread P is well-typed, its store σ and class table CT are ok in the same environment, and if all free classes in P as well as their superclasses (we denote this set by $\mathsf{fcl}(P)$) are locally available – the latter is guaranteed through the requirement $\mathsf{fcl}(P)\subseteq\mathsf{dom}(\mathsf{CT})$ and the last condition.

TN-Conf

$$\frac{\begin{array}{l}\Gamma\vdash P:\mathbf{thread} \quad \Gamma\vdash\sigma:\mathsf{ok} \quad \Gamma\vdash\mathsf{CT}:\mathsf{ok} \quad \mathsf{fcl}(P)\subseteq\mathsf{dom}(\mathsf{CT})\\ \forall C\in\mathsf{dom}(\mathsf{CT}).\,C<:D\vee D\in\mathsf{fcl}(C,\mathsf{CT}) \implies D\in\mathsf{dom}(\mathsf{CT})\end{array}}{\Gamma\vdash l[P,\sigma,\mathsf{CT}]:\mathbf{net}}$$

6 Type Safety and Communication Safety

As expected, the type system of Section 5 satisfies the subject reduction property.This is formulated as follows.

Theorem 1 (Subject Reduction).

– *If* $\Gamma;\Sigma\vdash\mathsf{e}:\mathsf{t};\Sigma'$, *and* $\Gamma\vdash\sigma:\mathsf{ok}$, *and* $\Gamma\vdash\mathsf{CT}:\mathsf{ok}$ *and* $\mathsf{e},\sigma,\mathsf{CT}\longrightarrow(\nu\mathsf{u}:\mathsf{t}')(\mathsf{e}',\sigma',\mathsf{CT})$ *then* $\Gamma,\mathsf{u}:\mathsf{t}';\Sigma\vdash\mathsf{e}':\mathsf{t}';\Sigma'$ *with* $\mathsf{t}'<:\mathsf{t}$ *and* $\Gamma,\mathsf{u}:\mathsf{t}'\vdash\sigma':\mathsf{ok}$.

- *If* $\Gamma \vdash P$:**thread**, *and* $\Gamma \vdash \sigma$: ok, *and* $\Gamma \vdash$ CT: ok *and* $P, \sigma, \mathtt{CT} \longrightarrow (\nu \mathtt{u} : \mathtt{t}')(P', \sigma', \mathtt{CT})$ *then* $\Gamma, \mathtt{u} : \mathtt{t}' \vdash P'$:**thread** *and* $\Gamma, \mathtt{u} : \mathtt{t}' \vdash \sigma'$: ok.
- *If* $\Gamma \vdash N$:**net**, *and* $N \longrightarrow N'$ *then* $\Gamma \vdash N'$:**net**.

The proof is based on generation lemmas, substitution lemmas and a detailed analysis of channel use.

Even more interesting than subject reduction, are the following properties of $\mathcal{L}_{doos}$:

P1 no *connection error* can occur, *i.e.* request and accept on the same channel must have the same session type;
P2 no *communication error* can occur, *i.e.* in the same net there cannot be two sends or two receives on the same channel;
P3 after a session has begun *the required communications are always executed in the expected order*;
P4 after a session has begun *all the required communications are executed* unless one of the following situations occurs:
  - a null pointer exception is thrown;
  - the computation diverges; or
  - there is a request or accept instruction waiting for the dual instruction.

These properties hold for a network obtained by reduction from an initial network. We say that a network N is *initial* if (writing $\prod_{0 \leq i < n} N_i$ for $N_0 \| N_1 \| \ldots \| N_{n-1}$):

- $\vdash N$:**net** is derivable using rule **TT-Start** with empty session environments in the premises;
- $N \equiv (\nu \mathtt{c} : \mathtt{s})(\prod_{0 \leq i < n} l_i [\mathtt{e}_i, \emptyset, \mathtt{CT}_i])$, where each $\mathtt{e}_i$ is a user expression; and
- N is closed.

Notice that the condition on the use of rule **TT-Start** is satisfied whenever all send and receive instructions are inside method bodies, a natural choice in the object-oriented paradigm.

In order to formulate properties **P1** and **P2**, we add a new constant ConmErr (*connection or communication error*) to the network and the following rule:

$$l_1 [E_1[\mathtt{e}] \mid Q_1, \sigma_1, \mathtt{CT}_1] \,\|\, l_2 [E_2[\mathtt{e}'] \mid Q_2, \sigma_2, \mathtt{CT}_2] \longrightarrow \mathsf{ConmErr}$$

if e *clashes* with e′, where e clashes with e′ when

$$\mathtt{e}, \mathtt{e}' \in \{\mathtt{c}.\mathbf{receive}, \mathtt{c}.\mathbf{send}(\ldots), \mathtt{c}.\mathbf{receiveIf}\{\ldots\}\{\ldots\}, \mathtt{c}.\mathbf{sendIf}(\ldots)\{\ldots\}\{\ldots\}, \mathtt{c}.\mathbf{receiveWhile}\{\ldots\}, \mathtt{c}.\mathbf{sendWhile}(\ldots)\{\ldots\}, \mathbf{request}\ \mathtt{c}\ \mathtt{s}\{\ldots\}, \mathbf{accept}\ \mathtt{c}\ \mathtt{s}\{\ldots\}\}$$

and they do not occur both in the premise of one of the rules in Fig. 4. In other words when e and e′ belong both to the above set they do not clash if $\mathtt{e} = \mathtt{c}.\mathbf{receive}$ and $\mathtt{e}' = \mathtt{c}.\mathbf{send}(\mathtt{e}'_0)$, or $\mathtt{e} = \mathtt{c}.\mathbf{receiveIf}\{\mathtt{e}_0\}\{\mathtt{e}_1\}$ and $\mathtt{e}' = \mathtt{c}.\mathbf{sendIf}(\mathtt{e}'_0)\{\mathtt{e}'_1\}\{\mathtt{e}'_2\}$, or $\mathtt{e} = \mathtt{c}.\mathbf{receiveWhile}\{\mathtt{e}_0\}$ and $\mathtt{e}' = \mathtt{c}.\mathbf{sendWhile}(\mathtt{e}'_0)\{\mathtt{e}'_1\}$, or $\mathtt{e} = \mathbf{request}\ \mathtt{c}\ \mathtt{s}\{\mathtt{e}_0\}$ and $\mathtt{e}' = \mathbf{accept}\ \mathtt{c}\ \mathtt{s}\{\mathtt{e}'_0\}$ or vice versa.

We can now prove that from initial nets, we never reach a configuration containing clashing expressions.

Theorem 2 (ConmErr **Freedom).** *Suppose that* N_0 *is an initial net and* $N_0 \longrightarrow\!\!\!\!\rightarrow N$. *Then* N *does not contain* ConmErr, *i.e. there does not exist* N' *such that* $N \equiv N' \parallel \mathsf{ConmErr}$.

The proof of the above theorem is straightforward from the subject reduction theorem.

For properties **P3** and **P4** we formulate the following soundness theorem:

Theorem 3 (Soundness). *Let* N_0 *be an initial net,* $N_0 \longrightarrow\!\!\!\!\rightarrow (\nu \mathsf{u} : \mathsf{t})N$, *and* $(\nu \mathsf{u} : \mathsf{t})N \longrightarrow (\nu \mathsf{c} : \mathsf{s})(\nu \mathsf{u} : \mathsf{t})N' \stackrel{\text{def}}{=} (\nu \mathsf{c} : \mathsf{s})N_1$ *by rule* **RN-ReqAcc** *with* $\mathsf{s} = \pi_1.\pi.\pi_2.\mathbf{end}$. *If* $(\nu \mathsf{c} : \mathsf{s})N_1$ *does not*

- *produce* NullExc *or*
- *diverge or*
- *stop on a request or accept instruction waiting for the dual instruction*

then

$$(\nu \mathsf{c} : \mathsf{s})N_1 \longrightarrow\!\!\!\!\rightarrow (\nu \mathsf{c} : \pi.\pi_2.\mathbf{end})N_2 \longrightarrow\!\!\!\!\rightarrow (\nu \mathsf{c} : \pi_2.\mathbf{end})N_3 \longrightarrow\!\!\!\!\rightarrow (\nu \mathsf{c} : \mathbf{end})N_4$$

with $\mathsf{c} \notin \mathsf{fn}(N_4)$, *where:*

- *if* $\pi = \dagger\mathsf{t}$ *then* $(\nu \mathsf{c} : \pi.\pi_2.\mathbf{end})N_2 \longrightarrow\!\!\!\!\rightarrow (\nu \mathsf{c} : \pi_2.\mathbf{end})N_3$ *with exactly one application of rule* **RN-CommSess** *on channel* c*;*
- *if* $\pi = \dagger\langle\pi', \pi''\rangle$ *then the first rule involving channel* c *is*
  - *either* **RN-CommSessIf-true** *and the application of this rules gives* $(\nu \mathsf{c} : \pi'.\pi_2.\mathbf{end})N_2'$ *and* $(\nu \mathsf{c} : \pi'.\pi_2.\mathbf{end})N_2' \longrightarrow\!\!\!\!\rightarrow (\nu \mathsf{c} : \pi_2.\mathbf{end})N_3$*;*
  - *or* **RN-CommSessIf-false** *and the application of this rules gives* $(\nu \mathsf{c} : \pi''.\pi_2.\mathbf{end})N_2'$ *and* $(\nu \mathsf{c} : \pi''.\pi_2.\mathbf{end})N_2' \longrightarrow\!\!\!\!\rightarrow (\nu \mathsf{c} : \pi_2.\mathbf{end})N_3$*;*
- *if* $\pi = \dagger\langle\pi'\rangle^*$ *then the first rule involving channel* c *is* **RN-CommSessWhile** *and the application of this rules gives* $(\nu \mathsf{c} : \pi_3.\pi_2.\mathbf{end})N_2'$ *with* $\pi_3 \in \{\dagger\langle\pi'\rangle^*, \varepsilon\}$ *and* $(\nu \mathsf{c} : \pi_3.\pi_2.\mathbf{end})N_2' \longrightarrow\!\!\!\!\rightarrow (\nu \mathsf{c} : \pi_2.\mathbf{end})N_3$.

The soundness proof requires careful analysis of the evaluation order and invariant properties of networks.

Finally we get:

Theorem 4 (Completion of Sessions). *Suppose* N_0 *is an initial net,* $N_0 \longrightarrow\!\!\!\!\rightarrow N \equiv (\nu \mathsf{u} : \mathsf{t})\prod_{0 \leq \mathsf{i} < \mathsf{n}} l_\mathsf{i}[\mathsf{e}_\mathsf{i}, \sigma_\mathsf{i}, \mathsf{CT}_\mathsf{i}]$ *and* N *is irreducible. Then either all* e_i *are values* $(0 \leq \mathsf{i} < \mathsf{n})$ *or there is* j $(0 \leq \mathsf{j} < \mathsf{n})$ *such that* $\mathsf{e}_\mathsf{j} \in \{\mathsf{NullExc}, E[\mathbf{request}\ \mathsf{c}\ \mathsf{s}\{\mathsf{e}'\}], E[\mathbf{accept}\ \mathsf{c}\ \mathsf{s}\{\mathsf{e}'\}]\}$.

7 Conclusions and Further Work

Session types have been successfully applied to theoretical settings such as the π-calculus [4, 5, 13, 15, 17, 25], a multi-threaded functional language [27], to practical settings such as CORBA [26] and a web-services description language [29]. With $\mathcal{L}_{doos}$ we aimed to link language development to engineering and standardisation practice.

To our knowledge $\mathcal{L}_{doos}$ is the first application of session types to a distributed, object-oriented class-based programming language. Our design aims were to restrict the number of novel features introduced into the object-oriented language (we added only four pairs of primitives for standard session communication in the user syntax), and to obtain a simple typing system by extending class and method signatures to contain the usage of channels assigned by session types. We have written several example programs, demonstrating that $\mathcal{L}_{doos}$ can express communication in a style that is natural for programmers from the object-oriented community.

It is worthwhile to notice that our session types are regular expressions of a limited shape, which can also be denoted by sum and recursion. Branching types instead are variant types, and therefore the recursive session types of [13, 14, 17, 26] are richer than ours.

The subtyping relation on session types considered in [13, 26] is covariant for input, contravariant for output as in [24] and moreover allow to change the number of branches in branching types. As our session types are regular expressions, the inclusion of regular languages induces a natural notion of subtyping which is simple but not interesting, because it lacks covariance and contravariance of inputs and outputs.

We plan to investigate extensions that would allow channels to carry channels, and channels to be passed as parameters to methods. In particular, we want to allow the passing of linear channels, through the use of π-types as parameter types; on the other hand, in order to ensure linearity, we will forbid π-types as the types of local variables or fields.

Furthermore, we will re-evaluate our design decision of omitting selection primitives from the $\mathcal{L}_{doos}$-session types. While in traditional session types, function names are included in types (*e.g.* sell:?**float**.?**float**.$\langle$!**float**$\rangle^*$.**end** would be the session type of the seller), in $\mathcal{L}_{doos}$ they are not included (*e.g.* ?**float**.?**float**.$\langle$!**float**$\rangle^*$.**end** is the type of a *channel* used by sell). With this design decision the structure of the program is primarily reflected in the classes and their methods, and therefore method names were not a part of the sessions types.

Finally, we wish to evaluate the various designs through a sequence of case studies and to develop type checking algorithms following [4].

Acknowledgements. We are grateful to the anonymous referees, to Kohei Honda, and to Simon Gay for pointing out some errors in the examples, and some weaknesses in the presentation. We are indebted to Dimitris Mostrous for many insightful comments. During and after the presentation at TGC-05 we had many interesting questions and suggestions from the participants, in particular from Rocco De Nicola, Mark Miller, Eugenio Moggi, and Davide Sangiorgi. Surely our future work on this subject will be strongly influenced by this useful interaction.

References

1. Alexander Ahern and Nobuko Yoshida. Formalising Java RMI with Explicit Code Mobility. In *OOPSLA '05 (to appear), the 20th Annual ACM SIGPLAN Conference on Object-Oriented Programming, Systems, Languages and Applications*. ACM Press, 2005.

2. Davide Ancona, Giovanni Lagorio, and Elena Zucca. Simplifying Types in a Calculus for Java Exceptions. Technical report, DISI - Università di Genova, 2002.
3. Gavin Bierman, Matthew Parkinson, and Andrew Pitts. MJ: An Imperative Core Calculus for Java and Java with Effects. Technical Report 563, University of Cambridge Computer Laboratory, April 2003.
4. Eduardo Bonelli, Adriana Compagnoni, and Elsa Gunter. Typechecking Safe Process Synchronization. In *FGUC 2004*, ENTCS, 2004.
5. Eduardo Bonelli, Adriana Compagnoni, and Elsa Gunter. Correspondence Assertions for Process Synchronization in Concurrent Communications. *To appear in JFP*, 2005.
6. Gilad Bracha, Martin Odersky, David Stoutamire, and Philip Wadler. Making the Future Safe for the Past: Adding Genericity to the Java Programming Language. In *OOPSLA'98*, pages 183–200. ACM Press, 1998.
7. Luca Cardelli and Andrew D. Gordon. Mobile Ambients. *Theoretical Computer Science*, 240(1):177–213, 2000. Special Issue on Coordination, D. Le Métayer Editor.
8. Mariangiola Dezani, Nobuko Yoshida, Alexander Ahern, and Sophia Drossopoulou. A Distributed Object Oriented Language with Session Types. In *Preliminary Proceedings of TGC'05*, 2005. http://www.cs.unibo.it/ sangio/TGC05/.
9. Edsger W. Dijkstra. *A Discipline of Programming*. Prentice-Hall, 1976.
10. Sophia Drossopoulou. Advanced Issues in Object Oriented Languages Course Notes. http://www.doc.ic.ac.uk/~scd/Teaching/AdvOO.html.
11. Sophia Drossopoulou, Giovanni Lagorio, and Susan Eisenbach. Flexible Models for Dynamic Linking. In *ESOP'03*, volume 2618 of *LNCS*, pages 38–53. Springer-Verlag, 2003.
12. Manuel Fahndrich and Robert DeLine. Adoption and Focus: Practical Linear Types for Imperative Programming. In *PLDI '02*, pages 13–24. ACM Press, 2002.
13. Simon Gay and Malcolm Hole. Types and Subtypes for Client-Server Interactions. In *ESOP'99*, volume 1576 of *LNCS*, pages 74–90. Springer-Verlag, 1999.
14. Simon Gay, Vasco T. Vasconcelos, and António Ravara. Session Types for Inter-process Communication. TR 2003–133, Department of Computing, University of Glasgow, March 2003.
15. Kohei Honda. Types for Dyadic Interaction. In *CONCUR'93*, volume 715 of *LNCS*, pages 509–523. Springer-Verlag, 1993.
16. Kohei Honda. Composing Processes. In *POPL'96*, pages 344–357. ACM Press, 1996.
17. Kohei Honda, Vasco T. Vasconcelos, and Makoto Kubo. Language Primitives and Type Disciplines for Structured Communication-based Programming. In *ESOP'98*, volume 1381 of *LNCS*, pages 22–138. Springer-Verlag, 1998.
18. Atsushi Igarashi, Benjamin C. Pierce, and Philip Wadler. Featherweight Java: a Minimal Core Calculus for Java and GJ. *ACM Transactions on Programming Languages and Systems*, 23(3):396–450, 2001.
19. Naoki Kobayashi, Benjamin Pierce, and David Turner. Linear Types and π-calculus. In *POPL'96*, pages 358–371. ACM Press, 1996.
20. Sun Microsystems Inc. Java home page. http://www.javasoft.com/.
21. Sun Microsystems Inc. The Java Tutorial: All About Sockets. http://java.sun.com/docs/books/tutorial/networking/sockets/.
22. Robin Milner, Joachim Parrow, and David Walker. A Calculus of Mobile Processes, Parts I and II. *Information and Computation*, 100(1), 1992.
23. Benjamin C. Pierce. *Types and Programming Languages*. MIT Press, 2002.
24. Benjamin C. Pierce and Davide Sangiorgi. Typing and Subtyping for Mobile Processes. In *Logic in Computer Science*, 1993. Full version in *Mathematical Structures in Computer Science* , Vol. 6, No. 5, 1996.
25. Kaku Takeuchi, Kohei Honda, and Makoto Kubo. An Interaction-based Language and its Typing System. In *PARLE'94*, volume 817 of *LNCS*, pages 398–413. Springer-Verlag, 1994.

26. Antonio Vallecillo, Vasco T. Vasconcelos, and António Ravara. Typing the Behavior of Objects and Components using Session Types. In *Foclasa 2002*, volume 68(3) of *ENTCS*. Elsevier, 2002.
27. Vasco T. Vasconcelos, António Ravara, and Simon Gay. Session Types for Functional Multithreading. In *CONCUR'04*, volume 3170 of *LNCS*, pages 497–511. Springer-Verlag, 2004.
28. Jan Vitek and Giuseppe Castagna. Seal: A Framework for Secure Mobile Computations. In *Internet Programming Languages*, volume 1686 of *LNCS*, pages 47–77, 1999.
29. Web Services Choreography Working Group. Web Services Choreography Description Language. http://www.w3.org/2002/ws/chor/.

Engineering Runtime Requirements-Monitoring Systems Using MDA Technologies*

James Skene and Wolfgang Emmerich

Dept. of Computer Science, University College London,
Gower St, London, WC1E 6BT, UK
{j.skene, w.emmerich}@cs.ucl.ac.uk

Abstract. The Model-Driven Architecture (MDA) technology toolset includes a language for describing the structure of meta-data, the MOF, and a language for describing consistency properties that data must exhibit, the OCL. Off-the-shelf tools can generate meta-data repositories and perform consistency checking over the data they contain. In this paper we describe how these tools can be used to implement runtime requirements monitoring of systems by modelling the required behaviour of the system, implementing a meta-data repository to collect system data, and consistency checking the repository to discover violations. We evaluate the approach by implementing a contract checker for the SLAng service-level agreement language, a language defined using a MOF metamodel, and integrating the checker into an Enterprise JavaBeans application. We discuss scalability issues resulting from immaturities in the applied technologies, leading to recommendations for their future development.

1 Introduction

Run-time monitoring of systems is useful in a variety of situations in which the behaviour of a system cannot be guaranteed in advance. Such situations include testing a system against its requirements if it cannot be proven to meet them by construction, or monitoring the behaviour of a system where the actions of external agents, such as its users, is the actual object of scrutiny. Such monitoring can be used in conjunction with a contractual agreement to establish a strong basis for trust in a system: the owners of the system agree that it will behave in a particular way, and the system is monitored to ensure that deviations from the desired behaviour are detected and properly compensated for.

In the past, several approaches to the automatic implementation of runtime requirements-monitoring systems have been proposed. Such automatic implementation is intended to provide control over the specification of monitoring, improve the accuracy of monitoring and reduce the cost of its implementation. This paper presents a novel approach to runtime requirements monitoring that has arisen out of work to develop a contract checker for a service-level agreement

* This work was partially funded by the TAPAS project, IST-2001-34069.

R. De Nicola and D. Sangiorgi (Eds.): TGC 2005, LNCS 3705, pp. 319–333, 2005.

(SLA) language, SLAng. The approach relies on several standards published by the Object Management Group (OMG), and appears to be particularly suitable for comparing the behaviour of a system to sets of requirements that can be selected dynamically at runtime from a range of possible options, as is typical in SLAs.

The Model-Driven Architecture (MDA) technology toolset includes a language for describing the structure of meta-data, the Meta-Object Facility (MOF), and a language for describing consistency properties that data must exhibit, the Object Constraint Language (OCL). The Java Meta-Data (JMI) standard prescribes patterns for implementing programmatic access to MOF defined meta-data repositories. These patterns can be implemented in a generative programming tool to generate implementations of repositories, which can in turn be integrated with off-the-shelf tools to perform consistency checking over the data they contain.

The SLAng SLA language is defined using a MOF meta-model that models the required behaviour of electronic services governed by SLAs. The model is divided into two parts, the first describing the syntactic structure of SLAng contracts, the second describing the behaviour of the services that the contracts govern. Associations and OCL constraints between the two parts serve to specify the semantics of the language, both by associating SLAs with the services to which they apply, and by describing the restrictions on the behaviour of those services that the SLAs imply. The original intent of this approach was to provide a precise definition of the language. However, in combination with the JMI mapping and an OCL interpreter, the meta-model serves as a specification from which a contract checker can be generated. This contract checker can be combined with simple hand-implemented software instruments to form a complete runtime monitoring system.

In this paper we describe the approach, critically discuss it as an alternative to previous work on runtime monitoring, and report on our practical experience with the technologies involved. The paper includes an overview of the approach in Section 2. In Section 3 we briefly review the features of the SLAng language and its specification. In Section 4 we discuss the design and implementation of a tool for generating the checker. In Section 5 we describe the architecture of the resulting checker. In Section 6 we describe the deployment of the checker to monitor an Enterprise JavaBeans application, and evaluate the practicality of the approach. In Section 7 we compare the approach to other work on run-time monitoring. Finally, in Section 8 we make some concluding remarks, and discuss future work.

2 Runtime Requirements Monitoring Using MOF and OCL

Runtime requirements monitoring systems typically consist of a set of software instruments for gathering the raw event data pertinent to the properties of interest, some logic for checking that this data meets requirements, and possibly a repository for data if requirements checking requires data gathered over an extended period. In the approach outlined in this paper the requirements checking logic and repository are implemented using a combination of automatic code generation from a MOF model and a reusable OCL checker component. Generating software instruments is discussed below.

MOF models are very similar to UML class models [22]. They include sets of classes, the data they contain, and their relationships. Constraints on the model that cannot be represented graphically are expressed using the OCL. OCL is a typed-expression language similar to the expressions parts of Java or C++, and is used to describe class invariants in the model.

The classes in a MOF model can be interpreted as directly modelling objects in the real world, as is the case in the SLAng meta-model which describes the way that services should behave in the presence of SLAs. Requirements can be expressed directly as constraints over the behaviour of services, which will generally be modelled as classes of events arising during the execution of the service. Alternatively they can be expressed in the context of a model of a requirements language associated with the service. Instances of this model are requirements that may be expressed in the language at runtime and associated with services. Constraints between the model of the requirements language and the model of the service describe how the service must act in the presence of the requirements. In this manner the semantics of the SLAng SLA language are defined in terms of constraints over the performance of services that only apply when SLAs are present.

The meta-model can alternatively be interpreted as a model of data describing the world, and the set of conditions necessary for those data to meet some set of requirements. If we interpret the meta-model in this way, then we can produce a computer program capable of holding those data and checking them, to see whether services are behaving in the way that we want them to.

This approach is shown in Figure 1 in which thick arrows represent code generation, and thin arrows represent data flow. The figure represents the case in which a requirements language is being used to specify requirements at runtime.

To implement the approach we found it necessary to develop a JMI generator. (As discussed in Section 4, this was needed because previous generators did not offer adequate flexibility over the type of code generated. However, this component may be considered 'off-the-shelf' as it is a standard MDA component independent of the particular application.) We combined the resulting generated data structures with the OCL2 interpreter implemented at Kent University [12], which features an extension allowing it to evaluate OCL constraints over plain Java objects using Java reflection. The design of the JMI generator is discussed in more detail in the next section. The design of the resulting checker is discussed in detail in Section 5. The performance of the checker is described in 6.

A complete requirements monitoring system also includes software instruments to gather the event data included in the service model. The implementation of these instruments requires the interpretation of the service model in the context of the particular system being instrumented. If the service model is de-

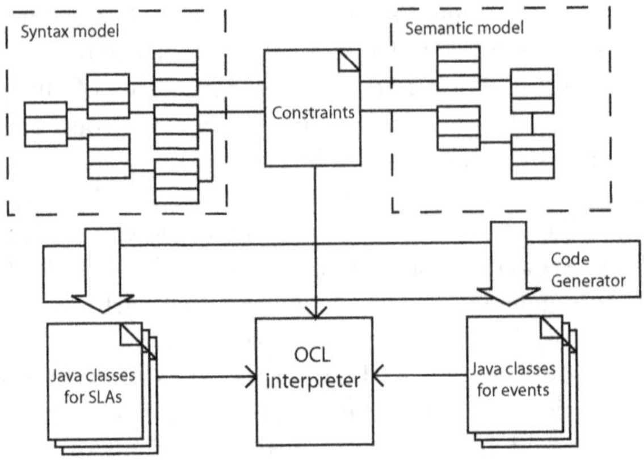

Fig. 1. Generating an SLA checker from the SLAng meta-model

scribed in the same terms as the system being monitored, for example in terms of particular Java classes and operations present in the implementation, then it will be possible to implement a generator for the instruments directly for the model. However, it may be that the service model is at a higher level of abstraction, and intended to apply to services with a range of designs and implementation technologies, as is the case with the SLAng language used as an example in this paper. In this case the instruments must be implemented manually, although the explicit nature of the service model provides considerable guidance in this process. In summary, the possibility of generating the instruments automatically depends on the level of abstraction of the MOF model, although we have not yet investigated the generation of instruments in practice.

3 The SLAng Language

The SLAng language syntax and semantics are defined by a MOF (version 1.1) model [20]. The model provides a formal definition of the structure of the syntax of the language, and of the semantic domain in which SLAs apply. These are modelled in terms of classes of objects with attributes and associations. Constraints in the model restrict the sets of objects described so that SLAs are only ever associated with services that are consistent with their terms and which meet their conditions. In this way the semantics of the language are formally defined. This approach was inspired by the work of the Precise UML group (pUML), who used the approach to define the semantics for their UML 2 submissions [13].

A view of the meta-model showing the syntax of the Electronic Service (ES) SLA is shown in Figure 2. The SLA is divided into a section for defining terms, and another for conditions. The conditions section is further subdivided between conditions on the behaviour of the service provider, and conditions on the behaviour of the client.

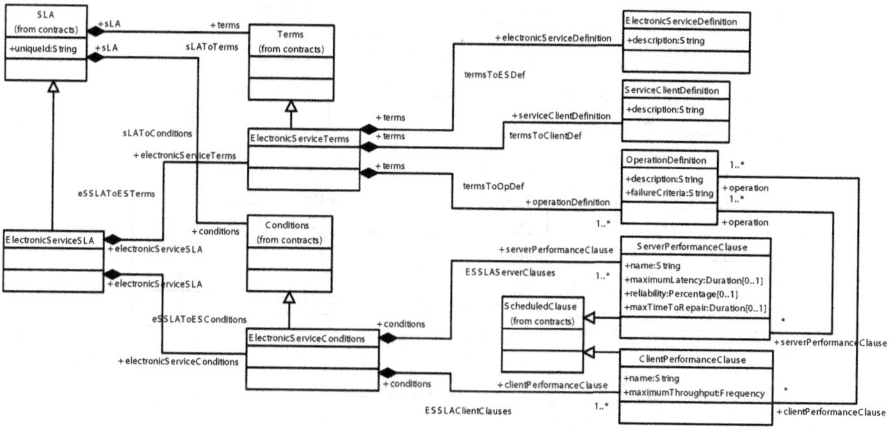

Fig. 2. Model of the syntax of SLAng electronic-service contracts

The use of a MOF meta-model to define the syntax of SLAng confers the advantages of the XML Metadata Interchange (XMI) [21] standard, a standard for serialising MOF-defined metadata. The XMI mapping of the SLAng syntactic model constitutes the concrete syntax of the language.

The semantic model of electronic service provision is shown in Figure 3. Service usages are events, occurring over a period, with the possibility of failure. They are associated with an operation, which forms part of an electronic service. They are also associated with the client that caused the usage. The syntactic and semantic models are co-located in a single model, and the terms in the syntactic model are associated with elements in the semantic model in order to define their meaning.

As stated above, the SLAng meta-model also includes OCL constraints that give meaning to condition statements in the language. The following is the top-level invariant defining the meaning of performance and reliability for Electronic Service SLAs:

```
context contracts::es::ServerPerformanceClause inv:
operation→collect(o : contracts::asp::OperationDefinition |
  o.operation
)→forAll(o : services::Operation |
  observedDowntime(o) < (timeRemaining(-1) ⋆ (1 - reliability)))
```

This expression is explained in detail in [23][1]. It relies on a number of function definitions, such as `observedDowntime` defined in the specification. The total amount of OCL for this constraint runs to about 50 lines.

[1] The expression is slightly modified from [23] as a result of testing and developing the meta-model and constraints using the generated SLA checker. However, its intent is the same and its structure is quite similar.

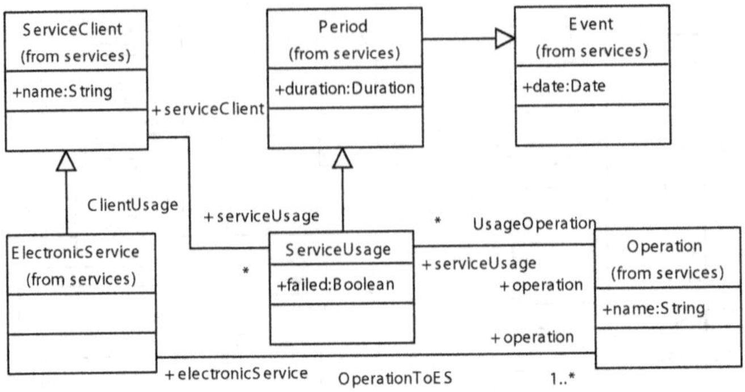

Fig. 3. Model of electronic service usage

In this section we have presented an overview of the SLAng language and its specification. For a more detailed discussion of the language, including a discussion of design decisions and objectives, and a comparison to other SLA languages and technologies, please refer to [23].

4 A JMI Generator

The JMI generator is implemented in Java, and follows the design shown in Figure 4. It is heavily dependent on the Velocity Template Engine (VTE) [11], developed as part of the Apache project. Similar to Java Server Pages (JSP) [5], or PHP [7], Velocity is a tool for generating text from predefined templates. These templates are text files that include fields delimited using special characters. The VTE is configured with these templates, and also extra data called 'context'. The templates are parsed by the VTE: ordinary text is passed straight through; the fields in the templates either control the order of parsing, for example by specifying optional or repeated sections, or indicate that data from the context should be inserted. By varying the context, several outputs can be produced from the same template.

The templates in our implementation are taken from the JMI specification, and translated into Velocity's template syntax. The JMI specification requires Java types to be produced corresponding to elements in the metamodel: for each class, a 'class proxy' interface, for creating and finding instances of the class, and an 'instance' interface, for editing properties and invoking operations of instances of the class, are required; for associations, an 'association proxy' interface for creating and querying pairs of associated instances; for each package, 'package proxy' interface enabling the discovery of class proxies, association proxies and subpackage proxies; for enumerations, an interface type for enumeration values and a class containing static exemplars of enumeration values. The JMI standard also specifies XMI reader and writer interfaces.

The generator includes a template for each of these types. Except in the case of enumerations, the JMI specification only defines interfaces, but does not

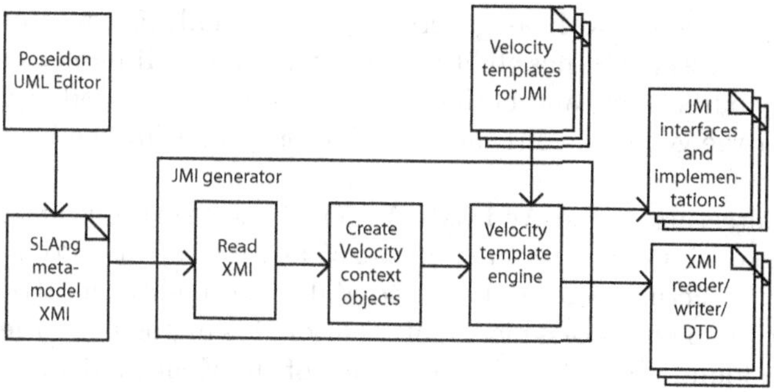

Fig. 4. Design of the JMI generator

indicate how they are to be implemented. The generator therefore also includes templates for implementations of each of the above elements. The generator also has a template to produce an XMI DTD following the pattern described in the XMI standard.

The context for each of these templates is drawn from the particular MOF model for which a set of JMI interfaces is being generated. In our case this is the SLAng meta-model. The meta-model is exported from a modelling tool in an XMI format file. The first stage of the JMI generator reads this file and creates an in-memory representation of it.

This initial in-memory representation of the API is not a suitable context for the Velocity templates, as it reflects the structure of the XMI file, rather than the structure of the templates. Velocity templates can only perform quite simple data manipulation (they lack recursion, for example, which makes it difficult to navigate data structures in the context). They must therefore be supplied with their context data in a form that closely reflects the way it is used in the template. The second stage of the generator creates a number of different context objects, appropriate to the Java files that must be generated, using the data from the in-memory representation of the XMI file.

In the third stage of its operation, the VTE is invoked using the generated context objects and the JMI templates, in order to generate the requisite JMI Java code. This is placed in the appropriate places in a package directory hierarchy on the file system.

Generating program code from UML diagrams is an important step in the Model Driven Architecture (MDA) methodology. A number of systems to achieve this have been developed with varying degrees of flexibility in the specification of their output. However, we found none to be ideal for our purposes, and elected to implement a generator by hand instead. We evaluated a number of tools in the autumn of 2003 before deciding on this course. These included the Netbeans Meta-Data Repository (MDR) [10], the Eclipse Modelling Framework (EMF) [8], and Novosoft's NSUML [6]. The EMF was rejected because it generates non-standard code from a non-standard meta-model (i.e. not JMI from MOF). The MDR and Novosoft were rejected because at the time they manifested problems reading standard XMI as generated by our modelling tool of choice. We also wished to reserve the possibility of modifying the JMI implementation code generated by our system, and both of these systems require code-level modifications to alter the generated JMI implementations, reducing the benefits of reuse considerably.

The architecture of the AndroMDA tool [1] is essentially identical to that presented here. However, as stated above, Velocity templates do not have powerful control structures and without the ability to modify the structure of the context objects to preprocess model information it is impossible to generate some outputs. We found the OCL-based approach of the Kent Modelling Framework, version 3 [9] to be adequately expressive. However, the OCL expressions are hard to write when a 'generation state' has to be maintained, containing things like a list of unique identifiers used. For this reason we preferred to use more conventional templates.

The decision not to reuse an existing modelling framework was an engineering decision. In principle any of the systems mentioned above could be adapted to our approach with some degree of effort. However, our requirement of flexibility in the generation of the implementation of the system will probably turn out to be a general requirement, because, as discussed in the evaluation section of this paper, modelling frameworks of this kind will need be adaptable to meet application-specific scalability requirements.

5 Architecture of the SLA Checker

The SLA checker consists of three major components:

1. The automatically generated JMI interfaces and implementation for holding SLAs and event data.
2. The Kent OCL implementation, with SLAng constraints loaded, for checking whether SLAs have been violated.
3. An API wrapper, that allows checks to be requested, and returns lists of violations that have been found. This part is hand-written in our implementation, because it is independent of the structure and semantics of the SLAng language.

The checker may be incorporated in electronic service systems wherever SLAs need to be monitored. It is used as follows:

1. The checker is instantiated.
2. The static elements from the semantic model are instantiated or loaded from an XMI file. These elements, with types such as `ElectronicService`, `ServiceClient` and `Operation` represent knowledge that the checker has about the service or services being monitored. The model is manipulated using the generated JMI interfaces.
3. One or more SLAs are instantiated or loaded from an XMI file, again using the JMI interfaces.

4. Associations are established between the service components defined in the SLAs and those components in the service model created in Step 2.
5. Monitoring data is provided to the component by invoking the various 'create' methods found on the JMI API (e.g. `createServiceUsage()` on the `ServiceUsage` class proxy interface). These data are associated with the relevant static elements in the service model, created in Step 2.
6. Periodically, the `check` methods on the violations API may be invoked. These return lists of violations, if any exist.

To demonstrate the SLA checker and to assist in the development of the SLAng semantics, we have implemented a browser that allows the editing of SLA and event data, via a tree-view of the model.

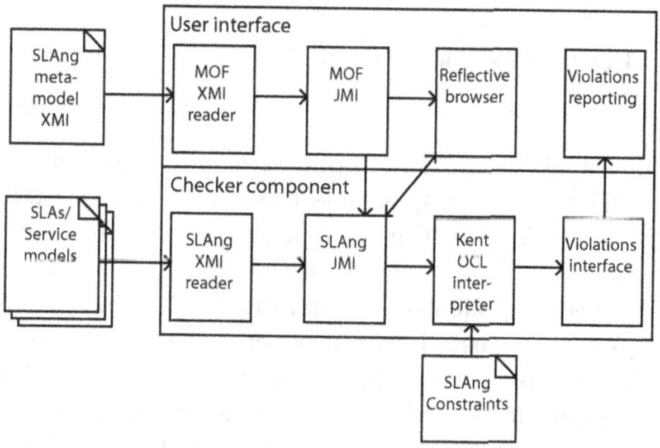

Fig. 5. Design of the SLA checker

The user-interface also allows interactive editing and checking of the constraints over the SLAng model, possible because the OCL constraints are interpreted at runtime, rather than compiled into the implementation language, Java.. The design of the checker is shown in Figure 5. A screenshot of the user interface is shown in Figure 6. The leftmost panel in the user interface contains the tree representing the SLAng model (SLAs and events). The middle panel lists the constraints over the model, and the rightmost panel allows the editing of constraints.

6 Evaluation

6.1 Deployment of the SLA Checker

We tested the SLA checker by deploying it to monitor the performance of an EJB application. The application is an auction management system developed

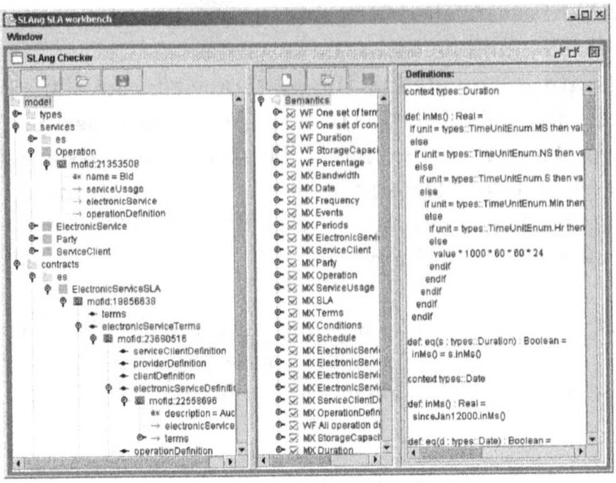

Fig. 6. Screenshot of the SLA checker user interface

by an industrial collaborator. The application is deployed in the popular application server JBoss, which implements the Java 2 Enterprise Edition (J2EE) specification [4], using Apache Tomcat to serve the web front-end [2].

The architecture of JBoss is based on the Java Management eXtensions library (JMX). In this component-based architecture, all functionality is deployed as 'managed beans' (MBeans), Java components that expose meta-data, configurable properties and lifecycle management methods. The JBoss distribution and default configuration includes MBeans implementing EJB containers, JNDI naming services, transactions, and many other services. We have deployed the SLA checker as an MBean, meaning that it has one instance per instance of the JBoss server. It is made available to other MBeans and to deployed EJBs via the JNDI naming repository.

To provide external access to the SLA checker, we implemented a small J2EE application called 'The SLAng Control Panel'. This consists of a single JSP page providing an interface to a stateless session bean. This bean in turn delegates operations to the SLAng checker. The main operation provided by the checker over this interface is `checkAll()`, which causes the component to evaluate the SLAng constraints over its internal model of SLAs and service data, and return a list of violations, if any exist.

Service performance information is passed to the SLAng service by a server-side interceptor configured as an option of the JBoss container configuration. JBoss remoting operates using a stack of interceptors on both the client and server side. These allow different types of functionality to be added to the communication channel independently, such as transaction management, security, and the communication protocol itself, which is managed by the outermost interceptor on client and server sides. For the purposes of evaluating the SLAng component, we added an interceptor on the server side to measure time spent processing EJB requests. The interceptor accesses the SLAng service using JNDI

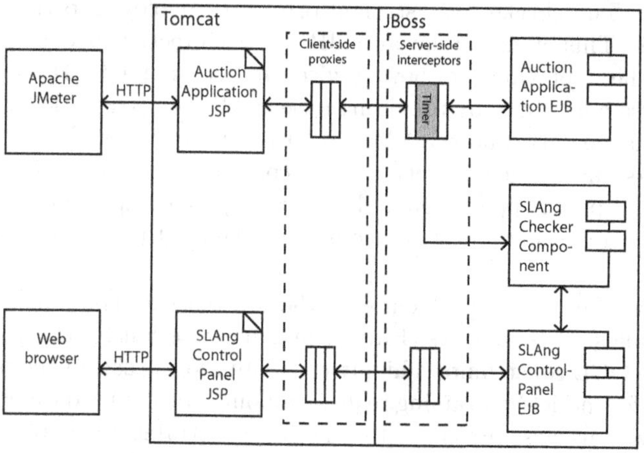

Fig. 7. The SLA checker component deployed to monitor an EJB application

and invokes the `createServiceUsage()`, method on its JMI interface to record the measured time. Apache JMeter was used to generate a variety of loads on the service [3].

6.2 Results

In this section we evaluate the SLA checker on three points: The ease of implementation of the checker; the ease of deployment of the checker in its intended context (in this case to monitor the auction application); and the performance of the checker.

Implementation: Effort in implementing the checker falls into three categories: implementing the JMI generator; implementing the SLAng language specification that is the input to the generator; and implementing the remaining code for the component, which mainly involves the integration of the OCL evaluator component and the provision of an API for requesting checks and reporting violations. Of these three categories, the first two could be speciously discounted on the grounds that they are separate efforts from the implementation of the actual component. If this were the case, then implementing the component would have taken around 1 man-week of labour. In fact, the total amount of labour has been closer to 1 man-year, and JMI generator, language and component have co-evolved to some extent. Indeed, as discussed below, the JMI generator, or at least it's templates will have to continue to adapt in the face of performance requirements that are somewhat related to the domain of the application, i.e. checking SLAng contracts. The SLA checker consists of approximately 115,000 lines of code (including blank lines and comments) outside of standard libraries of which 77,000 were generated, 36,500 form the implementation of the OCL evaluator and 1,500 were hand written.

Deployment: The checker was straightforward to deploy into the JBoss application server. This is mainly because JBoss's architecture is expressly designed to support the deployment of new services and components. However, the JMI interfaces also contribute by providing a clear API through which to deliver service performance data, and the XMI reader interface and implementation makes loading SLAs and service models into the component simple. Implementing the SLAng control panel application and integrating the component into JBoss took 2 weeks for a programmer not previously intimate with the workings of JBoss.

Performance: The major problem with the SLA checker is its inability to scale. This is manifest in two ways: Firstly, and most seriously, the time taken to evaluate the OCL constraints is highly correlated to the size of the model, and is far too long for models containing realistic amounts of service data. For a data set of 1000 service usages, the client throughput constraint compares every pair of usages to determine if they occur too closely together. If none do, this results in a million comparisons, and takes 20 minutes on a PC with 1.7GHz Intel Pentium 4 processor. The evaluation is slow due to a combination of factors: The OCL interpreter performs almost no optimisations, the interpretation of the OCL is innately expensive, and the data model over which the expressions are evaluated offers no shortcuts, such as indices.

The second issue is related. In our current implementation of the JMI interfaces all data is represented as Java objects stored in main memory. Since we have implemented no policy for removing or persisting old data, this leads inevitably to memory exhaustion as the application continues to be used. The amount of service usage data that can be checked is restricted by the amount of main memory available to the virtual machine in which the component is deployed.

To correct these issues without discarding the approach altogether requires some reengineering. The data model needs to be backed by a database. This could be either object oriented, or the translation to a more conventional model could be managed by the generated Java code for a particular model. Clearly not all data can be assumed to be in memory at the same time, and this may need to be reflected in the interface to the model data. The evaluation speed of the OCL constraints could be improved by translating it to Java, or possibly SQL (with some reduction in expressive power), rather than interpreting it. We gained some improvement in evaluation time by adding results caching to the OCL interpreter. Further optimisation of evaluation is required, and if the constraints are still to be evaluated across a generated interface, the generated interface may have to provide indices to assist in evaluation, possibly resulting in a closer coupling between interface standard and OCL evaluator.

Clearly these refinements should be the subject of further research.

7 Related Work

In [23] we provide a detailed comparison of SLAng with previous SLA languages, focusing on the extent to which these languages provide explicit definitions of their terms and conditions. Our use of an explicit model for this seems to be quite novel, and it is this feature of the language that allows us to generate the checker automatically.

A similar approach has been proposed in [19], a position paper that begins to elaborate the requirements for specifications supporting the use of contracts in an MDA process. The paper proposes that contracts can be transformed into one or more meta-models whose semantics are ultimately those of the Buisiness Contract Language (BCL) [18], a very flexible contract definition language based on the notion of 'communities', a kind of modelling template for collaborations described in the RM-ODP. It is proposed that these models could then be processed in various ways, including implementing monitors, by tools that implement the BCL semantics. It is unclear how the transformation of contracts into these metamodels provides a benefit over simply defining a contract in BCL directly, since the expressiveness of the contract and the meta-models is likely to be equivalent. However, it is correct to identify BCL as an alternative to MOF/OCL to describe runtime requirements. In cases where requirements are primarily related to the ordering of events, BCL provides considerable semantic assistance. In more general cases, the contract-oriented nature of BCL may be hinderance to the expression of the requirements.

Various other systems effectively define their own meta-models for requirements. Representative examples are: the Java-MaC system [16] which automatically embeds monitors in Java code from a requirements specification written in a language called PEDL/MEDL; Java PathExplorer [15] which does the same, but allows requirements to be specified in any high-level logic compatible with the Maude rewriting engine; and the KAOS-FLEA [14] system in which requirements specified using the KAOS methodology are monitored using the FLEA monitoring system coupled with manually implemented event detectors. These approaches are of comparable expressive power to the use of MOF/OCL to describe constraints on a system. JavaMaC and Java PathExplorer are examples of systems capable of generating software instruments thanks to the fact that their semantics are at least partially defined in terms of the structure of Java programs.

MOF/OCL offers the possibility to defer the specification of some requirements until runtime, by specifying requirements in terms of consistency relationships between the system and a model of a requirements language. In this way, the approach can be used to engineer a range of monitoring solutions, each with a language appropriate to their particular needs. This is in contrast to the approaches mentioned above, which prescribe a language for requirements, with the exception of Java PathExplorer which prescribes that a logic be used.

Choosing between systems for runtime requirements management requires at least two questions to be answered: in what form do I wish to represent my requirements? and, which monitoring technology will be practical? In comparison to other approaches, the use of MOF/OCL is very general, but also quite well aligned with conventional software engineering practice in that it is very similar to the use of UML. It is practical in the sense that it can be implemented using off-the-shelf technologies, but impractical in the sense that those technologies currently do not scale well (they may do in the future). In contrast, the approaches listed above assume the existence of a bespoke module implementing the logic for checking for violations. Engineering this module seperately may assist in scalability, although a more efficient OCL interpreter could equally easily be assumed. In terms of investigating the run-time performance of performance monitors, useful work has been done in [17], which demonstrates that the evaluation of requirements can be intractable, depending on the type of the requirement. A more comprehensive survey of the performance and practicality of available technologies would be desirable future work.

8 Conclusion

This paper has described the use of MDA technologies (although not necessarily an MDA approach) to produce runtime requirements monitoring systems. This has been exemplified by our implementation of an SLA checker, automatically, from the specification of our SLA language, SLAng.

In situations in which systems must be monitored against requirements specified at runtime designers may wish to consider adopting the approach as it offers the possibility to generate all or part of an interpreter for a requirements specification language (such as an SLA language) automatically. Where an explicit representation of the semantic primitives of such a language is practical, an OCL interpreter can be employed to check that these semantic elements are consistent with statements in the language, thereby implementing the logical part of a runtime requirements monitoring system. The approach is equally applicable in cases in which the requirements are invariant at runtime – the constraints in the model of the service are simply specified independently of any language model.

Our evaluation of the checker revealed some serious practical issues arising from immaturities in the technologies employed. Although for restricted numbers of objects the implementation serves its purpose, it seems that to achieve scalability both the mapping to implementation and the implementation of off-the-shelf components such as the OCL interpreter must be considerably more sophisticated. This is a consideration beyond SLA checking, as it is reasonable to assume that large software development efforts will wish to maintain and check consistency within large repositories of models. Future research should investigate this mapping further to produce implementation prescriptions to complement interface standards such as the JMI.[2]

References

1. AndroMDA code generation tool. `http://www.andromda.org/`.
2. Apache Jakarta Tomcat servlet container. `http://jakarta.apache.org/tomcat/`.

[2] Thanks to Werner Beckmann and Addesso, Inc. for the auction application. Also thanks to our TAPAS partners for their input into this work, and to Marc Fleury for his advice concerning JBoss.

3. Apache JMeter. `http://jakarta.apache.org/jmeter/`.
4. Java 2 Enterprise Edition. `http://java.sun.com/j2ee/index.jsp`.
5. Java Server Pages JSP v. 2.0 specification. `http://java.sun.com/products/jsp/`.
6. Novosoft Metadata Framework and UML Library (NSUML). `http://nsuml.sourceforge.net/`.
7. PHP: PHP Hypertext Preprocessor. `http://www.php.net/`.
8. The Eclipse Modelling Framework (EMF). `http://www.eclipse.org/emf/`.
9. The Kent Modelling Framework (KMF). `http://www.cs.kent.ac.uk/projects/kmf/documents.html`
10. The Netbeans Meta-Data Repository (MDR) Project. `http://mdr.netbeans.` hrefhttp://mdr.netbeans.org/`org/`.
11. The Velocity Template Engine v1.4. `http://jakarta.apache.org/velocity/`.
12. David Akehurst, Peter Linington, and Octavian Patrascoiu. OCL 2.0: Implementing the Standard. Technical report, Computer Laboratory, University of Kent, November 2003.
13. A. S Evans and S. Kent. Meta-modelling semantics of UML: the pUML approach. In *2nd International Conference on the Unified Modeling Language*, volume 1723 of *Lecture Notes in Computer Science (LNCS)*, pages 140 – 155, Colorado, USA, 1999. Springer-Verlag.
14. M. S. Feather, S. Fickas, A. van Lamsweerde, and C. Ponsard. Reconciling system requirements and runtime behavior. In *Proceedings of the 9th International Workshop on Software Specification and Design*, pages 50–59, 1998.
15. Klaus Havelund and Grigore Rosu. Monitoring java programs with java pathexplorer. In *Electronic Notes in Theoretical Computer Science*, volume 55. Elsevier Science Publishers, 2001.
16. Moonjoo Kim, Sampath Kannan, Insup Lee, Oleg Sokolsky, and Mahesh Viswanathan. Java-mac: a run-time assurance tool for java programs. In Klaus Havelund and Grigore Rosu, editors, *Electronic Notes in Theoretical Computer Science*, volume 55. Elsevier Science Publishers, 2001.
17. Moonjoo Kim, Sampath Kannan, Insup Lee, Oleg Sokolsky, and Mahesh Viswanathan. Computational analysis of run-time monitoring - fundamentals of java-mac. In *Electronic Notes in Theoretical Computer Science*, volume 70. Elsevier Science Publishers, 2002.
18. P. F. Linington, Z. Milosevic, J. Cole, S. Gibson, S. Kilkarni, and S. Neal. A unified behavioural model and a contract for extended enterprise. In *Data and Knowledge Engineering*, volume 51. Elsevier Science Publishers, 2004.
19. Peter F. Linington. Automating support for e-business contracts. In *Proc. of the EDOC 2004 Workshop on Contract Architectures and Languages, Monterey, California*. IEEE Computer Society Press, 2004.
20. The Object Management Group (OMG). *The Meta-Object Facility v1.4*, formal/2002-04-03 edition, April 2002.
21. The Object Management Group (OMG). *XML Metadata Interchange (XMI), v1.2*, formal/02-01-01 edition, January 2002.
22. The Object Management Group (OMG). *The Unified Modelling Language v1.5*, formal/2003-03-01 edition, March 2003.
23. J. Skene, D. Lamanna, and W. Emmerich. Precise service level agreements. In *Proc. of the 26th Int. Conference on Software Engineering, Edinburgh, UK*, pages 179–188. IEEE Computer Society Press, May 2004.

Automated Analysis of Infinite Scenarios

Mikael Buchholtz*

Informatics and Mathematical Modelling, Technical University of Denmark,
Richard Petersens Plads, bldg. 321, 1 DK-2800 Kgs. Lyngby
mib@imm.dtu.dk

Abstract. The security of a network protocol crucially relies on the scenario in which the protocol is deployed. This paper describes syntactic constructs for modelling network scenarios and presents an automated analysis tool, which can guarantee that security properties hold in all of the (infinitely many) instances of a scenario. The tool is based on control flow analysis of the process calculus LySa and is applied to the Bauer, Berson, and Feiertag protocol where is reveals a previously undocumented problem, which occurs in some scenarios but not in other.

1 Introduction

The security of any network protocol is not only determined by the behaviour the protocol itself. The security additionally relies upon the scenario in which the protocol is deployed. A protocol that suffers from a parallel session attack is an example of this: It may be possible to show that the protocol is secure — even when it is under attack — in the case that only a single session of the protocol is deployed on the network. However, when multiple session are present on the network, the parallel session attack can occur because the attacker uses messages from one session to perform the attack on another session.

This paper presents an automated analysis tool that focuses on deployment scenarios for security protocols. Protocols will be modelled in the process calculus LySa [4] and analysed with a control flow analysis that can guarantee confidentiality and authentication properties. The syntax of a LySa process, P, has features for modelling cryptography, nonce generation, message passing, etc. These features are well-suited to model the internal behaviour of individual principals. In this paper, we furthermore want to model the scenarios in which these principals appear. To this end, LySa is extended with a meta-level that contains various indexing constructs. For example, the meta-level has an indexing parallel composition, $|_{i \in S}\ M$, that describes a number of meta-level processes M in parallel. These processes only differ in their index i and, thus, the construct can be used to describe principals $A_1, A_2, A_3, \ldots$ that only differ in their identity but otherwise follow the same protocol.

* This work is funded by the Information Society Technologies programme of the European Commission, Future and Emerging Technologies, under the IST-2001-32072 project DEGAS.

R. De Nicola and D. Sangiorgi (Eds.): TGC 2005, LNCS 3705, pp. 334–352, 2005.

A key idea in having the meta-level is that it should *not* simply be a syntactic shorthand for succinct modelling of *one* specific instance of a scenario. Instead, a meta-level process specifies all the different instances that a protocol may be deployed in. Each instance of a scenario will be described by an object-level process P, which is an ordinary LySa process without indexing constructs. Instantiation is described by an instantiation relation, $M \Rrightarrow P$, and meta-level process may instantiate many different object-level processes. In fact, a meta-level is allowed to instantiate to infinitely many different object-level processes, thus, describing an infinitely large scenario.

A second step is to extend the control flow analysis from [4] to cover also meta-level processes. The control flow analysis is an automatable analysis technique that works by over-approximating the behaviour of a process. Thus, the extended meta-level analysis provides an automated analysis of scenarios and even copes with the fact that they may be infinitely large.

1.1 Contribution of This Paper

This paper contributes with version 2 of the LySatool. Version 1 of the tool [8] is the implementation of the control flow analysis of object-level LySa [4]. The second version of the LySatool includes the analysis of the meta-level and, hence, caters for analysis of arbitrarily large scenarios. The overall idea of adding an analysable meta-level was first suggested in [9] but for a different calculus. This paper extends that work in several respects: it (1) gives an implementation of a meta-level analysis. To take advantage of an existing implementation of an object-level analysis the idea of a meta-level has been applied on the LySa calculus; (2) gives a more detailed treatment of the correctness of the meta-level analysis. The simpler format of LySa over the calculus in [9] simplifies the work needed to do this; (3) makes the meta-level useful both to check confidentiality *and* authentication properties; and (4) uses the LySatool to find a previously undiscovered problem in a classical key establishment protocol [2].

2 LySa and the Meta-level

The process calculus LySa [4] is tailored to model network protocols that attain their security by means of cryptography. LySa models perfect cryptography, i.e. that successful decryption of ciphertext is only possible if the correct key is known. As of [5], LySa caters for both symmetric and asymmetric key cryptography. To keep the presentation simple, only symmetric key cryptography is presented in this paper. However, all the results in this paper, including the LySatool implementation, work also for asymmetric cryptography.

2.1 Syntax

The syntax of LySa is given in Figure 1. The syntax of expression $E \in Expr$ and processes $M \in MProc$ up until the horizontal double line corresponds closely

$$
\begin{array}{lll}
mx & ::= & x_{\bar{i}} \\
E & ::= & n_{\bar{i}} \quad | \quad mx \quad | \quad \{E_1, \ldots, E_k\}_{E_0} \\
M & ::= & \langle E_1, \ldots, E_k \rangle.M \quad | \quad (E_1, \ldots, E_j;\ mx_{j+1}, \ldots, mx_k).M \quad | \\
 & & \mathsf{decrypt}\ E\ \mathsf{as}\ \{E_1, \ldots, E_j;\ mx_{j+1}, \ldots, mx_k\}_{E_0}\ \mathsf{in}\ M \quad | \\
 & & (\nu\, n_{\bar{i}})\, M \quad | \quad !M \quad | \quad M_1 \mid M_2 \quad | \quad 0 \quad | \\
\hline\hline
 & & \mathsf{let}\ X \subseteq S\ \mathsf{in}\ M \quad | \quad |_{i \in S}\ M \quad | \quad (\nu_{\bar{i} \in \bar{S}}\ n_{\bar{a}\bar{i}})M
\end{array}
$$

Fig. 1. The syntax of LySa including the meta-level

to the syntax of LySa presented in [4]. This subset of processes is sometimes referred to as *object-level* processes taken from the set *Proc* and is ranged over by P. The syntax below the horizontal double line describes the new meta-level constructs.

The basic building blocks of LySa are values, which syntactically are described by expressions built over distinct countable sets of indexed names $n_{\bar{i}} \in \mathit{Name}$ and indexed variables $x_{\bar{i}} \in \mathit{Var}$. A sequence of indexes $\bar{i} = i_1 \ldots i_k$ (for $k \geq 0$) has each index i taken from a countable set *Index*. At the object-level, the indices are simply seen as a syntactic concatenation of $\bar{i}$ to n or x. At the meta-level, on the other hand, indices play a crucial role for the indexing constructs. A k-tuple of expressions, $E_1, \ldots, E_k$, may be encrypted under a key E_0 by the encryption expression $\{E_1, \ldots, E_k\}_{E_0}$.

2.2 Object-Level Semantics

Only the object-level of LySa has a dynamic semantics. This semantics describes how an object-level process, P, evolves in a step-by-step fashion. The semantics is formalised by a reduction relation, $P \rightarrow P'$, defined as the smallest relation satisfying the rules in Figure 2. The semantics ranges over values $V \in \mathit{Val}$, which are expressions without variables. The meaning of the object-level constructs and their formal semantics is explained in the following.

In LySa a tuple of values can be communicated over a global network. Sending a messages is done by synchronous output $\langle V_1, \ldots, V_k \rangle.P_1$ that matches a pattern-matching input $(V_1, \ldots, V_j;\ mx_{j+1}, \ldots mx_k).P_2$ as described by the rule (Com). If the first j values in output and input (until the semi-colon) are identical then last $k-j$ values in output are component-wise bound to the variables in input. This binding takes place through a substitution, which may apply α-renaming to avoid capturing bound names. An encrypted value may be decrypted as described by the rule (SDec). The key V_0 used for encryption and decryption must be the same and the first j values inside the encryption are pattern-matched. The process $(\nu\, n_{\bar{i}})\, P$ restricts the scope of $n_{\bar{i}}$ to be P, only. Apart from communication, parallel composition is interleaved as described by (Par). The inactive process, 0, cannot evolve and consequently it is not men-

$$(\text{Com})\ \langle V_1,\ldots,V_k\rangle.P_1 \mid (V_1,\ldots,V_j;\ mx_{j+1},\ldots,mx_k).P_2 \rightarrow P_1 \mid P_2[mx_{j+1} \overset{\alpha}{\mapsto} V_{j+1},\ldots,mx_k \overset{\alpha}{\mapsto} V_k]$$

$$(\text{SDec})\ \mathsf{decrypt}\ \{V_1,\ldots,V_k\}_{V_0}\ \mathsf{as}\ \{V_1,\ldots,V_j;\ mx_{j+1},\ldots,mx_k\}_{V_0}\ \mathsf{in}\ P \rightarrow P[mx_{j+1} \overset{\alpha}{\mapsto} V_{j+1},\ldots,mx_k \overset{\alpha}{\mapsto} V_k]$$

$$(\text{New})\ \frac{P \rightarrow P'}{(\nu\, n_{\bar{i}})\, P \rightarrow (\nu\, n_{\bar{i}})\, P'} \qquad (\text{Par})\ \frac{P_1 \rightarrow P_1'}{P_1 \mid P_2 \rightarrow P_1' \mid P_2}$$

$$(\text{Congr})\ \frac{P \equiv P'' \quad P'' \rightarrow P''' \quad P''' \equiv P'}{P \rightarrow P'}$$

Fig. 2. The reduction relation; $P \rightarrow P'$

tioned in Figure 2. Finally, the rule (Congr) may bring processes on a form where they match the other rules by applying the structural congruence $P \equiv P'$. This relation is as usual the least congruence on object-level processes where

- parallel composition is associative, commutative with $\mathsf{0}$ as neutral element,
- $!P$ describes replication of P i.e. $!P \equiv\ !P \mid P$,
- restriction has capture-avoiding scope extrusion, and
- names may undergo disciplined α-conversion.

The notion of *disciplined* α-conversion is used solely for the benefit of the analysis as discussed in Section 3. For the sake of the analysis, the set of names will be partitioned into equivalences classes. *Disciplined α-conversion* requires that α-conversion only takes place within the same equivalence class. Each of these classes contain countably many elements and consequently disciplining does not affect the expressive power of the semantics.

Example 1. A repeated nonce handshake between two principals A and B that initially share a key K may be modelled in LySa as the object-level process

$$\begin{array}{ll}(\nu\, K)\, (& !(\nu\, n)\, \langle A, B, n\rangle.(B, A;\ x).\mathsf{decrypt}\ x\ \mathsf{as}\ \{n;\ \}_K\ \mathsf{in}\ \mathsf{0} \\ & \mid\ !(A, B;\ y).\langle B, A, \{y\}_K\rangle.\mathsf{0}\ \ )\end{array}$$

Note in particular that the semi-colon is placed *after* the nonce n when the variable x is decrypted. This means pattern-matching takes place and decryption only succeeds if x is indeed bound to the nonce n encrypted under the key K.

2.3 Meta-level Semantics

The meta-level has no dynamic semantics as such. Instead, a meta-level process M specifies a scenario, which is made up of a set of object-level processes. The meta-level process M is said to *instantiate to* an object-level process P, written

$$\text{(IOut)}\ \frac{M \Rrightarrow P}{\langle E_1,\ldots,E_k\rangle.M \Rrightarrow \langle E_1,\ldots,E_k\rangle.P}$$

$$\text{(IInp)}\ \frac{M \Rrightarrow P}{(E_1,\ldots,E_j;\ mx_{j+1},\ldots,mx_k).M \Rrightarrow (E_1,\ldots,E_j;\ mx_{j+1},\ldots,mx_k).P}$$

$$\text{(ISDec)}\ \frac{M \Rrightarrow P}{\begin{array}{l}\mathsf{decrypt}\ E\ \mathsf{as}\ \{E_1,\ldots,E_j;\ mx_{j+1},\ldots,mx_k\}_{E_0}\ \mathsf{in}\ M \Rrightarrow\\ \mathsf{decrypt}\ E\ \mathsf{as}\ \{E_1,\ldots,E_j;\ mx_{j+1},\ldots,mx_k\}_{E_0}\ \mathsf{in}\ P\end{array}}$$

$$\text{(INew)}\ \frac{M \Rrightarrow P}{(\nu\, n_{\overline{a}})\ M \Rrightarrow (\nu\, n_{\overline{a}})\ P} \qquad \text{(IRep)}\ \frac{M \Rrightarrow P}{!M \Rrightarrow !P}$$

$$\text{(IPar)}\ \frac{M_1 \Rrightarrow P_1 \qquad M_2 \Rrightarrow P_2}{M_1 \mid M_2 \Rrightarrow P_1 \mid P_2} \qquad \text{(INil)}\ 0 \Rrightarrow 0$$

$$\text{(ILet)}\ \frac{M[X \mapsto S'] \Rrightarrow P}{\mathsf{let}\ X \subseteq S\ \mathsf{in}\ M \Rrightarrow P} \qquad \text{if } S' \subseteq_{\mathit{fin}} S$$

$$\text{(IIPar)}\ \frac{M[i \mapsto a_1] \Rrightarrow P_1 \quad \ldots \quad M[i \mapsto a_k] \Rrightarrow P_k}{|_{i\in\{a_1,\ldots,a_k\}}\ M \Rrightarrow P_1 \mid \ldots \mid P_k}$$

$$\text{(IINew)}\ \frac{M \Rrightarrow P}{(\nu_{\overline{i}\in\{\overline{a_1},\ldots,\overline{a_k}\}}\ n_{\overline{a}\overline{i}})\ M \Rrightarrow (\nu\, n_{\overline{a}\overline{a_1}})\ \ldots (\nu\, n_{\overline{a}\overline{a_k}})\ P}$$

Fig. 3. The instantiation relation; $M \Rrightarrow P$

$M \Rrightarrow P$, whenever P is in the set described by M. This set of object-level processes may be an infinite set.

The instantiation relation is defined in Figure 3. All object-level processes instantiate to themselves with any subprocesses instantiated as well. In the indexing meta-level constructs S is a set of indexes from $\mathcal{P}(\mathit{Index})$. The syntax of index sets, S, is left unspecified but include set identifiers $X \in \mathit{SetId}$ as placeholder for an index set. The process $\mathsf{let}\ X \subseteq S\ \mathsf{in}\ M$ declares such a set identifier X to stand for some arbitrary subset of S for use inside M. This is the key mechanism, which lets instantiation describe *sets* of object-level processes. Note that the rule (ILet) requires X to become bound to a *finite* subset of S. This is done to ensure that all object-level processes are syntactically finite when instantiation is performed. The rule (IPar) instantiates an indexed parallel to the parallel composition of the a finite number of processes that have the index i taken from the index set $\{a_1,\ldots,a_k\}$. This index set is required to be finite, which is again done to attain a finite object-level process. Finally, the indexed restriction $(\nu_{\overline{i}\in\overline{S}}\ n_{\overline{a}\overline{i}})M$ instantiates to restrictions of all the names $n_{\overline{a}\overline{i}}$ where $\overline{i}$ is substituted with elements from $\overline{S}$ as described by the rule (IINew).

Example 2. The nonce handshake in Example 1 describes scenario where precisely two principals are present. Below the meta-level constructs are used to describe the same nonce handshake but this time in a more general scenario:

$$\begin{array}{l} \mathsf{let}\ X \subseteq \mathbb{N}\ \mathsf{in}\ \mathsf{let}\ Y \subseteq \mathbb{N}\ \mathsf{in}\ (\nu_{ij \in X \times Y}\ K_{ij})(\\ \quad |_{i \in X}\ |_{j \in Y}\ !(\nu\, n_{ij})\, \langle A_i, B_j, n_{ij}\rangle.(B_j, A_i;\ x_{ij}).\mathsf{decrypt}\ x_{ij}\ \mathsf{as}\ \{n_{ij};\ \}_{K_{ij}}\ \mathsf{in}\ 0 \\ \quad |\ |_{j \in Y}\ |_{i \in X}\ !(A_i, B_j;\ y_{ij}).\langle B_j, A_i, \{y_{ij}\}_{K_{ij}}\rangle.0\ ) \end{array}$$

The first line declares the set identifiers X and Y to be subset of the natural numbers and, thus, the meta-level process describes all instances where *any* number of A_i's initiates a nonce handshake with any number of B_j's. Note also that the parts that describe the internals of each A_i and B_j closely correspond to the object-level processes in Example 1. The scenario, on the other hand is described by the meta-level constructs.

2.4 Binders and Substitution

The restriction operator $(\nu\, n_{\bar{i}})\, M$ is a *binder* of the name $n_{\bar{i}}$. In general, any kind of substitution of elements in the syntax respects binders and only substitutes free (i.e. unbound) instances of elements. Also input and decryption are binders of variables, the let-construct a binder of set identifiers, indexed parallel is a binder of the index i, and indexed restriction too is a binder of names.

Names that are not bound by any binder are said to be *free* names and they play an important role in the analysis attackers as discussed in Section 4. It is completely standard to define a function $\text{fn}(P)$ that finds the free names of the object-level process P. For the meta-level, we define a function, $\text{mfn}(M)$ that returns the most free names there can be in any instance of M. That is, mfn satisfies that if $M \Rrightarrow P$ then $\text{fn}(P) \subseteq \text{mfn}(M)$.

Names in $\text{mfn}(M)$ do not need to be free in every instance of M but will not be a problem with the way $\text{mfn}(M)$ is use in Section 4. This is as oppose to [9], where only a restricted class of processes were treated, namely the ones where names are either free in all instances or in none. Thus, the approach taken here considers a more general class of processes than in [9].

3 The Control Flow Analysis

The aim of a control flow analysis is to statically predict the behaviour of a process. Since the behaviour of an object-level process is given by its reduction semantics, the correctness of the analysis of object-level processes will as usual be given by a subject reduction result. A meta-level process, on the other hand, has no dynamic behaviour in itself. Instead, the control flow analysis will predict the behaviour of all the object-level processes that a meta-level process instantiates to. The correctness of the meta-level analysis will therefore show that the analysis is preserved by instantiation.

The control flow analysis can also be used to analyse processes under attack but the discussion of this is postponed until Section 4. An overall trademark of the analysis is that it works by finding conservative over-approximations to the behaviour of a process. This means that *any* actual behaviour of a process will be reflected in the analysis result but the converse does not necessarily hold. With respect to security, this means that the analysis can be used to *guarantee the absence of attacks.* However, the analysis cannot be used to guarantee the presence of an attack because a possible attack reported by the analysis may be a consequences of approximation.

3.1 Equivalence Classes for Dealing with Infinities

One of the challenges when making an efficiently computable, automated analysis of the behaviour of a process is the infinity of values that may occur in the execution of the process. For example, at the object-level a replicated restriction, such as in $!(\nu\, n)\,\langle n\rangle.P$, may semantically produce an infinity of names by α-converting the name n. Also, at the meta-level an indexing parallel, such as $|_{i\in X}\ \langle n_i\rangle.P$, may instantiate to infinitely different names if X represents an infinite set.

To deal with this infinity, the set of values, *Val*, will be partitioned into *finitely* many equivalence classes written $\lfloor \mathit{Val} \rfloor$. The partitioning of the value domain is fixed by the user of the analysis prior to analysing a process. The partitioning is made by assigning a canonical element $\lfloor n \rfloor$ to each name n, $\lfloor x \rfloor$ to each variable x, and $\lfloor i \rfloor$ to each index i. These assignments carry through to indexed names such that $\lfloor n_i \rfloor = \lfloor n'_{i'} \rfloor$ if and only if $\lfloor n \rfloor = \lfloor n' \rfloor$ and $\lfloor i \rfloor = \lfloor i' \rfloor$ and similarly for indexed variables. Finally, the canonical assignments are extended homomorphically over encryptions and thereby partition all of the value domain.

It is important to stress, that the partitioning is made purely for the benefit of the analysis and will in no way affect the semantic behaviour a process. The analysis records representatives of the equivalence classes i.e. the canonical values written $\lfloor V \rfloor$. As a consequence, the analysis is only capable of distinguishing two values V_1 and V_2 if they belong to different equivalence classes i.e. if $\lfloor V_1 \rfloor \neq \lfloor V_2 \rfloor$. The analysis is carefully designed such that any "mistakes" that arise because it cannot correctly distinguish two values will lead to over-approximation.

The choice of the partitioning is a parameter for controlling the precision of the analysis: The more distinct elements there are in the equivalence classes, the more elements the analysis may be able to distinguish between. A fine granularity in the partitioning will, on the other hand, also mean that the analysis has to consider more elements, thereby making the analysis result more expensive to compute. The analysis correctly over-approximates the behaviour of a process for *any* partitioning though in practice a very coarse partitioning often results in too significant over-approximation, which makes the analysis result uninformative.

3.2 The Object-Level Analysis

The object-level control flow analysis aims at giving an account of the messages communicated on the network during any execution of an object-level process.

$$
\begin{array}{lll}
\text{(AN)} & \rho \models n_{\bar{i}} : \vartheta & \text{iff } \lfloor n_{\bar{i}} \rfloor \in \vartheta \\
\text{(AVar)} & \rho \models x_{\bar{i}} : \vartheta & \text{iff } \rho(\lfloor x_{\bar{i}} \rfloor) \subseteq \vartheta \\
\text{(ASEnc)} & \rho \models \{E_1, \ldots, E_k\}_{E_0} : \vartheta & \text{iff } \wedge_{i=0}^{k} \rho \models E_i : \vartheta_i \wedge \\
 & & \quad \forall U_0 \in \vartheta_0 \ldots U_k \in \vartheta_k : \{U_1, \ldots, U_k\}_{U_0} \in \vartheta \\
\text{(AOut)} & \rho, \kappa \models_\Gamma \langle E_1, \ldots, E_k \rangle.M & \text{iff } \wedge_{i=1}^{k} \rho \models E_i : \vartheta_i \wedge \\
 & & \quad \forall U_1 \in \vartheta_1 \ldots U_k \in \vartheta_k : U_1 \ldots U_k \in \kappa \wedge \\
 & & \quad \rho, \kappa \models_\Gamma M \\
\text{(AInp)} & \rho, \kappa \models_\Gamma (E_1, \ldots, E_j;\, mx_{j+1}, \ldots, mx_k).M & \\
 & & \text{iff } \wedge_{i=1}^{j} \rho \models E_i : \vartheta_i \wedge \\
 & & \quad \forall U_1 \ldots U_k \in \kappa : \wedge_{i=1}^{j} U_i \in \vartheta_i \Rightarrow \\
 & & \qquad (\wedge_{i=j+1}^{k} U_i \in \rho(\lfloor mx_i \rfloor) \wedge \rho, \kappa \models_\Gamma M) \\
\text{(ASDec)} & \rho, \kappa \models_\Gamma \mathsf{decrypt}\ E\ \mathsf{as}\ \{E_1, \ldots, E_j;\, mx_{j+1}, \ldots, mx_k\}_{E_0}\ \mathsf{in}\ M & \\
 & & \text{iff } \rho \models E : \vartheta \wedge \wedge_{i=0}^{j} \rho \models E_i : \vartheta_i \wedge \\
 & & \quad \forall \{U_1, \ldots, U_k\}_{U_0} \in \vartheta : \wedge_{i=0}^{j} U_i \in \vartheta_i \Rightarrow \\
 & & \qquad (\wedge_{i=j+1}^{k} U_i \in \rho(\lfloor mx_i \rfloor) \wedge \rho, \kappa \models_\Gamma M) \\
\text{(ANew)} & \rho, \kappa \models_\Gamma (\nu\, n_{\bar{i}})\, M & \text{iff } \rho, \kappa \models_\Gamma M \\
\text{(ARep)} & \rho, \kappa \models_\Gamma !M & \text{iff } \rho, \kappa \models_\Gamma M \\
\text{(APar)} & \rho, \kappa \models_\Gamma M_1 \mid M_2 & \text{iff } \rho, \kappa \models_\Gamma M_1 \wedge \rho, \kappa \models_\Gamma M_2 \\
\text{(ANil)} & \rho, \kappa \models_\Gamma \mathsf{0} & \text{iff true}
\end{array}
$$

$$
\begin{array}{lll}
\text{(ALet)} & \rho, \kappa \models_\Gamma \mathsf{let}\ X \subseteq S\ \mathsf{in}\ M & \text{iff } \rho, \kappa \models_{\Gamma[X \mapsto S']} M \\
 & & \quad \text{where } S' \subseteq_{fin} \Gamma(S) \text{ and } \lfloor S' \rfloor = \lfloor \Gamma(S) \rfloor \\
\text{(AIPar)} & \rho, \kappa \models_\Gamma |_{i \in S}\ M & \text{iff } \wedge_{a \in \Gamma(S)} \rho, \kappa \models_\Gamma M[i \mapsto a] \\
\text{(AINew)} & \rho, \kappa \models_\Gamma (\nu_{\bar{i} \in \bar{S}}\ n_{\bar{a}\bar{i}})M & \text{iff } \rho, \kappa \models_\Gamma M
\end{array}
$$

Fig. 4. Analysis of LySa expressions, $\rho \models E : \vartheta$, and object-level and meta-level processes $\rho, \kappa \models_\Gamma M$

Messages communicate by the polyadic output are recorded in an analysis component $\kappa \in \mathcal{P}(\lfloor Val \rfloor^*)$ by a set of tuples of *canonical* values, thereby, benefitting from the finite partitioning of the value domain. It is also practical to have an analysis component $\rho : \lfloor Var \rfloor \rightarrow \mathcal{P}(\lfloor Val \rfloor)$ that records the set of values that variables may become bound to during the execution of a process. The control flow analysis is specified using the Flow Logic [20] framework as a predicate

$$\rho, \kappa \models_\Gamma P$$

that holds precisely when ρ, κ is an analysis result that correctly describes the behaviour of the object-level process P. The predicate is defined inductively in the structure of processes in Figure 4. The predicate may be seen as a specification of which analysis results, ρ, κ, that describe the behaviour of P. In practice, on the other hand, we will typically be interested in computing such an analysis result for a given process, P, and this the topic of Section 3.4. The last three rules in Figure 4 describe the meta-level analysis and they will be discussed in Section 3.3. These rules are the only ones that really use the environment Γ and this environment is often ignored when discussing the object-level analysis.

The object-level part of the analysis in Figure 4 is essentially the control flow analysis from [4]. It relies on an auxiliary predicate $\rho \models E : \vartheta$ defined on expression. Conceptually, $\vartheta \in \mathcal{P}(\lfloor Val \rfloor)$ contains the set of values that E may evaluate to in some execution: (AN) names may evaluate to their canonical name; (AVar) variables may evaluate to the values recorded in the analysis component ρ; and (ASEnc) encryption expression may evaluate to any encryption generated by recursive evaluation of subexpressions.

The rule for k-ary output (AOut) evaluates all expressions using the auxiliary predicate $\rho \models E_i : \vartheta_i$ and ensures that all combinations of their evaluations are recorded as k-tuples in κ. Correspondingly, k-ary input succeeds according to the analysis rule (AInp) for all k-tuples in κ where the first j values correspond to what the j first expressions may evaluate to. This takes care of the analysis of pattern-matching. If it is deemed successful then the remaining $k - j$ values are required to be component-wise recorded in $\rho(\lfloor mx_i \rfloor)$ thereby ensuring that the analysis records possible variable bindings. The rule (ASDec) for decryption follows the same idea as for pattern-matching input though here the candidates are found by evaluating the expression E. The remaining rules for the object-level analysis are standard. One may capture the fact that the analysis only distinguished names up to their canonical assignment — a similar result holds for variables.

Lemma 1 (Invariance of canonical names). *If $\rho, \kappa \models P$ and $\lfloor n_i \rfloor = \lfloor n'_{i'} \rfloor$ then $\rho, \kappa \models P[n_i \mapsto n'_{i'}]$.*

Proof. The lemma is a direct consequence of the fact that the analysis only records canonical names. The proof proceeds by straightforward by induction in the definition of the analysis with the only interesting case being the rule (AN) though it too is straightforward because $\lfloor n_i \rfloor = \lfloor n_i[n_i \mapsto n'_{i'}] \rfloor = \lfloor n'_{i'} \rfloor$.

The main technical result about the correctness of the object-level analysis is that the analysis correctly captures the behaviour of all executions of an object-level process. This is formulated as a standard subject reduction result:

Lemma 2 (Subject reduction). *If $\rho, \kappa \models P$ and $P \to P'$ then $\rho, \kappa \models P'$.*

Proof. The proof proceeds by structural induction in the reduction step $P \to P'$. The proof uses auxiliary lemmata about invariance of structural congruence and substitution of variables for values in ρ. The details may be found in [4].

3.3 The Meta-level

The analysis of the meta-level constructs are given in the last three rules in Figure 4. The rules makes use of the environment $\Gamma : (SetId \cup \mathcal{P}(Index)) \to$

$\mathcal{P}(Index)$ to record declarations of set identifiers. It is implicitly assumed that every index set S maps to itself i.e. that $\Gamma(S) = S$ for all $S \in \mathcal{P}(Index)$. The environment Γ also serves as a substitution. For example, taking $\Gamma = [X \mapsto S]$ then $M\Gamma$ is as M where every occurrence of X has been replaced by S.

The rule (ALet) updates Γ for the set identifier X declared in the let-construct. However, the analysis only keeps track of indices up to a finite, canonical partitioning of the index sets. Therefore it suffices to update Γ with a finite subset S' that belongs to the same equivalence class as the set S, which is declared in the let-construct. Thus, Γ will map all set identifiers to finite sets, which makes it easy to implement Γ. The rule (AIPar) makes the conjunction of the analysis of the process M where i has been substituted for the indexes in $\Gamma(S)$. This substitution corresponds to what happens semantically in (IIPar) while the conjunction is analogue to the analysis of binary parallel composition in (APar). The rule (AINew) ignores the restriction similarly to the rule (ANew).

The fact that the meta-level analysis is invariant up to the canonical partitioning of index sets is captured by the following lemma:

Lemma 3 (Invariance of canonical indices). *Let* $\lfloor a_1 \rfloor = \lfloor a_2 \rfloor$. *Then* $\rho, \kappa \models_\Gamma M[i \mapsto a_1]$ *if and only if* $\rho, \kappa \models_\Gamma M[i \mapsto a_2]$.

Proof. The substitution only modifies names and variables so it is sufficient to note that the analysis uses their canonical representatives and that $\lfloor n_{\bar{i}}[i \mapsto a_1] \rfloor = \lfloor n_{\bar{i}}[i \mapsto a_2] \rfloor$ as well as $\lfloor x_{\bar{i}}[i \mapsto a_1] \rfloor = \lfloor x_{\bar{i}}[i \mapsto a_2] \rfloor$. Thus, the analysis of $M[i \mapsto a_1]$ and $M[i \mapsto a_2]$ will be equivalent for all M.

The analysis of the let-construct uses the *largest* set of canonical indices. It suffices to use this set for the analysis because then all scenarios where smaller subsets are chosen will also be covered by this analysis. This can formally be stated as the lemma:

Lemma 4 (Subset in let-declaration). *If* $\lfloor S_2 \rfloor \subseteq \lfloor S_1 \rfloor$ *then* $\rho, \kappa \models_{\Gamma[X \mapsto S_1]} M$ *implies* $\rho, \kappa \models_{\Gamma[X \mapsto S_2]} M$.

Proof. The proof proceeds by induction in the structure of M.
Case $\mathsf{let}\ X' \subseteq S\ \mathsf{in}\ M$. Assume that $\rho, \kappa \models_{\Gamma[X \mapsto S_1]} \mathsf{let}\ X' \subseteq S\ \mathsf{in}\ M$ i.e. by (ALet)

$$\rho, \kappa \models_{\Gamma[X \mapsto S_1][X' \mapsto S']} M$$

for some S' such that $S' \subseteq_{fin} \Gamma(S)$ and $\lfloor S' \rfloor = \lfloor \Gamma(S) \rfloor$. Now assume that $X = X'$. Then the inner substitution of X is overwritten by $[X' \mapsto S']$ so

$$\begin{aligned} \rho, \kappa \models_{\Gamma[X \mapsto S_1][X' \mapsto S']} M \text{ iff } & \rho, \kappa \models_{\Gamma[X \mapsto S_2][X' \mapsto S']} M \\ \text{iff } & \rho, \kappa \models_{\Gamma[X \mapsto S_2]} \mathsf{let}\ X' \subseteq S\ \mathsf{in}\ M \end{aligned}$$

as required. Alternatively assume that $X \neq X'$. Then the order of substitutions does not matter. Using this and the induction hypothesis (IH) one may derive

$$\begin{aligned} \rho, \kappa \models_{\Gamma[X \mapsto S_1][X' \mapsto S']} M \text{ iff } \quad & \rho, \kappa \models_{\Gamma[X' \mapsto S'][X \mapsto S_1]} M \\ \text{implies } & \rho, \kappa \models_{\Gamma[X' \mapsto S'][X \mapsto S_2]} M \text{ (by IH)} \\ \text{iff } \quad & \rho, \kappa \models_{\Gamma[X \mapsto S_2][X' \mapsto S']} M \end{aligned}$$

which allows to conclude that $\rho, \kappa \models_{\Gamma[X \mapsto S_2]} \mathsf{let}\ X' \subseteq S\ \mathsf{in}\ M$ as required.

Case $|_{i \in S}\ M$. First notice that if $S \neq X$ then $\rho, \kappa \models_{\Gamma[X \mapsto S_1]} |_{i \in S}\ M$ implies $\rho, \kappa \models_{\Gamma[X \mapsto S_2]} |_{i \in S}\ M$ simply by applying the induction hypothesis for the analysis of M. Next assume that $S = X$, which gives that

$$\rho, \kappa \models_{\Gamma[X \mapsto S_1]} |_{i \in S}\ M \quad \text{iff} \quad \wedge_{a_1 \in S_1}\ \rho, \kappa \models_{\Gamma[X \mapsto S_1]} M[i \mapsto a_1]$$

From the assumption that $\lfloor S_2 \rfloor \subseteq \lfloor S_1 \rfloor$ it is known that for every $a_2 \in S_2$ there is a corresponding $a_1 \in S_1$ such that $\lfloor a_2 \rfloor = \lfloor a_1 \rfloor$. By Lemma 3 then it holds that $\rho, \kappa \models_{\Gamma[X \mapsto S_1]} M[i \mapsto a_2]$ for all $a_2 \in S_2$. This together with the induction hypothesis allows to conclude

$$\wedge_{a_2 \in S_2}\ \rho, \kappa \models_{\Gamma[X \mapsto S_2]} M[i \mapsto a_2]$$

which is precisely $\rho, \kappa \models_{\Gamma[X \mapsto S_2]} |_{i \in S}\ M$ as required.

The remaining cases are straightforward and follow by applying the induction hypothesis because the analysis does not directly use Γ in these cases.

Using this lemma, we can now prove the main result about the correctness of the meta-level analysis, namely that the meta-level analysis of a process M covers the analysis of all object-level processes that M instantiate to.

Theorem 1 (Correctness of instantiation). *If* $\rho, \kappa \models_\Gamma M$ *and* $M\Gamma \Rrightarrow P$ *then* $\rho, \kappa \models P$.

Proof. The proof proceeds by induction in the structure of M.
Case $\mathsf{let}\ X \subseteq S\ \mathsf{in}\ M$. First, calculate

$$(\mathsf{let}\ X \subseteq S\ \mathsf{in}\ M)\Gamma = \mathsf{let}\ X \subseteq \Gamma(S)\ \mathsf{in}\ M(\Gamma \setminus X)$$

where $\Gamma \setminus X$ is as Γ except that $\Gamma(X)$ is undefined. Next, assume that $(\mathsf{let}\ X \subseteq S\ \mathsf{in}\ M)\Gamma \Rrightarrow P$ which according to (ILet) in Table 3 happens because

$$(M(\Gamma \setminus X))[X \mapsto S'] \Rrightarrow P$$

for some $S' \subseteq_{fin} \Gamma(S)$. Because X is undefined in $\Gamma \setminus X$ this is the same as

$$M(\Gamma[X \mapsto S']) \Rrightarrow P$$

Next, assume that $\rho, \kappa \models_\Gamma \mathsf{let}\ X \subseteq S\ \mathsf{in}\ M$ i.e. from (ALet) that

$$\rho, \kappa \models_{\Gamma[X \mapsto S'']} M$$

where $S'' \subseteq_{fin} \Gamma(S)$ and $\lfloor S'' \rfloor = \lfloor \Gamma(S) \rfloor$. Notice that $\lfloor S' \rfloor \subseteq \lfloor S'' \rfloor$ so by Lemma 4

$$\rho, \kappa \models_{\Gamma[X \mapsto S']} M$$

From the induction hypothesis it then follows that $\rho, \kappa \models P$ as required.
Case $|_{i \in S}\ M$. Assume $\rho, \kappa \models_\Gamma |_{i \in S}\ M$ i.e. from (AIPar) that

$$\wedge_{a \in \Gamma(S)}\ \rho, \kappa \models_\Gamma M[i \mapsto a]$$

Furthermore, let $\Gamma(S) = \{a_1, \ldots, a_k\}$ for some arbitrary set $\{a_1, \ldots, a_k\}$. Next, assume that $(|_{i \in S}\ M)\Gamma \Rrightarrow P_1 \mid \ldots \mid P_k$ by (IPar). Noting that $(|_{i \in S}\ M)\Gamma = |_{i \in \Gamma(S)}\ M\Gamma$ and using (IIPar) this means that

$$M\Gamma[i \mapsto a_j] \Rrightarrow P_j$$

for each $a_j \in \Gamma(S)$. Since the two substitutions Γ and $[i \mapsto a_j]$ range over different domains the order of the substitution of does not matter. Thus, it also holds that for all $a_j \in \Gamma(S)$ that

$$(M[i \mapsto a_j])\Gamma \Rrightarrow P_j$$

The induction hypothesis can be applied k times to establish that

$$\rho, \kappa \models P_1 \wedge \ldots \wedge \rho, \kappa \models P_k$$

which by (APar) from Table 4 applied k times give precisely $\rho, \kappa \models P_1 \mid \ldots \mid P_k$ as required.

Case $(\nu_{\overline{i} \in \overline{S}}\ n_{\overline{a}\overline{i}})M$. Assume that $\rho, \kappa \models_\Gamma (\nu_{\overline{i} \in \overline{S}}\ n_{\overline{a}\overline{i}})M$ i.e. that

$$\rho, \kappa \models_\Gamma M$$

Let $\Gamma(\overline{S}) = \{\overline{a_1}, \ldots, \overline{a_k}\}$ and note that $((\nu_{\overline{i} \in \overline{S}}\ n_{\overline{a}\overline{i}})M)\Gamma = (\nu_{\overline{i} \in \Gamma(\overline{S})}\ n_{\overline{a}\overline{i}})M\Gamma$. Next assume that $((\nu_{\overline{i} \in \overline{S}}\ n_{\overline{a}\overline{i}})M)\Gamma \Rrightarrow (\nu\, n_{\overline{a}\overline{a_1}}) \ldots (\nu\, n_{\overline{a}\overline{a_k}})\, P$, which according to (IINew) happens because

$$M\Gamma \Rrightarrow P$$

The induction hypothesis applies to give that $\rho, \kappa \models P$, which by (ANew) from Table 4 is the same as $\rho, \kappa \models (\nu\, n_{\overline{a}\overline{a_1}}) \ldots (\nu\, n_{\overline{a}\overline{a_k}})\, P$ as requires.

The remaining cases for the object-level syntax are straightforward because the substitution Γ does not modify anything in the object-level syntax.

3.4 Implementation

The goal of implementing the control flow analysis is to attain an analysis result for a process. That is, given a process M the implementation provides ρ, κ such that $\rho, \kappa \models_{[]} M$. The implementation of the control flow analysis in the LySatool works in two steps: (1) a generation function $\mathcal{G}(M)$ produces a formula that corresponds to the analysis predicate defined in Figure 4, and (2) a standard solver [19] is used to find an interpretation, which satisfies the formula.

The main challenge when the object-level analysis of [4] was implemented in the LySatool version 1 [8] was that the analysis is specified over infinite sets of terms (which denote encryption). The implementation solves this by encoding sets of terms as regular tree grammars and manipulates a finite number of grammar rules akin to the strategy proposed in [18].

The second version of the LySatool is based on version 1 and indeed much of the code is reused. The main modification is to extend the constraint generation function $\mathcal{G}$ from ranging over object-level processes, only, to range over meta-level constructs as well. The definition of this function closely follows the three last rules in Figure 4 by taking the left-hand side of the iff as an argument to the function and returning the right hand-side. In the case of the let $X \subseteq S$ in M, one has to choose a finite set that is within the same equivalence class as S. In the implementation this is the point where the partitioning of the indexing sets are important and serve as a parameter for controlling the precision of the meta-level analysis. The analysis results presented in Section 4 and Section 6 have been attained using this version 2 of the LySatool.

4 The Attacker

The goal of the LySatool is to validate security properties of a LySa process. Consequently, the main focus is on analysing process under attack from malicious parties also populating the network. The object-level of LySa has been designed such that this attack setup can be described as simple parallel composition: if P is an object-level process describing a protocol and $P_\bullet$ is an attacker then the behaviour of the process $P \mid P_\bullet$ comprises all the attacks that $P_\bullet$ may launch over the network on P.

Instead of having to analyse all the infinitely many attackers $P_\bullet$ in parallel with P we follow ideas from [17]: It suffices to analyse a *single* process, P_{hard}, to get an account of the behaviour of all attackers.

Lemma 5 (Existence of a hardest attacker). *There exists process P_{hard} with the property that: for all attacker processes $P_\bullet$*

$$\rho, \kappa \models P \mid P_{hard} \quad \textit{implies} \quad \rho, \kappa \models P \mid P_\bullet$$

Proof. The proof is by construction of P_{hard} and subsequent induction in $P_\bullet$. The proof also relies on restricting the attention to attackers that only use the same arities as P for communication and encryption. Details can be found in [4].

By the subject reduction result in Lemma 2 it then follows that $\rho, \kappa \models P \mid P_{hard}$ gives an account of how P behaves under attack from any possible attacker, which is allowed by the semantics of LySa. This analysis result gives an account of the behaviour of the attacker. Note also that because $P_\bullet$ is placed in parallel with P it has access to all the free names in P. The hardest attacker, P_{hard}, therefore takes $\mathrm{fn}(P)$ as a parameter.

When choosing the partitioning of names and variables, a special equivalence class is reserved for names and variables at the attacker. Representatives of these equivalence classes are denoted $n_\bullet$ and $x_\bullet$, respectively. For example, $\rho(x_\bullet)$ is an over-approximation of all the values that any variable in an attacker may become bound to i.e. it represents the knowledge of the attacker.

4.1 The Attacker at the Meta-level

When we want to evaluate the security of a scenario described by a meta-level process M we must consider the possibility that each of the object-level process

P, where $M \Rrightarrow P$, may be under attack. The aim of the analysis is, hence, to guarantee that no such attacks can occur on any instance of M.

In order to analyse all instances of a meta-level process under attack, we can once more rely directly on the hardest attacker P_{hard}. By design every object-level process instantiates to itself. Consequently, adding P_{hard} at the meta-level means that it always instantiates to be a hardest attacker at the object-level. This is made clear by the following theorem:

Theorem 2 (Attacker at the meta-level). *If* $\rho, \kappa \models_\Gamma M \mid P_{hard}$ *and* $M\Gamma \Rrightarrow P$ *then* $\rho, \kappa \models P \mid P_\bullet$ *for all attacker processes* $P_\bullet$.

Proof. From (APar) then $\rho, \kappa \models_\Gamma M$ and $\rho, \kappa \models_\Gamma P_{hard}$. By Theorem 1 then $\rho, \kappa \models P$. Furthermore, because P_{hard} is an object-level process then $P_{hard}\Gamma = P_{hard}$ and $P_{hard} \Rrightarrow P_{hard}$ so by Theorem 1 it follows that also $\rho, \kappa \models P_{hard}$. Consequently, by (APar) then $\rho, \kappa \models P \mid P_{hard}$ and finally by Lemma 5 $\rho, \kappa \models P \mid P_\bullet$ for all attackers $P_\bullet$.

At the meta-level, the function mfn(M) is used to provide the set of free names to P_{hard}. This set may actually be larger than the free names in some specific instance of M meaning that the attacker may increase its power because it has access to too many names compared to what occurs semantically. However, if no attacks are reported by the analysis when the attacker has this extra power then no attacks can occur semantically, either.

Example 3. We refer to the scenario for the nonce handshake from Example 2 as the process M. Taking $\lfloor \mathbb{N} \rfloor = \{1\}$ the analysis result of $\rho, \kappa \models_{[]} M \mid P_{hard}$ as reported by the LySatool reveals that

$$\rho(x_\bullet) \cap \mathit{Name} = \{\lfloor n_{11} \rfloor, \lfloor A_1 \rfloor, \lfloor B_1 \rfloor\}$$

The index 1 in the analysis result is a canonical representative of any element in $\mathbb{N}$. Thus, the attacker may learn any nonce n_{ij} as well as the identities of any principal A_i and B_j for $i, j \in \mathbb{N}$. On the other hand, the analysis guarantees that the keys K_{ij} are confidential because $\lfloor K_{11} \rfloor$ is not in $\rho(x_\bullet)$. Since the analysis is an over-approximation this means that no attacker can ever learn the keys.

5 Security Properties

As discussed in Example 3, the analysis can guarantee *confidentiality* properties. To find out whether a particular value V is confidential one simply inspects the analysis result. If $\lfloor V \rfloor$ is not in $\rho(x_\bullet)$ then the analysis guarantees that no attacker can ever bind V to any of its variables.

The analysis of [4] is furthermore able to guarantee destination and origin *authentication.* This property considers the places where cryptography is applied to ensure that a message can only reach a particular principal. The property of destination and origin authentication is specified by annotations of the form

$$[\mathsf{at}\; c\; \mathsf{dest}\; \mathcal{C}] \qquad \text{and} \qquad [\mathsf{at}\; c\; \mathsf{orig}\; \mathcal{C}]$$

at all points of encryption and decryption, respectively. Here $c \in CP$ is a crypto-point that marks the point in the syntax (akin to a line-number). Encryptions are furthermore annotated with a set $C \subseteq CP$ of destination crypto-points where the encrypted values are intended to be decrypted. Symmetrically, decryptions are annotated with a set C of crypto-points where successfully decrypted value are intended to have been encrypted.

Semantically annotations are void i.e. they do not interfere with the semantic behaviour of a process. A process P is said to *guarantee dynamic authentication* none of these intentions are broken in any execution of the process. That is, P guarantees dynamic authentication if there are no reduction steps derived using the rule (SDec) of the form $\mathsf{decrypt}\{V_1, \ldots, V_k\}_{V_0}[\mathsf{at}\, c' \;\mathsf{dest}\, C'\,]\ \mathsf{as}\{V_1, \ldots, V_j; mx_{j+1}, \ldots, mx_k\}_{V_0}[\mathsf{at}\, c\ \mathsf{orig}\, C\,]\ \mathsf{in}\, P \to P'$ such that $c \notin C'$ or $c' \notin C$.

The main result of [4] is that an extension of the object-level analysis presented in Figure 4 is capable of analysing whether an object-level process guarantees dynamic authentication. The extension of the analysis essentially boils down to adding a check of whether $c \notin C'$ or $c' \notin C$ in the rule (SDec) for analysis of decryption. If the analysis finds no errors in these checks then a process P is said to *guarantee static authentication.* The main result of [4] is that

Lemma 6. *If P guarantees static authentication then P guarantees dynamic authentication.*

Proof. The proof relies on the fact that the analysis over-approximates the dynamic behaviour of P and thereby also the potential authentication errors that may be reported. The details are [4].

5.1 Authentication at the Meta-level

To further refine the authentication property for the meta-level, crypto-points are equipped with indices analogue to indices on names and variables. That is, crypto-points will be of the form $c_{\vec{i}}$. Crypto-points are also made subject to a notion of canonicity because the meta-level analysis only distinguishes elements up to the canonical partitioning of index sets.

The meta-level analysis is now capable of checking destination and origin authentication up to the partitioning into equivalence classes. Conceptually, the analysis guarantees that messages only reach principals within a certain equivalence class. The meta-level analysis is extended by adding a check of whether $\lfloor c_{\vec{i}} \rfloor \notin \lfloor C' \rfloor$ or $\lfloor c'_{\vec{i}} \rfloor \notin \lfloor C \rfloor$ in the rule (SDec). If no violations of the authentication properties are found by these checks in the meta-level analysis of M then M *guarantees static authentication.* The check for static authentication by the meta-level analysis suffices guarantee the authentication properties for all object-level process that M instantiates to:

Theorem 3 (Authentication at the meta-level). *If M guarantees static authentication and $M\Gamma \Rrightarrow P$ then P guarantees dynamic authentication.*

Proof. The theorem follows immediately from Theorem 1, the fact that indexed crypto-points are subject to canonicity, as well as Lemma 6.

6 An Example Protocol

To illustrate the usefulness of the meta-level we analyse a protocol by Bauer, Berson, and Feiertag [2]. According to a recent survey [6] there are no known attacks on the protocol and, furthermore, the protocol is the basis one of the key establishment mechanisms in an ISO/IEC standard [15]. The protocol makes use of a server with which each principal initially shares a key KS_i. In the first two messages of the protocol, fresh nonces na_{ij} and nb_{ij} produced by principal I_i and I_j, respectively, are sent to the server along with the identities of the principals. The server generates a new session key K_{ij}, which is returned encrypted to each principal along with their own nonce and the identity of the other principal. The protocol may be encoded as a meta-level scenario in the following way:

$$
\begin{array}{ll}
\multicolumn{2}{l}{\mathsf{let}\ X \subseteq S_0\ \mathsf{in}\ \mathsf{let}\ Y \subseteq S_1\ \mathsf{in}\ (\nu_{i\in X\cup Y}\ KS_i)} \\
\quad |_{i\in X}\ |_{j\in Y} & !(\nu\, na_{ij})\,\langle I_i, na_{ij}\rangle. \\
 & (;\ xa_{ij}).\mathsf{decrypt}\ xa_{ij}\ \mathsf{as}\ \{I_j, na_{ij};\ xk_{ij}\}_{KS_i}[\mathsf{at}\ a_{ij}\ \mathsf{orig}\ \{s2_{ij}\}]\ \mathsf{in}\ 0 \\
|\ |_{j\in Y}\ |_{i\in X} & !(I_i;\ yn_{ij}). \\
 & (\nu\, nb_{ij})\,\langle I_j, I_i, yn_{ij}, nb_{ij}\rangle. \\
 & (;\ yb_{ij}, ya_{ij}).\mathsf{decrypt}\ yb_{ij}\ \mathsf{as}\ \{I_i, nb_{ij};\ yk_{ij}\}_{KS_j}[\mathsf{at}\ b_{ij}\ \mathsf{orig}\ \{s1_{ij}\}]\ \mathsf{in} \\
 & \langle ya_{ij}\rangle.0 \\
|\ |_{i\in X}\ |_{j\in Y} & !(I_j, I_i;\ za_{ij}, zb_{ij}).(\nu\, K_{ij})\,\langle \{I_i, zb_{ij}, K_{ij}\}_{KS_j}[\mathsf{at}\ s1_{ij}\ \mathsf{dest}\ \{b_{ij}\}], \\
 & \qquad\qquad \{I_j, za_{ij}, K_{ij}\}_{KS_i}[\mathsf{at}\ s2_{ij}\ \mathsf{dest}\ \{a_{ij}\}]\rangle.0
\end{array}
$$

Annotations are added to declare that the two encryptions made at the server are intended for the correct responder and initiator of the protocol, only.

One scenario can be described by taking $S_0 = \{0\}$ and $S_1 = \{1\}$. Then the meta-level process describes a scenario where principal I_0 repeatedly initiates the protocol with I_1. When choosing $\lfloor S_0 \rfloor = \{0\}$ and $\lfloor S_1 \rfloor = \{1\}$, the analysis guarantees static authentication. That is, the analysis guarantees that the messages containing the session keys will only be delivered to the correct principals.

Taking instead $S_0 = S_1 = \mathbb{N}$, the encoding represents a scenario where every principal I_i can use the protocol with every principal I_j for $i, j \in \mathbb{N}$. This scenario includes the case where a pair of principals uses the protocol in both directions at the same time. For this scenario, the analysis is no longer guarantees static authentication. For example, if we choose $\lfloor \mathbb{N} \rfloor = \{1\}$ the analysis reports possible cross-overs of messages where something encrypted at $\lfloor s1_{11} \rfloor$ may be decrypted at $\lfloor a_{11} \rfloor$ and also that something encrypted at $\lfloor s2_{11} \rfloor$ may be decrypted at $\lfloor b_{11} \rfloor$.

In fact, the scenario does not satisfy dynamic authentication i.e. the authentication property may also be violated semantically. The attack occurs precisely when the protocol is used in both directions at the same time. That this is the case is illustrated by the following message sequence where $A(\cdot)$ describes the behaviour of the attacker:

$$
\begin{array}{llcl}
1.1 & I_i & \rightarrow I_j & : I_i, na_i \\
1.2 & I_j & \rightarrow A(S) & : I_i, na_i, I_j, nb_j \\
2.1 & I_j & \rightarrow I_i & : I_j, na_j \\
2.2 & I_i & \rightarrow A(S) & : I_j, na_j, I_i, nb_i \\
1.2' & A(S) & \rightarrow S & : I_i, nb_i, I_j, nb_j
\end{array}
$$

$$\begin{array}{lll} 1.3\ S & \rightarrow A(I_j): & \{K_{ij}, I_i, nb_j\}_{K_j}, \{K_{ij}, I_j, nb_i\}_{K_i} \\ 1.3'\ A(S) \rightarrow I_j & : & \{K_{ij}, I_i, nb_j\}_{K_j}, garbage \\ 2.3'\ A(S) \rightarrow I_i & : & \{K_{ij}, I_j, nb_i\}_{K_i}, garbage \end{array}$$

The decryption of message $2.3'$ happens at I_i acting as a responder and, thus, represents an unintended cross-over of a message as reported by the analysis when "something encrypted at $\lfloor s2_{11} \rfloor$ was decrypted at $\lfloor b_{11} \rfloor$".

As an end result of the attack the two principals I_i and I_j end up sharing a session key K_{ij}. However, both of them will think that the key came from the protocol session that the other principal initiated. More precisely, they expect that the protocol provided two distinct keys K_{ij} and K_{ji} because they ran two session of the protocol. In fact, the protocol distributed only one key K_{ij}. The problem is easy to fix: one simply needs to ensure that the two encryptions made at the server do not have the same format. The analysis guarantees authentication when the messages in one of these encryptions are rearranged.

7 Conclusion

7.1 Related Work

The meta-level analysis bears some resemblance to a result shown by Comon-Lundh and Cortier [11] that says that it suffices to consider a limited number of principals when analysing a protocol. Their result is shown by projecting the semantic behaviour of all principals onto this limited number of principals. More precisely is suffices to consider $k + 1$ principals where k is the number of different parts that a principal can play in the protocol. One comment on this is that Stoller has shown that there exists protocols require exponentially many different principals [21] so k may be quite large. Our meta-level analysis can also be seen as projection the behaviour of different principals. However, the projection is onto the canonical values in the analysis result rather that onto the semantic behaviour as in [11]. Thus, our results are provided by a computable analysis that features a syntactic meta-level, which furthermore allows a flexible modelling of different scenarios.

The idea of having additional syntax that describes scenarios can also be found in frameworks such as Casper [16], CAPSL [12], CVS [13],and AVISS [1]. The main difference from our approach is that they use syntactic unfolding i.e. that their scenarios undergo a syntactic transformation (corresponding to our instantiation) *before* analysis takes place.

It is also be appropriate to mention that our object-level analysis is related to the approaches in [3,14,10]. However, since none of these approaches deal with scenarios, which are the topic of this paper, the reader is referred to [4,7] for a detailed comparison.

7.2 Summary

When discussing the security of a protocol it is vital to consider the scenario in which the protocol will be deployed. This paper puts the focus on these deployment scenarios by extending the process calculus LySa with a meta-level. This meta-level contains language primitives that caters for a flexible description of scenarios. We have shown that it is viable to make a control flow analysis directly on the meta-level that, also in practice, is capable of guaranteeing both confidentiality and authentication properties. The analysis has been implemented with relatively minor effort by relying on a previous implementation of the object-level analysis. The result is version 2 of the LySatool, which has proven its worth by finding a previously unreported problem in a classical security protocol. The LySatool is freely available at

http://www.imm.dtu.dk/cs_LySa/lysatool

where the full analysis results for examples in this paper can also be found.

Acknowledgements. The idea of having an analysable meta-level came up when writing [9] with Flemming Nielson and Hanne Riis Nielson. Many other ideas concerning LySa come from them as well as Chiara Bodei and Pierpaolo Degano.

References

1. A. Armando, D. Basin, M. Bouallagui, Y. Chevalier, L. Compagna, S. Mödersheim, M. Rusinowitch, M. Turuani, L. Viganò, and L. Vigneron. The AVISS security protocol analysis tool. In *CAV 2002*, volume 2404 of *LNCS*, pages 349–353. Springer, 2002.
2. R. K. Bauer, T. A. Berson, and R. J. Feiertag. A key distribution protocol using event markers. *ACM Transactions on Computer Systems*, 1(3):249 – 255, 1983.
3. B. Blanchet. An efficient cryptographic protocol verifier based on Prolog rules. In *CSFW 2001*, pages 82–96. IEEE, 2001.
4. C. Bodei, M. Buchholtz, P. Degano, F. Nielson, and H. Riis Nielson. Automatic validation of protocol narration. In *CSFW 2003*, pages 126–140. IEEE, 2003.
5. C. Bodei, M. Buchholtz, P. Degano, F. Nielson, and H. Riis Nielson. Static validation of security protocols. *JSC*, 2004. To appear. Preliminary version at www.imm.dtu.dk/pubdb/views/edoc_download.php/3199/pdf/imm3199.pdf.
6. C. Boyd and A. Mathuria. *Protocols for Authentication and Key Establishment.* Springer, 2003.
7. M. Buchholtz. Automated analysis of security in networking systems. Ph. D. thesis proposal. Available from http://www.imm.dtu.dk/~mib/thesis/, December 2004.
8. M. Buchholtz. Implementing control flow analysis for security protocols. DEGAS Report WP6-IMM-I00-Pub-003, Draft 2003.
9. M. Buchholtz, F. Nielson, and H. Riis Nielson. A calculus for control flow analysis of security protocols. *IJIS*, 2(3-4):145–167, 2004.
10. M. Bugliesi, R. Focardi, and M. Maffei. Compositional analysis of authentication protocols. In *ESOP 2004*, volume 2986 of *LNCS*, pages 140–154. Springer, 2004.
11. H. Comon-Lundh and V. Cortier. Security properties: Two agents are sufficient. In *ESOP 2003*, number 2618 in LNCS, pages 99–113. Springer, 2003.
12. G. Denker, J. Millen, and H. Rueß. The CAPSL integrated protocol environment. Technical Report SRI-CLS-2000-02, SRI International, 2000.
13. A. Durante, R. Focardi, and R. Gorrieri. A compiler for analyzing cryptographic protocols using noninterference. *TSEM*, 9(4):488–528, 2000.

14. A. D. Gordon and A. Jeffrey. Authenticity by Typing for Security Protocols. In *CSFW 2001*, pages 145 –159. IEEE, 2001.
15. Information technology - security techniques - key management - part 2. mechanisms using symmetric techniques ISO/IEC 11770-2. International Standard, 1996.
16. G. Lowe. Casper: A compiler for the analysis of security protocols. *JSC*, 6(1):53–84, 1998.
17. F. Nielson, H. Riis Nielson, and R. R. Hansen. Validating firewalls using Flow Logics. *TCS*, 283(2):381–418, 2002.
18. F. Nielson, H. Riis Nielson, and H. Seidl. Cryptographic analysis in cubic time. In *TOSCA 2001*, volume 62 of *ENTCS*. Elsevier, 2001.
19. F. Nielson, H. Riis Nielson, and H. Seidl. A succinct solver for ALFP. *NJC*, 9:335–372, 2002.
20. H. Riis Nielson and F. Nielson. Flow Logic: a multi-paradigmatic approach to static analysis. In *The Essence of Computation: Complexity, Analysis, Transformation*, volume 2566 of *LNCS*, pages 223–244. Springer, 2002.
21. S. D. Stoller. A bound on attacks on authentication protocols. In *Proceedings of the 2nd IFIP International Conference on Theoretical Computer Science (TCS 2002)*, pages 588–600. Kluwer, 2002.

Namespace Logic: A Logic for a Reflective Higher-Order Calculus

L.G. Meredith[1] and Matthias Radestock[2]

[1] CTO, Djinnisys Corporation,
505 N72nd St, Seattle, WA 98103, USA
lgreg.meredith@gmail.com
[2] CTO, LShift, Ltd.,
6 Rufus St, London N1 6PE, UK
matthias@lshift.net

Abstract. In [19] it was observed that a theory like the π-calculus, dependent on a theory of names, can be closed, through a mechanism of quoting, so that (quoted) processes provide the necessary notion of names. Here we expand on this theme by examining a construction for a Hennessy-Milner logic corresponding to an asynchronous message-passing calculus built on a notion of quoting.

Like standard Hennessy-Milner logics, the logic exhibits formulae corresponding to sets of processes, but a new class of formulae, corresponding to sets of names, also emerges. This feature provides for a number of interesting possible applications from security to data manipulation. Specifically, we illustrate formulae for controlling process response on ranges of names reminiscent of a (static) constraint on port access in a firewall configuration. Likewise, we exhibit formulae in a names-as-data paradigm corresponding to validation for fragment of `XML Schema`.

1 Introduction

Starting from the practical end of things, whether we consider MAC addresses, IP addresses, domain names or URL's it is clear that distributed computing is practiced, today, using names. Moreover, it is essential to the programs that administer as well as to the ones that compute over this distributed computing infrastructure that these names have structure. Thus, when we look to theory, especially a theory, like the π-calculus, of computing based on interaction over named channels, to help us with this practice some story must be told about how the structure of these names contributes to interaction and computation over (channels named by) them.

Starting from the theoretical end, nowhere in the tools available to the computer scientist is there a countably infinite set of *atomic* entities that might function as names. All such sets, e.g. the natural numbers, the set of strings of finite length on some alphabet, etc., are *generated* from a finite presentation, and as such the elements of these sets inherit *structure* from the generating procedure. As a theoretician focusing on some aspects of the theory of processes

R. De Nicola and D. Sangiorgi (Eds.): TGC 2005, LNCS 3705, pp. 353–369, 2005.

built from such a set, one may temporarily forget that structure, but it is there nonetheless, and comes to the fore the moment one tries to build *executable* models of these calculi.

Thus the fact that the π-calculus ([20]) is not a closed theory, but rather a theory dependent upon some theory of names is both enabling and limiting. This openness of the theory has been exploited, for example, in π-calculus implementations, like the execution engine in Microsoft's Biztalk [17], where an ancillary binding language providing a means of specifying a 'theory' of names; e.g., names may be tcp/ip ports or urls or object references, etc. Reasoning foundationally, however, when names have structure, name equality becomes a computation; but, if our theory of interaction is to provide a basis for a theory of computation – especially of *distributed* computation – then certainly this computation must be accounted for as well. Moreover, the fact that any realization of these name-based, mobile calculi of interaction must come to grips with names that have structure begs the question: would the theoretical account of interaction be more effective, both as a theory in its own right and as a guide for implementation, if it included an account of the relationships between the structure of names and the structure of processes?

1.1 Overview and Contributions

In [19] we presented a theory of an asynchronous message-passing calculus built on a notion of quoting in which names have the structure of quoted processes, and may be thought of as representing the code of some process, i.e. a reification of the syntactic structure of some process (up to some equivalence). Name-passing, as such, becomes a way of passing the code of a process as a message, and in the presence of a dequote operation, turning the code of a process into a running instance, this machinery yields higher-order characteristics without the introduction of process variables. [1] As is standard with higher-order calculi, replication and/or recursion is no longer required as a primitive operation. Somewhat more interestingly, the introduction of a process constructor to dynamically convert a process into its code is essential to obtain computational completeness, and simultaneously supplants the function of the ν operator. [2]

In this paper we take the idea a little further via an investigation of a Hennessy-Milner logic for this calculus. The logic is a form of spatial logic ([6], [7]) with operators detecting structural as well as behavioral content of process. Further, like many other logics for message-passing calculi it describes formulae denoting sets of such processes in a more or less standard manner, but the additional reflective structure on names also gives rise to a new class of formulae.

[1] Following the tradition started by Smith and des Rivieres, [10] we dubbed this ability to turn running code into data and back again, reflection; and hence, called the calculus the *r*eflective, *h*igher-*o*rder calculus, or rho-calculus, for short, or ρ-calculus for even shorter.

[2] In fact, [19] gives a compositional encoding of the ν operator into the calculus, making essential use of dynamic quote as well as dequote.

These formulae denote sets of *names*, referred to in the sequel as namespaces and causing us to dub the logic *namespace logic.*

These new formulae suggest approaches to various application domains, e.g. reasoning about security, or the structure of the data passed between processes, that differ somewhat from the current treatment of these domains using message-passing calculi. For example, the analytic framework was not designed with security in mind, and as such has no additional security-specific features like nonce construction or unpacking, as is found in Gordon's spi-calculus ([3]), and yet has very simple formulae to express such properties as that a process will only ever receive requests from a given range of ports. Moreover, these properties are expressed as *formulae*, not as process specifications, thus observance is measured by satisfaction not protocol equivalence. Further, while closer in spirit – ala the proposition-as-types paradigm – to type-based approaches like Gordon and Jeffrey's approach to typing correspondence assertions [14] or Abadi's various type systems for security ([2] [1]), it is a logic and not a type system with the attendent advantages and disadvantages. For example, a very broad range of properties may be expressed, but the system is only semi-decidable. Likewise, neither the calculus nor the logic were designed with any particular data analysis in mind, and yet we find relatively simple treatment of the semantics of validation for a fragment of `XML` schema.

While the main focus of the paper is the logic, and some suggestive examples, to provide a self-contained presentation, the paper also presents a concrete instance of a minimal reflective asynchronous message-passing calculus and the manner in which its processes and names witness the formulae of the logic. As in [19] where we took the view that the main contribution of the concrete machinery was to provide an instrument to bring to life a set of questions regarding the role of names in calculi of interaction, here we assert that the real contribution manifest by the logic is an instrument to better frame and sharpen those questions. These questions include the calculation of name equality as a computation to be considered within the framework of interaction and the roles of name equality in substitution versus synchronization. These questions don't really come to life, though, without the instruments in hand. So, we turn immediately to the formal presentation.

2 The Calculus

This presentation is essentially the same as the one found in [19].

Notation. We let P, Q, R range over processes and x, y, z range over names.

ρ-calculus	$P, Q ::= 0$	null process
	$\mid\ x(y)\,.\,P$	input
	$\mid\ x\langle\!|P|\!\rangle$	lift
	$\mid\ \urcorner x \ulcorner$	drop
	$\mid\ P \mid Q$	parallel
	$x, y ::= \ulcorner P \urcorner$	quote

Quote. Working in a bottom-up fashion, we begin with names. The technical detail corresponding to the π-calculus' parametricity in a theory of *names* shows up in standard presentations in the grammar describing terms of the language: there is no production for names; names are taken to be terminals in the grammar. Our first point of departure from a more standard presentation of an asynchronous mobile process calculus is here. The grammar for the terms of the language will include a production for names in the grammar. A name is a *quoted* process, $\ulcorner P \urcorner$.

Parallel. This constructor is the usual parallel composition, denoting concurrent execution of the composed processes.

Lift and Drop. Despite the fact that names are built from (the codes of) processes, we still maintain a careful disinction in kind between process and name; thus, name construction is not process construction. So, if one wants to be able to generate a name from a given process, there must be a process constructor for a term that creates a name from a process. This is the motivation for the production $x\langle\!| P |\!\rangle$, dubbed here the *lift* operator. The intuitive meaning of this term is that the process P will be packaged up as its code, $\ulcorner P \urcorner$, and ultimately made available as an output at the port x.

A more formal motivation for the introduction of this operator will become clear in the sequel. But, it will suffice to say now that $\ulcorner P \urcorner$ is impervious to substitution. In the ρ-calculus, substitution does not affect the process body between quote marks. On the other hand, $x\langle\!| P |\!\rangle$ is susceptible to substitution and as such constitutes a dynamic form of quoting because the process body ultimately quoted will be different depending on the context in which the $x\langle\!| P |\!\rangle$ expression occurs.

Of course, when a name is a quoted process, it is very handy to have a way of evaluating such an entity. Thus, the $\urcorner x \ulcorner$ operator, pronounced *drop* x, (eventually) extracts the process from a name. We say 'eventually' because this extraction only happens when a quoted process is substituted into this expression. A consequence of this behavior is that $\urcorner x \ulcorner$ is inert except under and input prefix. One way of saying this is that if you want to get something done, sometimes you need to drop a name, but it should be the name of an agent you know.

Remark 1. The lift operator turns out to play a role analogous to $(\nu\ x)P$. As mentioned in the introduction, it is essential to the computational completeness of the calculus, playing a key role in the implementation of replication. It also provides an essential ingredient in the compositional encoding of the ν operator.

Remark 2. It is well-known that replication is not required in a higher-order process algebra [23]. While our algebra is *not* higher-order in the traditional sense (there are not formal process variables of a different type from names) it has all the features of a higher-order process algebra. Thus, it turns out that there is no need for a term for recursion. To illustrate this we present below an encoding of $!P$ in this calculus. Intuitively, this will amount to receiving a quoted form of a process, evaluating it, while making the quoted form available again. The reader familiar with the λ-calculus will note the formal similarity between the crucial term in the encoding and the paradoxical combinator [4].

Input and Output. The input constructor is standard for an asynchronous name-passing calculus. Input blocks its continuation from execution until it receives a communication. Lift is a form of output which – because the calculus is asynchronous – is allowed no continuation. It also affords a convenient syntactic sugar, which we define here.

$$x\,[y] \triangleq x\langle\!|\, \urcorner y \ulcorner \,|\!\rangle$$

The Null Process. As we will see below, the null process has a more distinguished role in this calculus. It provides the sole atom out of which all other processes (and the names they use) arise much in the same way that the number 0 is the sole number out of which the natural numbers are constructed; or the empty set is the sole set out of which all sets are built in ZF-set theory [16]; or the empty game is the sole game out of which all games are built in Conway's theory of games and numbers [8]. This analogy to these other theories draws attention, in our opinion, to the foundational issues raised in the introduction regarding the design of calculi of interaction.

2.1 The Name Game

Before presenting some of the more standard features of a mobile process calculus, the calculation of free names, structural equivalence, etc., we wish to consider some examples of processes and names. In particular, if processes are built out of names, and names are built out of processes, is it ever possible to get off the ground? Fortunately, there is one process the construction of which involves no names, the null process, 0. Since we have at least one process, we can construct at least one name, namely $\ulcorner 0 \urcorner$ [3]. Armed with one name we can now construct at least two new processes that are evidently syntactically different from the 0, these are $\ulcorner 0 \urcorner\,[\ulcorner 0 \urcorner]$ and $\ulcorner 0 \urcorner(\ulcorner 0 \urcorner)\,.\,0$. As we might expect, the intuitive operational interpretation of these processes is also distinct from the null process. Intuitively, we expect that the first outputs the name $\ulcorner 0 \urcorner$ on the channel $\ulcorner 0 \urcorner$, much like the ordinary π-calculus process $x\,[x]$ outputs the name x on the channel x, and the second inputs on the channel $\ulcorner 0 \urcorner$, much like the ordinary π-calculus process $x\,(x)\,.\,0$ inputs on the channel x.

Of course, now that we have two more processes, we have two more names, $\ulcorner\ulcorner 0 \urcorner[\ulcorner 0 \urcorner]\urcorner$ and $\ulcorner\ulcorner 0 \urcorner(\ulcorner 0 \urcorner)\,.\,0\urcorner$. Having three names at our disposal we can construct a whole new supply of processes that generate a fresh supply of names, and we're off and running. It should be pointed out, though, that as soon as we

[3] Pun gratefully accepted ;-).

had the null process we also had $0 \mid 0$ and $0 \mid 0 \mid 0$ and consequently, we had the names $\ulcorner 0 \mid 0 \urcorner$, and $\ulcorner 0 \mid 0 \mid 0 \urcorner$, and .... But, since we ultimately wish to treat these compositions as merely other ways of writing the null process and not distinct from it, should we admit the codes of these processes as distinct from $\ulcorner 0 \urcorner$?

This question leads to several intriguing and apparently fundamental questions. Firstly, if names have structure, whether this derives from the structure of processes or something else, what is a reasonable notion of equality on names? How much computation, and of what kind, should go into ascertaining equality on names? Additionally, what roles should name equality play in a calculus of processes? In constructing this calculus we became conscious that substitution and synchronization identify two potentially very different roles for name equality to play in name-passing calculi. That these are very different roles is suggested by the fact that they may be carried out by very different mechanisms in a workable and effective theory. We offer one choice, but this is just one design choice among infinitely many. Most likely, the primary value of this proposal is to raise the question. Likewise, we offer a proposal regarding the calculation of name equality that is just one of many and whose real purpose is to make the question vivid. We wish to turn to the core mechanics of the calculus with these questions in mind.

2.2 Free and Bound Names

The syntax has been chosen so that a binding occurrence of a name is sandwiched between round braces, $(\cdot)$. Thus, the calculation of the free names of a process, P, denoted $\mathcal{FN}(P)$ is given recursively by

$$\begin{aligned}
\mathcal{FN}(0) &= \emptyset \\
\mathcal{FN}(x(y) \,.\, P) &= \{x\} \cup (\mathcal{FN}(P) \setminus \{y\}) \\
\mathcal{FN}(x\langle\!| P |\!\rangle) &= \{x\} \cup \mathcal{FN}(P) \\
\mathcal{FN}(P \mid Q) &= \mathcal{FN}(P) \cup \mathcal{FN}(Q) \\
\mathcal{FN}(\urcorner x \ulcorner) &= \{x\}
\end{aligned}$$

An occurrence of x in a process P is *bound* if it is not free. The set of names occurring in a process (bound or free) is denoted by $\mathcal{N}(P)$.

2.3 Structural Congruence

The *structural congruence* of processes, noted $\equiv$, is the least congruence, containing α-equivalence, $\equiv_\alpha$, that satisfies the following laws:

$$\begin{aligned}
P \mid 0 \equiv P &\equiv 0 \mid P \\
P \mid Q &\equiv Q \mid P \\
(P \mid Q) \mid R &\equiv P \mid (Q \mid R)
\end{aligned}$$

2.4 Name Equivalence

We now come to one of the first real subtleties of this calculus. Both the calculation of the free names of a process and the determination of structural congruence between processes critically depend on being able to establish whether two names are equal. In the case of the calculation of the free names of an input-guarded process, for example, to remove the bound name we must determine whether it is in the set of free names of the continuation. Likewise, structural congruence includes α-equivalence. But, establishing α-equivalence between the processes $x(z) \,.\, w\langle\!|y[z]|\!\rangle$ and $x(v) \,.\, w\langle\!|y[v]|\!\rangle$, for instance, requires calculating a substitution, e.g. $x(v) \,.\, w\langle\!|y[v]|\!\rangle\{z/v\}$. But this calculation requires, in turn, being able to determine whether two names, in this case the name in the object position of the output, and the name being substituted for, are equal.

As will be seen, the equality on names involves structural equivalence on processes, which in turn involves alpha equivalence, which involves name equivalence. This is a subtle mutual recursion, but one that turns out to be well-founded. Before presenting the technical details, the reader may note that the grammar above enforces a strict alternation between quotes and process constructors. Each question about a process that involves a question about names may in turn involve a question about processes, but the names in the processes the next level down, as it were, are under fewer quotes. To put it another way, each 'recursive call' to name equivalence will involve one less level of quoting, ultimately bottoming out in the quoted zero process.

Let us assume that we have an account of (syntactic) substitution and α-equivalence upon which we can rely to formulate a notion of name equivalence, and then bootstrap our notions of substitution and α-equivalence from that. We take name equivalence, written $\equiv_N$, to be the smallest equivalence relation generated by the following rules.

$$\frac{}{\ulcorner\urcorner x \ulcorner\urcorner \equiv_N x} \qquad \text{(QUOTE-DROP)}$$

$$\frac{P \equiv Q}{\ulcorner P \urcorner \equiv_N \ulcorner Q \urcorner} \qquad \text{(STRUCT-EQUIV)}$$

2.5 Syntactic Substitution

Now we build the substitution used by α-equivalence. We use *Proc* for the set of processes, $\ulcorner \mathit{Proc} \urcorner$ for the set of names, and $\{\boldsymbol{y}/\boldsymbol{x}\}$ to denote partial maps, $s : \ulcorner \mathit{Proc} \urcorner \to \ulcorner \mathit{Proc} \urcorner$. A map, s lifts, uniquely, to a map on process terms, $\widehat{s} : \mathit{Proc} \to \mathit{Proc}$ by the following equations.

$$\begin{aligned}
(0)\widehat{\{\ulcorner Q \urcorner / \ulcorner P \urcorner\}} &= 0 \\
(R \mid S)\widehat{\{\ulcorner Q \urcorner / \ulcorner P \urcorner\}} &= (R)\widehat{\{\ulcorner Q \urcorner / \ulcorner P \urcorner\}} \mid (S)\widehat{\{\ulcorner Q \urcorner / \ulcorner P \urcorner\}} \\
(x(y) \,.\, R)\widehat{\{\ulcorner Q \urcorner / \ulcorner P \urcorner\}} &= (x)\{\ulcorner Q \urcorner / \ulcorner P \urcorner\}(z) \,.\, ((R\widehat{\{z/y\}})\widehat{\{\ulcorner Q \urcorner / \ulcorner P \urcorner\}})
\end{aligned}$$

$$(x\langle\!|R|\!\rangle)\widehat{\{\ulcorner Q\urcorner/\ulcorner P\urcorner\}} = (x)\{\ulcorner Q\urcorner/\ulcorner P\urcorner\}\langle\!|R\widehat{\{\ulcorner Q\urcorner/\ulcorner P\urcorner\}}|\!\rangle$$
$$(\urcorner x\ulcorner)\widehat{\{\ulcorner Q\urcorner/\ulcorner P\urcorner\}} = \begin{cases} \urcorner\ulcorner Q\urcorner\ulcorner & x \equiv_N \ulcorner P\urcorner \\ \urcorner x\ulcorner & otherwise \end{cases}$$

where

$$(x)\{\ulcorner Q\urcorner/\ulcorner P\urcorner\} = \begin{cases} \ulcorner Q\urcorner & x \equiv_N \ulcorner P\urcorner \\ x & otherwise \end{cases}$$

and z is chosen distinct from $\ulcorner P\urcorner$, $\ulcorner Q\urcorner$, the free names in Q, and all the names in R. Our α-equivalence will be built in the standard way from this substitution.

But, given these mutual recursions, the question is whether the calculation of $\equiv_N$ (respectively, $\equiv$, $\equiv_\alpha$) terminates. To answer this question it suffices to formalize our intuitions regarding level of quotes, or quote depth, $\#(x)$, of a name x as follows.

$$\#(\ulcorner P\urcorner) = 1 + \#(P)$$
$$\#(P) = \begin{cases} max\{\#(x) : x \in \mathcal{N}(P)\} & \mathcal{N}(P) \neq \emptyset \\ 0 & otherwise \end{cases}$$

The grammar ensures that $\#(\ulcorner P\urcorner)$ is bounded. Then the termination of $\equiv_N$ (respectively, $\equiv$, $\equiv_\alpha$) is an easy induction on quote depth.

2.6 Dynamic Quote: An Example

Anticipating something of what's to come, consider applying the substitution, $\widehat{\{u/z\}}$, to the following pair of processes, $w\langle\!|y[z]|\!\rangle$ and $w[\ulcorner y[z]\urcorner]$.

$$w\langle\!|y[z]|\!\rangle\widehat{\{u/z\}} = w\langle\!|y[u]|\!\rangle$$
$$w[\ulcorner y[z]\urcorner]\widehat{\{u/z\}} = w[\ulcorner y[z]\urcorner]$$

Because the body of the process between quotes is impervious to substitution, we get radically different answers. In fact, by examining the first process in an input context, e.g. $x(z).w\langle\!|y[z]|\!\rangle$, we see that the process under the lift operator may be shaped by prefixed inputs binding a name inside it. In this sense, the lift operator will be seen as a way to dynamically construct processes before reifying them as names.

2.7 Semantic Substitution

The substitution used in α-equivalence is really only a device to formally recognize that binding occurrences do not depend on the specific names. It is not the engine of computation. The proposal here is that while synchronization is the driver of that engine, the real engine of computation is a semantic notion of substitution that recognizes that a dropped name is a request to run a process. Which process? Why the one whose code has been bound to the name being dropped. Formally, this amounts to a notion of substitution that differs from syntactic substitution in its application to a dropped name.

$$(\urcorner x \ulcorner)\widehat{\{\ulcorner Q \urcorner / \ulcorner P \urcorner\}} = \begin{cases} Q & x \equiv_N \ulcorner P \urcorner \\ \urcorner x \ulcorner & \mathit{otherwise} \end{cases}$$

In the remainder of the paper we will refer to semantic and syntactic substitutions simply as substitutions and rely on context to distinguish which is meant. Similarly, we will abuse notation and write $\{y/x\}$ for $\widehat{\{y/x\}}$.

Finally equipped with these standard features we can present the dynamics of the calculus.

2.8 Operational Semantics

The reduction rules for ρ-calculus are

$$\frac{x_0 \equiv_N x_1}{x_0 \langle\!| Q |\!\rangle \mid x_1(y)\,.\,P \rightarrow P\{\ulcorner Q \urcorner / y\}} \qquad (\textsc{Comm})$$

In addition, we have the following context rules:

$$\frac{P \rightarrow P'}{P \mid Q \rightarrow P' \mid Q} \qquad (\textsc{Par})$$

$$\frac{P \equiv P' \qquad P' \rightarrow Q' \qquad Q' \equiv Q}{P \rightarrow Q} \qquad (\textsc{Equiv})$$

The context rules are entirely standard and we do not say much about them, here. The communication rule does what was promised, namely make it possible for agents to synchronize and communicate processes packaged as names. For example, using the comm rule and name equivalence we can now justify our syntactic sugar for output.

$$\begin{aligned} & x[z] \mid x(y)\,.\,P \\ = {} & x\langle\!| \urcorner z \ulcorner |\!\rangle \mid x(y)\,.\,P \\ \rightarrow {} & P\{\ulcorner \urcorner z \ulcorner \urcorner / y\} \\ \equiv {} & P\{z/y\} \end{aligned}$$

But, it also provides a scheme that identifies the role of name equality in synchronization. There are other relationships between names with structure that could also mediate synchronization. Consider, for example, a calculus identical to the one presented above, but with an alternative rule governing communication.

$$\frac{\forall R.[P_{channel} \mid Q_{channel} \to^{*} R] \Rightarrow R \to^{*} 0}{\ulcorner Q_{channel} \urcorner \langle\!| Q |\!\rangle \mid \ulcorner P_{channel} \urcorner (y) \,.\, P \to P\{\ulcorner Q \urcorner / y\}}$$
(COMM-ANNIHILATION)

Intuitively, it says that the codes of a pair of processes, $P_{channel}$, $Q_{channel}$, stand in channel/co-channel relation just when the composition of the processes always eventually reduces to 0, that is, when the processes annihilate one another. This rule is well-founded, for observe that because $0 \equiv 0 \mid 0$, $0 \mid 0 \to^{*} 0$. Thus, $\ulcorner 0 \urcorner$ serves as its own co-channel. Analogous to our generation of names from 0, with one such channel/co-channel pair, we can find many such pairs. What we wish to point out about this rule is that we can see precisely an account of the calculation of the channel/co-channel relationship as deriving from the theory of interaction. We do not know if the computation of name equality has a similar presentation, driving home the potential difference of those two roles in calculi of interaction.

We mention, as a brief aside, that there is no reason why 0 is special in the scheme above. We posit a family of calculi, indexed by a set of processes $\{S_\alpha\}$, and differing only in their communication rule each of which conforms to the scheme below.

$$\frac{\forall R.[P_{channel} \mid Q_{channel} \to^{*} R] \Rightarrow R \to^{*} R' \equiv S_\alpha}{\ulcorner Q_{channel} \urcorner \langle\!| Q |\!\rangle \mid \ulcorner P_{channel} \urcorner (y) \,.\, P \to P\{\ulcorner Q \urcorner / y\}}$$
(COMM-ANNIHILATION-S)

We explore this family of calculi in a forthcoming paper. For the rest of this paper, however, we restrict our attention to the calculus with the less exotic communication rule, using $\to$ for reduction according to that system and $\Rightarrow$ for $\to^{*}$.

3 Replication

As mentioned before, it is known that replication (and hence recursion) can be implemented in a higher-order process algebra [23]. As our first example of calculation with the machinery thus far presented we give the construction explicitly in the ρ-calculus.

$$D(x) \triangleq x(y) \,.\, (x[y] \mid \urcorner y \ulcorner)$$
$$!P(x) \triangleq x\langle\!| D(x) \mid P |\!\rangle \mid D(x)$$

$$\begin{aligned}
&!P(x)\\
&= \quad x\langle\!| (x(y) \,.\, (x[y] \mid \urcorner y \ulcorner)) \mid P |\!\rangle \mid x(y) \,.\, (x[y] \mid \urcorner y \ulcorner)\\
&\to \quad (x[y] \mid \urcorner y \ulcorner)\{\ulcorner (x(y) \,.\, (\urcorner y \ulcorner \mid x[y])) \mid P \urcorner / y\}\\
&= x[\ulcorner (x(y) \,.\, (x[y] \mid \urcorner y \ulcorner)) \mid P \urcorner] \mid (x(y) \,.\, (x[y] \mid \urcorner y \ulcorner)) \mid P
\end{aligned}$$

$$\begin{array}{ll} \rightarrow & \dots \\ \rightarrow^* & P \mid P \mid \dots \end{array}$$

Of course, this encoding, as an implementation, runs away, unfolding $!P$ eagerly. As it is instructive to construct a lazier – and more implementable – replication operator, restricted to input-guarded processes we recommend this exercise to the reader interested in gaining further inside into the mechanics of the calculus.

4 Bisimulation

Having taken the notion of restriction out of the language, we carefully place it back into the notion of observation, and hence into the notion of program equality, i.e. bisimulation. That is, we parameterize the notion of barbed bisimulation by a set of names over which we are allowed to set the barbs. The motivation for this choice is really comparison with other calculi. The set of names of the ρ-calculus is *global*. It is impossible, in the grammar of processes, to guard terms from being placed into contexts that can potentially observe communication. So, we provide a place for reasoning about such limitations on the scope of observation in the theory of bisimulation.

Definition 1. *An* observation relation, $\downarrow_{\mathcal{N}}$, *over a set of names,* $\mathcal{N}$, *is the smallest relation satisfying the rules below.*

$$\frac{y \in \mathcal{N},\ x \equiv_N y}{x\,[v] \downarrow_{\mathcal{N}} x} \qquad (\text{OUT-BARB})$$

$$\frac{P \downarrow_{\mathcal{N}} x \text{ or } Q \downarrow_{\mathcal{N}} x}{P \mid Q \downarrow_{\mathcal{N}} x} \qquad (\text{PAR-BARB})$$

We write $P \Downarrow_{\mathcal{N}} x$ *if there is* Q *such that* $P \Rightarrow Q$ *and* $Q \downarrow_{\mathcal{N}} x$.

Notice that $x(y)\ .\ P$ has no barb. Indeed, in ρ-calculus as well as other asynchronous calculi, an observer has no direct means to detect if a message sent has been received or not.

Definition 2. *An* $\mathcal{N}$-barbed bisimulation *over a set of names,* $\mathcal{N}$, *is a symmetric binary relation* $\mathcal{S}_{\mathcal{N}}$ *between agents such that* $P\ \mathcal{S}_{\mathcal{N}} Q$ *implies:*

1. *If* $P \rightarrow P'$ *then* $Q \Rightarrow Q'$ *and* $P'\ \mathcal{S}_{\mathcal{N}} Q'$.
2. *If* $P \downarrow_{\mathcal{N}} x$, *then* $Q \Downarrow_{\mathcal{N}} x$.

P *is* $\mathcal{N}$*-barbed bisimilar to* Q, *written* $P \dot{\approx}_{\mathcal{N}} Q$, *if* $P\ \mathcal{S}_{\mathcal{N}} Q$ *for some* $\mathcal{N}$*-barbed bisimulation* $\mathcal{S}_{\mathcal{N}}$.

5 Logic

Namespace logic resides in the subfamily of Hennessy-Milner logics discovered by Caires and Cardelli and known as spatial logics [7]. Thus, as is seen below, in addition to the action modalities, we also find formulae for *separation*, corresponding, at the logical level, to the structural content of the parallel operator at the level of the calculus. Likewise, we have quantification over names.

In this connection, however, we find an interesting difference between spatial logics investigated heretofore and this one. As in the calculus, we find no need for an operator corresponding to the ν construction. However, revelation in spatial logic, is a structural notion [7]. It detects the *declaration* of a new name. No such information is available in the reflective calculus or in namespace logic. The calculus and the logic can arrange that names are used in a manner consistent with their being declared as new in the π-calculus, but it cannot detect the declaration itself. Seen from this perspective, revelation is a somewhat remarkable observation, as it seems to be about detecting the programmer's intent.

reflective logic	$\phi, \psi ::= true$	verity
	$\mid\ 0$	nullity
	$\mid\ \neg\phi$	negation
	$\mid\ \phi \& \psi$	conjunction
	$\mid\ \phi \mid \psi$	separation
	$\mid\ \urcorner b \ulcorner$	descent
	$\mid\ a \langle\!| \phi |\!\rangle$	elevation
	$\mid\ \langle a?b \rangle \phi$	activity
	$\mid\ \mathsf{rec}\ X . \phi$	greatest fix point
	$\mid\ \forall n : \psi . \phi$	quantification
	$a ::= \ulcorner \phi \urcorner$	indication
	$\mid\ b$	...
	$b ::= \ulcorner P \urcorner$	nomination
	$\mid\ n$	...

We let $PForm$ denote the set of formulae generated by the ϕ-production, $QForm$ denote the set of formulae generated by the a-production and $\mathcal{V}$ denote the set of propositional variables used in the rec production.

Inspired by Caires' presentation of spatial logic [5], we give the semantics in terms of sets of processes (and names). We need the notion of a valuation $v : \mathcal{V} \to \wp(Proc)$, and use the notation $v\{\mathcal{S}/X\}$ to mean

$$v\{\mathcal{S}/X\}(Y) = \begin{cases} \mathcal{S} & Y = X \\ v(Y) & otherwise \end{cases}$$

The meaning of formulae is given in terms of two mutually recursive functions,

$$[\![-]\!](-) : PForm \times [\mathcal{V} \to \wp(Proc)] \to \wp(Proc)$$
$$(\!(-)\!)(-) : QForm \times [\mathcal{V} \to \wp(Proc)] \to \wp(\ulcorner Proc \urcorner)$$

taking a formula of the appropriate type and a valuation, and returning a set of processes or a set of names, respectively.

$$
\begin{aligned}
[\![true]\!](v) &= Proc \\
[\![0]\!](v) &= \{P : P \equiv 0\} \\
[\![\neg\phi]\!](v) &= Proc/[\![\phi]\!](v) \\
[\![\phi \& \psi]\!](v) &= [\![\phi]\!](v) \cap [\![\psi]\!](v) \\
[\![\phi \mid \psi]\!](v) &= \{P : \exists P_0, P_1.P \equiv P_0 \mid P_1,\ P_0 \in [\![\phi]\!](v),\ P_1 \in [\![\psi]\!](v)\} \\
[\![\urcorner b \ulcorner]\!](v) &= \{P : \exists Q, P'.P \equiv Q \mid \urcorner x \ulcorner,\ x \in (\!(b)\!)(v)\} \\
[\![a\langle\!|\phi|\!\rangle]\!](v) &= \{P : \exists Q, P'.P \equiv Q \mid x\langle\!|P'|\!\rangle,\ x \in (\!(a)\!)(v),\ P' \in [\![\phi]\!](v)\} \\
[\![\langle a?b\rangle\phi]\!](v) &= \{P : \exists Q, P'.P \equiv Q \mid x(y)\,.\,P', x \in (\!(a)\!)(v), \\
&\qquad \forall c.\exists z.P'\{z/y\} \in [\![\phi\{c/b\}]\!](v)\} \\
[\![\mathsf{rec}\ X\,.\,\phi]\!](v) &= \cup\{\mathcal{S} \subseteq Proc : \mathcal{S} \subseteq [\![\phi]\!](v\{\mathcal{S}/X\})\} \\
[\![\forall n : \psi\,.\,\phi]\!](v) &= \cap_{x \in (\!(\ulcorner\psi\urcorner)\!)(v)} [\![\phi\{x/n\}]\!](v) \\
(\!(\ulcorner\phi\urcorner)\!)(v) &= \{x : x \equiv_N \ulcorner P \urcorner, P \in [\![\phi]\!](v)\} \\
(\!(\ulcorner P\urcorner)\!)(v) &= \{x : x \equiv_N \ulcorner P \urcorner\}
\end{aligned}
$$

We say P witnesses ϕ (resp., x witnesses $\ulcorner\phi\urcorner$), written $P \models \phi$ (resp., $x \models \ulcorner\phi\urcorner$) just when $\forall v.P \in [\![\phi]\!](v)$ (resp., $\forall v.x \in [\![\ulcorner\phi\urcorner]\!](v)$).

Theorem 1 (Equivalence). $P \dot{\approx} Q \Leftrightarrow \forall\phi.P \models \phi \Leftrightarrow Q \models \phi$.

The proof employs an adaptation of the standard strategy. As noted in the introduction, this theorem means that there is no algorithm guaranteeing that a check for the witness relation will terminate.

Syntactic Sugar. In the examples below, we freely employ the usual DeMorgan-based syntactic sugar. For example,

$$
\begin{aligned}
\phi \Rightarrow \psi &\triangleq \neg(\phi \& \neg\psi) \\
\phi \vee \psi &\triangleq \neg(\neg\phi \& \neg\psi)
\end{aligned}
$$

Also, when quantification ranges over all of $Proc$, as in $\forall n : \ulcorner true \urcorner\,.\,\phi$, we omit the typing for the quantification variable, writing $\forall n\,.\,\phi$.

5.1 Examples

Controlling Access to Namespaces. Suppose that $\ulcorner\phi\urcorner$ describes some namespace, i.e. some collection of names. We can insist that a process restrict its next input to names in that namespace by insisting that it witness the formula

$$\langle\ulcorner\phi\urcorner?b\rangle\, true\, \& \neg\langle\ulcorner\neg\phi\urcorner?b\rangle true$$

which simply says the the process is currently able to take input from a name in the namespace $\ulcorner\phi\urcorner$ and is not capable of input on any name not in that namespace. In a similar manner, we can limit a server to serving only inputs in $\ulcorner\phi\urcorner$ throughout the lifetime of its behavior [4]

$$\mathsf{rec}\ X\,.\,\langle\ulcorner\phi\urcorner?b\rangle X \& \neg\langle\ulcorner\neg\phi\urcorner?b\rangle true$$

This formula is reminiscent of the functionality of a firewall, except that it is a *static* check. A process witnessing this formula will behave as though it were behind a firewall admitting only access to the ports in $\ulcorner\phi\urcorner$ without the need for the additional overhead of the watchdog machinery.

Validating the Structure of Data. Of course, the previous example might make one wonder what a useful namespace looks like. The relevance of this question is further amplified when we observe that processes pass names as messages as well as use them to govern synchronization. The next example, therefore, considers a space of names that might be seen as well-suited to play the role of data, for their structure loosely mimics the structure of the infoset model [9] of XML (sans schema).

$$\phi_{info} = \ulcorner \mathsf{rec}\ X\,.\,(\forall m\,.\,m\langle\!|\forall n\,.\,0 \vee n\langle\!|X|\!\rangle \vee \mathsf{rec}\ Y\,.\,(\forall n'\,.\,\langle n'?b\rangle(X \vee Y)) \vee (X \mid X)|\!\rangle)\urcorner$$

The formula is essentially a recursive disjunction selecting names that are first of all rooted with an enclosing lift operation – reminiscent of the way an XML document has a single enclosing root; and then are either

- the empty 'document'; or
- an 'element'; or
- a sequence of documents each 'located' at an input action; or
- an unordered group.

Notice that it is possible to parameterize this namespace on names for rooting 'documents' or 'elements'. Currently, these are typed as coming from the whole namespace, $\ulcorner true\urcorner$, but they could come from any subspace.

Moreover, the formula is itself a template for the interpretation of schema specifications [24]. If we boil XSD schema down to its essential type constructors, we have a recursive specification in which a schema is a

- a sequence, or
- a choice, or
- a group, or
- a recursion, in which a type name is bound to a schema definition

of element-tagged schema or schema references, with the recursive specification bottoming out at the simple and builtin types. Abstractly, then essential structures of XSD schema are captured by the grammar

[4] Of course, this formula also says the server never goes down, either – or at least is always willing to take such input...;-).

schema

$$
\begin{array}{rll}
S ::= & \epsilon & \text{empty document} \\
| & ESequence & \text{sequence} \\
| & EChoice & \text{choice} \\
| & EGroup & \text{group} \\
| & \mathsf{rec}\ N \,.\, S & \text{recursion} \\
ESequence ::= & \epsilon \mid E, ESequence & \text{sequence of elements} \\
EChoice ::= & \epsilon \mid E + EChoice & \text{choice of elements} \\
EGroup ::= & \epsilon \mid E \mid EGroup & \text{group of elements} \\
E ::= & tag(N \mid S) & \text{element}
\end{array}
$$

We use s to range over schema, σ, χ and γ to range over sequences, choices and groups, respectively.

The encoding below, which for clarity makes liberal – but obvious – use of polymorphism and elides the standard machinery for treating recursion variables, illustrates that we can view this grammar as essentially providing a high-level language for carving out namespaces in which the names conform to the schema.

$$
\begin{aligned}
[\![\epsilon]\!] &= \ulcorner 0 \urcorner \\
[\![tag(s), \sigma]\!] &= \ulcorner \forall n : [\![tag]\!] \,.\, \langle n?b \rangle ([\![s]\!] \mid [\![\sigma]\!]) \urcorner \\
[\![tag(s) + \chi]\!] &= \ulcorner \forall n : [\![tag]\!] \,.\, (\langle n?b \rangle [\![s]\!]) \vee [\![\chi]\!] \urcorner \\
[\![tag(s) \mid \gamma]\!] &= \ulcorner \forall n : [\![tag]\!] \,.\, (\langle n?b \rangle [\![s]\!]) \mid [\![\gamma]\!] \urcorner \\
[\![\mathsf{rec}\ N \,.\, s]\!] &= \ulcorner \mathsf{rec}\ N \,.\, [\![s]\!] \urcorner
\end{aligned}
$$

We emphasize that the example is not meant to be a complete account of `XML` schema. Rather, it is intended to suggest that with the reflective capabilities the logic gives a fairly intuitive treatment of names as structured data. The simplicity and intuitiveness of the treatment is really brought home, however, when employing the framework analytically. As an example, from a commonsense perspective it should be the case that any `XML` document that observes a schema automatically also corresponds to an infoset. The reader is encouraged to try her hand at using the framework to establish that if s is a schema, then

$$x \models [\![s]\!] \Rightarrow x \models \phi'_{info}$$

where ϕ'_{info} a suitably modified version of ϕ_{info}.

6 Conclusions and Future Work

We introduced namespace logic, a spatial-style Hennessy-Milner logic for a reflective asynchronous message-passing calculus built out of a notion of quote. We introduced some examples highlighting potential applications to security and data analysis.

We note that this work is situated in the larger context of a growing investigation into naming and computation. Milner's studies of action calculi led not only to reflexive action calculi [21], but to Power's and Hermida's work on name-free accounts of action calculi [15] as well as Pavlovic's [22]. Somewhat farther afield, but still related, is Gabbay's theory of freshness [12] and the nominal logics [13]. Very close to the mark, Carbone and Maffeis observe a tower of expressiveness resulting from adding very simple structure to names [18]. In some sense, this may be viewed as approaching the phenomena of structured names 'from below'. By making names be processes, this work may be seen as approaching the same phenomena 'from above'. But, both investigations are really the beginnings of a much longer and deeper investigation of the relationship between process structure and name structure.

Beyond foundational questions concerning the theory of interaction, or applications to security and data analysis such an investigation may be highly warranted in light of the recent connection between concurrency theory and biology. In particular, despite the interesting results achieved by researchers in this field, there is a fundamental difference between the kind of synchronization observed in the π-calculus and the kind of synchronization observed between molecules at the bio-molecular level. The difference is that interactions in the latter case occur at sites with extension and behavior of their own [11]. An account of these kinds of phenomena may be revealed in a detailed study of the relationship between the structure of names and the structure of processes.

Acknowledgments. The authors wish to thank Robin Milner for his thoughtful and stimulating remarks regarding earlier work in this direction, and Cosimo Laneve for urging us to consider a version of the calculus without heating rules.

References

1. Martín Abadi and Bruno Blanchet. Analyzing security protocols with secrecy types and logic programs. In *POPL*, pages 33–44, 2002.
2. Martín Abadi and Bruno Blanchet. Secrecy types for asymmetric communication. *Theor. Comput. Sci.*, 3(298):387–415, 2003.
3. Martín Abadi and Andrew D. Gordon. A calculus for cryptographic protocols: The spi calculus. In *ACM Conference on Computer and Communications Security*, pages 36–47, 1997.
4. Hendrik Pieter Barendregt. *The Lambda Calculus – Its Syntax and Semantics*, volume 103 of *Studies in Logic and the Foundations of Mathematics*. North-Holland, 1984.
5. Luís Caires. Behavioral and spatial observations in a logic for the pi-calculus. In *FoSSaCS*, pages 72–89, 2004.
6. Luís Caires and Luca Cardelli. A spatial logic for concurrency (part i). *Inf. Comput.*, 186(2):194–235, 2003.
7. Luís Caires and Luca Cardelli. A spatial logic for concurrency - ii. *Theor. Comput. Sci.*, 322(3):517–565, 2004.
8. John Horton Conway. *On Numbers and Games*. Academic Press, 1976.
9. John Cowan and Richard Tobin. Xml information set. W3C, 2004.
10. J. des Rivieres and B. C. Smith. The implementation of procedurally reflective languages. In *ACM Symposium on Lisp and Functional Programming*, pages 331–347, 1984.

11. Walter Fontana. private conversation. 2004.
12. M. J. Gabbay. The π-calculus in FM. In Fairouz Kamareddine, editor, *Thirty-five years of Automath.* Kluwer, 2003.
13. Murdoch Gabbay and James Cheney. A sequent calculus for nominal logic. In *LICS*, pages 139–148, 2004.
14. Andrew D. Gordon and Alan Jeffrey. Typing correspondence assertions for communication protocols. *Theor. Comput. Sci.*, 1-3(300):379–409, 2003.
15. Claudio Hermida and John Power. Fibrational control structures. In *CONCUR*, pages 117–129, 1995.
16. Jean-Louis Krivine. The curry-howard correspondence in set theory. In Martin Abadi, editor, *Proceedings of the Fifteenth Annual IEEE Symp. on Logic in Computer Science, LICS 2000.* IEEE Computer Society Press, June 2000.
17. Microsoft Corporation. Microsoft biztalk server. microsoft.com/biztalk/default.asp.
18. M.Carbone and S.Maffeis. On the expressive power of polyadic synchronisation in pi-calculus. *Nordic Journal of Computing*, 10(2):70–98, 2003.
19. L.G. Meredith and Matthias Radestock. A reflective higher-order calculus. In Mirko Viroli, editor, *ETAPS 2005 Satellites.* Springer-Verlag, 2005.
20. Robin Milner. The polyadic π-calculus: A tutorial. *Logic and Algebra of Specification*, Springer-Verlag, 1993.
21. Robin Milner. Strong normalisation in higher-order action calculi. In *TACS*, pages 1–19, 1997.
22. Dusko Pavlovic. Categorical logic of names and abstraction in action calculus. *Math. Structures in Comp. Sci.*, 7:619–637, 1997.
23. David Sangiorgi and David Walker. *The π-Calculus: A Theory of Mobile Processes.* Cambridge University Press, 2001.
24. Henry S. Thompson, David Beech, Murray Maloney, and Noah Mendelsohn. Xml schema part i: Structures, second edition. W3C, 2004.

Author Index

Lecture Notes in Computer Science

For information about Vols. 1–3701

please contact your bookseller or Springer

Vol. 3835: G. Sutcliffe, A. Voronkov (Eds.), Logic for Programming, Artificial Intelligence, and Reasoning. XIV, 744 pages. 2005. (Subseries LNAI).

Vol. 3814: M. Maybury, O. Stock, W. Wahlster (Eds.), Intelligent Technologies for Interactive Entertainment. XV, 342 pages. 2005. (Subseries LNAI).

Vol. 3807: M. Dean, Y. Guo, W. Jun, R. Kaschek, S. Krishnaswamy, Z. Pan, Q.Z. Sheng (Eds.), Web Information Systems Engineering – WISE 2005 Workshops. XV, 275 pages. 2005.

Vol. 3806: A.H. H. Ngu, M. Kitsuregawa, E.J. Neuhold, J.-Y. Chung, Q.Z. Sheng (Eds.), Web Information Systems Engineering – WISE 2005. XXI, 771 pages. 2005.

Vol. 3799: M. A. Rodríguez, I.F. Cruz, S. Levashkin, M.J. Egenhofer (Eds.), GeoSpatial Semantics. X, 259 pages. 2005.

Vol. 3793: T. Conte, N. Navarro, W.-m.W. Hwu, M. Valero, T. Ungerer (Eds.), High Performance Embedded Architectures and Compilers. XIII, 317 pages. 2005.

Vol. 3792: I. Richardson, P. Abrahamsson, R. Messnarz (Eds.), Software Process Improvement. VIII, 215 pages. 2005.

Vol. 3791: A. Adi, S. Stoutenburg, S. Tabet (Eds.), Rules and Rule Markup Languages for the Semantic Web. X, 225 pages. 2005.

Vol. 3790: G. Alonso (Ed.), Middleware 2005. XIII, 443 pages. 2005.

Vol. 3789: A. Gelbukh, Á. de Albornoz, H. Terashima-Marín (Eds.), MICAI 2005: Advances in Artificial Intelligence. XXVI, 1198 pages. 2005. (Subseries LNAI).

Vol. 3785: K.-K. Lau, R. Banach (Eds.), Formal Methods and Software Engineering. XIV, 496 pages. 2005.

Vol. 3784: J. Tao, T. Tan, R.W. Picard (Eds.), Affective Computing and Intelligent Interaction. XIX, 1008 pages. 2005.

Vol. 3781: S.Z. Li, Z. Sun, T. Tan, S. Pankanti, G. Chollet, D. Zhang (Eds.), Advances in Biometric Person Authentication. XI, 250 pages. 2005.

Vol. 3780: K. Yi (Ed.), Programming Languages and Systems. XI, 435 pages. 2005.

Vol. 3779: H. Jin, D. Reed, W. Jiang (Eds.), Network and Parallel Computing. XV, 513 pages. 2005.

Vol. 3777: O.B. Lupanov, O.M. Kasim-Zade, A.V. Chaskin, K. Steinhöfel (Eds.), Stochastic Algorithms: Foundations and Applications. VIII, 239 pages. 2005.

Vol. 3775: J. Schönwälder, J. Serrat (Eds.), Ambient Networks. XIII, 281 pages. 2005.

Vol. 3773: A. Sanfeliu, M.L. Cortés (Eds.), Progress in Pattern Recognition, Image Analysis and Applications. XX, 1094 pages. 2005.

Vol. 3772: M. Consens, G. Navarro (Eds.), String Processing and Information Retrieval. XIV, 406 pages. 2005.

Vol. 3771: J.M.T. Romijn, G.P. Smith, J. van de Pol (Eds.), Integrated Formal Methods. XI, 407 pages. 2005.

Vol. 3770: J. Akoka, S.W. Liddle, I.-Y. Song, M. Bertolotto, I. Comyn-Wattiau, W.-J. van den Heuvel, M. Kolp, J. Trujillo, C. Kop, H.C. Mayr (Eds.), Perspectives in Conceptual Modeling. XXII, 476 pages. 2005.

Vol. 3768: Y.-S. Ho, H.J. Kim (Eds.), Advances in Mulitmedia Information Processing - PCM 2005, Part II. XXVIII, 1088 pages. 2005.

Vol. 3767: Y.-S. Ho, H.J. Kim (Eds.), Advances in Mulitmedia Information Processing - PCM 2005, Part I. XXVIII, 1022 pages. 2005.

Vol. 3766: N. Sebe, M.S. Lew, T.S. Huang (Eds.), Computer Vision in Human-Computer Interaction. X, 231 pages. 2005.

Vol. 3765: Y. Liu, T. Jiang, C. Zhang (Eds.), Computer Vision for Biomedical Image Applications. X, 563 pages. 2005.

Vol. 3764: S. Tixeuil, T. Herman (Eds.), Self-Stabilizing Systems. VIII, 229 pages. 2005.

Vol. 3762: R. Meersman, Z. Tari, P. Herrero (Eds.), On the Move to Meaningful Internet Systems 2005: OTM 2005 Workshops. XXXI, 1228 pages. 2005.

Vol. 3761: R. Meersman, Z. Tari (Eds.), On the Move to Meaningful Internet Systems 2005: CoopIS, DOA, and ODBASE, Part II. XXVII, 653 pages. 2005.

Vol. 3760: R. Meersman, Z. Tari (Eds.), On the Move to Meaningful Internet Systems 2005: CoopIS, DOA, and ODBASE, Part I. XXVII, 921 pages. 2005.

Vol. 3759: G. Chen, Y. Pan, M. Guo, J. Lu (Eds.), Parallel and Distributed Processing and Applications - ISPA 2005 Workshops. XIII, 669 pages. 2005.

Vol. 3758: Y. Pan, D.-x. Chen, M. Guo, J. Cao, J.J. Dongarra (Eds.), Parallel and Distributed Processing and Applications. XXIII, 1162 pages. 2005.

Vol. 3757: A. Rangarajan, B. Vemuri, A.L. Yuille (Eds.), Energy Minimization Methods in Computer Vision and Pattern Recognition. XII, 666 pages. 2005.

Vol. 3756: J. Cao, W. Nejdl, M. Xu (Eds.), Advanced Parallel Processing Technologies. XIV, 526 pages. 2005.

Vol. 3754: J. Dalmau Royo, G. Hasegawa (Eds.), Management of Multimedia Networks and Services. XII, 384 pages. 2005.

Vol. 3753: O.F. Olsen, L.M.J. Florack, A. Kuijper (Eds.), Deep Structure, Singularities, and Computer Vision. X, 259 pages. 2005.

Vol. 3752: N. Paragios, O. Faugeras, T. Chan, C. Schnörr (Eds.), Variational, Geometric, and Level Set Methods in Computer Vision. XI, 369 pages. 2005.

Vol. 3751: T. Magedanz, E.R. M. Madeira, P. Dini (Eds.), Operations and Management in IP-Based Networks. X, 213 pages. 2005.

Vol. 3750: J.S. Duncan, G. Gerig (Eds.), Medical Image Computing and Computer-Assisted Intervention – MICCAI 2005, Part II. XL, 1018 pages. 2005.

Vol. 3749: J.S. Duncan, G. Gerig (Eds.), Medical Image Computing and Computer-Assisted Intervention – MICCAI 2005, Part I. XXXIX, 942 pages. 2005.

Vol. 3748: A. Hartman, D. Kreische (Eds.), Model Driven Architecture – Foundations and Applications. IX, 349 pages. 2005.

Vol. 3747: C.A. Maziero, J.G. Silva, A.M.S. Andrade, F.M.d. Assis Silva (Eds.), Dependable Computing. XV, 267 pages. 2005.

Vol. 3746: P. Bozanis, E.N. Houstis (Eds.), Advances in Informatics. XIX, 879 pages. 2005.

Vol. 3745: J.L. Oliveira, V. Maojo, F. Martín-Sánchez, A.S. Pereira (Eds.), Biological and Medical Data Analysis. XII, 422 pages. 2005. (Subseries LNBI).

Vol. 3744: T. Magedanz, A. Karmouch, S. Pierre, I. Venieris (Eds.), Mobility Aware Technologies and Applications. XIV, 418 pages. 2005.

Vol. 3740: T. Srikanthan, J. Xue, C.-H. Chang (Eds.), Advances in Computer Systems Architecture. XVII, 833 pages. 2005.

Vol. 3739: W. Fan, Z.-h. Wu, J. Yang (Eds.), Advances in Web-Age Information Management. XXIV, 930 pages. 2005.

Vol. 3738: V.R. Syrotiuk, E. Chávez (Eds.), Ad-Hoc, Mobile, and Wireless Networks. XI, 360 pages. 2005.

Vol. 3735: A. Hoffmann, H. Motoda, T. Scheffer (Eds.), Discovery Science. XVI, 400 pages. 2005. (Subseries LNAI).

Vol. 3734: S. Jain, H.U. Simon, E. Tomita (Eds.), Algorithmic Learning Theory. XII, 490 pages. 2005. (Subseries LNAI).

Vol. 3733: P. Yolum, T. Güngör, F. Gürgen, C. Özturan (Eds.), Computer and Information Sciences - ISCIS 2005. XXI, 973 pages. 2005.

Vol. 3731: F. Wang (Ed.), Formal Techniques for Networked and Distributed Systems - FORTE 2005. XII, 558 pages. 2005.

Vol. 3729: Y. Gil, E. Motta, V. R. Benjamins, M.A. Musen (Eds.), The Semantic Web – ISWC 2005. XXIII, 1073 pages. 2005.

Vol. 3728: V. Paliouras, J. Vounckx, D. Verkest (Eds.), Integrated Circuit and System Design. XV, 753 pages. 2005.

Vol. 3726: L.T. Yang, O.F. Rana, B. Di Martino, J.J. Dongarra (Eds.), High Performance Computing and Communications. XXVI, 1116 pages. 2005.

Vol. 3725: D. Borrione, W. Paul (Eds.), Correct Hardware Design and Verification Methods. XII, 412 pages. 2005.

Vol. 3724: P. Fraigniaud (Ed.), Distributed Computing. XIV, 520 pages. 2005.

Vol. 3723: W. Zhao, S. Gong, X. Tang (Eds.), Analysis and Modelling of Faces and Gestures. XI, 4234 pages. 2005.

Vol. 3722: D. Van Hung, M. Wirsing (Eds.), Theoretical Aspects of Computing – ICTAC 2005. XIV, 614 pages. 2005.

Vol. 3721: A. Jorge, L. Torgo, P.B. Brazdil, R. Camacho, J. Gama (Eds.), Knowledge Discovery in Databases: PKDD 2005. XXIII, 719 pages. 2005. (Subseries LNAI).

Vol. 3720: J. Gama, R. Camacho, P.B. Brazdil, A. Jorge, L. Torgo (Eds.), Machine Learning: ECML 2005. XXIII, 769 pages. 2005. (Subseries LNAI).

Vol. 3719: M. Hobbs, A.M. Goscinski, W. Zhou (Eds.), Distributed and Parallel Computing. XI, 448 pages. 2005.

Vol. 3718: V.G. Ganzha, E.W. Mayr, E.V. Vorozhtsov (Eds.), Computer Algebra in Scientific Computing. XII, 502 pages. 2005.

Vol. 3717: B. Gramlich (Ed.), Frontiers of Combining Systems. X, 321 pages. 2005. (Subseries LNAI).

Vol. 3716: L. Delcambre, C. Kop, H.C. Mayr, J. Mylopoulos, Ó. Pastor (Eds.), Conceptual Modeling – ER 2005. XVI, 498 pages. 2005.

Vol. 3715: E. Dawson, S. Vaudenay (Eds.), Progress in Cryptology – Mycrypt 2005. XI, 329 pages. 2005.

Vol. 3714: H. Obbink, K. Pohl (Eds.), Software Product Lines. XIII, 235 pages. 2005.

Vol. 3713: L.C. Briand, C. Williams (Eds.), Model Driven Engineering Languages and Systems. XV, 722 pages. 2005.

Vol. 3712: R. Reussner, J. Mayer, J.A. Stafford, S. Overhage, S. Becker, P.J. Schroeder (Eds.), Quality of Software Architectures and Software Quality. XIII, 289 pages. 2005.

Vol. 3711: F. Kishino, Y. Kitamura, H. Kato, N. Nagata (Eds.), Entertainment Computing - ICEC 2005. XXIV, 540 pages. 2005.

Vol. 3710: M. Barni, I. Cox, T. Kalker, H.J. Kim (Eds.), Digital Watermarking. XII, 485 pages. 2005.

Vol. 3709: P. van Beek (Ed.), Principles and Practice of Constraint Programming - CP 2005. XX, 887 pages. 2005.

Vol. 3708: J. Blanc-Talon, W. Philips, D.C. Popescu, P. Scheunders (Eds.), Advanced Concepts for Intelligent Vision Systems. XXII, 725 pages. 2005.

Vol. 3707: D.A. Peled, Y.-K. Tsay (Eds.), Automated Technology for Verification and Analysis. XII, 506 pages. 2005.

Vol. 3706: H. Fukś, S. Lukosch, A.C. Salgado (Eds.), Groupware: Design, Implementation, and Use. XII, 378 pages. 2005.

Vol. 3705: R. De Nicola, D. Sangiorgi (Eds.), Trustworthy Global Computing. VIII, 371 pages. 2005.

Vol. 3704: M. De Gregorio, V. Di Maio, M. Frucci, C. Musio (Eds.), Brain, Vision, and Artificial Intelligence. XV, 556 pages. 2005.

Vol. 3703: F. Fages, S. Soliman (Eds.), Principles and Practice of Semantic Web Reasoning. VIII, 163 pages. 2005.

Vol. 3702: B. Beckert (Ed.), Automated Reasoning with Analytic Tableaux and Related Methods. XIII, 343 pages. 2005. (Subseries LNAI).